W9-DGB-861

Nabokov's *Butterflies*

Nabokov's

edited and annotated by

BRIAN BOYD and ROBERT MICHAEL PYLE

Butterflies

UNPUBLISHED AND UNCOLLECTED WRITINGS

new translations from the Russian by

DMITRI NABOKOV

BEACON PRESS

BOSTON

BEACON PRESS
25 Beacon Street
Boston, Massachusetts 02108-2892
www.beacon.org

*Beacon Press books are published under the auspices of the
Unitarian Universalist Association of Congregations.*

Excerpts from the novels and short stories, the novella *The Enchanter, The Annotated Lolita, Lolita: A Screenplay, Speak, Memory: An Autobiography Revisited*, and *Strong Opinions* by arrangement with Vintage Books, a division of Random House, Inc. Excerpts from *Lectures on Literature, Lectures on Russian Literature*, and *Selected Letters 1940–1977* by arrangement with Harcourt Brace & Company. Excerpts from *Nikolai Gogol* by arrangement with New Directions Publishing Company. All other excerpts of text by Vladimir Nabokov by arrangement with the Estate of Vladimir Nabokov.

05 04 03 02 01 00   8 7 6 5 4 3 2 1

This book is printed on acid-free paper that meets the uncoated paper
ANSI/NISO specifications for permanence as revised in 1992.

*Composition by Wilsted & Taylor Publishing Services
Book design by Lucinda L. Hitchcock*

LIBRARY OF CONGRESS CATALOGING-IN-PUBLICATION DATA
Nabokov, Vladimir Vladimirovich, 1899–1977.
Nabokov's butterflies : unpublished and uncollected writings /
edited and annotated by Brian Boyd and Robert Michael Pyle ;
new translations from the Russian by Dmitri Nabokov.
p. cm.
Includes scientific articles previously published in various journals
and excerpts from literary works. Previously unpublished works include
a translation of an appendix to the novel *The Gift*.
ISBN 0-8070-8540-5 (alk. paper : cloth)
1. Butterflies.   2. Butterflies – Literary collections.
3. Nabokov, Vladimir Vladimirovich, 1899–1977 – Contributions in
entomology.   I. Boyd, Brian, 1952–   II. Pyle, Robert Michael.
III. Nabokov, Vladimir Vladimirovich,
1899–1977. Dar.   IV. Title.
QL452.N33 1999   595.78'9 – DC21   98-42846

to Véra
to Bronwen
to Thea

Contents

Abbreviations

ALL BOOKS BY VLADIMIR NABOKOV

ADA	*Ada or Ardor: A Family Chronicle*
AMNH	American Museum of Natural History, New York
BB	Brian Boyd
BS	*Bend Sinister*
CE	*Conclusive Evidence*
COLUMBIA	Bakhmeteff Archive, Columbia University
CORNELL	Cornell University Archives
DB	*Drugie berega*
DN	Dmitri Nabokov
DS	*Details of a Sunset and Other Stories*
EO	Alexander Pushkin, *Eugene Onegin,* trans. and with commentary by VN
GIFT	*The Gift*
IB	*Invitation to a Beheading*
KQK	*King, Queen, Knave*
LATH	*Look at the Harlequins!*
LCNA	Nabokov Archives, Library of Congress
LD	*Laughter in the Dark*
LL	*Lectures on Literature*
LS	*Lolita: A Screenplay*
MCZ	*Museum of Comparative Zoology, Harvard University*
MS	Manuscript
ND	*Nabokov's Dozen*
NG	*Nikolay Gogol*
NWL	*Nabokov-Wilson Letters*
PF	*Pale Fire*
PN	*Poslednie Novosti*
PP	*Poems and Problems*
RB	*A Russian Beauty and Other Stories*
RLSK	*The Real Life of Sebastian Knight*
RP	Robert Michael Pyle
SL	*Selected Letters 1940–1977*
SM	*Speak, Memory: An Autobiography Revisited*

SO	*Strong Opinions*
STORIES	*The Stories of Vladimir Nabokov*
TD	*Tyrants Destroyed and Other Stories*
TS	Typescript
TT	*Transparent Things*
VN	Vladimir Nabokov
VNA	Vladimir Nabokov Archive, Henry W. and Albert A. Berg Collection, New York Public Library
VNA, MTRX	Vladimir Nabokov Archive, Montreux
VNAY	Brian Boyd, *Vladimir Nabokov: The American Years*
YALE	Beinecke Library, Yale University

Illustrations

Color Plates

Nabokov,
Literature, Lepidoptera

BRIAN BOYD

My pleasures are the most intense known to man: writing and butterfly hunting.
[VLADIMIR NABOKOV, *Strong Opinions*]

The problem is this. Scientists think of VN *as an important entomologist who*
wrote fiction. Literary critics think of VN *as one of the most important twentieth century*
literary figures who somehow fancied insects. [RONALD S. WILKINSON[1]]

L̲ET ME PIN VLADIMIR NABOKOV into place alongside several superficially
similar specimens.

Nabokov and Beckett seem likely to be remembered as the foremost
writers of the mid-twentieth century. Both published over six decades,
from just after the heyday of the great modernists, Joyce, Proust, and
Kafka, to the emergence of postmodernism as a fashion and a formula.
Both wrote major works in two languages (Russian and English, English
and French) and translated them from one language into the other. Both
wrote with great eloquence, intelligence, learning, wit, and originality. But
their visions were polar opposites.

Or rather, Beckett's was polar, Nabokov's tropical. Beckett saw life as a
terminal illness and human thought, speech, and action as a babble amid
meaninglessness. Nabokov saw life as "a great surprise"[2] amid possibly
greater surprises. Four years after the best friend of his childhood was shot

and he was himself forced to leave forever the country he loved, a year after the father he adored was murdered, he has a character, a man whose young son has recently died, speak for him: "Everything in the world is beautiful, but Man only recognizes beauty if he sees it either seldom or from afar" (STORIES 45). Nabokov looked at his world tirelessly and at close range, and for all the horrors he could evoke in his darker books, he found it swarming with inexhaustible diversity and delight. Not the least of his delights was Lepidoptera.

In a game that asked us to associate natural kinds and famous people, "butterflies" would yield the answer "Nabokov" as surely as "hemlock" would trigger "Socrates." But while Socrates did not *choose* to be forever linked with hemlock, Vladimir Nabokov made butterflies his lifelong personal mark. He succeeded more than he could ever have imagined at the time when St. Peterburg's best portrait photographer came to record him, a boy of eight, surrounded by butterfly books. Although those who know just one fact about Nabokov know him as the author of *Lolita*, the familiar icon of Sue Lyon as Lolita licking her lollipop never graces books about him. Yet designers who would not dream of picking hemlock for the cover of a new book on Socrates again and again pin butterflies to the lapel of Nabokovian jackets.

Nabokov's singular attraction to butterflies attracts us as an image and an enigma. Consider another contrast. In the margins of his manuscripts Pushkin sketched hundreds upon hundreds of human faces in profile, a high proportion of them a stylized and embellished version of his own striking silhouette. Nabokov drew thousands of butterflies, for his scientific papers, for his unfinished catalogue of the butterflies of Europe, on the title pages of dedication copies of his novels, and in signing off his most playful letters. Pushkin's case needs no explanation: we can expect poets to be interested in people, and a romantic poet to be interested in himself above all. But why should someone with Nabokov's great gift as a writer be so obsessed with something so peripheral as butterflies are to most readers?

Does his passion for *papillons* indicate that he is insufficiently interested in people? Or should we argue the opposite, that the way he wielded his net has no bearing on the way he flourished his pen? After all, Humbert pursued nymphets, not Nymphalids, Luzhin captured chessmen, not Checkerspots, Pnin accumulated sorrows, not Sulphurs. Why did butterflies so fascinate Nabokov, and why should that so fascinate us? He became the world's most famous lepidopterist, but was he a serious scientist or little more than an enthusiastic collector? Did he leave any legacy in lepidoptery as he did in literature? And are the butterflies and moths in his works no more than a sly authorial signature?

When Nabokov caught his first butterfly in 1906, at the age of seven, his mother showed him how to spread it. She herself had a passion for collecting mushrooms and came from a family long interested in science. Her mother's father had been president of the Russian Academy of Medicine, and her mother had arranged to have a chemical laboratory built for herself. But it was Nabokov's father who had been a keen lepidopterist in his youth. A man of exacting scholarly standards, he was one of Russia's leading criminologists, along with much else (in politics, publishing, public life) that left him little time to wield a net. Nabokov adored both of his parents and the family's summer estate of Vyra, forty miles south of St. Petersburg, where he caught and collected his first butterflies. His parents' example and encouragement, and the chance to see and savor Vyra in a new way, sparked an explosive interest in butterflies.

Other elements in his makeup kept the fire burning. Sharp-eyed, sure of hand and foot, a zealous and accomplished sportsman (soccer, tennis, boxing), he always enjoyed the physical thrill of the butterfly chase. But the intellectual challenge appealed just as much to this precocious child. A mathematical prodigy at five, he lost the capacity for complex computation during a bout of pneumonia before he was eight. As he recovered, his mother surrounded his bed with butterflies and butterfly books. Decades later Nabokov would rework that memory by having Humbert bring Lolita, convalescing from influenza, a bouquet of wild flowers collected from a mountain pass and a book called *Flowers of the Rockies. That* child, for good reason, is unresponsive to *that* "parent" and in fact escapes before Humbert can see her again, but Nabokov thrived on his mother's love, "and the longing to describe a new species completely replaced that of discovering a new prime number" (SM 123).

From this point on, literature and Lepidoptera dance an elaborate *pas de deux* through seventy years of Nabokov's life.

As a boy of nine, still enjoying Wild West games, Nabokov would write to the great lepidopterist Nikolay Kuznetsov proposing a new subspecies name for a Poplar Admirable he had found (Kuznetsov scribbled back a two-word reply, the existing subspecies name and the name of its author) and a year or two later would translate Mayne Reid's Western novel *The Headless Horseman* into French verse. In his twin passions exhilaration merged with ambition and determination. Even before he read and reread all of Tolstoy, Flaubert, and Shakespeare in the original languages as he entered his teens, he had mastered the known butterflies of Europe and "dreamed his way through" the volumes so far published of Adalbert Seitz's *Die Gross-Schmetterlinge der Erde*.[3]

"Few things indeed have I known in the way of emotion or appetite, ambition or achievement, that could surpass in richness and strength the excitement of entomological exploration," Nabokov writes in his autobiography (SM 126). His lepidopterological ambitions seemed more haunting than his literary aspirations because they took so much longer to realize. At twelve or so, he sent off a description of a "new" moth to the British journal *The Entomologist*, whose editor did not recognize the species but found out that it had already been described by Kretschmar. Twenty years later, Nabokov still had discovered no new species, but he had become the leading writer of the Russian emigration and would recoup his adolescent disappointment by assigning Kretschmar's name to the unfortunate hero of *Camera Obscura*, unwittingly preempted in his love for Magda by another, slyer lover.

At fourteen Nabokov had prepared and distributed to friends and family his first "publication," a romantic poem of which he could later recall only one line, evoking a Hawkmoth hovering over a rhododendron. Real publication soon followed. Just turned seventeen, he had a poem accepted by Russia's most august literary journal, *Vestnik Europy*. That same summer, 1916, he had his first book of poems privately printed, and after inheriting his uncle's considerable estate, he began to contemplate seriously an expedition to Central Asia, perhaps with the great explorer and naturalist Grigory Grum-Grzhimaylo.

But when the Bolshevik coup came, he had to flee Petrograd. He could take with him his manuscript albums of verse and the slim volumes of his favorite poets, but he had to leave his butterfly collection behind. In the Crimea with his family, his rhymes nostalgically mourned Vyra and northern Russia even as he exulted in the opportunity to explore the almost Asiatic fauna in the cliffs above Yalta and on the Crimean plateau.

In the spring of 1919 the advance of the Bolshevik army forced the Nabokovs to abandon Yalta, and another butterfly collection, and head for England. In his first term at Cambridge Nabokov compiled a record of his butterfly-collecting in the Crimea that, early in 1920, "at last" – he was all of twenty – earned him his first publication in *The Entomologist*. Like the literary work of his Cambridge years – a Russian essay on Rupert Brooke, a translation of a difficult Romain Rolland novel from French into Russian, and, day after day, his own Russian poems – the butterfly article bore no relation to his nominal course of study.

Installed from 1922 in Berlin, by then the center of the Russian emigration, Nabokov soon evolved from imitative poetry to increasingly original prose. Except during a stint as a farmworker at Solliès-Pont near Toulon in the summer of 1923, he had few chances to collect butterflies: writing and tutoring earned him only enough to keep him in Berlin, not to pay for travel farther afield. But imagination offered a passe-partout. At the end of 1924 his first story about Lepidoptera, "Christmas," drew on his early and very late memories of northern Russia: the collection he had been forced to forsake at Vyra, and the one exception, the Hawkmoth pupa that he had kept in a box for seven years and that hatched in the overheated railway carriage taking him from Petrograd down to Simferopol. Nabokov knew he could not overload and unbalance his fiction with entomological detail, but in "Christmas," the Atlas moth that unexpectedly emerges crowns a very human story. A father, presumably a widower, cannot cope with the death of his only child, a son, the little lepidopterist who yearned to see that moth emerge. Just as the father decides life is no longer worth living, the glorious moth cracks open its cocoon, and its huge wings dilate in a sign of hope, perhaps even of resurrection.

But neither literature nor life offered Nabokov other significant outlets for his love of Lepidoptera until, at the end of 1928, German translation and serial rights for his second novel, *King, Queen, Knave*, paid well enough for him to take his wife, Véra, on their first butterfly expedition together, in the eastern Pyrenees, from February to April 1929 at Le Boulou, then until June at Saurat.

As would often happen in later years, in seeking butterflies Nabokov also found inspiration. While collecting above Le Boulou, the idea for his first masterpiece, *The Defense*, suddenly sprang to mind.[4] Able to write in the late afternoons and evenings, or on wet or dull mornings, he finished the novel by August. Back in Berlin, he checked his new catches against the records of the Entomological Institute at Dahlem in preparation for a report of his finds that he published in *The Entomologist*. In the course of this research he came across a detail that evolved into a key image in his next novella, *The Eye*, and may even, it has been suggested, have provided the first spark for the story.[5]

Certainly the four-month expedition in the south of France seems to have awakened in Nabokov a sense that his science could play a larger part in his art. As soon as he had completed *The Eye*, in the spring of 1930, he started "The Aurelian," a story about the owner of a Berlin butterfly store, who, after selling his prize collection, hopes to escape his frustrating domestic life and fulfill his one dream, of a collecting expedition to Spain and beyond.

By the end of 1932 Nabokov prepared to climb new heights in his art as he moved toward *The Gift*. In this new novel, far longer, denser and wider in scope than anything he had yet written, he would fuse his passions for literature and Lepidoptera, art and nature, country and family, life and art; ten years after the assassination of his father, he felt ready to commemorate him in print. The novel is the story of the development of a young Russian émigré writer in Berlin, Fyodor Godunov, an ardent lepidopterist who as a youth dearly longed to join his father on the last of his entomological expeditions into Central Asia, from which Count Godunov never returned. In real life, Nabokov's father had been an amateur lepidopterist and a celebrated statesman. Fyodor's father, however, has no time for politics but is renowned as a scientist, yet to Elena Nabokov he seemed an exact portrait of her husband. Fyodor tries to write a biography of his father, and in recounting the expeditions gradually includes himself in the party, at last even taking over his father's voice.

For Fyodor, as for Nabokov, these imagined expeditions are both a wish-fulfillment compensation for a dream that history had forever quashed, and a product of painstaking research in the writings of actual Russian naturalists like Grum-Grzhimaylo and Nikolay Przhevalsky. Although he had been producing novels at the rate of one a year, Nabokov began research for *The Gift* early in 1933 and did not complete the book until five years later.

At the beginning of 1937, with much of its final draft still to write, he fled Germany for France. Living in Moulinet, high in the Alpes Maritimes, in the summer of 1938, he caught a butterfly that seemed the long-delayed realization of his thirty-year-old dream: a new butterfly species. Three years later he would be able to describe and assign a species name to his catch – which would eventually prove, as he himself suspected could be the case, to be a hybrid rather than a new species.

In the meantime, like the collecting on the 1929 Pyrenees expedition, the new find further intensified his desire to explore entomology within his art. Sometime in 1939, it seems, Nabokov wrote a long appendix to *The Gift*. Here Fyodor recounts his own early love for Lepidoptera and expounds his father's incisive but cryptic ideas on speciation and evolution, supposedly noted down in outline on the eve of his departure for his final expedition. This appendix, translated from the Russian by Dmitri Nabokov and published here for the first time in any language, is, with the exception of *The Enchanter* – also a fifty-page typescript, also written in 1939 and also left unpublished in the author's lifetime – the longest piece of Nabokov's fiction to appear since his death. Here Nabokov's art, science, and metaphysics meet more unguardedly than anywhere else. Perhaps he did not publish it at the time because his other plans for continuing or expanding *The Gift* were never realized after the outbreak of the Second

World War and his shift from Europe to America and from Russian to English; but perhaps too he had misgivings about mixing hard science with the kind of free speculation he had allowed himself from behind the mask of the Godunovs, father and son.

Nabokov ends his autobiography, *Speak, Memory*, with the image of himself and his wife walking their son through a park in St. Nazaire, the port where they boarded the *Champlain* in May 1940 to escape to the United States. They know that Dmitri is about to glimpse the ship, to feel "the blissful shock, the enchantment and glee . . . [of] discovering ahead the ungenuinely gigantic, the unrealistically real prototype of the various toy vessels he had doddled about in his bath . . . to make out, among the jumbled angles of roofs and walls, a splendid ship's funnel, showing from behind the clothesline as something in a scrambled picture – Find What the Sailor Has Hidden – that the finder cannot unsee once it has been seen" (SM 309–10). Nabokov sets that ship and the America it implies in this key position at the book's close as the solution to a much larger puzzle, his long experience of exile.

America solved another problem, realized another dream, in allowing him a chance to discover new species and to become not merely an informed amateur but a scientist who could make a lasting contribution to lepidopterology. He began to write his autobiography in 1947, just after completing the first draft of his major lepidopterological monograph. No wonder he makes America shine through, ahead of time, here and there in *Speak, Memory*, never more riddlingly or triumphantly than at the end of his chapter on butterflies. In Europe, and in his first two entomological publications, he had been merely a talented collector. After arriving in New York, he turned into a scientist, at the same time as – and partly because – he stopped writing in Russian.

In the fall of 1940, Nabokov approached the American Museum of Natural History (AMNH) and asked to be allowed to check the status of his Moulinet catches (almost everything else in his European collection, the third he had lost to history, he had been forced to leave behind in Paris as German tanks advanced). Although he was unfamiliar with microscopes and dissection, he learned as he went along. Two years earlier, in Paris, he had written his first novel in English, setting much of it in the England he knew from his Cambridge days. Then he had still hoped to find an academic or publishing job in Great Britain, but nothing turned up. Now, in the United States, he did not yet consider himself ready to begin writing fiction for an American audience but felt he had to renounce writing fiction in Russian if he was to develop as an American novelist. Meanwhile he spent the winter of 1940–41 preparing the lectures he would give at Stanford that summer and anywhere else that might hire him as a Russian lecturer. But he happily took time off to work for nothing at the AMNH. This resulted in another short paper in the issue of the *Journal of the New York Entomological Society* that published his description of the Moulinet butterfly, which he now named *Lysandra cormion.*

He supported his family over his first winter in America partly by giving Russian tuition to several women associated with Columbia University. One, Dorothy Leuthold, offered to drive the Nabokovs across the continent to Stanford. Delighted, Nabokov collected all along the way. On June 7, 1941, he discovered a butterfly he recognized as new and would name in Dorothy Leuthold's honor *Neonympha dorothea* (subsequent work has reclassified it as a subspecies, *Cyllopsis pertepida dorothea,* of a species that had not been known to extend from Mexico into the United States). Here, on the south rim of the Grand Canyon, he realized his dream of discovery even more vividly than he had in Moulinet.

After the summer, Nabokov returned east to a one-year engagement as Visiting Lecturer in Comparative Literature at Wellesley College, near Boston. From October 1941 he began to work, unpaid, setting in order the butterfly collections of the Harvard Museum of Comparative Zoology (MCZ). By the middle of 1942 he had written his first major paper, on the genus *Neonympha,* and was appointed to a one-year position as Research Fellow at the MCZ, an appointment that would be extended a year at a time until he left Cambridge for Cornell in 1948.

During these six years he became the MCZ's *de facto* curator of Lepidoptera and one of the authorities on South and especially North American polyommatine butterflies, the "Blues." He wrote four key papers. In the fifteen-page "Nearctic Forms of *Lycaeides Hüb[ner]*," completed over the winter and spring of 1943, he established principles still used in analyzing the genitalia of the Blues. Between the fall of 1943 and the fall of 1944 he completed a thirty-five-page paper on the morphology of the genus *Lycaeides* that drew on the collection he had built up at the MCZ, now the most representative series of American *Lycaeides* anywhere; here for the first time he developed the technique of describing wing-markings by counting scale rows under the microscope. His sixty-page paper on the Blues of Central and South America, "Notes on Neotropical Plebejinae" (written 1944–45), constituted what taxonomists call a "first revision" – a comprehensive reconsideration – of what he called the subfamily Plebejinae and is now known as the tribe Polyommatini. His final and longest paper, the ninety-page monograph on the Nearctic members of the genus *Lycaeides*, took him from 1945 to 1948, since during this time he also wrote most of *Bend Sinister* and added a course in Russian literature to his two Russian language courses at Wellesley. His paper, in the words of another entomologist, "entirely rearranged the classification of this genus."[6]

The long paper on Neotropical Plebejinae stands out from the rest for several reasons. Nabokov often dreamed of chasing tropical butterflies but never had the opportunity. He did, on the other hand, collect zealously in North America. Why then did he choose to write a paper on *South* American Blues? Most likely for the simple reason that he had already mastered North American Blues and wished to compare the northern groups, as he now understood their relationships, with their southern counterparts. A colleague he greatly respected, Paul Grey, felt a similar impulse with Fritillaries, and borrowed all the AMNH's specimens of South American Fritillaries to see how they compared under the microscope with the North American species he knew so well. "He came to a grinding halt, however," notes Kurt Johnson, "when he saw how complex the southern stuff was. Nabokov saw how complex the southern stuff was and chose to do a seminal (generic) nomenclature for it."[7]

Nabokov's work on North American *Lycaeides* transformed the understanding of a particularly difficult genus and has proved extremely durable, but there are many scientists who have undertaken such intrageneric revisions within the well-known Nearctic and Palearctic butterfly fauna. But his work on South American Blues constitutes the first revision of a whole tribe of butterflies. As such, it took him to the frontiers of lepidopterological knowledge and would prove "seminal" even if the seeds took another half-century to sprout, in the recent work of Zsolt Bálint, Kurt Johnson, and their colleagues.

Nabokov worked as a laboratory scientist in the 1940s in a way he would never do again. Why did he feel driven to spend up to fourteen hours a day at the microscope? Chiefly because he could not stop. He found it bliss to be able to make far-reaching discoveries that he had in one sense long dreamed about but in another hardly anticipated, since his earlier work had been so confined to collecting. He was piecing together a whole new world. Those who have worked at the microscope with butterfly genitalia are inclined to say, "Show me a butterfly and I can't tell you what it is, but show me the genitalia and I'll identify anything you have." Nabokov learned to enjoy the deceptiveness and the difficulty of genitalic identification almost as much as the thrill of exploration and the triumph of discovery.

He also had few demands from the job that provided his basic income, teaching Russian language at Wellesley, until the fall term of 1946, when he was able to add his first Russian literature course. And for once his science could advance because his art retreated. Although he began writing *Bend Sinister*, his first American novel, in 1941, he found it agony to renounce his Russian prose. Rather than suffer the throes of writing a full-length work of fiction in a language other than Russian – although he was also writing stories in English and a critical book on Gogol – he could return to entomology, where his working language had always been English and where his sense of mastery, far from being diminished, was now vastly expanded.

At the end of *Bend Sinister* he pictures himself as both the author of the novel we are reading and as a lepidopterist. "Twang," the book ends, "A good night for mothing," as another moth hits the wire screen over his window and he closes down his hero's painful life. In the season the novel was published, its author, now an *Atlantic Monthly* and *New Yorker* regular, was photographed by *Time* and *Vogue* at his desk in Room 402 of the MCZ. That year, 1947, he began to write his autobiography and to build into it an explicit celebration of his life as a lepidopterist and its pattern of a dream fulfilled, if not in Europe then in the America that *Speak, Memory* foreshadows.

Although he had been eager to explore the fauna of as many states as he could from the moment he arrived in the United States, Nabokov had no car and little money during his first eight years in the country and had to depend on the offers of others. His friend Mikhail Karpovich of Harvard invited him to his summer home in Vermont in 1940 and 1942; Dorothy Leuthold drove him across the country in 1941; a whistle-stop lecture tour by train in late 1942 took him through much of the South; James Laughlin, his publisher, let him have low-cost accommodation at his alpine lodge above Sandy, Utah, in 1943, where he caught a number of previously unknown species of moths for his colleague James McDunnough, who in gratitude named one of them *Eupithecia nabokovi*. Not until 1947 did the advance for *Bend Sinister* again provide enough money to allow the family to travel west by train, to Estes Park, Colorado, where they were able to stay until September only because of the *New Yorker*'s enthusiastic response to the first installment of Nabokov's autobiography.

That year things began to change. Late in the fall Nabokov was offered a permanent position at Cornell. Taking it up for the fall term of 1948, he would now have no leisure for serious entomological work, but needed, and could afford, a car. Never a driver himself, he was chauffeured west by Véra every summer between 1949 and 1959 except for the three years (1950, 1955, 1957) when the pressure of work ruled it out. The motels where they stayed would provide material for *Lolita*, which he began writing in 1950, and his success at discovering the first known female of *Lycaeides sublivens* above Telluride, Colorado, in the summer of 1951, led him to commemorate the locale in the celebrated "final" scene in the novel, Humbert's vision from a mountain road of the mining town below, its tranquility broken only by the sounds of children at play.[8]

Even before *Lolita* made him famous, the image of Nabokov as lepidopterist was becoming well known. His autobiography, with its evocation of the onset of his "obsession," was extremely popular in its *New Yorker* instar, and when *Pnin* began to appear there too, in serial form, he had a character point out a score of small blue butterflies – actually the rare northeastern subspecies of *Lycaeides melissa*, identified and named *samuelis* by Nabokov from museum specimens and encountered by him in the wild in upstate New York in June 1950 – and remark, "Pity Vladimir Vladimirovich is not here. He would have told us all about these enchanting insects." Nabokov wryly has Pnin reply, "I have always had the impression that his entomology was merely a pose."[9]

In the wake of his autobiography, *Life* approached Nabokov for a photo-essay on his butterfly hunting. He was asked to review butterfly books for the *New York Times* and to send along what he could to the rather more modest *Lepidopterists' News*. He was even approached by Edmund Wilson's daughter, Rosalind, to write a book on mimicry for Houghton Mifflin, for whom she worked. In all cases he was happy to oblige, although in the first and last the very scale of his enthusiasm frightened the proposals away. But apart from the short pieces in the *Times* and the *News* he published nothing more on butterflies throughout the 1950s. His research interests had shifted to the enormous project of translating and annotating Pushkin's *Eugene Onegin*. Arising out of the needs of his Russian literature students and serving also as a means of establishing his academic credentials, this project, like his butterfly work in the 1940s, drew him deeper and deeper as the sheer excitement of discovery intensified. The whole effort took seven years (1950–57) and produced four five-hundred-page volumes before he was through.

When *Lolita* caught the attention of America in 1958, Nabokov had just finished his work on *Eugene Onegin* and now had the first opportunity in many seasons to spread the thousands of butterflies he had caught in his summer hunts since 1952. As he did so, he hit on an idea for a new story, "The Admirable Anglewing," his first purely entomological tale since "The Aurelian" in 1930 and the last short story he ever worked on. Although abandoned at the pupal stage despite several years of on-and-off work, it is published here for the first time and offers remarkable glimpses of Nabokov at both writing desk and laboratory bench.

Lolita allowed Nabokov to take a leave from Cornell early in 1959, which soon solidified into retirement. His novel's triumph also prompted Doubleday to issue his *Poems*, with a butterfly on the cover and title page in honor of the poem "A Discovery" and of his image as lepidopterist, more widespread than ever now that his afterword to *Lolita* ("Every summer my wife and I go butterfly hunting . . .") appeared in every copy of the novel. He was horrified at the designer's sketches, "as meaningless in the present case as would be a picture of a tuna fish on the jacket of *Moby Dick*" (SL 285). When he traveled west for the summer, reporter Robert H. Boyle was sent by Time-Life to cover Nabokov the lepidopterist for *Sports Illustrated*. His write-up provides the best minute-by-minute account we have of Nabokov the man and certainly of Nabokov the collector.

In the fall of 1959, Nabokov left with his wife for what they thought would be a short visit to Europe, primarily to be near their son, Dmitri, who was training as an opera singer in Milan. As it happened, apart from seven unexpected months in Hollywood in 1960 to write the *Lolita* screenplay and, of course, to resample Californian butterflies while there, they would never again live in the United States. After two decades away, Nabokov found Europe unappealing and overrun with cars, but once he had his first successful butterfly hunting there (he spent four hours in April 1961, chasing *Callophrys avis* Chapman in the south of France on behalf of the AMNH), and especially once he had his first taste of collecting in the High Alps in 1962, he settled comfortably back into a part of the world that he had never felt to be a proper home during the émigré years, when he could so rarely afford to pursue his passion.

In early 1948, just as he was putting the last touches to his longest lepidopterological monograph, Nabokov had suggested to Cyril dos Passos and Paul Grey that the three of them write a guide to the butterflies of North America. With his teaching at Cornell about to start and the *Onegin* project it spawned not far off, Nabokov would in fact have almost no time to pursue Lepidoptera research for the next fifteen years, let alone something on this scale. But in the early 1960s, after finishing *Pale Fire*, Nabokov found that his next novel – still tentatively entitled *The Texture of Time* and a long way from the *Ada* it would become – posed problems he could not yet solve. With no financial worries, no teaching duties, and for once no pressure from his muse, he was free to think of other projects.

His English publisher, George Weidenfeld, whose firm had been virtually *made* by the staggering success of *Lolita*, agreed at the end of 1962 to publish his complete catalogue of the *Butterflies of Europe*, covering all species and significant subspecies. From late 1963 through late 1964, Nabokov worked hard on what would have been his lepidopterological magnum opus. Like *Eugene Onegin*, it continued to expand as he worked, to the point where Weidenfeld became daunted by its size and could not guarantee publication even if it became a multinational, multilingual venture. Unable to settle to a new novel while the uncertainty persisted, Nabokov regretfully called off the project late in 1965. Had he been able to complete it, it would have been a work of natural history without parallel in the way it fused art and science through both its layout and its text. Left unfinished, and now obsolete, it can never be published in the form Nabokov envisaged, but his plans and the samples of the text included here hint at its magic.

As the *Butterflies of Europe* stepped back, *Ada* could advance. A first flash of inspiration in December 1965, apparently unconnected to the *Texture of Time* project, and another in February 1966, which established the connection, soon had Nabokov writing at a rapid rate. Occupying a place within his English works like that of *The Gift* within his Russian oeuvre, *Ada* was long in gestation, large in scale, and voracious in its curiosity, except that this time, everything was lighter, more playful, more disruptive. In *The Gift* Nabokov represented his sense of dislocation between Russia and Berlin almost literally, with meticulous realism; in *Ada* the dislocation of two worlds, Europe and America, becomes the disjunction between Terra and Antiterra, marked by disconcertingly or delightfully detailed distortions of our everyday world. As if he had reflected in the crazy mirror of the imagination his short-lived hopes of co-authoring a *Butterflies of North America* and his recent plans for the *Butterflies of Europe*, Nabokov places Ada on an Old World estate somewhere in New England, then makes her a precocious naturalist, an ardent lepidopterist, whose world of

Antiterra he stocks with invented but possible species belonging to real genera.

By the mid-1960s, Nabokov had begun to contemplate another project, *Butterflies in Art*. Ever since 1942, when Florence Read, the president of Spelman College in Atlanta, had given him a reproduction of a Theban wall fresco in honor of his love of butterflies, he had considered one day using the representation of butterflies in art to test whether evolutionary changes had been recorded within the span of human history. In his travels around Italy and its museums in the early 1960s, the idea had returned, and in 1965 he began a more systematic search. Although he deeply cherished as an ideal the fusing of art and science, this project too failed to materialize, even if he never quite abandoned it. But it permeated *Ada*, where Nabokov straddles the boundaries of art and life, art and nature, by making Ada a flower-painter and Lucette a student of art history who stumbles on some of her own creator's discoveries about butterflies in art.

In the 1970s, now in his seventies, Nabokov still collected butterflies every summer, still hoped to complete his *Butterflies in Art*, still dreamed of writing a *Speak on, Memory* or a *Speak, America* that would devote a chapter to his researches at the MCZ. Instead of continuing his autobiography, however, he ended his career with a savagely inverted fictional autobiography, *Look at the Harlequins!*, whose hero, a novelist called Vadim Vadimych, is a reduced shadow of himself:

> I spent what remained of the summer exploring the incredibly lyrical Rocky Mountain states, getting drunk on whiffs of Oriental Russia in the sagebrush zone and on the Northern Russian fragrances so faithfully reproduced above timberline by certain small bogs along trickles of sky between the snowbank and the orchid. And yet – was that all? What form of mysterious pursuit caused me to get my feet wet like a child, to pant up a talus, to stare every dandelion in the face, to start at every colored mote passing just beyond my field of vision? What was the dream sensation of having come empty-handed – without what? A gun? A wand?
> [LATH 155–56]

In 1975, at seventy-six, he was still working assiduously, starting at six o'clock every morning, to revamp the French translation of *Ada*, still chasing butterflies in the Alps. That summer, sapped of strength by the rush to transpose *Ada*, he had a serious fall down a steep slope at Davos. His butterfly net slipped still further, lodging on the branch of a fir, as he said, "like Ovid's lyre" (SL 552).

That image seems a perfect emblem of the link between literature and Lepidoptera that lasted to the end. For after this fall, Nabokov was never the same. He spent much of the next two years in hospital, in the summer of 1976 reading with delight, when his delirium lifted, the new Doubleday *Butterflies of North America*, and mentally rereading, as it were, the still unwritten text of his own next novel, *The Original of Laura*. But a year later, as another summer approached and he sank toward death, *Laura* remained largely unwritten, and in his last recorded words, he told his son tearfully that he knew "a certain butterfly was already on the wing; and his eyes told me he no longer hoped that he would live to pursue it again."

How fitting, then, that Dmitri Nabokov should now compensate for the twin plans his father's death cut short by translating from Russian into English his father's most intense amalgam of literature and Lepidoptera, his afterword to *The Gift*, itself cut short by his shift from Russian to English and from Europe to America at the midpoint of his life.

I have retold Nabokov's life as a dance in which science suavely partners art, but it would be perfectly possible to read a thousand pages of his best fiction – *The Defense, Invitation to a Beheading, The Real Life of Sebastian Knight, Lolita* less its afterword, *Pale Fire*, and *Transparent Things* – and another five hundred pages of his short stories and not even realize he was a lepidopterist. What, then, can his passion for butterflies explain in his art? How did it reflect or affect his mind, his thinking, his writing?

From as far back as we can see, Nabokov had a love of both detail and design, of precise, unpredictable particulars and intricate, often concealed patterns. Aware of how little most people know about nature, of how much effort it took to master all he himself knew about the butterflies of the world, and of how much more there always was to discover even about the Blues he specialized in, he disliked the impulse to impose easy meaning – a generalization, an allegorization, a handy quick-stick label – on a complex and recalcitrant reality. "As an artist and a scholar," he once proclaimed, "I prefer the specific detail to the generalization,[10] images to ideas, obscure facts to clear symbols, and the discovered wild fruit to the synthetic jam" (SO 7).

But if he rejected anything that quashed the live independence of things, he nevertheless, like any scientist, delighted in the patterns that ordered their relationship. Pattern has its purely esthetic side, of course, and Nabokov is celebrated for his mastery of phonic and fictive design. But understanding pattern also allows us some degree of control over the unruliness of life, and in Nabokov that urge to control was powerfully developed: witness his refusal to submit to interviews unless he could have the questions in advance, write out his answers, and check the final text; or his insistence that his characters were his "galley slaves"; or his famous comparison of the relationship between author and reader to that between chess problemist and problem solver; or his command of form at all levels, from phrase to finished fiction. Not for him the world as a big, booming, buzzing confusion. The world is there to be teased out by the inquiring mind, as in his fiction it is there to be shaped by the imaginative one.

Nabokov nevertheless had a strong sense of the limits of human knowledge: no matter how much we can find out, there is always more behind things – beyond our human sense of space and time, beyond the limits of personality and mortality, beyond our ignorance of ultimate origins and ends – that consciousness as we know it seems unable to penetrate. He had a lifelong urge to probe "the beyond," which Véra Nabokov has gone so far as to call – a slight overstatement in my judgment – "the main theme" of his work.[11]

This impulse may have derived from his mother's unconventional religious sense, even before he could be aware of the the antipositivism in the air in the Europe, and especially in the Russia, of his childhood (Bergson, Blok, Bely). But his passion for butterflies attests to and surely helped develop his respect for *this* world, no matter how strong his curiosity about what might lie beyond it. As he wrote rather gnomically in his last novel, "*this* was the simple solution, that the brook and the boughs and the beauty of the Beyond all began with the initial of Being" (LATH 16).

His love of Lepidoptera drew upon and further sharpened his love of the particular and the habits of detailed observation that gave him such fictional command over the physical world – biologically (birds, flowers, trees), geographically (localities, landscapes, ecologies), socially (manorial Russia, boardinghouse Berlin, motel America), and bodily (gesture, anatomy, sensation). He thought that only the ridiculously unobservant could be pessimists in a world as full of surprising specificity as ours, and he arranged his own art accordingly.

Still deeper than the pleasures of immediate observation were the delights of discovery. As a child exploring on his own his parents' butterfly books, he preferred the small type to the main text, the obscure to the obvious, the thrill of finding for himself what was not common knowledge. That impulse became a positive addiction as he peered into the microscope in Harvard's laboratories in the 1940s or prowled the stacks of its libraries while compiling his *Onegin* commentary in the 1950s. His fiction had always invited readers to discover things for themselves, but from the time he began *Bend Sinister* in 1941, he encouraged his readers more and more to become researchers in increasingly intricate labyrinths of internal and external references and relationships.

Nabokov's science gave him a sense of the endless elusiveness of reality that should not be confused with modern (or "postmodern") epistemological nihilism. Dissecting and deciphering the genitalic structure of lycaenids, or counting scale rows on their wings, he realized that the further we inquire, the more we can discover, yet the more we find that we do not know, not because truth is an illusion or a matter of mere convention but because the world is infinitely detailed, complex, and deceptive, "an infinite succession of steps, levels of perception, false bottoms" (SO 11).

He found this not frustrating but challenging, not niggardly of nature, in hoarding its secrets, but fantastically generous, in burying such an endless series of treasures for the human mind to unearth. This sense of design deeply embedded in nature's detail, of a playful deceptiveness behind things, of some kind of conscious cosmic hide-and-seek, is fundamental to Nabokov, though hardly unique to him. Almost three thousand years ago the Bible declared, "It is the glory of God to hide a thing, but the glory of kings to search things out" (Proverbs 5:2); at the dawn of modern science,

Francis Bacon liked to repeat and refashion the phrase; and in *Bend Sinister* Nabokov playfully half reveals and half conceals both sources for us to rediscover as he cites, "not for the first time," "the glory of God is to hide a thing, and the glory of man is to find it" (BS 106).

Throughout his later fiction Nabokov shapes his own worlds to match the munificence he senses behind our world's complexity. But although this feeling arose in good measure out of his science, he could not express it there. Only in mimicry did he suspect that the design behind things was apparent enough and explicit enough to be treated as science. No wonder, as he writes in his autobiography, "The mysteries of mimicry had a special attraction for me" (124), no wonder he has Konstantin Godunov-Cherdyntsev in *The Gift* expound to his son "about the incredible artistic wit of mimetic disguise, which was not explainable by the struggle for existence . . . and seemed to have been invented by some waggish artist precisely for the intelligent eyes of man" (122). Although he reported in the fall of 1941 that he was "writing a rather ambitious work on mimetic phenomena," and although he leaped at the chance to write a whole book on the subject a decade later, the first does not survive and the second was never written. It seems likely that, had he begun serious work on mimicry, he would have found sufficient evidence of purely physical explanations to be forced to abandon his dearly held metaphysical speculations.

Just as Nabokov suspected that there was some conscious design behind the world, so he also thought it likely that there was some transformation of human consciousness beyond death. Insect metamorphosis hardly provided a model, yet it seems strikingly apt that the journal in which his lepidopterological writings appeared most frequently, *Psyche*, was named after the Greek for "butterfly, moth, soul." Nabokov adverted often to the immemorial association between overcoming gravity and transcending death, and the change of form from a caterpillar's earthbound beginnings to the winged freedom and beauty of its final transformation at least offered an appealing image of the soul's expansion beyond death. He could use it half-playfully ("we are the caterpillars of angels," he wrote in a 1923 poem). He could also rudely reject it as a symbol: when a Russian Orthodox archbishop suggested that his interest in butterflies might be linked with the highest state of the soul, he retorted that a butterfly is not at all a half-angelic being and "will settle even on corpses." But in a series of stories, although increasingly more obliquely – in "Christmas," "The Aurelian," *Invitation to a Beheading, The Gift*,[12] and *Pale Fire*[13] – Nabokov repeatedly linked butterflies with the transcending of death.

Although the possibility of a metamorphosis beyond death had everything to do with Nabokov's art, it bore little relation to his science. What was – and is – his position as a scientist?

Nabokov had a reputation for arrogance. In literature he was supremely sure of himself and greatly enjoyed the shock value of his strong opinions about other writers. But as a lepidopterist he was different, if hardly diffident.

As a boy, he mastered butterflies and moths very early and developed a complementary interest in beetles, the most diverse animal order of all, but at Cambridge he had only brief exposure to zoology and none at all to entomology, and he remained little more than an ardent and ambitious collector, an encyclopedic amateur, until his arrival in the United States. There he had much to learn even from veteran collectors like Don Eff and Don Stallings, from the most efficient way of killing his catch (pinching the thorax immediately, rather than putting the butterfly in a carbona-soaked jar) to the most efficient way of finding it.

In the laboratory he had everything to learn, but he learned it quickly. He worked happily with other lepidopterists, especially William Comstock and Cyril dos Passos, and was eager to share information and propose collaboration. If in his work on *Eugene Onegin* he insisted on his own findings and poured scorn on his rivals, in his entomology, although still frank in disagreement, he could be generous in praise, even of those who had completed projects he would dearly have liked to undertake himself (see his reviews of Klots [1951] and Higgins and Riley [1970], and his acclaim, in the year before his death, for Doubleday's *Butterflies of North America*, illustrated and edited by William Howe).[14]

Nabokov's laboratory work focused almost entirely on the American representatives of one tribe, the Polyommatini, or Blues (in his day, classified as the subfamily Plebejinae) of the Lycaenidae, the largest of butterfly families, which includes Coppers and Hairstreaks as well as Blues. Although his output as a lepidopterist is small compared with that of scientists who spend a lifetime in the laboratory and the field, it is of lasting importance and value within its domain.

His methods were advanced for his time: more than most, he insisted on dissection rather than on superficial characteristics, and in a group as notoriously difficult as the Polyommatini, this stance was particularly well justified. His own findings at the microscope confirmed for him the modern recognition that the genitalia "differed in shape from species to species" and so "offered tremendous utility for taxonomy."[15] Writing his "Second Addendum to *The Gift*" in 1938, before he had worked in a laboratory himself, he had seemed to share Count Godunov-Cherdyntsev's dismissal of those the Count

> subtly berated . . . [as] "genitalists": it was just the time when it became fashionable to accept as an unerring and adequate sign of species differentiation distinctions in the chitinoid structure of the male organ, which represented, as it were, the "skeleton" of a species, a kind of "vertebra." "How simply various discussions would be resolved," [the Count] wrote, "if those who concentrated on splitting similar species according to this one criterion, whose absolute stability has, moreover, never been proven, turned their attention, in the first place, to the entire radiation of doubtful forms in their overall Palearctic aspect instead of concentrating on a handful of long-suffering French *départements* . . ."[16]

Five years later, working with as wide a range of samples as he could obtain, and at an entirely new level of detail, Nabokov himself had become one of the most advanced of "genitalists." Where others tended to consider "only the general features of the clasping parts of the male organ," he emphasized "the multiple differences in all the parts of the genital anatomy, in females as well as males. And by being extremely specific about the shapes of the various structures along the contour of the male clasper, as well as many other organs, Nabokov introduced many new structures into the study of Blues."[17] He named new micro-organs, developed new techniques to analyze the genitalia and offered new interpretations of the diagnostic value of their structure. He was "among the first researchers to picture more than a single genital illustration for each species," his "multiple illustrations buttressing his hypotheses concerning ranges of variation in one species and the hiatuses, or breaks, in those characters that distinguished different species."[18]

Since he also analyzed wing markings more minutely than anybody else had done in any group of butterflies, even counting the numbers of scale rows, "it was clear that no one else was applying such detailed analysis to Blue butterflies in the 1940s."[19] Although he was working in and just after the Second World War and had fewer specimens, less advanced equipment and techniques, and fewer diagnostic characters than would be available to modern researchers, he had a superb eye for relationships, and his classifications have stood the test of time.

His work in clarifying Nearctic (North American) Polyommatini was immediately appreciated by lepidopterists of the caliber of Don Stallings ("We name this distinctive race after V. Nabokov who is contributing so much to our American literature on Lepidoptera"),[20] Alexander Klots ("The recent work of Nabokov has entirely rearranged the classification of this genus"),[21] Cyril dos Passos ("I have followed . . . Prof. VLADIMIR NABOKOV in the PLEBEJINAE to the extent that he has revised the genera and species"),[22] and John Downey.

As a student driving a truck for a summer job in Utah in 1943, Downey, already a keen lepidopterist, chanced to meet Nabokov out with his net and was taken by him to the haunt of the curious subspecies *L. melissa annetta*. He later stressed that Nabokov "strongly influenced me to take up the study of the 'blues' and their relatives."[23] By the late 1960s, Downey had become the authority on the Blues, and found Nabokov's research indispensable: "Nabokov had put the study of North American Blues on a strong taxonomic footing, and the work he had produced had created a context for researching the evolution of this group in the complex environs characterizing the Rocky Mountains and Great Basin regions."[24] Downey's former graduate student Kurt Johnson recalls Downey in 1968 discussing the section on the Blues he was writing for Howe's *Butterflies of*

North America (which Nabokov would read and reread with such pleasure in his hospital bed, in the interstices between delirium, during his last full summer). They were considering the problem of whether *Everes comyntas* (the Eastern Tailed Blue) and *Everes amyntula* (the Western Tailed Blue) were separate species. Johnson suggested writing to Harry Clench, the associate curator of entomology at the Carnegie Museum of Natural History in Pittsburgh. Clench, who by this time had become a prominent Hairstreak authority and a specialist in the Blues, had been Nabokov's benchmate at the MCZ as a student in the early 1940s, and was influenced by his colleague's example in choosing his areas of specialization.[25] Downey snapped: "Clench doesn't know. If anybody knows, Nabokov would know!" Although Clench named a large number of new species, and as Johnson later judged, had come to fancy himself the authority on the Blues, he thought that little more needed to be done and therefore did not dissect much. Nabokov, by contrast, in Johnson's estimate, was a meticulous morphologist whose detailed work on wing patterns and genitalic structure showed a rigor and a range Clench lacked, despite being a professional with graduate training in zoology.[26]

Although Nabokov's North American work was drawn on immediately, there was little further research for many years on Neotropical (Central and South American) Polyommatini. The recent collaborative studies of Kurt Johnson of the AMNH and Zsolt Bálint of the Hungarian Museum of Natural History amply testify to the high regard in which Nabokov's single major paper on Neotropical Polyommatini is held. In the 1940s Nabokov was often thought to be a generic "splitter"—or as Johnson explains from the standpoint of the present: "His good eye had brought him to a level of taxonomic sophistication beyond that of many of his contemporaries, but in a sense it also made it easier for his work to be overlooked or misunderstood by those who weren't disposed to look quite as deeply."[27] He wrote his 1945 paper only a couple of years after two well-established AMNH lepidopterists, William Comstock and E. Irving Huntington, published *Lycaenidae of the Antilles*. "Unlike Nabokov two years later, Comstock and Huntington brought nothing new to the general taxonomy for the region; in the case of the Neotropical Blues, they deviated little from Draudt's rudimentary arrangement from 1921," yet because of their established names, their work was considered authoritative for decades to come.[28] As late as 1975 the distinguished lepidopterist Norman Riley, longtime editor of *The Entomologist* and Keeper of the Department of Entomology at the British Museum, could follow the lead of Comstock and Huntington and sink the genus *Cyclargus*, which Nabokov had proposed in 1945, back into *Hemiargus*, because to his expert eye, wing patterns in both groups looked too much the same; others in turn followed Riley. But scientists have recently reinstated Nabokov's *Cyclargus* after cladistic analysis of many anatomical features revealed that *Cyclargus* and *Hemiargus* are not even immediate sister genera, despite their apparent resemblance.[29] The many new species and specimens Johnson and Bálint have recorded in Latin America, especially in the Andes, confirm all Nabokov's generic divisions (although not all his names) and show that far from its being the case that he was an excessive splitter, there are, in fact, more lycaenid genera and many more species than even he could have suspected.

Bálint and Johnson announce that they "follow the methods of NABOKOV (1945) (the first reviser of the Neotropical polyommatines), who underlined the taxonomic importance of the genitalic armatures in lycaenid systematics,"[30] and Bálint declares his paper "the cornerstone of modern knowledge concerning polyommatine butterflies occurring in Latin America."[31] In honor of Nabokov's work as first reviser, Bálint and Johnson have named many new species after people, places, and things in his life and art, lately in consultation with leading Nabokov scholars (for example, *Itylos luzhin, Pseudolucia vera, Nabokovia ada, Paralycaeides shade, Madeleinea vokoban, Polytheclus cincinnatus, Leptotes krug*), and plan to dedicate their forthcoming volume on the Blues in the *Atlas of Tropical Lepidoptera* to his memory. So much for the idea that Nabokov was a mere dilettante and no serious scientist.

To write his papers on the Polyommatini Nabokov needed to clarify his sense of species, a seemingly natural notion – until nature confronts one with the complexities of the particular case. His agonized tussles with the problems of identity and relationship involved in speciation produced some of his most fascinating scientific writing, apparently prepared for a talk before the Cambridge Entomological Club and hitherto unpublished. Attacking the biological species concept then being advanced by the ornithologist Ernst Mayr, also of the MCZ, he not only rejects it as more suitable for birds than for butterflies and rightly insists on the logical priority of distinguishing on morphological grounds exactly *which* population one is counting, but goes so far as to suggest that the sense of specific distinction in Lycaenidae might need to be different from that of even other closely related families. Elsewhere, after suggesting possible courses of divergence within the genus *Lycaeides*, he comments: "This scheme of course is not a phylogenetic tree but merely its shadow on a plane surface, since a sequence in time is not really deducible from a synchronous series."[32] He could not foresee the theoretical advances leading to modern phylogenetic systematics, or the multiplication of characteristics of Lepidoptera anatomy that researchers would learn to consider, or the power of computer-assisted cladistic analyses that could factor in all these diagnostic variables and make it possible to construct species lines reflecting or suggesting evolutionary descent, but he shows himself to be acutely aware of the issues and brilliantly up to the task of articulating them.[33]

With only something like two full working years at the microscope, Nabokov had become a major lepidopterist, and a first-rate one. "He was *the* authority on Blues," attests Johnson.[34]

If scientists are measured in part by their ability to inspire new generations of workers in their field, Nabokov's achievement again seems remarkable. Never a professor of entomology, but only a research fellow in Lepidoptera, and then only from 1942 to 1948 – a position without power, renewed on a year-by-year basis, and competing for his time with his fiction, verse, and criticism and Russian language and literature classes – he nevertheless influenced Downey and Clench, two of the leading figures in the next generation of specialists in the Blues, and through Downey, Johnson, a leading figure in the generation after that.

Normally experts are more captious and begrudging of one another than outsiders. It seems telling that the sheer quality of Nabokov's lepidopterology has been appreciated most by those working closest to his particular field. In tribute to his work, colleagues at other American museums began to name butterflies after him in the late 1940s, soon after his first major papers appeared, and he would have been thrilled by the recent spate of species names that celebrates his contribution to both literature and Lepidoptera.

He seems in fact to have had a curiously intense desire for – and an exaggerated sense of – the fame accruing to those whose names become part of the taxonomic record. From childhood he had dreamed of discovering a new species, and when he thought he had, with his Moulinet catch,[35] he exulted in print:

> I found it and I named it, being versed
> in taxonomic Latin; thus became
> godfather to an insect and its first
> describer – and I want no other fame.
>
> Wide open on its pin (though fast asleep).
> and safe from creeping relatives and rust,
> in the secluded stronghold where we keep
> type specimens it will transcend its dust.
>
> Dark pictures, thrones, the stones that pilgrims kiss,
> poems that take a thousand years to die
> but ape the immortality of this
> red label on a little butterfly.[36]

He was never anxious about literary fame because he knew by the age of thirty that he had done enough to assure it, but he prized immortality as a lepidopterist precisely because it seemed so unattainable. Yet the mere naming of a single taxon hardly constitutes fame when there are, so far, about a million-and-a-half known biological species, and current estimates suggest there may be ten – perhaps even fifty – times as many names still to bestow.[37]

Although in his adult years Nabokov's collecting often led to or arose naturally from his papers, and was always guided by an instinct for the scientifically revealing, it is Nabokov's major papers of the 1940s, more than any of his catches, that will ensure his niche in entomological history. But if within the science of Lepidoptera his collecting was of secondary importance, it was one of his most intense and lasting pleasures throughout his years in Russia, in a few short seasons in his émigré years, and again throughout his American and final European years. In his first seasons in America, he searched for butterflies and moths wherever he could. From the late 1940s, with a car of his own, he repeatedly chose the Rockies, partly because altitude increases the variety of butterfly species one is likely to encounter and partly because the alpine vegetation reminded him of old Russia. He particularly sought out localities likely to yield lycaenids, especially those he had described from museum specimens but not caught for himself, those for which only one sex had so far been found, or those that might reveal an intergrade between one subspecies and the next.

Since he had lost three collections in Europe and now moved from house to house in America, he had no desire to keep his new collections himself. He gave them to the institutions with which he was associated, first the AMNH, then the MCZ, and finally Cornell. In Europe he continued to confine himself to collecting in montane areas, regularly in Switzerland, often in Italy (including Sicily), occasionally in France (including Corsica), once in Portugal. He would spend long stretches at a single mountain resort, a summer holiday for his wife and a writing retreat and a hunting ground for himself. Although he would catch anything uncommon, he still sought out lycaenids above all, managing, for instance, to net ninety percent of Swiss lycaenids from only five (the most alpine) of the twenty-two cantons. Knowing exactly what he wanted, he would collect long series only in genera where species were difficult to distinguish except in the laboratory. He bequeathed his European collection to the Musée Cantonal de Zoologie in Lausanne.

Exhibitions of his butterfly collections have been held in Milan and Lausanne as well as at Harvard and Cornell. Had Nabokov not been famous as a novelist, these commemorations would never have taken place. But had he not become a writer, he repeatedly said – had, for instance, he not been able to escape from Soviet Russia – he would have spent his life as a lepidopterist. As it was, other professionals have rated as extraordinary his achievement in the small time he was working professionally in the field.

As a lepidopterist he hoped to do much that he never achieved: neither the expedition to Central Asia he envisaged in his teens nor, fifty years later, the forays to Peru, Iran, or Israel "before I pupate"; neither the *Butterflies of North America* nor the book on mimicry that he contemplated in the United States; neither the *Butterflies of Europe* nor the *Butterflies in Art* that he began in Europe came to fruition. But in his seventies he replied to an interviewer's question, "My life thus far has surpassed splendidly the ambitions of my boyhood and youth. . . . At the age of twelve my fondest dream was a visit to the Karakorum range in search of butterflies. Twenty-five years later I successfully sent myself, in the part of my hero's father (see my novel *The Gift*) to explore, net in hand, the mountains of Central Asia. At fifteen I visualized myself as a world-famous author of seventy with a mane of wavy white hair. Today I am practically bald" (SO 177–78). Literature may have prevented him from realizing some of his dreams as a lepidopterist, but it also provided a way of realizing others far more fully than he could have imagined as a child.

Why this additional commemoration of literature's lepidopterist? Why *Nabokov's Butterflies*?

In the first place, a great deal of what follows either has not been previously published or, if published, has not been easily accessible.

Nabokov's technical articles, known to entomologists for half a century and still playing their part in lycaenid systematics, are here made available to the general reader for the first time, the shorter ones *in toto*, the longer ones generously and thoughtfully excerpted, by distinguished lepidopterist and nature writer Robert Michael Pyle, in such a way as to leave both the structure of their argument and the texture of their detail fully visible. As readers will soon discover, these articles have little in common with, for instance, the entomological memoirs of Jean-Henri Fabre, which so delighted writers from Maurice Maeterlinck to Marianne Moore, but which

Nabokov's Fyodor dismisses as "popular works, full of chitchat, inaccurate observations and downright mistakes" (GIFT 120).

It is one thing to know of Nabokov the lepidopterist from his superbly poetic evocation of his passion in *Speak, Memory*. It is another thing entirely to see the results of his research, so rigorous and painstaking, vivid proof of a whole side of his life and a whole sphere of knowledge remote from most of us but home to him. He knows our world, he can even describe parts of it better than those who have lived there all their lives; but most of us exploring this part of *his* world will find it another planet, where we can never directly breathe its air or palpate its soil.

Even the lepidopterists who know Nabokov's articles of the 1940s have been unaware of the prodigious amount of work he expended on the much larger scale of his *Butterflies of Europe*. Unlike the laboratory studies, this project describes a world where most of us can feel like fellow explorers, though we may not know the species involved. The outlines and samples offered in this collection suggest the shape and color of the book Nabokov planned, which, because of the acuteness of his eye and the astonishing precision of his memory, so evident in the text, would have made it unlike any other species guide ever written. Among the other unpublished material, the appendix to *The Gift*, the longest single item of all, shows him blending scientific detail and speculative fancy in a way he would never allow himself again.

Apart from all this new material, *Nabokov's Butterflies* also offers old passages that reveal new colors in this unfamiliar environment. The entire selection of Nabokov's work, published and unpublished, scientific and literary, polished and provisional, can be read as a singular case study in specialization and diversity, in development and metamorphosis.

The long chronological sequence, from a letter written by Nabokov's father two years after the boy discovered butterflies to a memoir by Dmitri Nabokov two years after his father's death, lets us track the development of the writer's art, the evolution of the naturalist's science, and the interplay between the two.

The shifts of scale, from microscopic samples to entire organisms, from a line or two to fifty pages of continuous text, also serve their purpose. Removed from their old haunts, the scores of short excerpts refocus the part and refresh the whole. Whenever a butterfly or moth plucked from its natural habitat in a particular novel demands attention, identification, and explanation, the anthologist's net suddenly becomes the reader's lens.

Not only in date and scope, but also in genre: no other volume of Nabokov's writing encompasses such variety, from novels, stories, poems, a screenplay, autobiography, criticism, lectures and articles to annotations, reviews, interviews, letters, drafts, notes, diaries, drawings. The very restrictedness of subject matter throws into striking relief the range of Nabokov's styles, strategies, contexts, and mental modes: troubled reflections, painstaking descriptions, lovingly fanciful sketches, comradely exchanges; the surreally false flatness of the world of *Invitation to a Beheading*, the majestic exoticism of *The Gift*, the lyric evocativeness of *Speak, Memory*, the haunting charms of *Pale Fire*, the dizzy density of *Ada*. And when we remember that outside his scientific work Nabokov limits severely what he allows himself to write about butterflies, it seems staggering that he can ring so many changes on this one theme. Exactly what he might have said about "that other V.N., Visible Nature."[38]

Between Climb and Cloud

Nabokov among the Lepidopterists

ROBERT MICHAEL PYLE

WHAT I REMEMBER MOST about that damp Swiss morning is the vibrancy of new beech leaves. Not long out of their buds, they were the essence of fragility, the very definition of spring green. Beneath the beeches, by the steep path down to the lake, early purple orchids were just now at their peak. Together with last year's leaf-copper, the soft leaflets, and fresh mud, they painted the path in colors richer than the wet April day gave any reason to expect. When the fog thinned and the rain came more heavily, the beeches and orchids glowed in the dull damp light. I brachiated downhill like some anxious ape, swinging from beech to smooth wet gray beech. I was on my way to see Nabokov.

Or, at least, to see where he lived. I'd been attending a conservation meeting at Morges, west of Lausanne on Lake Geneva. The meeting finished, I had a couple of days before I was due back in England, where I lived at the time. I had recently read *Speak, Memory* and I was aware that its author, Vladimir Nabokov, lived up-lake at Montreux. I didn't know much of Nabokov's literary writings at the time (having read, besides the memoir, only *Lolita*), but I had long been aware of his Lepidoptera work. Besides, I had recently concluded postgraduate studies with Charles L. Remington at Yale University, who had known Nabokov in earlier years and spoke of him often. Nabokov was the author, or namer, of the Karner Blue. Some of us working to conserve this endangered butterfly had approached Nabokov for his personal support, and he gave it. I wanted to thank him directly if possible. With the brash confidence of one still in his twenties, I thought perhaps if I just showed up I might meet him. Maybe if I invoke the name of Remington, I thought, I can gain entry long enough to say hello and pay my respects.

All I knew of Montreux was the jazz festival and Chillon Castle, the latter an image drawn from my grandmother and great-aunt's slides taken during a trip many years before. (Reading *Speak, Memory* I had found the same image on a postcard lodged on the fussy writing desk of Nabokov's governess, Mademoiselle O.) I knew the town was supposed to be a pricey place, and the name of Nabokov's residence – the Montreux Palace Hotel – was somewhat intimidating. When my train arrived, my impression was confirmed: the hotel was a baroque fortress. It was early evening and I thought of walking there right away, but I didn't want to arrive at dinnertime. Hungry myself and concerned about lodgings, I found a small pizza and a glass of wine for seven francs and, by phone, located a room for eighteen francs in a small hotel up on the mountainside at Caux. Reaching it entailed taking the Montreux Oberland Bernois, a funicular train. The ticket and a footpath map took another seven francs, leaving me with twelve undedicated francs in my wallet.

The last rail car of the evening was about to depart, so I jumped aboard and scaled the steep mountainside on the same cog railway that Dick Diver had fatefully taken in *Tender Is the Night*, a book Nabokov thought "magnificent." Just as F. Scott Fitzgerald had described, "After it cleared the low roofs, the skies of Vaud, Valais, Swiss Savoy, and Geneva spread around the passengers in cyclorama," only now those skies were slaty dark. I looked out the pine-framed windows and watched the lights of Montreux recede. The other passengers disembarked at Glion and I arrived at my aerie, the station hotel at Caux, by myself. Dr. Diver had been bound for a Caux hotel too, a rather fancier one, where he found the orchestra playing "Poor Butterfly." My simple lodging had no orchestra, but it did have a lake view and fresh, cold air from the forest all around. Warm beneath a huge duvet, I resolved to approach the Palace on the morrow. At worst I would be turned away; at best, I might meet the man who described and helped to save the Karner Blue.

The morning view took in a forested ravine and a spruce-clad, snow-dotted mountain. Alpine meadows, more brown than green, stretched away uphill. I imagined the butterflies summer would bring: Parnassians, Alpines, Fritillaries; no doubt Nabokov knew them well. Nothing was visible below through the thickset fog, but I imagined him down there, at his breakfast. Perhaps if we did meet, he would tell me where to seek the rarer *Erebia* on some future visit. In spite of the deadpan rain, I set out with high hopes.

Maybe my mistake was deciding to hike back down that day instead of taking the railway. The descent was exhilarating, through the beeches and orchids, and my spirits rose for the potential encounter. But then the rain picked up, and it fell hard and solid all the way down. When I struck the lakeshore, wet through, I found myself at the castle, and I knew I mustn't go home and tell Aunt Helen I had skipped it. I couldn't afford the stiff admission, nor had I the time for a tour, so I walked around the grounds of the romantic pile plunked onto the shores of Lake Geneva, backed by glaciated alps and high white valleys. The heavy round turret of Chillon seemed to hold down the wave-lapped stones at its base. My *petit déjeuner* at the hotel had been mighty *petit*, so I bought a small snack and ate it by the chateau portcullis, wondering if the Nabokovs' Palace would prove as impenetrable as Château de Chillon.

But I was stalling. I walked the Quai, the lakeshore promenade, spotted my first Pied Flycatcher, and continued past the hotel and on to the station. Checking the schedule, I found that a train was about to leave for Geneva. I had no place to stay another night, and if I went to Geneva right away I might be able to get a standby seat to London a day early. I was soaked, muddy, and chilled; disheveled, hungry, and broke; fresh out of the morning's ebullience. Surely the liveried doorman would sneer at my long beard, rude clothing, and muttered English, and turn me away. Or if I did gain entrance to the sanctum, what would I say to Mr. and Mrs. Nabokov, after I had thanked them for writing on behalf of the Karner Blue and given them the Remingtons' greetings? My knowledge of his specific butterfly work was sketchy, and of his fiction and poetry, even sketchier.

Of course I should have had faith in the ability of any two lepists to talk about butterflies and moths until the cows come home. I should have expected that his civility toward someone he saw as a "fellow sufferer" of the *morbus et passio aureliani* would overcome his storied hauteur and my obvious ignorance. At least I should have tried. But I didn't. I boarded the train and left, perhaps the first time I had ever ventured nothing when adventure beckoned. I rolled off toward Geneva, dripping in my seat, in the certain knowledge that my twenties were about over. Hell, I figured; I'll be back – there will be more meetings in Morges. Next time, I'll ask Remington to write in advance, and I'll have read more of Nabokov's work.

Two months later, in a Cambridge teashop, I opened a copy of the *Guardian* and read that Vladimir Nabokov was dead.

Many people know that Nabokov had something to do with butterflies, although they usually misunderstand the connection. I frequently hear some earnest student, reader, or critic say that Nabokov was "a butterfly buff," or insist that he had "an incurable obsession" with butterflies. The one hopelessly trivializes a great passion; the other conflates abiding love with neurosis. Or I'll hear ill-informed comments likening Nabokov's affinity for Lepidoptera with some sick tangency to female exploitation, à la John Fowles's *The Collector* or Thomas Harris's *The Silence of the Lambs*. Still others settle for cheap shots about his fixation on butterfly genitalia – for example, this egregious idiocy from a draft manuscript for a national magazine, which I was asked to read and was fortunately able to derail: "[Butterflies] are sexy, too. Besides their beauty, the insects' mating habits seem to hold a strong fascination for aficionados. Nabokov, author of *Lolita* and other best sellers, was proud of his collection of Lycaenid [*sic*] male genitalia, which he kept, coated in glycerin and meticulously labeled, in vials in his office." As if his attention to butterfly genitalia had anything prurient about it!

An old story has Nabokov working on specimen preparations at Harvard, when he is called away to conduct visiting alumni around the museum. With his genitalic preps sitting in potassium hydroxide, he grows impatient and says, "Excuse me, I must go play with my genitalia." One can almost imagine him making such a crack out of sheer, punning irreverence.

But the doltish linking of Nabokov's interest in butterfly genitalia – reliable taxonomic clues for the species he worked on – with the subject matter of his prose, reveals only the ignorance of those who have read neither his books nor his papers.[1]

His work with his beloved Blues was far more than play. While many are aware of Nabokov's interest in the Lepidoptera, few realize that he was a lepidopterist of consequence, or even understand what that implies. Even other lepidopterists sometimes think of him as a dilettante or a dabbler, of little lasting impact on the field. This is an equally mistaken impression. Butterflies and moths represented far more to Nabokov than a hobby or an eccentricity. But for the breaks, they could have been his true milieu. I know of no piece of writing that better expresses what it is to be enchanted by these insects than Chapter 6 of *Speak, Memory*, sometimes reprinted under the title "Butterflies," which we include as the first selection in this book. The essay thrillingly evokes the awakening of this particular passion in his young life, and how it carried him into the future. The lepidopterist Ronald Wilkinson writes that he regularly reread this chapter every spring, as a way of savoring the collecting season in advance before the first butterflies emerged and he could actually get out there. No one can read the concluding passage without sensing what these glittering insects meant to Nabokov, and no one should read anything else by him without this knowledge. The fact is that his devotion to butterflies and moths colored all the rest of his life: where he went, what he did, whom he knew, and how he wrote. As the pieces collected here abundantly show, butterflies constantly flit in and out of his awareness, often alighting on the paper and remaining there, immortal specimens pressed between the pages.

Nabokov analysts innocent of any knowledge of butterflies are always trying to make them into something else. Exegetists who think that butterflies are merely symbols not only clutter the critical literature with flimsy fancy, they also miss one of the author's most important characteristics. Nabokov wrote on many levels, incorporating his diverse knowledge liberally. His genius sustains the story apart from specialized facts, but a working knowledge of French, Russian, Russian poets, chess, or a dozen other topics can enhance the reader's picture. One of the most important of these subtexts is Lepidoptera.

Lepidopterists, and those readers who take the trouble to acquaint themselves with the field, can appreciate Nabokov's corpus on a level that most will miss. In certain of the poems, several of the stories, and many of the novels, butterflies and moths impinge on the text dramatically. Even in works that seem devoid of any lepidopteral theme, allusions or images or tropes pop up from that compendious file in the writer's mind. This book hopes to illuminate the master's butterfly-love for readers who, closing one of his books, notice a shimmer of iridescent scales in a shaft of light, and long to know what they imply. Likewise, those who know Nabokov chiefly as a lepidopterist may find themselves drawn into realms of literature they never expected to hazard.

As *Speak, Memory* makes clear, sun and butterflies defined a good day for the young Nabokov at Vyra, his family's country estate: "From the age of seven, everything I felt in connection with a rectangle of framed sunlight was dominated by a single passion. If my first glance of the morning was for the sun, my first thought was for the butterflies it would engender." Besides a supple intelligence, he had advantages that enabled him to become a learned lepidopterist by the age of nine. His father had been a collector and was able to pass on to him the basics of lepidopterology and the local fauna, as well as invaluable encouragement for the pursuit. Parental indifference or discouragement ordinarily vie with adolescent peer pressure to terminate a young entomologist's career before it begins, as butterfly nets become social liabilities. Tutored at home and nurtured in his outdoor enthusiasms by both parents, the boy had no such impediments. Summer travels with his family and tutors took him to exotic locales such as Biarritz, where he was able to expand his collection of butterflies. In the attic at Vyra, he discovered "armloads of fantastically attractive volumes," including Maria Sibylla Merian's seventeenth-century paintings of Surinamese insects, "Esper's noble *Die Schmetterlinge*" of 1777, and Adalbert Seitz's compendious *Die Gross-Schmetterlinge der Erde*, which Nabokov called "a prodigious picture book."

Soon, discovering a new species became the young Nabokov's fondest fantasy. His first proposal of a new name for an unfamiliar variety, sent to the great Russian specialist Kuznetsov, yielded only a "gruff reference to 'schoolboys who keep naming minute varieties of the Poplar Nymph!'"

The rebuke failed to dampen his ardor, though he little knew then that he would one day name a butterfly for his idol, Samuel Scudder, nor that he would live and collect in the territory so ably covered by what he called "Scudder's stupendous work on the *Butterflies of New England*."

Nabokov's idyll at Vyra, along with his relatively carefree occupations as a young poet and lepidopterist, came to an abrupt end with the Bolshevik Revolution and the family's dislocations. Their rustication in the Crimea, however, led to his first scientific publication on the area he considered entomologically to be "the connecting link between the Balkan and Caucasian districts." "A Few Notes on Crimean Lepidoptera" (1920) listed the species found as well as their botanical and landscape associations, setting a pattern for several papers in which he would narrate the results of memorable field trips. While the paper was chiefly an annotated list, Nabokov introduced a hint of the fine descriptive prose that would flower in later papers. *Erebia afra*, the sole species seen of a genus he loved, elicited a lyrical portrait; and Nabokov allowed himself an elegiacal note at the end, likening a Crimean hawkmoth to one he used to find at the foot of aspens at home "in happier days." The enchanted days of summery treks across the butterfly-filled bogs near Vyra were finished forever, and the pain of that loss would never fade.

Nabokov soon became an undergraduate at Trinity College, Cambridge. Here, I think, his path bifurcated. Had he come under the sway of the zoologists at Cambridge he might have pursued natural history professionally. But as Brian Boyd tells it in his splendid *Vladimir Nabokov: The Russian Years*, the Cantabrigian period (1919–22) was curiously light on scientific involvement. His zoology lectures on fish dissection, likely delivered by Professor Stanley Gardiner, left him cold, and he switched his major (as we would say) to French and Russian language and literature. Already familiar with the material, he was able to sail to a quick honors degree while concentrating on sports, poetry, and mild revelry. In *Speak, Memory*, he listed "the things I went in for" other than literature as "entomology, practical jokes, girls, and, especially, athletics," but that is the sole mention of entomology in his account of his three years at Cambridge.

Professor Stanley Gardiner is best known today for his book on the natural history of Wicken Fen, later a famous reserve for the British Swallowtail butterfly. Nabokov was aware of the area's rare butterflies: his character Sebastian Knight, arriving in Cambridge, compares the pending disappearance of the hansom-cab with that of the extinct Large Copper of the Cambridgeshire Fens. When Charles Darwin went up to Cambridge, ninety years before Nabokov, he often skipped classes to collect beetles at Wicken Fen, and soon found himself appointed naturalist aboard H.M.S. *Beagle.* But though Nabokov had also loved beetles as a boy, that nearby remnant of the once-great English marshlands failed to turn his eye from the soccer fields. And even though he was offered a job as a field assistant on an entomological expedition to Ceylon (which, one imagines, could have been his Galapagos), he scorned it in a letter to his father.

Why not more natural history? For one thing, and this is apparent in Boyd's biography, Nabokov's preoccupation with his lost home in the delicious countryside at Vyra led to a constant flow of poetry concerned almost exclusively with Russia. For another, he threw himself into sport and socializing to an extent that left little time for butterflies. He admired the Cambridge poet Rupert Brooke and recognized his "heart's attachment" to the local countryside, but to Nabokov the same scenery suggested only "humble humdrumness." He would later call the routine New England butterflies "pathetically dull" compared to the delights of the West, "rather like a garden in Cambridgeshire after a summer in the mountains of Spain." But he also spent summers in London and Berlin, and springs largely taking exams, so it might be that in Cambridge he simply never had much chance to swing a net.

In *The Gift*, Nabokov gives Fyodor's father, Konstantin Godunov-Cherdyntsev, a sympathetic mentor at Cambridge, where "he studied biology under Professor Bright" in the 1870s. When I was living in Cambridge in the early 1970s, I often met an emeritus biology don in the morning on the bridge from Cherry Hinton into the city. We would pause and chat about the condition of local butterflies and habitats. Though he was chiefly a student of flies, he had a strong interest in butterflies and their conservation, and I had first met him at one of the entomological societies' meetings. This man's name was John Smart. Professor Bright, Professor Smart: a perfectly Nabokovian coincidence.

John Smart did not come to Cambridge until well after Nabokov's period there in the 1920s, but the Cambridge entomologist Brian Gardiner (the long-time editor of *The Entomologist*, the journal in which Nabokov published his first Lepidoptera paper, and no relation to Stanley) told me that Cambridge would have been "crawling with entomologists" during Nabokov's time. Yet he seems not to have connected with them much. I can't help wondering what his life might have been had *he*, like Fyodor's father, come under the sway of a Bright or a Smart in his own English days.

Instead, upon graduation he was off to the continent; and soon, to life with Véra and Dmitri in expatriate literary colonies. Collecting for the first time in a decade, he published an account of a productive trip to the Pyrénées Orientales and the Ariège in southern France (1931), full of the wonder of new habitats and fresh fauna known to him previously only in books. By now he had thrown off any constraints at expressing his feelings and perceptions in an entomological article, and portions of it read no differently from his fiction. The piece opens with a "pleasant though silly dream" involving what he thought was a sardine, but was actually the moth-mimic of a flying fish. There is the hallmark attention to detail, both of the scene: "a bright little lamp," "people intent on the process of digestion . . . strolling up and down in the darkness with glowing cigars," "a pathetic wing in a spider's web"; and the butterflies: "fine specimens of a milk chocolate colour," "The fulvous band between the inner and outer lines is very conspicuous and the lunules are perfectly distinct." The elegy remains ("I was charmed to see together two insects that are seldom met with together . . . *P. aegeria* and *Aglia tau*, so remindful of boyhood and spring in Northern Russia)," yet it was "heartbreaking to leave Saurat." Butterflies were still intensely evocative and exciting, but literature had superseded science overall, a pattern that would seldom be fully reversed.

When the Nabokovs moved to the United States in 1940, Nabokov resumed his involvement in lepidopterology with zeal. At first, living in New York City while seeking employment, he connected with the American Museum of Natural History (AMNH). William P. Comstock, a member of the museum's entomology department, was his first real advocate as an entomologist in this country. Comstock gave the obviously talented immigrant full access to the collection and working space, and taught him the fundamentals of genitalic dissection. Here Nabokov also became acquainted with James H. McDunnough, the Grand Old Man of American Lepidoptera and author of the *Checklist of the Lepidoptera of Canada and the United States of America* of 1938; also research associates Cyril dos Passos, who would compile *A Synonymic List of the Nearctic Rhopalocera* in 1964, and Alexander B. Klots, future author of the 1951 Peterson series *A Field Guide to the Butterflies of North America, East of the Great Plains*, which Nabokov would review enthusiastically. Both dos Passos's and Klots's works warmly acknowledged Nabokov's contributions.

Nabokov began his long-term work on the genus of Blues known as *Lycaeides* in the great collections at the AMNH. Charles Remington feels that Comstock (a lycaenid man) reinforced his "thinking Blue." Dr. Frederick Rindge, now Curator Emeritus of the museum's collections and a great authority on geometrid (inchworm) moths, has grown understandably weary of dealing with inquiries about the famous Nabokov, but recognizes his contributions to the institution. Returning from his earliest American forays, he deposited his specimens in the museum's trays. Forced to leave one collection in St. Petersburg and another in Yalta, Nabokov never maintained a large personal butterfly collection in this country, but donated his prepared material to whichever museum he happened to be associated with at the time. During this unsettled New York period, as contemporary letters show, Nabokov found an intellectual and emotional anchor at the AMNH, where Comstock, McDunnough, and others extended collegiality and fueled his hopes that he might make a solid contribution of his own.

The Nabokovs' move to Wellesley in 1941 for a lectureship was followed by a succession of temporary positions there and at Harvard. In the "other" Cambridge, Nabokov became a part-time research fellow in Entomology and curator of Lepidoptera at Harvard's Museum of Comparative Zoology (MCZ) – the institution that has hosted such prominent biologists as Ernst Mayr, P. J. Darlington, William Morton Wheeler, Edward O. Wilson, Stephen Jay Gould, and the present Hessel Professor of Biology and Curator of Lepidoptera Naomi Pierce, a specialist on Blues and ants. His time at the MCZ was not particularly collegial, since most of the entomologists specialized in other insect groups, and as Charles Remington told me,

Nabokov never proclaimed any interest in or knowledge of insects in general. Frank Morton Carpenter, the ranking entomologist and a specialist in fossil insects in the footsteps of Scudder (of whom more later), thought of Nabokov as "a queer duck" and regarded him as not quite kindred with the other entomologists.

In *Speak, Memory,* Nabokov wrote that it was a long time before he met a "fellow sufferer" of the Lepidoptera pursuit. At Harvard he met two: Harry Clench, son of the MCZ mollusk curator, who was soon to leave for graduate study in Michigan; and then-graduate student Charles Remington. These were real lepidopterists; together they cofounded the Lepidopterists' Society in 1947. Nabokov became a charter member of this confederacy. Having Remington on hand at Harvard was important to Nabokov. When he would go off on collecting trips and come back with novelties, he needed someone with whom he could share his excitement and pore over the catch. Returning from Vermont after his first encounter with the sought-after Northern Hairstreak (*Euristrymon ontario*), for example, he pounced on Remington to tell him about it. Remington later spoke of "the joy we had" at such times, a joy known by all butterfly hunters who have ever shared their bag with one another. Remington has recorded his recollections of this period in his valuable contribution to *The Garland Companion to Vladimir Nabokov.*[2] On the whole, as Nabokov wrote in *Strong Opinions*, "The years at the Harvard Museum remain the most delightful and thrilling in all my adult life."

One often-told anecdote from the MCZ years has Nabokov pulling a prank on Harry Clench. According to Lee D. Miller, Clench's eulogist,[3] it went like this: "Harry spent much of his formative years in the friendly confines of the MCZ, where he began his systematic work. One of those who influenced him greatly during the MCZ days was Vladimir Nabokov. He was the source of one of Harry's favorite stories on himself. Harry had agonized over a small *'Thecla'* [hairstreak] from southern Brasil, and his frustration was well known to Nabokov. One evening Harry left the specimen in a box on his work bench, and went home; the following morning when he returned, Nabokov was nowhere to be seen, but the specimen had a neatly printed determination label on it from Nabokov proclaiming it to be '*Thecla caramba* Hewitson.' One has but to know how many Neotropical Theclinae Hewitson described (Comstock and Huntington's list had not yet been published) to imagine Harry's frantic search through the literature to find the original description of '*Thecla caramba.*' It is a tribute to Nabokov's puckish sense of humor that Clench never found the description he sought, because Hewitson had written no such description. Harry liked the name, however, and adopted it. It now stands as the valid name of a Neotropical thecline, despite the admonition of one of the elder Clench's Latin American graduate students: 'You shouldn't use that name, Harry, it is just like calling your butterfly *Thecla hell!*' "

Nabokov scattered apocryphal butterfly names here and there. Even at Wellesley College, where he taught Russian, although he spent as much time as he could at Harvard setting and dissecting butterflies, he left a butterfly mark. When I visited the archives and rare books collections at Wellesley, I found copies of a number of Nabokov's novels personally inscribed for faculty friends with colored-pencil drawings of fanciful butterflies he would often name for the dedicatee. He inscribed a copy of *Bend Sinister* to his close Wellesley colleague Sylvia Berkman with *Danaus sylvia*, a made-up relative of the Monarch. The fine drawing has a black outline and veins, a pink wash, and blue trailing edges with eyespots. Other first editions of Professor Berkman's, since donated to Wellesley, include illuminated inscriptions for *Pieris sylvia*, *Sphinx sylvia*, and *Morpho sylvia* (see color plates 15–17). A copy of *Nikolai Gogol* signed for Sarah Jane Manley bears a butterfly in three pastel colors, blue with pink veins and a yellow tinge. It is labeled in Nabokov's hand *Wellesleyana browningi* Nabokov in honor of Elizabeth Barrett Browning's door, which is preserved in the Wellesley Library.

Another biologist with memories of Nabokov in Cambridge is Ken Christiansen, now Professor Emeritus at Grinnell College in Iowa. During high school he worked as a volunteer at the MCZ, where he later completed graduate studies and "frequently ran into" Nabokov. Christiansen's unpublished memoir describes his close friendship with Harry Clench and acquaintance with Nabokov. "Being a curious teen-ager," he wrote, "I soon began spending some time with Nabokov discovering what he was working on. . . . He was a brilliant conversationalist and always seemed to have a fund of interesting stories and excitement about his work. I remember that he was working with the family Lycaenidae and at that time was enamored of a new taxonomic tool he had discovered that he called the 'magic triangles.' This involved the angles of certain structures in the male genitalia and he had many drawings of these and greatly enjoyed expounding their taxonomic utility and Euclidean harmony. . . . I soon discovered that his greeting was determined by how well he knew you. If he only remembered that he should know you but didn't remember your name he always gave a very expansive 'HELLO-O-O.' When he got to know you better the greetings were much more subdued."

"I also remember," wrote Christiansen, "that whenever I saw him again he always seemed to have a new funny story, usually about some book he had just reviewed. He also had a knack for illuminating the beauty of a small butterfly. Many times when I came in to visit him he would say, 'Ken, let me show you this,' and he would then pick up a small butterfly and say something like, 'Notice the lovely way the small silver lacings of the hind wing are illuminated by the dark blue borders,' and so the specimen would always seem more beautiful than it had before. In his room there were a number of cartoons he had tacked to the specimen cabinets. The one I remember most clearly was from *Punch*. It showed a clearly entomological explorer in the middle of what appeared to be the Gobi desert with a few assistants. On the horizon a Tyrannosaur could be seen chasing a Duckbilled Dinosaur. Below it was the caption, 'This is all very interesting, but I MUST remember I am a specialist in Lepidoptera.' "

Ken had met his future wife in the MCZ work room, where she was employed as Nabokov's assistant, mounting butterflies. Phyllis gained a rare familiarity with her boss, through hours of sheer proximity at the worktable. She also baby-sat for Dmitri and was "very friendly" with Véra, "a sweet, unassuming woman of great presence and charm." On an early spring visit, Ken bicycled back from his lab for coffee with me and his Grinnell colleague David Campbell. Gnomishly hooded against the sleet, he occupied David's daughter Tatiana with stories while Phyllis shared memories of her days in the lab with Nabokov. She kindly furnished me with her notes for an oral review of *Speak, Memory* she had once given to a circle of friends, touching on her experience with the Nabokov family.

"We worked side by side," Phyllis noted, "and my work was largely mechanical, so when he felt like talking, he talked. I did not at the time appreciate my position, but I grew to love him as a person, and as [his books] were published, one by one, of course we were very interested." Nabokov presented them with *Bend Sinister* as a wedding gift, inscribed it "To Phyllis and Kenny from V. and V. Nabokov wishing you a century of happiness," and drew a little dragonfly, Ken's special interest at the time. They also possess a *Real Life of Sebastian Knight* signed "For Phyllis" with a blue ink butterfly. In July, 1946, Phyllis got a letter from Nabokov penned in Bristol, New Hampshire, bemoaning their miserable vacation in a site plagued with unrewarding collecting, highway intrusion, and the everpresent odor of fried clams. After employing this letter in her 1973 talk, Phyllis returned it to Nabokov as a seventy-fifth birthday greeting.

Phyllis's notes confirm that in a place full of eccentric characters, "he stood out as one of the most colorful. Uninhibited, unselfconscious – sometimes quiet, sometimes *loud*" (usually in explosive laughter at some joke). He "*Loved* puzzles, jokes, games – especially games with *words*, memory, time." He talked about our sense of time, and about books, such as *Moby-Dick*. "He had an *intense* interest in human relationships, and what did I think of this or that? Questions, *questions!* Adjusting to U.S. customs and collecting always toward a new book." Phyllis recalls him as a very loving husband and father, but the family living in "genteel poverty," since he earned around $1,200 plus what he made through lectures. "I realize now," she wrote, "how much alone they were."

When the Christiansens visited Montreux in 1967, Phyllis found Nabokov full of probing questions about everything from MCZ gossip to the health of the family dog. "They were the very same people," her notes recalled. "He still calls her Darling; clearly they still adore each other." Dmitri, the boy she had baby-sat for, was now a six-foot, five-inch opera singer who also remembered intimate details of those years. Nabokov was playful and jocular. When they parted, he kissed her hand in mock solemnity, saying "This has been really nice . . . *huh!* – Well, that's *not* a cliché. I just coined that phrase: *Reeeeally* nice!" Phyllis's paper noted her astonishment at "how well he had known me."

Leaving Cambridge in 1948, Vladimir, Véra, and Dmitri moved to Ithaca, New York, for a professorship of Russian literature at Cornell, another institution with a long and robust history of scientific butterfly studies. John H. and Anna Botsford Comstock, unrelated to W. P. Comstock at the AMNH, had been popular entomologists and teachers of natural history. John had written a handbook of American butterflies, and Anna the most widely used nature study textbook in the country. They were long gone, but they had left an indelible stamp of hospitality on the place for the likes of Nabokov, who found a friendly reception in Comstock Hall among professors John Franclemont and W. T. M. Forbes, the author of *The Lepidoptera of New York State*.

Franclemont told Remington that Nabokov and Forbes were "always buddy-buddy." But while he enjoyed talking butterflies with the "pink-pated," "carp-shaped" Forbes, Nabokov may have felt more at ease with the unassuming Franclemont – one of the world's foremost students of noctuid moths (commonly known as "millers"), and now Professor Emeritus at Cornell. I asked him recently if he ever went afield with Nabokov. "Oh yes, I took him out to McLean Bogs twice looking for *Pieris virginiensis*," he replied. "Though we didn't find it, I was happy to take the time off on a sunny May day, and it gave Véra a day off. When we'd come back, he'd always insist I come in for a drink. It would be Scotch; I never heard vodka mentioned." (Nabokov eventually found the West Virginia White. As he wrote to Franclemont on the last day of May, 1959, he'd had "a delightful time with *Pieris virginiensis* in the Great Smokies of Tennessee.")

"We discussed many things. He was mostly down in the collections." I asked Franclemont if he was comfortable in conversation. "Yes," he said. "Some said it might have been my European name. But one got the impression that it was advisable to accept his statements as true – not to challenge – you wouldn't get anywhere." Even so, he enjoyed ribbing Nabokov. "I told him, after his *Lycaeides* paper, that if he carried his [taxonomic splitting] methods to their logical conclusion, butterflies would become their own phylum. He thought that was a pretty good joke." Franclemont is an aficionado of wordplay, and recalled swapping puns and word games with Nabokov. He enjoyed this, but did not discuss literature in the laboratory. "At his home and in the field," Franclemont said, "conversation ranged more widely. But when Nabokov crossed campus, he became a lepidopterist."

During his twenty years in America, Nabokov crossed the country as well as the campus in search of Lepidoptera. With Véra and usually Dmitri, he journeyed west almost every summer to collect butterflies and work on his books. Remington has summarized these travels,[4] and Boyd's biography elaborates on several of the summers. Nabokov did not drive, so at first they accepted rides or took public transportation to a destination near the lodge or motel where they established headquarters; then he ranged out mostly on foot to check out the countryside and collect. Dorothy Leuthold, who drove the family to the Grand Canyon and beyond in 1941, was rewarded by having an actual butterfly (not just a frontispiece fancy) named for her by the grateful Nabokov: *Neonympha dorothea dorothea*, now known as *Cyllopsis pertepida dorothea*.

Later, Véra learned to drive and chauffeured her husband to the butterfly grounds. Several of these trips were directed toward specific populations of orange-bordered Blues that he needed to examine for his classic studies on these bright insects. Others involved lectures, readings, or teaching. Their first American summer (1941) took them to Stanford University and Yosemite National Park. For collecting advice in California, he contacted yet another Comstock, John A., the venerable author of *California Butterflies*. In 1953 they stayed at the Tole cabin in lower Cave Creek Canyon near Portal, Arizona, which proved rainy and cold; but in Ashland, Oregon, his collecting "became a genuine mania," as he wrote his sister.

Destinations in Colorado, Wyoming, and Utah were butterfly Valhallas. Short papers published in Remington's *Lepidopterists' News*, such as "Butterfly Collecting in Wyoming" (1953), commented on the countryside, general conditions, and scientific questions that arose from the ramble, as his earlier notes on Crimea and the Pyrénées had done, while listing and describing the species encountered: one Fritillary was "fresh but frayed," one sulphur "slightly tinged with peach." His personal thoughts during the field trips, and the events surrounding them, often ended up in letters to the literary critic and at that time close friend, Edmund Wilson, such as this written from Teton Pass Ranch: "Dear Bunny, We have had some wonderful adventures in Utah and Wyoming and are driving back next week. I have lost many pounds and found many butterflies."[5]

Priding himself on curiosity toward all things, Wilson took a rough interest in Lepidoptera. But he did not fully share his friend's passion, possibly the very reason Nabokov loaded his letters with butterfly references. When Wilson did attempt to respond in kind, he was likely to get it wrong. In the autumn of 1953, he wrote to Nabokov "a story that you ought to be told." It concerned Paul Brooks, then editor-in-chief at Houghton Mifflin, and his encounter with a persistent moth. For three days, Wilson wrote, a "Polyphemus" moth came into Brooks's house, "flew through some of the rooms and then departed." Finally Brooks remembered a cocoon he'd left in a drawer; he found that the moth, a female, had emerged, and placed her outside "on the sundial, and the male came at once and got her. They left him a little note," Wilson concluded, "saying that if at any time he should get into trouble with dragons or ogres, he had only to call upon them."[6]

During a recent visit, Paul Brooks corrected the story for me. Actually, it was two male Promethea moths trying to get *in* his front door. Once admitted, they flew upstairs, out an open window, and back around to the front door. Brooks had collected a cocoon, but the female had emerged in the coat pocket where he'd left it, forgotten. The males had detected the expired female's pheromones from outside the house, which is remarkable enough without Wilson's fairy-tale flourish.

Although Edmund Wilson wasn't the naturalist Nabokov was, a watershed in natural history publishing came about because of an event at his summer home, and it is possible that Nabokov was involved. When Wilson's daughter, Rosalind, who then worked at Houghton Mifflin, was out walking with her father and several literary friends on Cape Cod, she joined with the others in attempting to save what they thought were stranded horseshoe crabs by tossing them back into the sea. The one member of the party versed in natural history berated their ill-informed efforts as counterproductive – the animals had hauled out to breed. Rosalind was appalled. Back in Boston, she announced to Paul Brooks that there ought to be a book to inform people about seashore life. Brooks agreed. Shortly thereafter he met Rachel Carson and asked her to write it. *The Edge of the Sea* resulted, and eventually, *Silent Spring*. When Brooks told me that story, I wondered, Who was that naturalist? Rosalind Wilson did know Nabokov; she later pitched a mimicry book for him, which never came to be.

The summer breaks were extremely important for Nabokov, since, between teaching and writing, he often felt overworked during the school year. He developed schemes for spending as much time afield as possible. During bad weather, he would remain in the lodge or motel room writing, ready to dart out with first rays of the sun. His method of writing – on index cards – according to Boyd grew out of the practice of keeping butterfly notes on such cards. When I viewed Nabokov's butterfly archive in the Berg Collection at the New York Public Library, I saw the remarkable tool he'd made to enhance his understanding of certain western butterflies. Dissatisfied with available references, he had constructed his own field guide to the troublesome and variable Fritillaries by cutting out the good color plates from W. J. Holland's *Butterfly Book*, a source he considered meretricious but well illustrated, and combining them with learned papers on the genus *Speyeria* by C. F. dos Passos, L. P. Grey, and A. H. Moeck.

Nabokov often walked ten or twenty miles in a day's collecting, becoming well acquainted with the vicinity of his lodgings. Remington told me how proud Nabokov was to be able to find *Mitoura spinetorum*, the uncommon Thicket Hairstreak, by going out early when the mistletoe-feeding, tree-top butterfly alighted on the road in numbers. Most collectors, who cover the ground more superficially, had less luck.

Remington also went afield with Nabokov in the West and observed him in action. During the summer of 1947, Vladimir, Véra, and Dmitri stayed at Columbine Lodge near Rocky Mountain National Park. At the time, Remington was conducting summer research not far away at the University of Colorado's Science Lodge near Ward. On an agreed morning, Remington picked up Nabokov at his lodge and took him "for a day-long collecting excursion to a fabulous montane butterfly locality, the great Tolland bogs east of the Moffat tunnel." As Remington recalled,[7] they were "talking animatedly the whole two-way drive. I was under the vague impression that he was a writer of novels, presumably erudite works for a special readership, but we never talked about that side of his productivity." Nabokov was more interested in the special bog Fritillaries (such as the silver-bordered *Boloria selene tollandensis*, described from specimens taken at that very site), and pink-edged willow Sulfurs named for the much-admired Samuel Scudder (*Colias scudderi*). Other treats of Tolland resembled butterflies he had known in the bogs near Vyra thirty years before. They found the Fritillaries, but the Sulfurs had to wait for a later day's collecting at Longs Peak Inn, a venerable hostelry built by the well-known nature writer Enos Mills just north of Columbine Lodge.

Nabokov's days afield near Longs Peak were among his most prized. The astonishing bit of time-travel woven into the end of Chapter 6 in *Speak, Memory*, when he sets out on a morning's expedition on the bogs beyond Vyra and ends up among the Ponderosa Pines and Mariposa Lilies in the shadow of Longs Peak some forty years later, comes as close to expressing the magic of his passion as anything he ever wrote.

One recent summer I located the piney old place once known as Columbine Lodge, from which Remington and Nabokov had set out. Now called High Peak Camp and owned by the Salvation Army, it is used for mountain retreats and outings for urban children who might otherwise never know the balm of the high country. I perched on a pine railing beside a patch of Colorado Blue Columbines in bloom and imagined the meeting between the young Remington, then twenty-five, and Nabokov, forty-eight, that morning during the month and year when I was born. Rising up behind the weathered main lodge, whose gable mimics its form, was the immense, stony peak of Mount Meeker (13,311 feet).

My novel-in-progress, *Magdalena Mountain*, which involves the sought-after, all-black Magdalena Alpine butterfly resident among the rockslides of the Colorado high country, is set at Mount Meeker. I began it, renaming the peak Magdalena Mountain, years before I learned that when Nabokov first collected *Erebia magdalena*, it was here. I wrote the early drafts in another rustic hostelry, Meeker Park Lodge, just a few miles down the Peak-to-Peak Highway from Columbine Lodge. No wonder I can see him in my mind's eye outlined against the thin blue Colorado sky, leaner than when he began his summer's search, swinging his net as the dusky form of a Magdalena Alpine volplanes down the talus toward him. And it did make an impression on him: in *Look at the Harlequins*, Vadim spends a month at Lupine Lodge near Longs Peak, and relates a poem by Bel describing their hike past the "Boulderfield, and its Black Butterfly."

Thus we know that Nabokov's initial encounter with this butterfly did not occur in the manner described by biographer Andrew Field in an anecdote linking their names:[8] "Once, when Nabokov was afield doing his farmwork, an old Englishman came by on horseback, dismounted, and asked him to hold his horse. The old man, who had a butterfly net and was in pursuit of a two-tailed Pasha flying around a fig tree, was startled when the bronzed young *paysan* dressed in blue denim pants inquired in taxonomically perfect Latin about what species he had been able to find in the region, which nicely parallels what happened to Nabokov himself some twenty years later, while collecting in the mountains of Utah, when he was offered a lift by a young truck driver who breezily called out: – **Hop in, entomologist! Have you gotten a Magdalena?**"

The "young truck driver" was John Downey, as I learned from Utah lepidopterist Clyde Gillette. Downey, a retired professor of biology from Iowa now resident in Florida, is another highly renowned expert on the Blue butterflies that Nabokov adored; his master's thesis, finished not long after he got to know Nabokov, concerned Boisduval's Blue (*Icaricia icarioides*) a common species of western Lupine fields. But the summer he met Nabokov, he was indeed a young laborer in the Utah mountains. Downey gave me the following audiotape account of his meeting with Nabokov:

> In the early part of the 1940's, in my late teens, I worked in the summer for Wasatch National Forest in Utah. I had a variety of tasks, from forest guard to fire lookout, assistant dispatcher and truck driver. While working as the latter – as a

truck driver – I hauled a bunch of different things to guard stations in the hinter-lands, mostly on a must-have basis, when they radioed the dispatcher's office that things were needed, or requested by rangers. On the day of our eventful meeting, I was hauling coal from the Salt Lake Valley to the western guard station at Alta, Utah, now a well-known ski resort. The old dumptruck I was using tended to overheat on the steep climb up Cottonwood Canyon, and always required me to stop a couple times, especially with a full load.

She was steaming up mightily as I rounded a gentle curve and noted some dis-tance ahead, coming down-canyon, a man with a butterfly net. I had plenty of time to pull to the side of the road, dismount, and open the hood to let it cool off before the unknown man reached the truck area. I came across the road to meet him, saying something like, as I recall, "Hullo. Whatcha doing? Collecting in-sects?" A rather obvious activity with a net in hand, I guess. He gave me a sharp glance but said nothing and continued on down the road at the same pace. I rather forgot how I might have looked to him, covered in coal dust and getting out of a belching truck and attempting an approach. Of course I must tell you how he looked to me at that time.

He was dressed, undressed might be a better term, in yellow track shorts, slit up the side, two low-cut canvas shoes, no socks, no shirt, and in place of a hat a handkerchief knotted in each corner and fitted to the top of his head like a French tam. He also had a thin collecting storage belt around the middle with a little package on it he could put specimens in. Now in those days, the heyday of macho-ism, men always wore long-legged pants, except perhaps for swimming or tennis, and shirts, and usually even an undershirt beneath the shirt. A man without pants and shirt would be considered dang near nude, and especially suspect when thus dressed with a butterfly net in hand. I really only reflected on these things later. At the moment I was so surprised and happy to have come across another collector that meeting him was the big issue. He no doubt held some thoughts about the rather bold approach of a grimy truck driver as well. Anyhow, he continued down the road at the same pace, and I dutifully fell in behind him.

I continued the one-sided conversation: "I'm a collector too!" This got a milli-second glance, and one raised eyebrow, as he strolled along. "I collect *butterflies*." (Usually while trucking I brought along my net and collecting gear, and would stop at likely locales and passes for a collecting lunch hour. This day, with coal on board, I left my gear at home. The meeting might have taken a different course if

I had exited the truck with a net in hand instead of just coal dust.) This statement rated me another raised eyebrow though, if not a slight nod of the head; but still no sound from him, nor slowing of his pace as he continued down-canyon.

Finally, a nymphalid, as I recall, flitted across the road. "What's that?" he asked. I gave him the scientific name as best I could remember, not having used the terms before with obvious professionals, and fresh out of Holland's *Butterfly Book*. His pace didn't slacken, but an eyebrow stayed higher a little longer this time. Yet another butterfly crossed the road. "What's that?" says he. I gave him a name, a little less sure of myself now, particularly since he had not confirmed the correctness of my first identification. "Hm!" was his only response. A third test specimen crossed his vision, and "What's that?" I gave him my best idea and to my surprise he stopped, put out his arm, and said, "Hello! I'm Vladimir Nabokov." And thus we met. What a way to meet my first famous lepidopterist, having to pass a practical exam before he would talk with me!

It turns out he and his family were staying at Alta, where he was studying the Blues of the genus *Lycaeides*. He was hiking about nine miles down-canyon each day to satisfy himself that the subspecies *annetta* was not flying there, but only at higher elevations. This nine-mile hike is referred to in his paper on his *Lycaeides* work.

I offered to take him up-canyon, back to his hotel diggings, but of all things I can't remember whether he took me up on the offer. At any rate we made arrangements to meet again the next day. You can rest assured I brought my net along. I met his wife and son at lunch that day. Nabokov visited Utah at least two more times, when he came to the university to teach at a writers' conference. At that time I was going to the university. I met him again on both of these occasions, and we took to the field at least once. We kept up a correspondence until his eye doctor limited his work on butterflies for a time. In fact in one exchange he told me he was going to have to give up work on Blues. But subsequently his eyes improved, and he got back to work on them at a later date.

Oh – I forgot about the *magdalena* reference quoted by Field. I don't recall our using this name during our first meeting. I knew *Erebia magdalena* of course, and its occurrence in the Uinta Mountains far to the east of the Wasatch Range where the original meeting transpired. Since we talked about much though, I don't know if it was brought up, but my memory will not confirm that it happened at our first encounter, as alluded to by Field.

This chance meeting in a Utah canyon of two future global authorities in the arcane field of lycaenology would be dismissed, if it appeared in a novel, as hopelessly contrived. In fact, their joint enthusiasm was not entirely a coincidence. As John Downey wrote to Kurt Johnson in 1996, "my encounter with Nabokov in Little Cottonwood Canyon . . . had more than a little effect on my picking the blues as a specialty. . . . he subsequently sent me a whole bunch of 3 × 4 cards (about a 1 to 1½ inches-high stack) with morphological sketches of the blues of interest, and indicated he was turning over his interest to me after his doctor told him to give up the microscope work and he was having severe eye problems. It must have worked . . . Nabokov strongly influenced me to take up the study of blues and their relatives."

If Nabokov never "got a *magdalena*" in Utah, a pin label for a female *Erebia magdalena* lodged in the Cornell University collection shows that he did find it again in Colorado. Andrew Warren copied the label for me after the two of us located the specimen in Comstock Hall. It reads: **Telluride, COLO.** / Alt. 10,000 ft. / July 15, 1951 / V. Nabokov. In his extended footnote "On a Book Entitled *Lolita*" (which refers to Telluride), Nabokov wrote that "the locality labels pinned under these butterflies will be a boon to some twenty-first century scholar with a taste for recondite biography." The pin labels on his specimens at Cornell, the MCZ, and the AMNH map a part of his life in telegraphic form (Alta, Utah, 30 June 43; Tolland Bog, Colo., July 47; Bighorn Mtns., Wyo., nr. Granite Pass, 17 July 58). They also imply something of the plants, the soils, the elevations, the cohort of other living things, and the skies, horizons, and topography of their habitats – something, in fact, of where and how he passed his days between writing the books for which he is mostly known. In summer, that often meant striding the West.

That random canyon rendezvous between John Downey and Vladimir Nabokov affected my course as well. One of Downey's papers, documenting the 1943 extinction of the Xerces Blue, inspired me to found the Xerces Society for the conservation of butterflies, other invertebrates, and their habitats, in 1971. John Downey became an early advisor to the society, whose first cause célèbre was Nabokov's Karner Blue. According to Boyd, the Lepidopterists' Society was Nabokov's only formal affiliation with any organization. But Dmitri Nabokov has written that his father also belonged to the Xerces Society.[9] Naturally I was eager to confirm this. The Berg Collection of the New York Public Library, where Dmitri and Véra Nabokov presciently decided to lodge the personal papers (under Boyd's curatorial oversight), contains a number of Xerces Society publications. These include an issue of the journal *Atala* devoted to the conservation of Blues, and a 1974 roster naming Nabokov as a member. The late Joan De-Wind, Xerces secretary at the time, could not recall his actually joining and guessed that he might have been given an honorary membership. But since he turned down many proffered honors and all gratuitous affiliations, yet kept the Xerces journals, the only such publications in his archive besides early issues of the *Lepidopterists' News* and individual reprints, the connection strikes me as authentic.

Nabokov did not, apparently, attend meetings of societies other than the Cambridge (Mass.) Entomological Club, whose gatherings he and Véra enjoyed. Records of the first several Lepidopterists' Society meetings in the early 1950s document the presence of friends such as Alexander Klots and Cyril dos Passos, but not of Nabokov, and Charles Remington does not recall his attendance at such conventions. On the whole, Nabokov told interviewers, he abhorred meetings. But if he didn't frequent their gatherings, Nabokov did carry on cordial visits and correspondence with a wide array of lepidopterists, and was well liked among them. Professor Charles V. Covell, Jr., a past-president of the Lepidopterists' Society and one of that organization's most contributory and admired members for many years, encountered Nabokov at Cornell, early in his career. "Nabokov seemed to me to be quite ordinary, pleasant and unprepossessing," Covell told me. "I hardly felt I was in the company of such a great man."

Nabokov's postal exchanges, many examples of which appear in this collection, were often vigorous and sprinkled with humor or vivid description. To dos Passos he wrote in friendly disagreement over Fritillary names. To Klots he sent a request for tips on lodging and collecting sites in the Tetons. And with Remington he exchanged drafts and ideas for his notes in the *Lepidopterists' News*, including an exchange of views with the Colorado teacher and lepidopterist F. Martin Brown, in which Nabokov demonstrated his willingness to stick to a position and argue trenchantly for it.[10] The debate concerned numerical analysis of butterfly variation. In the first volley, Brown complained of lepidopterists' reluctance to employ statistical methods to demonstrate the validity of their conclusions, singling out one of Nabokov's papers as a "chaotic mass of information" that could be improved by better statistics.

Nabokov, who regarded his precise measurements with special pleasure and pride, did not take kindly to Brown's criticism. In a reply to the *News*, he clarified his intent in the paper and explained how he felt Brown had misunderstood and misused him, while explaining in pungent terms his philosophy of taxonomy and statistics. Remington gave Dr. Brown the last word on the matter, and in the end, he admitted that Nabokov's subspecies was sound and his paper "excellent" on the whole. In many retellings among lepidopterists, the Nabokov/Brown debate took on heroic proportions. But in a videotaped interview given shortly before his death at ninety in 1993, Brown told lepidopterist Boyce Drummond that his relationship with Nabokov was friendlier than the notes in the *News* might suggest, and that they had collected together in the Thousand Islands in New York. Despite their statistical row, Brown thought highly of Nabokov, dubbing one species Nabokov's Satyr and another Nabokov's Blue in his great *Colorado Butterflies*. Nabokov in turn admired some of Brown's work, such as his painstaking papers on the stagecoach lepidopterist Theodore Mead's collecting itineraries in Colorado.

Nabokov was not one to hide his opinion of those with whom he disagreed or whose work he found shoddy. His butterfly papers at the Berg Collection contain these strong opinions: William J. Holland's "Blunderfly Book," which was "hopelessly unreliable"; Embrik Strand's "farcical nomenclatorial methods"; Walter Forster's work, "full of the most preposterous blunders"; Shyônen Matsamura, "as incompetent as he was prolific"; and Ben Leighton's "incredibly naive paper." But he could also dish out praise, sometimes for the very person he was roasting: William Henry Edwards gave a "very poor description" of *Colias scudderi*, but his *Butterflies of North America* was "one of the best butterfly books ever."

Nabokov also thought highly of the Peterson field guide for eastern North America by Alexander Klots (the 1951 democratic successor to Edward's rare nineteenth-century tome) and the equivalent Collins guide for Europe written by Lionel Higgins and Norman Riley. His reviews of these books, in the *New York Times* and *The Times* of London respectively (possibly the only butterfly field guides ever to be reviewed in these papers) are included in this volume. Klots, says Nabokov, wrote "the finest book on American butterflies to be published" since Scudder "inaugurated a new era in lepidopterology." The European guide earned Nabokov's praise for its "aura of authority and honesty, conciseness and completeness," and he spoke of the "glory of Higgins' and Riley's unique and indispensable manual."

Higgins's opinion of Nabokov, however, was not as uniformly generous. While recognizing Nabokov's "many contributions" to the study of *Lycaeides*, Higgins differed strongly with some of his methods and names, especially his use of the species epithet *L. argyrognomon* for what should be *L. idas*, as Nabokov later agreed. Corresponding with the Oregon lepidopterist John Hinchliff about the proper names for Northwest Blues of the genus *Lycaeides*, Higgins wrote, "I shall try very hard to show up the mistake without treading on too many tender American toes too hard!" Professor Higgins, then in his nineties, was preparing a paper summarizing his own work on these Blues. Hinchliff asked his opinion of papers by the two other recent writers on the genus, Jon Shepard and Vladimir Nabokov. Perhaps forgetting the grace of Nabokov's 1970 review, Higgins wrote that while both papers were "invaluable," Shepard's is "comprehensible but unconvincing," while Nabokov's "of course is incomprehensible but not without great interest."

Nabokov did not feel the need to detract from other lepidopterists who accomplished what he only hoped to do. This is clear in his kind reviews when he himself had contemplated writing works on the butterflies of both North America and Europe. It is almost as if, seeing the work done well, he was relieved of a self-imposed responsibility for doing it himself. Not that the Higgins and Riley handbook accomplished everything Nabokov had aimed to do in the illustrated catalogue he projected, which would have been much more ambitious. Time, the demands of literature, and the unwillingness of publishers to finance it properly did the book in, not competitors he did not see as such. And when someone else (actually twenty-two others) succeeded in producing a North American book to replace Holland's *Butterfly Book*, once an ambition of his own, he greeted it with great warmth and read it, according to Boyd, "with rapture." The way to be on Nabokov's good side as a "lepist" was to do solid, conscientious, and thorough work. Agreeing with him helped, but he often disagreed with others and still admired them. He had no patience for sloppiness, and his own judgments, even when later superseded, were never capricious or unseasoned.

What, then, were Nabokov's actual contributions to the science of lepidopterology? First, his technique of measuring the patterns of scales by counting, numbering, and quantitatively comparing their rows was a novel and ingenious new method. The fact that few if any others have taken advantage of it says more about the conservatism of science than the shortcomings of the technique. Nabokov made beautiful drawings of scale patterns, some of which are included here. Because he did not employ the complex mathematics of the modern morphometricians and numerical taxonomists, his results are sometimes pooh-poohed. In some degree, Nabokov was influenced in his studies of scale patterns by a series of papers published by B. N. Schwanwitsch, who studied the evolution of prototypical butterfly patterns at the Universities of Perm, Petrograd, and Leningrad in the 1920s and 1930s. But his method was his own, and no one before or since has undertaken the almost incredibly precise, scale-by-scale mapping that enabled Nabokov to untangle the relationships of pattern development and geographic variation in the orange-bordered Blues. As the robustness of his taxonomic work suggests, this painstaking labor proved much more than a fussy fixation with form and natural artistry. New genetic tools and statistical applications may mean he will remain the sole practitioner of these remarkable techniques.

In biology, those who classify animals and plants are known as taxonomists and systematists. Their work is essential if we are to make anything coherent out of the complexity of life. As Nabokov once wrote in the margin of a paper on butterfly genera by another worker, with whom he disagreed, "It is easier to handle things that have names." Imagine running a big city, or a world, without telephone books. Taxonomists study the characters that organisms have in common, furnish their names, and assign them to categories (= *taxa*). These include orders (Lepidoptera: all butterflies and moths; Primata: humans and their relatives); families (cats, or thrushes, or Swallowtails); genera (the genus *Canis* contains dogs; *Speyeria* includes the large Fritillary butterflies of North America, *Argynnis* those of Eurasia); species, the actual *kinds* of plants and animals, whose members are distinctive in a like manner and can interbreed and produce viable offspring (*Canis lupus* is the Gray Wolf; *Speyeria nokomis* is the Nokomis Fritillary); and subspecies (*Cyllopsis pyracmon nabokovi*), recognizeable varieties produced through geographic isolation. Systematists organize these taxa into theoretical phylogenies, or evolutionary lines of relationship.

Teasing out the details in the taxonomic puzzle was Nabokov's passion in the lab. He relished the extreme attention to detail – "the tactile delights of precise delineation" – that taxonomy required, not unlike that required by an intricate plot or an elegant chess problem. Yet Nabokov entertained no illusions about his field's fallibility. In a 1965 letter to E. P. Wiltshire, he wrote, "taxonomy is human, nature demonian." In particular, he chose to unravel the knot of names used for the orange-bordered Blues (genus *Lycaeides*) of the Northern Hemisphere, the Blues of the New World tropics, and a group of Satyrs then called *Neonympha*. In so doing he named a number of taxa and revised (= defined) these groups as he understood them. Nabokov's classification of Blues and Satyrs was perceptive and has profoundly affected all modern work on the same groups.

"As someone who always valued the individuating detail," Brian Boyd has written, Nabokov was "temperamentally a splitter," a taxonomist who recognizes and elevates distinct differences between types. (Those who tend to blur such differences into more generalized types are called "lumpers.") Nabokov was no arbitrary splitter, however – his separations were based on a keen discrimination of meaningful traits. Especially in later years, he deplored the proliferation of meaningless names for local variants, and sharply scorned the naming of "subspecies" based merely on locality labels rather than on actual, precisely observed morphology, a common practice of certain German dealers who named "different" Parnassians from nearly every valley in the Alps.

In an appraisal of Nabokov's work, Kurt Johnson wrote that "Taxonomists use the phrase 'a good eye' to refer to early workers whose care and discrimination allowed them, even at a time of relatively primitive taxonomic methods, to recognize distinctions between groups of organisms that are eventually borne out by the more complex methods of modern science. Nabokov possessed such a 'good eye,' and his strict adherence to characteristics of anatomy . . . [helped him] recognize what scientists now call 'natural groups,' that is, actual relatives."[11]

Nabokov augmented his "good eye" for drawing dissections of genitalia with what he called "the silent paradise" of the camera lucida, a double-reflection prism developed by William Hyde Wollaston in the early nineteenth century for drawing in perspective. When I visited Dr. Lionel Higgins in Surrey in 1982, he was making genitalic preparations and drawings of the same kinds of Blues that Nabokov labored over, his camera lucida still as serviceable as in Dr. Wollaston's day. A more complex device, roughed out by Leonardo da Vinci but dating from even earlier, is the camera obscura, which gives an actual image of the reflected object instead of the virtual image of the camera lucida. Nabokov did not use this instrument, but took its name for a 1931 novel written in Russian and later translated into English as *Laughter in the Dark*.

When Harvard University mounted an exhibition in 1988 to celebrate Nabokov's work, one of the descriptive labels reported that "His scientific contributions were primarily descriptive, rather than synthetic." In a *Harvard Magazine* article about the man and his butterflies, Philip Zaleski quotes professors Deanne Bowers and Frank Carpenter ascribing Nabokov's work to the realm of the amateur.[12] But it would be wrong to read "amateur" as a pejorative. As Carpenter himself noted, amateur natural history draws on an aristocratic Old World tradition: "Indeed, if you go back far enough, almost all the work was done by amateurs." Not only is this becoming the case again today, as systematics falls out of fashion and museum retirees go unreplaced, but it wasn't that rare in Nabokov's time:

an informal "head count" conducted by Kurt Johnson of the AMNH showed that fewer than ten percent of the curators of major institutions with active Lepidoptera collections had Ph.D.s when Nabokov was there and at Harvard. And if the definition of "professional" implies being paid, it is worth remembering that Nabokov was indeed employed at the MCZ.

Yet Professor Bowers, a chemical ecologist and the curator of the exhibit, described Nabokov to the *Boston Globe* as "a great amateur collector and a scientific naif." If some lepidopterists working in modern laboratories, unversed in the details of Nabokov's research, hold his accomplishment in lower regard than it deserves, those who take time to acquaint themselves with his results know that he used the tools of his time to their best advantage. And because those tools required close personal attention to the organisms themselves, both in the field and in the lab, Nabokov emerges as far more sophisticated in the lives of actual butterflies than many modern workers, who often treat leps as "systems" and deal in abstractions such as cladograms and electrophoretic gels. Dr. Robert Robbins, curator of butterflies at the Smithsonian Institution and a lycaenid specialist, told me that "given what he had, Nabokov did a very nice job – as good or better than most of the professionals of his time." According to Robbins, when there is "a close correspondence between the evidence and your conclusions, that's good work. Klots, Bell, and Williams had it," he said, "and Nabokov had it."

Charles Remington, once a graduate student of Carpenter's, also believes a more respectful measure of Nabokov is in order than Bowers's comments would suggest. According to Brian Boyd, "In his two years at the MCZ and subsequently as editor of the *Lepidopterists' News*, Remington could see better than anyone else the place of Nabokov's work in lepidopterology. He thought Nabokov's contribution to the subject 'extraordinary' in a mere six years as a research scientist – six years also shared between teaching Russian and the writing of four books. . . . Nabokov's reclassifications, his analysis of the diagnostic significance of the genitalia of the blues, and the unprecedented detail of his work on wing markings are all a matter of record in his published articles, but what particularly impressed Remington was the way Nabokov's quick intelligence and his wide knowledge of European butterflies allowed him to spot phenomena in North American [L]epidoptera that were new to American scholars."[13]

Nabokov noticed, for example, that many species regularly immigrated into the north from southern climes, where they were able to overwinter, not in two-way migrations like the Monarch's but in irregular irruptive waves. Wandering and breeding in temperate latitudes throughout the summer, these species had long been taken as part of the resident fauna of North America. Recalling the way that Painted Ladies and certain Blues and Sulfurs emigrate from North Africa into Europe, Nabokov deduced that a similar phenomenon was much more widespread here than indigenous collectors had appreciated. As Remington commented, "His long experience in Europe and now North America, coupled with his brainy approach to everything in life, made him an intuitive, skillful master at field work."[14]

Lee D. Miller, curator at the Allyn Museum of Entomology in the Florida State Museum, thinks equally highly of Nabokov's lab work. Miller is the foremost reviser of the satyrine tribe Euptychiini, a group of subtle but beautifully gemmed Browns in which fall Dorothy's and Nabokov's Satyrs. In his 1974 paper revising the genus *Cyllopsis* (formerly included in *Neonympha*), Dr. Miller had this to say in naming a new subspecies of *C. pyracmon* after Nabokov: "This subspecies is named for Dr. [*sic*] Vladimir Nabokov who first pointed out that both *pyracmon* and *henshawi* occurred in the desert southwest of the U.S. His papers, as with all of his literary endeavors, are highly entertaining and informative, and his work on the United States *Cyllopsis* . . . , as *Neonympha*, too long has been ignored."[15] I followed his lead by assigning *Cyllopsis pyracmon* the English name Nabokov's Satyr in the *Audubon Society Field Guide to North American Butterflies*.

It is true that Nabokov was reluctant to apply life history or ecology to questions of taxonomy, which he felt should be based on the "all-important morphological moment:" As he said of one skipper, "The egg is said to be different – but museum specimens do not lay eggs." Yet he certainly paid great attention to the overall natural history of his animals afield. The Harvard label describing Nabokov's work as "descriptive rather than synthetic" failed to properly assess the results of his labors in that very laboratory. His great appraisal of the *Lycaeides* Blues is indeed expertly descriptive, but it also tightly assimilates masses of experience on the insects' ecology, biogeography, phenology, life history, and evolution: precisely, in a word, synthetic.

But the opinions of his surviving peers and successors provide only one measure of the man as lepidopterist. In their summary of Nabokov's over-all performance in the field, Kurt Johnson, G. Warren Whitaker, and Zsolt Bálint point out that evaluations of one scientist's work by others are bound to change as styles shift in biology, so "any attempts to be authoritative when evaluating the quality of Nabokov's contributions to Entomology are ephemeral."[16] For example, Bálint, trained in the "phylogenetic" school of systematics, considers "Nabokov's concept of the species . . . very close to the modern one," while those from other schools might not frame the questions of speciation just as Nabokov did. In calling for "a more solid ground upon which to evaluate Nabokov's achievement in Lepidopterology," they identify two "unvarying standards": the International Code of Zoological Nomenclature and "the historical context within which systematic biology was performed in Nabokov's time."

As for the latter, Johnson and his co-authors conclude that, "To anyone familiar with the immediate post-War seminal systematic work on tropical lycaenid butterflies [Blues, Coppers, Hairstreaks, and Metalmarks] of the New World, which comprise perhaps a quarter of all the world's butterflies, Nabokov is one of the four major names that come to mind, together with Comstock, Huntington and Clench." This is all the more remarkable because his major field was Nearctic lycaenids, and he spent less than half a year on the neotropical species.

And as far as the Code goes, while many authors erected large numbers of scientific names, few attempted anything as ambitious as Nabokov undertook when he became "first reviser" of the Latin American Blues. Fewer still enjoyed such survivorship among the names they gave as Nabokov. A detailed checklist of all the names proposed by and for Nabokov, with their current status, follows at the end of the volume. In short, he named ten new species or subspecies, renamed another, and erected nine genera of American Blues. Of the twenty names to which his name is affixed as author, fifteen remain valid, a fine batting average for any taxonomist. When Nabokov made mistakes, they came from incomplete collections and inadequate literature. Lacking the pertinent journals, for example, he misapplied the preoccupied name *Pseudothecla* to a new genus. Out of high respect for his work, Francis Hemming renamed it *Nabokovia* in his honor.

As Johnson et al. stress in their appraisal, "Nabokov was not, and never attempted to be, a theoretical biologist . . . he was a 'taxonomist' who categorized specimens, not a 'systematist' who deals with questions of theory and methodology." In "Cetology," Chapter 32 of *Moby-Dick*, Herman Melville nicely exemplifies this distinction in a fanciful classification of whales that concludes they are fish yet serves his purpose. "I shall not pretend to a minute anatomical description of the various species," he writes. "My object here is simply to project the draught of a systematization of cetology. I am the architect, not the builder." From that perspective, Nabokov was a master builder. Melville also called classification "a ponderous task; no ordinary letter-sorter in the Post-office is equal to it." From the extracts of Nabokov's scientific papers presented here, readers will be able to judge the utter industry and exactitude that he brought to the task, the sheer amount of hard work his revisions required, and the depth of thought that went into them. The edifice he built, a house of blue butterflies, has stood up well.

Nabokov had a problem with natural selection. He stated repeatedly in *Speak, Memory* and elsewhere that he found natural selection inadequate to the task of explaining protective devices when developed to a degree of "mimetic subtlety, exuberance, and luxury far in excess of a predator's power of appreciation." Not that he was a creationist by any stretch: in his science as in his literature he often and explicitly celebrated the exuberance and wonder of organic evolution. Nabokov, like Darwin, was fascinated by mimicry in nature and by the astonishing array of protective adaptations in the survival repertoire of butterflies. But he doubted that Darwinian selection could tell the whole story. Evolutionary biologists may differ on the exact mechanism and rate of evolution, but they agree that these mimetic characters elegantly demonstrate selective forces at work in nature.

That elaborations seem disproportionate to their purpose is not unusual in evolution, where not every structure *has* to have an obvious function, and where the fine-tuning of adaptation often exceeds our own powers of discrimination.

Perhaps because the subterfuges of mimicry so resembled his own favorite tools as literary trickster, Nabokov was loath to consign their wonderment to strictly mechanical causes. He suspected a subtle intelligence was at work. Remington believes it was Nabokov's "strong metaphysical investment in his challenge to selection" that made him unsatisfied with a Darwinian explanation. "He was an excellent naturalist and could cite for himself very many examples of perfect resemblances, but he may have been too untrained in the complexities of modern population genetics," Remington wrote.[17] He later told me that in his view, had Nabokov possessed such training, he would have quickly grasped the essential nature of selection as the key to mimicry. Brian Boyd is not so sure, suspecting Nabokov might well have counter-argued in ways no one would have guessed.

But Nabokov did not pass over the subject superficially. He gave selection and mimicry a great deal of careful thought, took issue with the species concepts of the leading evolutionary biologists of the day (his Harvard contemporaries Ernst Mayr and Theodosius Dobzhansky), and wrote provocatively on mimicry. It may even be that some of his objections foreshadowed current debate among different schools of selectionists. But Nabokov withheld his assent for a universe fully ruled by chance, and this may have permitted his temperamental preference for mystery and convolution to overwhelm the parsimony of natural selection in wholly accounting for the miracles made manifest in butterflies. These ideas survive most fully in "Father's Butterflies," his addendum to *The Gift*. By no measure, however, does this diminish his legacy as a scientist.

Nabokov envisioned several books devoted solely to butterflies – the European and North American works mentioned above, a treatment of butterflies in art, and a blend of "science, art, and entertainment" touching on mimetic adaptation as well as his "adventures with leps" here and there. As Remington writes, "None came to fruition; but what fascination there would have been in his versions of any of these!" The inclusion here of selections from some of the unfinished books, and of notes that would have gone into others, should help to quell (or sharpen!) our disappointment over their abandonment.

Even with those projects uncompleted, Nabokov remains the foremost literary interpreter of butterflies and moths. Of the writers who have addressed both insects and literature – Jean-Henri Fabre, Edwin Way Teale, William Beebe, Don Marquis, Vincent Dethier, Howard Ensign Evans, Edward O. Wilson, Bernd Heinrich, John Alcock, Sue Hubbell, and A. S. Byatt come to mind – only Miriam Rothschild, John Burns, and a few others have been lepidopterists. No one approaches Nabokov's dual expertise in fiction and lepidopterology. Brian Boyd's introductory essay explores Nabokov's wide-ranging use of Lepidoptera in his literary corpus, and the selections in this volume demonstrate again and again that fecund pairing.

Nabokov also left his mark on conservation. The Karner Blue Project drew great sustenance from his personal support in a letter to the then director of the Xerces Society, Robert Dirig. Even more than that, he gave the butterfly its name. His own taxonomic work revealed that the species name *scudderi*, then used for a highly restricted subspecies of the Melissa Blue in the Northeast, properly applied to a subspecies of the Northern Blue in Manitoba. That left the northeastern Melissa Blue without a valid scientific name, so Nabokov named it *samuelis*, thus doubly honoring Samuel Scudder, whose classic *Butterflies of New England* he admired immensely.

Lycaeides melissa samuelis gained the common name Karner Blue from a village near its stronghold in New York's Albany Pine Bush. In recent decades, as its habitats from the Upper Midwest to New England have been altered by commercial development and fire suppression, the Karner Blue and its lupine host plant have grown rarer and rarer. Sparked by a Xerces Society campaign, public concern led to its listing first as a state endangered species in New York and then, in 1994, as a federal endangered species. According to Robert Dirig of Cornell University, a major player in Karner Blue conservation efforts, "It is fortunate that this butterfly was described by Vladimir Nabokov (1943), a literary genius of this century, whose celebrity has enhanced preservation efforts."[18]

Professor Pnin encountered the butterfly, which "fluttered around like blue snowflakes." Professor Nabokov finally collected it at Karner on June 2, 1950, eight years after he had described it from specimens reared by Scudder some eight decades before. In his *New York Times* review of Klots's field guide in 1952, he wrote, "the lupines and *Lycaeides samuelis* Nab. are still doing as fine under those old gnarled pines along the railroad as they did ninety years ago." Now, after the passing of half again as many years, the Karner Blues and their "sandy and flowery little paradise," as he described the habitat to Dirig, are not doing as well. Would Nabokov be amazed or amused to learn that the butterfly he shared with his admired antecedent Scudder has come under federal protection, and that he has helped give it whatever chance it has to survive into the next millennium?

In his note cards for his projected *Butterflies of Europe*, Nabokov expressed concern about the spectacular Apollo Parnassian, "steadily dying out in a number of its western European habitats," but stated clearly that "this phenomenon is seldom due to overcollecting." He anticipated a major contemporary issue in butterfly conservation by expressing equal disdain for commercial collectors of the delicate green, stained glass-like, long-tailed Isabella Silkmoth (*Graellsia isabellae*) in its few endangered colonies in France; and for officious wardens who would "forbid an old naturalist to move about with his old net" in the habitat of the Iolas Blue (*Iolana iolas*), where collecting could have no impact, but where the unnecessary destruction of its vineyard host plants will surely wipe it out." His conclusion, pegging "the real culprits" as habitat destroyers rather than collectors, speaks for many lepidopterists today. So does his contempt for "ignorance and pedantry," drawing attention away from habitats while frustrating "the scientist without whom a policeman could not tell a butterfly from an angel or a bat."

Not that collectors never deserve reining in. A recent, highly publicized case involved overavid commercial collectors who were sentenced in federal court for poaching vulnerable species such as the Kaibab Swallowtail of the Grand Canyon—modern counterparts of the French curio seekers Nabokov deplored, whose arrogant cupidity could reduce rare and protected species. Nabokov followed the rules and was attentive to proper protocol for sampling specimens. A letter I received from Vladimir Krivda, a former ranger in Riding Mountain Provincial Park in Canada, recalled that Nabokov had written him about the proper procedure for obtaining permission to collect in the park. When he collected in Grand Canyon and Yosemite national parks, he held the required permits by virtue of his institutional association with museums. He sampled selectively, took good care of his specimens, and made the best scientific use of the ones he brought back to the lab and museum. In later interviews, Nabokov frequently condemned the indiscriminant use of pesticides. Yet by nature he was optimistic about butterflies' chances in the long run against inept humanity.

A series of serendipitous events that might have delighted Nabokov has surrounded the publication of this collection. First, Brian Boyd's great two-volume biography appeared, providing a much clearer context for the butterfly work. Then Dieter Zimmer compiled, published, and later revised his meticulous "Nabokov's Lepidoptera: An Annotated Multilingual Checklist," in connection with a public exhibition around the donation of Nabokov's European butterfly collection, assembled in his later years, to the Museum of Natural History in Lausanne. Charles Remington wrote his reminiscences for the *Garland Companion to Vladimir Nabokov*. And throughout this period, Kurt Johnson of the American Museum of Natural History has been collaborating with Zsolt Bálint of Hungary to update the systematics of several groups of neotropical Blues on which Nabokov worked in addition to the *Lycaeides*. Their ambitious and timely work greatly strengthened this compilation, and they christened their new species with inspired Nabokovian names, such as *Itylos pnin, Nabokovia ada*, and *Madeleinea lolita*.

Yet, had it not been for a truly Nabokovian turn of events, this might not have come about. As Johnson and Bálint were writing their first paper, Dr. Emilio Balletto of Italy was investigating the same fauna. Balletto changed a number of Nabokov's generic assignments, named some of the same new species with pedestrian monikers, and published just a scant month before Johnson and Bálint's paper appeared. Although Balletto was not actively trying to scoop them, the usual application of the Code would give him priority, thus dooming the more appropriate Nabokovian names to the limbo of taxonomic synonymy.

However, a saving plot twist occurred. The American/Hungarian results were both more comprehensive and more conservative than the Italian. While Balletto, referring to few specimens, split Nabokov's genus names into numerous new genera, Johnson and Bálint, referring to many more, preserved most of Nabokov's judgments. A Solomon arose from the Neotropics in the person of Dr. Gerardo Llamas, director of the Peruvian National Museum, the preeminent Latin American lepidopterist, and the editor of the official South American checklist. Dr. Llamas ruled that Balletto had violated the Code by specifying in his etymologies that his new generic names were adjectival, whereas the Code unbendingly demands the nominative form. Balletto salvaged three of his new names, but the bulk of the Johnson/Bálint roster was given priority. This had the triple benefit of basing the revision on better biology, appropriately preserving the correct generic distinctions made by Nabokov himself, and validating a slew of superbly suitable new names. Thus will Vladimir Nabokov's contribution be graven in whatever kind of eternity taxonomy might allow.[19]

Butterflies weave in and out of Nabokov's life and his writing. In a *Boston Globe* column, Chet Raymo wrote that for Nabokov, "lepidopteral details – patterns, shapes, colors, textures – . . . resonated everywhere – in language, literature, love and life – enriching and deepening his experience in a way that scientists seldom share."[20] As a happy result, the language in his scientific writing is often indistinguishable from that of his "literary" prose. It was the genius of the young Charles Remington, as founding editor of the *News of the Lepidopterists' Society*, not to constrain his fellow sufferer's American English within the bounds of standard scientific language. Thus Nabokov's papers in the *News* include images like "Plunging into the forest . . . on the western slopes of the Snowy Range, I found [bog Fritillaries] on a small richly flowered marsh"; and "acting on a hunch, I visited a remarkably repulsive-looking willowbog, full of cowmerds and barbed wire," among the precise accounts of species found and their characteristics.

Elsewhere, Nabokov sometimes slipped lyrical language and informal prose into ordinarily stolid journals: "this clinches the matter"; "the smaller, dapper *atrapraetextus*"; "well formed, fattish falx"; "locality wiggle" for a place label; genitalic processes shaped "fish-like," "asparagus-like," "shoe-shaped," or "whip-like," with hatchets and hooks, or like "a headless dromedary." Even his most functionally descriptive paragraphs show the glister of the natural verbal colorist: "The *scintillant pulvis*: structural scales more or less extensively dusting with metallic greenish blue . . . or turquoise . . . leaving the scintillae as seapools are left by the sea at low tide." And "*Lacrimae*: two or four streamlets of blurred auroral pigment . . . 'trickling' distad across the terminal space."

It seems to me that Nabokov sometimes began a treatise with his good-faith idea of scientific writing – passive verbs, third person, impartial and unornamented phrasing – then picked up lyric momentum, and concluded in full flower. Thus "Notes of the Morphology of the Genus *Lycaeides*" begins "Out of the hundred or so holarctic Lycaenids distributed among at least sixteen genera of the subfamily *Plebejinae* (definitely fixed by Stempffer, 1937, Bull. soc. ent. France 42:211, etc.; *not* covering the superficial concept of 'Blues' for which no systematic term or division can exist)," and concludes with a memorable sentence at home among any of his literary works, invoking "the whole of China, the whole of the Moon" and a nameless collector situated "between climb and cloud on some mountain thousands of miles away from the describer's desk."

Nabokov himself felt that the gulf between scientific and artistic expression was not insuperable, that they could even meet. In his lecture on Charles Dickens's *Bleak House*, he wrote, "All we have to do when reading *Bleak House* is to relax and let our spines take over. Although we read with our minds, the seat of artistic delight is between the shoulder blades. That little shiver behind is quite certainly the highest form of emotion that humanity has attained when evolving pure art and pure science. Let us worship the spine and its tingle. Let us be proud of being vertebrates, for we are vertebrates tipped at the head with a divine flame." And later, "What is the joint impression that a great work of art produces upon us? . . . The Precision of Poetry and the Excitement of Science." For an interview with *Satur-*

day Review, he wrote that he was "certainly not afraid to bore readers with nature notes worked into a memoir or story. I am afraid to trim my science to size or – what is much the same – not to take full advantage of my art in speaking of 'scientific' details."[21] Ultimately, the writer/biologist yearned to reconcile his competing, collaborating talents and desires. In a tough review of a book on Audubon's butterflies, he asked, "Does there not exist a high ridge where the mountainside of 'scientific' knowledge joins the opposite slope of 'artistic' imagination?" As well as anywhere, that territory may be sought in Nabokov's ambidextrous work.

By now it should be clear that the dialectic between Lepidoptera and literature that critics and compulsive splitters of hairs love to worry about did not really exist in Nabokov's own mind. Thus, the biographer Andrew Field's statement that Nabokov's butterflies "sometimes seem an amazing stylistic mannerism" comes across as especially silly. Perhaps such a striking misapprehension should not be surprising from someone who had a "loathing for Lepidoptera," as Nabokov said of Field when writing him in 1966. But I would think it difficult to know anything at all about Nabokov's life and not see that butterflies and moths lived at the center of his soul.

Readers who mistake Nabokov's passion for a wild whim tend to be oblivious to butterflies. As he wrote in *Speak, Memory*, "it is astounding how little the ordinary person notices butterflies." Taking notice is the first step toward knowing, and knowing can lead to love. However they are approached – with camera, microscope, or binoculars, in a garden patch or a gossamer net – butterflies make for enchanting company, and there is no better introduction to them than this collection. Likewise, lepidopterists are often all but unaware of Nabokov's fiction and poetry. I don't know the personal reading habits of all my fellow leppers, but of the many meetings I've attended, only one produced a lively conversation on Nabokov's books, and there were just two participants. I hope this collection will lead more butterfly lovers to Nabokov the novelist, even as it brings rapturous readers of his prose and poetry to a fuller appreciation of butterflies.

In any discussion of Nabokov and butterflies, *Lolita* inevitably comes up. This is partly because *Lolita* is the only thing many people know about

Nabokov, if they have heard of him at all. Comparing Humbert's pursuit of Dolores and Quilty to a butterfly hunt is a cliché that few commentators or magazine writers have managed to avoid. Diana Butler, in a clever but overimagined essay entitled "Lolita Lepidoptera,"[22] makes the novel into a direct parallel of Nabokov's search for the female of the butterfly he named *Lycaeides*[now *idas*] *sublivens*. She pointed out the similar language in Nabokov's loving descriptions of the sad Dolores Haze and of the type specimen of the female *L. i. sublivens* . . . the soft brown appendages, the fine downy pelage. The two are not without obvious ties, but Butler takes the linkage much too far, finding butterfly and moth symbols beneath every host plant leaf.

No doubt the novel's construction contains elements of the lepidopterist's outing, tracking desirable prey from habitat to preferred or deduced habitat. More interesting is the fact that he wrote much of the book, by far his most commercially successful, on the road during actual butterfly-hunting expeditions in the West with Véra and often Dmitri. A BBC television documentary on the writing of *Lolita* staged an imaginary scene in which Véra is driving and Vladimir is revising text, tossing rejected manuscript cards out the car window. No holographic manuscript of the book exists, only a stack of these cards on which he stored his notes for the book. (I imagine finding a cache of the discards, yellowed and nibbled, in a Bushy-tailed Woodrat's nest—now *that* would be a catch!) The image of the tossed-out words floating across the Wyoming countryside like big white butterflies is to me a much more compelling connection than the facile one often made. As Brian Boyd pointed out to me, it also echoes a scene in *Look at the Harlequins*, when a wind-whipped piece of yellow paper seems to metamorphose into a Sulfur butterfly on a clover head.

Nabokov vigorously maintained that there was no connection between his science and his characters' sometimes dark lives. But of connections between entomology and literature, there were many. The names of dozens of lepidopterists are scattered throughout the corpus: the fictional post-editor of *Lolita* is named for John Ray, an important seventeenth century systematist; Bill Uhler, "the dragonfly man" in "The Admirable Angle-wing," recalls the namesake of Uhler's Arctic, *Oeneis uhleri*, a butterfly he knew from Colorado. Both real lepidopterists (himself in cameo in *Pnin*, Gregory Grum-Grzhimaylo in *The Gift*) and fictional ones (Paul Pilgram in "The Aurelian") appear in Nabokov's tales.

Butterfly names are also sprinkled liberally throughout the works. Nabokov took special pleasure in mingling the nomenclature of the creatures and their discoverers in his fictional landscapes. Ladoga, the birthplace of Ada's mother in the state of Mayne, is the subgenus of the European White Admirable butterfly. Lolita and Humbert spend time in Colorado between "Snow" and "Elphinstone." These reflect Snow's Copper (*Lycaena cupreus snowi*) and *Elphinstonia charlonia* (the Greenish Black-tip), both at home among high-altitude cliffs and rocky places. The former, brilliant as a molten ingot, Nabokov in fact collected near Telluride. The latter, a lovely lemony Sulfur, he had hoped to collect in the Atlas Mountains. Besides these that I've spotted, Nabokov left hundreds of such gifts for lepidopterist-readers, many of which Joann Karges teases out in her book, *Nabokov's Lepidoptera: Genres and Genera*.[23]

Besides name play, the author injected his fiction with substantial doses of actual, robust natural history. In one scene in *The Gift*, for example, Fyodor records the precourtship behavior of violet-tinged Coppers as they "tangled in lightning-swift flight in midair," while an Amandus Blue, a Freya Fritillary that "flicked among the Selenas," and a small hummingbird moth went about their business. The whole company told him the progress of the season and affected him deeply. When he tucked these wonderful layers of detail and esoteric references into his creations, Nabokov was having fun, but he was also blending his two driving passions in a manner that respected and celebrated both. As he wrote of Fyodor, "The divine meaning of his wood meadow was expressed in its butterflies" (GIFT 132) – and the whole world was his wood meadow.

One of Nabokov's loveliest poems may shadow back to his first thrill of lepidopterological discovery. In *Speak, Memory*, he tells of coming across a handsome little moth when he was ten years old, which he took for a new species. He wrote up his find and submitted it to Professor Richard South of London, who replied with the disappointing news that the moth had previously been described as *Plusia excelsa* from specimens taken at St. Petersburg. The eager young lepidopterist had been gazumped. His disappointment later made ripples in both *Laughter in the Dark* (where he names a blind man "Kretschmar" after the person who had named "his" moth) and *The Gift* (in which Fyodor's father undergoes a similar disappointment). I believe that fundamental episode also colored the poem "Lines Written in Oregon," inspired by a mountain outing during the summer of 1953, which the Nabokovs spent mostly in Ashland.

The poem begins with "Esmeralda! Now we rest / Here, in the bewitched and blest / Mountain forests of the West," mentions a "peacock moth on picnic table," and concludes with the line "Esmeralda, *immer, immer.*" Brian Boyd explains the enchanted theme in terms of "the magic of the Europe Nabokov derived from and rediscovers here in the American West." And, as lepidopteran images in Nabokov are seldom casual, I think the appearance of the picnic-table moth adds to the bewitchment.

While there has been much speculation as to the identity of "Esmeralda," my investigation of the lepidopteran candidates by that name convinces me that it may well refer to an Oregon moth closely related and similar to the one Nabokov had "discovered" as a boy. If so, although the Oregon moth is actually two or three species removed from the original, *Plusia esmeralda* is the nearest name Nabokov would have found for it in McDunnough's checklist at the time. When the poet wrote "Esmeralda, *immer, immer,*" he may have sighed for his own first, sweet discovery, and its sheer intensity and savor.

Still, something of that original thrill would revive when Nabokov, as a young man, found a striking Alpine novelty, which he described in "A Discovery." This poem has incorrectly been cited as applying to both the Karner Blue and Dorothy's Satyr, but it clearly pertains to *Lysandra cormion*, which later turned out to be a hybrid of two other species. The poet claims to "want no other fame" than the label designating him as its first describer. As shown by the checklist of Nabokovian names, it was a distinction he would achieve many times in the years to come, if never with quite the poignance of that first fresh moth.

Of his two devotions, literature and Lepidoptera, the latter – although this may seem heretical news to some literary Nabokovians – may have

been the greater. Several passages in *Speak, Memory*, and various statements in interviews, seem to suggest the primacy of this particular passion.
In fact, had things gone differently, Nabokov might have become better
known as an entomologist than a writer. As he told the *Paris Review*, "It is
not improbable that had there been no revolution in Russia, I would have
devoted myself entirely to lepidopterology and never have written any
novels at all."[24] But the Revolution did take place, dashing any hopes of
financing a great Asiatic expedition with his inherited fortune. Instead, he
created the lepidopterist that he would have liked to become in the person
of Konstantin Godunov-Cherdyntsev in *The Gift*.

The *Boston Globe* columnist Chet Raymo has expressed the belief that
"Nabokov never achieved the scientist's unity of vision" because of his "inability to un-see what had once been seen. He was a prisoner of particulars. . . . For Nabokov, seeing and knowing were one." Raymo concludes,
"I suspect he was inevitably destined to become a novelist, not an entomologist – his biographer and the Revolution notwithstanding."[25] I am not so
sure. At least for a time, Nabokov dwelled on that "high ridge where the
mountainside of scientific knowledge joins the opposite slope of artistic
imagination," the habitat of *Erebia* and *Elphinstonia*, place of rarefied air,
science, poetry, and sublime fiction, and thrived there. As Joann Karges
writes, he blended "the science, art, and sport of Lepidoptera" and "the art
and game of Literature" into "the ultimate spiral."[26] Clearly, he cherished
both, more than anything but his family, and perhaps the distant memory
of Vyra – where the butterfly hunt had begun.

Although I failed to meet Nabokov in Montreux that distant spring ago, it
is good that I went. As I later learned, the attempt was doomed from the
start. Nabokov was very ill at the time, at a hospital down the lake in Lausanne. Even had he been home, he was too weak to have considered receiving a casual caller. Yet it was not after all a case of nothing ventured, nothing gained. I ventured little but I gained much, for there is something to be
said for mere propinquity in a pilgrimage. Just being in the gravitational
field of the admired figure, among the landscapes and buildings that he or

she has known and loved, lends the seeker a sense of association that books and artifacts alone cannot provide. At this remove, writing about Nabokov, I feel that I know him better for having traveled to his final home.

Besides, I have in another sense met the man many times. I have walked with him every time I've chased a Swallowtail in the shadow of Longs Peak among Ponderosa Pines and Mariposa Lilies, or watched a Magdalena Alpine float down the stony slope of Mount Meeker. I have followed soft brown Satyrs with him under Gambel Oaks after a fragrant rain at the Black Canyon of the Gunnison. We have both paused at dusk to "greet the pink hawks sampling our lilacs." And when I tracked hulky butterflies in a hot Turkmenian canyon, erupting from the dusty road or vanishing onto tree bark, they were the same Great Banded Graylings that Nabokov stalked in Crimea.

I encountered Nabokov in the Chiricahua Mountains of southeast Arizona, up above the spectacular orange rhyolite formations of Cave Creek Canyon, when I walked into the pines and found the butterfly known today as Nabokov's Satyr – he had gone there especially to challenge another worker's (incorrect) sinking of this butterfly into the species he had earlier discovered at the Grand Canyon – and in Yankee Boy Basin in Colorado's San Juan Mountains, where I found Nabokov's Blue, a shred of the sky's thin air blowing across the alpine fellfields. Nabokov eventually discovered the first female of *Lycaeides idas sublivens* near here, and it was the crowning achievement in his pursuit of these scintillated and lunuled Blues across the miles and the years.

Vladimir Nabokov knew what all butterfly folk know: the rhapsodic thrall in which one may be held by butterflies and moths. Konstantin Godunov-Cherdyntsev knew it, and Ada Veen knew it too, though Lolita never quite got it. No simple whim, Nabokov's butterflies were the wings of a passion that many have known, but none have named as well as he: "a momentary vacuum into which rushes all that I love."

Nabokov's *Butterflies*

SELECTED WRITINGS

1908–1977

A Note on the Texts

ORDER: *The selections have been arranged chronologically. All texts by Nabokov after "Butterflies," Chapter 6 of* Speak, Memory: An Autobiography Revisited *(1966), which describes the onset of his passion, occur in the order in which they were written. Those few by others, such as letters to Nabokov or memoirs about him, appear at the appropriate place in the chronological sequence.*

TEXTS: *Nabokov usually prepared his texts thoroughly before publication and rarely revised later. Nevertheless, he substantially revamped the novel* King, Queen, Knave *when he translated it into English and also expanded his autobiography when transforming it from periodical essays to book form, and then from English into Russian and back again into English.*

Wherever butterflies appear in any passage in an earlier version of these two works, the relevant passage is placed at the year the text was first written (1928 for King, Queen, Knave; *late 1940s for the autobiography) but the text of these passages is taken from the later version. In the case of* King, Queen, Knave, *this is Nabokov's only English version; in the case of* Speak, Memory, *the later version is more accurate or better phrased or both, although the differences tend to be minor. When butterflies feature for the first time in a passage only in a later version, the passage appears under the date of the revision (1968 for* King, Queen, Knave; *1954 for the Russian version of the autobiography,* Drugie berega; *and 1966 for* Speak, Memory: An Autobiography Revisited). *This arrangement allows readers to encounter each text at its best without obscuring the early appearance of butterflies in Nabokov's literary work or the fact that, especially in the 1960s, as his fame as a writer – and a lepidopterist – grew, he went back to earlier texts to add more lepidopteral details.*

Since Nabokov planned each of his books in considerable detail before he began to write, he could work on any part, early or late, knowing where it would stand in the finished work. He wrote his autobiography in this way, a chapter at a time and not necessarily in sequence, between 1947 and 1950, and published the chapters, in the New Yorker *and elsewhere, as they were ready. Only then did he collect them in book form:* Conclusive Evidence, *the first American edition, was published in 1951; the British edition, under the title* Speak, Memory, *appeared later that year. Because Nabokov had the eventual sequence in mind from the first and regarded the periodical versions as provisional, the butterfly passages in the early version of the autobiography, except, as noted, for Chapter 6, follow the sequence in the book and are placed at the end of the 1940s.*

SELECTION: *While the selections do not include all Nabokov's nature writing – his trees, flowers, birds, and beasts, his landscapes, cloudscapes and lightscapes – they do feature examples of his writing on taxonomy and on insects other than butterflies and moths when these appear particularly apt.*

All selections are by Vladimir Nabokov and were originally written in English unless otherwise noted. Translations are by Brian Boyd unless otherwise noted.

BB

Butterflies

Autobiography. Written in November–early December 1947. Published in the *New Yorker*, June 12, 1948. Revised as Chapter 6 of *Conclusive Evidence/Speak, Memory* (1951).

1

On a summer morning, in the legendary Russia of my boyhood, my first glance upon awakening was for the chink between the white inner shutters. If it disclosed a watery pallor, one had better not open them at all, and so be spared the sight of a sullen day sitting for its picture in a puddle. How resentfully one would deduce, from a line of dull light, the leaden sky, the sodden sand, the gruel-like mess of broken brown blossoms under the lilacs – and that flat, fallow leaf (the first casualty of the season) pasted upon a wet garden bench!

But if the chink was a long glint of dewy brilliancy, then I made haste to have the window yield its treasure. With one blow, the room would be cleft into light and shade. The foliage of birches moving in the sun had the translucent green tone of grapes, and in contrast to this there was the dark velvet of fir trees against a blue of extraordinary intensity, the like of which I rediscovered only many years later, in the montane zone of Colorado.

From the age of seven, everything I felt in connection with a rectangle of framed sunlight was dominated by a single passion. If my first glance of the morning was for the sun, my first thought was for the butterflies it would engender. The original event had been banal enough. On the honeysuckle, overhanging the carved back of a bench just opposite the main entrance,

my guiding angel (whose wings, except for the absence of a Florentine lim-
bus, resemble those of Fra Angelico's Gabriel) pointed out to me a rare visitor, a splendid, pale-yellow creature with black blotches, blue crenels, and
a cinnabar eyespot above each chrome-rimmed black tail. As it probed the
inclined flower from which it hung, its powdery body slightly bent, it kept
restlessly jerking its great wings, and my desire for it was one of the most
intense I have ever experienced. Agile Ustin, our town-house janitor, who
for a comic reason (explained elsewhere) happened to be that summer in
the country with us, somehow managed to catch it in my cap, after which
it was transferred, cap and all, to a wardrobe, where domestic naphthalene
was fondly expected by Mademoiselle to kill it overnight. On the following
morning, however, when she unlocked the wardrobe to take something
out, my Swallowtail, with a mighty rustle, flew into her face, then made for
the open window, and presently was but a golden fleck dipping and dodg-
ing and soaring eastward, over timber and tundra, to Vologda, Viatka and
Perm, and beyond the gaunt Ural range to Yakutsk and Verkhne Kolymsk,
and from Verkhne Kolymsk, where it lost a tail, to the fair Island of St.
Lawrence, and across Alaska to Dawson, and southward along the Rocky
Mountains – to be finally overtaken and captured, after a forty-year race,
on an immigrant dandelion under an endemic aspen near Boulder. In a letter from Mr. Brune to Mr. Rawlins, June 14, 1735, in the Bodleian collection, he states that one Mr. Vernon followed a butterfly nine miles before
he could catch him (*The Recreative Review or Eccentricities of Literature
and Life*. Vol. 1, p. 144, London, 1821).

Soon after the wardrobe affair I found a spectacular moth, marooned in
a corner of a vestibule window, and my mother dispatched it with ether. In
later years, I used many killing agents, but the least contact with the initial
stuff would always cause the porch of the past to light up and attract that
blundering beauty. Once, as a grown man, I was under ether during appen-
dectomy, and with the vividness of a decalcomania picture I saw my own
self in a sailor suit mounting a freshly emerged Emperor moth under the
guidance of a Chinese lady who I knew was my mother. It was all there,
brilliantly reproduced in my dream, while my own vitals were being exposed: the soaking, ice-cold absorbent cotton pressed to the insect's le-

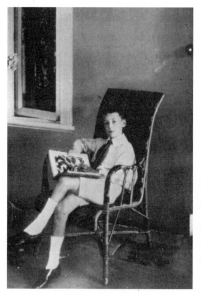 

Left: VN at eight, posed with
butterfly book, Vyra, 1907.
Photographed by the leading
St. Petersburg photographer,
Karl Bulla.
Right: VN with butterfly book
and his mother, Elena Nabokov,
a passionate mushroom
collector, Vyra, 1907.

murian head; the subsiding spasms of its body; the satisfying crackle produced by the pin penetrating the hard crust of its thorax; the careful
insertion of the point of the pin in the cork-bottomed groove of the spreading board; the symmetrical adjustment of the thick, strong-veined wings
under neatly affixed strips of semitransparent paper.

2

I must have been eight when, in a storeroom of our country house, among
all kinds of dusty objects, I discovered some wonderful books acquired in
the days when my mother's mother had been interested in natural science
and had had a famous university professor of zoology (Shimkevich) give
private lessons to her daughter. Some of these books were mere curios, such
as the four huge brown folios of Albertus Seba's work (*Locupletissimi Re-
rum Naturalium Thesauri Accurata Descriptio . . .*), printed in Amster-
dam around 1750. On their coarse-grained pages I found woodcuts of ser-
pents and butterflies and embryos. The fetus of an Ethiopian female child
hanging by the neck in a glass jar used to give me a nasty shock every time
I came across it; nor did I much care for the stuffed hydra on plate CII, with

its seven lion-toothed turtleheads on seven serpentine necks and its strange, bloated body which bore buttonlike tubercules along the sides and ended in a knotted tail.

Other books I found in that attic, among herbariums full of alpine columbines, and blue palemoniums, and Jove's campions, and orange-red lilies, and other Davos flowers, came closer to my subject. I took in my arms and carried downstairs glorious loads of fantastically attractive volumes: Maria Sibylla Merian's (1647–1717) lovely plates of Surinam insects, and Esper's noble *Die Schmetterlinge* (Erlangen, 1777), and Boisduval's *Icones Historiques de Lépidoptères Nouveaux ou Peu Connus* (Paris, begun in 1832). Still more exciting were the products of the latter half of the century – Newman's *Natural History of British Butterflies and Moths*, Hofmann's *Die Gross-Schmetterlinge Europas,* the Grand Duke Nikolay Mihailovich's *Mémoires* on Asiatic lepidoptera (with incomparably beautiful figures painted by Kavrigin, Rybakov, Lang), Scudder's stupendous work on the *Butterflies of New England.*

Retrospectively, the summer of 1905, though quite vivid in many ways, is not animated yet by a single bit of quick flutter or colored fluff around or across the walks with the village schoolmaster: the Swallowtail of June, 1906, was still in the larval stage on a roadside umbellifer; but in the course of that month I became acquainted with a score or so of common things, and Mademoiselle was already referring to a certain forest road that culminated in a marshy meadow full of Small Pearl-bordered Fritillaries (thus called in my first unforgettable and unfadingly magical little manual, Richard South's *The Butterflies of the British Isles* which had just come out at the time) as *le chemin des papillons bruns*. The following year I became aware that many of our butterflies and moths did not occur in England or Central Europe, and more complete atlases helped me to determine them. A severe illness (pneumonia, with fever up to 41° centigrade), in the beginning of 1907, mysteriously abolished the rather monstrous gift of numbers that had made of me a child prodigy during a few months (today I cannot multiply 13 by 17 without pencil and paper; I can add them up, though, in a trice, the teeth of the three fitting in neatly); but the butterflies survived. My mother accumulated a library and a museum around my bed, and the longing to describe a new species completely replaced that of discovering a new prime number. A trip to Biarritz, in August 1907, added new wonders (though not as lucid and numerous as they were to be in 1909). By 1908, I had gained absolute control over the European lepidoptera as known to Hofmann. By 1910, I had dreamed my way through the first volumes of Seitz's prodigious picture book *Die Gross-Schmetterlinge der Erde*, had purchased a number of rarities recently described, and was voraciously reading entomological periodicals, especially English and Russian ones. Great upheavals were taking place in the development of systematics. Since the middle of the century, Continental lepidopterology had been, on the whole, a simple and stable affair, smoothly run by the Germans. Its high priest, Dr. Staudinger, was also the head of the largest firm of insect dealers. Even now, half a century after his death, German lepidopterists have not quite managed to shake off the hypnotic spell occasioned by his authority. He was still alive when his school began to lose ground as a scientific force in the world. While he and his followers stuck to specific and generic names sanctioned by long usage and were content to classify butterflies by characters visible to the naked eye, English-speaking authors were introducing nomenclatorial changes as a result of a strict application of the law of priority and taxonomic changes based on the microscopic study of organs. The Germans did their best to ignore the new trends and continued to cherish the philately-like side of entomology. Their solicitude for the "average collector who should not be made to dissect" is comparable to the way nervous publishers of popular novels pamper the "average reader" – who should not be made to think.

There was another more general change, which coincided with my ardent adolescent interest in butterflies and moths. The Victorian and Staudingerian kind of species, hermetic and homogeneous, with sundry (alpine, polar, insular, etc.) "varieties" affixed to it from the outside, as it were, like incidental appendages, was replaced by a new, multiform and fluid kind of species, organically *consisting* of geographical races or subspecies. The evolutional aspects of the case were thus brought out more clearly, by means of more flexible methods of classification, and further links between butterflies and the central problems of nature were provided by biological investigations.

The mysteries of mimicry had a special attraction for me. Its phenomena showed an artistic perfection usually associated with man-wrought things. Consider the imitation of oozing poison by bubblelike macules on a wing (complete with pseudo-refraction) or by glossy yellow knobs on a chrysalis ("Don't eat me – I have already been squashed, sampled and rejected"). Consider the tricks of an acrobatic caterpillar (of the Lobster Moth) which in infancy looks like bird's dung, but after molting develops scrabbly hymenopteroid appendages and baroque characteristics, allowing the extraordinary fellow to play two parts at once (like the actor in Oriental shows who *becomes* a pair of intertwisted wrestlers): that of a writhing larva and that of a big ant seemingly harrowing it. When a certain moth resembles a certain wasp in shape and color, it also walks and moves its antennae in a waspish, unmothlike manner. When a butterfly has to look like a leaf, not only are all the details of a leaf beautifully rendered but markings mimicking grub-bored holes are generously thrown in. "Natural selection," in the Darwinian sense, could not explain the miraculous coincidence of imitative aspect and imitative behavior, nor could one appeal to the theory of "the struggle for life" when a protective device was carried to a point of mimetic subtlety, exuberance, and luxury far in excess of a predator's power of appreciation. I discovered in nature the nonutilitarian delights that I sought in art. Both were a form of magic, both were a game of intricate enchantment and deception.

3

I have hunted butterflies in various climes and disguises: as a pretty boy in knickerbockers and sailor cap; as a lanky cosmopolitan expatriate in flannel bags and beret; as a fat hatless old man in shorts. Most of my cabinets have shared the fate of our Vyra house. Those in our town house and the small addendum I left in the Yalta Museum have been destroyed, no doubt, by carpet beetles and other pests. A collection of South European stuff that I started in exile vanished in Paris during World War Two. All my American captures from 1940 to 1960 (several thousands of specimens including great rarities and types) are in the Mus. of Comp. Zoology, the Am. Nat. Hist. Mus., and the Cornell Univ. Mus. of Entomology, where they are safer than they would be in Tomsk or Atomsk. Incredibly happy memories, quite comparable, in fact, to those of my Russian boyhood, are associated with my research work at the MCZ, Cambridge, Mass. (1941–1948). No less happy have been the many collecting trips taken almost every summer, during twenty years, through most of the states of my adopted country.

In Jackson Hole and in the Grand Canyon, on the mountain slopes above Telluride, Colo., and on a celebrated pine barren near Albany, N.Y., dwell, and will dwell, in generations more numerous than editions, the butterflies I have described as new. Several of my finds have been dealt with by other workers; some have been named after me. One of these, Nabokov's Pug (*Eupithecia nabokovi* McDunnough), which I boxed one night in 1943 on a picture window of James Laughlin's Alta Lodge in Utah, fits most philosophically into the thematic spiral that began in a wood on the Oredezh around 1910 – or perhaps even earlier, on that Nova Zemblan river a century and a half ago.

Few things indeed have I known in the way of emotion or appetite, ambition or achievement, that could surpass in richness and strength the excitement of entomological exploration. From the very first it had a great many intertwinkling facets. One of them was the acute desire to be alone, since any companion, no matter how quiet, interfered with the concentrated enjoyment of my mania. Its gratification admitted of no compromise or exception. Already when I was ten, tutors and governesses knew that the morning was mine and cautiously kept away.

In this connection, I remember the visit of a schoolmate, a boy of whom I was very fond and with whom I had excellent fun. He arrived one summer night – in 1913, I think – from a town some twenty-five miles away. His father had recently perished in an accident, the family was ruined and the stouthearted lad, not being able to afford the price of a railway ticket, had bicycled all those miles to spend a few days with me.

On the morning following his arrival, I did everything I could to get out of the house for my morning hike without his knowing where I had gone. Breakfastless, with hysterical haste, I gathered my net, pill boxes, killing jar, and escaped through the window. Once in the forest, I was safe; but still I walked on, my calves quaking, my eyes full of scalding tears, the whole of me twitching with shame and self-disgust, as I visualized my poor friend, with his long pale face and black tie, moping in the hot garden – patting the panting dogs for want of something better to do, and trying hard to justify my absence to himself.

Let me look at my demon objectively. With the exception of my parents, no one really understood my obsession, and it was many years before I met a fellow sufferer. One of the first things I learned was not to depend on others for the growth of my collection. One summer afternoon, in 1911, Mademoiselle came into my room, book in hand, started to say she wanted to show me how wittily Rousseau denounced zoology (in favor of botany), and by then was too far gone in the gravitational process of lowering her bulk into an armchair to be stopped by my howl of anguish: on that seat I had happened to leave a glass-lidded cabinet tray with long, lovely series of the Large White. Her first reaction was one of stung vanity: her weight, surely, could not be accused of damaging what in fact it had demolished; her second was to console me: *Allons donc, ce ne sont que des papillons de potager!* – which only made matters worse. A Sicilian pair recently purchased from Staudinger had been crushed and bruised. A huge Biarritz example was utterly mangled. Smashed, too, were some of my choicest local captures. Of these, an aberration resembling the Canarian race of the species might have been mended with a few drops of glue; but a precious gynandromorph, left side male, right side female, whose abdomen could not be traced and whose wings had come off, was lost forever: one might reattach the wings but one could not prove that all four belonged to that headless thorax on its bent pin. Next morning, with an air of great mystery, poor Mademoiselle set off for St. Petersburg and came back in the evening bringing me ("something better than your cabbage butterflies") a banal Urania moth mounted on plaster. "How you hugged me, how you danced with joy!" she exclaimed ten years later in the course of inventing a brand-new past.

Our country doctor, with whom I had left the pupae of a rare moth when I went on a journey abroad, wrote me that everything had hatched finely; but in reality a mouse had got at the precious pupae, and upon my return the deceitful old man produced some common Tortoiseshell butterflies, which, I presume, he had hurriedly caught in his garden and popped into the breeding cage as plausible substitutes (so *he* thought). Better than he, was an enthusiastic kitchen boy who would sometimes borrow my equipment and come back two hours later in triumph with a bagful of seething invertebrate life and several additional items. Loosening the mouth of the net which he had tied up with a string, he would pour out his cornucopian spoil – a mass of grasshoppers, some sand, the two parts of a mushroom he had thriftily plucked on the way home, more grasshoppers, more sand, and one battered Small White.

In the works of major Russian poets I can discover only two lepidop-teral images of genuinely sensuous quality: Bunin's impeccable evocation of what is certainly a Tortoiseshell:

> And there will fly into the room
> A colored butterfly in silk
> To flutter, rustle and pit-pat
> On the blue ceiling . . .

and Fet's "Butterfly" soliloquizing:

> Whence have I come and whither am I hasting
> Do not inquire;
> Now on a graceful flower I have settled
> And now respire.

In French poetry one is struck by Musset's well-known lines (in *Le Saule*):

> *Le phalène doré dans sa course légère*
> *Traverse les prés embaumés*

which is an absolutely exact description of the crepuscular flight of the male of the geometrid called in England the Orange moth; and there is Fargue's fascinatingly apt phrase (in *Les Quatres Journées*) about a garden which, at nightfall, *se glace de bleu comme l'aile du grand Sylvain* (the Poplar Admirable). And among the very few genuine lepidopterological images in English poetry, my favorite is Browning's

> On our other side is the straight-up rock;
> And a path is kept 'twixt the gorge and it
> By boulder-stones where lichens mock
> The marks on a moth, and small ferns fit
> Their teeth to the polished block
>
> ("By the Fire-side")

It is astounding how little the ordinary person notices butterflies. "None," calmly replied that sturdy Swiss hiker with Camus in his rucksack when purposely asked by me for the benefit of my incredulous companion if he had seen any butterflies while descending the trail where, a moment before, you and I had been delighting in swarms of them. It is also true that when I call up the image of a particular path remembered in minute detail but pertaining to a summer before that of 1906, preceding, that is, the date on my first locality label, and never revisited, I fail to make out one wing, one wingbeat, one azure flash, one moth-gemmed flower, as if an evil spell had been cast on the Adriatic coast making all its "leps" (as the slangier among us say) invisible. Exactly thus an entomologist may feel some day when plodding beside a jubilant, and already helmetless botanist amid the hideous flora of a parallel planet, with not a single insect in sight; and thus (in odd proof of the odd fact that whenever possible the scenery of our infancy is used by an economically minded producer as a ready-made setting for our adult dreams) the seaside hilltop of a certain recurrent nightmare of mine, whereinto I smuggle a collapsible net from my waking state, is gay with thyme and melilot, but incomprehensibly devoid of all the butterflies that should be there.

I also found out very soon that a "lepist" indulging in his quiet quest was apt to provoke strange reactions in other creatures. How often, when a picnic had been arranged, and I would be self-consciously trying to get my humble implements unnoticed into the tar-smelling charabanc (a tar preparation was used to keep flies away from the horses) or the tea-smelling

Opel convertible (benzine forty years ago smelled that way), some cousin or aunt of mine would remark: "Must you *really* take that net with you? Can't you enjoy yourself like a normal boy? Don't you think you are spoiling everybody's pleasure?" Near a sign NACH BODENLAUBE, at Bad Kissingen, Bavaria, just as I was about to join for a long walk my father and majestic old Muromtsev (who, four years before, in 1906, had been President of the first Russian Parliament), the latter turned his marble head toward me, a vulnerable boy of eleven, and said with his famous solemnity: "Come with us by all means, but do not chase butterflies, child. It spoils the rhythm of the walk." On a path above the Black Sea, in the Crimea, among shrubs in waxy bloom, in March 1918, a bow-legged Bolshevik sentry attempted to arrest me for signaling (with my net, he said) to a British warship. In the summer of 1929, every time I walked through a village in the Eastern Pyrenees, and happened to look back, I would see in my wake the villagers frozen in the various attitudes my passage had caught them in, as if I were Sodom and they Lot's wife. A decade later, in the Maritime Alps, I once noticed the grass undulate in a serpentine way behind me because a fat rural policeman was wriggling after me on his belly to find out if I were not trapping songbirds. America has shown even more of this morbid interest in my retiary activities than other countries have – perhaps because I was in my forties when I came there to live, and the older the man, the queerer he looks with a butterfly net in his hand. Stern farmers have drawn my attention to NO FISHING signs; from cars passing me on the highway have come wild howls of derision; sleepy dogs, though unmindful of the worst bum, have perked up and come at me, snarling; tiny tots have pointed me out to their puzzled mamas; broad-minded vacationists have asked me whether I was catching bugs for bait; and one morning on a wasteland, lit by tall yuccas in bloom, near Santa Fe, a big black mare followed me for more than a mile.

4

When, having shaken off all pursuers, I took the rough, red road that ran from our Vyra house toward field and forest, the animation and luster of the day seemed like a tremor of sympathy around me.

Very fresh, very dark Arran Browns, which emerged only every second year (conveniently, retrospection has fallen here into line), flitted among the firs or revealed their red markings and checkered fringes as they sunned themselves on the roadside bracken. Hopping above the grass, a diminutive Ringlet called Hero dodged my net. Several moths, too, were flying – gaudy sun lovers that sail from flower to flower like painted flies, or male insomniacs in search of hidden females, such as that rust-colored Oak Eggar hurtling across the shrubbery. I noticed (one of the major mysteries of my childhood) a soft pale green wing caught in a spider's web (by then I knew what it was: part of a Large Emerald). The tremendous larva of the Goat Moth, ostentatiously segmented, flat-headed, flesh-colored and glossily flushed, a strange creature "as naked as a worm" to use a French comparison, crossed my path in frantic search for a place to pupate (the awful pressure of metamorphosis, the aura of a disgraceful fit in a public place). On the bark of that birch tree, the stout one near the park wicket, I had found last spring a dark aberration of Sievers' Carmelite (just another gray moth to the reader). In the ditch, under the bridgelet, a bright-yellow Silvius Skipper hobnobbed with a dragonfly (just a blue libellula to me). From a flower head two male Coppers rose to a tremendous height, fighting all the way up – and then, after a while, came the downward flash of one of them returning to his thistle. These were familiar insects, but at any moment something better might cause me to stop with a quick intake of breath. I remember one day when I warily brought my net closer and closer to an uncommon Hairstreak that had daintily settled on a sprig. I could clearly see the white W on its chocolate-brown underside. Its wings were closed and the inferior ones were rubbing against each other in a curious circular motion – possibly producing some small, blithe crepitation pitched too high for a human ear to catch. I had long wanted that particular species, and, when near enough, I struck. You have heard champion tennis players moan after muffing an easy shot. You may have seen the face of the world-famous grandmaster Wilhelm Edmundson when, during a simultaneous display in a Minsk café, he lost his rook, by an absurd oversight, to the local amateur and pediatrician, Dr. Schach, who eventually won. But that day nobody (except my older self) could see me shake out a piece of twig from an otherwise empty net and stare at a hole in the tarlatan.

5

Near the intersection of two carriage roads (one, well-kept, running north-south in between our "old" and "new" parks, and the other, muddy and rutty, leading, if you turned west, to Batovo) at a spot where aspens crowded on both sides of a dip, I would be sure to find in the third week of June great blue-black nymphalids striped with pure white, gliding and wheeling low above the rich clay which matched the tint of their undersides when they settled and closed their wings. Those were the dung-loving males of what the old Aurelians used to call the Poplar Admirable, or, more exactly, they belonged to its Bucovinan subspecies. As a boy of nine, not knowing that race, I noticed how much our North Russian specimens differed from the Central European form figured in Hofmann, and rashly wrote to Kuznetsov, one of the greatest Russian, or indeed world, lepidopterists of all time, naming my new subspecies "*Limenitis populi rossica.*" A long month later he returned my description and aquarelle of "*rossica* Nabokov" with only two words scribbled on the back of my letter: "*bucovinensis* Hormuzaki." How I hated Hormuzaki! And how hurt I was when in one of Kuznetsov's later papers I found a gruff reference to "schoolboys who keep naming minute varieties of the Poplar Nymph!" Undaunted, however, by the *populi* flop, I "discovered" the following year a "new" moth. That summer I had been collecting assiduously on moonless nights, in a glade of the park, by spreading a bedsheet over the grass and its annoyed glow-worms, and casting upon it the light of an acytelene lamp (which, six years later, was to shine on Tamara). Into that arena of radiance, moths would come drifting out of the solid blackness around me, and it was in that manner, upon that magic sheet, that I took a beautiful *Plusia* (now *Phytometra*) which, as I saw at once, differed from its closest ally by its mauve-and-maroon (instead of golden-brown) forewings, and narrower bractea mark and was not recognizably figured in any of my books. I sent its description and picture to Richard South, for publication in *The Entomologist.* He did not know it either, but with the utmost kindness checked it in the British Museum collection – and found it had been described long ago as *Plusia excelsa* by Kretschmar. I received the sad news, which was most sympathetically worded (". . . should be congratu-

lated for obtaining . . . very rare Volgan thing . . . admirable figure . . .")
with the utmost stoicism; but many years later, by a pretty fluke (I know I
should not point out these plums to people), I got even with the first discoverer of *my* moth by giving his own name to a blind man in a novel.

Let me also evoke the hawkmoths, the jets of my boyhood! Colors
would die a long death on June evenings. The lilac shrubs in full bloom before which I stood, net in hand, displayed clusters of a fluffy gray in the
dusk – the ghost of purple. A moist young moon hung above the mist of a
neighboring meadow. In many a garden have I stood thus in later years – in
Athens, Antibes, Atlanta – but never have I waited with such a keen desire
as before those darkening lilacs. And suddenly it would come, the low buzz
passing from flower to flower, the vibrational halo around the streamlined
body of an olive and pink Hummingbird moth poised in the air above the
corolla into which it had dipped its long tongue. Its handsome black larva
(resembling a diminutive cobra when it puffed out its ocellated front segments) could be found on dank willow herb two months later. Thus every
hour and season had its delights. And, finally, on cold, or even frosty, autumn nights, one could sugar for moths by painting tree trunks with a mixture of molasses, beer, and rum. Through the gusty blackness, one's lantern
would illumine the stickily glistening furrows of the bark and two or three
large moths upon it imbibing the sweets, their nervous wings half open
butterfly fashion, the lower ones exhibiting their incredible crimson silk
from beneath the lichen-gray primaries. "*Catocala adultera!*" I would triumphantly shriek in the direction of the lighted windows of the house as I
stumbled home to show my captures to my father.

6

The "English" park that separated our house from the hayfields was an extensive and elaborate affair with labyrinthine paths, Turgenevian benches,
and imported oaks among the endemic firs and birches. The struggle that
had gone on since my grandfather's time to keep the park from reverting to
the wild state always fell short of complete success. No gardener could
cope with the hillocks of frizzly black earth that the pink hands of moles
kept heaping on the tidy sand of the main walk. Weeds and fungi, and

ridgelike tree roots crossed and recrossed the sun-flecked trails. Bears had been eliminated in the eighties, but an occasional moose still visited the grounds. On a picturesque boulder, a little mountain ash and a still smaller aspen had climbed, holding hands, like two clumsy, shy children. Other, more elusive trespassers – lost picnickers or merry villagers – would drive our hoary gamekeeper Ivan crazy by scrawling ribald words on the benches and gates. The disintegrating process continues still, in a different sense, for when, nowadays, I attempt to follow in memory the winding paths from one given point to another, I notice with alarm that there are many gaps, due to oblivion or ignorance, akin to the terra-incognita blanks map makers of old used to call "sleeping beauties."

Beyond the park, there were fields, with a continuous shimmer of butterfly wings over a shimmer of flowers – daisies, bluebells, scabious, and others – which now rapidly pass by me in a kind of colored haze like those lovely, lush meadows, never to be explored, that one sees from the diner on a transcontinental journey. At the end of this grassy wonderland, the forest rose like a wall. There I roamed, scanning the tree trunks (the enchanted, the silent part of a tree) for certain tiny moths, called Pugs in England – delicate little creatures that cling in the daytime to speckled surfaces, with which their flat wings and turned-up abdomens blend. There, at the bottom of that sea of sunshot greenery, I slowly spun round the great boles. Nothing in the world would have seemed sweeter to me than to be able to add, by a stroke of luck, some remarkable new species to the long list of Pugs already named by others. And my pied imagination, ostensibly, and almost grotesquely, groveling to my desire (but all the time, in ghostly conspiracies behind the scenes, coolly planning the most distant events of my destiny), kept providing me with hallucinatory samples of small print: ". . . the only specimen so far known . . ." ". . . the only specimen known of *Eupithecia petropolitanata* was taken by a Russian schoolboy . . ." ". . . by a young Russian collector . . ." ". . . by myself in the Government of St. Petersburg, Tsarskoe Selo District, in 1910 . . . 1911 . . . 1912 . . . 1913 . . ." And then, thirty years later, that blessed black night in the Wasatch Range.

At first – when I was, say, eight or nine – I seldom roamed farther than the fields and woods between Vyra and Batovo. Later, when aiming at a particular spot half-a-dozen miles or more distant, I would use a bicycle to get there with my net strapped to the frame; but not many forest paths were passable on wheels; it was possible to ride there on horseback, of course, but, because of our ferocious Russian tabanids, one could not leave a horse haltered in a wood for any length of time: my spirited bay almost climbed up the tree it was tied to one day trying to elude them: big fellows with watered-silk eyes and tiger bodies, and gray little runts with an even more painful proboscis, but much more sluggish: to dispatch two or three of these dingy tipplers with one crush of the gloved hand as they glued themselves to the neck of my mount afforded me a wonderful empathic relief (which a dipterist might not appreciate). Anyway, on my butterfly hunts I always preferred hiking to any other form of locomotion (except, naturally, a flying seat gliding leisurely over the plant mats and rocks of an unexplored mountain, or hovering just above the flowery roof of a rain forest); for when you walk, especially in a region you have studied well, there is an exquisite pleasure in departing from one's itinerary to visit, here and there by the wayside, this glade, that glen, this or that combination of soil and flora – to drop in, as it were, on a familiar butterfly in his particular habitat, in order to see if he has emerged, and if so, how he is doing.

There came a July day – around 1910, I suppose – when I felt the urge to explore the vast marshland beyond the Oredezh. After skirting the river for three or four miles, I found a rickety footbridge. While crossing over, I could see the huts of a hamlet on my left, apple trees, rows of tawny pine logs lying on a green bank, and the bright patches made on the turf by the scattered clothes of peasant girls, who, stark naked in shallow water, romped and yelled, heeding me as little as if I were the discarnate carrier of my present reminiscences.

On the other side of the river, a dense crowd of small, bright blue male butterflies that had been tippling on the rich, trampled mud and cow dung through which I trudged rose all together into the spangled air and settled again as soon as I had passed.

After making my way through some pine groves and alder scrub I came to the bog. No sooner had my ear caught the hum of diptera around me, the guttural cry of a snipe overhead, the gulping sound of the morass under my foot, than I knew I would find here quite special arctic butterflies, whose pictures, or, still better, nonillustrated descriptions I had worshiped for several seasons. And the next moment I was among them. Over the small shrubs of bog bilberry with fruit of a dim, dreamy blue, over the brown eye of stagnant water, over moss and mire, over the flower spikes of the fragrant bog orchid (the *nochnaya fialka* of Russian poets), a dusky little Fritillary bearing the name of a Norse goddess passed in low, skimming flight. Pretty Cordigera, a gemlike moth, buzzed all over its uliginose food plant. I pursued rose-margined Sulphurs, gray-marbled Satyrs. Unmindful of the mosquitoes that furred my forearms, I stooped with a grunt of delight to snuff out the life of some silver-studded lepidopteron throbbing in the folds of my net. Through the smells of the bog, I caught the subtle perfume of butterfly wings on my fingers, a perfume which varies with the species – vanilla, or lemon, or musk, or a musty, sweetish odor difficult to define. Still unsated, I pressed forward. At last I saw I had come to the end of the marsh. The rising ground beyond was a paradise of lupines, columbines, and penstemons. Mariposa lilies bloomed under Ponderosa pines. In the distance, fleeting cloud shadows dappled the dull green of slopes above timber line, and the gray and white of Longs Peak.

I confess I do not believe in time. I like to fold my magic carpet, after use, in such a way as to superimpose one part of the pattern upon another. Let visitors trip. And the highest enjoyment of timelessness – in a landscape selected at random – is when I stand among rare butterflies and their food plants. This is ecstasy, and behind the ecstasy is something else, which is hard to explain. It is like a momentary vacuum into which rushes all that I love. A sense of oneness with sun and stone. A thrill of gratitude to whom it may concern – to the contrapuntal genius of human fate or to tender ghosts humoring a lucky mortal.[1]   [CE 79–92, SM 119–39]

From letter from V. D. Nabokov (father) to his wife, June 7, 1908

From Kresty Prison,[2] St. Petersburg. In Russian.

Have just received your dear little letter with the butterfly from Volodya. I was very touched. Tell him that there are no butterflies here in the prison yard except *rhamni* and *P. brassicae*. Have you found any *egerias*?

[*Vozdushnye puti* 4 (1965): 272]

A Few Notes on Crimean Lepidoptera

Lepidoptera paper. Written at Cambridge, October 1919. Published in 1920.

By V. V. Nabokoff.

Russia offers a wide and fruitful field of research to the entomologist. Just as in its north-western part the Scandinavian and Central European fauna mingle together, producing in the same place species of quite different haunts, such as *Brenthis freija* and *Apatura iris*, *Oeneis jutta* and *Pontia daplidice*, Crimea, from the zoological point of view, seems to be the connecting-link between the Balkan and Caucasian districts. The region of steppes in the north of Crimea (districts of Eupatoria, Perekop, and partly of Simferopol and Theodosia) forms geographically a continuation of the so-called Novorossian steppes and is distinguished by the very same peculiarities – lack of water, scanty vegetation, and, moreover, extreme heat and dryness in summer, snow-storms in winter. Only for a short time in spring these plains are covered with flowers, and the fresh grass delicately waves in the soft sunshine. The steppes, gradually ascending, form in the south a chain of mountains stretching from Theodosia to the Cape of Khersones. On the gentle northern slopes, facing the barren plain, begins the woodland (oak, beech, lime, elm, ash, mountain ash, poplar, willow, etc.). Southwards, on the steeper side, the commonest tree is a Crimean variety of *Pinus sylvestris,* while further on, in the narrow space between the mountains and the sea, cypress, pomegranates, laurel, olive and fig trees give a touch of Italy to the landscape. Few interesting insects occur, however, in the beautiful gardens and parks of the coast. My chief collecting-grounds were the rocky southern slopes of the mountain Ai Petri and the Yaila – hilly pastures on the northern side. Moreover, I made half-a-dozen excursions to the central part of Crimea. I give below a list of butterflies noted from November, 1917, to August, 1918.

HESPERIIDÆ.

Carcharodus alcææ: Very abundant everywhere, in two broods. *C. lavateræ*: A few specimens captured in May. *Hesperia carthami*: One female, May 20th, at the foot of Ai Petri. *H. alveus* (*? armoricanus*, Obthr.): Common in June on the Yaila. *H. malvæ*: Appeared April 10th. *Pyrgus proto*: One male, August 7th, near Bakchisarai. *P. orbifer*: Appeared April 19th. The most abundant of all. *P. sao*: Appeared May 20th. Scarce. *P. protheon*: A beautiful female, July 13th, in a pine-wood. *Nisoniades tages*: 1st gen. April 13th, 2nd gen. June 30th. *Augiades comma*: Abundant in August in Central Crimea. The females are very dark. *A. sylvanus*: Appeared May 31st. *Adopæa flava*: Appeared May 30th.

LYCÆNIDÆ.

Chrysophanus thersamen: I captured only two examples – a tattered one of the 1st gen., June 7th, and a fresh one July 3rd. Both are males. *C. phlæas*: Scarce.

Plebeius ægon: One male, June 18th. *Scolitantides orion*: First seen June 27th. Rare. *S. baton*, var. *clara*: Appeared April 13th. Very abundant in some places. *Aricia medon*, var. *sarmatis*: Appeared April 23rd. Common everywhere. *Polyommatus icarus*: Very abundant in several broods. *Agriades bellargus*: First seen May 27th. Common in fields at the foot of Ai Petri. Large specimens. Males tinged with purple – very different from the western ones. *A. meleager*: Appeared June 18th. Very abundant. In the southern part of Crimea the females are ab. *steeveni*; on the plains of the inland, typical. *A. corydon*: Appeared June 30th. *Cupido minimus*: One, June 3rd, at the top of Ai Petri. *Nomiades semiargus*: Appeared June 27th. *N. cyllarus*, var. *æruginosa*: Appeared June 30th. Common for a short time in parks. *Lycæna euphemus*: In woods of the inland. *Thecla w-album*:

Plentiful in beech-woods. Once, on a sunny day, I found scores of specimens settled on some nettles. When disturbed they flew off, but immediately returned again to their resting-place. *T. acaciæ*: First seen, June 18th. Abundant here and there, on lawns, fluttering about like a small *Lycæna*. Some specimens seem to be var. *abdominalis*. *Callophrys rubi*: Appeared April 16th. Large specimens. Underside pale green, with only one white dot – the lower one – on hind wings. *Celastrina argiolus*: 1st gen. March 27th, 2nd gen. June 9th. The commonest butterfly in spring.

PAPILIONIDÆ.

Iphiclides podalirius: Plentiful in gardens. First brood appeared at the end of March, the second at the end of June. Worn specimens of the first generation were on the wing as late as June 15th. *Papilio machaon*: I captured only one example (June 3rd). In this specimen the two upper lunules on the outer margin of hind wings are tinged with orange. This is an unusual aberration.

    Parnassius apollo, var. ?: Said to occur near Simferopol. I have seen specimens in local collections.

    Thais polyxena: Abundant on the plains of the inland in March. I have not noticed it in the south of Crimea. This also refers to the next species.

PIERIDÆ.

Aporia cratægi: Two faded females, July 18th. *Pieris rapæ*: 1st gen. April 1st, 2nd gen. June 16th. *P. napi*: 1st gen. March 27th, 2nd gen. June 2nd. *Pontia daplidice*: 1st gen. March 23rd (ab. *bellidice*), 2nd gen. June 10th.

    Euchlöe belia var. *uralensis*: In one gen. First appeared April 6th. This is a common butterfly in the parks and gardens of the coast. *E. cardamines*: Appeared March 3rd.

    Leptidia sinapis: 1st gen. March 23rd. The males have pale grey tips and the space between the inner margin and vein vii on the underside of hind wings is suffused with greyish-green, which reminds me of *duponcheli*. That species, as much as I know, has never been observed in Crimea. 2nd gen. July 3rd. Black tips and very pale – nearly white – underside of hind wings, ab. *diniensis*?

    Colias hyale: Single specimens throughout the summer. I have a couple of males in which the dark markings are nearly absent. *C. edusa*: Extremely abundant from March to late November, in several broods. Ab. *pallida* (*helice*) and intermediate forms are frequent.

Gonepteryx rhamni: Appeared June 20th, but was rarely seen. Much more abundant in the spring.

NYMPHALIDÆ.

Dryas paphia: Not common. *D. pandora*: Appeared June 30th. Abundant for a week or so near Yalta. It was delightful to watch, as it sailed to and fro, over roadside thistles.

Argynnis aglaia: One specimen, July 13th, on a mountain road. *A. adippe*: One male (ab. *cleodoxa*), June 2nd.

Issoria lathonia: 1st gen. April 10th, 2nd gen. June 6th.

Brenthis dia: Appeared June 3rd. Scarce.

Melitæa cinxia: Appeared April 28th. *M. didyma*, var. *neæra*: 1st gen. June 7th, 2nd gen. August 1st. Abundant with *cinxia* on mountain slopes. A pretty, well-defined variety. *M. athalia*: In woods on the northern side of Ai-Petri. Small, dark specimens.

Pyrameis cardui: A great quantity of fresh specimens appeared April 26th, and then again June 6th. It is the most abundant butterfly in Crimea. In August on the plains of the inland it is to be met in thousands – the only butterfly for miles around. *P. atalanta*: Very common, too, chiefly in spring. On sunny days in winter I have noticed numerous examples sailing and fluttering among oak-trees. *Vanessa io*: Now and then in gardens. *Aglais urticæ*: Abundant on the Yaila. Fine, warm-coloured specimens. *Eugonia xanthomelas*: One male July 2nd. *E. polychloros*: Plentiful in parks.

Polygonia c-album: Rarely seen. *P. egea*: One female February 2nd, in a Tartarian village on the coast.

LIBYTHEIDÆ.

Libythea celtis: 1st gen. March 23rd, 2nd gen. June 9th. Abundant in gardens and on the outskirts of pine-woods at the foot of Ai Petri. It flits and glides over bushes, somewhat resembling a *Melitæa maturna*, often settles with closed wings on twigs and stones, and has a habit of darting in unexpected directions when pursued. Examples of the second generation are of a deeper orange hue with darker and stronger markings, which give the butterfly when on the wing a bluish-black, glossy appearance.

SATYRIDÆ.

Pararge roxelana: I saw one male June 20th, in a park by the sea. *P. megaera*: 1st gen. April 13th, 2nd gen. June 30th. *P. egeria* var. *intermedia?*: 1st gen. March 31st, 2nd gen. June 27th. Common in shady nooks. Much paler than the Mediterranean form, but not quite so pale as the northern variety.

Satyrus circe: Appeared June 18th. *S. anthe*: One specimen, a fresh but somewhat deformed female, in a mountain gorge July 13th. *S. statilinus*: Very abundant everywhere in autumn.

Hipparchia semele: Appeared June 1st. Very common. The females are exceedingly large. *H. hippolyte*: July 13th, at the very summit of Ai-Petri. Gently flutters among rocks, often settling with closed wings on the ground. The examples I obtained are bigger and brighter than Andalusian specimens.

Enodia dryas: Common in central Crimea. I captured some fine specimens in August near Bakchisarai – the former residence of the Khans.

Epinephele jurtina: Appeared May 16th. *E. lycaon*: Appeared June 23rd. Very common in the mountains. Small examples.

Cœnonympha pamphilus: Very scarce.

Erebia afer: I found this butterfly locally abundant on the Yaila June 3rd. There were no males about and most of the females were faded. They rise from out of the grass when disturbed, float for a short time in the wind, and languidly drop again with outspread wings on stones and blossoms. This butterfly, when flying, bears a striking resemblance to *E. janira* ♂.

Melanargia galathea: Appeared June 9th. Very common in grassy places at the foot of Ai-Petri. Ground-colour of underside of hind wings ranges from pearly-white to ochre-yellow.

This makes 77 species in all. It is obvious that many others are found in Crimea, for I have included in this list only those that I have seen myself. The absence of *Pieris brassicæ* is strange, while on the other hand I was disappointed in not finding *H. euxinus* – a new species lately described by

Kuznetzoff. My collection, which, unfortunately, I was compelled to leave in Yalta, includes also about a hundred different species of moths, many of which are unknown to me.

Sphinx convolvuli, Daphnis nerii, Deilephila livornica and *D. euphorbiæ* were all common at dusk on honeysuckle. *Pterogon gorgoniades* also occurs now and then near Yalta. On June 3rd I detected a fine female on a window-pane. When at rest with protruding hind wings it resembles a very small specimen of that handsome grey-marbled moth *Smerinthus tremulæ* (*amurensis*, Stdr.), which, in happier days, I used to find at the foot of aspens in the neighbourhood of Petrograd. Among other interesting things I may mention *Acronycta pontica, Gnophos stevenaria* and *Endagria salicicola*, a pearly-white, black-dotted little moth that is confined to the shores of the Black Sea.

> Trinity College,
>> R. Great Court,
>>> Cambridge.   [*The Entomologist* 53 (1920): 29–33]

From letter to V. D. Nabokov (father), June 10, 1920

From Cambridge. In Russian. Unpublished.

I would desperately like to find for the summer something, *some job*, which might give me a little income. When I spoke about this here, they gave me the most incredible propositions, one of which consisted of going to Ceylon as an assistant entomologist.   [VNA]

A Butterfly (*Vanessa antiopa*)[3]

Poem in Russian ("Babochka (*Vanessa antiopa*)"). Written at Cambridge, January 10, 1921. Published in *Gorniy put'* (1923). Translated by Gavriel Shapiro with DN.

> Velvety-black, with a warm tint of ripe plum,
> here it opened wide; through this live velvet
> delightfully gleams a row of cornflower-azure grains,
> along a circular fringe, yellow as the rippling rye.

It has perched on a trunk, and its jagged tender wings breathe,
now pressing themselves to bark, now turning toward the rays . . .
Oh, how they exult, how divinely they shimmer! One would say:
a blue-eyed night is framed by two pale-yellow dawns.
Greetings, oh greetings, reverie of a northern birch grove!
Thrill, and laughter, and love of my eternal youth.
Yes, I'll recognize you in a Seraph at the wondrous meeting,
I'll recognize your wings, their sacrosanct design.

[*Stikhi* 60]

I think of her, that girl, that distant girl

Poem in Russian ("Ya dumayu o ney, o devochke, o dal'ney"). Written at Cambridge, June 4, 1921.
Published in *Gomii put'* (1923). Translated by BB and DN.

I think of her, that girl, that distant girl,
and see the white water-lily on the river,
and the soaring martins, and in a broken bathing house
    a little dragonfly on a board.

There, there we would meet and gaily thence
go down to roam through whispering woods,
where a ray in the green gloom revealed wonder after wonder,
    shining on the leaves.

We rummaged in all God's treasure-houses;
she and I would search out in a willow bush
now lacquered beetles, now caterpillars like
    chess knights.

And we knew all the dear little paths,
and gave all the little birches names,
and called the youngest of them: Mary
    Holy White.

O God! I am ready beyond the eternal walls

to undergo incalculable sufferings

but grant us, grant us a sole instant

      beneath those trees again to stand.

                                                    [*Stikhi* 63]

Moths

Poem in Russian ("Nochnye babochki"). Published in *Rul'*, March 15, 1922. Translated by DN.

I remember evenings at the start of the fall,

the night depth of the melancholy garden,

where the leaves of a single oak are still thick;

and the thick hazy darkness under its branches

swoons, and downy moths

still fly to it at the dreamy lilac hour;

unseen eyelashes tremble in the dark,

puffy ghosts flutter . . .

                For you,

moths, I prepare a lure:

anticipating since morning a successful hunt,

I mix flat beer half and half

with warmed molasses, then add rum.

And I go out into the garden, to its mists and wonders,

and I smear the damp oak trunk

with sticky gold, and juice drips from the brush,

trickles down into the cracks, gleaming and heady. . . .

The saffron globe of the moon sails out from behind the cloud,

and the oak, my accomplice, looms tall and ample.

It has soaked up many an earthly dream;

I wait in the lilac gloom, and it waits with me.

And here, mysterious and sudden as shooting

stars, pensively, soundlessly, like the flight of

flowery fluff, one and then another
little shadow slips, white and flickering:
grey moths are born in the dark.

On the trunk I train the circle of a pocket lamp
and see five moths soak up the intoxicating juice,
blissfully unfurling their coiled proboscises,
and raising their wings, grey with pink lining,
freeze – and suddenly, flapping their wings,
disappear into the dark – and again fly lightly down
to the sweet smell. I stand before the trunk,
attentively follow their finery, half visible,
their color and pattern, and choosing a moth
over the very bark I smoothly swing
the whitish muslin of the wide-mouthed net.

Enchanted hours! Rapture of recollection!
My soul seethes. . . . Latin names
turn around in my head – and the night is warm and hazy . . .
The moon's huge lemon hangs in a swollen gloom.
In the distance, between the branches, beyond the flowerbeds, behind the dark
lawn, three lights burn in the manor.
From there they can call me at the proper hour,
tell me that it's time for bed and, looking out the window,
see the dark garden, a cautious little lamp,
the whitish spot of the fleeting net . . .

And I return with my airy prey:
Life still knocks at the walls of the box,
I pour cold, sweet-stifling ether on cotton-wool;
under its thorax I hold the baby moth, –
it weakens, it expires, little winged person,
and into the cork crack between linden boards
I carefully pin my catches in a row.

Sleep, little wings, eyed heads, tiniest antennae! . . .
                Here is a puffy silkmoth,
speckled, like a fallen leaf; here are the wings of a black hawk-moth
with a pearl V on the knotty vein;
here is a tiny fan with a lucent fringe;
here's a meek old man, a monk in a dark cassock;
– and here is their empress, the bride of the breeze:
two ribbons of velvet on pink satin,
flamingo dust at the end of its abdomen . . .

Thanks, my tender ones! Years upon years have gone by
and you have thawed with the warmth and flared up again.
I have experienced an inexplicable love,
dreamily bending over your rows
in fragrant, dry glass drawers,
like the thin leaves of big, faded Bibles
with faded flowers placed inside . . .
I don't know, moths, maybe you have perished,
mould or larvae have got in, small worms have nibbled at you,
your little wings and feet and antennae have broken,
or rough hands the sacred cupboard opened
and crunched the glass – and you have turned into
a colored handful of sweet-smelling dust.

I don't know, tender ones – but from another land
I look into the depth of a melancholy garden;
I remember evenings at the start of fall,
and my oak on the meadow, and the honey smell,
and the yellow moon over black branches –
and I cry, and I fly, and in the twilight with you
I soar and breathe beneath the gentle foliage.

                                  [*Grozd'* (1923), 51–54]

Letters

Poem in Russian ("Pis'ma"). Written in Berlin, January 23, 1923. Translated by BB and DN.

> Here are letters, all yours (already on the folds
> their traces of jerky pencil are fading). By day,
> folded up, they sleep, amid dry flowers, in my
> fragrant drawer, but at night they fly out,
> semitransparent and weak, they glide
> and flutter over me, like butterflies: one
> I may catch in my fingers, and at the night blue
> I look through it, and in it the stars shine through.

[*Stikhi* 85]

Painted Wood

Excerpt from article. Written in Berlin over pseudonym "V. Cantaboff." Commissioned for *Karussel*, a trilingual (German-French-English) journal dedicated to Berlin's new Russian cabarets.

Japanese butterflies, those splendid tailed creatures with splashes and ripples of colour on their delicately veined wings, always seem to have fluttered off Japanese fans or screens, just as the dove-grey volcano of that country looks as if it were acutely aware of its pencilled image. And there is something in the fat little bronze idols, in their placid curves and eastern chubbiness – that makes one think of those round staring fishes that dream in a rainbow haze – gleaming ghosts of a tropical sea. Thus, art and nature mingle together – in such a wonderful way that it is difficult to say for instance whether sunsets made Claude Lorrain, or Claude Lorrain made sunsets.

[*Karussel* 2 (1923): 9]

No, life is no quivering quandary!

Poem in Russian ("Net, bytiyo – ne zybkaya zagadka"). Written in Berlin, May 6, 1923. Translated by BB and DN.

No, life is no quivering quandary!
Here under the moon things are bright and dewy.
We are the caterpillars of angels; and sweet
It is to eat from the edge into the tender leaf.

Dress yourself up in thorns, crawl, bend, grow strong –
and the greedier was your green track,
the more velvety and splendid
the tails of your liberated wings.

[*Stikhi* 105]

The Gods

Excerpt from story in Russian ("Bogi"). Written in Berlin, October 1923. Published first in French translation, *La Vénitienne*, 1990. Translated by DN.

[The narrator walks through Berlin with his wife toward the cemetery where their young son lies.]

They are leading camels along the street, on the way from the circus to the zoo. Their plump humps list and sway. Their long, gentle faces are turned up a little, dreamily. How can death exist when they lead camels along a springtime street? At the corner, an unexpected whiff of Russian foliage; a beggar, a divine monstrosity, turned all inside out, feet growing out of armpits, proffers, with a wet, shaggy paw, a bunch of greenish lilies-of-the-val . . . I bump a passerby with my shoulder. . . . Momentary collision of two giants. Merrily, magnificently, he swings at me with his lacquered cane. The tip, on the back-swing, breaks a shopwindow behind him. Zigzags shoot across the shiny glass. No – it's only the splash of mirrored sunlight in my eyes. Butterfly, butterfly! Black with scarlet bands. . . . A scrap of velvet. . . . It swoops above the asphalt, soars over a speeding car and a tall building, into the humid azure of the April sky. Another, identical butterfly once settled on the white border of an arena; Lesbia, senator's daughter, gracile, dark-eyed, with a gold ribbon on her forehead, entranced by the palpitating wings, missed the split second, the whirlwind of blinding dust, in which the bull-like neck of one combatant crunched under the other's naked knee. [STORIES 46–47]

From letter to Véra Slonim,[4] July 19, 1924

From Prague. In Russian. Unpublished. Translated by BB and DN.

All day long I wandered about the hills, searching out wonderful paths, bowing warmly to familiar butterflies. [VNA]

Evening

Poem in Russian ("Vecher"). Written July 10, 1924. Published *Stikhi*. Translated by DN.

> I heaved from my shoulder my pick and shovel
> into a corner of the barn
> mopped my brow and walked slowly outside toward the sunset
> a bonfire cool and rosy-hued.
>
> It peacefully blazed beyond the high-reaching beeches,
> in between funereal boughs,
> where burst forth for an instant sounds that were priceless
> from a vibrant nightingale.
>
> And a guttural din, choirs of toads gutta-perchalike
> sang resilient on the pond.
> It broke off. My forehead was trustingly, downily
> brushed by the flight of a passing moth.

The hills grew more somber: there, flashed reassuringly
    a twinkle of nocturnal lights.
In the distance, a train chugged and vanished. A lingering
    whistle, lingeringly stilled. . . .

The air smelled of grass. And I stood without thinking.
    And when the nebulous note died down,
I saw night had fallen, and stars loomed suspended,
    and tears were streaming down my face.

[Gibian and Parker, *The Achievements*
of Vladimir Nabokov (1984), 168–69]

Laughter

Poem in Russian ("Smekh" in manuscript, mistitled "Stikhi"). Written early 1924. Translated by DN.

While wandering through a neglected garden,
I spied, at midday, in the sightless air,
two oculated butterflies, collapsing
with laughter above the velvet navel of
a sunflower. And I saw, once, in the city,
a building with an air suggesting that
it was restraining laughter; twice I passed it,
and then, with a dismissing wave, I yielded
to laughter of my own. The building, though,
did not burst forth. A wily, fleeting glint
through windows flashed, and that was all. All this
my soul recalls, and in it sees a hint
that, in the sky, God laughs with childlike laughter
while watching as a barefoot seraph stoops
to reach far down and give our world a tickle
with but a single azure plume of his.

[*Rul'*, April 3, 1924]

vn with hand-drawn insignia,
Berlin, c. 1924.

Christmas

Story in Russian ("Rozhdestvo"). Written in Berlin, December 1924. Published in *Rul'*, January 6 and 8, 1925. Translated by DN with VN.

I

After walking back from the village to his manor across the dimming snows, Sleptsov sat down in a corner, on a plush-covered chair which he never remembered using before. It was the kind of thing that happens after some great calamity. Not your brother but a chance acquaintance, a vague country neighbor to whom you never paid much attention, with whom in normal times you exchange scarcely a word, is the one who comforts you wisely and gently, and hands you your dropped hat after the funeral service is over, and you are reeling from grief, your teeth chattering, your eyes blinded by tears. The same can be said of inanimate objects. Any room, even the coziest and the most absurdly small, in the little-used wing of a great country house has an unlived-in corner. And it was such a corner in which Sleptsov sat.

The wing was connected by a wooden gallery, now encumbered with our huge north Russian snowdrifts, to the master house, used only in summer. There was no need to awaken it, to heat it: the master had come from Petersburg for only a couple of days and had settled in the annex, where it was a simple matter to get the stoves of white Dutch tile going.

The master sat in his corner, on that plush chair, as in a doctor's waiting room. The room floated in darkness; the dense blue of early evening filtered through the crystal feathers of frost on the window-pane. Ivan, the quiet, portly valet, who had recently shaved off his mustache and now looked like his late father, the family butler, brought in a kerosene lamp, all trimmed and brimming with light. He set it on a small table, and noiselessly caged it within its pink silk shade. For an instant a tilted mirror reflected his lit ear and cropped gray hair. Then he withdrew and the door gave a subdued creak.

Sleptsov raised his hand from his knee and slowly examined it. A drop of candle wax had stuck and hardened in the thin fold of skin between two fingers. He spread his fingers and the little white scale cracked.

2

The following morning, after a night spent in nonsensical, fragmentary dreams totally unrelated to his grief, as Sleptsov stepped out into the cold veranda, a floorboard emitted a merry pistol crack underfoot, and the reflections of the many-colored panes formed paradisal lozenges on the whitewashed cushionless window seats. The outer door resisted at first, then opened with a luscious crunch, and the dazzling frost hit his face. The reddish sand providently sprinkled on the ice coating the porch steps resembled cinnamon, and thick icicles shot with greenish blue hung from the eaves. The snowdrifts reached all the way to the windows of the annex, tightly gripping the snug little wooden structure in their frosty clutches. The creamy white mounds of what were flower beds in summer swelled slightly above the level snow in front of the porch, and farther off loomed the radiance of the park, where every black branchlet was rimmed with silver, and the firs seemed to draw in their green paws under their bright plump load.

Wearing high felt boots and a short fur-lined coat with a karakul collar, Sleptsov strode off slowly along a straight path, the only one cleared of snow, into that blinding distant landscape. He was amazed to be still alive, and able to perceive the brilliance of the snow and feel his front teeth ache from the cold. He even noticed that a snow-covered bush resembled a fountain and that a dog had left a series of saffron marks on the slope of a snowdrift, which had burned through its crust. A little farther, the supports of a footbridge stuck out of the snow, and there Sleptsov stopped. Bitterly, angrily, he pushed the thick, fluffy covering off the parapet. He vividly recalled how this bridge looked in summer. There was his son walking along the slippery planks, flecked with aments, and deftly plucking off with his net a butterfly that had settled on the railing. Now the boy sees his father. Forever-lost laughter plays on his face, under the turned-down brim of a straw hat burned dark by the sun; his hand toys with the chainlet of the leather purse attached to his belt, his dear, smooth, suntanned legs in their serge shorts and soaked sandals assume their usual cheerful widespread stance. Just recently, in Petersburg, after having babbled in his delirium about school, about his bicycle, about some great Oriental moth, he died, and yesterday Sleptsov had taken the coffin – weighed down, it seemed, with an entire lifetime – to the country, into the family vault near the village church.

It was quiet as it can only be on a bright, frosty day. Sleptsov raised his leg high, stepped off the path and, leaving blue pits behind him in the snow, made his way among the trunks of amazingly white trees to the spot where the park dropped off toward the river. Far below, ice blocks sparkled near a hole cut in the smooth expanse of white and, on the opposite bank, very straight columns of pink smoke stood above the snowy roofs of log cabins. Sleptsov took off his karakul cap and leaned against a tree trunk. Somewhere far away peasants were chopping wood – every blow bounced resonantly skyward – and beyond the light silver mist of trees, high above the squat isbas, the sun caught the equanimous radiance of the cross on the church.

3

That was where he headed after lunch, in an old sleigh with a high straight back. The cod of the black stallion clacked strongly in the frosty air, the white plumes of low branches glided overhead, and the ruts in front gave off a silvery blue sheen. When he arrived he sat for an hour or so by the grave, resting a heavy, woolen-gloved hand on the iron of the railing that burned his hand through the wool. He came home with a slight sense of disappointment, as if there, in the burial vault, he had been even further removed from his son than here, where the countless summer tracks of his rapid sandals were preserved beneath the snow.

In the evening, overcome by a fit of intense sadness, he had the main house unlocked. When the door swung open with a weighty wail, and a whiff of special, unwintery coolness came from the sonorous iron-barred vestibule, Sleptsov took the lamp with its tin reflector from the watchman's hand and entered the house alone. The parquet floors crackled eerily under his step. Room after room filled with yellow light, and the shrouded furniture seemed unfamiliar; instead of a tinkling chandelier, a soundless bag hung from the ceiling; and Sleptsov's enormous shadow, slowly extending one arm, floated across the wall and over the gray squares of curtained paintings.

He went into the room which had been his son's study in summer, set the lamp on the window ledge, and, breaking his fingernails as he did so, opened the folding shutters, even though all was darkness outside. In the blue glass the yellow flame of the slightly smoky lamp appeared, and his large, bearded face showed momentarily.

He sat down at the bare desk and sternly, from under bent brows, examined the pale wallpaper with its garlands of bluish roses; a narrow officelike cabinet, with sliding drawers from top to bottom; the couch and armchairs under slipcovers; and suddenly, dropping his head onto the desk, he started to shake, passionately, noisily, pressing first his lips, then his wet cheek, to the cold, dusty wood and clutching at its far corners.

In the desk he found a notebook, spreading boards, supplies of black pins, and an English biscuit tin that contained a large exotic cocoon which had cost three rubles. It was papery to the touch and seemed made of a brown folded leaf. His son had remembered it during his sickness, regretting that he had left it behind, but consoling himself with the thought that the chrysalid inside was probably dead. He also found a torn net: a tarlatan bag on a collapsible hoop (and the muslin still smelled of summer and sun-hot grass).

Then, bending lower and lower and sobbing with his whole body, he began pulling out one by one the glass-topped drawers of the cabinet. In the dim lamplight the even files of specimens shone silklike under the glass. Here, in this room, on that very desk, his son had spread the wings of his captures. He would first pin the carefully killed insect in the cork-bottomed groove of the setting board, between the adjustable strips of wood, and fasten down flat with pinned strips of paper the still fresh, soft wings. They had now dried long ago and been transferred to the cabinet – those spectacular Swallowtails, those dazzling Coppers and Blues, and the various Fritillaries, some mounted in a supine position to display the mother-of-pearl undersides. His son used to pronounce their Latin names with a moan of triumph or in an arch aside of disdain. And the moths, the moths, the first Aspen Hawk of five summers ago!

4

The night was smoke-blue and moonlit; thin clouds were scattered about the sky but did not touch the delicate, icy moon. The trees, masses of gray frost, cast dark shadows on the drifts, which scintillated here and there with metallic sparks. In the plush-upholstered, well-heated room of the annex Ivan had placed a two-foot fir tree in a clay pot on the table, and was just attaching a candle to its cruciform tip when Sleptsov returned from the main house, chilled, red-eyed, with gray dust smears on his cheek, carrying a wooden case under his arm. Seeing the Christmas tree on the table, he asked absently: "What's that?"

Relieving him of the case, Ivan answered in a low, mellow voice: "There's a holiday coming up tomorrow."

"No, take it away," said Sleptsov with a frown, while thinking, Can this be Christmas Eve? How could I have forgotten?

Ivan gently insisted: "It's nice and green. Let it stand for a while."

"Please take it away," repeated Sleptsov, and bent over the case he had brought. In it he had gathered his son's belongings – the folding butterfly net, the biscuit tin with the pear-shaped cocoon, the spreading board, the pins in their lacquered box, the blue notebook. Half of the first page had been torn out, and its remaining fragment contained part of a French dictation. There followed daily entries, names of captured butterflies, and other notes:

"Walked across the bog as far as Borovichi, . . ."

"Raining today. Played checkers with Father, then read Goncharov's Frigate, *a deadly bore."*

"Marvelous hot day. Rode my bike in the evening. A midge got in my eye. Deliberately rode by her dacha twice, but didn't see her . . ."

Sleptsov raised his head, swallowed something hot and huge. Of whom was his son writing?

"Rode my bike as usual," he read on, *"Our eyes nearly met. My darling, my love . . ."*

"This is unthinkable," whispered Sleptsov. "I'll never know. . . ."

He bent over again, avidly deciphering the childish handwriting that slanted up then curved down in the margin.

"Saw a fresh specimen of the Camberwell Beauty today. That means autumn is here. Rain in the evening. She has probably left, and we didn't even get acquainted. Farewell, my darling. I feel terribly sad. . . ."

"He never said anything to me. . . ." Sleptsov tried to remember, rubbing his forehead with his palm.

On the last page there was an ink drawing: the hind view of an elephant – two thick pillars, the corners of two ears, and a tiny tail.

Sleptsov got up. He shook his head, restraining yet another onrush of hideous sobs.

"I-can't-bear-it-any-longer," he drawled between groans, repeating even more slowly, "I – can't – bear – it – any – longer. . . ."

"It's Christmas tomorrow," came the abrupt reminder, "and I'm going to die. Of course. It's so simple. This very night . . ."

He pulled out a handkerchief and dried his eyes, his beard, his cheeks. Dark streaks remained on the handkerchief.

". . . death," Sleptsov said softly, as if concluding a long sentence.

The clock ticked. Frost patterns overlapped on the blue glass of the window. The open notebook shone radiantly on the table; next to it the light went through the muslin of the butterfly net, and glistened on a corner of the open tin. Sleptsov pressed his eyes shut, and had a fleeting sensation that earthly life lay before him, totally bared and comprehensible – and ghastly in its sadness, humiliatingly pointless, sterile, devoid of miracles. . . .

At that instant there was a sudden snap – a thin sound like that of an overstretched rubber band breaking. Sleptsov opened his eyes. The cocoon in the biscuit tin had burst at its tip, and a black, wrinkled creature the size of a mouse was crawling up the wall above the table. It stopped, holding on to the surface with six black furry feet, and started palpitating strangely. It had emerged from the chrysalid because a man overcome with grief had transferred a tin box to his warm room, and the warmth had penetrated its taut leaf-and-silk envelope; it had awaited this moment so long, had collected its strength so tensely, and now, having broken out, it was slowly and miraculously expanding. Gradually the wrinkled tissues, the velvety fringes, unfurled; the fan-pleated veins grew firmer as they filled with air.

It became a winged thing imperceptibly, as a maturing face imperceptibly becomes beautiful. And its wings – still feeble, still moist – kept growing and unfolding, and now they were developed to the limit set for them by God, and there, on the wall, instead of a little lump of life, instead of a dark mouse, was a great *Attacus* moth like those that fly, birdlike, around lamps in the Indian dusk.

And then those thick black wings, with a glazy eyespot on each and a purplish bloom dusting their hooked foretips, took a full breath under the impulse of tender, ravishing, almost human happiness.   [STORIES 131–36]

From letter to Elena Nabokov, September 28, 1925

From Berlin. In Russian. Unpublished.

Oh, I had an enchanting, utterly sweet adventure. Going to the Saks' in the morning, I found on a linden tree near Charlottenburg station a wonderfully rare moth[5] – the dream of German collectors (it's rather large, with soft-emerald forewings marked with brown). I immediately took it off to the owner of a butterfly shop on Motzstrasse. He was amazed – and really it is a great rarity – and offered to spread it himself.   [VNA]

Mary

Excerpts from novel in Russian (*Mashen'ka*). Written in Berlin, spring-fall 1925. Published in 1926. Translated by Michael Glenny with VN.

[Ganin, living in Berlin in 1924, recalls Mary, his first love, whom he has not seen since 1917 in Russia.]

For a moment Ganin stopped recollecting and wondered how he had been able to live for so many years without thinking about Mary – and then he caught up with her again: she was running along a dark, rustling path, her black bow looking in flight like a huge Camberwell Beauty. Suddenly Mary pulled up, gripped him by the shoulder, lifted her foot and started to rub her sand-dusted shoe against the stocking of her other leg, higher up, under the hem of her blue skirt.   [*Mary* 60]

[Ganin recollects receiving an unexpected letter from Mary in January 1918, nearly two years after their love affair had ended, and after he had fled from the revolution in Petrograd to the Crimea. A precarious correspondence ensued.]

Duty kept him in Yalta – the civil war was under way – but there were moments when he decided to give up everything to go and look for Mary among the farms of the Ukraine.

There was something touching and wonderful about the way their letters managed to pass across the terrible Russia of that time – like a cabbage white butterfly flying over the trenches. His answer to her second letter was very delayed, and Mary simply could not understand what had happened, as she was convinced that where their letters were concerned the usual obstacles of those days somehow did not exist.   [*Mary* 90–91]

From letter to Elena Nabokov, April 23, 1926

From Berlin. In Russian. Unpublished.

Yesterday I was with Kardakov[6] at the Entomological Institute in Dahlem. There I met one famous scientist,[7] who spoke so wonderfully, so touchingly, so romantically about butterflies, that tears came right into my eyes. The Institute is a charming little building among flower gardens, very quiet and light, smells not quite of a laboratory, not quite of the tropics. I was shown all sorts of very curious collections – and I fell utterly in love with this old, fat, red-cheeked scientist, watched him with a dead cigar in his teeth as he casually and dextrously picked through butterflies, cartons, glass boxes, and thought that only two months ago he was catching huge green butterflies on Java. "Look," he said, "at this female – she could simply take your heart away." Or: "This isn't a pupa, but a whole doll,[8] although you could give it to a child to play with." Or again: "Yes, this variation of spots happens in the best of families." And all this in a guttural

Russian (he is of German stock), with a wheeze, as he chews his cigar and clicks his fat fingers – and with such love. Oh it was so good, mummy . . . I will go back and bliss out again in a few days. . . . [VNA]

Butterflies

Excerpt from long poem in Russian ("Babochki").[9] Written c. 1926–29. Unpublished. Translated by DN.

to dear Nikolay Ivanovich Kardakov from the author

> . . . From afar you recognize the swallowtail
> by its sunny, tropical color:
> it rushed along an ant slope
> and settled on a highway dandelion.
> A blow of the net – and a loud rustle in the gauze.
> O, yellow demon, how you tremble!
> I am afraid to tear its little toothed borders
> and its black tails, as delicate as can be.
> But at times, in the willow park,
> some happy noon, windy and hot,
> I stand, in ecstasy at the fragrance,
> before a tall crumbly lilac,
> almost raspberry in comparison
> with the sky's deep blue;
> and a swallowtail hangs down from the cluster, breathes,
> getting drunk, gold-winged guest,
> and the wind blindingly sways
> both the butterfly and the sweet cluster.
> You aim – but the branches get in the way;
> you sweep – but it flashed and was off;
> and from the turned out net fall out
> only the torn-off crests of flowers.

[Terry Myers Collection]

VN's manuscript of an excerpt from the long poem "Butterflies" (otherwise unknown), sent to lepidopterist Nikolay Kardakov. (*Terry Myers Collection*)

Дорогому Николаю Ивановичу Кардакову
от автора.

(Отрывокъ изъ поэмы "Бабочки")

... Издалека узнаешь махаона
по солнечной, тропической красѣ:
пронесся вдоль муравчатаго склона
и сѣлъ на одуванчикъ у шоссе.
Ударъ сачка, — и въ сѣткѣ шелестъ громкій.
О, желтый демонъ, какъ трепещешь ты!
Боюсь порвать зубчатыя каемки
и черные тончайшіе хвосты.
А то бывало, въ иволговомъ паркѣ,
въ счастливый полдень, вѣтреный и жаркій,
стою, отъ благовонья самъ не свой,
передъ высокой рыхлою сиренью,
почти малиновою по сравненью
съ глубокою небесной синевой;
и махаонъ свисаетъ съ грозди, дышитъ,
пьянѣетъ онъ, золотокрылый гость,
и вѣтеръ ослѣпительно колышетъ
и бабочку и сладостную гроздь.
Нацѣлишься, — но помѣшаютъ вѣтки;
взмахнешь, — но онъ блеснулъ, и былъ таковъ;
и сыплются изъ вывернутой сѣтки
лишь сорванные крестики цвѣтовъ ...

В. Набоковъ-Сиринъ

In Paradise

Poem in Russian ("K dushe" ["To My Soul"], retitled "V rayu"). Written September 25, 1927. Published in *Rul'*, March 18, 1928. Translated by VN.

My soul, beyond distant death
your image I see like this:
a provincial naturalist,
an eccentric lost in paradise.

There, in a glade, a wild angel slumbers,
a semi-pavonian creature.[10]
Poke at it curiously
with your green umbrella,

speculating how, first of all,
you will write a paper on it,
then – But there are no learned journals,
nor any readers in paradise!

And there you stand, not yet believing
your wordless woe.
About that blue somnolent animal
whom will you tell, whom?

Where is the world and the labeled roses,
the museum and the stuffed birds?
And you look and look through your tears
at those unnamable wings.

[PP 45]

From letter to Elena Nabokov, February 18, 1928

From Berlin. In Russian. Unpublished.

I am leading a mole-like existence, i.e. seeing no one except my pupils and am sweating, sweating over my novel until my head spins. The fourth chapter is almost finished – I'll probably finish it today. It's so boring for me without Russians in the novel that I wanted to compensate by introducing an entomologist, but killed him in time, in the muse's womb. Boredom of course is hardly the right word – in fact it is bliss to be in a medium I create, but I am also tired out putting it all in order.   [VNA]

King, Queen, Knave

Excerpts from novel in Russian (*Korol', dama, valet*). Written in 1927–28, published in 1928, translated and revised by VN in 1966–67. For material added in translation, see pp. 644–45.

[Dreyer sits at a chair on his terrace, observing.]

Out of nowhere came a Red Admirable butterfly,[11] settled on the edge of the table, opened its wings and began to fan them slowly as if breathing. The dark-brown ground was bruised here and there, the scarlet band had faded, the fringes were frayed – but the creature was still so lovely, so festive. . . .   [KQK 44]

[A beach; Franz and Martha and Dreyer are no longer there.]

A white butterfly went by, battling the breeze. Flags flapped. The photographer's shout approached. Bathers entering the shallow water moved their long legs like skiers without their poles.   [KQK 260]

The Defense

Excerpts from novel in Russian (*Zashchita Luzhina*). Written in 1929. Published in *Sovremennye zapiski* 40–42 (1929–30). Translated by Michael Scammell with VN.

[Luzhin's father returns to his country house late after a day in St. Petersburg with his mistress, his wife's sister, who has told him of his son's passion for chess. Luzhin Senior cannot resist testing him out immediately and discovers his difficult son's brilliance at the chessboard.]

His son put away the board and the box on a wicker table in the corner and having blurted a phlegmatic "good night" softly closed the door behind him.

Left: VN with net, late 1920s(?).
Right: In *Speak, Memory*, VN supplies this caption: "My wife took, unnoticed, this picture, unposed, of me in the act of writing a novel in our hotel room. The hotel is the Etablissement Thermal at Le Boulou, in the East Pyrenees. The date (discernible on the captured calendar) is February 27, 1929. The novel, *Zashchita Luzhina (The Defense)*, deals with the defense invented by an insane chess player. Note the pattern of the tablecloth. A half-empty pack of Gauloises cigarettes can be made out between the ink bottle and an overful ashtray. Family photos are propped against the four volumes of Dahl's Russian dictionary. The end of my robust, dark-brown penholder (a beloved tool of young oak that I used during all my twenty years of literary labors in Europe and may rediscover yet in one of the trunks stored at Dean's, Ithaca, N.Y.) is already well chewed. My writing hand partly conceals a stack of setting boards. Spring moths would float in through the open window on overcast nights and settle upon the lighted wall on my left. In that way we collected a number of rare Pugs and spread them at once (they are now in an American museum). Seldom does a snapshot compendiate a life so precisely."

"Oh well, I should have expected something like this," said Luzhin senior, wiping the tips of his fingers with a handkerchief. "He's not just amusing himself with chess, he's performing a sacred rite."

A fat-bodied, fluffy moth with glowing eyes fell on the table after colliding with the lamp. A breeze stirred lightly through the garden. The clock in the drawing room started to chime daintily and struck twelve.

"Nonsense," he said, "stupid imagination. Many youngsters are excellent chess players. Nothing surprising in that. The whole affair is getting on my nerves, that's all. Bad of her – she shouldn't have encouraged him. Well, no matter. . . ."

He thought drearily that in a moment he would have to lie, to remonstrate, to soothe, and it was midnight already. . . .   [*Defense* 66]

From letter to Elena Nabokov, August 15, 1929

From Kolbsheim. In Russian. Unpublished.

The weather continues very tasty. It's charming swimming here, especially from our little plot. There's tennis here too, I'm giving Véra lessons and she's already playing not at all badly. The only drawback is the toilet, where you sit over a hole full of filth and get tickled by flies. So it's best to do one's business in the pine thickets. Lots of butterflies – and my soul convulses when I remember the recent fairy-scene in the Pyrenees and at times, especially at night, looking out (still about the same business) into the garden and seeing how behind the fence, around the lantern, moths loom in pale patches, I feel drawn south again, into wild, fragrant places.   [VNA]

From letter to Elena Nabokov, October 18, 1929

From Berlin. In Russian. Unpublished.

I am spending hours working in the museum to identify rare butterflies, moving and exciting work. What collections they have there!   [VNA]

Notes on the Lepidoptera of the Pyrénées Orientales and the Ariège

Lepidoptera paper. Researched October 1929, written in late 1929–early 1930? Published in 1931.

By V. Nabokoff.

I had done no collecting at all for more than ten years, and then quite suddenly a stroke of luck enabled me to visit in the spring and early summer of 1929 the Pyrénées Orientales and the Ariège. The night journey from Paris to Perpignan was marked by a pleasant though silly dream in which I was offered what looked uncommonly like a sardine, but was really a tropical moth, the mimic – *mirabile dictu* – of a flying fish. Next day the motor-bus, starting from Perpignan, rapidly covered the thirteen miles between that town and the village of Boulou, crossed the bridge over the Tech, and after another mile's run put me down at the Hôtel Thermal du Boulou. Further on the road forks, one branch going to Maureillas, the other to Perthus on the Spanish frontier. My collecting was mostly done either along those two roads, or on the low hills of the usual southern type – *Ulex*, broom, heather, oak-bushes, etc. – in the immediate vicinity of the hotel. The weather dur-

VN in the East Pyrenees, spring 1929, on his first extended butterfly hunt since the Crimean summer of 1918, paid for by the advance for the German translation of *King, Queen, Knave.*

ing the whole of my stay, from February 8th to April 24th, was somewhat annoying, for whenever the sun shone, which it did fairly often, a fierce wind sprang up, blowing in two equally disgusting varieties – the Spanish one and the Northern. This appears to be a usual feature of spring in that part of the Roussillon. The window-panes quivered, the foliage of the olive and cork trees in the brilliant sunshine gleamed, rustled and tumbled about in a most distressing fashion and Mount Canigou shone bitterly white in the distance.

Things began quietly with two weak and tattered *Macroglossa stellatarum* on a window. Then on February 10th a couple of *Pararge aegeria* were observed fluttering over some rocks, and a *Vanessa polychloros* flew by. After supper I went out to have a look at the lights in the hotel court, and stood for a while near the garage, where there was a bright little lamp above the entrance. Some people intent on the process of digestion kept strolling up and down in the darkness with glowing cigars. It was very cold. My net and attitude were commented upon, and I heard someone explain in rich Catalonian accents that he had once seen at Vernet an old gentleman similarly engaged. At that moment a male *Chaemerina caliginearia* appeared whirling wildly round and round the lamp and I promptly netted it. This fascinating species continued coming to light throughout February and March, but all the males taken in that way are worthless as cabinet specimens, for they have a habit of dashing themselves against the lamps so furiously that they lose at once their lovely and very delicate bloom, tear their long fringes and assume a blurred, dingy aspect.

It was fairly warm on February 18th and I noted fresh *Pieris rapae, Gonepteryx cleopatra*, which was afterwards very common, flopping about everywhere, and *Pararge megera*. The hibernated Vanessids, once *Vanessa polychloros* had given the lead, appeared in the following order: *atalanta* February 20th, *io* February 26th, *antiopa* March 11th, *urticae* and *Polygonia c-album* March 12th. *Pontia daplidice* gen. *bellidice* was first seen on February 22nd, and next day was already found *in cop*. On the same day I saw in a leafy tunnel pierced by a sunbeam a *Libythea celtis* poised wings spread on a twig, and a few *Colias croceus* gen. *vernalis* were flying along the roads. Three days later near a brook I took a beautifully fresh *Ch. caliginearia*, male, silvery grey and pink, which fluttered weakly out of a bush, and when in the net crawled about with its wings held rather in the manner of a *Hypena*. Subsequently I got other male examples by beating bushes, and also found a pathetic wing in a spider's web.

Orthosia ruticilla, ranging from reddish to leaden grey, and other spring moths began coming to light in the last days of February. March started with *Lycaenopsis argiolus, Chrysophanus phlaeas* and *Euchloë belia* March 8th. The latter was rather local – in fact, I found it common only on a stretch of waste ground among olive trees near the hotel. I saw nothing of female *caliginearia* till March 10th, when four perfect specimens floated into the room one after the other and quietly settled on the wall above my writing-desk. The female varies considerably in markings, colouring – I have one nearly white – and the development of its quaintly shaped wings. On the same night the first *Eupithecia* species arrived – *pumilata* var. *temperstivata*, and its dwarf form *parvularia*.

Next day was fine and less windy. *Pieris napi* appeared. The sallow in full blossom attracted hundreds of bees and dozens of *L. celtis*, which afterwards, in the late afternoon, I observed looking for places to roost high up in an old oak tree together with a large friendly *polychloros*. On March 12th in a warm, sheltered spot on the road to Perthus I got a couple of *Pieris manni* of the small first brood. On March 13th *Callophrys rubi* var. *fervida* appeared at sallow – fine specimens of a milk-chocolate colour. It soon became extraordinarily abundant, remaining so till the end of my stay, though by then very worn. On certain days when the wind was exceptionally furious this game little creature, with perhaps a few *cleopatra*, was the only butterfly on the wing, flickering among the broom and gorse on the slopes. In some specimens the white markings on the hind-wing underside assume the form of bars; these tend to unite, forming a line, which, however, never takes on the special curve and tint found in *avis*. I saw nothing of the latter species, though I was on the look-out for its rich glow. It could hardly have been expected to stand the weather conditions at Boulou, which are quite different from those of Amélie-les-Bains.

Small fresh specimens of *Issoria latonia* and colonies of *Lycaena baton* var. *albonotata* appeared on March 15th near Perthus, and there I got several *Oreopsyche muscella* gently flying a foot or so above the road in the afternoon sun and looking like big dark flies. I also took three examples of another Psychid, similar to some small specimens labelled "*pulla,*" from Barcelona, in the Püngeler Collection. It flew, a minute black speck, over stones and heather on the hill just behind the hotel between two and four o'clock. Geometrids were by now getting common in bushy places and soon I captured *Fidonia famula* flying in the sun like a *Chrysophanus*, and some splendid *Gnophos asperaria* with its ab. *pithyata*. *Coenonympha pamphilus* and *Carcharodus alceae* were first seen on March 17th, and on the following days *Papilio podalirius* var. *feisthamelii* gen. *miegii* became abundant among almond trees on a hill; I took a freakish specimen, dark and small, with the long brown abdominal part of the pupa-case firmly adhering to its body, this giving the insect a weird, moth-like appearance, but hardly impeding its flight. At light Noctuids, as well as *Larentia* and *Eupithecia* species, came freely; among the latter I may mention a single example of the strange, dusky *E. semitinctaria*, April 1st.

On March 22nd I observed hibernated *Gonepteryx rhamni*, one *Colias hyale*, some fresh *atalanta*, a single fresh *cardui* – no more seen afterwards – several fine *Pararge maera* var. *adrasta* among rocks, a worn *edusa* ab. *helice*, small, like all the specimens of the first spring brood, and netted three very diminutive examples of *belia*. I had not seen much of *manni*, it did not like the wind, and hid in bushes, till March 28th, a fine day, when it was fairly common round the hotel. Large very fresh specimens of *croceus* and numerous *Leptidia sinapis* – a sun-loving species in these parts – were also noticed, while *Lycaena melanops*, males only, cropped up on one spot near the hotel. The end of March was marked by the appearance of *Papilio machaon, Euchloë cardamines, Lycaena icarus* and *Hesperia malvoides*, and at light I took one last very small *caliginearia* female, half-a-dozen males of a dark form of *Lycia hirtaria*, again similar to Barcelona specimens, some fine *Exaereta ulmi* of both sexes, many *Mamestra* and *Dianthoecia* species, and a single example of *Trichoclea sociabilis*.

On April 9th I caught a fresh *Melitaea deione* and saw one or two others, all on one spot by the side of a brook near the hotel. The specimen I took appeared to be intermediate between the type and var. *rondoui*, the lunules in the outer band (hind wing underside) being squared, though not so unicoloured as in specimens from Gèdre I had seen. I tried the next day to get some more in order to ascertain whether the specimen was simply an aberration or represented a local race, but saw none, and then there was a week of wind and cold. On April 18th I set out for a long tramp, and beyond the village of Maureillas saw *Tortrix pronubana* flying in the morning sun and hundreds of freshly hatched *deione*, plain this time, except for a certain thickness of markings, their chrysalids noticeable on the rocks bordering the road. Further on towards Las Ilas, in a ravine near a stream, a greasy-grey looking butterfly that floated low above the ground turned out to be a small, slightly faded female of *Thais rumina* var. *medesicaste*, but no more were found. On April 20th *Lycaena medon* and fresh *Pieris manni* with very yellow underside, second spring brood, appeared, and the beautiful *Leucanitis cailino* was common on a stony bank flying in dashing style for short stretches and settling again, when its light colouring made it difficult to detect among the white stones.

Four days later I left for the Ariège and stopped at Saurat near Tarascon. Saurat is a large village, altitude about 2000 ft., snugly cradled between mountains which rise up to 6000 ft. all around it. The lepidopterous fauna at Saurat proved to be mellower than at hard, dry Boulou. On a sunny day, April 28th, after rain I saw or took in the luscious meadows near the village the following butterflies: *P. podalirius*, typical, *P. machaon, P. brassicae, P. rapae, P. napi, Pontia daplidice*, very worn, *E. cardamines, E. euphenoides*, the tips, in the female, varying in tint from lemon to apricot with more or less dark suffusion, *L. sinapis, C. hyale, C. edusa, G. rhamni, C. rubi*, in rags, *Chrysophanus dorilis* – I noticed a male courting *Euclidia glyphica* in the most persistent manner – *Ch. phlaeas, Everes argiades* gen. *polysperchon, L. icarus* – no *thersites* noticed – *L. bellargus, L. cyllarus, P. c-album, V. urticae*, already fresh, *V. io, V. antiopa, Melitaea cinxia, M. phoebe, I. latonia, Brenthis dia, P. megera, Coenonympha pamphilus, Carcharodus alceae, C. altheae, H. serratulae, H. sao, H. malvoides, Nisoniades tages*, and a little higher up in a birch wood I was charmed to see together two insects that are rarely met with in the same place – the Southern *P. aegeria* and males of *Aglia tau*, so remindful of boyhood and spring in Northern Russia.

After that there was a week of rain and then again a radiant day which added to the list: *L. medon, Cupido minimus, M. parthenie, B. euphrosyne* – a fine warm coloured form – *H. onopordi* and *H. armoricanus. Parthenie* varied greatly, the usual tendency of the markings, especially of the border and the inner lines on both wings, being to disappear; I got, however, an aberration with the fore wing completely chocolate brown except for a fulvous subterminal band. On the top of a rocky peak, 3000 ft., scores of *podalirius* were swiftly circling and chasing each other, and a few *P. maera*, tending to var. *adrasta*, were noted. Next day at Carlong, 3500 ft., I found *Nemeobius lucina* and some very fresh *C. rubi*, looking strangely dark after var. *fervida*, among which was an example with white androconial brand. On May 17th, after another spell of rain, the damp meadows and muddy paths yielded *Everes alcetas, L. semiargus, L. sebrus, Limenitis rivularis, Melitaea aurinia*, tending to var. *provincialis*, and *deione*, these ranging from very bright fulvous specimens with very thin border to dullish and rather heavily marked ones similar to my Maureillas specimens; none approached var. *rondoui*.

Among numerous *deione* gliding to and fro over a grassy slope, near the village, I got a few males of a very fine *Melitaea* which certainly belongs to the *dictynna* group, and is most probably var. *vernetensis*, or an allied race. (*Vernetensis* is not represented in the collections here, nor have I been able to get at Oberthür's description, so that my knowledge of *vernetensis* is founded on later – and very short – descriptions, and with these my specimens seem to agree.) I took the first one on May 22nd; this, however, proved to be a rather singular extreme ab. of the Saurat race, specimens of which only appeared three weeks later, June 14th, on the same spot. This race is far larger and stronger than any form of *dictynna* I know. Though the markings are very black, much darker than in *dictynna*, still it looks a brighter insect owing first to the rich shade of the fulvous ground-colour, secondly to the narrowness of the markings, especially so in the case of the "inner subterminal line" – Wheeler's definition – and thirdly to the fact of the basal suffusion, though very black, being much reduced, as if wiped away, leaving beautifully clear the costal marks and elbowed line on the fore wing and the light ground-colour between the extra line and the inner one on the hind wing, as well as the basal spot and some other light patches in the discal cell. The fulvous band between the inner and outer lines is very conspicuous and the lunules are perfectly distinct. On the underside, however, I can find no essential difference from the type, except perhaps that the outer band is less reddish than in most specimens of *dictynna*. Now comes the specimen of the extreme ab. above mentioned. In this the markings and the basal suffusion are not only reduced as in "*vernetensis*," but are, moreover, of a dull brownish colour. The elbowed line is thin and dim in its middle part, the lunules are very large, and the outer subterminal line curves out towards the inner one owing to the development of the third lunule. The white fringes seem to cut deeper than usually into the border between the veins, and there is a slight angulation in the curve of the fore wing about a third of the way down the outer margin. On the hind wing underside the line dividing the pale central band is visible only near the costa and the five rusty dots in the outer band are very small.

On May 22nd I noted the first *Erebia evias*, which, together with *Euchloë euphenoides*, a black butterfly and a golden one, became abundant on the loose scree of the small mountain Calamès just beyond the village, and later on at a greater elevation. *Evias* pops out from nowhere, flies straight and low, rarely settling, and seems easy to net, but is not. On May 23rd *Aporia crataegi* appeared, and then on May 28th typical *L. baton*, followed by fresh *C. argiolus, Plebeius argus (argyrognomon)*, fresh *G. cleopatra* and *Epinephele jurtina*. On June 6th after yet another rainy period I met, a little lower, with *P. cardui*, one specimen, *Argynnis cydippe, Melanargia galathea, Coenonympha arcania* – in a shady, swampy spot – *Thymelicus lineola* and *T. thaumas*. The next day on the Roc des Iregges (pronounced "Ye wretches") at an elevation of 3000 ft. I took a male *E. stygne* with the hind wing underside of a uniform glossy brown, and with the wings longer and smarter than the dark roundish *stygne* which appeared commonly a week later in the same place – in company with *Lampides boeticus* and *Augiades sylvanus*.

The only *Parnassius – mnemosyne* var. *pyrenaica* – a female with pouch, was taken on the Chemin des Lanes, 2,500 ft., on June 16th. Next day a walk up to the Col-du-Port, about 5000 ft., resulted in *Erebia epiphron* (very common among the rhododendrons – dark specimens with hardly any ocelli visible on hind wing underside), and some delightful Geometrids, *Larentia turbata* var. *pyrenaearia* among others.

It was heartbreaking to leave Saurat – "le pays des eaux folles," as the tourist booklet has it – on June 24th when things were getting really lively, *Thecla spini, T. ilicis, Chrysophanus gordius, Everes argiades, L. hylas, L. arion, Satyrus circe* and *Aphantopus hyperanthus*, all emerging together on a cloudless day.

The electric light was so weak at Saurat that I could scarcely do any night collecting. Still, I managed to lure in a few good things, as, for instance, a fine race of *Eupithecia pumilata*, June 10th, with a very light greenish-grey tinge, or so it seems when compared with var. *tempestivata*, which is itself much less brown than the type, numerous examples of the frail pearly *E. liguriata* coming with miraculous punctuality just after eleven every night from May 19th till the middle of June; and a single *Chesias isabella* May 13th, which in its way is perhaps still lovelier than *rufata*.

In conclusion my sincerest thanks are due to Dr. W. Horn, of the Entomological Institute, Dahlem, and Dr. M. Hering, of the Natural Science Museum, Berlin, for kindly allowing me to consult the collections in their charge.

27, Luitpoldstr.,

Berlin W.

[*The Entomologist* 64 (1931): 255–57; 268–71]

The Eye

Excerpt from novella in Russian (*Soglyadatay*). Written in early 1930. Published in *Sovremennye zapiski* 44 (October 1930). Translated by DN with VN.

[The strange narrator has become obsessed with a character called Smurov and the conflicting images others have of him.]

The situation was becoming a curious one. I could already count three versions of Smurov, while the original remained unknown. This occurs in scientific classification. Long ago, Linnaeus described a common species of butterfly, adding the laconic note *"in pratis Westmanniae."* Time passes, and in the laudable pursuit of accuracy, new investigators name the various southern and Alpine races of this common species, so that soon there is not a spot left in Europe where one finds the nominal race and not a local subspecies. Where is the type, the model, the original? Then, at last, a grave entomologist discusses in a detailed paper the whole complex of named races and accepts as the representative of the typical one the almost 200-year-old, faded Scandinavian specimen collected by Linnaeus; and this identification sets everything right.[12]

In the same way I resolved to dig up the true Smurov, being already aware that his image was influenced by the climatic conditions prevailing in various souls – that within a cold soul he assumed one aspect but in a glowing one had a different coloration. I was beginning to enjoy this game.

[*Eye* 63–64]

The Aurelian

Story in Russian ("Pil'gram"). Written in March 1930. Published in *Sovremennye zapiski* 43 (July 1930). Translated by VN and Peter Pertzoff.

I

Luring aside one of the trolley-car numbers, the street started at the corner of a crowded avenue. For a long time it crept on in obscurity, with no shop-windows or any such joys. Then came a small square (four benches, a bed of pansies) round which the trolley steered with rasping disapproval. Here the street changed its name, and a new life began. Along the right side, shops appeared: a fruiterer's, with vivid pyramids of oranges; a tobacco-nist's, with the picture of a voluptuous Turk; a delicatessen, with fat brown and gray coils of sausages; and then, all of a sudden, a butterfly store. At night, and especially when it was damp, with the asphalt shining like the back of a seal, passersby would stop for a second before that symbol of fair weather. The insects on exhibit were huge and gorgeous. People would say to themselves, "What colors – amazing!" and plod on through the drizzle. Eyed wings wide-open in wonder, shimmering blue satin, black magic – these lingered for a while floating in one's vision, until one boarded the trolley or bought a newspaper. And, just because they were together with the butterflies, a few other objects would remain in one's memory: a globe, pencils, and a monkey's skull on a pile of copybooks.

As the street blinked and ran on, there followed again a succession of ordinary shops – soap, coal, bread – with another pause at the corner where there was a small bar. The bartender, a dashing fellow in a starched collar and green sweater, was deft at shaving off with one stroke the foam topping the glass under the beer tap; he also had a well-earned reputation as a wit. Every night, at a round table by the window, the fruiterer, the baker, an unemployed man, and the bartender's first cousin played cards with great gusto. As the winner of the current stake immediately ordered four drinks, none of the players could ever get rich.

On Saturdays, at an adjacent table, there would sit a flabby elderly man with a florid face, lank hair, and a grayish mustache, carelessly clipped. When he appeared, the players greeted him noisily without looking up from their cards. He invariably ordered rum, filled his pipe, and gazed at the game with pink-rimmed watery eyes. The left eyelid drooped slightly.

Occasionally someone turned to him, and asked how his shop was doing; he would be slow to answer, and often did not answer at all. If the bartender's daughter, a pretty freckled girl in a polka-dotted frock, happened to pass close enough, he had a go at her elusive hip, and, whether the slap succeeded or not, his gloomy expression never changed, although the veins on his temple grew purple. Mine host very humorously called him "Herr Professor." "Well, how is the Herr Professor tonight?" he would ask, coming over to him, and the man would ponder for some time in silence and then, with a wet underlip pushing out from under the pipe like that of a feeding elephant, he would answer something neither funny nor polite. The bartender would counter briskly, which made the players at the next table, though seemingly absorbed in their cards, rock with ugly glee.

The man wore a roomy gray suit with great exaggeration of the vest motif, and when the cuckoo popped out of the clock he ponderously extracted a thick silver watch and gazed at it askance, holding it in the palm of his hand and squinting because of the smoke. Punctually at eleven he knocked out his pipe, paid for his rum, and, after extending a flaccid hand to anyone who might choose to shake it, silently left.

He walked awkwardly, with a slight limp. His legs seemed too thin for his body. Just before the window of his shop he turned into a passage, where there was a door on the right with a brass plate: PAUL PILGRAM. This door led into his tiny dingy apartment, which could also be reached by an inner corridor at the back of the shop. Eleanor was usually asleep when he came home on those festive nights. Half a dozen faded photographs of the same clumsy ship, taken from different angles, and of a palm tree that looked as bleak as if it were growing on Helgoland hung in black frames above the double bed. Muttering to himself, Pilgram limped away into bulbless darkness with a lighted candle, came back with his suspenders dangling, and kept muttering while sitting on the edge of the bed and slowly, painfully, taking off his shoes. His wife, half-waking, moaned into her pillow and offered to help him; and then with a threatening rumble in his voice, he would tell her to keep quiet, and repeated that guttural "*Ruhe!*" several times, more and more fiercely.

After the stroke which had almost killed him some time ago (like a mountain falling upon him from behind just as he had bent toward his shoestrings), he now undressed reluctantly, growling until he got safely into bed, and then growling again if the faucet happened to drip in the adjoining kitchen. Eleanor would roll out of bed and totter into the kitchen and totter back with a dazed sigh, her small face wax-pale and shiny, and the plastered corns on her feet showing from under her dismally long nightgown. They had married in 1905, almost a quarter of a century before, and were childless because Pilgram had always thought that children would be merely a hindrance to the realization of what had been in his youth a delightfully exciting plan but had now gradually become a dark, passionate obsession.

He slept on his back with an old-fashioned nightcap coming down on his forehead; it was to all appearances the solid and sonorous sleep that might be expected in an elderly German shopkeeper, and one could readily suppose that his quilted torpor was entirely devoid of visions; but actually this churlish, heavy man, who fed mainly on *Erbswurst* and boiled potatoes, placidly believing in his newspaper and quite ignorant of the world (insofar as his secret passion was not involved), dreamed of things that would have seemed utterly unintelligible to his wife or his neighbors; for Pilgram belonged, or rather was meant to belong (something – the place, the time, the man – had been ill-chosen), to a special breed of dreamers, such dreamers as used to be called in the old days "Aurelians" – perhaps on account of those chrysalids, those "jewels of nature," which they loved to find hanging on fences above the dusty nettles of country lanes.

On Sundays he drank his morning coffee in several sloppy sessions, and then went out for a walk with his wife, a slow silent stroll which Eleanor looked forward to all week. On workdays he opened his shop as early as possible because of the children who passed by on their way to school; for lately he had been keeping school supplies in addition to his basic stock. Some small boy, swinging his satchel and chewing a sandwich, would slouch past the tobacconist's (where a certain brand of cigarettes offered airplane pictures), past the delicatessen (which rebuked one for having eaten that sandwich long before lunchtime), and then, remembering he wanted an eraser, would enter the next shop. Pilgram would mumble something, sticking out his lower lip from under the stem of his pipe and, after a listless search, would plump down an open carton on the counter. The boy would feel and squeeze the virgin-pale India rubber, would not find the sort he favored, and would leave without even noticing the principal wares in the store.

These modern children! Pilgram would think with disgust and he recalled his own boyhood. His father – a sailor, a rover, a bit of a rogue – married late in life a sallow-skinned, light-eyed Dutch girl whom he brought from Java to Berlin, and opened a shop of exotic curios. Pilgram could not remember now when, exactly, butterflies had begun to oust the stuffed birds of paradise, the stale talismans, the fans with dragons, and the like; but as a boy he already feverishly swapped specimens with collectors, and after his parents died butterflies reigned supreme in the dim little shop. Up to 1914 there were enough amateurs and professionals about to keep things going in a mild, very mild, way; later on, however, it became necessary to make concessions, a display case with the biography of the silkworm furnishing a transition to school supplies, just as in the old days pictures ignominiously composed of sparkling wings had probably been a first step toward lepidopterology.

Now the window contained, apart from penholders, mainly showy insects, popular stars among butterflies, some of them set on plaster and framed – intended merely for ornamenting the home. In the shop itself, permeated with the pungent odor of a disinfectant, the real, the precious collections were kept. The whole place was littered with various cases, cartons, cigar boxes. Tall cabinets contained numerous glass-lidded drawers filled with ordered series of perfect specimens impeccably spread and labeled. A dusty old shield or something (last remnant of the original wares) stood in a dark corner. Now and then live stock would appear: loaded brown pupae with a symmetrical confluence of delicate lines and grooves on the thorax, showing how the rudimentary wings, feet, antennae, and proboscis were packed. If one touched such a pupa as it lay on its bed of moss, the tapering end of the segmented abdomen would start jerking this way and that like the swathed limbs of a baby. The pupae cost a reichsmark apiece and in due time yielded a limp, bedraggled, miraculously expanding moth. And sometimes other creatures would be temporarily on sale: just then there happened to be a dozen lizards, natives of Majorca, cold, black, blue-bellied things, which Pilgram fed on mealworms for the main course and grapes for dessert.

2

He had spent all his life in Berlin and its suburbs; had never traveled farther than Peacock Island on a neighboring lake. He was a first-class entomologist. Dr. Rebel, of Vienna, had named a certain rare moth *Agrotis pilgrami*; and Pilgram himself had published several descriptions. His boxes contained most of the countries of the world, but all he had ever seen of it was the dull sand-and-pine scenery of an occasional Sunday trip; and he would be reminded of captures that had seemed to him so miraculous in his boyhood as he melancholically gazed at the familiar fauna about him, limited by a familiar landscape, to which it corresponded as hopelessly as he to his street. From a roadside shrub he would pick up a large turquoise-green caterpillar with a china-blue horn on the last ring; there it lay quite stiff on the palm of his hand, and presently, with a sigh, he would put it back on its twig as if it were some dead trinket.

Although once or twice he had had the chance to switch to a more profitable business – selling cloth, for instance, instead of moths – he stubbornly held on to his shop as the symbolic link between his dreary existence and the phantom of perfect happiness. What he craved for, with a fierce, almost morbid intensity, was *himself* to net the rarest butterflies of distant countries, to see them in flight with his own eyes, to stand waist-deep in lush grass and feel the follow-through of the swishing net and then the furious throbbing of wings through a clutched fold of the gauze.

Every year it seemed to him stranger that the year before he had not managed somehow to lay aside enough money for at least a fortnight's collecting trip abroad, but he had never been thrifty, business had always been slack, there was always a gap somewhere, and, even if luck did come his way now and then, something was sure to go wrong at the last moment. He had married counting heavily on a share in his father-in-law's business, but a month later the man had died, leaving nothing but debts. Just before

World War I an unexpected deal brought a journey to Algeria so near that he even acquired a sun helmet. When all travel stopped, he still consoled himself with the hope that he might be sent to some exciting place as a soldier; but he was clumsy, sickly, not very young, and thus saw neither active service nor exotic lepidoptera. Then, after the war, when he had managed again to save a little money (for a week in Zermatt, this time), the inflation suddenly turned his meager hoard into something less than the price of a trolley-car ticket.

After that he gave up trying. He grew more and more depressed as his passion grew stronger. When some entomological acquaintance happened to drop in, Pilgram was only annoyed. That fellow, he would think, may be as learned as the late Dr. Staudinger, but he has no more imagination than a stamp collector. The glass-lidded trays over which both were bending gradually took up the whole counter, and the pipe in Pilgram's sucking lips kept emitting a wistful squeak. Pensively he gazed at the serried rows of delicate insects, all alike to you or me, and now and then he tapped on the glass with a stubby forefinger, stressing some special rarity. "That's a curiously dark aberration," the learned visitor might say. "Eisner got one like that at an auction in London, but it was not so dark, and it cost him fourteen pounds." Painfully sniffling with his extinguished pipe, Pilgram would raise the box to the light, which made the shadows of the butterflies slip from beneath them across the papered bottom; then he would put it down again and, working in his nails under the tight edges of the lid, would shake it loose with a jerk and smoothly remove it. "And Eisner's female was not so fresh," the visitor would add, and some eavesdroppers coming in for a copybook or a postage stamp might well wonder what on earth these two were talking about.

Grunting, Pilgram plucked at the gilded head of the black pin upon which the silky little creature was crucified, and took the specimen out of the box. Turning it this way and that, he peered at the label pinned under the body. "Yes – 'Tatsienlu, East Tibet,'" he read. "'Taken by the native collectors of Father Dejean'" (which sounded almost like "Prester John") – and he would stick the butterfly back again, right into the same pinhole. His motions seemed casual, even careless, but this was the unerring nonchalance of the specialist: the pin, with the precious insect, and Pilgram's fat fingers were the correlated parts of one and the same flawless machine. It might happen, however, that some open box, having been brushed by the elbow of the visitor, would stealthily begin to slide off the counter – to be stopped just in the nick of time by Pilgram, who would then calmly go on lighting his pipe; only much later, when busy elsewhere, he would suddenly produce a moan of retrospective anguish.

But not only averted crashes made him moan. Father Dejean, stout-hearted missionary climbing among the rhododendrons and snows, how enviable was thy lot! And Pilgram would stare at his boxes and puff and brood and reflect that he need not go so far: that there were thousands of hunting grounds all over Europe. Out of localities cited in entomological works he had built up a special world of his own, to which his science was a most detailed guidebook. In that world there were no casinos, no old churches, nothing that might attract a normal tourist. Digne in southern France, Ragusa in Dalmatia, Sarepta on the Volga, Abisko in Lapland – those were the famous sites dear to butterfly collectors, and this is where they had poked about, on and off, since the fifties of the last century (always greatly perplexing the local inhabitants). And as clearly as if it were a reminiscence Pilgram saw himself troubling the sleep of a little hotel by stamping and jumping about a room through the wide-open window of which, out of the black generous night, a whitish moth had dashed in and, in an audible bob dance, was kissing its shadow all over the ceiling.

In these impossible dreams of his he visited the Islands of the Blessed, where in the hot ravines that cut the lower slopes of the chestnut- and laurel-clad mountains there occurs a weird local race of the cabbage white; and also that other island, those railway banks near Vizzavona and the pine woods farther up, which are the haunts of the squat and dusky Corsican swallow-tail. He visited the far North, the arctic bogs that produced such delicate downy butterflies. He knew the high alpine pastures, with those flat stones lying here and there among the slippery matted grass; for there is no greater delight than to lift such a stone and find beneath it a plump sleepy moth of a still undescribed species. He saw glazed Apollo butterflies, ocellated with red, float in the mountain draft across the mule track that ran between a steep cliff and an abyss of wild white waters. In Italian gardens in the summer dusk, the gravel crunched invitingly underfoot, and Pilgram gazed through the growing darkness at clusters of blossoms in front of which suddenly there appeared an oleander hawk, which passed from flower to flower, humming intently and stopping at the corolla, its wings vibrating so rapidly that nothing but a ghostly nimbus was visible about its streamlined body. And best of all, perhaps, were the white heathered hills near Madrid, the valleys of Andalusia, fertile and wooded Albarracin, whither a little bus driven by the forest guard's brother groaned up a twisted road.

He had more difficulty in imagining the tropics, but experienced still keener pangs when he did, for never would he catch the loftily flapping Brazilian morphos, so ample and radiant that they cast an azure reflection upon one's hand, never come upon those crowds of African butterflies closely stuck like innumerable fancy flags into the rich black mud and rising in a colored cloud when his shadow approached – a long, very long, shadow.

3

"*Ja, ja, ja,*" he would mutter, nodding his heavy head, and holding the case before him as if it were a beloved portrait. The bell over the door would tinkle, his wife would come in with a wet umbrella and a shopping bag, and slowly he would turn his back to her as he inserted the case into the cabinet. So it went on, that obsession and that despair and that nightmarish impossibility to swindle destiny, until a certain first of April, of all dates. For more than a year he had had in his keeping a cabinet devoted solely to the genus of those small clear-winged moths that mimic wasps or mosquitoes. The widow of a great authority on that particular group had given Pilgram her husband's collection to sell on commission. He hastened to tell the silly woman that he would not be able to get more than 75 marks for it, although he knew very well that, according to catalogue prices, it was worth fifty times more, so that the amateur to whom he would sell the lot for, say,

a thousand marks would consider it a good bargain. The amateur, however, did not appear, though Pilgram had written to all the wealthiest collectors. So he had locked up the cabinet, and stopped thinking about it.

That April morning a sunburned, bespectacled man in an old mackintosh
and without any hat on his brown bald head sauntered in, and asked for
some carbon paper. Pilgram slipped the small coins paid for the sticky violet stuff he so hated to handle into the slit of a small clay money pot and,
sucking on his pipe, fixed his stare into space. The man cast a rapid glance
round the shop, and remarked upon the extravagant brilliancy of an iridescent green insect with many tails. Pilgram mumbled something about
Madagascar. "And that – that's not a butterfly, is it?" said the man, indicating another specimen. Pilgram slowly replied that he had a whole collection of that special kind. "*Ach, was!*" said the man. Pilgram scratched his
bristly chin, and limped into a recess of the shop. He pulled out a glass-
topped tray, and laid it on the counter. The man pored over those tiny vitre-
ous creatures with bright orange feet and belted bodies. Pilgram pointed
with the stem of his pipe to one of the rows, and simultaneously the man
exclaimed: "Good God – *uralensis*!" and that ejaculation gave him away.
Pilgram heaped case after case on the counter as it dawned upon him that
the visitor knew perfectly well of the existence of this collection, had come
for its sake, was as a matter of fact the rich amateur Sommer, to whom he
had written and who had just returned from a trip to Venezuela; and finally,
when the question was carelessly put – "Well, and what would the price
be?" – Pilgram smiled.

He knew it was madness; he knew he was leaving a helpless Eleanor,
debts, unpaid taxes, a store at which only trash was bought; he knew that
the 950 marks he might get would permit him to travel for no longer than
a few months; and still he accepted it all as a man who felt that tomorrow
would bring dreary old age and that the good fortune which now beckoned
would never again repeat its invitation.

When finally Sommer said that on the fourth he would give a definite
answer, Pilgram decided that the dream of his life was about to break at
last from its old crinkly cocoon. He spent several hours examining a map,

choosing a route, estimating the time of appearance of this or that species, and suddenly something black and blinding welled before his eyes, and he stumbled about his shop for quite a while before he felt better. The fourth came and Sommer failed to turn up, and, after waiting all day, Pilgram retired to his bedroom and silently lay down. He refused his supper, and for several minutes, with his eyes closed, nagged his wife, thinking she was still standing near; then he heard her sobbing softly in the kitchen, and toyed with the idea of taking an axe and splitting her pale-haired head. Next day he stayed in bed, and Eleanor took his place in the shop and sold a box of watercolors. And after still another day, when the whole thing seemed merely delirium, Sommer, a carnation in his buttonhole and his mackintosh on his arm, entered the store. And when he took out a wad, and the banknotes rustled, Pilgram's nose began to bleed violently.

The delivery of the cabinet and a visit to the credulous old woman, to whom he reluctantly gave 50 marks, were his last business in town. The much more expensive visit to the travel agency already referred to his new existence, where only butterflies mattered. Eleanor, though not familiar with her husband's transactions, looked happy, feeling that he had made a good profit, but fearing to ask how much. That afternoon a neighbor dropped in to remind them that tomorrow was the wedding of his daughter. So next morning Eleanor busied herself with brightening up her silk dress and pressing her husband's best suit. She would go there about five, she thought, and he would follow later, after closing time. When he looked up at her with a puzzled frown and then flatly refused to go, it did not surprise her, for she had long become used to all sorts of disappointments. "There might be champagne," she said, when already standing in the doorway. No answer – only the shuffling of boxes. She looked thoughtfully at the nice clean gloves on her hands, and went out.

Pilgram, having put the more valuable collections in order, looked at his watch and saw it was time to pack: his train left at 8:29. He locked the shop, dragged out of the corridor his father's old checkered suitcase, and packed the hunting implements first: a folding net, killing jars, pillboxes, a lantern for mothing at night on the sierras, and a few packages of pins. As an afterthought he put in a couple of spreading boards and a cork-bottomed box, though in general he intended to keep his captures in papers, as is usually done when going from place to place. Then he took the suitcase into the bedroom and threw in some thick socks and underwear. He added two or three things that might be sold in an extremity, such as, for instance, a silver tumbler and a bronze medal in a velvet case, which had belonged to his father-in-law.

Again he looked at his watch, and then decided it was time to start for the station. "Eleanor!" he called loudly, getting into his overcoat. As she did not reply, he looked into the kitchen. No, she was not there; and then vaguely he remembered something about a wedding. Hurriedly he got a scrap of paper and scribbled a few words in pencil. He left the note and the keys in a conspicuous place, and with a chill of excitement, a sinking feeling in the pit of the stomach, verified for the last time whether the money and tickets were in his wallet. "*Also los!*" said Pilgram, and gripped the suitcase.

But, as it was his first journey, he still kept worrying nervously whether there was anything he might have forgotten; then it occurred to him that he had no small change, and he remembered the clay money pot where there might be a few coins. Groaning and knocking the heavy suitcase against corners, he returned to his counter. In the twilight of the strangely still shop, eyed wings stared at him from all sides, and Pilgram perceived something almost appalling in the richness of the huge happiness that was leaning toward him like a mountain. Trying to avoid the knowing looks of those numberless eyes, he drew a deep breath and, catching sight of the hazy money pot, which seemed to hang in midair, reached quickly for it. The pot slipped from his moist grasp and broke on the floor with a dizzy spinning of twinkling coins; and Pilgram bent low to pick them up.

4

Night came; a slippery polished moon sped, without the least friction, in between chinchilla clouds, and Eleanor, returning from the wedding supper, and still all atingle from the wine and the juicy jokes, recalled her own wedding day as she leisurely walked home. Somehow all the thoughts now passing through her brain kept turning so as to show their moon-bright, attractive side; she felt almost lighthearted as she entered the gateway and proceeded to open the door, and she caught herself thinking that it was surely a great thing to have an apartment of one's own, stuffy and dark though it might be. Smiling, she turned on the light in her bedroom, and saw at once that all the drawers had been pulled open: she hardly had time to imagine burglars, for there were those keys on the night table and a bit of paper propped against the alarm clock. The note was brief: "*Off to Spain. Don't touch anything till I write. Borrow from Sch. or W. Feed the lizards.*"

The faucet was dripping in the kitchen. Unconsciously she picked up her silver bag where she had dropped it, and kept on sitting on the edge of the bed, quite straight and still, with her hands in her lap as if she were having her photograph taken. After a time someone got up, walked across the room, inspected the bolted window, came back again, while she watched with indifference, not realizing that it was she who was moving. The drops of water plopped in slow succession, and suddenly she felt terrified at being alone in the house. The man whom she had loved for his mute omniscience, stolid coarseness, grim perseverance in work, had stolen away. . . . She felt like howling, running to the police, showing her marriage certificate, insisting, pleading; but still she kept on sitting, her hair slightly ruffled, her hands in white gloves.

Yes, Pilgram had gone far, very far. Most probably he visited Granada and Murcia and Albarracin, and then traveled farther still, to Surinam or Taprobane; and one can hardly doubt that he saw all the glorious bugs he had longed to see – velvety black butterflies soaring over the jungles, and a tiny moth in Tasmania, and that Chinese "skipper" said to smell of crushed roses when alive, and the short-clubbed beauty that a Mr. Baron had just discovered in Mexico. So, in a certain sense, it is quite irrelevant that some time later, upon wandering into the shop, Eleanor saw the checkered suitcase, and then her husband, sprawling on the floor with his back to the counter, among scattered coins, his livid face knocked out of shape by death. [STORIES 244–54]

From letter to Véra Nabokov, May 12, 1930

From Prague. In Russian. Unpublished.

Today I was sorting through some dusty books to take something with me, and gnawed into old numbers of *The Entomologist*. I'm striking it lucky, the first guest to arrive on Sunday[13] turned out to be an entomologist, imagine how white-hot we became. On Thursday he will show me the museum and a famous collection of *Papilios*. In the province of Podolsk he caught a perfectly wonderful *Podalirius*, a match for the black *machaon* of Püngeler's collection. . . . [Mother] and E.K.[14] arranged everything marvelously for me, volumes of *The Entomologist* lay on my bedside table, and they had bought me stamps, new pens and paper for my letters to you.   [VNA, MTRX]

From Nikolay Raevsky reminiscence,
"Vospominaniya o Vladimire Nabokove"

Published in 1989.

In one of our conversations I said to him something like this: "Vladimir Vladimirovich, it's a great happiness for Russian literature that you aren't earning much yet. If you were well off, I'm afraid you'd rush anywhere there were wonderful butterflies, where the climate was vile and dangerous for the health. Nabokov the writer could die there prematurely."

Nabokov with rapturous enthusiasm told me that he did indeed dream of travelling to New Guinea, to French Equatorial Africa, or, say, the Solomon Islands. "The climate is vile in all these places, but I am young, healthy, fit, so maybe I'd stay alive to bring back fabulous collections."

[*Prostor* 2 (1989): 115–16]

From letter to Véra Nabokov, May 17, 1930

From Prague. In Russian. Unpublished.

Went to the museum yesterday. They showed me their excellent collections, not of course as full as in Berlin, though you can't say that to the

Czechs. . . . Fyodorov, about whom I wrote you, was just here. He strongly advises going to Varna, where it's extremely cheap and there are lots of butterflies. The trip from here costs 20 marks, so from Berlin forty all told. For two persons or beasts 80. There and back 160. And you can fit two animals per room. The food costs two marks a day and for a month we'd need for travel and living costs roughly only 250 marks. I think we'll go at the start of June. There are no snakes there. [VNA, MTRX]

From letter to Véra Nabokov, c. May 20, 1930

From Prague. In Russian. Unpublished.

I went to see Obenberger at the entomological museum again. [VNA, MTRX]

From letter to Véra Nabokov, May 22, 1930

From Prague. In Russian. Unpublished.

By the way I'll copy this out for you from Kipling:

> Do you know the pile-built village where the sago dealers trade –
> Do you know the reek of fish and wet bamboo?
> Do you know the steaming stillness of the orchid-scented glade
> When the blazoned, bird-winged butterflies flap through?
> It is there that I am going with my camphor, net and boxes,
> To a gentle yellow pirate that I know –
> To my little wailing lemurs, to my palms and flying-foxes,
> For the Red Gods call me out and I must go![15]

"Flap" is especially good. . . . And here's something about us:

> She was queen of Sabaea
> And he was Asia's lord
> But they both of them talked to the butterflies
> When they took their walks abroad.[16]

[VNA, MTRX]

Glory

Excerpts from novel in Russian (*Podvig*). Written May–October 1930. Published in *Sovremennye zapiski* 45–48 (February 1931–January 1932). Translated by DN with VN.

[Martin, in the Crimea, has just heard that his father has died.]

It was hot, even though a rainstorm had raged a short time before. Blow-flies buzzed around the glossy medlar shrubs. An ill-tempered black swan floated in the pool, moving from side to side its bill which was so crimson that it seemed painted. Petals had fallen from the almond trees, and stood out pale on the dark earth of the damp path, like almonds in gingerbread. Not far from some enormous cedars of Lebanon grew a lone birch tree, with that particular slant to its foliage that only a birch has (as if a girl had let her hair down on one side to be combed, and stood still). A zebra-striped swallowtail glided past, its tails extended and joined. The sparkling air, the shadows of the cypresses (old trees, with a rusty cast, their small cones half-hidden under their cloaks); the black glass of the pool, where concentric circles spread around the swan; the radiant blue into which serrated Mount Petri rose wearing a broad belt of karakul-like pine – everything was permeated with agonizing bliss, and it seemed to Martin that somehow his father played a part in the distribution of shadow and shine.

[*Glory* 9]

[In the south of France, Martin wakes up from his wagon-lit when the train stops.]

Martin once again crawled over to the window: he saw a lighted station platform; a man passed trundling an iron baggage cart with a muffled clatter, and on the cart was a crate with the mysterious inscription "FRAGILE." Several midges and one large moth circled around a gas lantern; shadowy people shuffled along the platform conversing about unknown things as they went; then there was a jangle of buffers and the train glided off.

[*Glory* 21]

[At a hotel above Lausanne, Switzerland, Martin has lost at tennis.]

On the way home he mentally replayed every shot, transforming defeat into victory, and then shaking his head: how very, very hard it was to capture happiness! Brooks burbled, concealed among the foliage; blue butterflies fluttered up from damp spots on the road; birds bustled in the bushes: everything was depressingly sunny and carefree. That evening after dinner they sat as usual in the drawing room; the door to the piazza was wide open, and, since there had been a power failure, candles burned in the chandeliers. [*Glory* 47–48]

[*Back again in Switzerland, Martin cannot resist the impulse to climb a precipitous hill and finds himself on a cliff ledge.*]

He experienced faintness, dizziness, sickening fear, yet at the same time he observed himself from the outside, noting with odd lucidity his open-collared flannel shirt, his clumsy clinging position on the ledge, the thistle ball that had attached itself to his stocking and the entirely black butterfly that fluttered by with enviable casualness like a quiet little devil and began to rise along the rock face; and though there was no one around to make showing off worth while, Martin began to whistle; then he vowed to himself that he would pay no attention to the invitation of the abyss and began to displace his feet slowly, as he moved to the left. [*Glory* 86]

[*Another impulse leads him suddenly to rush off a train in the middle of the night, at an unknown station somewhere in the south of France, to explore lights in the distance.*]

Still panting, Martin traversed the platform. A porter who was pushing a luggage cart with a big box labeled "*Fragile*" said to him gaily, with the metallic accent peculiar to Provence: "You woke up at the right moment, Monsieur." "Tell me," Martin inquired, "what's in that box?" The porter looked at it as if he had only just noticed its presence, and read out the address: "Museum of Natural Science." "Ah yes, a collection of insects, no doubt," said Martin, and walked toward the little group of tables at the entrance of the dimly lit buffet.

The air was velvety and warm; around a milky white arc light swirled pale midges and one ample dark moth with hoary margins. A six-foot poster adorned the wall: it was an attempt on the part of the War Department to picture for the benefit of young men the allurements of military service: in the foreground, a valiant French soldier; in the back, a date palm, a dromedary, and a burnoosed Arab; and in the corner, two opulent forms in charshafs. [*Glory* 158]

Thus, sitting on a rock and listening to the brook's gurgling, Martin enjoyed his fill of viatic freedom from all concerns: he was a wanderer, alone and lost in a marvelous world, completely indifferent toward him, in which butterflies danced, lizards darted, and leaves glistened – the same way as they glisten in a Russian or African wood.   [*Glory* 161]

From letter to Elena Nabokov, May 18, 1931

From Berlin. Unpublished. In Russian.

I am waiting for "The Entomologist" with my article. . . .

Good God, how I long for butterflies. Patience is the distinguishing characteristic of the Russian people.   [VNA]

From letter to Elena Nabokov, May 26, 1931

From Berlin. Unpublished. In Russian.

A very nice *machaon*. . . . It turned up around the last week of May (old style), liked the roadside dandelions and the lilac in the garden. Today I was lying in the blazing Grunewald sun and counted eleven species of butterfly, including a very fresh *machaon*.[17]   [VNA]

Terra Incognita

Excerpts from story in Russian ("Terra Incognita"). Written in late 1931. Published in PN, November 22, 1931. Translated by DN with VN.

[A feverish narrator is uncertain whether he is a botanist approaching a delirious death on a jungle expedition or an invalid in a snug bedroom somewhere in Europe.]

Gregson strode on beside me, sinewy, lanky, with bare, bony knees. He held a long-handled green butterfly net like a banner.   [STORIES 293]

We were now alone. Cook and all eight of the natives, with tent, folding boat, supplies, and collections, had deserted us and vanished noiselessly while we busied ourselves in the thick bush, chasing fascinating insects. I think we tried to catch up with the fugitives – I do not recall clearly, but, in any case, we failed. We had to decide whether to return to Zonraki or continue our projected itinerary, across as yet unknown country, toward the Gurano Hills. The unknown won out. We moved on. I was already shivering all over and deafened by quinine, but still went on collecting nameless plants, while Gregson, though fully realizing the danger of our situation, continued catching butterflies and diptera as avidly as ever.

[STORIES 294]

The noonday sky, now freed of its leafy veils, hung oppressively over us with its blinding darkness – yes, its blinding darkness, for there is no other way to describe it. I tried not to look up; but in this sky, at the very verge of my field of vision, there floated, always keeping up with me, whitish phantoms of plaster, stucco curlicues and rosettes, like those used to adorn European ceilings; however, I had only to look directly at them and they would vanish, and again the tropical sky would boom, as it were, with even, dense blueness. We were still walking along the rocky promontory, but it kept tapering and betraying us. Around it grew golden marsh reeds, like a million bared swords gleaming in the sun. Here and there flashed elongated pools, and over them hung dark swarms of midges. A large swamp flower, presumably an orchid, stretched toward me its drooping, downy lip, which seemed smeared with egg yolk. Gregson swung his net – and sank to his hips in the brocaded ooze as a gigantic swallowtail, with a flap of its satin wing, sailed away from him over the reeds, toward the shimmer of pale emanations where the indistinct folds of a window curtain seemed to hang. *I must not*, I said to myself, *I must not*. . . . I shifted my gaze and walked on beside Gregson, now over rock, now across hissing and lip-smacking soil.

[STORIES 295]

Glossy birds flew through the haze of the marsh and, as they settled, one turned into the wooden knob of a bedpost, another into a decanter. Gathering all my will power, I focused my gaze and drove off this dangerous trash. Above the reeds flew real birds with long flame-colored tails. The air buzzed with insects. Gregson was waving away a varicolored fly, and at the same time trying to determine its species. Finally he could contain himself no longer and caught it in his net. [STORIES 298]

Then I thought about our discoveries, our precious finds, the rare, still undescribed plants and animals that now would never be named by us. I was alone. Hazier flashed the reeds, dimmer flamed the sky. My eyes followed an exquisite beetle that was crawling across a stone, but I had no strength left to catch it. Everything around me was fading, leaving bare the scenery of death – a few pieces of realistic furniture and four walls. My last motion was to open the book, which was damp with sweat, for I absolutely had to make a note of something; but, alas, it slipped out of my hand. I groped all along the blanket, but it was no longer there. [STORIES 299]

Perfection

Excerpts from story in Russian ("Sovershenstvo"). Written May–June 1932. Published in PN, July 3, 1932. Translated by DN with VN.

[Ivanov, an impoverished tutor, tries to stir the imagination of his young charge, whom he chaperones on a Pomeranian beach.]

The forest was dense. Geometrid moths, matching the bark in coloration, flew off the tree trunks. Silent David walked reluctantly. "We should cherish the woods," Ivanov said in an attempt to divert his pupil. "It was the first habitat of man. One fine day man left the jungle of primitive intimations for the sunlit glade of reason. Those bilberries appear to be ripe, you have my permission to taste them. Why do you sulk? Try to understand: one should vary one's pleasures. And one should not overindulge in sea bathing. How often it happens that a careless bather dies of sun stroke or heart failure!"

Ivanov rubbed his unbearably burning and itching back against a tree trunk and continued pensively: "While admiring nature at a given locality, I cannot help thinking of countries that I shall never see. Try to imagine, David, that this is not Pomerania but a Malayan forest. Look about you:

you'll presently see the rarest of birds fly past, Prince Albert's paradise bird, whose head is adorned with a pair of long plumes consisting of blue oriflammes." "*Ach, quatsch*," responded David dejectedly.

"In Russian you ought to say '*erundá*.' Of course, it's nonsense, we are not in the mountains of New Guinea. But the point is that with a bit of imagination – if, God forbid, you were someday to go blind or be imprisoned, or were merely forced to perform, in appalling poverty, some hopeless, distasteful task, you might remember this walk we are taking today in an ordinary forest as if it had been – how shall I say? – fairy-tale ecstasy."

[STORIES 340–41]

[*When David feigns drowning, Ivanov rushes in to help him. After a struggle with the waves, he comes out to a gray landscape, and cannot see David.*]

It is not my fault, I did all I could to save him, but I am a poor swimmer, and I have a bad heart, and he drowned. But there was something amiss about these thoughts, and when he looked around once more and saw himself in the desolate mist all alone with no David beside him, he understood that if David was not with him, David was not dead.

Only then were the clouded glasses removed. The dull mist immediately broke, blossomed with marvelous colors, all kinds of sounds burst forth – the rote of the sea, the clapping of the wind, human cries – and there was David standing, up to his ankles in bright water, not knowing what to do, shaking with fear, not daring to explain that he had not been drowning, that he had struggled in jest – and farther out people were diving, groping through the water, then looking at each other with bulging eyes, and diving anew, and returning empty-handed, while others shouted to them from the shore, advising them to search a little to the left; and a fellow with a Red Cross armband was running along the beach, and three men in sweaters were pushing into the water a boat grinding against the shingle; and a bewildered David was being led away by a fat woman in a pince-nez, the wife of a veterinarian, who had been expected to arrive on Friday but had had to postpone his vacation, and the Baltic Sea sparkled from end to end, and, in the thinned-out forest, across a green country road, there lay, still breathing, freshly cut aspens; and a youth, smeared with soot, gradually turned white as he washed under the kitchen tap, and black parakeets flew above the eternal snows of the New Zealand mountains; and a fisherman, squinting in the sun, was solemnly predicting that not until the ninth day would the waves surrender the corpse.   [STORIES 343]

Despair

Excerpt from novel in Russian (*Otchayanie*). Written in late 1932. Published in *Sovremennye zapiski* 54–56 (January–October 1934). Translated by VN 1938, revised 1966.

A silence. Small blue butterflies settling on thyme.   [*Despair* 38]

From letter to Véra Nabokov, October 29[?], 1932

From Paris. Unpublished. In Russian.

"And again with all four colored wings on an aster a butterfly settles flat." This is a verse about Kolbsheim. I sent it to Nika and Natasha.[18] I wrote them twice, but no reply.   [VNA, MTRX]

From letter to Elena Nabokov, March 5, 1934

From Berlin. Unpublished. In Russian.

Spring, spring, – and the Pilgram[19] in me pines and longs for action.   [VNA]

How I Love You

Poem in Russian ("Kak ya lyublyu tebya"). Written April 17, 1934. Published in *Poslednie novosti*, May 3, 1934. Translated by VN.

> Kind of green, kind of gray, i.e.,
> striated all over with rain,
> and the linden fragrance, so heady,

that I can hardly — Let's go!
Let's go and abandon this garden
and the rain that seethes on its paths
between the flowers grown heavy,
kissing the sticky loam.
Let's go, let's go before it's too late,
quick, under one cloak, come home,
while you still are unrecognized,
my mad one, my mad one!

Self-control, silence. But with each year,
to the murmur of trees and the clamor of birds,
the separation seems more offenseful
and the offense more absurd.
And I fear ever more that rashly
I may blab and interrupt
the course of the quiet, difficult speech
long since penetrating my life.

Above red-cheeked slaves
the blue sky looks all lacquered,
and pumped-up clouds
with scarcely discernible jerks
    move across.
I wonder, is there nowhere a place there,
to lie low – some dark nook
where the darkness might merge
with a wing's cryptic markings?
(A geometrid thus does not stir
spread flat on a lichened trunk)

What a sunset! And once more tomorrow
and for a long time the heat is to last,
a forecast faultlessly based
on the stillness and on the gnats:

hanging up in an evening sunbeam,
their swarmlet ceaselessly jiggles,
reminding one of a golden toy
in the hands of a mute peddler.

How I love you! In this
evening air, now and then,
the spirit finds loopholes, translucences
in the world's finest texture.
The beams pass between tree trunks.

How I love you! The beams
pass between tree trunks; they band
the tree trunks with flame. Do not speak.
Stand motionless under the flowering branch,
inhale – what a spreading, what flowing! –
Close your eyes, and diminish, and stealthily
into the eternal pass through.

[PP 79–81]

Invitation to a Beheading

Excerpts from novel in Russian, *Priglashenie na kazn'*. Written June–December 1934. Published in *Sovremennye zapiski* 58–60 (June 1935–February 1936). Translated by DN with VN.

[*Cincinnatus is in prison, under sentence of death for the crime of being opaque in a world of transparent souls. In this insufficiently real world, the jailer brings insects for the obligatory prison spider to feed on.*]

Of the three items of furniture – cot, table, chair – only the last was movable. The spider also moved. Up above, where the sloping window recess began, the well-nourished black beastie had found points of support for a first-rate web with the same resourcefulness as Marthe displayed when she would find, in what seemed the most unsuitable corner, a place and a method for hanging out laundry to dry. Its paws folded so that the furry elbows stuck out at the sides, it would gaze with round hazel eyes at the hand with the pencil extended toward it, and would begin to back away, without taking its eyes off it. It was most eager however, to take a fly, or a moth from the large fingers of Rodion – and now, for example, in the southwest part of the web there hung a butterfly's orphaned hind wing, cherry-red, with a silky shading, and with blue lozenges along its crenelated edge. It stirred slightly in a delicate draft.   [IB 119]

[Later.]

Let us be calm. The spider had sucked dry a small downy moth with marbled forewings, and three houseflies, but was still hungry and kept glancing at the door. Let us be calm. Cincinnatus was a mass of scrapes and bruises. Be calm; nothing had happened.   [IB 169]

"What a treat you are getting today," said Rodion, not to Cincinnatus but to the spider.

In both hands, most carefully, but at the same time squeamishly (care prompted him to press it to his chest, distaste made him hold it away) he carried a towel gathered together in a lump in which something large stirred and rustled.

"Got it on a window pane in the tower. The monster! See how it flops and flaps – you can hardly hold it . . ."

He was going to pull up the chair, as he always did, in order to stand up on it and deliver the victim to the voracious spider on his solid web (the beast was already puffing himself up, sensing the prey) but something went wrong – his gnarled, fearful fingers happened to release the main fold of the towel, and he immediately cried out and cringed, as people cry out and cringe whom not a bat but an ordinary house mouse inspires with revulsion and terror. Something large, dark, and furnished with feelers, disengaged itself from the towel, and Rodion emitted a loud yell, tramping in one place, afraid to let the thing escape but not daring to grab it. The towel fell; and the fair captive clung to Rodion's cuff, clutching it with all six of its adhesive feet.

It was only a moth, but what a moth! It was as large as a man's hand; it had thick, dark-brown wings with a hoary lining and gray-dusted margins; each wing was adorned in the center with an eye-spot, shining like steel.

Its segmented limbs, in fluffy muffs, now clung, now unstuck themselves, and the upraised vanes of its wings, through whose underside the
same staring spots and wavy gray pattern showed, oscillated slowly, as the
moth, groping its way, crawled up the sleeve, while Rodion, quite panic-
stricken, rolling his eyes, throwing away, and forsaking his own arm,
wailed, "Take it off'n me! take it off'n me!"

Upon reaching his elbow, the moth began noiselessly flapping its heavy
wings; they seemed to outbalance its body, and on Rodion's elbow joint,
the creature turned over, wings hanging down, still tenaciously clinging to
the sleeve – and now one could see its brown, white-dappled abdomen, its
squirrel face, the black globules of its eyes and its feathery antennae resembling pointed ears.

"Take it away!" implored Rodion, beside himself, and his frantic ges-
turing caused the splendid insect to fall off; it struck the table, paused on it
in mighty vibration, and suddenly took off from its edge.

But to me your daytime is dark, why did you disturb my slumber? Its
flight, swooping and lumbering, lasted only a short time. Rodion picked
up the towel and, swinging wildly, attempted to knock down the blind
flyer; but suddenly it disappeared as if the very air had swallowed it.

Rodion searched for a while, did not find it, and stopped in the center of
the cell, turning toward Cincinnatus, arms akimbo. "Eh? What a rascal!"
he ejaculated after an expressive silence. He spat; he shook his head and
pulled out a throbbing match box with spare flies, with which the disappointed animal had to be satisfied. Cincinnatus, however, had seen perfectly well where the moth had settled.   [IB 202–4]

"... But now, when I am hardened, when I am almost fearless of ..."

Here the page ended, and Cincinnatus realized that he was out of paper.
However he managed to dig up one more sheet.

"... death," he wrote on it, continuing his sentence, but he immediately
crossed out that word; he must say it differently, with greater precision:
"execution," perhaps, "pain" or "parting" – something like that; twirling
the stunted pencil in his fingers, he paused in thought, and a little brown
fuzz had stuck to the edge of the table where the moth had quivered only a
short time ago, and Cincinnatus, remembering it, walked away from the

table, leaving on it the blank sheet with only the one solitary word on it, and that one crossed out, and bent down (pretending that he was fixing the back of his slipper) by the cot, on whose iron leg, quite near the floor, it was settled, asleep, its visionary wings spread in solemn invulnerable torpor; only he was sorry for the downy back where the fuzz had rubbed off leaving a bald spot, as shiny as a chestnut – but the great dark wings, with their ashen edges and perpetually open eyes, were inviolable – the forewings, lowered slightly, lapped over the hind ones, and this drooping attitude might have been one of somnolent fragility, were it not for the monolithic straightness of the upper margins and the perfect symmetry of all the diverging lines – and this was so enchanting that Cincinnatus, unable to restrain himself, stroked with his fingertip the hoary ridge near the base of the right wing, then the ridge of the left one (what gentle firmness! what unyielding gentleness!); the moth, however, did not awaken, and he straightened up and, sighing slightly, moved away; he was about to sit down at the table again when suddenly the key scraped in the lock and the door opened, whining, rattling and groaning in keeping with all the rules of carceral counterpoint. Rosy M'sieur Pierre, in a pea-green hunting habit, first inserted his head and then came in completely, and behind him came two others, whom it was almost impossible to recognize as the director and the lawyer.   [IB 205–7]

[The executioner, Monsieur Pierre, about to lead Cincinnatus off to his death, wants the cell tidied.]
A broom was handed Rodrig through the door and he set to work.

First of all, with the end of the broom, he knocked out the whole grating in the recess of the window; there came a distant, feeble "hurrah," as if from an abyss, and a gust of fresh air entered the cell – the sheets of paper flew off the table, and Rodrig scuffed them into a corner. Then, with the broom, he pulled down the thick gray cobweb and with it the spider, which he had once nursed with such care. To while away the time Roman picked up the spider. Crudely but cleverly made, it consisted of a round plush body with twitching legs made of springs, and, there was, attached to the middle of its back, a long elastic, by the end of which Roman was holding it suspended, moving his hand up and down so that the elastic alternately contracted and extended and the spider rose and fell. M'sieur Pierre cast a sidelong cold glance at the toy and Roman, raising his eyebrows, hastily pocketed it. Rod, meanwhile, wanted to pull out the drawer of the table, tugged with all his strength, budged it, and the table split in two. At the same time the chair on which M'sieur Pierre was seated emitted a plaintive sound, something gave, and M'sieur Pierre nearly dropped his watch. Plaster began to fall from the ceiling. A crack described a tortuous course across the wall. The cell, no longer needed, was quite obviously disintegrating.

". . . Fifty-eight, fifty-nine, sixty," counted M'sieur Pierre. "That's all. Up, please. It's a fine day, the ride will be most enjoyable, anyone else in your place would be in a hurry to start."

"Just an instant more. I find it ludicrous and disgraceful that my hands should tremble so – but I can neither stop nor hide it, and, yes, they tremble and that's all. My papers you will destroy, the rubbish you will sweep out, the moth will fly away at night through the broken window, so that nothing of me will remain within these four walls, which are already about to crumble. But now dust and oblivion are nothing to me; I feel only one thing – fear, fear, shameful, futile fear . . ." Actually Cincinnatus did not say all this; he was silently changing his shoes. [IB 210–11]

From letter to Elena Nabokov, September 8, 1935

From Berlin. In Russian. Unpublished.

I am working a lot amid the entrancing chore of attending to Mityenka.[20] He calls stones[21] "ka-ka" and stretches out for bright autumn butterflies.

[VNA]

Mademoiselle O

Excerpt from an autobiographical sketch in French. Written in January 1936. Published in *Mesures* 2 (1936). Translated by VN with Hilda Ward.

[The young Vladimir's governess reads to him in French on the verandah of the family summer home.]
Presently my attention would wander still farther, and it was then, perhaps, that the rare purity of her rhythmic voice accomplished its true pur-

pose. I looked at a cloud and years later was able to visualize its exact shape. The gardener was pottering among the peonies. A wagtail took a few steps, stopped as if it had remembered something – and then walked on, enacting its name. Coming from nowhere, a comma butterfly settled on the threshold, basked in the sun with its angular fulvous wings spread, suddenly closed them just to show the tiny initial chalked on their underside, and as suddenly darted away. But the most constant source of enchantment during those readings came from the harlequin pattern of colored panes inset in a white-washed framework on either side of the veranda. The garden when viewed through these magic glasses grew strangely still and aloof. If one looked through blue glass, the sand turned to cinders while inky trees swam in a tropical sky. The yellow created an amber world infused with an extra strong brew of sunshine. The red made the foliage drip ruby dark upon a coral-tinted footpath. The green soaked greenery in a greener green. And when, after such richness, one turned to a small square of normal, savorless glass, with its lone mosquito or lame daddy longlegs, it was like taking a draft of water when one is not thirsty, and one saw a matter-of-fact white bench under familiar trees. But of all the windows this is the pane through which in later years parched nostalgia longed to peer.   [STORIES 482–83]

Spring in Fialta

Excerpt from story in Russian ("Vesna v Fial'te"). Written in April 1936. Published in *Sovremennye zapiski* 61 (1936). Translated by VN and Peter Pertzov.

[Four friends converse in a sidewalk café and notice someone seated next to them.]
Meanwhile the big Englishman suddenly made up his mind, got up on a chair, stepped from there onto the windowsill, and stretched up till he reached that coveted corner of the frame where rested a compact furry moth, which he deftly slipped into a pillbox.   [STORIES 423–24]

From letter to Véra Nabokov, February 20, 1937

From Paris. In Russian.

And on April 1 we shall meet in Toulon. *Incidentally, I am not particularly interested in the butterflies of that department – Var –* for I have already collected there and am familiar with everything, so that I shall take care of my little one all day long and write in the evenings. And in May we'll find a cheaper arrangement. I think this time common sense is on my side.

[SL 19]

Cloud, Castle, Lake

Excerpt from story in Russian ("Oblako, ozero, bashnya"). Written in late June 1937. Published in *Russkie zapiski* 2 (1937). Translated by VN and Peter Pertzov.

They spent the night in a tumble-down inn. A mature bedbug is awful, but there is a certain grace in the motions of silky silverfish. The post-office clerk was separated from his wife, who was put with the widow; he was given to Vasiliy Ivanovich for the night. The two beds took up the whole room. Quilt on top, chamber pot below. The clerk said that somehow he did not feel sleepy, and began to talk of his Russian adventures, rather more circumstantially than in the train. He was a great bully of a man, thorough and obstinate, clad in long cotton drawers, with mother-of-pearl claws on his dirty toes, and bear's fur between fat breasts. A moth dashed about the ceiling, hobnobbing with its shadow. "In Tsaritsyn," the clerk was saying, "there are now three schools, a German, a Czech, and a Chinese one. At any rate, that is what my brother-in-law says; he went there to build tractors."

[STORIES 430]

From letter to Irina Guadanini,[22] July 28, 1937

From Cannes. In Russian. Unpublished.

The Esterel hills seem like cigarette paper. I got lost in some wild spots there a few days ago (red sheer cliffs, the screech of cicadas, fiery smells, interesting butterflies) and returned only towards evening, in a truck with heart trouble. "Alors, monsieur, vous faîtes l'élévage des papillons?"[23]

[Private Collection]

From letter to Irina Guadanini, August 2, 1937

From Cannes. In Russian. Unpublished.

I am writing this letter in an amazing thicket that I reached chasing butter-flies. No, I'm not collecting them, but only rereading them, because I know them all in these localities. They've all been studied here – and I collected here myself in 1923.

[Private Collection]

The Gift

Excerpts from novel in Russian (*Dar*). Written 1933–38. Published, except for Chapter 4, in *Sovre-mennye zapiski* 63–67 (April 1937–October 1938) and complete, in book form, in 1952. Translated Michael Scammell and DN with VN.

[On the occasion of the publication of his first slim book of poems, Fyodor Godunov-Cherdynstev, the hero and narrator, casts his mind back over his series of poems about childhood.]

Meanwhile the air in the poems has grown warmer and we are preparing to return to the country, where we might move as early as April in the years before I began school (I began it only at the age of twelve).

> The snow, gone from the slopes, lurks in ravines,
> And the Petersburg spring
> Is full of excitement and of anemones
> And of the first butterflies.
> But I don't need last year's Vanessas,
> Those bleached hibernators,
> Or those utterly battered Brimstones,
> Through transparent woods flying.
> I shall not fail, though, to detect

The four lovely gauze wings

Of the softest Geometrid moth in the world

Spread flat on a mottled pale birchtrunk.

This poem is the author's own favorite, but he did not include it in the collection because, once again, the theme is connected with that of his father and economy of art advised him not to touch that theme before the right time came. Instead he reproduced such spring impressions as the first sensation immediately upon walking out of the station: the softness of the ground, its kindred proximity to your foot, and around your head the totally unrestrained flow of air. [GIFT 24]

[Summer in Fyodor's Berlin.]

In a quiet lane behind the church the locust trees shed their petals on a gray June day, and the dark asphalt next to the sidewalk looked as if cream of wheat had been spilled on it. In the rose beds around the statue of a bronze runner the Dutch Glory disengaged the corners of its red petals and was followed by General Arnold Janssen. One happy and cloudless day in July, a very successful ant flight was staged: the females would take to the air, and the sparrows, also taking to the air, would devour them; and in places where nobody bothered them they kept crawling along the gravel and shedding their feeble prop-room wings. From Denmark the papers reported that as a result of a heat wave there, numerous cases of insanity were being observed: people were tearing off their clothes and jumping into the canals. Male gypsy moths dashed about in wild zigzags. The lindens went through all their involved, aromatic, messy metamorphoses. [GIFT 59–60]

[Fyodor at an émigré literary soirée.]

Tamara was indicating a vacant chair to him, and as he made his way to it he again thought he heard the sonorous ring of his name. When young people of his age, lovers of poetry, followed him on occasion with that special gaze that glides like a swallow across a poet's mirrory heart, he would feel inside him the chill of a quickening, bracing pride; it was the forerunner of his future fame; but there was also another, earthly fame – the faithful echo of the past: he was proud of the attention of his young coevals, but no less proud of the curiosity of older people, who saw in him the son of a great explorer, a courageous eccentric who had discovered new animals in Tibet, the Pamirs and other blue lands. [GIFT 65]

[Fyodor relives a scene of his youth.]

The rainbow was already fading. The rain had quite stopped, it was scorching hot, a horsefly with satiny eyes settled on his sleeve. A cuckoo began to call in a copse, listlessly, almost questioningly: the sound swelled like a cupule, and again, like a cupule, unable to find a solution. The poor, fat bird probably flew further away, for everything was repeated from the beginning in the manner of a reduced reflection (it sought, who knows, a place for the best, the saddest effect). A huge butterfly, flat in flight, bluish-black with a white band, described a supernaturally smooth arc, settled on the damp earth, closed its wings and with that disappeared. This is the kind that now and then a panting peasant lad brings one, cramming it with both hands into his cap. This is the kind that soars up from under the mincing hooves of the doctor's well-behaved little pony, when the doctor, holding the almost superflous reins in his lap or else simply tying them to the front board, pensively drives along the shady road to the hospital. But on occasion you find four black-and-white wings with brick-colored undersides scattered like playing cards over a forest footpath: the rest, eaten by an unknown bird. [GIFT 77–78]

[Fyodor emerges from his memories.]

Meanwhile, around him everything that had just been imagined with such pictorial clarity (which in itself was suspicious, like the vividness of dreams at the wrong time of day or after a soporific) paled, corroded, disintegrated, and if one looked around, then (as in a fairy tale the stairs disappear behind the back of whoever is mounting them) everything collapsed and disappeared, a farewell configuration of trees, standing like people come to see someone off and already swept away, a scrap of rainbow faded in the wash, the path, of which there remained only the gesture of a turn, a butterfly on a pin with only three wings and no abdomen, a carnation in the sand, by the shade of the bench, the very last most persistent odds and ends, and in another moment all this yielded Fyodor without a struggle to his present, and straight out of his reminiscence (swift and senseless, visiting him like an attack of a fatal illness at any hour, in any place), straight from the hothouse paradise of the past, he stepped onto a Berlin tramcar.   [GIFT 80]

[Fyodor's mother visits him from Paris.]

On the eve of her departure they both sat up late in his room, she, in the armchair, easily and skillfully (whereas formerly she could not sew a button on) darning and mending his pitiful things, while he, on the sofa, biting his nails, was reading a thick battered book;[24] earlier, in his youth, he had skipped some of the pages – "Angelo," "Journey to Arzrum" – but lately it was precisely in these that he had found particular pleasure. He had only just got to the words: "The frontier held something mysterious for me; to travel had been my favorite dream since childhood," when suddenly he felt a sweet, strong stab from somewhere. Still not understanding, he put the book to one side and slipped blind fingers into a boxful of homemade cigarettes. At that moment his mother said without raising her head: "What did I just remember! Those funny rhymes about butterflies and moths which you and he composed together when we were out walking, you remember. 'Your blue stripe, Catocalid, shows from under its gray lid.'" "Yes," replied Fyodor, "some were downright epics: 'A dead leaf is not hoarier than a newborn *arborea*.'" (What a surprise it had been! Father had only just brought back the very first specimen from his travels, having found it during the initial trek through Siberia – he had not even had time to describe it yet – and on the first day after his return, in the Leshino park, two paces from the house, with no thought of lepidoptera, while strolling with his wife and children, throwing a tennis ball for the fox terriers, basking in his return, in the balmy weather and the health and gaiety of his family, but unconsciously noting with the experienced eye of a hunter every insect along his path, he had suddenly pointed out to Fyodor with the tip of his cane a plump reddish-gray *Epicnaptera* moth, with sinuate margins, of the leaf-mimicking kind, hanging asleep from a stalk under a bush; he had been about to walk on (the members of this genus look very much alike) but then squatted down, wrinkled his forehead, inspected his find and suddenly said in a bright voice: "*Well, I'm damned!* I need not have gone so far!" "I always said so," interposed his wife with a laugh. The furry little monster in his hand belonged to the new species he had just brought back – and now it had cropped up here, in the Province of St. Petersburg, whose fauna had been so well investigated! But, as often happens, the momentum of mighty coincidence did not stop there, it was good for one more stage: only a few days later his father learned that this new moth had just been described from St. Petersburg specimens by a fellow scientist, and Fyodor cried all night long: they had beaten Father to it!   [GIFT 94–95]

[The sudden impulse on his mother's last night in Berlin has developed in Fyodor into the idea for a biography of his father.]

Pensive, abstracted, vaguely tormented by the thought that somehow in his talks with his mother he had left the main thing untold, Fyodor returned home, took off his shoes, broke off the corner of a chocolate bar together with its silver paper, moved the book left open on the sofa closer. . . . "The harvest rippled, awaiting the sickle." Again that divine stab! And how it called, how it *prompted* him, the sentence about the Terek ("In faith, the river was awesome!") or – even more fitly, more intimately – about the Tartar women: "They were sitting on horseback, swathed in yashmaks: all one could see were their eyes and the heels of their shoes."

Thus did he hearken to the purest sound from Pushkin's tuning fork – and he already knew exactly what this sound required of him. Two weeks after his mother's departure he wrote her about what he had conceived, what he had been helped to conceive by the transparent rhythm of "Arzrum," and she replied as if she had already known about it:

> It is a long time since I have been as happy as I was with you in Berlin, but watch out, this is no easy undertaking. I feel in my heart that you will accomplish it wonderfully, but remember that you need a great deal of exact information and very little family sentimentality. If you need anything I'll tell you all I can, but take care of the special research where you are, and this is most important, take all his books and those of Grigoriy Efimovich,[25] and those of the Grand Duke,[26] and lots

more; of course you know how to obtain all this, and be sure to get into touch with Vasiliy Germanovich Krüger, search him out if he's still in Berlin, they once traveled together, I remember, and approach other people, you know whom better than I, write to Avinov,[27] to Verity,[28] write to that German who used to visit us before the war, Benhaas? Banhaas?[29] Write to Stuttgart, to London, to Tring,[30] in Oxford, everywhere, *débrouille-toi* because I know nothing of these matters and all these names merely sing in my ears, but how certain I am that you will manage, my darling.

He continued, however, to wait – the planned work was a wafture of bliss, and he was afraid to spoil that bliss by haste and moreover the complex responsibility of the work frightened him, he was not ready for it yet. Continuing his training program during the whole of spring, he fed on Pushkin, inhaled Pushkin (the reader of Pushkin has the capacity of his lungs enlarged). [GIFT 96–97]

[Early preparations for the biography.]

Pushkin entered his blood. With Pushkin's voice merged the voice of his father. He kissed Pushkin's hot little hand, taking it for another, large hand smelling of the breakfast *kalach* (a blond roll). He remembered that his and Tanya's nurse hailed from the same place that Pushkin's Arina came from – namely Suyda, just beyond Gatchina: this had been within an hour's ride of their area – and she had also spoken "singsong like." He heard his father on a fresh summer morning as they walked down to the river bathhouse, on whose plank wall shimmered the golden reflection of the water, repeating with classic fervor what he considered to be the most beautiful not only of Pushkin's lines but of all the verses ever written in the world: "*Tut Apollon-ideal, tam Niobeya-pechal'*"[31] (Here is Apollo-ideal, there is Niobe-grief) and the russet wing and mother-of-pearl of a Niobe fritillary flashed over the scabiosas of the riverside meadow, where, during the first days of June, there occurred sparsely the small Black Apollo.

Indefatigably, in ecstasy, he was really preparing his work now (in Berlin with an adjustment of thirteen days it was also the first days of June), collected material, read until dawn, studied maps, wrote letters and met with the necessary people. From Pushkin's prose he had passed to his life, so that in the beginning the rhythm of Pushkin's era commingled with the rhythm of his father's life. Scientific books (with the Berlin Library's stamp always on the ninety-ninth page), such as the familiar volumes of *The Travels of a Naturalist* in unfamiliar black and green bindings, lay side by side with the old Russian journals in which he sought Pushkin's reflected light. [GIFT 98]

[Advanced preparations for the biography, including some details on his father's father.]

He returned to Russia in 1883, no longer a Louisiana duelist but a Russian dignitary, and on a July day, on the leather sofa in the little blue corner room where I later kept my collection of butterflies, he expired without suffering, talking all the while in his deathbed delirium about a big river and the music and lights.

My father was born in 1860. A love of lepidoptera was inculcated into him by his German tutor. (By the way: what has happened to those originals who used to teach natural history to Russian children – green net, tin box on a sling, hat stuck with pinned butterflies, long, learned nose, candid eyes behind spectacles – where are they all, where are their frail skeletons – or was this a special breed of Germans, for export to Russia, or am I not looking properly?) After completing early (in 1876) his schooling in St. Petersburg, he received his university education in England, at Cambridge, where he studied biology under Professor Bright. His first journey, around the world, he made while my grandfather was still alive, and from then until 1918 his whole life consisted of traveling and the writing of scientific works. The main ones among them are: *Lepidoptera Asiatica* (8 volumes published in parts from 1890 to 1917), *The Butterflies and Moths of the Russian Empire* (the first four out of six proposed volumes came out 1912–1916) and, best known to the general public, *The Travels of a Naturalist* (7 volumes 1892–1912). These works were unanimously recognized as classics and he was still a young man when his name occupied one of the first places in the study of the Russo-Asiatic fauna, side by side with the names of its pioneers, Fischer von Waldheim,[32] Menetriés,[33] Eversmann.[34]

He worked in close touch with his remarkable Russian contemporaries.

Kholodkovski[35] calls him "the conquistador of Russian entomology." He collaborated with Charles Oberthur,[36] Grand Duke Nikolai Mihailovich, Leech[37] and Seitz.[38] Scattered throughout entomological journals are hundreds of his papers, of which the first – "On the peculiarities of the occurrence of certain butterflies in the Province of St. Petersburg" (Horae Soc. Ent. Ross.) – is dated 1877, and the last – "*Austautia simonoides* n. sp., a Geometrid Moth Mimicking a Small Parnassius" (Trans. Ent. Soc. London) – is dated 1916. He conducted a weighty and acrimonious polemic with Staudinger,[39] author of the notorious *Katalog*. He was vice-president of the Russian Entomological Society, Full Member of the Moscow Soc. of Investigators of Nature, Member of the Imperial Russian Geographical Soc., and Honorary Member of a multitude of learned societies abroad.

Between 1885 and 1918 he covered an incredible amount of territory, making surveys of his route on a three-mile scale for a distance of many thousands of miles and forming astounding collections. During these years he completed eight major expeditions which in all lasted eighteen years; but between them there was also a multitude of minor journeys, "diversions" as he called them, considering as part of these minutiae not only his trips to the less-well-investigated countries of Europe but also the journey around the world he had made in his youth. Tackling Asia in earnest he investigated Eastern Siberia, Altai, Fergana, the Pamirs, Western China, "the islands of the Gobi Sea and its coasts," Mongolia, and "the incorrigible continent" of Tibet – and described his travels in precise, weighty words.

Such is the general scheme of my father's life, copied out of an encyclopedia. It still does not sing, but I can already hear a living voice within it. It remains to be said that in 1898, at thirty-eight years of age, he married Elizaveta Pavlovna Vezhin, the twenty-year-old daughter of a well-known statesman; that he had two children by her; that in the intervals between his journeys. . . .

An agonizing, somehow sacrilegious question, hardly expressible in words: was her life with him happy, together and apart? Shall we disturb this inner world or shall we limit ourselves to a mere description of routes– *arida quaedam viarum descripto?* "Dear Mamma, I now have a great favor to ask of you. Today is the 8th of July, his birthday. On any other day I could never bring myself to ask you. Tell me something about you and him. Not the sort of thing I can find in our shared memories but the sort of thing you alone have gone through and preserved." And here is part of the reply:

> . . . imagine – a honeymoon trip, the Pyrenees, the divine bliss of everything, of the sun, the brooks, the flowers, the snowy summits, even the flies in the hotels – and of being every moment together. And then, one morning, I had a headache or something, or the heat was too much for me. He said he would go for a half hour's stroll before lunch. With odd clearness I remember sitting on a hotel balcony (around me peace, the mountains, the wonderful cliffs of Gavarnie) and reading for the first time a book not intended for young girls, *Une Vie* by Maupassant. I remember I liked it very much at the time. I look at my little watch and I see that it is already lunchtime, more than an hour has passed since he left. I wait. At first I am a little cross, then I begin to worry. Lunch is served on the terrace and I am unable to eat. I go out onto the lawn in front of the hotel, I return to my room, I go outside again. In another hour I was in an indescribable state of terror, agitation, God knows what. I was traveling for the first time, I was inexperienced and easily frightened, and then there was *Une Vie*. . . . I decided that he had abandoned me, the most stupid and terrible thoughts kept getting into my head, the day was passing, it seemed to me that the servants were gloating at me – oh, I cannot convey to you what it was like! I had even begun to thrust some dresses into a suitcase in order to return immediately to Russia, and then I suddenly decided he was dead, I ran out and began to babble something crazy and to send for the police. Suddenly I saw him walking across the lawn, his face more cheerful than I had ever seen it before, although he had been cheerful the whole time; there he came, waving his hand to me as if nothing had happened, and his light trousers had wet green spots on them, his panama had gone, his jacket was torn on one side. . . . I expect you have already guessed what had happened. Thank God at least that he finally caught it after all – in his handkerchief, on a sheer cliff – if not he would have spent the night in the mountains, as he coolly explained to me. . . . But now I want to tell you about something else, from a slightly later period, when I already knew what a really good separation could be. You were quite small then, coming up to three, you can't remember. That spring he went off to Tashkent. From there he was due to set off on a journey on the first of June and to be away

for not less than two years. That was already the second big absence during our time together. I often think now that if all the years he spent without me from the day of our wedding were added together they would amount in all to no more than his present absence. And I also think of the fact that it sometimes seemed to me then that I was unhappy, but now I know that I was always happy, that that unhappiness was one of the colors of happiness. In short, I don't know what came over me that spring, I had always been sort of batty when he went away, but that time I was quite disgracefully so. I suddenly decided that I would catch up with him and travel with him at least till autumn. Secretly I gathered a thousand things together; I had absolutely no idea what was needed, but it seemed to me that I was stocking up everything well and properly. I remember binoculars, and an alpenstock, and a camp-bed, and a sun helmet, and a hareskin coat straight out of *The Captain's Daughter*,[40] and a little mother-of-pearl revolver, and some great tarpaulin affair that I was afraid of, and a complicated water bottle that I couldn't unscrew. In short, think of the equipment of Tartarin de Tarascon.[41] How I managed to leave you little ones, how I said good-by to you – that's in a kind of mist, and I don't remember any more how I slipped out from Uncle Oleg's surveillance, how I got to the station. But I was both frightened and cheerful, I felt myself a heroine, and on the stations everyone looked at my English traveling costume with its short (*entendons-nous:* to the ankle) checked skirt, with the binoculars over one shoulder and a kind of purse over the other. That's how I looked when I jumped out of the tarantass in a settlement just outside of Tashkent, when in the brilliant sunlight, I shall never forget it, I caught sight of your father within a hundred yards of the road: he was standing with one foot resting on a white stone, one elbow on a fence, and talking to two Cossacks. I ran across the gravel, shouting and laughing; he turned slowly, and when I suddenly stopped in front of him like a fool, he looked me all over, slit his eyes, and in a horribly unexpected voice spoke three words: "You go home." And I immediately turned, and went back to my carriage, and got in it, and saw he had put his foot in exactly the same place and had again propped his elbow, continuing his conversation with the Cossacks. And now I was driving back, in a trance, petrified, and only somewhere deep within me preparations had started for a storm of tears. But then after a couple of miles [and here a smile broke through the written line] he overtook me, in a cloud of dust, on a white horse, and we parted this time quite differently, so that I resumed my way to St. Petersburg almost as cheerfully as I had left it, only that I kept worrying about you two, wondering how you were, but no matter, you were in good health.

No – somehow it seems to me that I do remember all this, perhaps because it was subsequently often mentioned. In general our whole daily life was permeated with stories about Father, with worry about him, expectations of his return, the hidden sorrow of farewells and the wild joy of welcomings. His passion was reflected in all of us, colored in different ways, apprehended in different ways, but permanent and habitual. His home museum, in which stood rows of oak cabinets with glassed drawers, full of crucified butterflies (the rest – the plants, beetles, birds, rodents and reptiles – he gave to his colleagues to study), where it smelled as it probably smells in Paradise, and where the laboratory assistants worked at tables along the one-piece windows, was a kind of mysterious central hearth, illuminating from inside the whole of our St. Petersburg house – and only the noonday roar of the Petropavlovsk cannon could invade its quiet. Our relatives, non-entomological friends, the servants and the meekly touchy Yvonna Ivanovna talked of butterflies not as of something really existing but as of a certain attribute of my father, which existed only insofar as he existed, or as of an ailment with which everybody had long since got used to coping, so that with us entomology turned into some sort of routinary hallucination, like a harmless domestic ghost that sits down, no longer surprising anyone, every evening by the fireside. At the same time, none of our countless uncles and aunts took any interest in his science and had hardly even read his popular work, read and reread by dozens of thousands of cultured Russians. Of course Tanya and I had learned to appreciate Father from earliest childhood and he seemed even more enchanting to us than, say, that Harold about whom he told stories to us, Harold who fought with the lions in the Byzantine arena, who pursued brigands in Syria, bathed in the Jordan, took eighty fortresses by storm in Africa, "the Blue Land," saved the Icelanders from starvation – and was famed from Norway to Sicily, from Yorkshire to Novgorod. Then, when I fell under the spell of butterflies, something unfolded in my soul and I relived all my father's journeys, as if I myself had made them: in my dreams I saw the winding road, the caravan, the many-hued mountains, and envied my father madly, agonizingly, to the point of tears – hot and violent tears that would suddenly gush out of me at table as we discussed his letters from the road or even at the simple mention of a far, far place. Every year, with the approach of spring, before moving to the country, I would feel within me a pitiful fraction of what I would have felt before departing for Tibet. On the Nevski Avenue, during the last days of March, when the wooden blocks of the spacious street pavements gleamed dark blue from the damp and the sun, one might see, flying high over the carriages, along the façades of the houses, past the city hall, past the lindens in the square, past the statue of Catherine, the first yellow butterfly. In the classroom the large window was open, sparrows perched on the windowsill and teachers let lessons go by, leaving in their stead squares of blue sky, with footballs falling down out of the blueness. For some reason I always had bad marks in geography and what an expression our geography teacher would have when he used to mention my father's name, how the inquisitive eyes of my comrades turned on me at this point and how within me the blood rose and fell from suppressed rapture and from fear of expressing that rapture – and now I think of how little I know, how easy it is for me to make some idiotic blunder in describing my father's researches.

At the beginning of April, to open the season, the members of the Russian Entomological Society used to make a traditional trip to the other side of Black River, in a suburb of St. Petersburg, where in a birch grove which was still naked and wet, still showing patches of holey snow, there occurred on the trunks, its feeble transparent wings pressed flat against the papery bark, our favorite rarity, a specialty of the province. Once or twice they took me with them too. Among these elderly family men cautiously, tensely practicing sorcery in an April wood, there was an old theater critic, a gynecologist, a professor of international law and a general – for some reason I can recall especially clearly the figure of this general (X. B. Lambovski – there was something Paschal about him), his fat back bending low, with one arm placed behind it, next to the figure of my father, who had sunk on his haunches with a kind of Oriental ease – both were carefully examining in search of pupae a handful of reddish earth dug up with a trowel – and even to this day I am wondering what the coachmen waiting on the road made of all this.

Sometimes, in the country, Grandmother would sail into our school-room, Olga Ivanovna Vezhin, plump, fresh-complexioned, in mittens and lace: "*Bonjour les enfants,*" she would sing out sonorously and then, heavily accenting the prepositions, she informed us: "*Je viens de voir* DANS *le jardin,* PRÈS *du cèdre,* SUR *une rose un papillon de toute beauté: il était bleu, vert, pourpre, doré – et grand comme ça.*[42] Quickly take your net," she continued, turning to me, "and go into the garden. Perhaps you can still catch it." And she sailed out, completely oblivious to the fact that if such a fabulous insect were to come my way (it was not even worth a guess as to what banal garden visitor her imagination had so adorned), I would have died of heartbreak. Sometimes, to give me special pleasure, our French governess would choose a certain fable of Florian's for me to learn by heart, about another impossibly gaudy *petit-maître* butterfly.[43] Sometimes some aunt or other would give me a book by Fabre,[44] whose popular works, full of chitchat, inaccurate observations and downright mistakes, my father treated with scorn. I also remember this: one day, upon missing my net I went out to look for it on the veranda and met my uncle's orderly returning from somewhere with it on his shoulder, all flushed and with a kindly and shy smile on his rosy lips: "Just see what I've caught for you," he proclaimed in a satisfied voice, dumping the net on the floor; the mesh was secured near the frame by a bit of string, so that a bag was formed in which a variety of live matter swarmed and rustled – and good heavens, what rubbish there was in it: thirty-odd grasshoppers, the head of a daisy, a couple of dragonflies, ears of wheat, some sand, a cabbage butterfly crushed out of all recognition, and finally, an edible toadstool noticed on the way and added just in case. The Russian common people know and love their country's nature. How many jeers, how many conjectures and questions have I had occasion to hear when, overcoming my embar-rassment, I walked through the village with my net! "Well, that's nothing," said my father, "you should have seen the faces of the Chinese when I was collecting once on some holy mountain, or the look the progressive schoolmistress in a Volga town gave me when I explained to her what I was doing in that ravine."

How to describe the bliss of our walks with Father through the woods, the fields and the peat bogs, or the constant summer thought of him if he was away, the eternal dream of making some discovery and of meeting him with this discovery – How to describe the feeling I experienced when he showed me all the spots where in his own childhood he had caught this and that – the beam of a half-rotted little bridge where he had caught his first peacock butterfly in '71, the slope of the road down to the river where he had once fallen on his knees, weeping and praying (he had bungled his stroke, it had flown for ever!). And what fascination there was in his words, in the kind of special fluency and grace of his style when he spoke about his subject, what affectionate precision in the movements of his fingers turning the screw of a spreading board or a microscope, what a truly enchanting world was unfolded in his lessons! Yes, I know this is not the way to write – these exclamations won't take me very deep – but my pen is not yet accustomed to following the outlines of his image, and I myself abominate these accessory curlicues. Oh, don't look at me, my childhood, with such big, frightened eyes.

The sweetness of the lessons! On a warm evening he would take me to a certain small pond to watch the aspen hawk moth swing over the very water, dipping in it the tip of its body. He showed me how to prepare genital armatures to determine species which were externally indistinguishable. With a special smile he brought to my attention the black Ringlet butterflies in our park which with mysterious and elegant unexpectedness appeared only in even years. He mixed beer with treacle for me on a dreadfully cold, dreadfully rainy autumn night in order to catch at the smeared tree trunks that glistened in the light of a kerosene lamp a multitude of large, banded moths, silently diving and hurrying toward the bait. He variously warmed and cooled the golden chrysalids of my tortoiseshells so that I was able to get from them Corsican, arctic and entirely unusual forms looking as if they had been dipped in tar and had silky fuzz sticking to them. He taught me how to take apart an ant-hill and find the caterpillar of a Blue[45] which had concluded a barbaric pact with its inhabitants, and I saw how an ant, greedily tickling a hind segment of that caterpillar's clumsy, sluglike little body, forced it to excrete a drop of intoxicant juice, which it swallowed immediately. In compensation it offered its own larvae as food; it was as if cows gave us Chartreuse and we gave them our infants to eat. But the strong caterpillar of one exotic species of Blue will not stoop to this exchange, brazenly devouring the infant ants and then turning into an impenetrable chrysalis which finally, at the time of hatching, is surrounded by ants (those failures in the school of experience) awaiting the emergence of the helplessly crumpled butterfly in order to attack it; they attack – and nevertheless she does not perish: "I have never laughed so much," said my father, "as when I realized that nature had supplied her with a sticky substance which caused the feelers and feet of those zealous ants to get stuck together, so that they rolled and writhed all around her while she herself, calm and invulnerable, let her wings strengthen and dry."

He told me about the odors of butterflies – musk and vanilla; about the voices of butterflies; about the piercing sound given out by the monstrous caterpillar of a Malayan hawkmoth, an improvement on the mouselike squeak of our Death's Head moth; about the small resonant tympanum of certain tiger moths; about the cunning butterfly in the Brazilian forest which imitates the whir of a local bird. He told me about the incredible artistic wit of mimetic disguise, which was not explainable by the struggle for existence (the rough haste of evolution's unskilled forces), was too refined for the mere deceiving of accidental predators, feathered, scaled and otherwise (not very fastidious, but then not too fond of butterflies), and seemed to have been invented by some waggish artist precisely for the intelligent eyes of man (a hypothesis that may lead far an evolutionist who observes apes feeding on butterflies); he told me about these magic masks of mimicry; about the enormous moth which in a state of repose assumes the image of a snake looking at you; of a tropical geometrid colored in perfect imitation of a species of butterfly infinitely removed from it in nature's system, the illusion of the orange abdomen possessed by one being humorously reproduced in the other by the orange-colored inner margins of the secondaries; and about the curious harem of that famous African swallowtail, whose variously disguised females copy in color, shape and even flight half a dozen different species (apparently inedible), which are also the models of numerous other mimics. He told me about migrations, about the long cloud consisting of myriads of white pierids that moves through the sky, indifferent to the direction of the wind, always at the same level above the ground, rising softly and smoothly over hills and sinking again into valleys, meeting perhaps another cloud of butterflies, yellow, filtering through it without stopping and without soiling its own whiteness – and floating further, to settle on trees toward nighttime which stand until morning as if bestrewn with snow – and then taking off again to continue their journey – whither? Why? A tale not yet finished by nature or else forgotten. "Our thistle butterfly," he said, "the 'painted lady' of the English, the '*belle dame*' of the French, does not hibernate in Europe as related species do; it is born on the African plains; there, at dawn, the lucky traveler may hear the whole steppe, glistening in the first rays, crackle with an incalculable number of hatching chrysalids." From there, without delay it begins its journey north, reaching the shores of Europe in early spring, suddenly enlivening the gardens of the Crimea and the terraces of the Riviera; without lingering, but leaving individuals everywhere for summer breeding, it proceeds further north and by the end of May, by now in single specimens, it reaches Scotland, Heligoland, our parts and even the extreme north of the earth: it has been caught in Iceland! With a strange crazy flight unlike anything else the bleached, hardly recognizable butterfly, choosing a dry glade, "wheels" in and out of the Leshino firs, and by the end of the summer, on thistleheads, on asters, its lovely pink-flushed offspring is already reveling in life. "Most moving of all," added my father, "is that on the first cold days a reverse phenomenon is observed, the ebb: the butterfly hastens southward, for the winter, but of course it perishes before it reaches the warmth."

Simultaneously with the Englishman Tutt,[46] who observed the same thing in the Swiss Alps as he in the Pamirs, my father discovered the true nature of the corneal formation appearing beneath the abdomen in the impregnated females of Parnassians,[47] and explained how her mate, working with a pair of spatulate appendages, places and molds on her a chastity belt of his own manufacture, shaped differently in every species of this genus, being sometimes a little boat, sometimes a helical shell, sometimes – as in the case of the exceptionally rare dark-cinder gray *orpheus* Godunov – a replica of a tiny lyre. And as a frontispiece to my present work I think I would like to display precisely this butterfly – for I can hear him talk about it, can see the way he took the six specimens he had brought back out of their six thick triangular envelopes, the way he lowered his eyes with the field magnifier close to the abdomen of the only female – and how reverently his laboratory assistant relaxed in a damp jar the dry, glossy, tightly folded wings in order later to drive a pin smoothly through the insect's thorax, stick it in the cork groove of the spreading board, hold down flat upon it by means of broad strips of semitransparent paper its open, defenseless, gracefully expanded beauty, then slip a bit of cotton wool under its abdomen and straighten its black antennae – so that it dried that way forever. Forever? In the Berlin museum there are many of my father's captures and these are as fresh today as they were in the eighties and nineties. Butterflies from Linnaeus' collection now in London have subsisted since the eighteenth century. In the Prague museum one can see that same example of the showy Atlas moth that Catherine the Great admired. Why then do I feel so sad?

His captures, his observations, the sound of his voice in scientific words, all this, I think, I will preserve. But that is still so little. With the same relative permanence I would like to retain what it was, perhaps, that I loved most of all about him: his live masculinity, inflexibility and independence, the chill and the warmth of his personality, his power over everything that he undertook. As if playing a game, as if wishing in passing to imprint his force on everything, he would pick out here and there something from a field outside entomology and thus he left his mark upon almost all branches of natural science: there is only one plant described by him out of all those he collected, but that one is a spectacular species of birch; one bird – a most fabulous pheasant; one bat – but the biggest one in the world. And in all parts of nature our name echoes a countless number of times, for other naturalists gave his name either to a spider, or to a rhododendron, or to a mountain ridge – the latter, by the way, made him angry: "To ascertain and preserve the ancient native name of a pass," he wrote, "is always both more scientific and more noble than to saddle it with the name of a good acquaintance." [GIFT 102–13]

[Fyodor's character sketch of his father flows into a description of one of his expeditions.]

He who in his time had slaughtered countless multitudes of birds, he who had once brought the newly wed botanist Berg the *complete* vegetable covering of a motley little mountain meadow in one piece, the size of a room in area (I imagined it rolled up in a case like a Persian carpet), which he had found somewhere at some fantastic height among bare cliffs and snow – he could not forgive me a Leshino sparrow wantonly shot down with a Montecristo rifle or the young pondside aspen I had slashed with a sword. He could not stand procrastination, hesitation, the blinking eyes of a lie, could not stand hypocrisy or syrupiness – and I am sure that had he caught me out in physical cowardice he would have laid a curse on me.

I have not said everything yet; I am coming up to what is perhaps most important. In and around my father, around this clear and direct strength, there was something difficult to convey in words, a haze, a mystery, an enigmatic reserve which made itself felt sometimes more, sometimes less. It was as if this genuine, very genuine man possessed an aura of something still unknown but which was perhaps the most genuine of all. It had no direct connection either with us, or with my mother, or with the externals of life, or even with butterflies (the closest of all to him, I daresay); it was neither pensiveness nor melancholy – and I have no means of explaining the impression his face made on me when I looked through his study window from outside and saw how, having suddenly forgotten his work (I could feel inside me how he had forgotten it – as if something had fallen through or trailed off), his large wise head turned slightly away from the desk and resting on his fist, so that a wide crease was raised from his cheek to his temple, he sat for a minute without moving. It sometimes seems to me nowadays that – who knows – he might go off on his journeys not so much to seek something as to flee something, and that on returning, he would realize that it was still with him, inside him, unriddable, inexhaustible. I cannot track down a name for his secret, but I only know that that was the source of that special – neither glad nor morose, having indeed no connection with the outward appearance of human emotions – solitude to which neither my mother nor all the entomologists of the world had any admittance. And strange: perhaps the estate watchman, a crooked old man who had twice been singed by night lightning, the sole person among our rural retainers who had learned without my father's help (who had taught it to a whole regiment of Asian hunters) to catch and kill a butterfly without mangling it (which, of course, did not stop him advising me with a businesslike air not to be in a hurry to catch small butterflies, "tiddlers" as he expressed it, in spring, but to wait till summer when they would have grown up), namely he, who frankly and with no fear or surprise considered that my father knew a thing or two that nobody else knew, was in his own way right.

However that may have been, I am convinced now that our life then really was imbued with a magic unknown in other families. From conversations with my father, from daydreams in his absence, from the neighborhood of thousands of books full of drawings of animals, from the precious shimmer of the collections, from the maps, from all the heraldry of nature and the cabbalism of Latin names, life took on a kind of bewitching lightness that made me feel as if my own travels were about to begin. Thence, I borrow my wings today. Among the old, tranquil, velvet-framed family photographs in my father's study there hung a copy of the picture: Marco Polo leaving Venice. She was rosy, this Venice, and the water of her lagoon was azure, with swans twice the size of the boats, into one of which tiny violet men were descending by way of a plank, in order to board a ship which was waiting a little way off with sails furled – and I cannot tear myself away from this mysterious beauty, these ancient colors which swim before the eyes as if seeking new shapes, when I now imagine the outfitting of my father's caravan in Przhevalsk, where he used to go with post-horses from Tashkent, having dispatched in advance by slow convoy a store of supplies for three years. His Cossacks went round the neighboring villages buying horses, mules and camels; they prepared the pack boxes and pouches (what was there not in these Sartish yagtans and leather bags tried by centuries, from cognac to pulverized peas, from ingots of silver to nails for horseshoes); and after a requiem on the shore of the lake by the burial rock of the explorer Przhevalski, crowned with a bronze eagle – around which the intrepid local pheasants were wont to roost – the caravan took the road.

After that I see the caravan, before it gets drawn into the mountains, winding among hills of a paradisean green shade, depending both on their grassy raiment and on the apple-bright epidotic rock, of which they are composed. The compact, sturdy Kalmuk ponies walk in single file forming echelons: the paired packloads of equal weight are seized twice with lariats so that nothing can shift and a Cossack leads every echelon by the bridle. In front of the caravan, a Berdan rifle over his shoulder and a butterfly net at the ready, wearing spectacles and a nankin blouse, Father rides on his white trotter accompanied by a native horseman. Closing the detachment comes the geodesist Kunitsyn (this is the way I see it), a majestic old man who has spent half a lifetime in imperturable wanderings, with his instruments in cases – chronometers, surveying compasses, an artificial horizon – and when he stops to take a bearing or to note down azimuths in his journal, his horse is held by an assistant, a small anemic German, Ivan Ivanovich Viskott, formerly chemist at Gatchina, whom my father had once taught to prepare bird skins and who took part from then on in all the expeditions, until he died of gangrene in the summer of 1903 in Dyn-Kou.

Further I see the mountains: the Tyan-Shan range. In search of passes (marked on the map according to oral data but first explored by my father) the caravan ascended over steep slopes and narrow ledges, slipped down to the north, to the steppe teeming with saigas, ascended again to the south, here fording torrents, there trying to get across high water – and up, up, along almost impassable trails. How the sunlight played! The dryness of the air produced an amazing contrast between light and shadow: in the light there were such flashes, such a wealth of brilliance, that at times it became impossible to look at a rock, at a stream; and in the shadow a darkness which absorbed all detail, so that every color lived a magically multiplied life and the coats of the horses changed as they entered the cool of the poplars. [GIFT 114–17]

I can conjure up with particular clarity – in this transparent and changeable setting – my father's principal and constant occupation, the occupation for whose only sake he undertook these tremendous journeys. I see him leaning down from the saddle amid a clatter of sliding stones to sweep in with a swing of his net on the end of its long handle (a twist of the wrist causing the end of the muslin bag, full of rustling and throbbing, to flip across the ring, thus preventing escape) some royal relative of our Apollos, which had been skimming with a ranging flight over the dangerous screes; and not only he but also the other riders (the Cossack corporal Semyon Zharkoy, for example, or the Buryat Buyantuyev, or else that representative of mine whom I sent in the wake of my father throughout my boyhood) work their way fearlessly up the rocks, in pursuit of the white, richly ocellated butterfly which they catch at last; and here it is in my father's fingers, dead, its hairy yellowish incurved body resembling a willow catkin, and the glazy underside of its crisp folded wings showing the blood-red maculation at their roots. [GIFT 117–18]

In the darkling air the clear ring of shoeing resounds above the ample noise of water. It has grown quite dark. Father has climbed a rock looking for a place to suit his calcium lamp for catching moths. Thence one can see in Chinese perspective (from above), in a deep gully, the redness, transparent in the darkness, of the campfire; through the edges of its breathing flame seem to float the broad-shouldered shadows of men, endlessly changing their outlines, and a red reflection trembles, without moving from the spot, on the seething water of the river. But above, all is quiet and dark, only rarely does a bell tinkle: the horses, who have already stood to receive their portion of dry fodder, are now roaming among the granite debris. Overhead, frighteningly and entrancingly close, the stars have come out, each conspicuous, each a live orbicle, clearly revealing its globular essence. Moths begin to come to the lure of the lamp: they describe crazy circles around it, hitting the reflector with a ping; they fall, they crawl over the spread sheet into the circle of light, gray, with eyes like burning coals, vibrating, flying up and falling again – and a large, brightly illumined, unhurriedly skillful hand, with almond-shaped fingernails, rakes noctuid after noctuid into the killing jar.

Sometimes he was quite alone, without even this nearness of men sleeping in camp tents, on felt mattresses, around the camel bedded down on the campfire ashes. Taking advantage of lengthy halts in places with abundant food for the caravan animals, Father would go away for several days on reconnaissance, and in doing so, carried away by some new pierid, more than once ignored the rule of mountain hunting: never to follow a path of no return. And now I continually ask myself what did he use to think about in the solitary night: I try fervently in the darkness to divine the current of his thoughts, and I have much less success with this than with my mental visits to places which I have never seen. What did he think about? About a recent catch? About my mother, about us? About the innate strangeness of human life, a sense of which he mysteriously transmitted to me? Or perhaps I am wrong in retrospectively forcing upon him the secret which he carries now, when newly gloomy and preoccupied, concealing the pain of an unknown wound, concealing death as something shameful, he appears in my dreams, but which then he did not have – but simply was happy in that incompletely named world in which at every step he named the nameless.   [GIFT 118–19]

[By now Fyodor imagines himself as accompanying his father, as he would so much have liked to do.] Spring awaited us in the mountains of Nan-Shan. Everything foretold it: the babbling of the water in the brooks, the distant thunder of the rivers, the whistle of the creepers which lived in holes on the slippery wet hillsides, the delightful singing of the local larks, and "a mass of noises whose origins are hard to explain" (a phrase from the notes of a friend of my father's, Grigoriy Efimovich Grum-Grzhimaylo, which is fixed in my mind forever and full of the amazing music of truth because written not by an ignorant poet but by a naturalist of genius). On the southern slopes we had already met our first interesting butterfly – Potanin's subspecies of Butler's pierid – and in the valley to which we descended by way of a torrent bed we found real summer. All the slopes were studded with anemones and primulae. Przhevalski's gazelle and Strauch's pheasant tempted the hunters. And what sunrises there were! Only in China is the early mist so enchanting, causing everything to vibrate, the fantastic outlines of hovels, the dawning crags.

[GIFT 120–21]

There were the times when going up the Yellow River and its tributaries, on some splendid September morning, in the lily thickets and hollows on the banks, he and I would take Elwes' Swallowtail – a black wonder with tails in the shape of hooves.   [GIFT 122]

[By now Fyodor imagines himself as his father.]

In Tatsien-Lu shaven-headed lamas roamed about the crooked, narrow streets spreading the rumor that I was catching children in order to brew their eyes into a potion for the belly of my Kodak. There on the slopes of a snowy range, which were drowned in the rich, rosy foam of great rhododendrons (we used their branches at night for our campfires), I looked in May for the slate-gray, orange-spotted larvae of the Imperatorial Apollo and for its chrysalis, fastened by means of a silk thread to the underside of a stone. That same day, I remember, we glimpsed a white Tibetan bear and discovered a new snake: it fed on mice, and the mouse I extracted from its stomach also turned out to be an undescribed species. From the rhododendrons and from the pines draped in lacy lichen came a heady smell of resin. In my vicinity some witch doctors with the wary and crafty look of competitors were collecting for their mercenary needs Chinese rhubarb, whose root bears an extraordinary resemblance to a caterpillar, right down to its prolegs and spiracles – while I, in the meantime, found under a stone the caterpillar of an unknown moth, which represented not in a general way but with absolute concreteness a copy of that root, so that it was not quite clear which was impersonating which – or why.   [GIFT 122–23]

Having explored the uplands of Tibet I headed for Lob-Nor in order to return from there to Russia. The Tarym, overcome by the desert, exhausted, forms with its last waters an extensive reedy swamp, the present-day Kara-Koshuk-Kul, Przhevalski's Lob-Nor – and Lob-Nor at the time of the Khans, whatever Ritthofen might say. It is fringed with salt marshes but the water is salt only at the edges – for those rushes would not grow around a salt lake. One spring I was five days going round it. There in twenty-foot-high reeds I had the luck to discover a remarkable semi-aquatic moth with a rudimentary system of veins. The bunchy salt marsh was strewn with the shells of mollusks. In the evenings the harmonious, melodic sounds of swan flights reverberated through the silence; the yellow of the rushes distinctly brought out the lusterless white of the birds. In 1862, sixty Russian Old-Believers with their wives and children lived for half a year in these parts, after which they went to Turfan, and where they went thence nobody knows.

Further on comes the desert of Lob: a stony plain, tiers of clay preci-
pices, glassy salt ponds; that pale fleck in the gray air is a lone individual of
Roborovski's White,[48] carried away by the wind. In this desert are preserved traces of an ancient road along which Marco Polo passed six centuries before I did: its markers are piles of stones.   [GIFT 124]

[The vision ends.]

All this lingered bewitchingly, full of color and air, with lively movement in
the foreground and a convincing backdrop; then, like smoke from a breeze,
it shifted and dispersed – and Fyodor saw again the dead and impossible
tulips of his wallpaper, the crumbling mound of cigarette butts in the ashtray, and the lamp's reflection in the black windowpane. . . .

He remembered with incredible vividness, as if he had preserved that
sunny day in a velvet case, his father's last return, in July 1912. Elizaveta
Pavlovna had already gone the six miles to the station to meet her husband:
she always met him alone and it always happened that no one knew with
any clearness which side they would return on, to the right or left of the
house, since there were two roads, one longer and smoother – along the
highway and through the village; the other shorter and bumpier – through
Peshchanka. Fyodor put on his riding breeches just in case and ordered his
horse saddled, but nonetheless he could not make up his mind to ride out
and meet his father because he was afraid of missing him. He tried vainly
to come to terms with inflated, exaggerated time. A rare butterfly taken a
day or two before among the blueberries of a peat bog had not yet dried on
the spreading board: he kept touching its abdomen with the end of a pin –
alas it was still soft, and this meant it was impossible to take off the paper
strips completely covering the wings which he was so keen to show his father in all their beauty. He loafed about the manor, feeling the weight and
pain of his agitation, and envying the way the others got through these big,
empty minutes.   [GIFT 125–26]

[Fyodor sums up his father's preparation for his fateful last expedition.]

The following year, busy with scientific work, he did not go anywhere, but
by the spring of 1914 he had already begun to prepare for a new expedition

to Tibet together with the ornithologist Petrov and the English botanist Ross. War with Germany suddenly canceled all this.

He looked upon the war as a tiresome obstacle which became more and more tiresome as time went on. His kinsfolk were for some reason certain that Konstantin Kirillovich would volunteer and set off right away at the head of a detachment: they considered him an eccentric, but a manly eccentric. Actually, Konstantin Kirillovich, who was now over fifty but had retained untapped reserves of health, agility, freshness and strength–and perhaps was even more ready than before to overcome mountains, Tanguts, bad weather and a thousand other dangers undreamt of by stay-at-homes– now not only stayed at home but tried not to notice the war, and if he ever spoke about it, he did so only with angry contempt.   [GIFT 127]

Elizaveta Pavlovna was drawn into Red Cross work, which had people comment that her energy "was making up for her husband's idleness," he being "more concerned with Asian bugs than with the glory of Russian arms" as was actually pointed out, by the way, in one jaunty newspaper.

[GIFT 128]

In the spring of 1915, instead of getting ready to move from St Petersburg to Leshino, which always seemed as natural and unshakable as the succession of months in the calendar, we went for the summer to our Crimean estate–on the coast between Yalta and Alupka. On the sloping lawns of the heavenly-green garden, his face distorted with anguish, his hands trembling with happiness, Fyodor boxed southern butterflies; but the genuine Crimean rarities were to be found not here among the myrtles, wax shrubs, and magnolias but much higher, in the mountains, among the rocks of Ai-Petri and on the grassy plateau of the Yayla; more than once that summer his father accompanied him up a trail through the pinewoods in order to show him, with a smile of condescension for this European trifle, the Satyrid recently described by Kuznetsov, which was flitting from stone to stone in the very place where some vulgar daredevil had carved his name in the sheer rock. These walks were Konstantin Kirillovich's only distraction. It was not that he was gloomy or irritable (these limited epithets did not tally with his spiritual style) but that, putting it simply, he was fretting – and Elizaveta Pavlovna and the children were perfectly aware of what it was he wanted. Suddenly in August he went away for a short time; where he went no one except those closest to him knew; he covered up his journey so thoroughly as to excite the envy of any traveling terrorist; it was funny and frightening to imagine how Russian public opinion would have wrung its little hands had it learned that at the height of the war Godunov-Cherdyntsev had traveled to Geneva to meet a fat, bald, extraordinarily jovial German professor (a third conspirator was also present, an old Englishman wearing thin-rimmed spectacles and a roomy gray suit), that they had come together there in a small room in a modest hotel for a scientific consultation, and that having discussed what was necessary (the subject was a work of many volumes, stubbornly continuing publication in Stuttgart with longstanding cooperation of foreign specialists on separate groups of butterflies) they peaceably parted – each in his own direction. But this trip did not cheer him up; on the contrary, the constant dream weighing on him even increased its secret pressure. In the autumn they returned to St. Petersburg; he worked strenuously on the fifth volume of *Butterflies and Moths of the Russian Empire,* went out rarely and – fuming more at his opponent's blunders than at his own – played chess with the recently widowed botanist Berg. He would look through the daily papers with an ironical smile; he would take Tanya on his knees, then lapse into pensiveness, and his hand on Tanya's round shoulder would grow pensive too.   [GIFT 128–30]

[The stalled expedition restarts.]

And then something suddenly changed in Konstantin Kirillovich's mood: his eyes came to life and softened, one again heard that musical humming which he used to emit on the move when he was particularly pleased about something, he went off somewhere, certain boxes arrived and departed and in the house, around all this mysterious gaiety of the master's, one could sense a growing feeling of indefinite, expectant perplexity – and once when Fyodor happened to be passing through the gilt reception hall, bathed in spring sunshine, he suddenly noticed the brass handle of the white door leading into Father's study jiggle but not turn, as if someone was limply fingering it without opening the door; but then it quietly opened and Mother came out with a vague meek smile on her tear-stained face, making an odd gesture of helplessness as she went past Fyodor. He knocked on his father's door and entered the study. "What do you want?" asked Konstantin Kirillovich without looking up or stopping writing. "Take me with you," said Fyodor.

The fact that at the most alarming time, when Russia's borders were crumbling and her inner flesh was being eaten away, Konstantin Kirillovich suddenly planned to abandon his family for two years for the sake of a scientific expedition into a remote country, struck most people as a wild caprice, a monstrous frivolity. There was even talk that the government "would not permit purchase of provision," that "the madman" would get neither traveling companions nor pack animals. But no further away than in Turkestan the peculiar smell of the epoch was hardly perceptible; practically the only reminder of it was a reception organized by some district administrators to which the guests brought gifts to aid the war (a little later a rebellion broke out among the Kirghiz and the Cossacks in connection with the summons to do war work). Just before his departure in June 1916, Godunov-Cherdyntsev came from town to Leshino to bid his family farewell. Until the very last minute Fyodor dreamed that his father would take him with him – once he had said he would do so as soon as his son was fifteen – "At any other time I would take you," he said now, as if forgetting that for him time was always *another* one.

In itself this last farewell was in no way different from preceding ones.

[GIFT 131]

[After his father's final departure.]

Fyodor walked across the park, opened the tuneful wicket gate and cut across the road where the thick tires had just imprinted their tracks. A familiar black-and-white beauty rose smoothly off the ground and described a wide circle, also taking part in the seeing-off. He turned into the trees and came by way of a shady path, where golden flies hung aquiver in transversal sunbeams, to his favorite clearing, boggy, blooming, moistly glistening in the hot sun. The divine meaning of this wood meadow was expressed in its butterflies. Everyone might have found something here. The holidaymaker might have rested on a stump. The artist might have screwed up his eyes. But its truth would have been probed somewhat deeper by knowledge-amplified love: by its "wide-open orbs"[49] – to paraphrase Pushkin.

Freshly emerged and because of their fresh, almost orange coloration, merry-looking Selene Fritillaries floated with a kind of enchanting demureness on outstretched wings, flashing ever so rarely, like the fins on a goldfish. An already rather bedraggled but still powerful Swallowtail, minus one spur and flapping its panoply, descended on a camomile, took off as if backing from it, and the flower it left straightened up and started to sway. A few Black-veined Whites flew about lazily; one or two were spattered with bloodlike pupal discharge (spots of which on the white walls of cities predicted to our ancestors the fall of Troy, plagues, earthquakes). The first chocolate *Aphantopus* Ringlets were already fluttering, with a bouncy, unsteady motion over the grass, and pale micros rose from it, immediately falling again. A blue-and-red Burnet moth with blue antennae, resembling a beetle in fancy dress, was settled on a scabiosa in company with a midge. Hastily abandoning the meadow to alight on an alder leaf, a female cabbage butterfly by means of an odd upturn of her abdomen and the flat spread of her wings (somewhat reminiscent of flattened-back ears), informed her badly rubbed pursuer that she was already impregnated. Two violet-tinged Coppers (*their* females were not yet out) tangled in lightning-swift flight in midair, zoomed, spinning one around the other, scrapping furiously, ascending ever higher and higher – and suddenly shot apart, returning to the flowers. An Amandus Blue in passing annoyed a bee. A dusky Freya Fritillary flicked by among the Selenas. A small hummingbird moth with a bumblebee's body and glasslike wings, beating invisibly, tried from the air a flower with its long proboscis, darted to another and then to a third. All this fascinating life, by whose present blend one could infallibly tell both the age of the summer (with an accuracy almost to within one day), the geographical location of the area, and the vegetal composition of the clearing – all this that was living, genuine and eternally dear to him, Fyodor perceived in a flash, with one penetrating and experienced glance. Suddenly he placed a fist against the trunk of a birch tree and leaning on it, burst into tears. [GIFT 132–33]

[He ponders the mystery of his father's failure to return from this last expedition.]

Did they shoot him in the ladies' room of some godforsaken station (broken looking glass, tattered plush), or did they lead him out into some kitchen garden one dark night and wait for the moon to peep out? How did he wait with them in the dark? With a smile of disdain? And if a whitish moth had hovered among the shadowy burdocks he would, even at that moment, I *know*, have followed it with that same glance of encouragement with which, on occasion, after evening tea, smoking his pipe in our Leshino garden, he used to greet the pink hawks sampling our lilacs. [GIFT 137]

[Two years after abandoning his biography of his father, and just after having published a biography of writer Nikolay Chernyshevsky, Fyodor relaxes in the summer in Berlin's Grunewald park.]

Farther on it became very nice: the pines had come into their own, and between their pinkish, scaly trunks the feathery foliage of low rowans and the vigorous greenery of oaks broke the stripiness of the pinewood sun into an animated dapple. In the density of an oak, when you looked from below, the overlapping of shaded and illumined leaves, dark green and bright emerald, seemed to be a jigsaw fitting together of their wavy edges, and on these leaves, now letting the sun caress its yellow-brown silk and now tightly closing its wings, there settled an Angle Wing butterfly with a white bracket on its dark mottled underside; suddenly taking off it alighted on my bare chest, attracted by human sweat. And still higher above my upturned face, the summits and trunks of the pines participated in a complex exchange of shadows, and their leafage reminded me of algae swaying in transparent water. [GIFT 332]

[He strips off to sunbathe in the Grunewald.]

To move around naked was astonishing bliss – the freedom around his loins especially pleased him. He walked between the bushes, listening to the vibration of insects and the rustling of the birds. A wren crept like a mouse through the foliage of a small oak; a sand wasp flew by low down, carrying a benumbed caterpillar. The squirrel he had just seen climbed up the bark of a tree with a spasmodic, scrabbly sound. Somewhere in the vicinity sounded girlish voices, and he stopped in a pattern of shadow, which stayed motionless along his arm but palpitated rhythmically on his left side, between the ribs. A golden, stumpy little butterfly, equipped with two black commas, alighted on an oak leaf, half opening its slanting wings, and suddenly shot away like a golden fly. And as often happened on these woodland days, especially when he glimpsed familiar butterflies, Fyodor imagined his father's isolation in other forests – gigantic, infinitely distant, in comparison with which this one was but brushwood, a tree stump, rubbish. And yet he experienced something akin to that Asiatic freedom spreading wide on the maps, to the spirit of his father's peregrinations – and here it was most difficult of all to believe that despite the freedom, despite the greenery and the happy, sun-shot dark shade, his father was nonetheless dead. [GIFT 334–35]

[On the eve of the last day of the novel's action, Fyodor dreams that he returns to the apartment where he had tried to write the biography of his father. He meets his old landlady.]

"Go to your room and wait there. You must be prepared for anything," she added with a vibrant note in her voice and pushed him into the room which he had thought he would never in his life enter again. He grasped her by the elbow, losing control over himself, but she shook him off. "Somebody has come to see you," said Stoboy, "he's resting . . . Wait a couple of minutes." The door banged shut. The room was exactly as if he had been still living in it: the same swans and lilies on the wallpaper, the same painted ceiling wonderfully ornamented with Tibetan butterflies (there, for example, was *Thecla bieti*). Expectancy, awe, the frost of happiness, the surge of sobs merged into a single blinding agitation as he stood in the middle of the room incapable of movement, listening and looking at the door. He knew *who* would enter in a moment, and was amazed now that he had doubted this return: doubt now seemed to him to be the obtuse obstinacy of one half-witted, the distrust of a barbarian, the self-satisfaction of an ignoramus. His heart was bursting like that of a man before execution, but at the same time this execution was such a joy that life faded before it, and he was unable to understand the disgust he had been wont to experience when, in hastily constructed dreams, he had evoked what was now taking place in real life. Suddenly, the door shuddered (another, remote one had opened somewhere beyond it) and he heard a familiar tread, an indoor Morocco-padded step. Noiselessly but with terrible force the door flew open, and on the threshold stood his father.   [GIFT 353–54]

Laughter in the Dark

Excerpt from novel in Russian (*Kamera obskura*). Written early 1931. Published in *Sovremennye zapiski* 49–52 (May 1932–May 1933). Translated, revised, and retitled by VN, fall 1937. He added the meadow browns here only in this revision.

[Albinus and his mistress Margot take a holiday from Germany down through France, driven by Margot's lover Rex.]

Roads bordered with apple trees, and then roads with plum trees, were lapped up by the front tires – endlessly. The weather was fine, and toward night the steel cells of the radiator were crammed with dead bees, and dragon-flies, and meadow-browns. Rex drove wonderfully, reclining lazily on the very low seat and manipulating the steering wheel with a tender and almost dreamy touch. In the back-window hung a plush monkey, gazing toward the North from which they were speeding away.   [LD 201]

Answer to publisher's questionnaire, early 1938

Unpublished.

18. *Hobbies, collections, etc.*

The study and collection of butterflies and moths.   [TS, VNA]

The Real Life of Sebastian Knight

Excerpts from novel. Written late 1938–early 1939. Published in 1941.

[Novelist Sebastian Knight's half-brother describes Sebastian's mother.]

Virginia reappeared in 1908. She was an inveterate traveller, always on the move and alike at home in any small pension or expensive hotel, home only meaning to her the comfort of constant change; from her, Sebastian inherited that strange, almost romantic, passion for sleeping-cars and Great European Express Trains, "the soft crackle of polished panels in the blue-shaded night, the long sad sigh of brakes at dimly surmised stations, the upward slide of an embossed leather blind disclosing a platform, a man wheeling luggage, the milky globe of a lamp with a pale moth whirling around it; the clank of an invisible hammer testing wheels; the gliding move into darkness; the passing glimpse of a lone woman touching silver-bright things in her travelling-case on the blue plush of a lighted compartment." [RLSK 7–8]

[After Sebastian's death, his brother sorts through his papers.]

After a while I went on with my business, examining and roughly classifying the contents of the drawers. There were many letters. These I set aside to be gone through later. Newspaper cuttings in a gaudy book, an impossible butterfly on its cover. No, none of them were reviews of his own books: Sebastian was much too vain to collect them; nor would his sense of humour allow him to paste them in patiently when they did come his way. Still, as I say, there was an album with cuttings, all of them referring (as I found out later when perusing them at leisure) to incongruous or dream-absurd incidents which had occurred in the most trivial places and conditions. Mixed metaphors too, I perceived, met with his approval, as he probably considered them to belong to the same faintly nightmare category. [RLSK 37]

Sebastian Knight's college years were not particularly happy. To be sure he enjoyed many of the things he found at Cambridge – he was in fact quite overcome at first to see and smell and feel the country for which he had al-

ways longed. A real hansom-cab took him from the station to Trinity College: the vehicle, it seemed, had been waiting there especially for him, desperately holding out against extinction till that moment, and then gladly
dying out to join side whiskers and the Large Copper.[50]   [RLSK 41]

[Sebastian Knight's secretary-agent, Mr. Goodman, writes a hack biography of the writer.]
For Mr. Goodman, young Sebastian Knight "freshly emerged from the
carved chrysalid of Cambridge" is a youth of acute sensibility in a cruel
cold world.   [RLSK 54]

[Sebastian Knight's novel Success *traces the way two separate lines of fate, a man's and a woman's,
are made to converge.]*
We learn a number of curious things. The two lines which have finally ta-
pered to the point of meeting are really not the straight lines of a triangle
which diverge steadily towards an unknown base, but wavy lines, now
running wide apart, now almost touching. In other words there have been
at least two occasions in these two peoples' lives when unknowingly to one
another they all but met. In each case fate seemed to have prepared such a
meeting with the utmost care; touching up now this possibility now that
one; screening exits and repainting signposts; narrowing in its creeping
grasp the bag of the net where the butterflies were flapping; timing the least
detail and leaving nothing to chance. The disclosure of these secret preparations is a fascinating one and the author seems argus-eyed as he takes into
account all the colours of place and circumstance. But, every time, a minute
mistake (the shadow of a flaw, the stopped hole of an unwatched possibility, a caprice of free will) spoils the necessitarian's pleasure and the two
lives are diverging again with increased rapidity.   [RLSK 95]

[His brother imagines the end of Sebastian's first love, at the end of a Russian summer.]
"Must you go?" asks his voice.
    A last change: a V-shaped flight of migrating cranes; their tender moan
melting in a turquoise-blue sky high above a tawny birch-grove. Sebastian,
still not alone, is seated on the white-and-cinder-grey trunk of a felled tree.
His bicycle rests, its spokes a-glitter among the bracken. A Camberwell

Beauty skims past and settles on the kerf, fanning its velvety wings. Back to town to-morrow, school beginning on Monday.

"Is this the end? Why do you say that we shall not see each other this winter?" he asks for the second or third time. No answer.   [RLSK 137]

[V. describes Sebastian's last novel.]

A man is dying, and he is the hero of the tale; but whereas the lives of other people in the book seem perfectly realistic (or at least realistic in a Knightian sense), the reader is kept ignorant as to who the dying man is, and where his deathbed stands or floats, or whether it is a bed at all. The man is the book; the book itself is heaving and dying, and drawing up a ghostly knee. One thought-image, then another breaks upon the shore of consciousness, and we follow the thing or the being that has been evoked: stray remnants of a wrecked life; sluggish fancies which crawl and then unfurl eyed wings. They are, these lives, but commentaries to the main subject.   [RLSK 173]

[In a disturbing dream, V. sees himself and his mother waiting for Sebastian.]

Our wait was uneasy, laden with obscure forebodings, and I felt that they knew more than I, but I dreaded to inquire why my mother worried so much about a muddy bicycle which refused to be crammed into the wardrobe: its doors kept opening. There was the picture of a steamer on the wall, and the waves on the picture moved like a procession of caterpillars, and the steamer rocked and this annoyed me – until I remembered that the hanging of such a picture was an old and commonplace custom, when awaiting a traveller's return. He might arrive at any moment, and the wooden floor near the door had been sprinkled with sand, so that he might not slip.   [RLSK 185–86]

Father's Butterflies

Second Addendum to *The Gift*

A Note on the Translation of "Father's Butterflies" *by Dmitri Nabokov*

This unpublished fragment points to only one of the ways Nabokov had considered of continuing *Dar* (*The Gift*). Another was a different, smaller "satellite" (as my father called it), "*Krug*," which he and I translated and published as a short story under the title "Triangle in a Circle." Yet another path, as Brian Boyd has also suggested, would have been to enlarge on *Dar*'s Pushkinian conclusion and use VN's completion of Pushkin's *Rusalka* (*The Mermaid*) as a transition to a sequel, in which Zina Mertz would die and Fyodor Godunov-Cherdyntsev would, as a consequence, withdraw into himself. But by that time Nabokov was turning his thoughts to *The Enchanter*, *The Real Life of Sebastian Knight*, and the never-finished *Solus Rex*. Hitler's rumble was approaching Paris, and one of his bombs would even hit our apartment house on rue Boileau. It was time to head for St. Nazaire and embark on the *Champlain* for newer shores. We were as lucky with the ship as with the building: on its next sailing, for which we had originally been booked, it was sunk with all aboard. *Dar* would remain as it was, with its existing complement of poems and butterflies, and, when finally published in book form in 1952, with the reinstated chapter on Chernyshevski that timid editors had dropped from the initial version in a noted émigré periodical, *Sovremennye zapiski*. In the meantime, the "completion" of Pushkin's *Rusalka* had already swum separately into print, in *Novy zhurnal*, X, 1942.

   The present fragment has been conserved at the Library of Congress since the 1950s, and consists of fifty-two manuscript pages. Five initial sheets were typed by Véra Nabokov many years ago on our old Russian-language Adler, through whose ribbons many Nabokov works had passed. The remaining, handwritten material is not altogether legible. In many places the text proved impervious even to the most expert eyes. I am particularly grateful to Boyd and to Dr. Jane Grayson for their gallant deciphering efforts. The problem was eventually resolved by Prof. Alexander Dolinin, who analyzed the illegible portions, with the help of the Library's sophisticated equipment, in a way that allowed one to peek under the refractory palimpsest's edges, and to identify with considerable confidence what was on the layers beneath.

A typescript of extremely high quality finally arrived from Dolinin. This marvel inspired me to tug a remaining weed or two from the densest thickets. Again I received help from Boyd, who culled needed lepidopterological references from Dieter E. Zimmer's ingenious synopticon of popular and taxonomic-Latin butterfly names; from the ever-watchful Serena Vitale; and from Peter Lubin, who crossed the Atlantic to engage in amicable skirmishes over longish sentences and convoluted locutions. Very few puzzles remain.

Story (additional chapter for novel) in Russian ("Vtoroe prilozhenie k *Daru*").
Written early 1939? Unpublished. Translated by DN.

THE NOTORIOUS *Schmetterlingsbücher*, those German entomological tomes that accompanied me through my childhood, gave pride of place to that colorful Third Estate of the butterfly realm, the popular, quintessentially Central European *Tierchen* ("little animals"). Intended as much for the run-of-the-mill amateur as for the impassioned neophyte (for whom the supreme joy is the capture of a "Death's Head" moth), these sturdy atlases with their crude and glossy illustration plates, together with the utterly crass pocket classifiers, representing a stagnant mix of preconception and obsolescence, shunned the extraordinary – in the same way as one could find in our school anthologies Tyutchev's "Storm" (minus the final stanza, it is true), but naturally not the same poet's *"mglisto-lileynoe"* ("duskily-lily").[51]

Everything indigenous to the east of Hungary, north of Jutland, and south of the Pyrenees was ignored by the small atlases (understandably so, inasmuch as their avowed purpose was to deal only with German fauna), while the large ones, i.e., those that were supposed to give an overview of all of Europe from Iceland to Baku, from New "Zemblya" to Gibraltar, if they did mention it, did so not only haphazardly, incompletely, and inaccurately, and in the dark to boot, i.e., minus accompanying illustrations (or else, in the relatively superior Hofmann, the depiction of a diminutive rarity bore as much resemblance to the original as an oleograph of General Skobelev[52] did to the general himself).

Things would not have been so bad if the reticence and laconicism had been the result of ignorance or justified by the impossibility of keeping up with each year's discoveries through annual revisions of a voluminous work. But no – the compilers simply found it unnecessary to burden collectors who devoted their summer leisure to the joys of natural science with detailed classifications of species and varieties known to specialists, but legendarily local, or else present only on the fringes of the readily accessible areas of Europe, and therefore hardly likely to catch the eyeglasses of a schoolboy; the calculation is awful in itself, based as it is on the popularizer's principle of simultaneously goading and bridling human curiosity, regulating its satisfaction by the norms of a median level or the demands of a restrictive system, and, in practice, an erroneous one at that – for in reality those summering collectors, as they matured and developed a taste for it, made it to some pretty distant places: this one to Lapland, that one to Sicily, i.e., to areas where the atlas they had brought along lost its scientific weight, and gradually turned into a simple burden at the bottom of the suitcase. Meanwhile, from a trusting distance came pathetic orders for a type of edition produced almost exclusively by the Germans; these *Schmetterlingsbücher* were sometimes even translated and, as also happened with German encyclopedias, the tentative attempts at adaptation proved ineffectual before the triumphal skeleton of the text.

Sometimes, also, a note on an exceptional butterfly would be set in brevier – and it was precisely the small print that had always been my passion, wherever I found it, even in chemistry or history textbooks, bored as I was by anything meant to be accessible to all, which of course I failed to assimilate for the very reason that what I selected for my reveries, often quite unconnected with the subject, were the sacrosanct thickets of brevier, whence, consequently, I also emerged with a feverish evening chill and a firebird's flea in my game-bag. But, just as the young son of a genius may instinctively make sense of certain professional matters beyond the ken of his father's colleagues, I would delve into the small print of a *Schmetterlingsbuch* not only to inflame my own passion but also with a sense of superiority and of chagrin. How I fumed at some *"bis jetzt im Wallis beobachtet,"** devoid of an illustration of that tender-violet butterfly, copiously represented, of course, in my father's collection, but confiscated from me, so to speak, by the compiler, as if the window through which it could have smiled at me were shuttered – and how many things I wanted to learn about it, beginning with the circumstances of its discovery and ending with its table manners.

Yet what irked me even more (and here I reveal the crucial theme of these notes, i.e., the impossibility in former times of visualizing the fauna of Russia – of European Russia at least – by consulting all these *Gross-Schmetterlinge Europas*) was the patently erroneous conception of the butterfly itself resulting from the circumscription of its habits within the geographical space in the German compiler's focus. Nor, say, the fact that some frankly primitive Lampert – or that other one, I forget his name, who was so poetically and ridiculously translated by Kholodkovski – but illustrated reference works (that no foreign entomological library could do without) comparatively rich in quantity but shoddy in quality, such as Hofmann's or Berge's famous atlases, unabashedly riveted to mountains, even to geewhiz-mountains, species of Lepidoptera (belonging to the *Parnassius* or *Plusia* genus), that occurred right in the meadows of my Russian plain; but inasmuch as the putative user, your average collector, within the limits of his putative peregrinations, might encounter those butterflies predominantly in the mountains, there was no need to remind him, for instance, that an Apollo in the environs of Moscow had no need for Alpine air.

The same complaints most emphatically apply to the less numerous and less familiar works that covered "Europe" for an English or French audience; but in both those countries the compilational flaws, even more vulgar

---

*Heretofore observed only in the [Swiss Canton of] Valais.

than in the German (although resulting less from preconceptions than from lack of information), were more than compensated for by the elegance and thoroughness of specialized studies – qualities not common in analogous scientific works by Germans, "masterful collectors, but wretched classifiers," as my father once put it. Incidentally, it should be noted that various *British Butterflies and Moths*, intended to give the insular collector a notion of his native (admittedly very limited) fauna, are also substantially more complete and detailed than compilations devoted solely to German or French butterflies. Atlases of this kind for Russian butterflies, i.e., works more or less consistent with the degree to which lepidopterology had evolved by the end of the nineteenth century, were not published at all; and since, given the above considerations and conditions, the thickest *Schmetterlingsbücher* excluded Russia, she remained an inconspicuous terra incognita, a hopeless void, a situation which, incidentally, had dire effects on the attempts of some monographers to research the real links between Palearctic forms.

But then, we do exaggerate. Three – at least three – specific Russian localities were invariably cited in the *Schmetterlingsbücher*: Petersburg, Kazan, Sarepta, most often the last. We might conclude that, on one hand, all three sites were, entomologically speaking, extraordinarily pampered; and, on the other, that such a definite, if succinct, indication as "Sarepta, period" excluded the probability of finding a given species in a multitude of other locations. But it can all be explained much more charmingly, namely by the fact that the indicated habitats were natural observation centers for the first German entomologists who studied our country and presented the results in journals of the day or in long-outdated surveys. Half a century, perhaps, or more, had elapsed since those labels were inscribed; over those years specialists and simple collectors (not to mention that vile breed, butterfly merchants who, in the preradiogramophone days of the past when lepidopterology was a fashion, literally stamped out certain local rarities) had had ample time to convince themselves that a Petersburg or Kazan orphan was also found both in Ryazan and the Dnieper. Yet the old labels were lovingly transferred by the compilers into their editions. . . . And this applied not only to butterflies: similarly, a notorious atlas of beetles, analogous to the Hofmann, gives the reader the interesting impression that an extraordinary number of rare beetles reside prevalently in Volhynia. From which we deduce that very often the insect's place of origin is simply the insectologist's place of residence.

During my adolescence, the butterfly enthusiast ("*le curieux,*" as the *honnêtes gens* used to put it in judicious France, "*the aurelian,*" as the poets said in grove-rich England, the "fly doctor," as they wisecracked in advanced Russian circles) who wished to acquire from books a general notion of the fauna of Europe, including Russia, was compelled to scrabble for his crumbs of information in entomological journals in six languages and in multivolume, hard-to-find editions such as the Oberthür books or those of Grand Duke Nikolai Mikhailovich. The absence or utter inadequacy of "references" in the atlases *ad usum Delphini,* the tedious perusal of the index of names enclosed with an annual volume of a monthly journal, the sheer number of these journals and volumes (in my father's library there were more than a thousand of the latter alone, representing a good hundred journals) – all this had to be overcome in order to hunt down the necessary reference, if it existed at all. Nonetheless, even in my exceptionally propitious situation things were not easy: Russia, particularly in the north, dwelt in a mist, while the local lists, scattered through the journals, totally haphazard, scanty, and cruelly inaccurate in nomenclature, only maddened me when at last I ferreted them out. My father was the preeminent entomologist of his time, and very well off to boot, but the ordinary amateur, unable to dispatch his scouts throughout Russia, and denied the opportunity – or not knowing how – to gain access to specialized collections and libraries (and an accidental boon, the hasty inspection of collections at a lepidopterological society or in the cellar of some museum, does not satisfy the true enthusiast, who needs to have the boon always at hand), had no choice but to hope for a miracle. And that miracle dawned in 1912 with the appearance of my father's four-volume work *The Butterflies and Moths of the Russian Empire.*

Although in a hall adjoining the library dark-red cabinets contained my father's supremely rich collections, consisting of specimens complete with thoroughly accurate names, dates, and places of capture, I personally belonged to the category of *curieux* who, in order to acquaint themselves properly with a butterfly and to visualize it, require three things; its artistic depiction, a compendium of all that has been written about it, and its insertion within the general system of classification. With no words and no art, without a penetrating and synthesizing process of thought, for me a butterfly would remain incomplete. Only one thing could wholly replace these three demands: if I had caught it myself, if the expression of the given specimen's wings corresponded to the individual particulars of a familiar habitat (with its smells, hues, and sounds) where I would have lived through all that impassioned, insane joy of the hunt, when as I climb the rock, my face contorted, gasping, shouting voluptuously senseless words, I do not notice thorn or precipice, and see neither the viper under my feet nor the shepherd, yonder, observing with the irritation of ignorance the spasms of the madman with his green net as he approaches his heretofore undescribed prey. In other words, it was impossible to reconcile the creative contact between me and the countless rarities collected by others and not defined in the journals, or hopelessly buried in them. And, even though, through the glass top and bottom of the ultra-sleek sliding cases of my father's collection (lowering my gaze for hours down endless rows of thickset, small Hesperidae [skippers], in various hues of black with specks from hydrochloric acid and checkered fringes, and turning the case upside down to examine pearlescent cabalistic markings – little kegs, hourglasses, trapezes, on the rowan-tinged or sulphury-grayish undersides of the hind wings), aided by the inscriptions on the labels, I could make a meticulous study of the local mutability of forms, it was only when I found those species and races assembled, researched, and especially, illustrated in the just-published *Butterflies and Moths of the Russian Empire* that a fascinating, lifelike portrait would reveal to me the mystery of the prepared lepidopteron: henceforth it was mine.

I knew what labors, what tender care, and what diligence had been required of the miniaturist painters working under the supervision of my father (who himself also participated in this task: for instance, both the *Triphysa zemphyra* Godun. and the *phryne* Pall.,[53] on plate 34 of Volume I are the work of his own hand), for what I saw as an initation into the mystery.

I knew that, first, a photographic transparency was made of the butterfly; that this perfect outline awaited the press and caress of color from supremely refined brushes; that the butterfly itself, in greatly enlarged form, was projected like a sunrise before the artist, who, separated by a magic lens from his own enormous pink fingers, would color the pattern, photographed in actual size, but enlarged by the lens to the size of the projected model. I no longer remember the details of the method (I have always been ridiculously devoid of a technical bent). . . . It may turn out that I have missed the very essence that would have transformed the prismatically radiant muddle of light, lens, and color into a meaningful image. . . . Be that as it may, through the conjunction of three factors – tracing under the magnifying glass, the special solution of the pigments found thanks to experiments on the chromatism of the scales, and finally, the diabolical spark of the individual artist (at various times my father had working for him such masters as Mastakov, Frenkel, Innokentiy Petrov, Rukayishnikov, and others) – truly bewitching beauty was achieved. Today, after an interval of many years, as I examine anew those magnificent, velvety plates, I not only relish with greater maturity of perception their perfection, unattained by anyone else from Hübner to Culot, the silky, flower-dusty, vividly hazy delicacy of those colors (that last epithet contains no contradiction for one who has feasted on the pinkishness of a freshly emerged sphingid, or an auroral cloudlet, or the rainbow at the opening of the second chapter), but, in addition, I relive in my temples, oppressive and intense to the point of making them buzz, that swarthy winter morning with the lamp's reflection on the lacquered wood of the screen adorned with Chinese birds, when I was in bed recovering from one of the childhood illnesses across whose deserts I kept pursuing my father's caravan, and my mother brought me, with a special play of her features – as if to say, oh, I'm holding something not especially interesting – as she slyly, lovingly replied to the moans of my yearning, to the frenzied groping of my outstretched hands, sharing beforehand all the quiver, all the goose-pimpled nakedness of my soul, the joy that would have bounced me out of my bed had she waited another second, a magnificently solid, boxed, freshly printed, first volume of *Butterflies and Moths of the Russian Empire*.

The preciousness of that dark-blue book, furiously, carefully withdrawn from its case, consisted for me in the revelation of beauty and the poetry of perception that it presaged, for I was at last on the verge of possessing what I could get neither from Spuler or Rebel, who had haphazardly retouched Hofmann, nor even from the very first (still bearable) issues of Seitz's *Palearctica*. The lepidopterological fauna of my vast homeland was being offered to me in toto, with classic finality. Even ordinary European butterflies, some Red Admirable or Mourning Cloak, gained a special charm when their portraits were painted from Russian specimens. Everything was transformed by the new geographical situation – Asia brought with it amazing changes to the modest contents of the "European" atlases. New interrelations, the surprises of Siberian fauna, the uncanny relatives to Spanish, American, and Indo-Chinese forms, enigmatically gazed at me from the glossy plates. The illustrations, of unprecedented generosity, gave both the upper- and undersides, not only of both sexes of the type, but also of its local deviations; meticulous reproductions of the initial stages, certain details of structure, and, last but not least, delightful instant snapshots interspersed in the text (how I remember the Eversmann's Apollo napping on a flower!) completed the picture. Moreover, these Russian marvels now took their place securely in the system, the family, and I found it laughable to recall all my hunting for them in the remote thickets of journals, where they had been yanked out of their natural environment, where the "first description" was often given without benefit of an illustration. And even if a search uncovered it in some other work, the description would turn out to be hopelessly clumsy, or would economically include only the two right wings and no body, a practice reminiscent of a child's cruelty or spiders' feasts, the barbarous incompetence of Japanese preparers, who revoltingly averted their gaze and failed to see the butterfly behind its carnival mask or saw only the severed half.

There, there it is, this picture gallery of the genius of Russian nature, the splendid blue cast of the black "Cavalier," with a tiger in the background to lend a tropical flavor to the Far Eastern fauna; the orange wingtips, almost in keeping with fashion, of the African pierids, the neat and graceful [Chazara briseis] *pirata*, the beauty of the spring steppes; the fiery silk of Romanoff's [Colias caucasica] *olga*, so fleet-winged that no *dzhigit* (crack

Caucasian horseman) could keep up with it; the dusky mosaic of the *Brenthis* [Lesser Fritillaries] from the Gulf of Khaipudirsk; the celestially innocent Volga Blues. The unwrapped copy was so close to the locked-up original that even chance flaws in appearance or spreading are reproduced here, and I, who am so repelled by Seitz's artificial tatterdemalions, am especially captivated by an accurate portrayal of the priceless, utterly frayed and faded, single specimen of "Godunov's Erebia" ever found on the face of the earth, "amid dense leafy woods, July 8, 1903," Father quotes from a letter sent him by Moltrecht, "in the stifling heat at verst twenty of the old Aimsk road."

Consider the charm of remarkable aberrations encountered only within the confines of Russia, the Sooty Swallowtail (Avinov's [Iphlicides podalirius] *lucifer*), or an [Argynnis] Paphia with a continuous pearlescent smear . . . and what about Orlov's strain of *Limenitis*! . . . And the lacework of Suvarov's Melanargia. . . .

"*Le glorieux chef-d'oeuvre du grand maître des lépidopt[érologues]*" exclaims Charles Oberthür (always such a staunch partisan of the "*la bonne figure*") in Volume X of *La Lépidoptérologie comparée*. "As far as we can judge, without knowing the language, nothing comparable to this work, especially in respect of the wealth and beauty of illustration, has ever been attempted before," wrote Rowland-Brown in *The Entomologist*, citing his favorite example of "the iridescence of truth":

> Many black-colored diurnal butterflies, when very fresh, have a striking metallic or moiré, blue-green sheen, which does not survive in prepared specimens; nonetheless, illustrators have succeeded not only in making the wings of the iridescent *Apaturas* [Purple Emperors] iridesce with a warm ("*rich*") violet cast depending on how the page angled toward the light (so that the right or the left half of the *Apatura* displays its August "*purple*"), but certain black satyrids [wood nymphs] as well, when struck by the light, suddenly glow with the gloss of green inks and thus the master's portrait expresses the essence of the butterfly better than the specimen itself in the collection.

My initiation into the mystery of a species was not limited to the imago; I penetrated further and saw, alongside the already mentioned delicate

Steppe Aurora, its slender, olivaceous caterpillar, first found by my father and drawn by Petrov with a jeweler's precision. A partisan of research in the definition of metamorphoses, he subtly berated those whom he called "genitalists": it was just the time when it became fashionable to accept as an unerring and adequate sign of species differentiation distinctions in the chitinoid structure of the male organ, which represented, as it were, the "skeleton" of a species, a kind of "vertebra." "How simply various discussions would be resolved," he wrote, "if those who concentrate on splitting similar species according to this one criterion, whose absolute stability has, moreover, never been proven, turned their attention, in the first place, to the entire radiation of doubtful forms in their overall Palearctic aspect instead of concentrating on a handful of long-suffering French *départements*; and, secondly, made an attempt (as did Chapman and . . .)[54] to define the initial stages of the now 'isolated' species in order to compare them to the same stages of the species that formerly 'contained' it." And in fact my father's discovery of the Terzit caterpillar made it possible to adopt an entirely new, quite unexpected approach in juxtaposing "Terzit" with "Icarus" [the Common Blue] and Escher's Blue.

I recall my irritation, in the atlases, with the "*Raupe unbekannt*" that followed a butterfly's description – and especially the fact that, indeed, one of the inherent attributes of a species was the ratio between these "*unbekannt*" and the number of species in a genus (and sometimes they even coincided!). For the diurnal butterflies of Europe this percentage (about forty) was reduced by my father to fifteen, and would likely have decreased by as much again had he devoted two or three seasons to indigenously western species. I had seen, right in our village, with what perseverance and success he would sometimes seek out a "patrolling" female (i.e., one in search of a spot for oviposition), establish its food plant, and then breed the caterpillar on it, always keeping in mind potential problems arising as the fodder changed with age, or the whims of symbiosis and hibernation; I knew how assiduously he collected during his journeys all that could touch upon the biography of this or that butterfly, while, in every region of Russia, his collectors would seek out locally, breed, sketch, and prepare laboratory samples. Hence, even if at the end of the description of this or that butterfly in *Butterflies and Moths of the Russian Empire* the notation "caterpillar unknown" appeared, I would understand that hitherto the obstacles had been truly insurmountable (extreme rarity of species; its extremely recent discovery; extraordinarily arduous conditions and circumstances of observation), but that, at the least opportunity, at the smallest lapse in the watchfulness of the powers guarding nature's mysteries, the thief's light of Father's lamp would snatch out of the dewy chaos of the steppe grasses some little fishlike, perhaps seminocturnal larva.

In this explosive sequence of revived impressions, I limit myself to Volume I, "Diurnal Butterflies." In the following three, as in the last installments of "Lep. Asiat.," the illustrations are still more perfect – the downy, velvety texture, the blurry translucence of various families of "moths" are rendered so delicately that you would be afraid to run your finger across the paper . . . but the first volume remains the most precious of all in my memory. How I luxuriated in it in the blissfully languorous days of my convalescence, with a crumb of toast tormenting my buttock, weakness in my shoulders, a constantly filling bladder, and a cottony haze in my nape. . . . I liked the solidity of my father's method, for I liked sturdy toys. For every genus there was a supplementary list of Palearctic species that did not occur within the confines under examination, complete with precise "references" to textual location. Each Russian butterfly was allocated from one to five pages of small print, depending on its obscurity or variability, i.e., the more mysterious or changeable, the more attention it received. In places a small map helped to assimilate the detailed description of a species' or its subspecies' distribution, just as an oval photograph in the text added something to the careful exposition of observations of the habits observed in a given butterfly. The "leak" of a species westward as far as Andalusia was followed just as attentively as its adventures in the mountains of Central Asia. Corrections of old errors were enlivened by polemic thrusts, and I can picture the author's laughing eyes, as I read today, "When I dropped in on this genus [*Syrichtus*, an old name for the Grizzled Skippers] I found it in an awful state after a half-century of classifiers' struggles," or, when I come upon the good-humored demolition of some "discovery" by that German muddler who recklessly let loose with names (all mythological to boot, even Walpurgian), creating along the way, countless local, often imaginary races, even disrupting his own priority, such as it was, with secondary descriptions of the same subspecies from a different location – but his entomological fervor and his splendidly assembled collections allowed him to be forgiven everything.

Today, as I reread these four plump volumes (of a different color, alas, than the blue gifts brought for my childhood), not only do I find in them my fondest recollections, and revel in information that, at the time, was not as comprehensible, but the very body, flow, and structure of the whole work touches me in the professional sense of a craft handed down. I suddenly recognize in my father's words the wellsprings of my own prose: squeamishness toward fudging and smudging, the reciprocal dovetailing of thought and word, the inchworm progress of a sentence – and even some embryos of my own parentheses. To these traits must be added my father's predilection for the semicolon (often preceding a conjunction – something one does find in the language of his university tutors: "*that scholarly pause*," an echo of unhurried English logic – but at the same time related to Montaigne whom he regarded so highly); and I doubt that the development of these traits under my frequently willful pen was a conscious act.

I copy out the following full-blooded, flowing periods (from his preface to the genus *Lycaena*):

> During the blaze of noon, between two sumptuous thunderstorms, the mud of Russian roads serves as a drinking establishment for the male Blues, but not every damp spot is suitable; the intensity of visitation is determined by a certain average saturation of the soil as well as the greater evenness of its surface. On an attractive spot like this, with a round, runny border and a relatively limited diameter (rarely exceeding two feet), a group of butterflies settles at close quarters; if one startles the gathering, it rises en masse and remains suspended in a "sorting" hover over the given spot on the road, descending to it anew with mathematical precision. . . . Only the air cooling toward evening, or the arrival of clouds, puts an end to the banquet. I have had occasion to observe the presence of one and the same specimen of Meleager's Blue sitting from eleven in the morning until a quarter to six in the evening, when the long shadow of a nearby oak had reached the very spot where, besides my friend and a few other engrossed Blues and a handful of

golden *adonis*, there remained (from three in the afternoon) a small cluster of *bo-yarishnitsa* (Black-veined Whites), whose general appearance was reminiscent either of little paper cockerels or a regatta of sailboats heeling this way and that. In all those hours the composition and size of the gathering would vary and more than once I inadvertently shooed away my Meleager while fishing out some trifle I needed from the general heap. Now, with the onset of shade, it would soar with elastic grace and, having chosen a bough to perch on – a choice not at all typical for *Lycaena* in a normal state, but quite characteristic as a temporizing maneuver for a butterfly that has left a "drinking place" – would settle on a *Rubus* leaf, as if hoping that the dusk and the chill were but the passing influence of a cloud and that, in a moment, one could return. In a few minutes I noticed that it had dozed off; with that, the observation ended.

I would like to cite many more such artistic and scientific sapphires, but I do not know what to pick out – the account of the extraordinary difficulties (in Volume III) involved in the capture of the salt-marsh [owlet moth] *Plusia rosanovi*, which darted like lightning from place to place, vanishing each time among the pebbles, so that the only chance of catching it (light fails to lure it) was to take advantage of the split second when, before squirting out, it "came to a boil" at the feet of the stealthy hunter. How lovely it is, by the way, how one's eye is caressed by, the dark-cherry forewing, traversed by a mauve-pink stripe and adorned at its center by the golden emblem of its genus, in this instance a tapering, bowed half-moon – and if it is hard to render the flowery velvet of the background, what is one to say of the "emblem," which, on the actual moth, resembles a dab of gilt redolent of turpentine, and must therefore be copied (and recopied!) in such a way that the painter's work transmits, besides all the rest, a resemblance to the work of a painter! Or else such trifles, unforgettable for me, as the line referring to a pair of a new species of *Acidalia* [a former name for the inchworm genus *Scopula*] "once brought to me by Dr. P. P. Paradizov, who had taken them off a wall in the Astrakhan railroad station on October 11, 1889"? Or the discovery in northern Finland of a stunning blue-black *Arctia* [a genus of Tiger Moths] covered with slender red figure eights?

Or, finally, the epic of how the author found, on a cliff in the Altai, a

Tephroclystia [an inchworm genus, Eupthecia] that, until then, had only been identified in the Maritime Alps and on California summits – the "Madonna's window" as it is fondly called by old hunters in aurelian clubs when they secretly gather, and fragments of recollections float in the undulating smoke: *"Once in Uganda where I was collecting for Rothschild, I saw and missed . . ." – ". . . Und war es schön in Moulinet, Hans – schöner als auf Sumatra?" – ". . . Moi, qui a chassé le* Callimuchus dobrugensis *avec le roi de Bulgarie" – ". . . Come, come, von Nolte, I'd give a good deal to have seen your face on that particular summer morning* auf dem *Campolungo Pass . . ." – ". . . Car je soutiens qu'il existe entre celle de la rave et celle de Mann* [the Small white and Mann's white] *une espèce méditerranéenne, à l'abdomen fin et poudré, non encore reconnue . . ." ". . .* Here, Walsingham, how's this for a pursuer of moths – a species that's been found on the Island of Chuma, an unattractive but touching creature . . ." ". . . Now, Professor, tell us about your dog, how, a hundred years ago, it went into a point under some Castilian pines before the first *isabella* (sitting on a stump, green with russet eyespots). . . ."

". . . Oh, to be dying again in the rich reek of that hot steaming swamp among the snakes and the orchids, and with those dear flies flapping about me . . ."

Butterflies and Moths of the Russian Empire, published fifteen years ago [Fyodor was writing in 1927], was at the same time translated, under the author's supervision, into English, as was done with the most important sections of *Lep. Asiat.*, but the author died, publication of the translation was delayed, and I have no idea where the manuscript is now. The independence and proud stubbornness that had made my father write his work in his mother tongue, devoid even of the Latin synopses that, for the benefit of foreigners, were included in Russian scientific journals, did much to slow the book's westward penetration – which was a pity, for, in passing, it resolves a good number of problems regarding western fauna. Nonetheless, even if very slowly, and thanks more to illustrations than text, my father's views of relationships among species within various "difficult" genera have to a degree already made their mark on the literature in the West.

Things would speed up considerably if the English translation appeared at last.

When, on one occasion, Count B., the governor of one of our central provinces, a boyhood friend and distant relative of my father's, addressed to him an official, friendly request for a radical means of dealing with some highly energetic caterpillar that had suddenly gone on a rampage against the province's forests, my father replied, "I sympathize with you, but do not find it possible to meddle in the private life of an insect when science does not require it." He detested applied entomology – and I cannot imagine how he could work in present-day Russia, where his beloved science is wholly reduced to anti-locust campaigns or class struggles against agricultural saboteurs. This horrid debasement of "sublime curiosity" and its hybridization with unnatural factors (social ones, for instance) explain (apart from the general numbing of Russia) the artificial oblivion that has befallen his work in his homeland. No wonder that even the crowning achievement among his biological reflections, that wonderful theory of "natural classification," to which we must now turn, has so far found no followers in Russia, and has penetrated abroad rather haphazardly and in incomplete, muddled form.

This theory, which even today strikes the dominant factions in the scientific world as lawless fantasy, a knight's move off the board into space (a consequence of the utter failure to assimilate the author's premises), came to my father in his last year of scientific activity. Densely set forth on only thirty pages, as a supplement to his last published volume, *Lep. Asiat.*, it retroactively reduced generally accepted classification to trivial absurdity. The fact that, in his own writings, he mechanically contented himself with that classification (apart from minor changes, incidentally very different in spirit from the research of his contemporaries in this field, who had busied themselves for some time with the artificial proliferation of generic names) is explained by the concentration of his scientific attention mainly on the structure and mores of creatures he found in the wild and by the consideration that the description of his catches, i.e, the incessant introduction of new members into the traditional system, did not permit him to dwell on the validity of the system itself, even if the reassignment of certain species required by new observations already hinted at its inadequacies. In addition, prolonged contact with animate nature placed at his mind's disposal not only a succession of scenes, but the repetition of those scenes and the series in which they occurred. It is little wonder he was always so interested in "imitation of one's neighbor, imitation of one's surroundings." Something lurking behind the mental capabilities he called on for the straightforward investigation of haphazardly accumulating materials suddenly manifested itself, like the meekest employee who suddenly appears before his employer with a plan that casts a whole new light on a deal the tycoon had negotiated with reckless haste, proposing certain options, a new connection. In other words, the hour had come when my father suddenly sensed a truth had matured that he had not consciously sought but that had harmoniously grown out of an internal association of elements he had gathered. The mystery was only in the very act of association, and akin to capillary attraction – happening, as it were, independently of the gatherer's will. Yet his entire effort, it now turns out, was still imperceptibly propelled and directed by this very force, which, at the appropriate moment, suggested a method of stellar elegance for organizing the gathered materials. His study, brief but prodigiously original, was modestly and almost imperceptibly tucked into the volume of his purely descriptive work, still in progress. He entitled it merely "Supplement," which, basically, was misleading, since what he set forth in these thirty astonishing pages in no way "supplemented" the works of his predecessors in the fields of evolution, genetics, classification, and so forth, but was absolutely exact within the context of the author's own scientific work, which this material supplemented like the missing piece of a jigsaw puzzle, at last making it totally intelligible. So as to lay to rest the ruckus this study caused in scientific circles, let us say, first of all, that, under the impact of the political situation in Russia at the time (Volume VIII came out in 1917, when my father was no longer there), the response was belated and spasmodic. Only recently (in 1923) was the article in part translated and in part paraphrased, with accompanying barbed commentary from a biologist emeritus, in *The Zoological Review*. Secondly, entomologists were so perplexed and infuriated by the sample sketch of the new classification with which the article concluded, that the impression left by the author's arguments was almost totally obscured by professional outrage, and the theory itself relegated to inscrutable dust and fog, eclipsed by its own explosion. At first sight (to which, so far, commentators have limited themselves), the principles traced by the author of spherical classification, in the present instance employed for Lepidoptera, but, as was very coolly indicated in a footnote, applicable to all areas of nature, seemed mere confusion and delirium. But a similar impression of delirium and confusion would also have resulted from, say, the measurement of the earth or the laws linking it to the other planets, if humanity had not already had an inkling of its roundness and rotation. Of the few scientists who have so far turned their attention to my father's theory the majority have simply failed to understand it – and, in fact, the assimilation of its point of departure demands an extraordinary leap, an acrobatic movement of the brain. Personally, I would have gone astray in the fog (at the same time avoiding the perilous idylls of the dilettante and all of the punishments inflicted by unjustified self-confidence), had it not been for Murchison's "sensational" book, published last spring, in which this interpreter of the *Supplement* – until now the sole unbiased one – inarticulately, conscientiously, in a clumsily vulgarizing manner, but with occasional flashes as guiding mirages for my cerebration, explains in three hundred pages what my father expresses in thirty. Of course the author of the *Supplement* himself foresaw this difficulty of perception. At the outset of his presentation he warned, "I quite realize" – I am forced to translate back into Russian from the scraps of English translation in Z.R., since that very eighth volume of *Lep. Asiat.* is missing in libraries here, and so far I have not succeeded in ordering it from the British Museum – "I quite realize that the effort required to comprehend the basic tenets of this paper is not immediately accessible to a mind that has constructed, alongside the rules of logical thought, certain idols or habits of thought that, having rooted themselves and developed more by the rules of secondary mechanics than initial inspiration, have nevertheless acquired legislative power, leaving to logic only the executive. . . . One must renounce habit, one must have one's thought assume an uncommon pose that might, *a priori*, appear as difficult to achieve as the unnatural arm-and-leg motions of a floating human are to a beginner (*tyro*) at a swimming school. But as soon as this special approach (*the knack of the thing*) is seized – and if the author has succeeded in rendering it, then it is thanks more to happy chance than happy predisposition – what is set forth below will immediately become clear, and will even become so obvious and coherent that the reader's mind will involuntarily race ahead, and reproach the author for excessive elaboration."

Alas, as for what follows, namely the exposition itself of the "principles of natural classification," I do not know whether I correctly convey the author's reasoning, and dissect correctly the mysterious sentences (retranslated by me!). My main difficulty is that I am insufficiently versed in such matters as, for instance, paleontology or genetics, so that, as I step into the pitch-blackness, the labyrinth of ice, I lack even a lantern. And, if I nevertheless decide upon this adventure, it is only because of the abstruse kinship, that poetic bond that, independent of the scientific essence of the subject, connects me to the author.

Let us begin, as he did, by defining the concept of species. By "species" he intends the original of a being, nonexistent in our reality but unique and definite in concept, that recurs ad infinitum in the mirror of nature, creating countless reflections; each one of them perceived by our intelligence, reflected in that selfsame glass and acquiring its reality solely within it, as a living individual of the given species. An aberration, or chance deviations are but the consequence of less "faithful" areas of the mirror, while the recurrent falling of a reflection on one and the same flaw may yield a stable local race, the idea of which tends toward the periphery of the circle, the center of which, in turn, is the idea of the species. These races remain on the circumference of the species insofar as the spatial link (i.e., one with a locus on earth at a given point in time) between the type (i.e., the most precise sample at a given moment) and a local variant is supported by intermediate variations (that can manifest themselves as local races or chance deviations), in other words, so far as the species circle remains unbroken. Potential interbreeding with the type, and the permanence of a certain basic scheme (in butterflies the veinage, scale shape, leg structure, and so forth) delineates boundaries within which the variety conforms to the species. In exactly the same way, the repetition of individual reflections in time (limited by the span during which a given species conserves its basic identity) may, if the process lasts long enough, generate certain modifications that, however, are just as unanchored as spatial variations, with which they may even coincide if we have come upon the species in its ideal period, i.e., at the moment of full harmony among its radial components. Here we must designate as the current type of a species not the first described individual (resolutely rejecting this sophism of nomenclature, which taints science with possessiveness, happenstance, and childish competition), but that form which represents either the obvious center of a species' variational boundaries, or (in the case of a severe distortion of the given species circle) can only be defined by analogy with the behavior of other species points on the circumference of the genus that controls each of them. Roughly speaking, if one imagines a sphere, then its equator will denote the spatial cycle of a species in its ideal period, and an average meridian the cycle of possible changes of the type in time. And at the center resides the heart of the species, its idea, its original.

When we affirm this conformity between the cycles of a species in time and in space, we are very far from the concept of evolution. In both time and space the development of variational distinctions is subordinate to the circle enclosing the species. One more step and we are out of the circle and have entered the domain, equally delineated and autonomous, of a different species. When a paleontologist aligns a row of progressively larger skeletons purporting to represent the evolution of the "horse," the deception is that, in reality, no hereditary connection exists; the concept of species is hopelessly confused here with those of genus and family; we are faced with such a number of different species of animals that *at one time* formed, with other species related to each of them, a specific spatial cycle of a particular genus, to which a particular cycle corresponds in time; all these spheres of species (and genera) have long ago disintegrated; and the various species of *Equus* that we currently encounter on earth in a far from typical period of the species' harmony, nonetheless represent more fully the "history of the horse" than a series of heterogeneous animals arranged on an evolutionary ladder. By this we certainly do not mean to say that the work of evolutionists has no scientific significance. The value of biological observations is in no sense diminished by the fact that deductions from them might have either been made a priori, or else have tempted thought into a vicious circle. By the same token, the value to a collector of a solid-black *hospiton* (Corsican Swallowtail) or of a pathological specimen of *avis* (Chapman's Green Hairstreak) with a white androconial almond spot is not diminished by the fact that one might unerringly predict the existence of deviations, as yet unobserved, in the given butterfly. The variety, precision, and logical consistency of experiments performed by this school of thought are worthy of the highest praise. It has evaluated with great subtlety such questions as the influence of environmental conditions or the mathematics of heredity. Its fallacy lies in the acceptance and even the encouragement of miracles. As soon as such miracles become compatible and systematic, the laws found to justify their repetition are powerless to explain each of them individually, to say nothing of the fact that these same laws may be imaginary, even if quite harmonious, in their mimicry of truth. One is tempted to compare the evolutionist to a passenger who, observing through a railroad-car window a series of phenomena that implies a certain logic of structure (such as the appearance of cultivated fields, followed by factory buildings as a city approaches), would discern in these results and illustrations of movement the reality and laws of the very force governing the shift of his gaze.

Yet that a certain development of forms, from which the "bubbles of species" arose, somehow grew, for some reason burst, is beyond doubt. It is this path that we must now explore.

Reaching again into the basket of generally accessible examples, let us recall the analogy noticeable between the development of individual and species. Here an examination of the human brain can be most fruitful. We emerge from darkness and infancy and regress into infancy and darkness, completing an entire circle of existence. In the course of life we learn, among other things, the concept of "species," unknown to the ancestors of our culture. Yet, not only is the history of mankind parodied by the developmental history of the writer of these and other lines, but the development of human ratiocination, in both the individual and historic senses, is extraordinarily linked to nature, the spirit of nature considered as the aggregate of all its manifestations, and all the modifications of them conditioned by time. How is it conceivable, in fact, that amid the huge jumble containing the embryos of countless organs (of which up to forty-three are currently represented), the magnificent chaos of nature never included *thought*? One can doubt the ability of a genius to animate marble, but one cannot doubt that one afflicted by idiocy will never create a Galatea. Human intelligence, with all its limitations and rights, inasmuch as it is a gift of nature, and a perpetually repeated one, cannot fail to exist in the warehouse of the bestower. It may, in that dark storehouse, differ from its species seen in sunlight as a marble god is distinct from the convolutions of the sculptor's brain – but still it *exists*. Certain whims of nature can be, if not appreciated, at least merely noticed only by a brain that has developed in a related manner, and the sense of these whims can only be that – like a code or a family joke – they are accessible only to the illuminated, i.e., human, mind, and have no other mission than to give it pleasure – we are speaking of the fantastic refinement of "protective mimicry," which, in a world lacking an appointed observer endowed with artistic sensitivity, imagination, and humor, would simply be useless (*lost upon the world*), like a small volume of Shakespeare lying open in the dust of a boundless desert. This fact, even taken alone, implies a silent, subtle, charmingly sly conspiracy between nature and the one who alone can understand, who alone has at last achieved this comprehension – a spiritual alliance concluded above and beyond all the seething, the stirring, the darkness of roaming reveilles, behind the back of all the world's organic life.

Just as an increase in the brain's complexity is accompanied by a multiplication of concepts, so the history of nature demonstrates a gradual development in nature herself of the basic concept of species and genus as they take form. We are right in saying quite literally, in the human, cerebral sense, that nature grows wiser as time passes, that in a given period it has reached this or that specific stage. The only nit that can be picked is that we do not know what we imply when we say "nature" or "the spirit of nature." But, as we shall see, this monstrous "X" to which, taking advantage of its infinite spaciousness, we ascribe responsibility even for our ignorance about its true countenance, does not avoid us in some inviolable mist, but merely does not turn our way. This particularity, in turn, opens the way toward identification, and strikes the first blow toward concrete comprehension, promising us what we, who were raised on the idea of orbits, can naturally expect, upon the sighting of anything revolving away from us, that it will keep rotating until it turns back to face us.

Until that happens we must be content with the half-smile of averted lips, a conspiratorial sign, an elusive glance from narrowed eyes. In order to bring into focus the concrete subject that interests us – the formation of the species concept in nature's mind – this sign should suffice; but the path of thought pursuing the given objective is such a mirror-slippery slope – follows, like any correct but barely passable path, such a narrow ledge above such a chasm of nonsense – that its very novelty can already give a sense of falling.

We must imagine a certain remote time on earth, when the concept of species (or genus) was as foreign to nature as it is foreign to the infancy of a human or of humanity. A three-year-old child thinks a cow is the wife of a stallion, and a dog the husband of a cat. Even the Stagirite, although he could distinguish between a "cabbage butterfly" and a moth that flew flamewards (that, apparently, was the extent of Aristotle's lepidopterological erudition), understood less about this distinction than a child or a layman today. Yet, long before the dawn of mankind, nature had already erected stage sets in expectation of future applause, the chrysalis of the Plum *Thecla* [Strymonidia pruni, the Black Hairstreak] was *already* made up to look like bird droppings, the whole play, performed nowadays with such subtle perfection, had been readied for production, only awaited the sitting down of the foreseen and inevitable spectator, our intelligence of today (for tomorrow's, a new show was in preparation).

However, in that most remote of times that we must now imagine, none of this had yet been conceived. Nature was ignorant of genera and species; the specimen reigned supreme. As a crude illustration of the position it occupied one might say that a squirrel that mated with a goose would give birth to a giraffe, a sturgeon, and a garden spider. In reality, of course, such common creatures did not yet exist and, if so clamorous an example is given, it is only to jar the reader's imagination from its habitual stance. The example is misleading also because zoological selection of "specimen-species" presupposes at least the establishment of a distinction between the animal kingdom and, say, the vegetable one. But even this distinction did not yet exist. If a present-day naturalist with his particular methods of classificatory thinking were actually transported into that primordial age, into nature's preschool era, then, on the moving earth, where various forms of life were changing places, but were not differentiating (as a wave cannot be considered a differentiation of the element of water), in a hot and fat young world, under a sky that, at midday (according to the profound conjecture of the Dutch geologist Buning), was "gleaming black with the sun like the flame of a reflection in polished ebony," he would come upon billions of seething creatures, each of which would turn out to belong to a separate "species" (an empty concept in this case, given the exact correspondence of the number of individuals to the number of species), all of which would be linked not only by the family resemblance of being utterly unknown and incomparable with creatures familiar today (as the drawings of a deranged person share the naïveté of delirium), but also by the universalizing ambience of a given terrestrial era. This similarity could also be imagined as a multitude of different forms of life cut out of one and the same piece of material, bearing its own simple design, so that each creation would reveal its origins through parts of this material, no matter how hard the clothier tried to mask its unity with a variety of outlines, lest, by a chance repetition (such as cutting out two ostriches or two perch) he hint they were of the same stuff. Therefore any two specimens out of any found on earth by a researcher who navigated back to these upper reaches of earthly time would turn out to have such diverse traits that they would demand of him, raised as he was on present-day methods of classification, an assignment to various subdivisions, but at the same time would be marked by that mendacious similarity (a consequence of the "material") betrayed to us today by the atavistic phenomena of "protective mimicry" – those "rhymes of nature," in the author's ingenious words.

At this point we shall take the liberty of digressing somewhat, or, rather, of opening some parentheses, with a reminder that numerous accumulated observations had persuaded him, in the first place, of the absolute impossibility that given similarities were attained through evolution, through the gradual accumulation of resemblance, or through the fixation of magical mutations (the very thing that caused him to reexamine and reject the more "logical" theory of the origin of species); and, secondly, of the utter uselessness (which incidentally disproves the obtuse *lex parsimoniae* of the old-time naturalists) of such resplendent masks for the well-being of mimetic forms. Among the numerous illustrations of these blatant excesses of nature let us select the following curious example: the caterpillar of the quite local Siberian Owlet moth (*Pseudodemas tschumarae*) is found exclusively on the chumara plant (*Tschumara vitimensis*). Its outline, its dorsal pattern, and the coloring of its fetlocks make it resemble precisely the downy, yellow, rusty-hued inflorescence of that shrub. The curious thing is that, in conformity to the rules of its family, the caterpillar appears only at summer's end, while chumara blooms only in May, so that, against the dark green of the leaves, the caterpillar, uncircled by flowers, stands out in sharp contrast. The resulting impression (if one adheres to the illusory theory of "protective mimicry") is that there has been a hitch in fulfilling the agreement, or that, at the last minute, nature defrauded one of the parties. One could posit, for example, that, at one time, the chumara's bloom, because of a different climate, coincided with the appearance on it of the caterpillar, which thus was safe from some extraordinarily wily foe, against whom it was worthwhile to armor itself with correspondingly wily camouflage. Besides the fact that neither this coincidence nor subsequent divergences can be imagined (if only because a given insect, belonging to one of the purely polar types, is organically bound to today's climate in given localities, with all the attendant consequences regarding seasonal generation and flowering), the Siberian Owlet should by all rights have perished, having become visible to its enemy as soon as the décor changed. Instead that Owlet thrives to this day, and its caterpillar has no particular enemies. Its coarse hairs make it unpalatable to birds, and we should not deceive ourselves about the anthropomorphic capabilities of ichneumons. As for the eventuality of an unknown, long-extinct enemy, it introduces such a hypothetical element into our discourse that thought blurs – or else comes back at you from the wrong direction, and with a superfluous evolutionary onus as extraneous to the essence of the assumption as applied science is to the pure, namely to the fact that the villain of the play was a rational creature (thus Professor Dawson, in an outburst of despair familiar to many evolutionists but, in his own way, quite logically, posited that the mimetic niceties of certain Polynesian caterpillars were directed against the Malaysians who had, from time immemorial, been feeding on them!). But let us leave in peace the famous "struggle for survival": strugglers have no time for art. The happy impression of enchanting irrationality experienced by the observer at the sight of a disguised *tschumarae* – an imaginary flower, an impossible flower – that is what nature, our intelligent accomplice and witty mother wanted to achieve, and did.

Let us also consider that, through a natural concomitance of circumstances (and it could not be otherwise), we arrived in time for the main act of the comedy of mimicry. In nature as it exists today one does not note forms of half- or quarter-resemblance that would indicate that we are present as well at certain intermediate stages of the phenomenon in question, together with some closer to accomplishment. Obviously one cannot number among such approximations the ability of a certain caterpillar to assume, impromptu, the color of a plant or a net with which the experimenter has surrounded it. Perfection of color tonality is attained immediately. At the same time, though, this does not represent a "new" manifestation of protective coloration occurring before our eyes, but rather a play of the same nature-inspired possibilities inherent in the object under investigation, and withholding its secret from forced demonstration. Thus, not only the "aimlessness" of the accomplishment (the "aimlessness" of pure art), but also the absence of transitional forms, the ultimate clarity of observed phenomena, arouses strong doubts about the evolutionary progressive character of their genesis. The impossibility of achieving false similarities via a gradual accumulation of corresponding traits, whether by chance or as a consequence of "natural selection," is proven by a simple lack of time. If the former process occurred, then, by the most generous calculation, by the removal of the mime's birth date into the most distant depths of centuries, the line beyond which lie fossil species whose organic harmony coincides with the existence of other, extinct representatives of the animal kingdom could in no way harmonize with the existence of any species (or genus) familiar to us – that line confines its history to some kind of limits susceptible to some kind of calculable extremes. Yet a trillion light years would hardly be sufficient, even thanks to a series of happy coincidences, to disguise a multitude of disparate species by one and the same process (for instance, endowing a folded butterfly with the exact appearance of a certain variety of leaf with the artistic bonus of a realistic flaw: a small hole eaten through it by somebody's larva). As for the second method, the time span might be sufficient, but only on condition that the species developing a "protective mimicry" (especially since it might not be the decisive lure for the mime, for not every model is poisonous and not every poisonous one has a mime) were pursuing this goal consciously, having conferred beforehand with the model and determined that the latter, during the full number of centuries required by the toiler at evolution toward a gradual attainment of resemblance, would remain unchanged (in the kind of immobility that a painter demands of his model). The process would accelerate further if the model just as consciously indulged the imitator by mutating part way in proportion to the mime's mutations, or if the very goal of the imitator were to change concomitantly with the evolutionary metamorphoses of the model, in the same way a painter, having begun a nude of a young female model, might strive for a likeness with such ardor that, as he tirelessly recorded every trait, he would, in the end, find that he was depicting the old woman into which the model had evolved during her plurennial pose. Yet the concept of evolution in no way presupposes either the existence of a conscious and focused will within a developing creature, or a coordination of actions between two creatures or between a creature and its environment. As for the presumption that nature mesmerizes subjects selected for mimetic study, influencing them to perform specific roles, that notion must be relegated to fantasy, for where are the anchor points for the cobweb of hypnosis? The same variations that might result from a blind struggle for survival, no matter how credible their results may *appear* (for instance, winter coloration, bearing in mind that one must still prove that the monochrome white of rabbit and snow can truly deceive a predator), endlessly retard the putative course of a given evolutionary process, for it is here that the element of happenstance reappears. Simply because some dimwit creature employs it does not lessen its essential laziness – if, in fact, that beast actually does so. More complex examples of imitation, of one's neighbor or one's neighborhood, are by the same token even less plausible via mechanical maneuvers on the "place d'armes" of nature, which the corresponding theory presupposes, and we are propelled back into a domain of numbers so dizzying that no history of the earth can encompass them. To everything already set forth one would have to add the fatal damage inflicted on a given species' quintessence through its supposed impermanence in time, an impermanence infinitely surpassing the fluctuations of its spatial variations. Nonetheless (as we have already deduced from the principle of the sphericity of a species), there exists, for possible deviations from type in both time and space, a curve, a boundary beyond which a given species, as such, can no longer be considered authentic. The duration of a species, its sitting as a model, its presence before nature's mirror, cannot be measured in increments of time that would presuppose radical changes incompatible with the preservation of its idea. To say that, over the centuries, one species evolves into another by a genealogical line is to disrupt, to the same degree, the basic idea of species, as would admitting that between two extant species intermediate forms were to be represented as well. Yet the appearance of species is unarguable; and neither the evolutionist "how" nor the metaphysical "whence" can be answered until we agree to admit it was not species that evolved in nature, but the very concept of species.

To return to the question of the state of nature before the origin of this concept, and imagine the immeasurably distant times when "the specimen reigned supreme," we can, with the aid of parlor verse, if not of armchair science, indistinctly perceive this undulating, iridescent world, and nature's first attempts at stabilizing something. A crawling root, the extremity of a tropical creeper vivified by the wind, turned into a snake solely because nature, noticing movement, wished to reproduce it, as a child amused by the flight of a forest leaf picks it up and tosses it back up. But it is only in nature's fingers that the leaf could turn into a *Kallima*. It would be more accurate to say, though, that it was not the work of the wind, but some energizing, thought-engendering rotation – not just the earth's rotation, but the even force that so festively animates the Dance of the Planets that is the universe. The idea of rotation acting upon the ferment of life, and provoked by that ferment itself, is what gave rise in nature to the lawlike regularity of repetition, of recognition, and of logical responsibility, to which the apparatus of human ratiocination, the fruit of the same agitated woodlands, is subordinate. A reminder is in order: so far, all this is but an approximate image, in the same way as it would be purely allegorical for us to start affirming that the initial division of all earthly specimens into two groups were a separation of two halves under the influence of centrifugal force, and that the dual sexuality of today is a surviving signpost of that first separation, which, in itself, was not yet a differentiation of the sexes.

Here we traverse the most precarious part of the trail, where thought, with lowered gaze and aware of its direction, is therefore fearful of a superfluous nudge – the effort of double-checking, a flawed appellation, a misstep and a slip, the way the surrounding vista from the precarious path is liable to provoke, instead of a flow of reason and memory, a fatal vertigo. But what one must establish clearly for oneself, something that will, incidentally, lead us out onto relatively safe ground, is that all of nature's subsequent work on the differentiation and definition of the notion of species (as well as of genus and family), through a special property of its agitation, was fated to follow the laws of spherical entities burgeoning, disintegrating, and newly developing, out of the disintegrated elements, into newly intricate clusters. As we study this method of nature via reflections that have reached us, we involuntarily come away with the impression that in its implementation, at once obediently carefree and subtly rational (as a painter alternately whistles and narrows his eyes), nature found immense delight, whose exact quality is familiar to us in the joy we derive from a witty problem, from harmony, from creativity. At times nature found it amusing, or artistically valid, to retain, near a selected species, an elegant corollary, generically quite unrelated, but simply picked up from the ground simultaneously back in the times when a dragonfly might simultaneously be a butterfly. Or else it pained nature to disjoin two of its initial creations, which, despite the abyss of differences separating them, nonetheless modulated between one another. From one angle, you see a lichen; from another, an inchworm moth. Whatever subsequent alterations this plant and this insect underwent, the ripply-grayish something that, in the depths of ages, corresponded to them was conserved by nature (which had not given up mythogenesis for the sake of scientific system, but had cunningly united them). As soon as a creature capable of appreciating the unexpected resemblance, its poetry and magical antiquity, had matured on earth, this phenomenon was proffered to him by nature for admiration and amusement, as a precious symbol of the homogeneousness (*oneness*) in which she had once found the prime compound for the creation of the first denizens of her kindergarten. It is remarkable that, assuming the spatial classification proposed below, based on an annular principle and organized in a ringlike pattern forming new ringlike systems, mime and model perforce exchange glances from the nearest points of rings that pertain to totally disparate genera of butterflies. We are led to conjecture that, in respect to "protective coloration" as well, one can find similar juxtapositions, very hard to trace, of course, given the extravagantly heterogeneous objects of imitation and the appurtenance of the "shielded" and the "shield" (apparently quite heraldic in a practical sense) to totally different groups.

The gradual affirmation of the concept of species led to an even more vivid diversity among these new units of life, making the wheels spin and disintegrate with greater intensity – and here a certain role might also have been played by vacillations in the earth's temperature and the fruitful reciprocity between the phases of flora and fauna.*

Of course the basic spirit of development in no way depended on the chance cataclysms of a chance environment. The disintegration of a species, the explosion of a species ring, resulted when the given idea of a species grew impoverished – something that manifested itself in the extinction of the type or the weakening of its bonding force, which in turn entailed

---

*[In margins:] At the same time, however, the development from variety into species occurred in another way, for the concept of species was different.

abrupt leaps in the variation of peripheral forms and the disappearance of intermediate ones. The conclusion of this process became evident when these extreme variations, which, so to speak, had dispersed in every direction from the explosion of the species ring, began evolving their own cycles. Those that managed to endure became the centers of new ideas of species. The difficulty of visualizing these phenomena in concrete physical guise lies in that the gradual development of the very notion of species has, in nature, stipulated varying distinctness at varying points in time. This distinctness has finally reached a stage where any present-day attempt to imagine the emergence of one species from another (or, more precisely, from one or another of its peripheral variations) contradicts the limitations of the concept of species already discussed. Hence it is vitally important to take into account that interval, that leap (somewhat similar to what we find when we compare mechanical and animal motion), which separates the twilight of heteromorphism still present in the guidance of a species from the dawning of autonomous existence. The deeper we delve into the past, the less distinct appear the contours of the species concept, and the less noticeable is the interval of genesis. But if reason finds it hard to deal with this phenomenon, every *curieux* still knows that special hint of intuitive conviction inherent in its outcome, that certainty akin to revelation that we sharply experience as a leap, a turning point, when at the sight of two species of butterfly, one of which only yesterday had been reassigned to a separate species by a supremely keen-eyed entomologist, and, although during the 150 years since Linnaeus these two species had been regarded as one, now that the traits of arcane species differentiation have been unveiled by another's perspicacity, suddenly our eyes open wide, and how could one ever have overlooked those very traits that, with such elegant precision, now distinguish the two butterflies.

As for *genus*, in its present aspect it must be considered as a complete circle made up of species rings, its central nucleus expressed by the genus type. For a classifier who has learned to distinguish the necessary traits it is not hard to isolate this central type, provided he has caught up with the given genus during the period preceding its disintegration. It is sometimes possible to establish, as well, a circle of peripheral species represented in full. Then we say that we have found a genus in its ideal form, whereupon separate peripheral species may (in parallel with the disappearance of intermediate forms upon the breakup of species) vanish, or conversely, due to the heightened agitation of tumultuously disintegrating species rings, yield their place to new species (according to the aforementioned method), while the genus type disappears, allowing the active species rings to collect around the new genus center. Thus, the classifier is obliged to take into account not only the equatoriality of a genus, but also its meridians, i.e., the sphericity of the genus (like that of the species). This means that, as a basis for the distribution of species and genera, one must recognize not only the order in which the forms rotate around the center, but also the order of traits in the chronology of genus (and species). For a genus, for instance, it is essential to find an explanation for gaps in the circumference of a given species circle, or for the absence of a true genus type – that the genus either has not yet stabilized or has already disappeared. At the center of the whole system will be found the ideal cycles of genera, i.e., those that, in our time, are fully represented and hence have (temporarily) attained a perfect phase of development. At the same time it is curious to note that, given the mutability of a species in time (and also, although to an unknown but probably lesser degree, given the persistence of analogous concepts in the future of natural development as well – an exceedingly sluggish development, destined only for the earth's terminal phase, after having traversed all the most intolerable restrictions, to regress to the specimen idea), the very order (and, in part, the spirit) of classification will have to vary naturally through the ages. Thus an entomologist of the nth century, having encountered different ideal cycles of butterfly genera now familiar to us, will assign them a place in the system today occupied by cycles that then will be in the delirious throes of collapse and disintegration. The furious competition prevalent today, especially among British naturalists, to split up genera even to the point of burdening every member of a genus with a genus of its own, as if already hinting at the beginning of a partial collapse of the genus concept, might, of course, be a transitory phenomenon.

In examining the clusters of genus cycles of Lepidoptera currently represented on earth, we note, as confirmation of the pyrotechnic events accompanying the disintegration of genera just set forth, that genera comprising numerous species (*Erebia, Lycaena,* etc.) display eloquent signs of disintegrative ferment. The more species are present in a genus (both in a general sense and in the separation into subgroups of two or three species within a genus) the more they resemble each other, and the richer the variations within the limits of each species. Conversely, scarceness of species (e.g., in the genus *Libythea* [Snout Butterflies]) is associated with a minimal capability of a given species for racially aberrant variation. Let us note, by the way, that genus rotation, having attained its paroxysm, attains almost visible expression via the rapidly multiplying species of certain of these "bursting" genera, giving, as it were, a photographic image of the idea of its ferment or, like a fever, breaking out in a rash, pictorially resembling round spots, rings, eyespots. Striking examples of this feverish state (concurrent with spasmodic attempts to found new nuclei) can be seen in the current situation of such genera as RMP *Melitea* or *Syrichtus* [Checkerspots, Checkered Skippers]. It is worth noting that at any given period there appears to exist a characteristic limit to the number of species within represented genera (and of genera within a family), depending on the exactitude of the concept of genus (as well those of species, etc.). The average such number gives, so to speak, the temperature of the "pathology of development" of a given order of animals at a given time, and serves as a basis for fruitful juxtapositions in establishing the seniority of the various orders existing on earth.

Insofar as concrete characteristics illustrating both the periphery and the center of a genus are concerned, the author of the "Addendum" cautions the future classifier about the dangerous mental habit that mechanically seeks, first of all, gradations of forms. If, within the confines of a species, such a gradation ("intermediate variations of species") is natural and evident as an elementary expression of the unifying force of a type and its domain, then, in a corresponding attempt at distributing species within a genus, *such* a gradation (based on an assumption that happens to be incompatible with the very idea of intraspecies variation) is unacceptable in the methodological sense, even though it may be encountered as one of the symptoms of the disintegration of a genus. The case is analogous to that of the central species of a genus (i.e., the most accurate embodiment of the idea of a given genus), which is by no means obligated to incorporate traits of all the species within that genus, just as the species do not represent the full spectrum or scale of traits in the genera so much as the varied and harmonious utilization of possibilities stored within the nucleus species. The establishment of these laws of harmony (as characteristic for every genus as the appearance of every one of its species), the calculation of possibilities, the scrutiny of their manifestations at any given moment, their reciprocal relations and the gaps or clusters on the circumference of a genus – herein lie the fundamental problems for the classifier. The fact that the central species embodies the exact formula for the harmony of a given genus can serve as a guide. The number of members subsumed by this formula is limited in practice by the fact that all of them stand for known traits of equivalent classificatory importance and are irreducible integers. Hence, in instances where the basic schema is simple enough, it is possible to predict the number of species that comprise the ideal composition of a given genus. In studying the very few ideal genus circles extant in our era (according to a preliminary calculation, somewhat hindered by the artificial accumulation of "subspecies" referred to above, their number equals approximately one-eighth of one percent of the number of all the currently extant genera of Lepidoptera, while the number of those in the stages of formation and disintegration would at present seem to be in a state of reciprocal equilibrium), we observe that the number of satellites revolving around the central nucleus is expressed in the even numbers four, six, and eight – and, as far as it has yet been possible to determine, does not exceed the highest of those. In such genus rings, the harmony resides in the fact that all peripheral species perfectly complement each other in their embellishment and, conversely, in the degree of their diversity. These supplements and variations in precision are controlled by the proportion of those traits present in the central species, which "dictate to each of the peripheral species a special role in the play performed by the entire cast of the genus and uniting all the participants through the harmony expressed in the person of its hero (within its main character)." Thus, for example, in the Asiatic genus *Eurythemia*, each of the four species comprising its circumference has appropriated and developed ("elaborated") four of the sixteen traits characterizing the appearance of the genus, namely one of the four traits of pattern, one of the four traits of foot structure, one of the four genital traits, and one of the four traits of venation. This casting of roles is so distinct and thorough (satisfying) as to lend the impression of a crystalline structure's elegance. Given the unvarying distance that distinguishes the peripheral species from each other and the mathematical harmony of traits adopted for refinement by the central species, there can be no doubt that, at present, there does exist on our earth some sixth representative of the given genus.

All of this is with regard to ideal rings. In some cases, despite the presence of a central species, the peripheral ones indistinctly develop fundamental traits, with gaps to be filled or with localized crowding (for example, the persistence of relationships peculiar to aberrational deviations within the limits of a species such as blurring or increased definition of pattern), making allowance for "dotted tracing" or "local congestion," yet distributing themselves in ringlike fashion (as, for example, in the comparatively young genus *Pyrameis* [or Vanessa, the Painted Ladies] with its central species *indica*). In these cases we say that the genus is in its formative state and situate it at an appropriate point on the family meridian. The central species may be indefinable, with the peripheral ones greatly multiplied and so resembling each other that for decades one or another of them remains "under its neighbor's wing" – sometimes with "experimental species" being created and not surviving for more than three or four generations – then we say that the genus is disintegrating, and situate it on the opposite side of the equator of perfect periods. It follows that the ability to combine temporary traits (the degree of the rotational development of a genus) with spatial traits (the relationship of contemporary genera among themselves and the placement of species within them) is a direct indicator of correct spherical classification, in which the place of honor goes to the bubbles of genera that are most distinctly and harmoniously represented.

A preliminary outline of such a classification of Lepidoptera is presented by the author, concisely and without commentary, at the conclusion of the "Addendum" (where in many families even the parentheses of genera are not opened). It is only an illustration of principles, the assimilation of which will leave to the reader the pleasure of figuring out for himself the author's reasons for adopting this particular distribution. Here I shall get no help from Murchison, whose lepidopterological knowledge is very limited. My father's work interests him only for its biological-philosophical refraction. But the lapidary concision of the present schema probably gratified two senses highly developed in its author: that of proportion and that of humor. In an essay where, judging by excerpts, every sentence is like an opaquely glazed door with a sign to halt intruders, and inside everything is replete with knowledge that calls for bridges where the reader, notwithstanding the pesky prodding of the wayward Murchison, would otherwise sink into the murky ooze – in such an essay, where the author's goal, essentially, was to provide a minimum of words and a maximum of thought, an elaborate exposition of its deductions would have been uneconomical. At the same time, anticipating the perplexity, and even the irritation, that a conservative scientist must experience when faced with a blueprint for classification at the conclusion of an incomprehensible essay, caused its author no little amusement. But of course the main thing is that he had intended, at his leisure, to dedicate a separate study to the question raised here, and at the same time believed that, if the precariousness of human life, and the fog settling on Russia, and the danger of a new hunt far afield projected in such an unpropitious year thwarted it, a maximally accurate exposition of the principles of such a study would still allow minds that at last understood them a chance to consummate the plan outlined by the author. I like to think he was not mistaken here, and that, in time, men will appear who are more alert than Murchison, more educated than I, more talented and lively than the terrible turtles who direct learned journals, and that the elaboration of my father's thoughts, jotted in the hasty hand of a testament in the night preceding a dubious departure, when holster, gloves, and compass intrude momentarily on the sedentary life of the desk, and pursued here in a haze of filial love, piety, inspiration, and mental helplessness, will create a worthy monument to him, visible from every corner of natural science. The bitterness of interrupted life is nothing compared to the bitterness of interrupted work: the probability that the former may continue beyond the grave seems infinite when compared to the inexorable incompletion of the latter. There, perhaps, it will seem like nonsense, but here it still remains unfinished. Whatever may lie in store for the soul, however fully earthly mishaps may be resolved, there must remain a faint hum, vague as stardust, even if its source vanishes with the earth. That is why I cannot forgive the censorship of death, the prison officials of the other world, the veto imposed on the research envisioned by my father. It is not for me, alas, to complete it. Here I recall, with no connection to this eternal hurt or, at least, no rational connection, how, one warm summer night, a boy of fourteen, I sat on the veranda bench with some book – whose title, too, I shall surely recall in a moment, when it all comes into focus – and my mother, smiling as in a dream, was laying out on the illumined table cards that were particularly glossy against the thick, velvet heliotrope-soaked chasm into which the veranda glided. I had difficulty understanding what I read, for the book was difficult and strange, and the pages seemed out of order, and my father, with someone – with a guest, or with his brother, I cannot make out clearly – was walking across the lawn, slowly, judging by their softly moving voices. At a certain moment, as he passed beneath an open window, his voice drew nearer. Almost as if he were reciting a monologue, for, in the darkness of the fragrant black past, I have lost track of his chance interlocutor, my father declared emphatically and cheerfully, "Yes, of course it was in vain that I said 'accidental,' and accidental that I said 'in vain,' for here I agree with the clergy, especially since, for all the plants and animals I have had occasion to encounter, it is an unquestionable and authentic. . . ." The awaited final stress did not come. Laughing, the voice receded into the darkness – and now I have suddenly remembered the title of the book.

The Enchanter

Excerpts from novella in Russian (*Volshebnik*), an embryonic version of the *Lolita* story. Written October–November 1939. First published in English in 1986. Translated by DN.

[As he travels by train to meet her again, the central character imagines a future with the daughter of the woman whom he has married and who has just died.]

Against the light of that happiness, no matter what age she attained – seventeen, twenty – her present image would always transpire through her metamorphoses, nourishing their translucent strata from its internal fountainhead. And this very process would allow him, with no loss or diminishment, to savor each unblemished stage of her transformations. Besides, she herself, delineated and elongated into womanhood, would never again be free to dissociate, in her consciousness and her memory, her own development from that of their love, her childhood recollections from her recollections of male tenderness. Consequently, past, present, and future would appear to her as a single radiance whose source had emanated, as she had herself, from him, from her viviparous lover.

Thus they would live on – laughing, reading books, marveling at gilded fireflies, talking of the flowering walled prison of the world, and he would tell her tales and she would listen, his little Cordelia,[55] and nearby the sea would breathe beneath the moon. . . . And exceedingly slowly, at first with all the sensitivity of his lips, then in earnest, with all their weight, ever deeper, only thus – for the first time – into your inflamed heart, thus, forcing my way, thus, plunging into it, between its melting edges . . .

The lady who had been sitting across from him for some reason suddenly got up and went into another compartment; he glanced at the blank face of his wristwatch – it wouldn't be long now – and then he was already ascending next to a white wall crowned with blinding shards of glass as a multitude of swallows flew overhead. *[Enchanter 74–75]*

[He takes her away by car for a holiday during which he plans to possess her.]

On we go. He looked at the forest that kept approaching in undulating hops from hillside to hillside until it slid down an incline and tripped over the road, where it was counted and stored away. "Shall we take a break here?" he wondered. "We could have a short walk, sit for a while on the moss among the mushrooms and the butterflies. . . ." But he could not bring himself to stop the chauffeur: there was something unbearable about the idea of a suspicious car standing idle on the highway.   [*Enchanter* 79]

Interview with Nikolay All, June 1940

In New York. In Russian.

I was surprised even by the customs officers on the passenger wharf. [. . .] When they opened my suitcase and saw two pairs of boxing gloves, two officers put them on and began boxing. The third became interested in my collection of butterflies and even suggested one kind be called "captain." When the boxing and the conversation about butterflies finished, the customs men suggested I close the case and go. Doesn't this show how straightforward and kind Americans are?   [*Novoe Russkoe Slovo*, June 23, 1940]

From letter to Mikhail Karpovich,[56] c. mid-June 1940

From New York. In Russian. Unpublished.

Warmest thanks for your very kind offer, I accept with pleasure. If it's absolutely all right by you, we would come at the very beginning of July. [. . .] I can't think without a quiver – a sweet, torturing quiver – that my passion for entomology will also be satisfied in Vermont. I am writing Avinov about some of my scientific findings in this domain.   [COLUMBIA]

From letter to Elizaveta and Marussya Marinel,[57] August 25, 1940

From West Wardsboro, Vermont. In Russian. Translated DN.

We are staying amid marvelous green wilds with the wonderfully kind Karpoviches, where one can go around half-naked, write an English novel, and catch American butterflies (soon I'll have to start using your sweater: fall is near). My position is fatally undecided, so far nothing has worked out, and the thought of winter is rather frightening, but, by comparison, it is a genuine paradise here.[58]   [SL 33]

From letter to Tatiana and Mikhail Karpovich, September 15, 1940

From New York. In Russian. Unpublished.

After my marvelous summer mood I have had a strong reaction: anxiety and a slight flu. But it really was wonderfully good *chez vous*. I don't just mean the butterflies.   [COLUMBIA]

From American Museum of Natural History certificate, September 17, 1940

The American Museum of Natural History has received from Mr. V. Nabokov 22 Butterflies (family) Hesperidae.   [AMNH]

From letter to Mikhail Karpovich, October 7, 1940

From New York. In Russian. Unpublished.

I console myself with unpaid work in the museum, where *I joined the staff as volunteer worker.*[59]   [COLUMBIA]

From "Prof. Woodbridge in an Essay on Nature Postulates the Reality of the World"

Review of Frederick J. E. Woodbridge, *An Essay on Nature* (1940).

That philosophers are essentially diurnal creatures (no matter how late into the night their inkpots and spectacles glitter) and that space would not

VN's most distinctive European butterfly catch, a male (upperside on left, underside on right) two days after the one other catch (also a male) above the village of Moulinet, above Menton. He deposited this specimen, which he designated the holotype, and the other (the allotype) at the American Museum of Natural History, where he worked in 1941 on the article in which he described and named the species *Lysandra cormion*. A 1989 experiment showed the butterfly to be, as he had suggested could be the case, a cross between *Meleageria daphnis* and *Lysandra coridon*. See the article "*Lysandra cormion*, a New European Butterfly," this page; the poem "On Discovering a Butterfly," pp. 273–74; and the *Speak, Memory* caption for a photograph of both specimens, pp. 637–38.

be space if color and outline were not primarily perceived are suppositions that transcend the author's "naïve realism" just at the point where he seems to be most securely hugging the coast. But is visibility really as dominant as that in all imaginable knowledge of Nature? Though I personally would be satisfied to spend the whole of eternity gazing at a blue hill or a butterfly, I would feel the poorer if I accepted the idea of there not existing still more vivid means of knowing butterflies and hills.   [*New York Sun*, December 10, 1940]

Lysandra cormion,* a New European Butterfly

Lepidoptera paper. Researched and written December 1940–January 1941.

This peculiar insect is best described in terms of relation to *Lysandra coridon* Poda and *Polyommatus meleager* Esp. Roughly speaking, it is more like the former above, and more like the latter below. Its expanse is that of a slightly undersized *coridon*.

The upper side is a clear silky blue, comparable to the bluest varieties of *coridon* (and recalling yet another species, *Polyommatus eros* O.). Next to it *meleager* looks purplish and *coridon* silvery gray. The dark fuscous border of the primaries is broader than in *meleager*; less sharply defined than in *coridon*. The fringes belong to the double (*meleager*) type, with the inner line a pale fuscous on the fore wing, but unlike *meleager's* they are slightly checkered. The secondaries while rounder than in *coridon*, and with a

---

*See also figures of ♂ genitalia in *Psyche*, 1945 (26 Oct.) 52, p. 48–49, p. 54, Pl. 1, figs. 4 and 5. [VN note, *Lepidopterological Papers 1941–1953*.]

whiter abdominal fold, do not suggest *meleager's* ample contour; they have their subcostal vein curved in the *coridon* manner, *i.e.,* more arched than it is in *meleager*, and display a submarginal row of conspicuous black dots (that are generally wedge-shaped in *coridon* and absent in *meleager*).

On the under side, as in *meleager,* the primaries lack the two basal spots* found in *coridon,* but the first one of the submedian row seems advanced basally – a *coridon* feature. There is a *Lysandra*-like difference in tone between the wings; but the light tint of the primaries is of the *meleager* (whitish) shade, and this tint is merely deepened to a dunnish gray on the secondaries without any admixture of buff so frequently seen in *coridon*. All the ocelli are neatly accentuated, with their white rings especially distinct on the darker hind wing. This has a clear median streak (indiscernible in most males of *meleager* owing to the general bleached effect of the under side); the submarginal chevrons show no trace of orange, but are rather more strongly outlined than in *meleager,* and the base of the wing is dusted with metallic blue.

An examination of the genitalia reveals that the ædeagus of *cormion,* with its bulblike enlargement just before the tip, closely resembles that of *coridon* and has nothing to do with the elongated form and bottleneck terminal process seen in *meleager* and other *Polyommatus* species. In *cormion* this organ appears to be just a trifle thinner and its swelling rather less accentuated than is the case with *coridon;* but there can be no question of its forming any intermediate between *coridon* and *meleager;* it is quite unmistakably of the *Lysandra* type. On the other hand, the more perfectly rounded hump of the vinculum, the deeper notch beneath the terminal spur of the harpé and the irregular, less solid looking structure of the uncus seem to differ from the corresponding parts of *coridon* in a way approaching *meleager.*

The only two specimens known (holotype and paratype, both now in The American Museum of Natural History) are males and were taken by me on the 20th and 22nd of July, 1938, at an altitude of about 4,000 feet on the flowery slopes above Moulinet (Alpes Maritimes, France), a place

---

*They are faintly and incompletely present in the holotype as they are often in *coridon* and *meleager*. [VN note, *Lepidopterological Papers 1941–1953*.]

seldom visited by collectors though famed since Fruhstorfer's time for some remarkable "*Lycæna*" races (and the type locality of his *escheri* var. *balestrei* and *amandus* var. *isias*). Both specimens were netted because they looked so different on the wing from the rest of the "blues" present, and during the next two days I saw two more (or a third one twice) which I missed, bungling being encouraged by a strong wind and the steepness of the ground. Suitable females were also looked for, but in vain; nor did a subsequent search through the rich material of the British Museum yield any additional examples.

Had not the bulk of my collection remained in a basement in Paris, I should have liked to compare *cormion* not only with *coridon,* but with my series of the very closely allied *rezniceki* Bart., the Riviera representative of a Spanish species. I feel a puzzle here. Apart from the link hinted at by *cormion*, there seems to exist a curious mimetic affinity between *meleager* and the "*coridon*" group, thus the pale under side of sturdy *albicans* H.S. bears a striking resemblance to that of *meleager,* especially when, as often happens in the former's case, the fulvous fillings are greatly reduced.

There is also the question of interbreeding. Some of the "blues" have been suspected of unconventional pairings, and in connection with *meleager* one may mention that Rebel[60] described and figured (Verh. zool. bot. Ges. Wien, v. 70, *meledamon*) a *Polyommatus*-like *Agrodiætus* captured in 1919 in the vicinity of Vienna, which he assumed to be – with wholly unwarranted precision – a cross between *meleager* male and *damon* female. In the present case where *meleager* and *coridon* are examined it would be likewise poor science to suppose that *cormion*, not being a plausible mutation of either, ought to be the offspring of both. The powers responsible for the moulding of Mediterranean *Lycænidæ* seem to be in a state of hectic activity, issuing new forms by the hundred, some of which may be fixed and retained by the secret decrees of nature, others dismissed and lost the very next season. Whether *cormion* will have to be deemed the freakish outcome of such evolutionary gropings which fashioned a few specimens in the season of 1938, never to bring out that particular make again, or whether it will turn up here and there, to struggle for elbow room between *coridon* and *meleager,* somewhat in the way *thersites* does between *icarus* and *escheri*, is a matter for the future to settle. Personally I would have postponed describing this rarity were I ever likely to revisit its lovely haunts.

In conclusion, my thanks are due to Mr. W. P. Comstock[61] of The American Museum of Natural History for so very kindly placing all available material at my disposal and dissecting for me the genitalia of the three insects involved.   [*Journal of the New York Entomological Society* 49 (1941): 265–67]

On Some Asiatic Species of *Carterocephalus*

Lepidopterological paper. Researched and written winter–spring 1941.

1. The true *Carterocephalus* * *dieckmanni* Graeser.

In 1888 (Berl. Ent. Z.) Graeser described a new *Carterocephalus*, *dieckmanni* from two males taken near Vladivostok; in 1891 (Entmol. XXIV Suppl.) Leech named another Asiatic species, from Tibet, *gemmatus;* a month later, this was described and figured as *demea* by Oberthur (Etudes Entom.) who never forgave Leech for having hastily forestalled him after seeing a proof copy of the plate; and in 1897 Elwes and Edwards, revising the family (Trans. Zool. Soc.) cheerfully sank both *gemmatus* Leech and *demea* Obthr., as synonyms of Graeser's *dieckmanni*.

Little though Leech seems to have deserved it, his *gemmatus* (*demea* Obthr.) must now be restored. Elwes and Edwards' error was rather remarkable in view of Oberthur's perfect representation of his *demea* and of Graeser's detailed and beautifully accurate description of his *dieckmanni*; but more remarkable still is the fact that this confusion ("*dieckmanni*" Graeser = *gemmatus* Leech) has been kept up for half a century by other writers including of course Mabille, in his half-hearted, incredibly muddled survey (I volume of Seitz), and Gaede (Suppl. to "Seitz") who, however, was sufficiently acquainted with the facies of the alleged synonym to be bothered by the figure in Seitz, and no wonder he was; that figure hap-

---

*The "black-and-white" group merges into the "golden" so naturally that I do not see any reason for isolating the former in the subgenus *Aubertia* very vaguely proposed by Oberthur in 1896.

pens to represent the true *dieckmanni*! "The form illustrated in volume I," says Gaede (trying as it were to patch up the matter), "has two rows of white spots on underside of hind wings. Occasionally these are conjoined forming two bands as illustrated by Oberthur."

The simple reality of course is that *gemmatus* Leech (*demea* Obthr.) and *dieckmanni* Graeser are separate species, and incidentally, the latter is more seldom met with in collections than the former. On the underside of the secondaries the central silvery band of *gemmatus* is replaced in *dieckmanni* by three spots* with the general pattern recalling a "golden" species *argyrostigma* Ev. (as was noted by Graeser himself); and another striking feature is that, in *gemmatus*, the fringes of the secondaries are dark, the costal part alone being white, whereas in *dieckmanni* (as again Graeser notes) they are white throughout except for a short stretch between the upper angle and vein 2 where there is a peculiar shading not quite reaching the outer edge.

The only specimen of C. *dieckmanni* at the American Museum of Natural History is a male, from Sining.

2. *Carterocephalus canopunctatus* new species.
Upperside brownish black with small dull-white spots; these recall *flavomaculatus* Obthr. in size and *christophi* Gr.-Grsh† in disposition. Wings and abdomen have a slim elongated appearance.

Primaries above with two spots in the cell, the first near the base, wedge-shaped, surmounted by a small bluish-white patch, the other at one third from the end, bar-shaped across the cell; below this a slightly broader spot placed outwards; and four sub-apical spots, the first three from near the costa in a narrow band divided by the veins and the fourth placed outwards, with a hardly perceptible dot in a line below. Apex tipped with white even more slightly than in *niveomaculatus* Obthr. Fringes brownish.

---

*This is curiously paralleled in another Hesperid genus, *Pyrgus*, by the difference between *maculata* Brem. et Gr. and *malvae* L.

†Or rather *dulcis* Obthr. if the latter be considered as a form of *christophi* with slightly reduced spots. There is also *niveomaculatus var. tibetanus* South, but the author's meager description (Bomb. Nat. Hist. Soc. 1913) is worthless as the few characters he mentions might apply equally well to *christophi or dulcis.*

Secondaries with two spots, the first bar-shaped across the cell and the other below it less extended inwards than in *flavomaculatus*. Fringes shaded with brownish, except along the costa and at one point above the anal angle where they are white.

Primaries underside washed with olivaceous along the costa and on apical area, otherwise brown with the spots of the upperside reproduced and slightly enlarged.

Secondaries underside resembling *niveomaculatus* and, still more, *flavomaculatus*, olivaceous, with the usual pale pincer-shaped markings at the base, a yellow medial streak, a line of more or less distinct yellow dots along the margin and nine spots, silvery-white (except the small costal one, central series, which is yellowish as in *flavomaculatus*) and placed as follows: a sub-basal one, rounded, as large as in *flavomaculatus*; five forming a central series, the fifth being more extended inwards than in *flavomaculatus* or *niveomaculatus,* and a sub-marginal series represented by a small rounded spot at the upper angle, one below, extended outwards (not both ways as in the two other species), and two in the medium interspaces.

One male, holotype, in the American Museum of Natural History, labelled "Ta-Tsien-Lu, Ost Tibet" and coming from the collection of Mr. E. L. Bell who obtained it from the firm of Staudinger and Bang Haas.

[*Journal of the New York Entomological Society* 49 (1941): 221–23]

The Creative Writer

Excerpt from lecture/essay. Written c. spring 1941 for creative writing summer course that year at Stanford. Published in *Bulletin of the New England Modern Languages Association*, January 1942.

Then, as the thousands of centuries trickled by, and the gods retired on a more or less adequate pension, and human calculations grew more and more acrobatic, mathematics transcended their initial condition and became as it were a natural part of the world to which they had been merely applied. Instead of having numbers based on certain phenomena that they happened to fit because we ourselves happened to fit into the pattern we apprehended, the whole world gradually turned out to be based on numbers, and nobody seems to have been surprised at the queer fact of the outer network becoming an inner skeleton. Indeed, by digging a little deeper somewhere near the waistline of South America a lucky geologist may one day discover, as his spade rings against metal, the solid barrel hoop of the equator. There is a species of butterfly on the hind wing of which a large eyespot imitates a drop of liquid with such uncanny perfection that a line which crosses the wing is slightly displaced at the exact stretch where it passes through – or better say under – the spot: this part of the line seems shifted by refraction, as it would if a real globular drop had been there and we were looking through it at the pattern of the wing. In the light of the strange metamorphosis undergone by exact science from objective to subjective, what can prevent us from supposing that one day a real drop had fallen and had somehow been phylogenetically retained as a spot? But perhaps the funniest consequence of our extravagant belief in the organic being of mathematics was demonstrated some years ago when an enterprising and ingenious astronomer thought of attracting the attention of the inhabitants of Mars, if any, by having huge lines of light several miles long form some simple geometrical demonstration, the idea being that if they could perceive that we knew when our triangles behaved, and when they did not, the Martians would jump to the conclusion that it might be possible to establish contact with those oh so intelligent Tellurians.   [LL 374–75]

From letter to Edmund Wilson,[62] April 29, 1941

From New York.

Two more stories (longer ones, too) are now being translated for the *Monthly*[63] and seem to be shaping out rather well. You will appreciate this: Rakhmaninov has asked me to translate the words of his "Bells" into English.[64] . . . I have also translated some Lermontov poems for my lectures and will soon have to tackle Tute-chev.[65] I have sent a novel I wrote straight in English to New Directions, but I am afraid it may not click. I have described some new species of butterflies in the Museum and have had 8 teeth extracted – howlessly, but the pain *after* the drug stops acting is horrible. So you see I am fairly busy. . . .   [NWL 43–44]

VN with his Russian-language student Dorothy Leuthold, who drove the Nabokovs from New York to Palo Alto, where VN was to teach creative writing, in June 1941. At the Grand Canyon she "kicked up" the first specimen of the butterfly VN named *Neonympha dorothea*.

From letter to Edmund Wilson, May 25, 1941

From New York.

Dear Bunny,

I am driving off to California to-morrow with butterfly-nets, manuscripts and a new set of teeth. I shall be back by Septembre. [*sic*]   [NWL 45]

From letter to Edward Weeks,[66] June 16, 1941

From Palo Alto. Unpublished.

I have been collecting butterflies in deserts and on mountains and have had – and am still having – the time of my life.

[Weeks Collection, University of Texas, Austin]

From letter to Edmund Wilson, September 18, 1941

From Wellesley, Massachusetts.

I have been working a good deal lately in my special branch of entomology, two papers of mine have appeared in a scientific journal, I am describing a new butterfly from the Grand Canyon and am writing a rather ambitious work on mimetic phenomena.[67]   [NWL 48]

Vladimir, Véra, and Dmitri Nabokov and Dorothy Leuthold, traveling west. VN would hunt for butterflies at every suitable stop.

From letter to Edward Weeks, September 19, 1941

From Wellesley, Massachusetts.

It is pathetically dull to watch the good old eastern combination of butterflies on the college lawns here – after my Western orgies: rather like a garden in Cambridgeshire after a summer in the mountains of Spain.

[Weeks Collection, University of Texas, Austin]

From letter of Thomas Barbour[68] to VN, October 17, 1941

Unpublished.

I have been away or you should have heard from me before. Mr. Banks has told me of your visit here and of your interests. I may say that, since he saw you, he has managed to gather together fifty glass trays and only yesterday I placed an order that fifty more should be made. So that, if you see fit to come here and, in your spare time, help bring a little more order into our collection of Lepidoptera, some means will be at your disposal, to say nothing of a warm welcome.   [VNA]

From letter to Mark Aldanov,[69] October 20, 1941

From Wellesley, Massachusetts. In Russian. Unpublished.

I spend a good deal of time on butterflies, describing new species (I discovered a wonderful thing in the Grand Cañon!), working once a week at Harvard's Museum of Comp. Zool., and so on. . . . At the same time I am writing a work on mimicry (with a furious refutation of "natural selection" and the "struggle for life") and a new novel in English.　　　[COLUMBIA]

From letter to Andrey Avinov,[70] January 27, 1942

From Cambridge, Massachusetts. Unpublished.

I am still working on my expanding paper on the Neonympha and have just brought back with me from New York series loaned me by Dos Passos as well as the whole material lumped as "henshawi," from the A.M.N.H.

. . . I have no specimens from *central* Arizona or from Mexico. I am wondering whether you might consent to send me (Museum of Comp. Zool., Cambridge, c/o Dr. Banks) the Carnegie series of *henshawi*, Edwards' specimens included, or at least some from as many localities as possible? I am also badly in need of specimens of *pyracmon*. I would not keep them more than a week. This, I know, is a bothersome request, but both the A.M.N.H. and the M.C.Z. are as anxious as I am to have this 60-year-old muddle straightened out.　　　[VNA]

From letter to William Comstock, February 20, 1942

From Wellesley, Massachusetts. Unpublished.

I am sending you my paper on NEW OR LITTLE KNOWN NORTH AMERICAN NEONYMPHAE. . . .

At first, when examining the sixty specimens or so that had accumulated, I was puzzled to find not *two* different species among them (the new one and *henshawi*) but *three*, all occurring in Arizona. Eventually I realized that the third was *pyracmon* which you will see from the bibliography is also so little known as to have been confused with *henshawi* and which apparently has never been known to occur in the limits of the U.S.A.

Apart from color and the very distinctive markings on secondaries both sides, these three species are easily distinguishable from one another by the sexmark, the form of the wing and the course of the middle line primaries underside. These are absolutely constant characters and I have made the corresponding drawings which I think it would be quite necessary to publish with the article (the only thing that troubles me is the price – I am a poor man, as you know, with no definite income except what I get for this one year in Wellesley). . . .

You will observe that I have only named things when it was quite unavoidable. I have selected the Grand Cañon race as nymotypical not merely because I happened to take that little walk down the slushy mule track from the Bright Angel Lodge in company with a friend who motored my family and me across this Continent – and not only because I know the butterfly from fresh easily described specimens, – but because this form seems to express at their fullest all the characters of the species.

. . . Be sure to tell me whether anything in my paper offends any entomological susceptibilities (except Wiemer – who does not count) and whether my bibliographic references and noting of type specimens are clear enough. I have compressed my article to at least half of what it is in my notes, – but I had to give all the facts regarding original descriptions etc. I do not think it is necessary to wait for any more news about these species as the essentials are now well digested (though I still keep wondering now and then – mainly in trains between Boston and Wellesley – whether the simple distinctions I have brought out have not been made already in some very obscure or very obvious place). If my paper seems all right you will please pass it on to whatever Journal or Proceedings you think would publish it with the least delay. I am taking advantage of your kindness but it is your own fault if I have grown accustomed to it.   [VNA]

From letter to Walter Sweadner,[71] February 22, 1942

From Cambridge, Massachusetts. Unpublished.

I am really very very grateful to you and Dr. Avinov for sending me those Neonympha. They fit nicely with the conclusions I had arrived at on the strength of some 60 specimens I had already studied. It is a great thing to work at these matters when one gets such wonderful support.   [VNA]

Fame

Excerpt from poem in Russian ("Slava"). Written March 21–22, 1942. Published in *Novyy zhumal* 2
(1942). Translated by VN.

> . . . I kept changing countries like counterfeit money,
> hurrying on and afraid to look back,
> like a phantom dividing in two, like a candle
> between mirrors sailing into the sun.
>
> It is far to the meadows where I sobbed in my childhood
> having missed an Apollo,[72] and farther yet
> to the alley of firs where the midday sunlight
> glowed with fissures of fire between bands of jet.
>
> But my word, curved to form an aerial viaduct,
> spans the world, and across in a strobe-effect spin*
> of spokes I keep endlessly passing incognito
> into the flame-licked night of my native land.

[PP 105, 113]

From letter to James Laughlin,[73] April 9, 1942

From Wellesley, Massachusetts.

I am rather in low spirits lately because I have not the vaguest idea what is
going to happen to my family and me next. My Wellesley year[74] ends practically in June and I have not been able to find any academic post for the
next season. I do not know what plans to make for Summer or indeed what
kind of Summer we can afford. I feel a little tired because I seem to be doing

---

*The term renders exactly what I tried to express by the looser phrase in my [Russian] text "sequence of spokelike
shadows." The strobe effect causes wheels to look as if they revolved backward, and the crossing over to America (line
36 ["sailing into the sun"]) becomes an optical illusion of a return to Russia. [VN's note]

too many things at once – my new English novel, two short stories, translations for my lectures, some Russian stuff and a huge scientific paper about certain butterflies I have discovered.   [SL 40]

Some new or little known Nearctic *Neonympha* (Lepidoptera: Satyridae)*

Excerpts from Lepidoptera paper. Researched and written September 1941–April 1942. Published in *Psyche* 49 (September–December 1942 [Published February 1943]).

The capture in Arizona in June 1941 of what struck me as an undescribed species of *Neonympha* suggested certain investigations, the results of which are given in this paper. A study of about a hundred specimens labelled "*henshawi* Edw.," which I accumulated from different sources, revealed that two pairs of geminate[75] species, one pair unnamed, the other neglected, occurred in Arizona. Confusion has been due not so much to some chance obscurity in a great entomologist's description 66 years ago, as to the indifference and consequent lack of precision in regard to this section of *Neonympha* on the part of those who wrote after him. Somehow lepidopterists have never seemed overeager to obtain these delicately ornamented, quickly fading Satyrids that so quaintly combine a boreal-alpine aspect with a tropical-silvan one, the upperside quiet velvet of "browns" being accompanied by an almost Lycænid glitter on the under surface. There exists very little information concerning such things as the number of broods, possible seasonal variation, limits of distribution, allied Mexican and Central American forms, haunts, habits and early stages.

What follows is an attempt to set down the peculiarities of these four insects as a tentative basis for further research that would amplify the comparatively meager facts at my disposal. A definition of the species most usually confused with *henshawi* Edw. and a full description of its typical race, with comparative descriptions of two other races are followed by compar-

---

*Published with the aid of a grant from the Museum of Comparative Zoölogy of Harvard College. [VN's note]

ative descriptions of the three other species, listing their distinctive characters in the same order. The species to be discussed are:

Neonympha dorothea n. sp. (referred to by Edwards as "some specimens" etc., in conjoint description of *henshawi* Edw., 1887, Butt. N. Am., III, *Neonympha* I; reproduced from a female in Edwards' collection as "*henshawi* Edw., male," by Holland, 1898, and later editions, Butt. Book, Pl. 25, fig. 8, upperside.)

Neonympha maniola n. sp. (presumably figured, as "*henshawi*," by Wright, 1905, Butt. W. Coast, Pl. 25, fig. 226 a, b, c, male, upperside, female, both sides).

Neonympha pyracmon Butler (1866, Proc. Zool. Soc., London, p. 499, female; 1867, Proc. Zool. Soc., London, Pl. 11, fig. 11, female, underside; Godman 1901, Biol. Centr. Am. Rhop., II, p. 658; III, Pl. 107, figs. 11, 12, male, both sides, mislabelled "*hilaria*"; Weymer, 1911, in Seitz, Rhop. Am., p. 223).

Neonympha henshawi Edwards (1876, Trans. Am. Ent. Soc., p. 205, female; Godman, 1880, Biol. Centr. Am., Rhop., III, Pl. 8, fig. 27, female, underside, mislabelled "*pyracmon*"; Edwards, 1887, Butt. N. Am., III, Pl. 1, figs. 5–8, both sexes, both sides; Maynard, 1891, Mnl. N. Am. Butt., p. 108, female; fig. 35d, female, hind-wing underside).

Neonympha dorothea n. sp.

Sharing with the other three species such upperside characters as: brownish ground color in male, with more or less diffuse fulvous red; fine fulvous margin, mainly subanal in secondaries; androconial mark in male primaries; præterminal dark spots in secondaries of both sexes; and such underside characters as: more or less fulvous ground color of primaries; small discal button-spot on both wings; four transverse lines, to wit: first discal, crossing cell R + M; second discal, curving round cell (its course in primaries dependent upon specific outline of termen); subterminal, mostly striate in primaries (less adjusted there to differentiation of termen) and mostly incomplete and deformed in secondaries; præterminal, mostly punctate in primaries, and embossed with serrate silver in secondaries where it forms a silver W in Cu_1, passes through two double ocelli in M_3

and M_2 placed within a cinereous irroration, and produces two pairs of V-shaped dashes in M_1 and R_8.

Distinguished from its three congeners as follows: Primaries apically short and rather bluntly rounded, with straight termen; secondaries evenly rounded in both sexes, with very slight sinuation in female; præterminal spots rather blurred.

Androconial mark: medium sized, with fairly smooth outer edge coinciding, except in Cu_2 where it retreats basally, with second discal line as seen through wing; consisting of 5 patches (shading in 2A not included),

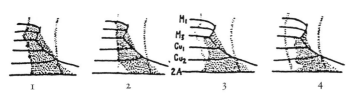

Figs. 1–4. Scheme of androconial patches in *Neonympha*.
1, *N. maniola*; 2, *N. dorothea*; 3, *N. henshawi*; 4, *N. pyracmon*.

adjoining cell and separated by veins, as follows: rhomboid, with sides slanting basally subparallel to cubitus, in Cu_2; two decreasing trapezoids, in Cu_1 and M_3; two wedges in M_2 and M_1; and of short triangle, in cell R + M, against inner side of cross vein, pointing basally and reaching down to about level of Cu_1. (See fig. 2.)

Female upperside: diffusely colored, with slight shadings.

Male and female underside: primaries: second discal line running subparallel to first discal line, curving from costa behind cell to slope down towards subterminal line and thus limiting with the latter a truncate upsilon-shaped area in middle of wing; subterminal line from dorsum up to about Cu_1 running closer to second discal than to termen but then, by retaining a primal course, diverging terminally to reach apex (which would have been costa, had the apex been longer, in which case the subterminal line would have been parallel to a primal, slanting, termen), thus enhancing the impression of the outward slope on the part of the second discal which in reality is subparallel to the straight termen (to which, contrary to the subterminal line, it has become adjusted); secondaries: heavily and completely bordered with dark cinereous which encloses ocelli and silver serration, and expands in M_2 and M_3 where the second discal line is thickly arched inversely to termen.

Neonympha dorothea dorothea n. subsp.

Male: expanse of left fore-wing 20.9 (from base to end of M_1). Upperside: deep brown with lighter veins; some dark fulvous red scales just discernible in between them; cilia fuscous; dark fuscous androconial mark. Primaries very finely edged with fulvous; secondaries more broadly so, but only to about Cu_1 from tornus, with four spots along termen: first one rather indistinct, in Cu_1; second and third subreniform, blotchy, blackish, in M_3 and M_2; and fourth, very weak, in M_1; a fine dark ray (interneural fold) through middle of each reaching the cilia from disc. Underside: primaries: flushed with deep warm red of Erebian ("*callias*") tone over lower part; thickly dusted with yellowish brown and traversed by reddish brown striæ over upper part; lines: chestnut brown; præterminal consisting of very indistinct sequence of dots; small brown discal spot above M_2 near cell $R + M$ on both wings, buttoning top of androconial mark in primaries (if viewed through wing). Secondaries: discally of darker shade of brown than subcostal and subapical areas of primaries; with some redder striæ and a sprinkling of fluffy hoary scales basally; discal lines: deep chestnut brown; the first irregularly crossing cell $R + M$; the second from tornus following serrated (on Cu_2) but fairly direct course up to Cu_1 beyond which it strongly thickens and arches inversely to termen in M_3–M_2, then narrows again, abruptly turns outward as if to end at M_1, just above a roughly V-shaped basally pointed combination of two silver præterminal dashes, but really swerves back again and up towards R_s in which interspace it is almost concealed by a second V-pair of silver dashes which seems superimposed. Subterminal line from tornus arches inversely to termen in Cu_2, dips terminally, then shoots up basally along middle of cell Cu_1 where it stops, forming a thickish chestnut brown bar which coincides with the terminal course of the interneural fold. A broad cinereous border heavily stippled with purplish black transverse striæ, merged with the cinereous underside of the fringe and limited inwardly by the arches of the second discal and subterminal lines, occupies the whole outer third (excepting a vineleaf-shaped, as viewed from base, fulvous brown space between second discal and subterminal lines in C_1–C_2), thus completely enclosing the ocelli and other markings to be mentioned. Examined in its action upon the discal and subterminal lines, it may be described as invading the termen from the tornus, with its inward edge causing the subterminal line to arch inversely to termen in Cu_2, then bursting through in Cu_1, diverting basally the broken end of the subterminal line and swelling strongly towards the second discal; beyond Cu_1 it pushes up even farther, touching (except for a few dusky scales in between) the second discal, which its pressure forces to arch in M_3–M_2, and then reaching the termination of R_8. This border, which produces a strong avian or "scaly" effect, encloses præterminally, in M_3 and M_2, two subreniform (twinned) ocelli, jet-black, each delicately rimmed and threaded through with light fulvous so as to form a capital "B" facing the termen, with the interneural folds faintly traced in a paler tint through the dark cinereous irroration; in each black cell of each "B" a bright silver "T" glitters, its stem projecting basally, its crossbar subparallel to the termen and neither stem nor bar touching the rim. The embossed silver of these four "T" marks is supplied by the breaking up of a silver line which starts from about Cu_2 (in continuation and sublimation of a vaguely discernible dark præterminal line from tornus); forms in Cu_1, upon the interneural ray and beneath the end of the subterminal line, a "W" (as viewed from base), where an ocellus, visible as a spot on the upperside, seems to be in the process of being built with the help of the dark pigment which is channelled terminally by the interneural fold from the end of the subterminal line; then traverses the kernels of the spots in M_3 and M_2 and produces farther up the V-shaped pairs of silver dashes already mentioned; the first pair of these suggests the formation of a rudimental fourth spot whose interneural ray looks like a terminal projection of the second discal line. There is a thin bright fulvous margin from tornus to middle of cell Cu_1, running between the cilia and the silver line (incidentally, in regard to these very *Coenonympha*-like markings, it should be noted that the ocelli in the latter genus are formed subterminally, not præterminally as in this section of *Neonympha*).

Female. Exp. 21.5. Upperside pale reddish brown with pinkish tone. Primaries: with faint adumbration post-cellularly and terminally, but on the whole producing a unicolorous impression. Secondaries: evenly rounded, as in male; with dim greyish shade surrounding the rather blurred and formless dark spots (in M_2, M_3 and Cu_1) and slightly deepening towards apex. Underside as in male.

Male, holotype, female, allotype, and two males, paratypes, placed in the American Museum of Natural History. Taken during a brief visit to Grand Cañon, Ariz., South Rim, on June 9th, 1941 (bright cold morning after snow and rain). They were weakly fluttering beside the trail together with a few *Coen. tullia furcae* – almost no other butterflies about. Named in honor of Miss Dorothy Leuthold who kindly kicked up the first specimen. Female, paratype, labelled "Grand Cy., June 11th '30", ex Coll. of C. F. dos Passos, Am. Mus. Nat. Hist.

Neonympha dorothea edwardsi n. subsp.

Male. Exp. 20.2. Upperside: brown tint somewhat lighter, with much greater amount of duller fulvous red diffused in both wings. Secondaries: spots reduced to two, in M_3 and M_2 (visible also in Cu_1 in some specimens). Underside: striæ somewhat more abundant and conspicuous on both wings. Primaries: pale fulvous brown with light reddish wash in lower part; præterminal line quite clear as a row of dots. Secondaries: fulvous brown; beyond second discal line correspondingly paler than in *dorothea dorothea*. Cinereous border somewhat less developed, i.e. not approaching as close to arched but slightly thinner second discal in M_3 and M_2, thus leaving a narrow but distinct stretch of ground color in between.

Female. Exp. 20.7. Upperside pale reddish brown but lacking the pinkish tone of *dorothea dorothea* – a slight but distinct character connecting it with transitions to the fulvous southern race or races.

Male, holotype, labelled: "Gila Co. Ariz. June 1902, O. C. Poling," ex A. G. Weeks Coll., Museum of Comparative Zoology, Cambridge, Mass.; female, allotype, "Ariz. 1892, C. J. Paine," Mus. Comp. Zool. Paratypes: 3 males "Gila Co. Ariz. June 1902, O. C. Poling," ex A. G. Weeks Coll., Mus. Comp. Zool.; 2 males and 1 female "Ariz. 1892, C. J. Paine," Mus. Comp. Zool.; male and female, from "Ariz\ª," wrongly labelled "*Henshawi* M" in Edwards' hand, ex Edwards' Coll., Carnegie Museum (it is the female of this pair that Holland figures as "*henshawi* Edw., male" with the remark "much like N. *gemma*, but considerably larger and decidedly reddish upon the upperside"; 1 male "Water Cañon, N. Mex., 5,000 ft. August '81, F. H. Snow" ex Edwards' Coll., Carn. Mus.; 1 male "Fort Wingate (N. Mex.), June '23, Marloff Coll.," Carn. Mus.; 2 males "Colorado" (one "Coll. Hy Edw."), 1 female "Colorado, Coll. Hy Edw.", Am. Mus. Nat. Hist.

(I should have preferred taking as holotype the male from Edwards' collection were it not for the awkwardness of having such a vague locality as "Ariz^a" for the type of a race.)

Neonympha dorothea avicula n. subsp.

Male. Exp. 17.6. Upperside: primaries, fuscous, less brown than *dorothea dorothea,* with the dark fuscous androconial shading standing out very clearly; two large bright fulvous red patches in Cu$_1$ and M$_3$ and a similar bright tint along the veins involved in this area. The fulvous is so conspicuous and the fuscous so vague (and so much lighter than the sexmark), that the eye is inclined to accept the former as ground color. Secondaries: somewhat darker than primaries with only a slight suggestion of fulvous red in disc and two indistinct præterminal spots in M$_3$ and M$_2$. Underside: ground color of both wings a dull dunnish brown, very different from the rich and contrasting shades in *dorothea dorothea,* and of a remarkably even appearance owing to the almost total lack of (brown) striæ, which are only faintly discernible about the costa and base of both wings. Primaries: lines very faint, with the first discal hardly differentiated from the striæ; but the discernible directions of the lines are naturally those of the species. Secondaries: first discal indistinct; second discal thickening and arching strongly, of a duller brown than in *dorothea dorothea* or *edwardsi.* Cinereous border as dark and rich as in typical race, but pressing against second discal in M$_3$–M$_2$ completely, without even the presence of a few dusky scales in between. Ocelli a trifle smaller than the smaller size of the insect might justify; silver serration and brown bar well developed; terminal fulvous line broader anally than in *dorothea dorothea.*

Female. Exp. 18.5. Upperside of a very *Cœnonympha*-like appearance stressed by small size and fulvous tone which slightly deepens in primaries in area corresponding to that limited by the discal lines beneath, but not showing any definite bands or lines, only a pale fuscous border merging with a similar shading along the costa. Secondaries: with a slight sinuation in termen unimpairing their "dorothean" roundness and correspondence to primaries; well shaded with greyish; light fulvous in disc and beyond that slightly irrorated with the trans-wing shadows of the heavily striated cinereous border beneath. Underside: rather more contrasty than in male. Primaries: yellowish with faint fulvous red flush over lower part; marked as in male. Secondaries: as in male except for a slight olivaceous brown deepening of the dull ground color.

Male, holotype, female, allotype, and female, paratype, all three labelled "Fort Davis, Texas, 3.VI.40," female, paratype, exp. 20.5, same label, with the addition "6,500 f." All these ex Coll. C. F. dos Passos, Am. Mus. Nat. Hist.

The fixation of these three definite racial points, *dorothea dorothea*, *dorothea edwardsi* and *dorothea avicula* is, I think, unavoidable, but one does not care to indulge in pursuing this course and giving names to the various transitions which occur between them, especially as some of these variations seem to be seasonal. It will be noted that the holotypes of all three races were taken in June. Fifteen smallish specimens, twelve males, three females (Carn. Mus.), from Paradise, Ariz. taken by Poling late in the season (August–October) represent a certain transition from *edwardsi* to *avicula*; another kind of transition between the same is represented by two males from Silver City, South New Mexico, ex coll. dos Passos, Am. Mus. Nat. Hist. . . .

[*Psyche* 49: 61–68]

Neonympha maniola n. sp.

. . . I have felt somewhat reluctant to fix this as a species, as there are no females in any of the collections I have examined. *Maniola* is closely allied to *dorothea*; but granted that androconial mark, wing shape, behavior of second discal and subterminal lines, and certain peculiarities of scaling, such as disclosed by the cinereous irroration, constitute specific characters in this group (if they do not, then one arrives at the absurd conclusion that there is only one "good" species, *gemma* Hübner, with ab. *pyracmon*, ab. *henshawi*, ab. *maniola*, ab. *dorothea* etc. not even as races, for they occur together in different combinations) I cannot very well see how *maniola* can be placed alongside the *dorothea* races described, which all have a system of common characters quite inapplicable to *maniola*.

The third species, *pyracmon* Butl., is newly added here to the fauna of North America, although for many years specimens, labelled "henshawi" in collections, have been coming from Arizona. The Biol. Centr. Am. figure of "*Pyracmon*" female underside, totally different from Butler's figure, refers obviously to a form of *henshawi,* while the beautifully executed portrait of *pyracmon* male, with underside, is designated as "*hilaria*" (an error corrected in the text). Butler's figure of the underside is coarsely colored, being, with the other butterflies on the plate, too dusky and though illustrating, as it purports to do, a female, produces a wrong impression, simulating a male. Thus, *pyracmon* is pretty well concealed from the collector. However, a careful examination of Butler's text and figure convinces me that the Biol. Centr. Am. does illustrate the male of Butler's species, and with this figure the Arizonian insect tallies nicely. Unfortunately, I have not been able to obtain Mexican specimens or to get a photograph of the type from England. . . .   [*Psyche* 49: 70]

It remains to tackle the fourth species. In 1876 W. H. Edwards, working, it may be assumed, in a bad light (note the "plumbaginous"), thus described a new "Euptychia":

"Euptychia henshawi, n. sp. male. Exp. 1.5 inch. Upperside light fuscous, immaculate. Underside of primaries russet, deepest along inner margin, brownish towards costa; crossed by four wavy ferruginous lines, one of which is parallel to the hind margin, midway between cell and margin, one just beyond cell and curving around it to costa, the third crosses middle of cell and the fourth is a demi-line ending at median nervure; there are also four transverse streaks near base of wing. Secondaries grey-brown, slightly russet tinted, crossed by two ferruginous lines, the outer one irregular, wavy towards margin, shaded on its inner side: the outer, near base, rather zigzag than wavy; some fine streaks on basal area; the hind margin ashy brown streaked with dark ferruginous; showing four black eyelets, small, equal, placed near the edge of the wing, in pairs on the upper median and next upper interspaces, each with a plumbaginous streak across the marginal side and through the middle, but not reaching quite across; irregular streaks or slight patches of dull silver in the interspaces both towards outer and inner angle; the margin next inner angle edged with ferruginous. Body above fuscous, beneath gray, the abdomen buff, legs gray; palpi gray with black hair in front; antennæ fuscous, imperfectly annulated with whitish; club fuscous above, russet below.

"Female. Exp. 1.7 inch. Both wings russet in disc, primaries most brightly. The margins fuscous as is also costal edge of primaries; on secondaries the eyelets of underside are indicated by small dark fuscous spots. Underside as in male.

"From Arizona and New Mexico, collected in 1874 by H. W. Henshaw of the Wheeler expedition in honor of whom I name the species, and in 1875 by Lieut. W. C. Carpenter."

The description of the male is worthless for all purposes of determination and I have ignored it in my bibliographical summary. A light fuscous Neonympha expanding 1.5 inch with no markings, red flush or androconial brand might be, for all one knows, an oversized *gemma* – although on the other hand it is possible to argue that the describer was merely in a hurry to get to the interesting underside. The "demi-line" obviously refers to some chance sequence of striæ (and what is further left without comment fits at least seven species of *Neonympha*). Size, ground color of underside and description of lines in secondaries underside apply perhaps better to *dorothea edwardsi* than to the species which I hold to be the true *henshawi* Edw. The words "New Mexico," where *henshawi* is not yet known to occur, suggest that there were some specimens of *edwardsi* (not however the one taken, much later, by Snow) among the series Edwards was examining as he wrote. On the other hand, the description of the lines in primaries upperside and of the cinereous scaling in secondaries underside does not fit *edwardsi* (or any race of *dorothea*) at all: it exactly fits *henshawi*. In fact, if this male were a hybrid between the two, with moreover a strain of *gemma*, it could not have been better described. Such a freak being unlikely, I am forced to dismiss this confused and composite picture altogether as not applying to any known insect.

The description of the female however is that of a fairly recognisable *henshawi* (a form of which was figured as *pyracmon* by Godman four years later) differing from the female of *dorothea* in the two main details cited: "russet in the disc, primaries most brightly" and "small dark fuscous spots" which in *dorothea* are comparatively large and dim. As the tint which Edwards calls "russet" seems to be on the yellow, rather than on the red side (for example, the costal yellowish brown of the primaries underside in *dorothea* or the ground color upperside in female *avicula*), "russet" cannot apply to the pale reddish female of *dorothea edwardsi*, a specimen of which Edwards had. "Underside as in male" merely suggests that when Edwards picked up the fresher female of the two he possessed, a *henshawi*, the general impression he had formed from the inspection of his mixed males was based less on his specimens of *dorothea*, than on those of *henshawi*. But again, the back of an entomologist's mind is not a very sound basis for the deciphering of his descriptions, and so a further accumulation of clues is necessary.

In 1887, 11 years later, Edwards, in one of the finest works on butterflies ever published, gave a lovely plate illustrating his species, the models being a male and female from his collection. These are before me as I write and are not *dorothea edwardsi*. Except that the termen in the female is perhaps not sinuated enough, these figures are admirable. The accompanying description, which is far superior to the original one, will be examined presently. Edwards adds that the resemblance of his species to *gemma* is close in regard to the markings, and describes the egg which Doll sent him from Arizona in 1881, but which did not hatch (thus leaving us in doubt as to which of four possible species laid the dome-shaped turquoise blue ovum Edwards figures). In 1891, Charles J. Maynard described *N. henshawi* Edw. ("Henshaw's Quaker") as follows: "About the size of the type *N. euritris*, but is more reddish or rusty above, a dark band crosses middle of both wings, and there are two black dots in middle of outer border. Beneath finely marked with minute lines between the common bands. On outer portion of fore wings there is a wavy band but no spots. In the middle of hind wing is a whitish space containing four dots in pairs, each with a silver center. Above and below these are silver markings." There is not a shadow of doubt that this blunt description refers to the species (though not to the same specimen) that Edwards figured, and the humble woodcut Maynard gives of the underside of a female right hind wing represents that species quite unmistakably – which is a highly important moment in the nomenclatorial history of this unfortunate butterfly, and which would have prevented me, if nothing else did, from switching the name *henshawi* to the species *dorothea* had I wished to retain the more familiar name for a butterfly which appears to be more widely distributed this side of the border. Godman's mention of "*henshawi*" (II, p. 658) may as well refer to *dorothea*; Weymer's description of "*henshawi*" in what Holland politely calls a "monograph" of the *Neonympha* is much too slapdash and muddled to be taken into any account at all.

But to return to Edwards' description in Butt. N. Am.:

"Male. Exp. 1.5 inch. Upperside dark brown, often with russet over the extra-discal areas of both wings; some examples have an ill defined patch of russet on the median interspaces of primaries, and there is usually a russet edging to hind margin secondaries next anal angle; on the middle of same margin two small black spots not always present; fringes dark grey. Underside either brown or russet, thickly dusted with yellow-white scales, more yellow beyond the discal band of secondaries; the whole surface finely streaked and dotted with red brown; primaries crossed by three wavy red brown lines, two of which enclose the discal band, the other lying nearly midway between the band and margin, often macular; some examples have a demi-line crossing cell to median; the discal lines are continued across secondaries, the outer one often projecting roundly on second subcostal nervule; a short sinuous line an anal angle; on middle of hind margin a large suboval patch, the ground of which is dark brown, sprinkled with whitish scales; within this, in upper median and discoidal interspaces, a pair of velvet black spots, each with an inverted "T" shaped patch of silver; in the interspaces towards outer angle a pair of silver dashes each, and in lower median a silver serration, and a bar in submedian. Body above dark brown, beneath grey brown; legs same; palpi grey with many black hairs; antennæ blackish, annulated with light; club black above, ferruginous at tip and beneath.

"Female. Exp. 1.7 inch.; russet, brown about the margin; spots on secondaries as in male. Underside of primaries russet, of secondaries yellow brown; marked like the male.

"New Mexico, Arizona, Colorado. First taken by H. W. Henshaw of the Wheeler Exploring Expedition, 1874. Morrison afterwards brought examples from Arizona and B. Neumoegen from Oak Creek Canon, Colorado."

It is evident that here again Edwards had a series of mixed specimens before him. Only the Arizona ones, and not all of them, were *henshawi*. The "patch of russet" coming directly after the "russet" of the first line is not mere repetition, but seems to imply the difference that Edwards might have noticed between Henshaw's specimens with diffuse fulvous and a fulvous patched New Mexican race of *dorothea*. The "not always present" is less an excuse for the "immaculate" of the original description than an impression produced by the contrast between the distinct spots of *henshawi* and the rather dim blotches of *dorothea*. The abundantly steaked yellow underside is *henshawi* all over; so is the continuation of the lines from primaries across secondaries. The "often roundly projecting" refers to specimens of *dorothea*. The "suboval patch" is again *henshawi*. The original description of the female has been slightly revised as Edwards was evidently puzzled at having such different specimens of females. But taken all in all, I think we can distinguish here, through the fade-out of *dorothea*, an elegant and correct delineation of both sexes of the species which in 1887 corresponded to Edwards' final concept of his *henshawi*, the butterfly figured.

An examination of the eight specimens which are labelled, I understand, by Edwards himself, and come from his collection (now in the Carnegie Museum) reveals that five of these are *dorothea edwardsi* while the other three (two males and one female) represent the insect which I here definitely fix as *Neonympha henshawi*. There is no doubt in my mind that the female belongs to the same colony as the two males, and there is a reasonable amount of probability that it is the exact specimen of the original description which in the corresponding passage conveys rather neatly the general impression produced by this remarkably well conserved female. This noted, the following summary of distinctive characters will settle the identity of N. *henshawi*. . . .

[*Psyche* 49: 73–77]

A few words may be added concerning the male armature of the four species under consideration. In *dorothea* the uncus looks straighter and the clasp broader (more arched dorsally and fuller ventrally) than in *maniola, pyracmon* or *henshawi*. I do not perceive much difference between the organs of *pyracmon* and *henshawi*, except perhaps a slightly thinner uncus in the latter. Of the four species, *maniola* seems to have the narrowest clasp (concave ventrally, with elongated spur). Partly because several superficial characters proved sufficient to easily separate the four species, and partly because the number of specimens representing each was not compatible with a long series of dissection, the examination of the male armature was limited to half a dozen preparations, two of which were made for me by Mr. W. P. Comstock at the American Museum of Natural History. For the genitalia of *maniola* I used a slide prepared in 1934 by Dr. Marson Bates. Judging by the fact that he prepared a slide of *dorothea* too, it seems fair to suppose that he had noticed the difference between these two insects long before I did. Further study might reveal whether the shape of the clasps is constant (it was identical in 3 specimens of *dorothea*), or, if not, what is the specific scope of its variation.

In conclusion, my thanks are due to Mr. W. P. Comstock of the American Museum of Natural History for his invariable assistance and advice, and for the loan of their material; to Mr. C. F. dos Passos for loaning me his specimens; to Prof. Nathan Banks for placing at my disposal the series of the Museum of Comparative Zoology; to Dr. C. T. Parsons of that institution for assisting me in several matters; to Dr. A. Avinoff and Dr. W. R. Sweadner of the Carnegie Museum who not only patiently answered my queries concerning the Edwards series, but did me the exceptional favor of sending me all the "*henshawi*" material of the Carnegie Museum.

[*Psyche* 49: 80]

From letter from Gladys McCosh,[76] April 20, 1942

Unpublished.

We are looking forward to your lecture on "The Theory and Practice of Mimicry" on Wednesday afternoon, April 29. It will be in room 100 Sage Hall at three-forty o'clock (3.40 P.M.) The lecture will be announced in the weekly bulletin.[77]   [VNA]

From letter to Edmund Wilson, April 30, 1942

From Wellesley, Massachusetts. Published in *Briefwechsel mit Edmund Wilson*.

Dear Bunny,
    I just want to tell you that I shall be coming[78] alone *Saturday.* . . .
    I am bringing Pushkin and my butterfly net.   [YALE]

From letter to Mark Aldanov, May 20, 1942

From Wellesley.

I have finished my big work on "Some New or Little Known Nearctic Neo-nympha," and the Am. Mus. of Nat. Hist. is paying for the drawings. I work two days a week in the Harvard Mus. of Comp. Zool., where I now rule alone over the Lepidoptera section, since my lab assistant has gone off to war.   [COLUMBIA]

From letter to Edmund Wilson, June 16, 1942

From Wellesley, Massachusetts.

Funny – to know Russian better than any living person – in America at least, – and more English than any Russian in America, – and to experience such difficulty in getting a university job. I am rather jittery about next year. The only thing I have managed to obtain is the position of research fellow, for one year (1200 dollars) beginning Sept. 1, at the Mus Comp Zool – three hours a day and all the butterflies at my disposal. If I could combine this with college lectures it would be perfect. And of course I would chuck it if I got a better position elsewhere.   [NWL 66]

From letter to Edmund Wilson, June 30, 1942

From West Wardsboro, Vermont. Published in *Briefwechsel mit Edmund Wilson*.

The io-moth and its elegant companion are in the museum labelled "Coll. Edm. Wilson, Cape Cod."   [YALE]

somebody left a pair of old shoes in the grass
as sometimes happens.

From letter to James Laughlin, July 16, 1942

From West Wardsboro, Vermont.

Vermont is very pleasant and beautiful – although beautiful in a kind of go-belin way, and of course lacking the floral versatility of the West. The other day I got a butterfly here which has never been recorded yet from this state: *Colias interior* Scudder which was first found by Agassiz on the North shore of Lake Superior.[79]   [SL 40–41]

From letter to Edmund Wilson, August 9, 1942

From West Wardsboro, Vermont.

I am going to Cambridge on the 31st of August as my duties at the Mus. Comp. Zool. begin on the 1st of Sept. We have taken a flat there – 8 Craigie

Circle. It is amusing to think that I managed to get into Harvard with a butterfly as my sole backer. I am capturing a good deal of them here, chiefly moths. It is one of the most perfect pleasures I know of – to open the window wide on a muggy night and watch them come. Each has its own lampside manner: one will settle quietly on the wall to be boxed in comfort, another will dash and bang against the lampshade before falling with quivering wings and burning eyes upon the table, a third will wander all over the ceiling. The system is to have several tumblers with a piece of "carbona" soaked cotton-wool stuck to the bottom, and you overturn the tumbler upon the bug. When stunned it is transferred to another jar to be pinned later. Tonight I shall sugar for them: you mix: a bottle of stale beer, two pounds of brown sugar (or treacle) and a little rum (added just before applying); then just before dusk you smear (with a clean paint brush) a score of tree trunks (preferably old lichened ones) with the concoction and wait. They will come from nowhere, settling on the glistening bark and showing their crimson underwings (especially brilliant in the flashlight) and you cover them with a tumbler beginning with the lower ones. Try, Bunny, it is the noblest sport in the world. [NWL 69]

From letter to Véra Nabokov, October 2–4, 1942

From Coker College, Hartsville, South Carolina. In Russian. Unpublished.

My darling,

A million butterflies and a thousand ovations (to make allowance for fervent Southern cordiality). About ten I came back with Mrs Coker, and after noticing some very interesting moths on the brightly lit columns of the pediment spent about an hour gathering them in a glass with carbona. You can imagine how tired I was after this mix-up of a day, but I had a marvelous sleep and the next morning read the Tragedy of Tragedy lecture (to finish with the lecture theme: today's, the third and last, also in the morning, was a reading of "Mlle O"; for all this I got a cheque today, a hundred dollars, which I'll change on Monday).

In front of the house is a huge garden, huge trees around, various kinds of live oaks, and in one corner flowerbeds and the surprising candy smell of "tea olive" – all this in the blue of a Crimean summer – with masses of butterflies. I caught them there after my lecture, and after lunch the biologist of the college (rather like Miss McCosh) drove me to the woods or rather coppices by the lake, where I caught wonderful Hesperids and various sorts of Pierids. I wanted to send to my dear Mityushenka one of the very broad local Papilios, but they are torn so I'll send *eubule*,[80] the most prominent local butterfly, which I'll soften and spread when I get back. . . . Today after The Tragedy of Tragedies I set off collecting again and again it was wonderful. And after lunch appeared a Presbyterian minister named Smythe, a passionate butterfly collector and the son of the well-known lepidopterist Smythe, whom I knew all about, he worked on Sphingids. Both of us, the clergyman and I, set off with our nets to a new locality several miles away and collected to 4:30. There I caught something for Banks, the fly *Chrysoptera*. . . .

I hope that at the next lecture stop there will be as many butterflies but less cordiality and less scotch on the rocks. I haven't spent a cent here so far and Fisher[81] writes me that in Valdosta they are ready to put me up as long as I want. Tomorrow apart from still another Coker dinner with the local gentry there don't seem to be any engagements, and I'll go off on a longer butterfly hunt. Here there is one large long-tailed Hesperid,[82] with a kind of peacock fluff on its body, charming. A great many here have read my little things in the *Atlantic* and the *New Yorker* and in general the atmosphere is the same middle-brow one as at Wellesley. . . . The minister and I collected many interesting caterpillars, which *he* will raise. I'd like a drink – all the glasses have carbona.

There you are, darling, a full account of Thursday-Friday-Saturday. I hope you've been at the museum too, I'll write Banks in a few days. I'll let him know I'm staying a few days more than I thought (by the way Fisher still hasn't sent me the next itinerary, only a postcard about Valdosta). I'm madly impatient to return to you and to the museum, and it's only when I'm shoving my way through the shrubbery after some *Thecla* that I feel it's been worth coming here. . . . One lady, who was complaining about a caterpillar in the garden, and to whom I said they give rise to swallowtailed butterflies, answered: "I don't think so. I have never seen them grow wings or anything."   [VNA, MTRX]

From letter to Véra Nabokov, October 11, 1942

From Spelman College, Atlanta, Georgia. In Russian. Unpublished.

Not many butterflies here, a thousand feet above sea level, I hope there are more in Valdosta. As before I am not spending a cent. My lecture on Pushkin and his Negro blood was greeted with almost comical enthusiasm. I decided to finish it too with a reading of "Mozart and Salieri." Apart from that, I spent some time in a biology class, spoke about mimicry, and the day before yesterday went with a woman teacher and a group of black girls, very intensely chewing gum in an open wooden motor-coach some 20 miles from here. . . . I am working on Gogol. Hot cloudless weather, and when I go out after butterflies my pants and shirt get covered with green armour: hooked seeds like tiny burdocks. . . . Store the prepared trays in with my Lycaenids but to the left of them. I caught some interesting flies for Banks and will write him in a few days.   [VNA, MTRX]

From letter to Véra Nabokov, October 12, 1942

From Atlanta. In Russian. Unpublished.

I am sending Mityushenka a wonderful longtailed Hesperid, and you a check for a hundred dollars, which they rather unexpectedly gave me here in Spelman, although it was agreed that my eloquence would earn only room and board.   [VNA, MTRX]

From letter to Véra Nabokov, October 14, 1942

From Georgia State College for Women, Valdosta, Georgia. In Russian. Unpublished.

After lunch I asked the president to take me to the fields, which he did. I caught charming butterflies for an hour and a half, then he picked me up and brought me back to my hotel. . . .

VN, with glass tray of butterflies and students of Georgia State College for Women, Valdosta, which he visited as part of a lecture tour in October 1942.

Thanks for going to the museum. Look after the Pierids (*Pieris, Colias, Euchloe*, and so on – ask Banks) when you have repinned all the Satyrids.

[VNA, MTRX]

From letter to Véra Nabokov, October 17–18, 1942

From Valdosta, Georgia. In Russian. Unpublished.

Yesterday I gave a reading of "Mademoiselle O," and in the evening talked to the biologists about mimicry. Today there was a meeting of the Readers' Forum, and I read "Mozart and Salieri." I collected butterflies, played tennis with President Reade, he is a perfectly dazzling man, with the irrationality of a Wilson and the knowledge of a Thompson.[83] . . . Today (it's now 11 P.M., Sunday) I was driven out by a biology teacher (when I mention women biologists, always think of Miss McCosh's features) into wonderful palmetto wilds and pine groves where I collected butterflies from 10 to 2. It was bliss, flowers I've never seen before (one of which I'm sending for Mityusha), violet berries of *Carocarpa americana, Myrica* bushes, palmettos, cypresses, hot sun, huge grasshoppers and lots of the most interesting butterflies (including one *Neonympha*). I got lost in these sunny thickets and don't know how I got out to the road again, where near the car the biologist was standing up to her knees in ditchwater collecting some of her watery small fry. The only torment is all the thorns that tear my net and gouge my legs. We are on the very border of Florida and the flora and fauna are the same, but I'd very much like to get (about 150 miles) to the Gulf of Mexico, where it's still warmer. This has been my best collecting. . . . Despite the butterflies, I miss you *terribly*, my dear darling.   [VNA, MTRX]

From letter to Véra Nabokov, October 20, 1942

Between Atlanta, Georgia, and Cowan, Tennessee. In Russian. Unpublished.

Please, drop Miss Read[84] a couple of lines: "My husband has been telling me so much about you in his letters that I almost feel as if I knew you," some such thing, and thank her for "all the kindness that you and your wonderful college showed him." She gave me for Mityushen'ka a real war compass, and gave me a huge image of a detail from an Egyptian fresco with butterflies, about which I'll write something.[85] All in all, it's hard to describe the attention she has surrounded me with.   [VNA, MTRX]

From letter to Edmund Wilson, November 3, 1942

From Cambridge, Massachusetts.

I have been working hard in my Museum these few days I have stolen from my tour; and I have been ill. I am not very eager to renew my jogging. There will not be any lepidoptera in Illinois and Minnesota. A child in Georgia called a butterfly a "flutter-by" – which almost solves the puzzling origin of that word (a good try was a "better fly" i.e. larger, brighter than other flies).

               [NWL 86]

From letter to Véra Nabokov, November 5, 1942

From Chicago. In Russian. Unpublished.

I had an ideal journey to Chicago and spent an ideal day in the wonderful museum here, the Field Museum. I found my *Neonymphas*, showed how to arrange them, talked and lunched with a very nice entomologist who somehow knew I was on a lecture tour, as if it was in some museum journal.

[VNA, MTRX]

From letter to Véra Nabokov, November 7, 1942

From Springfield, Illinois. In Russian. Unpublished.

I got on very well with the director of the state museum, MacGregor, a really wonderful museum with a wonderful collection of butterflies and undescribed fossil insects that will be sent to Carpenter[86] in my museum. . . .

[VNA, MTRX]

From letter to Edmund Wilson, November 25, 1942

From Cambridge, Massachusetts.

[From a catalog of curious encounters on his lecture tour.]

4) Man in shirtsleeves at my hotel.[87] Stuck out his pink head as I was walking along the passage to my room about 10 P.M. and suggested a night-cap. I did not want to offend him, so we sat on his bed and had some whiskey. He had been evidently bored to death and was now making much out of my skimpy company. Began telling me, with copious details, all about his sugar business in Florida, his reasons of coming to Valdosta (to hire colored labor) and lots of extravagant particularities about his factory. My whole body felt like one big yawn. I kept peeping at my watch – thought I'd give him another 10 minutes and then turn in. As I was fumbling in my pocket for matches, a little pill-box I used for collecting moths on lighted porches fell out and rolled on the floor. He picked it up and remarked:

"might be mine: I use these for collecting moths." He turned out to be an entomologist who had at one time been in touch with the Am. Mus. Nat. Hist. where I had worked. I did not look at my watch any more. It is the second time I have been fooled that way (first time was with Prof. Forbes[88] in a Boston subway).   [NWL 88]

From letter to Véra Nabokov, December 7, 1942

From Farmville, Virginia. In Russian. Unpublished.

I saw Moe,[89] and it turned out that he's a very close friend of Barbour. "Well, you must be a jolly good man if Tom Barbour took you!" . . . I saw Comstock, Sanford and Mitchener, who proved to be a very nice young man (it appears that it was he, not Comstock, who did those magnificent drawings for me). I had to do preparations and drawings of the genitalia of my *Lysandra cormion*, but it turned out that that and all the other types had been transferred to an entomological institute fifty miles from New York. The next morning (a Saturday) it was fetched for me from there and I devoted myself to it to my heart's content.   [VNA, MTRX]

A Discovery

Poem. Written December 1942. Published (as "On Discovering a Butterfly") in the *New Yorker*, May 15, 1943.

> I found it in a legendary land
> all rocks and lavender and tufted grass,
> where it was settled on some sodden sand
> hard by the torrent of a mountain pass.
>
> The features it combines mark it as new
> to science: shape and shade – the special tinge,
> akin to moonlight, tempering its blue,
> the dingy underside, the checquered fringe.

My needles have teased out its sculptured sex;
corroded tissues could no longer hide
that priceless mote now dimpling the convex
and limpid teardrop on a lighted slide.

Smoothly a screw is turned; out of the mist
two ambered hooks symmetrically slope,
or scales like battledores of amethyst
cross the charmed circle of the microscope.

I found it and I named it, being versed
in taxonomic Latin; thus became
godfather to an insect and its first
describer – and I want no other fame.

Wide open on its pin (though fast asleep),
and safe from creeping relatives and rust,
in the secluded stronghold where we keep
type specimens it will transcend its dust.

Dark pictures, thrones, the stones that pilgrims kiss,
poems that take a thousand years to die
but ape the immortality of this
red label on a little butterfly.[90]

[PP 155–56]

From letter to Edmund Wilson, December 13, 1942

From Cambridge, Massachusetts.

I loved the bit about languages – though personally I would not have compared <<ж>> to a butterfly – good as the resemblance is – for you see <<ж>> is most essentially the symbol of *beetle*, жукъ, жужжание, жудъ, etc., – and so when I look at that letter I see a coleopteron on its back with legs outspread – not having made up its mind whether to sham dead or perform the six-limbed passes that might help it to turn over. . . .

I envy so bitterly your intimacy with English words, tumbling them as you do, that it seems rather silly to send you the poem[91] you will find on a separate page. . . . I wrote it on my way to Washington where I went for the only purpose of sorting out some butterflies I had described (not the one referred to here, which is in New York and which I visited too – and also had a drink with Pierce[92]). Wars pass, bugs stay. Do please give it an expert look soon, because I want to send it [to] the *NYr*, and need money badly.

[NWL 90–91]

From letter to Edmund Wilson, January 12, 1943

From Cambridge, Massachusetts.

The Californian *Lycaeides anna* Edw. has proved to be a subspecies of *L. argyrognomon* Bergstr. of the Palaearctic region; and an unnamed subspecies of *cleobis* Brem., a Siberian butterfly, is distributed through Saskatchewan, Alberta, Idaho, Wyoming and Colorado. These are two of the many remarkable discoveries I am making by examining hundreds of ♂ genitalia. *Lycaeides melissa* Edw. is of course quite a separate species.   [NWL 94]

From letter to C. A. Pearce, c. January 18, 1943

From Cambridge, Massachusetts. Unpublished.

Yes, of course: "horny"[93] must go. I never really liked it. I had sculptured in one of my first drafts, and I think it is nearer to what I wanted to convey. . . .

I am most grateful to you for saving that line from an ignorance-is-bliss disaster. And that nightmare pun . . . This has somewhat subdued me – I was getting rather pleased with my English.   [VNA]

From letter to Edmund Wilson, March 7, 1943

From Cambridge, Massachusetts.

I hope you will enjoy reading my new paper on Lepidoptera,[94] which I am appending. Try reading it *between* the descriptions – though there are some fine bits in them too.   [NWL 96]

Letter to William Comstock, April 7, 1943

From Cambridge, Massachusetts. Unpublished.

Dear Mr. Comstock,

This is disappointing. I cannot postpone my trip, as I have some lectures to deliver in Virginia and am stopping in New York on my way there for one day. I must be back in Cambridge not later than the 19th. Briefly what I wanted to discuss with Mr. dos Passos amounts to the following:

the numerous forms of *Lycaeides* fall into *five* specific unities according to certain constant proportions between certain parts of the uncus & subunci? (sulunci): *argyrognomon* Bergstr.-Kirby, *ismenias* meig., *cleobis* Brem., *melissa* Edw. and *agnata* Stdgr. The first *four* are represented in America by various forms. Unfortunately a number of these are still unnamed or go under obviously wrong names in collections. I am mainly interested in following up the morphological affinities between the Palaearctic and Nearctic forms, – not in naming things; but on the other hand I find it very inconvenient to have no names – or doubtful names – for phylogenetically important forms. It would be for instance a boon and a blessing if Mr. dos Passos published a paper in which he would fix the Canadian (Winnipeg L.)[95] insect (which is a form of *cleobis*) as *scudderi* Edw. and give a name to the New York insect (which is a form of *melissa*) – calling it for instance "samuelis" in honor of the great entomologist who really discovered it and figured its armature half a century ago.

I feel that it is very difficult to discuss these matters by letter and therefore I think a personal interview with dos Passos highly necessary. I do not know when I shall be able to come to New York again. Anyway I am very much looking forward to seeing you on the 15th if possible, and perhaps we can then devise some plan.

Yours cordially,

(Signed) V. NABAKOV   [Dos Passos Collection, AMNH]

From letter from Cyril dos Passos to William Comstock, April 10, 1943

Mr. Nabakov's [*sic*] letter is very interesting and it may well be that there is something to it. We always felt that the Albany *scudderi* was different from typical *scudderi* but this is one of the many matters I have never been able to get to. Now that I am tied up with Grey[96] on the *Argynnis* matter and the summer is coming on with its long vacation, it is impossible to promise to take up the matter within the near future.

[Dos Passos Collection, AMNH]

The Female of *Neonympha maniola* Nabokov (Lepid.-Satyridae)

Lepidopterological note. Written in 1943. Published in *Psyche* 50 (March–June 1943) [Published March 6, 1944].

Since describing this species (1943, Psyche, **49**: 68), I have found three specimens of its female (two labelled, "Paradise, Ariz.," one "So. Ariz.") in the collection of the United States National Museum. My reference (l.c. pp. 62, 69, 70) to Wright's figures has proved to be correct.   [*Psyche* 50: 33]

From Minutes of the Cambridge Entomological Club, April 12, 1943

597th Meeting

The regular meeting of the Cambridge Entomological Club was held in the Biological Laboratories on Monday April 12, 1943 with ten members and guests present. Dr. Bequaert, in the absence of the President Banks, called the meeting to order at 8 o'clock. The secretary's minutes of the preceding meeting were accepted as read. The club taking note of the fact that on the morrow Mr. Banks would celebrate his seventy-fifth birthday, commended his long service to Entomology in general and to the Museum of

Comparative Zoology in particular and the hope was expressed that he would honor the club with an address on the occasion of the next meeting.

The scientific program of the evening was in the hands of Dr. Vladamir [*sic*] Nabokov who read from his as yet unpublished book a chapter entitled "Mimicry in Theory and Practice"[97] – a reading, the entertaining informativeness and clarity of which these prosaic minutes could hardly attempt to capture.

After considerable stimulating discussion the meeting adjourned at 9:15.

Respectfully submitted,

G.E. ERIKSON

(secretary)   [Harvard, MCZ]

From letter to Edmund Wilson, postmarked April 23, 1943

From Cambridge, Massachusetts.

The weather in Virginia was perfectly dreadful and except for a few *Everes comyntas* there was nothing on the wing; but Sweet Briar is a splendid place and my "contact with the audience" was absolutely perfect.

[NWL 101–2]

The Nearctic Forms of *Lycaeides* Hüb.
(Lycaenidae, Lepidoptera)*

Excerpts from lepidopterological paper. Researched and written late 1942–early 1943. Published in *Psyche* 50 (September–December 1943) [Published March 1944].

What follows is a brief summary of some conclusions mainly relative to the classification of the American forms of *Lycæides* Hübner, 1823 (Plebejinæ). This genus comprises at least half-a-dozen structural (genitalic)

---

*Published with the aid of a grant from the Museum of Comparative Zoology at Harvard College. [VN's note] unities which may be termed species, and a full account of its morphology will be published in due time. Except in one inevitable case, no new names are introduced, as it is felt that further study might result in some equilibrium of the variational scheme in *Lycæides*, so as to avoid a chaotic accumulation of poorly balanced "subspecies."

Owing to the abundant Holarctic material in the Museum of Comparative Zoölogy, and thanks to generous loans from the American Museum of Natural History and from private collections (I have especially to thank Mr. H.K. Clench and Mr. Don B. Stallings), a considerable number of specimens could be examined; of these, some 350 were dissected and measured.

Three specific categories may be distinguished as affecting the classification of the Nearctic forms:

> *argyrognomon* Bergsträsser, 1779, Nomencl. 2:76 (Tutt, 1909, Brit. Butt. 3 pl. 50, fig. 2, male genit.; *argus* [L.] Hübner, [1800], Samml. europ. Schmett. fig. 316, male; Scudder, 1872, 4th Ann. Rep. Peabody Acad. Sci. 1871:54; Reverdin, 1917, *in* Oberthur, Et. Lép. Comp. 14 pl. 1, 2, fig. 1, 1a, male genit.; *idas* L [*nom. præocc*], *auct., pro part.; non argyrognomon* Beuret, 1935, Forster, 1936).
>
> *scudderi* Edwards, 1861, Proc. Acad. Nat. Sci. Philadelphia, 1861:164 male; Scudder, 1889, Butt. N. Engl. 2:967, line 22; Stempffer, 1933, Bull. Soc. Ent. France 38:[98]110, 111, fig. 1, male genit.; *non scudderi auct.* [nec female *scudderi* Edw., 1861, l.c. = (*Agriades*) *aquilo* Boisduval, 1832]
>
> *melissa* Edwards, 1873, Trans. Amer. Ent. Soc. 4:346 (Mead, 1875, Rep. Lep. Colorado etc.:783, pl. 36, fig. 5, 6, male, 7, 8, female; Chapman, 1917, *in* Oberthur, Et. Lép. Comp. 14, pl. 9, fig. 25, male genit.).

Besides being dissimilar both in specific expression of generic external variation and in the basic shape of the male armature (e.g., the "retroussé" spur [processus superior of the valve] in *argyrognomon*, the spare tapering weakly hooked falx in *melissa*) these three unities are separated throughout the numerous forms that cluster around the three peaks of speciation by constant relations between certain parts of that organ when its dorsum is viewed from below. If F ("forearm") denotes the length of the falx from its distal point to its elbow; H ("humerulus") the length of the falx from elbow to shoulder point; and U the length of the uncus lobe from its tip to the shoulder of the falx, then the following three categories can be formulated:

(1)   argyrognomon: H greater than U, F/H smaller than in (2)

(2)   scudderi: H equal to U, F/H smaller than in (3)

(3)   melissa: H smaller than U.

The Palearctic and Nearctic forms of *argyrognomon* are not only absolutely conspecific, but in one or two cases are strikingly alike exteriorly. *Argyrognomon* was presumably derived from a form of which the Central Asiatic *agnata* Staudinger, 1889, is the closest image to-day. *Scudderi* and the Asiatic *cleobis* Bremer, 1861 (*?subsolanus* Eversmann, 1851*) are, except for a more robust build in the *cleobis* organ, practically identical in genitalic structure (and share at least two peculiar underside characters), but either have not been in touch for a longer time or are coincident species *i.e.*, separately evolved from initial *argyrognomon*-like structures (*scudderi* decreasing in the *argyrognomon* H while *cleobis* arrived at the same proportional result by an increase in the *argyrognomon* U). We find these two on parallel lines which after passing through two coincident stages have widely diverged to produce *melissa* on one hand and *ismenias* Meigen, 1830 (Heydemann, 1931; *insularis* Leech, Verity, 1921, *nec* Leech) on the other. This scheme of course is not a phylogenetic tree but merely its shadow on a plane surface, since a sequence in time is not really deducible from a synchronous series. What seems certain, however, is that *scudderi* in its actual structure stands about midway between *argyrognomon* and *melissa* – somewhat closer perhaps to the former than to the latter.

The *Lycæides* variation in color and pattern as expressed in more or less constant races of each species can only be briefly alluded to here. Its scope in regard to the male upperside does not seem so wide in the American *ar-*

---

*Eversmann's type of *subsolanus*, if it still exists, should be examined: his lucid description (grotesquely mistranslated by Rühl and thus copied by Seitz) seems to me to fit quite exactly the species known as *cleobis* Bremer.

gyrognomon and *scudderi* as it is in the palearctic *argyrognomon* and *cleobis*, in both of which the upperside may be, racially, almost or totally devoid of optical scales, thus leaving the richly pigmented fuscous surface intact. In the nearctic groups, both in *argyrognomon* and in *scudderi*, the optical spread transcends at least the subterminal limit so that the insulæ of the secondaries (the silhouetted in fuscous pigment counterparts of the underside præterminal spots), if not circumviated more or less completely by the violet blue, are left sometimes encased in a slightly less compact fuscous which the eye sees as a thick, sometimes crenulated, "black border." The effect of crenulation may be enhanced by the strong development of terminal triangles and cilian markings in both these species as well as in *ismenias*. In *melissa* the blue extends at least to the circumviating stage but more often swamps the insulæ to reach a terminal limit (that last bulwark of tenuous fuscous which is not crossed in any Blue) so that on the upperside the male *melissa* may be said to be (as far as is known) the least variable of the polymorphic Lycæides species.

On the underside, however, all three pass through a gamut of coloration just as wide as in the palearctic forms. Each of them goes racially from the nearest approach to the basic pigmentation of the upper surface, namely from brown or brownish fawn, through fawn, pale fawn and greyish fawn, to greyish and almost pure white. If a combination of characters does not produce in both sexes some striking and constant aspect in a more or less extensive population, and insofar as tangible objects, and not ecological or other causalities, should receive systematic names, it seems to me quite useless to separate a series of, say, pale underside Yakima *melissa* from equally pale Nevada series, or a darkish underside Texas series from a similar one collected in Saskatchewan.

The rhythms in the pigmentation of the spots, in the spread of the underside optical scaling and in the structure of the marginal ornamentation* cannot be treated here; but a few words in regard to the disposition of the extradiscal series as I understand it may be of use. What we see as a trans-

---

*The latter shows a tendency towards obliteration throughout the Nearctic *Lycæides* – a feature unknown racially (except perhaps in the case of the Corsican *argyrognomon bellieri* Obthr) among western Palæarctic forms and paralleled only by certain Central Asiatic ones.

verse, more or less sinuous "line" or "row" of spots seems to me to be the outcome of two unrelated phylogenetic phenomena. The "upper" part of the "row" (from the last radial interspace to the last median one) is formed by spots having radiated fanwise from the discoidal owing to an apicoid extension of the wing texture; the "lower" part (spot in Cu_1 and the two Cu_2 spots, separated by the memory of an A_1 nervule) have been pulled out from a subcellular position (in the proximal corners of their respective interspaces) presumably by a cubitoid extension which did not necessarily occur at the same time as the other. Had not a third phenomenon taken place – namely the appearance and expansion of subterminal ornamental markings ("caudæ pavonis") which held the advancing spots at bay – the latter might have gained the practically præterminal position which they reach in some *Glaucopsychinæ*. This is why the classical conception of a row of ocelli as the result of a statically placed line or band having broken up into spots, seems to me absolutely irrelevant to the understanding of the Lycænidæ pattern. Insofar as spots have been evolved in this family, they occupy different positions in different species or genera, and what we see is not the remnants of a definite band in a definite place, but this or that stage of a more or less coordinated longitudinal movement of spots distad along the interspaces (certain comet-tail traces of this progress are sometimes caught and fixed aberrationally). In a word it is not a row of squares on a chessboard, but a shifting line of attacking pawns.

Lycæides argyrognomon Bergsträsser

As represented by my material, the nearctic *argyrognomon* forms, contrary to those of *melissa*, may be for convenience's sake divided into groups A and B ("white underside" and "fawn underside") and each may be subdivided again into 1 and 2 ("weakly marked" and "strongly marked"). A1 to A2 is expressed by *argyrognomon anna* Edwards, 1861 (Proc. Ac. Nat. Sci. Phil. 1861: 163; Strecker, 1874, Lep.: 88, pl. 10, fig. 4, male, fig. 5., female; Stempffer, 1933, Bull. Soc. Ent. France 102: 111, fig. 2, male genit.).*

---

*In the case of this form, as in that of the *nom. sp. argyrognomon* and *melissa*, I give only the most pertinent biblio-

"Typical" fairly weak *anna* is represented by series from California (seven stations), Nevada and Oregon. A stronger *anna* comes from "Glacier Pt." (it is figured by Wright, 1906, Butt. W. Cst. fig. 384, *anna*), and a form of *anna* with all markings as well developed as in any *Lycæides* is provided by a pair from "Pt. Arena," Mendocino Co. What I suppose is *ricei* Cross (1937, Pan-Pacific Ent. 13:88) is represented by a small, very weak underside *anna* form with a uniformly brown female from Oregon ("Kirk") and by a series without locality data mislabeled "*annetta*." A form from "Yakima R." and another from "Vancouver Isl." may be also placed under *anna*.

The other, B group with fawn or whitish fawn underside, represented by long series, has apparently never been detected before and may eventually require a subspecific name to counterbalance the *anna* group. Of B1 I have a series from Washington ("Brewster"): these specimens, if I am American-minded, look like unusually dingy or dusty underside "*anna*" and if I am European-minded, curiously resemble certain weak Swiss forms. Of B2 I have series from Brit. Col. ("B.C.," "Fernie," "Cranbrook," "Michel," "Landsdowne") and from Alberta ("Calgary," "Didsbury," "Carbon," "Laggan"*), darkish "black-border" specimens (see above, discussion of *Lycæides* pattern), with an underside resembling series of *argyrognomon singularis* Heydemann, 1932, and other strong W. European races.

Lycæides argyrognomon, trans. ad *scudderi* Edwards

I have not yet examined Edwards' specimens of *kodiak* Edwards (1870, Trans. Am. Ent. Soc. 3:20). Judging by its O.D. and the colored photographs professing to illustrate it (Wright, 1906, *op. cit.*, fig. 365; Holland, 1930, Butt. Bk. pl. 66, fig. 14, 15), it seems somewhat similar to what I have as "*kodiak*" from Alaska ("McKinley").

In this series a twofold individual variation (on the general basis of a dingy underside tone with faint dull fulvous lunules) easily allows the eye to sort out the "*argyrognomon*" and the "*scudderi*" specimens. Genita-

---

graphic data. A fuller synonymy, as well as complete data and acknowledgments in regard to the series of specimens mentioned here, will be given in the main work.

* This [the Laggan specimen] belongs to ssp. *scudderi*. [VN note, *Lepidopterological Papers 1941–1953*.]

lically they do represent these two species but the twofold variation mentioned is shared by examples of structural *argyrognomon* and structural *scudderi* in such a way as not to correspond to the definite specific differences in the valve and the falx; so that not only are they inseparable by the shuttling external characters, but all the examples look as if they belonged on the whole to one "arctic" race of one and the same species. Here we put our finger on something very like the actual evolution of *scudderi* from *argyrognomon*, and I have discovered an analogical case in the Palearctic, where *cleobis kenteana* Staudinger, 1892, (*?ida* Grum Grshmaïlo, 1891)* is linked up with a most interesting (undescribed) "black" form of *argyrognomon* from North-Eastern Asia. Otherwise, throughout their nearctic distribution wherever a *scudderi* form comes from the same locality as an *argyrognomon* one, both series are correctly separable at a glance. On the other hand in the case of forms from widely separate regions, such as the distinctly marked Glacier Pt. form of *argyrognomon anna* and the ridiculously similar talcum white underside *scudderi* from Riding Mts., Manitoba (kindly loaned me by Dr. Gertsch of the Am. Mus. Nat. Hist. and by Don B. Stallings), the two can be distinguished externally only by the wider terminal space in the former.

Lycæides scudderi Edwards
scudderi Edwards.

The types are lost. The name is precariously poised on the brink of synonymity into which it is drawn by the alien *aquilo* female. The type locality is not the vague "Lake Winnipeg" as given by Edwards, but the more Western "mouth of the Saskatchewan" mentioned by Scudder who took the type specimen there in 1860. I find it just possible however to save the name by applying it to the *Lycæides* species the organ of which was figured by Stempffer in 1933 (from a Brit. Col. specimen). Up to now it has been confused by all authors with the Eastern subspecies of *melissa*, Ontario specimens of which Edwards misidentified as his *scudderi* in 1862 (Proc. Acad. Nat. Sci. Philadelphia 1862:225).

---

*I question the accepted identity of *kenteana* Staudinger with Grum Grshmaïlo's *ida* from Amdo.

Most of the Northern specimens are greyish, whitish-grey or white on the underside, but in some cases, when sympathetically examined, or when the whitish bloom has worn off, may be said to fit in with the "dark grey" of Edwards' very poor description. . . .

Lycæides melissa Edwards

Melissa is the commonest and most widely distributed nearctic Lycæides, or more exactly its structure seems to be the most popular achievement in the genus. There is some indication that in some form or other it reaches Labrador in the North-East. For the Palearctic, it has been reported from the Lower Volga (as *sareptensis* Chapman, 1917, *in* Oberthur, *op. cit.*, 14, pl. 12, male genit., *et* 1918. Ent. Rec. 30:2–5) on the basis of specimens collected by Sheldon and Jones (Sheldon, 1914, Ent. 47:273); the authenticity of the locality data has been criticised by Stempffer, 1931, who however was only aware of the brief mention of *sareptensis* in the 1917 paper. A pair of specimens has also been reported from Kamchatka by Forster (1936, Mitt. München. Ent. Ges. 26:81, slide 418, male genit.) and this might seem fairly plausible had not Forster's work been full of the most preposterous blunders.*

melissa melissa Edw.

Although different shades of underside coloration can be racially perceived, the intergradation is so complete and geographically so intricate that I do not hesitate to group all such specimens which only differ in the shade of fawn, from brownish fawn through greyish to almost white, under *melissa melissa*. I have series of this from nineteen stations in Colorado, eleven in California, six in Utah, five each in Idaho, Montana and Manitoba, four each in Washington and British Columbia, two each in Nevada and Wyoming, and from single localities in Saskatchewan, Alberta, Oregon, Arizona, Texas† and Kansas.

My material shows that at four points of its extensive Western range

---

*Such as assigning an alien *Lycæides* organ (Mitt. Münchner Ent. Ges. 26, slide 493) to *Plebejus argus* ssp. *tanerei* Græser (l.c. fig. 27) or confusing *Lycæna anna* Edwards with *Thecla anna* Druce (l.c.:141), etc.

†Taken by me near Dallas. [vn note, *Lepidopterological Papers 1941–1953*.]

melissa produces four striking local races embossed as it were on its rather monotonous morphological texture. These are:

1. A curious Colorado form from Pitkin Co. and Lake Co. which, owing to the narrowness of the underside ornamental band, bears a false resemblance to *scudderi*. Possibly referred to by Barnes and McDunnough *op. cit.*: 110.

2. A darkish form with discernible insulæ and a peculiar underside: hoary greyish fawn with a generous spread of pale greenish-blue dusting from base in secondaries and very large golden-green præterminal blotches. From Gold Lake and Mammoth Lake, California. Figured by Comstock, 1927 (Butt. Calif., Pl. 53, Fig. 21, *melissa* female).

3. A showy, rather light lilac blue form with a white underside, well developed and sometimes quite separate orange lunules, and a florid female. From several districts in California ("Bouquet Cn," "Owens Lake," "Tehachapi"; also apparently "Arrowhead," "Olancha," "Lebec"). This race is the "*lotis*" of authors (Barnes and McDunnough, 1916, *op. cit.*, pl. 11, fig. 12, male; Comstock, 1927, *op. cit.*, pl. 53, fig. 23, 24, male, 25, female; Stempffer, 1933, Bull. Soc. Ent. France 102:110).

4. *melissa annetta* [Mead in litt.] Edwards, 1882 (Papilio 2:48–49; Holland, 1898, *op. cit.*: 266–267, pl. 32, fig. 13, male, 14, female; et 1930, *ibid.* pl. 66, fig. 16, male). Sparse, weak or obsolescent markings on white ground of underside; pale greyish blue female. In 1943 I travelled to Utah with the express object of obtaining this little known form and found it in fair numbers, though very local, on lupine among firs at 9,000 ft. near Alta in the Wasatch Mts. A full account of its habits will be given later. The male armature is quite similar to that of the typical *melissa* which occurred at about 6,500 ft., some ten miles nearer to Salt Lake City (with intergrades especially in females cropping up among the *annetta* population). In some of the *annetta*, however, there is a slight increase above the *melissa* average in the H of the otherwise typical *melissa* organ, and this, together with a *scudderi lotis* aspect of some of the specimens, tends to diminish the hiatus between *melissa* and the Wyoming form of *scudderi*.

The production of such local forms with more or less fluid edges is characteristic of the other species too, but in one respect *melissa* seems to be unique among its American congeners, and, namely, in that it is completely replaced East of the Mississippi (from at least Southern N. Carolina to at least Ontario) by a remarkably constant form which might serve as an example of how a really good subspecies ought to behave. It is the best known *Lycæides* in America, but lacks a name.

Lycæides melissa subsp. *samuelis* nom. nov.
(*scudderi* Edwards, Scudder, 1889, Butt. N. Engl. 3, pl. 6, fig. 6, male, pl. 34, fig. 29, male genit., *non scudderi* Edw.; Holland, 1898, Butt. Book, pl. 30, fig. 48, male, fig. 49, female, *et* 1930, *op. cit.* pl. 66, fig. 12, male,* *non scudderi* Edwards, *nec* "type"; *melissa* Edwards, Chapman, 1917 *in* Oberthur, *Et. Lep. Comp.* 14, pl. 9, fig. 26, male, genit.; *et* 1918, Ent. Rec. 30:4).

Distinguished from all *melissa* forms by the following combination of characters: ampler (cubitoid) termen, especially noticeable in female. Upperside: optical scaling producing a duller violet effect in both sexes. Fulvous arches in female generally restricted to the secondaries and to the strong interspaces. Underside: colder tone of greyish fawn coloration which produces, in spite of the pronounced halos around the well-pigmented extradiscal spots, a uniform effect (recalling certain palearctic *Plebejus* species), this effect being due both to the broader wing space and to a peculiar reduction of the white arches which form mere rims to the thin fuscous arches (this distinguishes it also from *scudderi*); narrowness of subterminal ornamentation in contrast to spacious disc; spot in Cu_1 generally placed in a more distad advanced position due presumably to cubitoid wing shape, and thus not forming with the discoidal and the $Cu_2 + (A_1)$ spots a regularly slanting line as it does in most individuals of other *melissa* forms. Genitalically shows the highest differentiation of the *melissa* male organ from that of *scudderi*, in all specimens measured the fraction H/U being even smaller than is usual for most *melissa* forms (see p. 88).

Male, holotype, labelled "Orig. Pl. 6, fig. 6, Butt. N. Engl. Cab. S. H. Scudder, 306," Mus. Comp. Zool. Slide No. 338. Genitalia measurements: F = 0, 57mm., H = 0, 35mm., U = 0, 44mm. Female, allotype, labelled "Al-

---

*Dr. W. R. Sweadner of the Carnegie Museum, where this specimen (coll. Edwards) is preserved, obligingly sent me a replica of the locality wiggle. It reads: "N. York."

bany N.Y." ex coll. Scudder, Mus. Comp. Zool. Paratypes: 5 males, 1 female, "Albany N.Y."; 1 male, 1 female "Centre N.Y."; and 1 female "Canada, Saunders." [London, Ont.], all these ex coll. Scudder, Mus. Comp. Zool.; 2 males, 1 female "Centre N.Y.," 1 female "Detroit, Mich."; 1 male, 1 female "Pa." and 2 males, 1 female "N.Y. State," all these in Mus. Comp. Zool.; 22 males, 12 females "Albany N.Y." coll. H. K. Clench; 1 male "Albany, N.Y.," 6 males "Sylvania, Ohio" and two pairs "Toronto, Ont." coll. Don B. Stallings; four pairs "Albany, N.Y.," two pairs "Karner, N.Y., 1 male "Massach ex coll. Angus," and 2 females "Mass. ex coll Hy. Edwards ["from W. H. Edwards" – W. P. Comstock *in litt.*], Am. Mus. Nat. Hist.; one pair each "Sylvania, Ohio," "Ness Lake, Mich." and "Toronto, Ont." coll. T. N. Freeman and one male, two females "Nashua, N.H." coll. W. P. Comstock.   [*Psyche* 50: 87–91]

From letter to Mstislav Dobuzhinsky,[99] May 15, 1943

From Cambridge, Massachusetts. In Russian. Unpublished.

I have finished a book on Gogol. I am finishing a big study of the genitalia of one group of butterflies ("blues").   [COLUMBIA]

From letter to Edmund Wilson, June 11, 1943

From Cambridge, Massachusetts.

I am sure you will understand the thrill I experienced today when a series of microscopic manipulations proved that *lotis* was a *scudderi* form and not a *melissa* one as had been supposed for seventy years.   [NWL 103]

From letter to Edmund Wilson, postmarked July 15, 1943

From Sandy, Utah.

We had a very comfortable, cheap and wholly delightful journey. At Albany and Cleveland where we ночевали[100] we had not to bother about

porters or taxis because there were not any; and there was plenty of standing room in the trains. Never in my life, not even in the wilds of Asia, have
I had such good collecting as here. I climb easily to 12000 ft as our altitude
is 8600 (which incidentally has a disastrous effect on my pen). I screamed
when I got my first *Cercyonis behri* Grin. What are the joys of literature
compared to tracking an ovipositing *Callophrys sheridani* Edw. to its food
plant or boxing undescribed moths from the lobby windows of J. Laughlin's very pleasant though somewhat primitive hotel! The drawing you sent
me is a fairly recognizable one of a Sphyngid (hawkmoth) belonging to the
general genus *Smerinthus* and is probably *jamaicensis*. If so, it has eyespots
on the secondaries (hind wings) which it discloses with a jerk from under
its cryptic primaries (forewings) in order to frighten off such enemies as
would not be taken in by its resemblance to a leaf. . . .   [NWL 105–6]

I walk from 12 to 18 miles a day, wearing only shorts and tennis shoes. Curiously enough, in spite of the lepidoptera, my big novel is shaping out
quite satisfactorily. Véra is a little disappointed with the climate here –
there is *always* a cold wind blowing in this particular cañon. Dmitri has a
great time catching butterflies and gophers and building dams. Weekend-
ers come to inspect my captures and ask me whether butterflies *grow*.

[NWL 107]

From letter to Mark Aldanov, August 6, 1943

From Sandy, Utah. In Russian. Unpublished.

We are living in wild eagle country, terribly far from everything, terribly
high up. There used to be mines here, 5000 miners, shooting in bars and all
that a captain[101] unknown to the Americans regaled us with in our child-
hoods. Now there is no one, a rocky remoteness, a "ski" hotel on an open
slope (8600 feet high), the grey ripple of aspens amid black firs, bears crossing the roads, mint, Saffron crocus, lupin flowering, Uinta ground squirrels
(a kind of suslik) stand upright beside their burrows, and from morning till
night I collect the rarest butterflies and flies for my museum. I know you're

no nature lover, but all the same I tell you it's an incomparable pleasure to clamber up a virtual cliff at 12000 feet and there observe, "in the neighbourhood" of Pushkin's "God," the life of some wild insect stuck on this summit since the ice ages. The climate here is harsh, icy winds, loud thunder, and as soon as the sun beats down, painful blackflies stick to one – which they especially enjoy when you go dressed as I do in nothing but shorts and tennis shoes; but the collecting here is magnificent, and I have rarely felt so good.

[COLUMBIA]

Nikolay Gogol

Excerpts from critical book. Written 1942–43, published in 1944.

[Gogol's nightmare characters, his dream-brief figures.]

In *The Government Inspector* this manner is apparent from the start in the weird private letter which the Town-Mayor Skvoznik-Dmukhanovski reads aloud to his subordinates – School Inspector Khlopov, Judge Lyapkin-Tyapkin (Mr. Slap-Dash), Charity Commissioner Zemlyanika, (Mr. Strawberry – an overripe brown strawberry wounded by the lip of a frog) and so forth. Note the nightmare names so different from, say, the sleek "Hollywood Russian" pseudonyms Vronski, Oblonski, Bolkonski etc. used by Tolstoy. (The names Gogol invents are really nicknames which we surprise in the very act of turning into family names – and a metamorphosis is a thing always exciting to watch.)

[NG 43]

The difference between human vision and the image perceived by the faceted eye of an insect may be compared with the difference between a halftone block made with the very finest screen and the corresponding picture as represented by the very coarse screening used in common newspaper pictorial reproduction. The same comparison holds good between the way Gogol saw things and the way average readers and average writers see things. Before his and Pushkin's advent Russian literature was purblind. What form it perceived was an outline directed by reason: it did not see color for itself but merely used the hackneyed combinations of blind noun and dog-like adjective that Europe had inherited from the ancients. The sky was blue, the dawn red, the foliage green, the eyes of beauty black, the clouds grey, and so on. It was Gogol (and after him Lermontov and Tolstoy) who first saw yellow and violet at all. That the sky could be pale green at sunrise, or the snow a rich blue on a cloudless day, would have sounded like heretical nonsense to your so-called "classical" writer, accustomed as he was to the rigid conventional color-schemes of the Eighteenth Century French school of literature. Thus the development of the art of description throughout the centuries may be profitably treated in terms of vision, the faceted eye becoming a unified and prodigiously complex organ and the dead dim "accepted colors" (in the sense of "idées reçues") yielding gradually their subtle shades and allowing new wonders of application.

[NG 86–87]

– "WELL," – SAID MY PUBLISHER. . . .

A delicate sunset was framed in a golden gap between gaunt mountains. The remote rims of the gap were eyelashed with firs and still further, deep in the gap itself, one could distinguish the silhouettes of other, lesser and quite ethereal, mountains. We were in Utah, sitting in the lounge of an Alpine hotel. The slender aspens on the near slopes and the pale pyramids of ancient mine dumps took advantage of the plateglass window to participate silently in our talk – somewhat in the same way as the Byronic pictures did in regard to the dialogue in Sobakevich's house.

– "Well," – said my publisher, – "I like it – but I do think the student ought to be told what it is all about."

I said . . .

– "No," – he said, – "I don't mean that. I mean the student ought to be told more about Gogol's books. I mean the *plots*. He would want to know what those books are *about*."

I said . . .

– "No, you have not," – he said. – "I have gone through it carefully and so has my wife, and we have not found the plots. There should also be some kind of bibliography or chronology at the end. The student ought to be able to find his way, otherwise he would be puzzled and would not bother to read any further."

I said that an intelligent person could always look up dates and things in a good encyclopedia or in any manual of Russian literature. He said that a student would not be necessarily an intelligent person and anyway would resent the trouble of having to look up things. I said there were students and students. He said that from a publisher's point of view there was only one sort.

– "I have tried to explain," – I said, – "that in Gogol's books the real plots are behind the obvious ones. Those real plots I do give. His stories only mimic stories with plots. It is like a rare moth that departs from a moth-like appearance to mimic the superficial pattern of a structurally quite different thing – some popular butterfly, say."

– "That's all right," – he said.

– "Or rather unpopular, unpopular with lizards and birds."

– "Yes, I understand," – he said. – "I understand perfectly well. But after all a plot is a plot, and the student must be told what *happens*. For instance, until I read *The Government Inspector* myself I had not the slightest idea what it was all about although I had studied your manuscript."

[NG 151–52]

– "No," – said my publisher hastily. – "I don't think that a list of books on Gogol is necessary. What I meant, was a list of Gogol's own books with a sequence of dates and a chronology of his doings, and something about the plots and so on. You could easily do this. And we must have Gogol's picture."

– "I have been thinking of that myself," – I said. "Yes – let us have a picture of Gogol's nose. Not his face and shoulders, etc. but only his nose. A big solitary sharp nose – neatly outlined in ink like the enlarged figure of some important part of a curious zoological specimen. I might ask Dobuzhinski,[102] that unique master of the line, or perhaps a Museum artist . . ."

– "And it would kill the book," – said my publisher.

[NG 154]

From letter to Edmund Wilson,
postmarked August 23, 1943

From Sandy, Utah.

I have trudged and climbed some 600 miles in the Wasatch Mts and made some superb entomological discoveries. Lovely melmoths and bread-and-butterflies. A man was plugged in the dinner by an envious prospector the other day. I have some good stories for you.   [YALE]

From index card notes, c. September 1943

annetta

A few worn ♀ ♀ *melissa melissa* were observed at about 5000 ft in the suburbs of Salt Lake City in the last days of June. These were obviously the remnants of a first brood emerging probably about the middle of May. On August after a thunderstorm an emergence of ♂ ♂ occurred in the same spot, which was not revisited. It is thus clear that at this feeble altitude *melissa melissa* has two broods, a late spring and a late summer one. On July   a locality was found at about 6500 ft in the Wasatch Mts where a colony composed of fairly fresh ♂ ♂ was restricted to a growth of vetch near the highway leading to Alta. This locality, which lies in a belt of country where sage and oak are the most conspicuous types of vegetation was revisited during   when the ♂ ♂ were becoming very worn. Only on August   however, a solitary fairly fresh ♀ was found on that spot. Thus there would seem to be a summer brood at that altitude, corresponding to the early summer brood at the lower elevation, but it does not seem likely that a second brood, corresponding to the August one of the lowland might manage to squeeze into the season sometime in September. Higher up (7000ft) at some two miles distance from this last locality the country changes to the aspen and fir sort with open [illegible] slopes and keeps to it up to (and well above) Alta. In spite of assiduous search, nowhere along this stretch was a single *melissa* found, nor was any vetch noticed. On July *melissa annetta* was found on some lupine covered slopes near Alta at 8 500–9000 feet i.e. along the top of the Little Cottonwood Canyon. Several things were observed: that some specimens (♂ ♀) had already lost their fringes, others were just emerging; that although lupine grew abundantly all over the mountains, *annetta* never occurred on the open slopes, but was restricted to such spots where firs grew in groves; that at such spots anthills were common; and that oviposition occurred on lupine directly surrounding the anthills. It is also to be noted that whereas there was a considerable gap between the appearance of the sexes of *melissa melissa*, the ♀ ♀ of *annetta* appeared together with the ♂ ♂, a continuous emergence of both sexes taking place well into August. The locality was about 2¹/₂ miles long and less than a mile broad and was broken into two by a stretch of lower ground where firs were absent. In locality A¹ (at the top of the 9000ft canyon) the population consisted entirely of typical *annetta*, tending to and producing, as defined above, a certain per cent of almost spotless undersides and with the ♀ varying from pale blue to brown in the variation (also defined above). In locality A² (the slopes near the mayor of Alta's house, 8 500 feet), 2 ♂ ♂ were captured, among the typical *annetta*, which were very close to typical *melissa*, and two ♀ ♀ one of which was practically indistinguishable from *melissa melissa*. Slight intergradations (a strengthening of the dark pigment) were also noted. The peak of the emergence was reached early in August but a few presentable specimens (♂ ♀) might still be sorted out among waning and battered ones in the third week of August. It was never over common. During the 45 days that I held this colony under continual observation, I took 56 specimens, my son took another dozen and a very charming local collector John Downey who had never seen *annetta* and whom I once took to my haunts, took a few more. If I had taken all the specimens I saw, collecting an hour or so every day, I doubt whether I would have taken much more than 500. This is merely to give an approximate idea of what "fairly common" might mean.

Once or twice I saw a ♂ fluttering over a damp spot on a neighbouring path, but otherwise they kept to their weedy surroundings, flying very low and settling more often on grass blades and leaves than on flowers. The weather was generally windy and seldom quite cloudless. *Glaucopsyche oro* had been abundant on the same place earlier in the season. The main companions of *annetta* on that particular spot were the prodigiously common *heteronea*, the less abundant *Argynnis bischoffii* and a small moth in great numbers, which deceived the Lycaenid ♂, if not the entomologist, into pursuing them as plausible ♀ ♀. To the N. West (i.e. down the canyon) no *annetta* or *melissa* was, I have said, found in spite of assiduous search. To the North W., however, on the other side of a ridge over 10000 high, another small colony of *annetta* was found on July   in the neighbourhood of Brighton at some 9000 ft and in the same surrounding as in Alta. (discussed above) Although miles and miles of ground were explored in the intervening regions no trace of *annetta* – or *melissa* – was noted.

[the term "biological race" or "ecological race" or even "geographical race" may be convenient to define the exact aspect of the general case discussed, but are worse than useless when used taxonomically not only because they overlap, but because they drag in strings of hypothesis. The concept of species contains besides its main, morphological, sense (for an entomologist) the necessary geographical implication, and the geographical concept implied covers the others, as no ecological or biological race can exist without a spatial condition. The "geographical variety" was necessary to distinguish in the old days when individual forms and aberrations were reckoned as "varieties." Refer to "potentially interbreeding." In order to speak of a thing you must know that a thing is a thing – and that is why the morphological aspect has precedence. It is a question of gnossology, not a question of taxonomic or biological or ecological inclinations. Incidentally there is nothing so irritating as to find "geographical" generalisations based on faulty determination of particular species or forms.]

These are the facts, and it can be shown how easy it would be to evolve an ecological and biological explanation. Fire. Anthills. Ants. Myrmocophilous. *Annetta* is, *melissa* is not. Different larval and pupal life and/or exudation of "honey" produce bleaching, reduction of fulvous lunules, etc. But the next collector, now that *annetta* is discovered, may find it in different surroundings, or find *melissa* in the same.

Viewed as "geographical form" it seems to meet at this point, coming north or south along the canyons and lake banks of the mountains, *melissa* that comes from Nevada in sage brush country. There is slight reason to think (the *scudderi* like or dark *annetta* like *melissa* specimens from 11000 Colorado) that the range of *annetta* is long.   [VNA, Lepidoptera material, Box 6]

From Minutes of the Cambridge Entomological Club, October 19, 1943

Unpublished. Written by G. E. Erikson.

Dr. Vladamir [*sic*] Nabokov was nominated for membership in the club by Prof. Carpenter and Mr. Clench.   [Harvard, MCZ]

From letter to Edmund Wilson, November 23, 1943

From Cambridge, Massachusetts.

I was lying on my bed groaning as the frost of the drug gradually gave way to the heat of pain[103] – and as I could not work, I lay there yearning for a good detective story – and at that very moment the *Taste for Honey*[104] sailed in. Mary[105] was right, I enjoyed it hugely – though the entomological part is of course all wrong (in one passage he confuses the Purple Emperor, a butterfly, with the Emperor moth). But it is very nicely written. Did Mary see the point of the detective's *name* at the very end? I did.   [NWL 113]

From letter to Edmund Wilson, November 28, 1943

From Wellesley, Massachusetts.

A summary of part of my scientific work on the Blues (the *Lycaeides* genus – "Silver Studded Blues" in English) in which I correlate the nearctic and palaearctic representatives, is due to appear in a week or two. The labour involved has been immense; the number of my index cards exceeds a thousand references – for half a dozen (very polytypic) species; I have dissected and drawn the genitalia of 360 specimens and unraveled taxonomic adventures that read like a novel. This has been a wonderful bit of training in the use of our (if I may say so) wise, precise, plastic, beautiful English language. [NWL 116]

From draft letter, c. late 1943–1944

I must apologize for delaying so long my intention of sending you some notes and drawings related to *icarioides* and allied species. I am doing so now, and have mailed some specimens I took in Utah. . . .

The species is quite obviously in a state of furious evolution and one almost feels that one would like it to "settle down" before naming races. In connection with the Nearctic *Lycaeides* I have calculated that in order to treat local forms in a rational way I ought to have examined 1000 specimens of both sexes *per county* which would make quite an astronomical number for the whole of N. America. I am afraid that we must compromise and do what we can. [VNA, Lepidoptera material, Box 5]

From interview with Katherine Reese,[106] December 1943

[On people's reactions to his collecting.]
Obviously all they want to know is what the devil I am doing with a butterfly net! And in Arizona a horse, a total stranger, followed me for five miles. Then in New Mexico I was nearly arrested because I painted a farmer's trees with sugar to attract a certain type of moth.

[*We* (Wellesley College) 1–2 (December 1943): 32]

From letter to Edmund Wilson, January 3, 1944

From Cambridge, Massachusetts.

An obscure paper on some obscure butterflies in an obscure scientific journal is another sample of Nabokoviana which will soon be in your hands.
[. . .]

Papilio bunnyi

[NWL 121–22]

The Poem

Written in early January 1944. Published in the *New Yorker*, June 10, 1944.[107]

Not the sunset poem you make when you think
aloud,
with its linden tree in India ink
and the telegraph wires across its pink
cloud;

not the mirror in you and her delicate bare
shoulder still glimmering there;
not the lyrical click of a pocket rhyme –
the tiny music that tells the time;

and not the pennies and weights on those
evening papers piled up in the rain;
not the cacodemons of carnal pain;
not the things you can say so much better in plain
prose –

but the poem that hurtles from heights unknown
 – when you wait for the splash of the stone
deep below, and grope for your pen,
and then comes the shiver, and then –

in the tangle of sounds, the leopards of words,
the leaflike insects, the eye-spotted birds
fuse and form a silent, intense,
mimetic pattern of perfect sense.

[PP 157]

From letter to Edmund Wilson, January 18, 1944

From Cambridge, Massachusetts.

I have had lately a rather exhausting burst of literary activity and am now reverting with relief to my *Lycaenidae*. The novel will be completed by the end of June before a collecting trip I am contemplating to make to Mendocino Co, Cal. where I want to look for *Lycaeides scudderi lotis* which, so far, is known only in two specimens – the ♀ holotype and what I have fixed in my paper as the ♂ neotype. . . .

Some years ago Doubleday and Doran published Holland's *Butterfly Book*. I have been saying nasty things about the terrific blunders in that book in my last entomological papers. But the plates are good – and I intend – this is serious – suggesting to D.D. that I make complete revision of the last (1931) edition – practically rewriting the text and bringing the whole thing up to date. It first appeared in 1898 and sixty-five thousand copies were sold. The long-winded, misleading and hopelessly inadequate text consists of some 400 unnecessary pages – but it is the only comparatively inexpensive work (15 dollars, I think) which illustrates (although often under the wrong names) at least 90% of the butterfly-fauna of North America. Barbour, or Banks, or Comstock of the Am Mus Nat Hist N.Y. would tell them, if they do not know, that I am well qualified for this work. What do you think of this idea?   [NWL 126, 127]

From letter from Austin Clark,[108] March 22, 1944
Unpublished.

It was indeed a pleasure to read your most excellent discussion of the Near-ctic Forms of *Lycaeides* of which you were so very kind to send me a copy. What a joy it is to find that there is someone interested in our American butterflies who does not subconsciously entertain the concept that Bering Strait is an impassable line separating the fauna of North America from that of Asia! [VNA]

Evolution of specific idea
Notes written 1943–44.

We may imagine some mild lover of nature in the seventeenth century, somewhere in Europe, bringing home from a ramble half a dozen little blue butterflies and as many biggish tawny ones with black dots. He would say, being observant, that they belonged to two different *kinds* of butterflies. This difference in *kind* is at the basis of what later became known as specific difference, and insofar as nobody in his right mind can hope to find a living intergrade between say an elephant and an oyster the distinction will probably hold good as long as the idea of category exists. In the case of the ancient aurelian, a knowledge that a pig and a cow do not interbreed may have helped him to surmise that the offspring of his different kinds of butterflies would remain different in the same way; and at this point the idea of sex became vaguely involved in the idea of "different kind" and this combination produced the idea of species.

The next generation of lovers of nature were no more the "curieux" of the old days but naturalists with a method. The blue butterflies were found to be mutually different, and the tawny bunch also presented distinctions in pattern, but whereas the distinction between what we now call an Argynninae and a Plebejinae has remained as objective, obvious and real as the distinction between a cow and a pig, the comparatively minor distinctions between the butterflies in each bunch were from the very start apt to be misunderstood by their first observer and his arrangement misinterpreted by the next one.

It was moreover discovered that the sexual idea involved in that of species somewhat contradicted the idea of similarity and dissimilarity between individuals as characterising the "one species" and the two different "species." A small brown butterfly with orange markings was found to be the female of the blue fellow and thus, at the very outset of classification, it was seen that for the recognition of a sex-species certain structural affinities or differences were of more importance than superficial markings no matter how divergent. Simultaneously with this a thing called a "variety" was assigned the part of a poor relative in relation to the species and as the ranking of varietal differences was a completely subjective affair ~~when the breeding test had not been applied, the classification of butterflies which had started from the perfectly logical assumption that two butterflies of very different size, color and shape were two different kinds of butterflies, entered upon a course which at every new turn distorted the plain reality of "the different kind" idea.~~

By a queer paradox the theory of evolution which spoke of the formation of species in reality led to the disintegration of the species, and nowadays a species is only "safe" when it is a polytypic one generically distinct from any other constellation.   [vna, Lepidoptera material, Box 6]

[Notes on speciation]

Written apparently at the time Nabokov was preparing "Notes on the Morphology of the Genus *Lycaeides*," in late 1943 and early 1944.

A modern taxonomist straddling a Wellsian time machine to explore the cenozoic era would reach a point, presumably in the early Miocene, where he still might find butterflies classifiable on structural grounds as Lycaenids, but possibly would not be able to discover among them anything distinctly referable to the structural group he now diagnoses as *Plebejinae*. Indeed it is highly probable that by comparison with the orderly categories he has learnt to distinguish, the "blues" which he would collect (with the help of some bright Pithecanthropus boy) would reveal a strange confusion of structures some of them vaguely familiar (i.e. resembling perhaps his *Catochrysopinae* or *Everinae*) others having no niche in his system or showing complex mozaic intrusions on the part of other "families," and since it is quite possible that at different periods of phylogenetic time, nature stressed different aspects of structure in Lycaenids, the taxonomist would have to devise a completely new classification adapted to each given period.

If however he slowed and carefully retraced his steps from the Miocene to the recent and followed the development of a selected species rather than that of a group, then, granted he hit upon some *Lycaenid* that did not become extinct in the Pliocene or Pleistocene times,[109]

[VNA, Lepidoptera material, Box 11]

Kuznetsov (*l.c.*) in one of the profoundest [works] written on the subject has denied the logical or rather taxonomical existence of such conceptions as species, subspecies, etc.

I think that if [they] do exist they do so taxonomically as abstract conceptions, mummified ideas severed from and uninfluenced by the continuous evolution of data-perception, some historical stage of which may have endowed them at one time with a fugitive sense. To adopt them as logical realities in classification would be much the same as conceiving a journey in terms of stopping places.

its (present) distribution in space somehow corresponds to its (past) distribution in time[110]

By Lycaeides "form" I understand a morphological unity (except for aberrational differences) represented by any quantity of individuals quite similar to each other in appearance and structure, interbreeding in any given or not given point of time or points of space. It may thus mean one "colony" of indefinite size or any number of identical colonies spatially distributed in any kind of way. The particular combination of forms termed Lycaeides to be discussed are linked by certain unique characters, mainly of genitalic structure (define under 1). These characters are expressed in different ways (define under 2) unimpairing their Lycaeides nature, and these Lycaeides forms are grouped according to these differences under the term "species." In each species there is a fluctuation of character-expression which repeats in a minor way around its specific nature the general fluctuation throughout the whole combination. In the case of the particular butterflies here examined this combination is termed a genus of specific grouped forms or more exactly a "Plebeid genus" as it forms part of a larger unity, the Plebejinae subfamily. Neither the species, subgenus, genus, nor family have any real taxonomic meaning unless their relation to a given set of morphological unities (the forms of the species of the genus Lycaeides) is quite definitely expressed and that in other combinations of such sets the very conception of species, subgenus, genus and family must necessarily vary in exact proportion to the difference between a Lycaenid morphological unity and any other one while in the family Lycaenidae itself there are differences between the conception of one "genus" and another.

~~The task of the classificator implies the grouping of morphological unities in such [a] way as to have the "species" entering the "genus," all of exactly the same value in respect to the different fluctuations of characters that each contains. I have attempted this in the subgenus Lycaeides and failed, my failure proving of more value to the understanding of this particular group than the attaining of a forced harmony would have been. This inequality of "specific" values in the genus Lycaeides is in itself a particular generic character defining as it were the very conception of a genus in regard to these particular butterflies. And this relation of specific value is different in the Agriades, in the Agrodiaetus etc.~~

The Lycaeides is one of the most "natural genera" in existence, and when the unnatural conception of "genus" (that is when uncolored by a definite morphological reality each time modifying – and vitalising – the generic idea) seems "natural" in respect to a combination of given forms one begins to suspect that these organisms form one huge polytypic species, rather than a genus. The Lycaeides have proved to be linked in such a way as to represent rather the evolution of one combined species than the constancy of several.

1. Non-structural form (e.g. *melissa samuelis*) perfectly constant in known space (N. Amer. east of Mississippi R. between 41° and 44° lat.) and

known time (eighty years), the distribution area being fairly extensive and no intergrades in adjacent or other areas being known.

2. Same but with various intergradations (e.g. *argyrognomon anna*)

3. Same but of very limited distribution (e.g. represented only by specimens labelled "Gold Lake"), with or without known intergradation.

4. Extreme forms (e.g. altitudinal) of race A.

5. The "background" form (e.g. valley) of race A.

6. Race A as a whole = subspecies.

7. Form represented by one specimen of one or either sex. It is not true that in order to appreciate the difference between two allopatric series of specimens some of which cannot be distinguished from each other, these series should be "large." We can fix it as a law that if no expert in a group is able to sort out specimens correctly once their labels are removed, such specimens should not be assigned to different subspecies. It would need very little ability indeed to pick out correctly one specimen, ♂ or ♀ of, say, *argyrognomon anna* from a thousand specimens of other forms. In other cases a selection unclouded by doubt can be only arrived at by using the microscope, but in a number of cases no expert on earth would be able to pick out correctly unlabelled specimens say from two different "type" localities supposed to yield two different "subspecies." On the other hand however a certain repetition (in terms of specimens) is needed by the describer to make him feel sure that the sole individual he has from a region where no other representatives of a given species had been collected before, is a sound basis (both in quantity and quality of character) for the creation of a new subspecies. An aberration would not of course fool an experienced observer (for instance it can safely be affirmed that no Lycaeides characterised by a subspecific "radiation" of underside macules exists anywhere in the world), but there is always the possibility that some detail of pattern (size of macules or semimacules) had chanced to be more accentuated in that individual than is typical for the race.

8. Structural forms, where a superficial variation is allied to a structural one (e.g. the Colorado *scudderi*).

9. Parallel forms: A is a "background" form distributed through an area Z where there are two unconnected ranges of mountain X and Y (sepa-

rated by miles of desert) on both of which an altitudinal form, B, is produced. BX cannot be distinguished from BY but there would be students, especially in California, who would be inclined to make of them two different subspecies. Actually the subspecies comprises A and the two Bs.

[VNA, Lepidoptera material, Box 6]

Distinguish specific and generic aberrations.

The first – obsolescence, radiation etc – is of course common to all Blues – and the man who would bet the price of a trip to Tibet that he would bring back a spotless felicis or a . . . would not be risking much. The generic aberrational tendency is something else: the production of similar looking species in dissimilar groups or the repetition of certain specific characters in different groups. A species is a generic aberration.

[VNA, Lepidoptera material, Box 5]

There is *generic variation* not to be confused with *generic aberrations*

they show the way taxa [travel?] like the sunsets and sunbursts of hotel labels on a tourist's trunk [VNA, Lepidoptera material, Box 6]

The elevation of a form or forms to the rank of a subspecies is a purely subjective affair on the part of the worker so long as an exact definition of "form" "subspecies" and "species" is not given for a particular genus. However even the most rigorous application of such a definition cannot be absolutely flawless as a methodological approach, and this for the following reasons: 1) the selection of some particular indices (e.g. the proportion between uncus and humerulus in the Lycaeides and the form of the comb) as a basis for specific differentiation necessarily disregards certain other indices both of structure and pattern, which another worker may prefer to use. 2) new material may disclose both defects in the original definitions and new possibilities of classification. 3) If the separation of species is thus based on a rather precarious equilibrium of parts, definitions for unities lower than the species can still less be expected to be absolutely exact either in their relation to the species or among themselves. In other words there is always a gap through which subjectivity can creep in. Thus the very slight but absolutely constant difference in the male structure between the American *scudderi* and the Asiatic *cleobis* forms although negligible from the point of view adopted here for the separation of species is still an obvious fact and anyone applying another method than mine (or perfecting that method) is perfectly entitled to regard ~~cleobis~~/*subsolanus* and *scudderi* as different species. Again what I here call "subspecies" is a combination of forms ("local forms" etc) which all possess some obvious factor (e.g. *cleobis/subsolanus/scudderi*) but cannot be separated from another combination of forms (Asiatic *cleobis/subsolanus* forms) on the strength of the specific definition proposed. But new material may disclose the presence of intergrades that will necessitate a revision of the subspecific notion in this case. [VNA, Lepidoptera material, Box 6]

This disgusting jumble is due to the following major sins, each of which has several components

1) totally ignoring type-specimens, obediently following traditional determinations of the old (Staudinger) school and blindly adopting names on labels affixed by dealers

2) describing new forms in terms of privately owned *series* or of more or less imagined *populations* and geographical *distributions*, instead of fixing morphologically a definite holotype preserved in a museum.

3) avoiding the comparative method in descriptions, or comparing new forms to doubtfully determined ones

4) not illustrating descriptions with figures of genitalia or imagoes, or using for the illustration of the latter uncolored photographs

5) cluttering the nomenclature with poorly described "geographical subspecies" selected in complete ignorance of the generic variations in the group, without troubling to define what is meant by the word "subspecies" . . . [VNA, Lepidoptera material, Box 6]

Every systematic name has really two meanings, a particular and a general one; the former not only comes first, but from a purely taxonomic point of view is incomparably more important. When a racial name has been based on a single specimen known it may often happen that not only its particular (individual, or maximal) meaning does not apply to the population of the type locality, but that even when employed in a general (composite or minimal) sense it is in open contradiction with the general aspect of the race. If there is any real need of having a name for the actual race, the reviser may single out his own holotype, i.e. such a specimen, whose particular aspect easily allows a natural expansion and generalization of characters so as to apply, in its general meaning, to the race or colony or museal series. But if so another name must be used which restricts the earlier one either to a chance form – or to a special colony which the reviser has missed in his rambles within the type-locality limits. In other words what cannot be done, but what is constantly done by modern revisers of so-called "rassenkreise" is to retain the initial name because of its definite locality but to substitute for the original description a generalised one of the topotypical series at hand so as to stress a racial aspect absolutely incompatible with the character of the type-specimen, which the reviser does not even trouble to look up. I have taken an extreme case, but there are all kinds of gradations of this pernicious method.

The whole thing seems to be a consequence of the curious breach in the logic of modern systematics which simultaneously demand a holotype (the tangible individual object) and sanction a morphologically diffuse conception of a "population" with all the biological, geographical and ecological (more often than not purely hypothetical) implications which this important term conveys; and this leads gradually to the disregard of the[111]

[VNA, Lepidoptera material, Box 6]

[VN rejects]

Subspecific distinctions based solely on biological data with morphological data interchangeable. . . . Such biological data may be: differences in number of broods, of foodplants, of behaviour, of habitat, of color of larva and so on, while at the same time a series of one such form mixed (without locality data) with specimens of another is impossible to differentiate by any definite character or combination of characters. Here again although such biological differences are of interest and may lead to much more important discoveries than the mere comparison of dried specimens with which a certain type of museal worker prefers to field work, it is impossible, methodologically, to give such biological forms names of the same value as those given to morphological unities.   [VNA, Lepidoptera material, Box 6]

A too great concern with geographical, geophysical and such-like matters (generally theoretical and based on traditional hypotheses) has led to series of Lycaeides specimens being considered primarily as illustrations of more or less solid geographical or paleontological conceptions. There is no doubt that these little blue butterflies may to a certain degree reflect their surroundings, but more often than not the surrounding perceived in these blue mirrors are but one's own pet theories. Butterflies considered merely as appendages to their locality labels lose precisely those connections with natural surroundings that geographically minded workers are so keen upon and become mere pictures – in fact one worker has been actually known to name a series of "races" on the strength of pictures in Oberthür. With all due admiration for Coulot's art, I am quite certain that [such] names are based on nothing. Coulot is neither God nor a gene.

[VNA, Lepidoptera material, Box 6]

"Biological species" Parody

19448 (50% ♂ ♀) live specimens belonging, it had been believed, to one species were examined. All were exactly alike. But: the ♂ ♂ specimens A^1 to A^{4862} mated only with the ♀ ♀ A^{4863} to A^{9724} respectively, while the specimens B^1 to B^{4862} mated *only* with B^{4863} to B^{9724}. It is quite clear that *A and B belong to different biological species*

  This is the kind of nonsense that you finally get with these subtle experiments of the geneticists!   [VNA, Lepidoptera material, Box 10]

It is my firm opinion that in order to discuss a given population, from any point of view, the worker must have had actual field-experience throughout several seasons in the region discussed, must have tramped hundreds of miles and minutely examined hundreds of specimens, after which he is perfectly entitled to supplement the all-important morphological description with all such matters that may widen our knowledge of a natural object in its natural surroundings.   [VNA, Lepidoptera material, Box 9]

It is this concern with "geographic variation" seeking to lay the stress on the adjective and not upon the noun, that is highly detrimental to a true story of forms. A subspecies is a subspecies when it can be identified from the aspect of any individual – and not from a locality label affixed by a German dealer. The very interesting and very important matter of geographical variation can be only then reasonably tackled when the markings and structure of a butterfly are left to tell their own story.

[VNA, Lepidoptera material, Box 6]

GERMANS

The complete absurdity which the Germans attain through complete ignorance of the principles of modern taxonomy is perhaps best illustrated by a Herr Roth describing (22.VI. 1932, Ent. Zeitschrift 46 (6): 61–68) a new species of *Parnassius* (on the basis of one ♀ from Tib. occ. and performing the following taxonomic feat: . . .

In the eighties and nineties Russian entomologists, scientifically exploring Central Asia, got so annoyed by Staudinger's agents feverishly collecting specimens in the same regions (which specimens were promptly described, to be bundled into German sale catalogues – with weird locality data) that they adopted the course of publishing at once short Latin definitions of butterflies recognized as new in the field. In most cases these definitions were followed later on by leisurely and very complete descriptions, often with beautiful figures by Kavrigin and Lang (those rivals of Coulot) in Romanov's great work. Grum Grzhimailo who sometimes used this method, with great success, unfortunately in the case of the "argus" group postponed a full description and illustration of the forms he had collected and very perfunctorily described to the day when he could fulfil his lifelong desire of writing a monograph on the "Lycaena." This he never did, and we are left with most irritating and confusing "diagnoses" which lead nowhere. As however he was careful to send cotypes abroad, I have no doubt that this can be quite easily traced, apart from the fact that there is no reason to doubt that they are to be found in Leningrad, provided of course that during the revolution none of them were published by some thrifty German amateur as happened to the (then unique) specimen of that

most remarkable of pal[illegible] butterflies P. . . .   Avinov. On the
other hand as all allusions to Grum Grzhimaïlo forms in German journals are based on commercial specimens distributed under that name by
Staudinger and others, it is quite impossible to be sure of their being correctly named. For the same reason *all* the Asiatic forms attributed to Alph-
[eraky] and Grum Grzhimaïlo by Forster who never even troubles either to
mention the grounds he has for this or that identification, let alone having
these forms conform with the original description (which, being in Latin
or in French he could not have been able to read all the same) must be regarded with suspicion as based merely on commercial or . . . museal labels.

[VNA, Lepidoptera material, Box 10]

HOMOPSIS

I have not been able to use for the definition of this kind of resemblance the
term *isomorphism*, because, taken literally, it implies similitude of shape
whereas wing-shape is inessential and structural shape (e.g. of aedeagus or
valve or uncus or falx) is barred by definition, and (mainly) because the
term has been used in connection with mimetic forms[112] e.g. forms belonging as often as not to different families and moreover linked by a (still inexplicable, in my opinion) coincidence between mimetic aspect and mimetic
behaviour and mimetic habitat, this coincidence being as impossible to explain satisfactorily either by blind accidental causes or by the blind coordination of accidents termed natural selection (even if the protective value of
mimetic resemblance is proved). In homopsis, on the other hand, there is
nothing to suggest the train of thought usualy associated with the extraordinary facts of mimetic resemblance: homoptic forms by definition belong
to the same family and the various analogous characters grouped homopti-
cally are distributed in various ways throughout the family; there is moreover not the faintest suggestion of there being any protective value in these
complicated inter-generic resemblances of one definite form to another
definite form, even if (as in the case of development of ornament) we can
attribute to this or that character a protective (cryptic or warning) effect in
its general evolution: in other words it is logically impossible to assume
that a certain subtle specific aspect (which can be appreciated only in result

of study of a vast number of allopatric forms) is worth copying in this or that particular case, all the differences involved being extremely minute and thus not comparable to lurid patterns of the aposematic order.

[VNA, Lepidoptera material, Box 6]

IF MIMICRY MINDED

The pattern of the Blues (underside) may be considered as *cryptic* inasmuch as it resembles the flowerhead on which the butterfly sleeps, with the scintillae imitating dewdrops in the dangerous light of the morning. Or the ornamentation of the margin may be regarded as *pseudaposematic* (false warning, or *badge* markings in Porchinsky's sense) suggesting either the eye of a lizard or bird with its orange nictitating membrane and glossy pupil or (Porchinsky) the ooze of some unpalatable liquid (and the three badge-colours of the warning combination black-yellow-white), or again in some cases (tailed species) the head and eyes of the butterfly itself. All these enter the section of *apatetic* colours of Poulten [Porchinsky?] (i.e. resembling some part of the environment or another species [or another substance!]). Again the blue of the males has a faint *epigamic* suggestion.

[VNA, Lepidoptera material, Box 6]

From letter to Edmund Wilson, March 26, 1944

From Cambridge, Massachusetts.

I am sending you a copy of a preliminary paper on the classification of the holarctic Lycaeides forms. It has produced a tremendous stir in the butterfly-man world since it completely upsets the system of old conceptions. I am now busy preparing for publication my main work on this group, and as hundreds of drawings must be made, this takes a good deal of my time. It will be a monograph of some 250 pages. The taxonomic part reads like a *roman d'aventures* because it involves terrific feuds between entomologists and all kinds of interesting psychological matters. In 1938 there were five (5) people in the whole world who knew anything of the particular group I am discussing: one of them is dead by now and another, an Alsatian, has vanished. So that's that.   [NWL 131]

From letter to Edmund Wilson, May 8, 1944

From Cambridge, Massachusetts.

I know, however, quite well that the appalling condition of my purse (a few hundred dollars melting in the bank, my miserable museal salary and some 800 which I shall earn next semester at Wellesley) is my own fault i.e., I am devoting too much time to entomology (up to 14 hours per day) and although I am doing in this line something of far-reaching scientific importance I sometimes feel like a drunkard who in his moments of lucidity realizes that he is missing all sorts of wonderful opportunities.

Plan: to retire from butterflies to a cottage on the Atlantic O. for at least a couple of months and finish my novel.   [NWL 135]

From letter to Mstislav Dobuzhinsky, May 8, 1944

From Cambridge, Massachusetts. In Russian. Unpublished.

I drew with my own hand 450 drawings in india ink and about 50 in colored pencil for my extensive work on butterflies (which takes up more of my time than my pocket permits – in other words it would be far better if I spent more time on literature).   [COLUMBIA]

From letter to Robert C. Williams,[113] May 15, 1944

From Cambridge, Massachusetts. Unpublished.

I prefer keeping them[114] in vials because the "elbow" of the falx is liable to be a little distorted by the pressure of the cover, and sometimes the "spur" of the valve tends to be furled when mounted.   [VNA]

From notes for Cyril dos Passos,[115] c. May 30, 1944

Unpublished.

There is no locality given, besides the general heading "Lappland Butter-flies"; but [*Erebia*] *disa*,[116] with which it often flies, is reported by Schneider (op. cit.: 413) from the "most northern region of Tornoe Province, Lappland."

[Dos Passos Collection, AMNH]

From letter to Edmund Wilson, June 8, 1944

From Cambridge, Massachusetts. Unpublished.

Dear Bunny,

I got your letter at the hospital where I landed owing to the following curious circumstances:

On the day of the invasion[117] certain 'bacilli' mistook my innards for a beachhead. I had lunched on some Virginia ham in a little *Wursthaus* near Harvard Square and was happily examining the genitalia of a specimen from Havilah, Kern Co., Calif. at the Museum, when suddenly I felt a strange wave of nausea. Mind you, I had been most extravagantly well up to that point and had actually brought my tennis racket in order to play with my friend Clark (echinoderms – if you know what I mean) in the late afternoon. Suddenly, as I say, my stomach rose with an awful whoop. I managed somehow to reach the outside steps of the Museum, but before attaining the grassplot which was my pathetic goal, I threw up, or rather down, i.e. right on the steps, such sundry items as: pieces of ham, some spinach, a little mashed potatoes, a squirt of beer – in all 80 cents worth of food. Excruciating cramps racked me and I had just the strength to reach the toilet where a flow of brown blood rushed out of me from the opposite part of my miserable body. Since I have in me a heroic strain, I forced myself to climb the stairs, lock my lab, and leave a note in Clark's office cancelling the tennis game. Then, vomiting every three steps, I proceeded to stagger home, much to the amusement of passersby who thought I had been over-celebrating the invasion.

Now, you should note, dear Bunny and Mary, that the day before, Vera and Dmitri had gone to New York for the appendicitis operation (it was scheduled to take place [that] day, Wednesday the 7th, to-day is Thursday and I feel awfully worried not being able to get any news), so that when I finally crawled into my flat I was quite alone and helpless. . . .   [YALE]

From letter to Cyril dos Passos, June 13, 1944

From Cambridge, Massachusetts. Unpublished.

If there is anything you would like checked, I shall be always glad to do it.

[Dos Passos Collection, AMNH]

From letter to Edmund Wilson, postmarked June 15, 1944

From Cambridge, Massachusetts. Published in *Briefwechsel mit Edmund Wilson.*

Dear Bunny,
I am out of the hospital after my dreadful experience and am still very weak. . . .
My flutterbys have lost their grip during my illness and I am working again at my novel.   [YALE]

From letter to Edmund Wilson, June 29, 1944

From Cambridge, Massachusetts.

. . . as usually happens to me after seeing the Wilsons (Dmitri is still chuckling over your postcard – he especially appreciated the absence of the definite article) I have been blessed with a flow of inspiration and have composed another tremendous chapter of my novel. I think it will be finished by September. I have also translated three Pushkin poems. . . . A severe cold contracted while we were waiting for the taxi at S Station (and now shared by Véra and Dmitri) helped to segregate me from my bugs. You do not tell me how much you enjoyed my paper on the *Lycaeides*. Here is what they look like

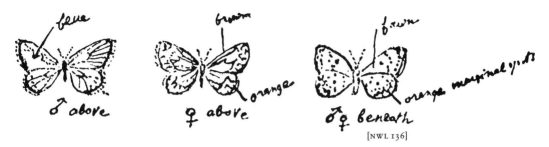

[NWL 136]

From letter to James Laughlin, July 10, 1944

From Cambridge, Massachusetts.

NB   10-VII-44

Ship it to: V. Nabokov

Museum of Comparative Zoology

Harvard   Room 402

Cambridge

Dear Laughlin,

I want you to do something for me. I noticed with dismay that I have somehow mislaid samples of plants which I brought from Utah – and namely the pabulum of two allied forms of butterflies – a thing I call *vetch* on which *melissa* breeds and the species of lupine – the food plant of *annetta*. I need these plants badly to identify them quite exactly. There are several species of lupine around Alta. I need the one growing in the haunts of *annetta* (Locality N° 2 on the chart I append). As *annetta* lives in symbiosis with ants I would also like to have a few, half-a-dozen, say, specimens of ants from the anthill (or anthills) shown on the map. Both lupine and ant must come from that precise spot. Kill the ants with alcohol or carbona or any other stuff handy (just drown them, do not squash) and put them into a small box with cotton wool. The plants can be mailed in a carton or in any other way,

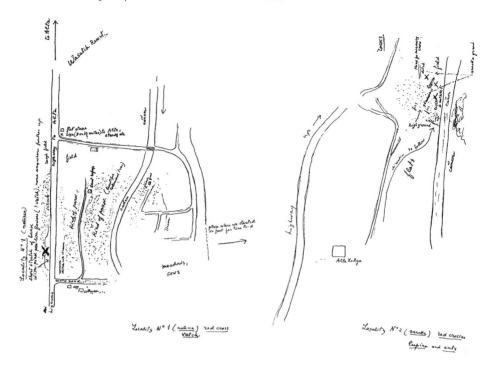

but try to keep them flat (they might also be placed in some book etc). The other plant, the "vetch" (I am not quite sure whether it is vetch, but it has pods), although growing in the vicinity of Walker's Lane, along the roads, *must come from the limited locality N°*. Mrs. Laughlin once saw me collecting there, and another time I pointed out these flowers to you on our way down. *Melissa* is well out and on the wane, little blue butterflies fluttering about that vetch, but nowhere else higher up. *Annetta* may be just emerging. It will be in full force towards the end of the month. You will do me a great favour if you can send me these plants (and a few ants)![118]

Sincerely yours V. NABOKOV

! Please, give me the approx. altitude of the *Vetch locality* (6000?) and its distance from Salt Lake City and Alta. Also, please, the altitude of *Walker's Lane* [where another form of *melissa* occurs in June and in August (also as "noted")].

[SL 50–53]

Time and Ebb

Excerpts from story. Written August–September 1944. Published in the *Atlantic Monthly*, January 1945.

[A scientist in the 2020s recalls New York's Central Park in the strangely remote early 1940s.]

Negro children sat quietly upon the artificial rocks. The trees had their Latin binomials displayed upon their trunks, just as the drivers of the squat, gaudy, scaraboid motorcabs (generically allied in my mind to certain equally gaudy automatic machines upon the musical constipation of which the insertion of a small coin used to act as a miraculous laxative) had their stale photographic pictures affixed to their backs; for we lived in the era of Identification and Tabulation; saw the personalities of men and things in terms of names and nicknames and did not believe in the existence of anything that was nameless.   [STORIES 579]

Notes on the Morphology of the genus *Lycaeides* (Lycaenidae, Lepidoptera)*

Excerpts from lepidopterological paper. Researched and written late 1943–October 1944. Published in *Psyche* 51 (September–December 1944) [Published February 1945].

Out of the hundred or so holarctic Lycænids distributed among at least sixteen genera of the subfamily *Plebejinæ* (definitely fixed by Stempffer, 1937, Bull. soc. ent. France **42**:211, etc.; *not* covering the superficial concept of "Blues" for which no systematic term or division can exist), only fourteen species or so, two of which are obvious invaders from the Tropics, occur in the nearctic region (north of the 30th parallel). These belong to seven genera, four of which (the first four in the list given below) are holarctic and contain together six species of which one half is common to both regions. All three exclusively American genera have the free portion of the ædeagus elongated; all the exclusively palearctic genera, except *Aricia* R. L. (and the, mainly tropical, *Chilades* Moore[†] and *Freyeria* Courvoisier) have

---

*Published with the aid of a grant from the Museum of Comparative Zoölogy at Harvard College. [VN's note]

[†]Unexpectedly represented by *speciosa* Staudinger in the Andes.

stubby or proximally "bulbous" free portions. Of the four genera common to both regions one half belongs to the first type and one half to the second. . . .

[Psyche 51: 104]

For some time I have been especially concerned with the genus *Lycæides*. In a preliminary paper (Nabokov, 1943 [March, 1944], Psyche 50:87 etc.) an attempt was made to clear up several taxonomic points mainly in regard to the nearctic section;* the palæarctic one is still badly confused taxonomically, especially because the type specimens of a number of races have never been examined structurally (German authors, for instance, blindly relying upon the haphazard commercial identifications of the Staudinger firm). These matters I shall discuss elsewhere, but it is necessary to make a few comments regarding the genotype.

This is the "*argus* Linn." of Hübner ([1823], Verz. bekannt. Schmett. 5:69), *nec* Linn., which was selected as the type by Scudder (1872, 4th Ann. Rep. Peabody Acad. Sci. 1871:54; 1875, Proc. Amer. Acad. Arts Sci., Boston 10:208), and since Hübner's *argus* is the "*Argus*" of Reverdin (1917, *in* Oberthur, Et. lép. comp. 14:22, fig. 3, uncus) it follows that it is also the "*argyrognomon* Bergsträsser" of Tutt [and Chapman] (1909, Brit. Butt. 3:205–208, pl. 50, fig. 2, uncus) and thus not the "*Ligurica*" of Reverdin (1917, op. cit.:22, fig. 4, uncus) which is the "*ismenias* Meigen" of Heydemann (1931, Int. ent. Zft. 25:129) and the "*argyrognomon* Bergsträsser" of Forster (1938, Mitt. Munchner ent. ges. 28:11), wrongly, and belatedly, selected by the latter author as "type" with the suggestion that readers look up for themselves Hübner's plate. They do, and find (Hübner, Samml. europ. Schmett. pl. 64 [1800]) that fig. 316, to which Scudder referred when selecting the type, can be easily matched by German males of the "*Argus*" of Reverdin and of the "*argyrognomon* Bergstr." of Tutt and, consequently, of Hemming (1934, Gen. names hol. butt. 1:108), who definitely fixed it (thus excluding the other species of *Lycæides* which he knew well) as the type of the genus, and this clinches the matter, whatever the two spe-

---

*With an incidental suggestion (*l.c.* : 88, *nota*) that *cleobis* Bremer falls to *subsolanus* Eversmann. I now find that Hemming (1938, Proc. R. Ent. Soc. London, 7(1), B : 5–7, fig., male, type) had already come to the same conclusion.

cies be called. The publication of Beuret's important paper (1935, Lambillonea 35:162, etc.) has led to attempts to transfer the name *argyrognomon* Bergsträsser (1779, Nomenclatur, 2:76–77, pl. 46, fig. 1,2) from the short-falx species (the genotype) to which it was applied by Tutt (1909) and which we shall term for the moment species X, to the long-falx species, *ismenias* Meigen, 1830 (Heydemann,* 1931) which we shall term species Y. These attempts have been prompted by the fact that female specimens apparently belonging to Y (Beuret, l.c., does not give the reasons for his determination), casually collected in the type locality of *argyrognomon* Bergstr., proved to be closer to Bergsträsser's equivocal figures than sympatric females of X. One cannot deny that the figures apply better to the general run of Y females than to the general run of X females; but pending further investigation, or some formal decision on the part of a special commission, I am compelled to use in this paper the name *argyrognomon* Bergstr. for X because of the following considerations: 1. As noted and illustrated by Beuret himself (1934, Lambillonea 34:119) at a time when he still called X by the name *argyrognomon*, absolute similarity to Bergsträsser's figures is exhibited by what he (inconsequently) named *argyrognomon rauraca* Beuret (*l.c.* pl. 5, 5a, fig. 9, 10. See also Beuret, 1928, Soc. Ent. 43, fig. 5, 10, uncus, *argyrognomon*, "Augst"). This, now extinct, colony was discovered on a plot of ground, a thousand feet long and 1/6 of this broad, near Augst in the Aargau, N. Switzerland, *i.e.*, some 200 miles south from the type locality (Bruchköbel Forest, in the Hesse-Nassau district, Central Germany) of *argyrognomon* Bergstr.; but morphologically, *i.e.*, apart from current geographic obsessions and notwithstanding the inconvenience of the thing not flying where it ought to fly, *rauraca* Beuret was when discovered, and in my opinion remains so now, an absolute synonym of *argyrognomon argyrognomon* Bergstr., since in genitalia it corresponds to Tutt's *argyrognomon* Bergstr. and in the appearance of the female to Bergsträsser's figures; 2. There is no guarantee that the next German, or British, collector in the Hesse-Nassau district will not come across chance specimens or a little colony of X, different from the race of X (*lycidasoides* Beuret,

---

*Whose clumsy fixation I reluctantly adopt.

1934), assigned to the general region, and similar to Beuret's Aargau series – in which case the whole question would have to be brought up again (Tutt remaining the first reviser*); and 3. It is not at all clear what name should be used for X if "*argyrognomon*" is switched to Y. The name *acreon* Fabricius (1787 Mantissa 2:76), on the basis of a worn specimen of *argus* auct (which combined at least X and Y) in the Banksian collection was assigned to the latter omnibus species by Butler (1869, Cat. Diurn.Lep., descr. by Fabricius, in coll. B. M.:171) which leaves us none the wiser, even if Butler did see "the type female in Copenhagen" as stated by Heydemann (1931, Int. ent. Zft. 25:150) who anyway had not seen it himself and thus was perfectly unjustified in using the name (l.c. pl. 1, fig. 4, 12) for a race of X. The name *calliopis* Boisduval ([1832] Ic. hist. lép. Europe 1:58, fig. 4,5) suggested by Hemming (1938, Proc. R. Ent. Soc. London 7,B:4) also cannot be used for X, until the female type (from Grenoble, France) and the Uriage male assigned to *calliopsis*† by Oberthur (1896, Et. ent. 20, pl. 5, fig. 64) are critically investigated in the B. M. collection. In view of the fantastic misadventures which names have undergone in this genus, pedantic care must be taken, so as to avoid some new nomenclatorial trouble in the future.

The genus *Lycæides,* of which *argyrognomon* Bergstr.-Tutt is the type, is characterized by an uncus (including the falces) exceedingly different from the corresponding structure found in other subdivisions of the *Plebejinæ,* and as I think it advisable to base specific unities upon the intrageneric variation of that character which intergenerically is responsible for the greatest hiatus, it is the uncus that I have selected (partly in development of Reverdin's, Chapman's, and Stempffer's views) for differentiating species in the *Lycæides.*

The male armature consists of a dorsal (in regard to the body) portion (the uncus) and of a ventral one (the valves – which have a constant fishlike shape in the *Plebejinæ*). The two are hinged to each other somewhat in the way of the lids of a shell and appear "closed" when viewed *in situ.* When

---

*In the sense that by figuring the male genitalia he first applied the name *argyrognomon* Bergstr. (which previously to 1909 had covered at least two *Lycæides* species and a form of *Plebejus argus* Linn.) to a definite species.
†*Calliopis.* [VN's correction, *Psyche* 52 (1945): n. 2; see p. 351].

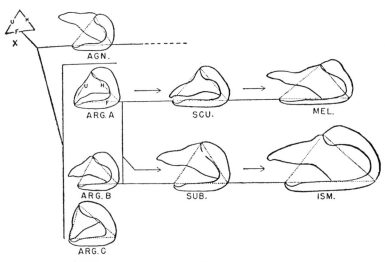

Plate I. Evolution and Speciation of Uncus in Lycæides

F   – length of forearm of falx.

H   – length of humerulus of falx.

U   – length of uncus lobe, equal to distance between apex of falx and apex of shoulder.

FHU   – triangle for measuring relative dimensions of parts.

X   – hypothetical ancestor; FHU = 0.25 + 0.22 + 0.22 = 0.69 mm.

AGN   – *agnata agnata* Staudinger, prep. 193, "Maralbaschi [Maralbashi, W. Sinkiang, Central Asia]" *ex* coll. Weeks, M.C.Z.; FHU = 0.33 + 0.26 + 0.30 = 0.89 mm.

ARG.A   – *argyrognomon* Bergstrasser ssp. (*ssp. anna* Edw. *prox.*), prep. 348, "Brewster, Washington [N. America], 18-VII-1940" coll. Stallings-Turner; FHU = 0.36 + 0.33 + 0.27 = 0.96 mm.

ARG.B   – *argyrognomon bellieri* Oberthuz, prep. 189, "Corsica [S. Europe]" *ex* coll. Weeks, M.C.Z.; FHU = 0.33 + 0.30 + 0.25 = 0.88 mm.

ARG.C   – *argyrognomon* Bengstr. ssp. (*ssp. opulenta* Verity *prox.*), prep. 211, "Alto Adigo [N. Italy] 3-VII-1930," *ex* coll. Weeks, M.C.Z.; FHU = 0.39 + 0.40 + 0.27 = 1.06 mm.

SCU   – *scudderi scudderi* Edwards, prep. 168, neotype, "Saskatchewan [N. America] [*leg.*] Kennicott," M.C.Z.; FHU = 0.45 + 0.34 + 0.34 = 1.13 mm.

SUB   – *subsolanus* Bremer *ssp.*, prep. 242, "Korea [E. Asia], 27-VII-1933, *leg.* Suk," M.C.Z.; FHU = 0.44 + 0.39 + 0.39 = 1.22 mm.

MEL   – *melissa samuelis* Nabokov, prep. 338, holotype, "[Albany, New York] Orig. Pl. 6, fig. 6, Butt. N. Engl. Cab. S. H. Scudder," M.C.Z.; FHU = 0.57 + 0.35 + 0.44 = 1.36 mm.

ISM   – *ismenias calabricola* Verity, prep. 152, "San Fili (Cosenza), Calabria [Italy] 17-VI-1920 [*leg.* fam.] Querci," *ex* coll. Weeks, M.C.Z.; FHU = 0.74 + 0.56 + 0.49 = 1.79 mm.

teased out of the tissues and viewed ventrally, *i.e.*, when the whole organ is forced open oysterwise so that its symmetrically extended valves continue to point down, whereas the uncus lobes point distad from the observer, the most conspicuous thing about the upper portion is the presence of a pair of formidable semi-translucent hooks (the subunci or falces – of a peculiar shape not found in allied genera), produced from the opposite side of the distally twinned uncus and facing each other in the manner of the stolidly raised fists of two pugilists (of the old school) with the uncus hoods lending a Ku-Klux Klan touch to the picture. The flame-shaped distal part of the candle-shaped ædeagus reaches a point between their elbows, while its proximal part is propped by the *fultura inferior* (furca) at the root of the valves.

In the paper already referred to, I introduced the following terms: F. for the length of the upright portion, or *forearm*, of the falx measured from its distal point to the apex of its elbow; H. for the length of the *humerulus* of the falx, from the apex of its elbow to the apex of its shoulder; and U. for the length of the *uncus lobe* from its distal point to the apex of the shoulder of the falx. In the majority of some 500 preparations, regardless of whether the elbow of the falx happened to be raised (in the follow-through of an "uppercut," to pursue the pugilistic image) as it is for instance in fig. ARG.A. of pl. 1, or whether it remained in its normal position (*i.e.* with the forearm parallel to the axis of the uncus lobe), a rather curious fact was noticed, namely that the distance between the tip of the falx and the apex of the shoulder exactly equalled U. This suggested the tracing of a triangle, FHU, its lines joining three points: apex of forearm, apex of elbow, and apex of shoulder. A glance at fig. 1 will show that, according to the dimensions of forearm, humerulus and uncus lobe, this triangle assumes a different size (showing the gradual generic development) and a different shape (showing the specific relative dimensions of parts).

I view evolution in *Lycæides* as a twofold process of growth: 1. as a generic growth – involving the whole of the male genitalic structure, so that the absolute size of the uncus (independently from the size of the wings) in its general graduation from the most primitive structures ($F + H + U =$ about 0.9 mm.) to the most specialized ones ($F + H + U =$ about 1.8 mm.) is doubled at the maximum limit of development; and 2. as a specific growth – a process acting upon the relation of parts F, H, and U, attacking one part more strongly than the other, whereupon the latter tends to catch up with the former, producing at a certain stage stabilization and equilibrium, which eventually are again broken by unequal growth. Details cannot be discussed here, but it may be noted that the generic growth produces more robust structures in the palearctic section than it does in the nearctic one; that there is also a difference in the rhythm of the specific growth (H being the part conspicuously affected in the palearctic branch, while it is the relation U/H which grows in the nearctic branch where H is more cramped and sluggish); and that throughout the general process stunted by-products occur (holarctically), reduction in absolute size of structure synchronizing here with reduction in size of wings.

I have separated the extremely numerous subspecies of which some 120, most of them badly chosen and poorly described, have names (with up to four synonyms in some cases) into six specific groups. In each there is a considerable range of racial fluctuation in the general size of the structure, and in F/U and a more limited individual fluctuation in H/U, but there is a convenient constance in the structural proportions (and in other structural details not mentioned here) of forms clustering around the main peaks of speciation. . . . [*Psyche* 51: 105–10]

It may be added that the genus is distributed from the polar regions to just below latitude 40° in Europe and eastern North America, and to at least 30° in western North America and Asia. Its cradle is a lost country of plenty beyond the Arctic circle of today; its nurseries are the mountains of central Asia, the Alps, and the Rockies. Seldom more than two and never more than three species are known to occur in a given geographical region, and so far as records go, not more than two species have ever been seen frequenting the same puddle or the same flowery bank.

When about to draw up detailed comparative descriptions of the numerous forms, some of them new, involved in my examination of this genus, I was confronted by the fact that the pattern of the Lycænidæ had never been adequately analyzed by systematists. On the other hand, none of the works especially devoted to schemes of stripes or lines deal with that family nor can I adapt anything they contain to my needs, since pattern development and correspondence in design values are discussed by authors (Eimer, Kusnezov, Schwanwitsch, and others) from a point of view with which I entirely disagree.* Thus I have been forced to devise a scheme of my own.

Before passing on to this scheme, certain methodological points must be explained. An extremely exact and simple method of mapping the wing characters has been suggested by the fact that the wing is crossed by a set of concentric scale lines of equal breadth (very constantly about 0.06 mm.; sinking to 0.05 only in dwarfs and rising to 0.07 only in giants). Although a few of these lines may fork† here and there, their curved course is, on the whole, remarkably regular, and easily followed from costa to dorsum. By stating the meridian of the scale line and the parallel of the vein, the position of any point on the wing can be given, and by counting the scale lines occupied by a marking, the extension of the latter can be adequately measured both in its absolute size and in relation to the whole expanse of the wing. At the root of the wing the scale lines are badly blurred, since the scales here are coarse and irregular. I have thus taken for 0 the scale line crossing the wing through the base of Cu, which is especially convenient as then the axis of the forewing discoidal macule (*i.e.* the two discales or cross veins) coincides more or less with the course of the hundredth scale line (from about the 95th in average sized specimens). Out of a great number of specimens examined and measured, an average looking *Lycæides* was selected the discoidal macule of which lay exactly upon the hundredth scale line (see pl. V, the model of which was a Colorado male of *melissa melissa* Edwards, to which macules R^2 and R^3 have been added from other individuals).

When prolonged beyond the wing, the scale lines are seen to form con-

---

*While deeply enjoying the profusion of fascinating figures provided by those authors; and of course Kusnezov's masterpiece (1915, Insectes lépidoptères (Nasekomye cheshuekrylye) 1 (1), *in* Faune de la Russie) is unsurpassed by any other general survey of the morphology of Lepidoptera.

†This seems to be a more frequent occurrence in large races than in small ones, and takes place more often distally than basally but I have not yet come to any conclusion regarding the morphological value of this character.

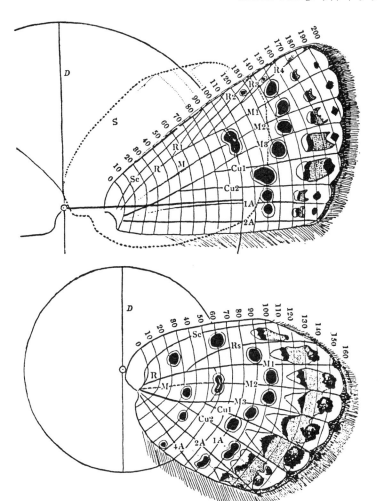

Plate V. Nabokov-Lycæides

centric circles (the curvature of the central and distal lines, forewing, and that of the distal ones, hindwing, showing almost geometrical regularity). These, however, are not concentric with the termen (especially in the forewing)* and thus the outline of the latter seems as it were carved out (as if somebody had taken a sheet of paper that happened to be neatly ruled and

---

*They are concentric to the termen in representatives of other subfamilies, *e.g.* in *Thecla* Fabricius (*s.s.*).

had cut out a butterfly, ignoring the lines), after which the transversal disposition of the markings was more or less adapted to the new shape (especially in the case of the more distal markings) in consequence of which they ceased to follow the curvature of the scale lines. Its center in regard to the forewing lies outside the root of the latter at a point corresponding to the root of the forewing on the opposite side of the thorax, *i.e.*, at a distance from the base of the wing equal to the breadth of the body at that point; the hindwing center, however, is situated at the very root of the wing (base of costa), so that in order to make the two curvatures coincide, the right hindwing must be placed upon the right forewing in such a way as to have its hub coincide with the root of the left forewing (see plate V). My ignorance of mathematical and mechanical matters is prodigious, and thus I am quite incapable of following up certain lines of thought which these curious facts suggest.

Four veins have been lost in the course of the development of the Lycænidæ or of their ancestors. The first to go was an additional radial nervule between ScR and Rs. The next to go was $3A$ of hindwing. Its more recent disappearance is suggested by the rather constant rheniform shape of macule $2A$ and by a slight halving of the cretule (*q.v.*) due to the occurrence of a line of weak scales (or a very slight scar) following the old $3A$ course upon a slightly darker ground. The last two veins to go were $1A$ and M, probably more or less simultaneously, their remnants being very similar. These remnants are: the still quite definite separation of first macule (*q.v.*) in $1A$ from that in Cu_2 (the oldest set), the somewhat less definite (in hindwing especially so) separation of the second macule (*q.v.*) in $1A$ from that in Cu_2 (a more recently evolved set) and the distinct scar of vein $1A$. I have treated it as an existing vein in my classification of macules. A similar scar is visible in cell RM, the intracellular macule of the hindwing being placed *under* that scar (in other genera there is also an upper macule), and consequently I call it M. The discoidal double macule (RM) placed upon two very weak and often partly obsolescent discales, is very like macules $Cu_2 + 1A$ (the + denoting their frequent fusion). It seems likely that the third macules in Sc and Cu_2 of the hindwing travelled to their present positions distad after the disappearance of the veins that had once halved their cells. In the forewing the last radial is numbered R_4 since I have not come to any conclusion as to which of the initial five veins disappeared. The stalking of R_3 and R_4 seems to have occurred after the (rare and weak) first and second macules in R_3 reached their present position from a point adjacent to cell RM; their weak condition seems due to the subsequent segregation in the prison of the shortened and narrowed interspace.

An examination of all known genera of Lycænidæ, clues provided by aberrational individuals and certain ontogenetic data suggest that the maculation of a given interspace develops phylogenetically in result of a series of recurrent waves or rays of pigment, each shorter than its predecessor. An initial wedge-like or gusset-like infuscation, in the proximal corner (against cell RM) of a neutrally colored interspace, grows distad, extending along the interneural fold. This ray broadens distally; the limit (and transverse breadth) it attains varies, and this variability is responsible for the variable position and interneural breadth (filled completely in "striped" forms) of the subsequent macule. The latter is formed by a gradual deepening and concentration of the fuscous pigment at its maximal distal limit, which in the case of the *first macule* to be evolved, is subterminal. The rest of the fuscous extension is weakened, owing to this local concentration, and finally degenerates and disappears, leaving only the residue of its distal limit and the initial wedge-shaped store of fuscous in the proximal corner, whereupon the whole process is repeated (in the majority of the Lycænidæ). It is repeated with a little less vigour but with more variety in the limit of the fuscous extension and hence in the position and size of the *second macule* which is formed discally in the same way as the first was formed subterminally. In some interspaces the number of which varies in the Lycænidæ, a proximal wedge still remains, even after the termination of the second process. At this point it may not have sufficient strength to extend again but a certain concentration of fuscous does occur, with the formation of a half halo distally, (see *halo*), this gusset-like macule appearing to the eye as a sessile *third macule* ready to emerge completely and creep in the wake of the second one. However, in certain interspaces a third wave of fuscous may extend as freely as it had done in the second process and a third macule is formed more or less discally. The occurrence of yet a fourth process has been noted only in a limited number of forms (*e.g.* in the Lycænidæ like patterns of certain Riodinidæ).

Having retained a certain vitality even after it has been formed (or owing to an extension of the wing membrane in the termen) the first macule splits, *i.e.,* the distal part stretches and snaps off and then a fissure is formed, within which very often the neutral ground undergoes an auroral andor structural differentiation. In certain species where the general process started very early (*e.g.* in *Tomares*) a splitting occurs too in the second macule of the interspace (and the resulting fissure is also differentiated aurorally from the ground, or, *e.g.* in *Cosmolyce boeticus* Linn. (*Catochrysopinæ*) is filled with white structural scales).

Thus the difference we see in the position of the same macule when comparing two specimens is really a matter of different limits attained by the sequence of initial rays. In comparing specimens, however, the eye sees those differences as the result of the actual "movement" of this or that macule distad and this is a true impression, inasmuch as a macule is formed at different limits of the distally progressing infuscations. On the other hand, the white cretule capping a semimacule proximally (and produced not only by a gradual draining of the ground on the part of the first macule but also by the force of the stretch attending the splitting of the latter), is not at all "growing basad" as one is tempted to see it in some forms: in direction of growth and in shape it adheres to the general standard, for it should be noted that the essential shape of a macule and its halo, of a semimacule and its cretule, of an interval and its aurora, of a præterminal mark and its scintilla, is obovate, sagittate, cordate, arcuate, with the wider part directed distad; this outline repeats that of a sessile macule which in its turn conforms to the shape of the apex of the cell; or in other words, the shape of any of these markings renders macrocosmically the shape of each distally broadening scale and microcosmically the general fanwise expansion of the wing and its cells, and is influenced in details of outline and direction by the apical andor cubito-anal development of the termen (alone the ciliary markings, lying as they do beyond the membrane of the wing, point distad). I see no trace or possibility of the basally directed development of markings postulated by authors to explain certain phenomena of pattern.

Pseudo-linear arrangements of markings, insofar as they occur in the

Lycænidæ, must be also briefly noted. The terminal line is the only sequence of interspatial markings for which I employ the word "line" at all, as it is the simplest term. Although it may be the remaining maximal limit of an infuscation preceding the formation of the first macule, its connection with ciliary elements places it in a separate class (submarkings) from the macules. It would not have mattered much had I called it "limbal" with Herrich Schäffer or "extreme" with Schröder, or "marginal" with the British authors. But if I called it "Line I" with Eimer (who has eleven of them numbered basad) or "XII" with Verity (who has twelve of them, numbered distad), or "22d" with Kusnezov (who has twenty-two) or "external I" with Schwanwitsch (who has three such external ones) or "Randbinde I" with Süffert (who has two such "Randbinden"), then I would be instantly involved in a wild confusion of manmade patterns. I fail to perceive in the Lycænid wing any suggestion whatsoever of initial transverse lines or stripes forming, or having formed, an integral part of the pattern and lending themselves to classification and "homologisation." In Lepidoptera generally, the limit of a lost ancestral infuscation in any place within a given cell, may produce, in combination with a similar limit occurring at more or less the same point in an adjacent cell, what may be loosely termed a line. When this occurs in several interspaces without a special macular differentiation in any, and is followed by various adjustments and adaptations to the distal outline of the wing in the course of more or less synchronized stages of posterior and anterior development of the termen, then the line may seem very perfect to the eye, but it is the *result* of those processes and not a "primitive" line which Mother Nature automatically traced with her brush on one butterfly after another as soon as she had stuck on the wings.

It is never the line as such that "breaks" into ocelloid macules. Such macules are formed by the initial spread of fuscous, or not at all; and sometimes when the latter had been strong enough interneurally to span that space, the resulting macule may be broad enough to "connect" with any other macule (not necessarily of its "own," *i.e.,* synchronous series) formed in an adjacent cell; or, more seldom, during the process of concentration + draining + isolation the macule may steal additional pigment from the ground of a neighboring unoccupied interspace and form therein part of its halo.

Even in the most zebroid species of *Catochrysopinæ* or *Theclinæ*, the macules peep through their linear disguise. If on the basis of some synthetic "prototype" we tried to classify these lines (say Lx, Ly, Lz), we would be continuously mistaking proximal and distal parts of split macules for components of different linear sets, or, in other cases, would come to the nonsensical conclusion that the same macules (*e.g.*, the second macules of the posterior interspaces) form the lower part of Lx in one species, the lower part of Lz in another, and an intermediate Ly in a third. The illusion of a stripe in the subfamilies mentioned is due to several variously combined factors. The macules in two or more adjacent cells may be bar-like, with halos formed only laterally. Sessile third macules (half haloed, *i.e.*, only distally) wedged proximally in their interspaces, *e.g.*, in R_4 (just above the outer part of a split discoidal macule) and in M_3 (just between the discoidal outer portion and the second macule in Cu_1), combined with a posterior sequence of second macules in Cu_1, Cu_2, and A_1 may complete the illusion of a stripe crossing the wing radianally. Moreover, when these macules are comparatively weakly pigmented, the eye tends to confuse them with portions of ground color; or a complete transverse section of brown ground between "white lines" (formed by the inversely in regard to each other directed half halos of two different macular series) may be mistaken for a "stripe." Remarkable cryptic phenomena in some genera produce yet other illusory patterns, and a "white line" that the eye follows across two cells may really consist of a proximal half-halo in one and a distal one in the other. Finally, it should be kept in mind that among the second macules *any* three may be *always* seen in line provided that two of them (such as A_1 and Cu_2 or M_1 and M_2) are those which, throughout the family, are more or less linked together in their movement distad. Although quite possibly my judgment may be affected by the fact that the genus which I have especially studied and to which we must now turn is most honestly "spotted" – and also by the fact that I am interested more in what happens within a given interspace than in the wing pattern as a whole, still I am quite sure that it would be a waste of time to try and twist this or that illusion created by a transverse combination of Lycænid macules into this or that "prototypical line."

THE WING-CHARACTERS OF THE GENUS LYCÆIDES

The categories to be discussed are: I. Size and shape. II. Ground. III. Cyanic overlay. IV. Vadosal elements. V. Scintillant elements. VI. Hairscales. VII. Terminal submarkings. VIII. Maculation. (Number of specimens of *Lycæides* forms examined: 959). . . .   [*Psyche* 51: 111–21]

II. GROUND.

Upperside, both sexes: ranging from neutral fuscous or weak brown to blackish. Costa in hindwing above Sc of a scaly neutral fuscous still weakened by the addition of colorless or very faintly iridescent scales. In a few female forms, with greatly developed upperside auroræ (see VIII 4), the fuscous ground may be intermixed with sparse auroral scales (the beginning of a brightening of the ground which in both sexes of *Plebulina* is well on the way to complete predominance, as occurring in *Lycæninæ*).

Underside, both sexes: ranging from fawn to brownish; or from white (colorless scales completely covering some, or all, neutral ground areas) to whitish fawn; or producing a greyish or bluish effect due to the even admixture of colorless or faintly iridescent scales with a more or less developed ground pigmentation. Occasionally the veins and the vein scars appear marked in a lighter shade. The forewing is generally of a slightly more diluted and smoother tone than the hindwing, and in one and same race the ground of the female is generally slightly richer than that of the male.

III. CYANIC OVERLAY.

Upperside, both sexes: structural scales invading the ground from the base with more or less vivid violet blue; partly (a) or almost completely (b); (a) clothing or dusting only certain areas (*i.e.*, absent discally, or only empurpling the cretules (*q.v.*) in the female) or reduced to a few scales at the base; (b) overlaying the ground evenly or more or less sparsely (*i.e.*, leaving out minute bald patches and the vadosal elements, *q.v.*) but always keeping clear of the costa in both wings, of most of the subcostal area in the hindwing (see further, V, 1 and IV, 5, 6) and reaching distad a maximum limit situated at a distance of about three scale-lines from the termen (see IV, 4) and less sharply defined in the female than in the corresponding male;

the intensity and tint of the violet blue depending upon the density of the scaling producing it, as well as upon the fundamental pigmentation of the wings.* Reduced or absent in the female considerably more often than in the male, where its complete absence occurs only in a few races. . . .

[*Psyche* 51: 122–23]

V. SCINTILLANT ELEMENTS.

1. The *scintillant pulvis*: structural scales more or less extensively dusting with metallic greenish blue (in strongly pigmented forms) or turquoise (in weakly pigmented or white forms) the ground at the base and in the anal interspaces of the underside; mainly in hindwing; sometimes quite absent or reduced to a few scales next to the body. Upperside: confined to the dorsum and to the proximal and posterior part of the subcostal interspace of the hindwing and intergrading there with the main overlay; in a few female forms, occurring also on the upperside of the forewing where it clothes the costa and lines the veins discally (*i.e.*, more or less corresponding to the distribution of short white hairscales in the male); consisting there of rather coarse scales of a dull turquoise tone suggesting "dead" parts of the cyanic overlay.

2. The *scintilla*:[†] a variable number of scintillant scales more or less thickly and evenly grouped, overlaying the pigment of each præterminal mark of hindwing underside; tending to be gradually reduced from M_3 or M_2 costad, and often lacking in the anterior interspaces, but seldom missing in the posterior ones; very poorly developed in some forms but only individually quite absent; in most cases placed rather proximally upon the mark, *i.e.,* not reaching its distal limit, so that the latter spreads out beard-

---

*Culling at random definitions of these shades from original descriptions of *Lycæides* forms, I find: dull violet, shiny blue, glossy violet blue, silky lilac blue, deep purple, hyssop violet, lavender blue, pruinose blue, pinky lilac, violet with a pink tinge, and at least two authors have found in their races a greenish cast. All these, more or less subjective, color impressions are worthless as racial characters unless the combination of the two factors producing the color effect (in fresh specimens) be carefully analyzed in comparison with fresh specimens of other races (of the same and of different species).

†Possibly remnants of a dense scintillant pulvis which had covered the whole of the hindwing, completely swamping all its markings, at some period in the evolution of the Lycænidae, as it still does in certain Asiatic species of *Albulina*, *Glaucopsyche*, *Lycæna*, and *Tomares*, and which subsequently had disappeared, leaving the scintillæ as seapools are left by the sea at low tide.

like from underneath the scintillant incrustation, if viewed from the termen; (the following more individual than racial variations in position are to be noted since any one of them can be stabilized specifically in other genera) sometimes coming in complete contact with the aurora (*q.v.*), but often well separated from it by a tendency to occupy a median, or even distal, position within the mark; sometimes absent from a more or less conspicuous point in the center (upon the interneural fold) which thus forms a blackish pupil; in some cases agglomerating band-like across the mark; or distributed unevenly, with patches and dots of black showing at different points; but in a few cases overlaying the mark completely (with or without a pupil), or, as it were, overlapping or replacing it in cases when the pigment of the mark tends to obsolescence or is quite gone; in shade varying (racially, inasmuch as the pigmentation varies racially) to the naked eye from turquoise (in poorly pigmented forms) through peacock blue (at an average or reduced development in well-pigmented forms) to golden green (when completely overlaying a strongly pigmented mark), but hardly distinguishable from the scintillant pulvis under lens (both sets of scales being turquoise), the aforesaid variations in color depending on the angle of light, the compactness of scales, the pigmental basis and frame – and a subjective approach on the part of the observer. . . .   [*Psyche* 51: 124-25]

When examining *Lycænidæ* patterns for systematic purposes, loose impressionistic descriptions will inevitably result (and I have erred myself in this respect) if the describer does not take into account the actual distances of the macules from the apices of their cells and from the termen, the actual and comparative positions of the split first macules, the extension of the split in comparison to the whole wing, the development of the terminal space, and the relation between the size of the macules and the entire number of scale-lines. . . .   [*Psyche* 51: 135]

In conclusion a few words may be said concerning the specific repetition, rhythm, scope, and expression of the generic characters supplied by the eight categories discussed. "Repetition" when affecting a conspicuous character or a great number of characters, produces striking resemblances between certain forms (which may be widely allopatric and associated with totally different surroundings) belonging to two or more different species of *Lycæides*, and this kind of resemblance I term *homopsis* since I cannot use "isomorphism" (the mimetic implications of which would be quite irrelevant in the case of this genus), or "parallelism" (which I restrict to resemblances in structural characters), or "analogy" (which is a minor form of homopsis affecting allopatric races of the same species); *interspecific homopsis* to be precise – for remarkable homoptic forms may be also supplied by *generically* and *tribally* different Lycænids. "Rhythm" depends on the following: if B, L, P, T represent in one species of *Lycæides* certain combinations of characters as revealed by definite subspecies, and if in another species the combination L fails to be represented at all, while on the other hand P is not represented by a single definite subspecies, but is spread over several, these omissions, gaps, fusions, and syncopatic jerks will produce in one species a variational rhythm different from that of another. "Scope" refers to range of variation in a species in comparison to that of another species and in its approach towards the generic range. A species may set a unique record in one character or category, while lagging behind in the others, or it may attain a good average in most characters. Finally, "expression" means the slight differences by which even the most strikingly homoptic forms (*i.e.*, belonging to different species) may be distinguished without an examination of the genitalic structure.

A priori, I had assumed that in the course of the combination and segregation of generic characters in various racial forms (and this is incidentally the meaning I attach to the term "form") each of the six structurally different groups (*i.e.*, species) of *Lycæides* would be seen to repeat certain stages of the same general (*i.e.*, generic) variation, but would reveal differences in rhythm, scope, and expression, the total of which would produce the synthetic character of one species as differing from the synthetic character of another. This has proved correct insofar as the species are known at present, although certain aspects of rhythm are exaggerated or, inversely, blurred by erratic taxonomy and by the tendency to create a new form not because of its marking some important combinational stage in the morphologic development of the species, but because of its coming from some new locality. New localities, however, are most welcome in themselves, for it should not be forgotten that immense areas, practically all of European and Asiatic Russia, as well as China, and numerous more limited areas in the palearctic and nearctic regions are more or less *terra incognita* in regard to these butterflies (although no doubt much precious material from there lies unsorted or misidentified in museums), so that one can still hope to obtain an *agnata* with white underside, a *subsolanus* as blue as *melissa,* and a *melissa* with a heavy vadum.

In delineating in this manner the principles I intend to follow in my subsequent discussion of racial variation in *Lycæides* species, I am guided among other things by the belief that the systematist may fare better when keeping to the all important morphological moment, than when giving comprehensive geographic names (the whole of China, the whole of the Moon) to hypothetical "populations" (a dreadfully misused term – and a hideous word, anyway) on the basis of half a dozen specimens taken by somebody between climb and cloud on some mountain thousands of miles away from the describer's desk.   [*Psyche* 51: 137–38]

[Reflections on the species concept]

Notes apparently written after the paper "Notes on the Morphology of the Genus *Lycaeidae*," and probably read as part of talk "A Genus of Blue Butterflies," Cambridge Entomological Club, October 10, 1944.

The probing of the structural mysteries of the Holarctic Blues and the scholastic but exhilarating sport of synonym hunting have somewhat obscured the main difficulty which must confront anybody trying to bring some order into this, or any other, chaotic group. I am referring to the variable vagueness of the very basis on which natural objects are being classified by the human mind.

The idea of "species" is the idea of difference; the idea of "genus" is the idea of similarity. What we do when trying to "erect a genus," as the saying goes, is really the paradoxical attempt to demonstrate that certain objects that are dissimilar in one way are similar in another. The first line of thought implies "specific distinction," the second "generic affinity."

Unfortunately the more we study a given "species" the less inclined we become to have it remain linked generically with another "species," because we notice that the idea of affinity while abundantly provided by the constellation of races (or "subspecies") forming the given species necessitates a loosening of the logical belt which we have taken such pains to tighten by one hole. In other words an increase of knowledge regarding the internal affairs of a "species" tends to apply to the organization of its different forms the old idea of "genus."

The orgy of generic splitting which has so distressed those lepidopterists who have somehow assumed that Dr. Staudinger in his sales catalog was merely reflecting a natural order of living things sanctioned by commonsense, is not the efflorescence of the generic idea, but its disintegration. (And a hundred and fifty years ago Latreille considered Fabricius a pernicious splitter.)

Up to here I have mentally agreed with myself that a "species" is something that actually (if only temporarily) exists and thus lends itself to a general definition to which it will always conform. I still believe that such a definition *can* be found although I am not satisfied either with those in current use or with those that I can supply myself. The idea of interbreeding is better left alone, not alone because nothing is definitely known whether say, a race of *Agr. pheretes* from the Swiss Alps will breed with a race of the same species from China, but also because the gap between the abstract idea of species and its concrete form as a "collection of individuals" remains most clumsily unbridged.

We can mentally visualize a given species as a unity even if we are aware of all its racial aspects, but we cannot do so with a "genus" unless it consists of very closely allied units, and in this case the generic idea will be merely an extension of the specific one, a constellation of constellations, with one serious drawback however: a "species" possesses certain limits (which though capable of being extended by the discovery of new forms and capable of being narrowed by the accordance of specific rank to former "varieties" are quite definitely perceptible to the mind); a genus possesses none, for the simple reason that it does not exist "in nature" but is merely a more or less artificial collection of specifically more or less close units. If you say that a "species" is a number of individuals that can or do interbreed, or usually do so (to avoid "hybrids"), you are stating a positive fact, no matter how ridiculous the definition is. But a "genus" cannot be defined by any such positive and factual statement. Its definition must rely either on the fluctuating philosophy of natural evolution, or on the assumption of the existence of "generic" characters as opposed to specific ones.

[vna, Lepidoptera material, Box 6]

A *species* is a relative category, at its tangible best represented by a number of interbreeding organisms which constantly differ in structure from and do not interbreed with any other organism inhabiting the same area. Two allopatric organisms (i.e. inhabiting non-communicating areas) as similar to each other in structure as two sympatric individuals but inhabiting non-communicating areas can be said to belong to one species only by analogy and this regardless of the fact whether or not they can be made to interbreed in the laboratory.

A *genus* is a combination of two or more species which are morphologically connected by some peculiar type of structure and separated by differences in the morphologically possible stages of the development of this structure within the limits of its kind. It must be stressed that the only really objective evidence of specific distinctness in the case of two or more organisms is their keeping morphologically and biologically apart from each other while breeding in the same territory or in intercommunicating areas.

Subspecies

A group of forms showing some slight but constant distinctive character of the genitalic structure in the limits of its specific range of fluctuation and a certain more or less subtle combination of superficial characters which in spite of individual or local variation separate the group from all other groups within the species. A subspecies is seldom monotypic unless it inhabits an island, or any other comparatively small, but isolated area. A quadrinomial nomenclature may be necessary to denote the local forms of a subspecies in its capacity of incipient species and it is my belief that all minor local forms worth describing owing to some special character can be and must be linked up with a group of related forms composing this or that subspecies. This is why so little is gained by random description of chance local forms without a profound study of the general variation of all the polytypic species in the genus. The term "race" is convenient to denote any geographic variation – whether subspecific or of a lower degree – on actual individuals of a butterfly. Whether his species or subspecies is "degraded" as the German name-mongers call it, to the position of a microcusp or to that of an "individual form," is of no importance whatever in the matter of the relationship between a name and an object. The thing that does matter is whether the description is clear or vague, detailed or hopelessly brief, comparative or not, based on actual specimens or based upon secondhand geographical notions. Clarity, precision and originality in morphological matters come first. The accumulation of names in entomological literature is of quite minor importance when compared to the accumulation of loose, totally unscientific, stereotype descriptions (mostly in the German language) of hypothetical populations. [VNA, Lepidoptera material, Box 6]

[Notes for talk "A Genus of Blue Butterflies," October 10, 1944]

Written in 1944.[119]

In the most recent definitions of species such as given for instance by Dobzhansky (1937, *Genetics and the Origin of Species*, N.Y.) or by Mayr (1942, *Systematics and the Origin of Species*, Columbia Univ. Press) the morphological criterion is consciously avoided, but is unconsciously retained in the queer euphemism implied by the term "potentially interbreeding." Mayr (op. cit.: 120) follows Dobzhansky and other authors in defining "species" as "groups of actually or potentially interbreeding natural populations, which are reproductively isolated from other such groups." Any person of course can pull any other person's definition to bits and substitute his own definition where again a loophole will be detected by a third party. This is the tragic fate of all generalizations. In the present

VN, with net and box for the day's folded catches, pauses on a walk with Dmitri, La Videmanette, above Rougemont, near Gstaad, August 1971.

(Dmitri Nabokov)

PLATE I

*All photographs in this section by
James Hamilton, courtesy Glenn Horowitz
Bookseller, Inc., unless otherwise noted.*

PL. 2 *Arlequinus arlequinus* male, drawn by VN for
Véra in Montreux, August 1974, in a copy of *Look at the
Harlequins!*, Nabokov's last completed novel, published
that month. The novel parodies Nabokov's autobiography
Speak, Memory, which was at first to have been called
Speak, Mnemosyne, after the Greek goddess of memory
and mother of the Muses, and the butterfly *Parnassius
mnemosyne*. *Look at the Harlequins!* continues the
lepidopteral title, since there several Caribbean butterflies called Harlequin. As prominent in *Speak, Memory*
as the butterflies is a pattern of images of rainbows,
spectra, and diamonds of colored glass, partly a private
harlequinade, since it seems that when VN first met Véra in
1923 she was wearing a harlequin mask.

PL. 3 *Adorata adorata*, drawn for Véra's sixty-eighth
birthday, January 5, 1970, in a copy of Nabokov's *Collected
Stories* (*Gesammelte Erzählungen*), edited by Dieter E.
Zimmer. An invented butterfly within the tailless *Battus
polydamas* Swallowtail group, which have this wing shape
and these toothed hindwings.

PL. 4 *Brenthis dozenita* Nab., which VN drew on receiving
this 1971 American edition of the 1958 short-story collection *Nabokov's Dozen* and presented to Véra on January
19, 1971. "Dozenita" combines the "dozen" of the volume
title with a Lolita-esque Spanish suffix, but also forms in
Russian *do zenita*, "to the zenith" (perhaps because *Lolita*
raced to the "zenith" of the best-seller charts in the month
Nabokov's Dozen was first published?). The Russian
underneath "Nabokov's Dozenita" reads "*dozenitnaya
perlamutrovka*," "Dozenita Fritillary." This invented
species resembles certain actual species in the genus *Brenthis* (now *Boloria*), especially *B. eunomia*, one of the
northern bog species adored by VN and described in the
opening selection from *Speak, Memory*.

PL. 5 A much more feminine variant on the rainbow-and-
spectrum theme in the drawing of *Arlequinus arlequinus*
above.

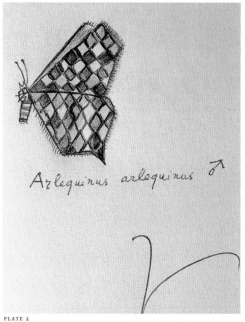

Arlequinus arlequinus ♂

PLATE 2

for Véra

Adorata adorata

PLATE 3

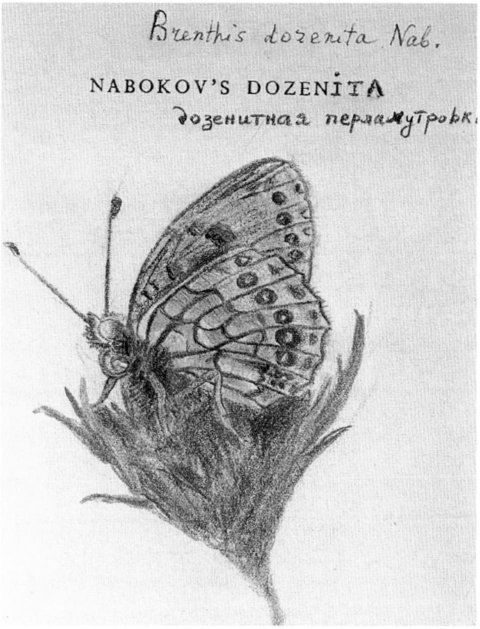

Brenthis dozenita Nab.

NABOKOV'S DOZENITA
дозенитная перламутровк

PLATE 4

PLATE 5

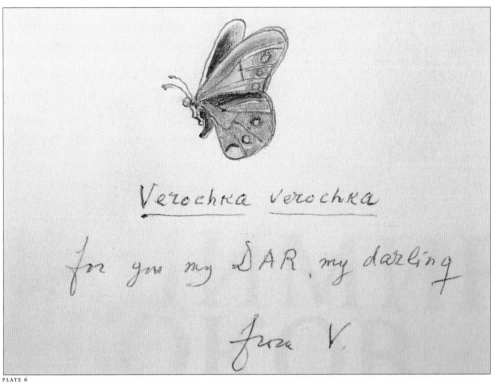

Verochka verochka

for you my DAR, my darling

fra V.

PLATE 6

LOLITA

PLATE 7

PL 6 *Verochka verochka*, drawn for Véra for Christmas 1975, on the second Russian-language edition of *Dar* (*The Gift*) (Ann Arbor: Ardis, 1975). A tropical Brushfoot in blue ink and colored pencil.

PL 7 Unlabeled butterflies on Nabokov's "official" corrected copy of the first American edition (1958) of *Lolita*. Kurt Johnson identifies these as probably from North American species, reflecting the journeys of Lolita and Humbert (and their maker while writing the novel.) The topmost recalls a stylized Variegated Fritillary; the second, with the eyespot row on its wings, an Appalachian Satyr, a species VN found in McLean Bog near Ithaca; the third a North American Tortoiseshell; and the fourth a Metalmark, some of which occur in the American West and "have 'maplike' designs on their wings resembling criss-crossed roads and highways" (Johnson).

Eugenia onegini

PLATE 8

PL 8 *Eugenia onegini*, on the front endpaper of *Conclusive Evidence* (1951), the first book version of VN's autobiography, inscribed on the dedication page in Russian: "*My darling 23.i.51.*" With this silver-green iridescence on its upper wings, the butterfly resembles the large-winged African Brushfoot genus *Panacea*. It is named for Aleksandr Pushkin's novel in verse, *Eugene Onegin*, the greatest long poem in Russian, which Nabokov had begun to translate, following a suggestion from Véra, the previous year (the four-volume translation with commentary was not published until 1964). Pushkin himself had African blood, by his great-grandfather, Abram Gannibal, whose murky origins VN traced in an appendix to his *Eugene Onegin* translation.

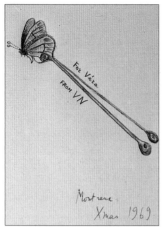

PLATE 9

PLATE 10

PLATE 11

Unnamed butterfly in a copy of *King, Queen, Knave*, translated by Dmitri Nabokov with his father (1968), in the publisher's presentation binding. An exaggerated fusion of a spectacular and celebrated Australian Lacewing, Neuroptera, which does have eyespots on bulbous tail ends, and the wings of a Hairstreak butterfly of the "Coronota" group, which are "vivid sky blue on their upperface and green beneath with large spots at the base of the tails" (Johnson).

Charaxes verae Nabokov, male, drawn on the endpaper of the first English edition of *The Gift* (1963), for the Nabokovs' forty-third wedding anniversary, April 15, 1968. *The Gift* celebrates the love and implied impending marriage of a young Russian writer and young Russian-Jewish reader in émigré Berlin who in some ways clearly resemble the Nabokovs; VN's anniversary gift to his wife belongs to the spectacular and popular African and Indo-Australian *Charaxes* genus of the Brushfoot family, and combines features of at least three groups, the arched double tails of one, the blue wing hues of another, the yellow margins of a third. The Russian inscription means "Here is the tenderest of butterflies, worthy of our anniversary."

Adorina verae Nab., drawn on a publisher's presentation copy of *Look at the Harlequins!*, Christmas 1974. The rainbow-and-stained glass motif of *Speak, Memory* (see caption to drawing of *Arlequinus arlequinus* above) recurs here in this butterfly that somewhat resembles *Ancyluris latisfasciata* Lathy, "perhaps the most extreme of the rainbow and stain-glass-like Metalmarks. They, like Nabokov's creation here, are arranged in window-like 'panes' within thickened black veins resembling lead dividers" (Johnson).

PLATE 12

PLATE 13

PLATE 14

An unnamed butterfly of the genus *Parnassius*, in a specially bound presentation copy of *Podvig* (*Glory*), given to Véra in December 1970, just after VN had put the final touches to Dmitri's translation (published 1971) of the last of the Russian novels to be turned into English. Nabokov collected Parnassians, a montane and arctic genus, in both Europe and North America. Butterflies in the genus are chalky or transparent white with red and black markings; apart from the blue of the eyespots, this could depict a real Parnassian.

Paradisia radugaleta, ovipositing, a drawing done for Véra's sixty-seventh birthday, January 5, 1969, in a specially conjoined binding of *Al'manakh: Dva puti* (*An Almanac: Two Paths*, 1918, poems by VN and his schoolmate Andrey Balashov) – the only known copy of this slim volume – and *Gorniy put'* (*The Empyrean Path*, 1923). Nabokov had just completed *Ada*, in which the locus of action, passion, and recollection is the family manor of narrator Van Veen's uncle Dan, Ardis, named after "paradise." Van's father and uncle share another estate, "Radugalet," the "other Ardis": from Russian *raduga*, "rainbow," and the English diminutive *-let*, this would mean "little rainbow" except that the *radugaleta* in the butterfly's name adds another twist, since *raduga leta* means "rainbow of summer." Here the rainbow and stained-glass motifs fuse, in a butterfly whose forewing recalls tropical Metalmarks and whose hindwing, with its eyespot and curvate, bulbed tail, suggests to Kurt Johnson the African *Abisara* Metalmarks, which have a tail like this, and an eyespot, although usually above the tail rather than, as here, below it.

Verina raduga Nab., Russian for "Véra's Rainbow." Drawn for Véra's sixty-ninth birthday. Resembles the gemmate Satyrs of the genus *Neonympha* (now *Cyllopsis*) that VN revised, sorting out several kinds in the American Southwest. The iridescence is exaggerated here, but it suggests the combination of auroral and scintillant elements with soft browns that VN so loved in this group of Satyr butterflies.

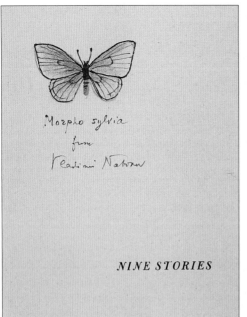

NINE STORIES

Morpho sylvia, for Nabokov's Wellesley College colleague, the short-story writer Sylvia Berkman, in *Nine Stories* (1947), published in VN's last year at Wellesley. *Morpho* is a genus (sometimes considered a family) of large, bright, remarkably metallic-blue South American butterflies.

(Wellesley College Library, Special Collections, gift of Sylvia Berkman. Photographed by Stephanie Wolf.)

TOP *Sphinx sylvia*, for Sylvia Berkman, in *Conclusive Evidence* (1951). *Sphinx* is the type genus of the Hawkmoth family VN so often evokes in his writings.

(Wellesley College Library, Special Collections, gift of Sylvia Berkman. Photographed by Stephanie Wolf.)

BOTTOM *Danaus sylvia*, on the front flyleaf of *Bend Sinister* (1947), for Sylvia Berkman, whose work Nabokov tried to promote. *Danaus*, a genus of large butterflies, especially of the tropics of Africa and the Far East, includes the well-known American butterfly, the Monarch (*Danaus plexippus*).

(Wellesley College Library, Special Collections, gift of Sylvia Berkman. Photographed by Stephanie Wolf.)

case however there is both a logical flaw in the reasoning and an error in the interpretation of known facts. Taking the factual error first it is clear to any entomologist that there are cases when two organisms connected by obvious intergrades in other regions – not necessarily intermediate regions – not only are prevented by geographical circumstances from meeting and mating, but cannot be said to be even potentially capable of interbreeding owing say to a constant difference in size, although the proportional relations between the different structural parts in each may be exactly similar. If copulation were attempted the dorsal armature of one would tear the bursa of the other and inversely the small valves of one kind of male would not be able to grip the big female of the other kind. If we still maintain that potentially these two forms can interbreed we presuppose the existence of a *morphological criterion* for instance we might say that if all the parts of one form were similarly diminished the bigger form *would be* able to copulate with the smaller one when made to meet in the breeding cage. And this brings us back to the logical flaw in the definition of species as proposed by those who attempt to supplant a definite conception of structure by biological generalizations.

Indeed on what grounds can we select the so-called "population" whose potential capacity of breeding with a given population we must judge? Quite obviously the process of reasoning here implies certain morphological conceptions which the definition attempts to avoid, but which it lets in by the back door and that is why the term "potential interbreeding" is a pathetic euphemism for "structural affinities." In Mayr's case, the author rather lamely adds that sometimes "we may have to apply the degree of morphological difference as a yardstick" but unless this yardstick is also a divining rod how on earth should we know *what* to measure since the definition does not allude to the species possessing any structure or visible shape at all and is solely concerned with biological and geographical causalities?

From the point of view of entomological systematics which incidentally are as different from ornithological systematics as a bird is different from an insect, the so-called biological definition of species alone is absolutely useless. Also incidentally, some of Mayr's references to Lepidoptera are based on utterly erroneous data supplied by quite unreliable authors (such as for instance the passage on p. 202 wherein "*Pieris napi, rapae* and *brassicae* among butterflies" are quoted as being "*well known* European examples of *sibling species*" which is pure nonsense), nor do he and other recent writers on speciation realize the importance of genitalic structures in modern entomology. I have also no use for the four kinds of species distinguished by Huxley (1938: 172), the successional, the geographical, the ecological and the genetic ones since the only one which is of interest to me is the morphological species. If a species cannot be based on morphological data, the concept must be dropped altogether insofar as it is linked up with the nomenclature and classification in use and some new kind of classification evolved, based say on function or environment or reaction to light or any thing of that kind.

The definition of species which I have arrived to runs on the following lines.

A species is a relative category, at its tangible best represented by a number of interbreeding organisms which constantly differ in structure from and do not interbreed with any other organism *inhabiting the same area.* Two organisms inhabiting *non-communicating* areas but resembling each other in structure as much as two sympatric individuals do, can be said to belong to one species only by *analogy* and thus regardless of the fact *whether or not they can be made to interbreed in the laboratory.* In other words *biology* helps *morphology* to establish a structural standard in the case of *sympatric* species, but from this point on *morphology alone* evaluates specific affinities and distinctions between *allopatric* organisms.

GENUS

The quality of a genus i.e. its natural or its artificial condition depends upon the gap between it and any other genus and also upon the interspecific gaps within it. The greater the intergeneric hiatus and the smaller the interspecific ones the more natural the genus appears.

But when – with a sigh of relief – we find a beautifully limited "natural" genus (~~Glaucopsyche~~ or ~~Scolitantides~~ ~~or the true~~ *Aricia*) which displays a number of species closely linked – and yet different – in pattern and structure, all having a most satisfactory *air de famille*, – we are, I am afraid, deceiving ourselves: this "natural" genus is but an extended species, and its representatives are so to speak fresh from the subspecific oven – they have just crossed the limit of specific alliance, of racial vassaldom – they are "good" species all right – but this rank has been acquired so recently that they still display exactly those conspecific features that we clutch at as being characteristics of a "natural" genus. The slender bridge between a species containing a number of well-defined subspecies and a well-defined genus containing a number of closely allied species is thrown over a stretch of very shallow water indeed.

The statistics relating to polytypic and monotypic species in Rensh and other authors are quite absurd – since a monotypic species can turn into a polytypic overnight – it is a case of bibliography not biology.

Passing now to lower categories we see that in practice there has been of late a definite trend to replace the morphological notion of subspecies or race by a purely geographical or geophysical one. It is amusing to note how reluctant some workers, especially the German workers, are to fix a holotype when proposing a new subspecific name. This is due to the fact of the name denoting not a definite morphological unit distinguishable at a glance from all other forms, but a certain variational tendency in a certain direction disclosed by the majority of individuals inhabiting a given area, this majority being deduced from the aspect of a chance series collected in a given locality. There have been cases mainly in Germany when a carefully described geographical subspecies on the basis of a single specimen was replaced next season in that particular locality by a totally different race or was found to be only a chance variation on the background of a subspecies really worth describing. This being so the modern worker is in mortal fear lest if he gives a too exact description of a selected specimen, the next batch of butterflies from the same region will not live up to subspecific expectations. There is, generally speaking, a curious breach in the logic of modern systematics which simultaneously demand a holotype (the tangible individual object) and allow a morphologically diffuse conception of a "population" with all the biological geographical and ecological (more often than not conjectural) implications which this most unfortunate term conveys, – and this leads to a gradual disregard of the actual aspect of an actual insect.

When a describer fixes his type on the basis of a good series, the assumption is that he chooses the most representative or average specimens – and hopes that nature will not contradict him. If however he thinks, as one reviser, P. Reese [name not clearly legible] does, that he can safeguard his ("geographic") average character by selecting for his allotype a specimen collected five hundred miles away from his holotype (with three or four "paratypes" sprinkled over the intervening region), he is wrong. Whatever the method employed and no matter the length and uniformity of his series, what he is describing is not an *a priori* geographical subspecies but the specimens he has before him. Only time assisted by several polemically minded first, second, third and Nth revisers, can settle the objective existence of this or that geographical subspecies, but this can in no way cancel or distort the particular meaning of a clear description based on the actual structure of any actual insect.   [VNA, Lepidoptera material, Box 9]

If a generalized definition of species given by one author can be successfully demolished by any other author, the case is different when the idea of species is limited to its morphological aspect in a given group of organisms. The main results of my study of such a given group are the following:

1) every species of Lycaeides is polytypic i.e. consists of a number of subspecies and local forms.

Suggested generalization:

Monotypic species are doomed. They exist only insofar as an expert has not had a go at this or that genus. A monotypic species can turn into a polytypic one overnight.

2) The conception of a Lycaeides species is purely morphological, being based on certain structural data perceptible when the whole group as now known is mathematically divided into certain smaller unities

3) the process of speciation is a phenomenon of [unusual?] growth on the basis of generic [derivation?] which is from regular growth

4) the peaks of speciation are governed by a certain stability of balance attained by certain proportions of certain parts of the sexual armature in the male

5) Generic variation is mirrored specifically i.e. every species repeats in its own way and more or less completely the range of pattern fluctuation particular to the whole genus. I have classified these variational characters.

6) There is a curious discrepancy not realized by workers in this line, between the idea of a species as a complex of forms on one hand and the sympatric moment on the other. That is, saying that two forms occurring together in a given locality *are* different species because structurally different and not interbreeding is not quite the same thing as saying that they *belong* to different specific groups some allopatric forms of which come very close to each other in structure and might be supposed to interbreed if they occurred together. This is a very important point. In all such cases where two forms occur on the same ground and do not nor can interbreed owing to difference in structure I consider them as representing different species. It is interesting to note in this respect that although there are at least six peaks of speciation in the genus in no locality so far known do more than two species occur together, except perhaps in central Asia where three may possibly occur together in certain localities. Since all the six species intergrade when viewed in their general polytypic aspect we have the paradox of two sympatric forms representing at the same time two different species in a given locality but coinciding with allopatric races expressing different intergrades between the same two species. I have illustrated this by what I call the spiral of speciation, which is not quite the same thing as the instances given by Rensch and by Huxley of the end members of a single chain of intergrading subspecies not breeding together since here it is *not* the meeting of an endemic form and a migratory one that I have in mind.

The idea of species in order to be workable in any given case must be based on objective fact and the only fact on which it can be based is the threefold phenomenon given in the definition: structural difference, biological breach, co-existence.

In the course of these remarks I have especially in view such cases where the sympatric organisms to be distinguished specifically reveal a great similarity in superficial pattern while the constant structural hiatus between them is provided by secondary differences in the parts of the very organ which in its general, primary, aspect, differs from the corresponding organ of all other groups of superficially more or less similar species. This is another tangible fact and gives the opportunity of defining the idea of genus.

The two or three organisms (superficially more or less similar, i.e. "closely allied") coexisting in one area and defined by us as belonging to different specific categories are endlessly repeated throughout an enormous geographical region. Their superficial aspect varies from colony to colony, and so does their sympatric combination. If in most localities it is A and B that occur together, in other localities A or B will occur alone, or else either A or B or both are replaced by something which is not quite A and something which is not at all B, or the combination A and B may be enriched by C or D. It is however a fact that the number of distinct sympatric units will always be (in the case of the particular group studied) at least half and generally less than half [*sic*] of the whole sum of species through the general distribution of the genus.

At this point there has occurred a breach of logic in our reasoning. We have evidence for separating specifically the sympatric units A and B from each other or the sympatric C and B from each other or again the sympatric A, B and D from each other. But it transpires that C and D and A and E never occur together.

Thus our definition of specific distinction is insufficient for handling these constantly allopatric units. As moreover, A and B or any other unit reveals certain slight variation in essential structure (A_1, A_2, A_3, etc., B_1, B_2, B_3 etc) through their geographical distribution we cannot appeal to analogy when attempting to distinguish C from allopatric D *because*, say, the latter is specifically distinguishable from sympatric A and B. In other words, there is nothing to prove that the difference between C and B is not of the same degree as say between A_1 and A_3.

To solve this question we must now turn away from the clearcut structural difference between sympatric units and examine the slight but p[ersistent?] structural variation of each unit through its geographic distribution (A_1, A_2, A_3, etc). We have also to abandon for the moment the idea of species, since its basic requirements are non existent in the examination of allopatric series.

We find that the structure providing variations has certain variational limits.

We find that a complete intergradation from one limit to another runs through the sequence of units in their geographical distribution.

But we also find that this sequence can be divided into several groups ("peaks of speciation") each showing the structural characters of A or B or C or D or E. We come back thus to the specific idea, since these groups are illustrated by the different units we indeed know in their various sympatric combinations. Or to put it otherwise, the grouping of these allopatric units is based by us on the means of the structural characters shown by sympatric units.

Summing up these various points my definition of a Lycaeides species would be: a group of structural forms which at the peak of development in this or that region definitely and constantly shows one of the six possible proportions between certain parts of the male armature and none of which interbreed with any representative of another such group when occurring on the same ground although one specific group of forms may merge into another in one of the valleys of speciation.

I shall now proceed to give a more detailed picture of the genus Lycaeides.

pereyti k stat'e[120]   [VNA, Lepidoptera material, Box 6]

From Minutes of the Cambridge Entomological Club, October 10, 1944

Unpublished. Written by G. E. Erikson.

The 606th Meeting of the Cambridge Entomological Club was held at the Harvard Faculty Club on Oct 10, 1944. Eleven members and guests were present. . . .

The scientific program of the evening was in the hands of Dr. Vladimir Nabokov who spoke on "A Genus of Blue Butterflies." Dr. Nabokov considered the concept of species & genus – criticizing the definitions of Huxley and of Mayr. He then proceeded to the problem of speciation in the genus *Lycaeides* of the Blue Butterflies – considering particularly the male genitalia and scale patterns on wings. These characters he illustrated clearly and entertainingly by means of a series of excellent crayon drawings – with delightful illusions [*sic*] to human attitudes seen in the structures by the artist's eye.

This was followed by a showing by Prof. Brues of a reel of film on Bot fly maggots.[121]   [HARVARD, MCZ]

From letter to Edmund Wilson, October 11, 1944

From Cambridge, Massachusetts.

I have spent a month in arranging Part I of my butterfly work for publication and have had a good deal of trouble with the drawings. It goes to the printers to-day and the trees are green and rusty brown, stepwise, like gobelins. Enfin – c'est fait. It is going to remain a wonderful and indispensable thing for some 25 years, after which another fellow will show how wrong I was in this and that. Herein lies the difference between science and art.

[NWL 143]

From letter from William Comstock, November 17, 1944

Unpublished.

Your note at hand and I am much delighted thereby. It is time someone went to work on the Lycaenid mess. I do not mind in the least being the goat. I am glad I put in the screwy references so you could jump on them.

[VNA]

From letter to Robert C. Williams, January 15, 1945

From Cambridge, Massachusetts. Unpublished.

My study of specific and racial fluctuation in this genus is nearing its end, but before I have finished, I constantly need *all* the specimens I have accumulated (about 1000) in order to follow the variational course of this or that component of the pattern whose turn it is to be checked.   [VNA]

From letter from Cyril dos Passos, January 31, 1945

Unpublished.

In case you have not yet noticed the recent article by Chermock[122] on "Some New North American *Lycaenidae*," 1944, The Canadian Entomologist, volume 76, page 213, I thought that you would like to have it called to your attention, since it proposes names for four races of *scudderi* and two races of *melissa*, insects in which I know you are interested.

I am not over-enthusiastic about the paper but it must, nevertheless, be taken into account. [VNA]

Letter to Cyril dos Passos, February 4, 1945

From Cambridge, Massachusetts. Unpublished.

4-I[123]-45

Dear Mr Dos Passos,

Thanks for your kind letter. I have not yet seen the Can. Ent. but know what mess to expect. Some time ago Stallings[124] informed me that Chermock was sending out specimens with new names. I wrote to Chermock and tried to tell him that – while holding no patent for American forms of *Lycaeides* – I was not sure whether, in view of the complex phylogenetic and distributional problems involved, it were wise at this stage to give subspecific names to chance series and morphological intergrades (the extremes of which I know, but he does not) without bothering about the genitalia etc. He answered very effusively, saying that he had thoroughly studied the whole question long before my notes in *Psyche* appeared and promised to send me specimens of his "new" races (I am still waiting for them). From his remarks on them I gathered he was merely interested in giving names to things and was far from possessing the true scientific spirit which for instance Paul Grey has.

My longish paper on certain questions concerning *Lycaeides* is to appear very soon and I shall at once forward you a copy.

I shall visit the A.M.N.H. on Monday, the 12th. Will you be there? I would very much like to see you.

Sincerely yours
V. NABOKOV   [AMNH]

From letter from Cyril dos Passos, February 6, 1945
Unpublished.

Yours of the fourth instant was received this morning.

I see therefrom that you have sized up Chermock correctly. You may receive paratypes of his new races and then again, you may not. So far as I am concerned I want nothing whatever to do with him.   [VNA]

From letter from William Comstock, March 14, 1945
Unpublished.

I have read your recent paper with considerable interest. As I have told you before I like your explanation of maculation better than that of Schwanwitsch and others. It appeals to me as being more logical but I can also see why a student examining banded species might get a different initial idea and develop from it the line theory.

Your paper is somewhat hard reading because of your almost telegraphic expression. I suppose this was necessary to keep the cost down in these war days but nevertheless I think it a detriment because everyone is busy and they are apt to pass over a paper if it is hard to read.   [VNA]

From letter to William Comstock, March 16, 1945
From Wellesley, Massachusetts. Unpublished.

Enclosed are the camera lucida drawings I made of *hanno hanno* and of *huntingtoni*. I am also contributing some notes which I would like to be published together with your paper and the figures, preferably as an addendum. I hope you have nothing against this arrangement.   [VNA]

Note on the male genitalia of *Hemiargus hanno* Stoll and *huntingtoni* Comstock, with two figures

Lepidopterological notes. Written March 1945. Unpublished.

An investigation of the male and female armature of neotropical *Plebejinae* (*sensu stricto*), a detailed account of which will be published in due course, has revealed that *Hemiargus* contains five species: 1. *hanno* Stoll (Comprising races *hanno* Stoll, *bogotana* Draudt, *watsoni* Comstock-Huntington and a few other namable forms) which ranges from S. Brasil and Bolivia to Haiti and Panama; 2. A species for which the correct name is probably *ramon* Dogrin, from Ecuador; 3. *ceraunus* Fabricius (comprising races *ceraunus* Fabricius, *filenus* Poey, *zachaina* Butler, *gyas* Edwards and *antibubastus* Hübner) which ranges from Hispaniola and Colombia to the eastern and western United States; 4. *huntingtoni* Comstock, from Trinidad, and 5. *isola* Reakirt which ranges, from an undetermined southern point, through Central America to favorable localities west of the Mississippi.

Of other species that have been assigned to *Hemiargus*, the remarkable *bornoi* Comstock-Huntington described from Haiti belongs to a new genus, and a third one contains four West Indian species, namely: 1. *ammon* Lucas; 2. *dominica* Moschler; 3. *woodruffi* Comstock-Huntington, and 4. *thomasi* Clench (comprising races *thomasi* Clench, *noeli* Comstock-Huntington and *bethune-bakeri* Comstock-Huntington, all of which have been incorrectly assigned to *ammon*), the last reaching Florida from Hispaniola via the Bahamas.

No other *Plebejinae* (s.s.) than those ten are known from the West Indies, Central America or eastern South America. The genus *Leptotes*, for instance, belongs to *Catochrysopinae* (holotropical) the cosmopolitan *Zizula gaika* Moore (*cyna* Edwards, *tulliola* Godman) together with the African and American genus *Brephidium* are in a quite separate group, *etc.* The Andes, however, yield no less than five additional genera of *Plebejinae* (four new, one revised), again containing ten species, some of which reveal striking Old World affinities of an ancestral kind. This brings the total of neotropical species of *Plebejinae* to twenty, which is a little more than the small nearctic total (see N., 1944 (1945), Psyche 51: 104–105, where incidentally the specific name "*hanno*" should be replaced by "*ceraunus*") and hardly one fourth of the large Central Asiatic and western palaearctic total, but as much as three times the number of species as yet known to inhabit the palaeotropical region.

In regard to the figures which Mr. W. P. Comstock permitted me to append to his paper, the following points are of interest:

Fig. 1: *Hemiargus hanno hanno* Stoll, ♂, neotype (as selected by Comstock and Huntington); T,U,F: left part of tegumen (T) with uncus lobe (U) and falx (F), ventral view; falx rather thick, blunt, with rounded shoulder. A: Aedeagus, lateral view: large, with long distal sheath terminating on the dorsal side in a double excurved little process (2); cornuti present on vesica. S: rudimentary fultura superior (sagum)1 T,t: fultura inferior (furca), very small, but efficiently holding the aedeagus in its forking. V,P: valve, small, with long curved trunk-like process (p) and curiously keeled lower margin.

Fig. 2: *Hemiargus huntingtoni* Comstock, ♂, paratype; T,U,F: left part of tegumen (T) with uncus lobe (U) and falx (F), ventral view; the whole uncus shorter than in *hanno*; falx much thinner, tapering, with high conical shoulder. A: aedeagus, lateral view; smaller than in *hanno*, unarmed, with comparatively short distal sheath (i.e. external portion of the penis). S,S: fultura superior (sagum) lateral view (S) *in situ*, and spread flat (S) with the aedeagus removed; peculiarly shaped, each of its ventrally directed ends with four teeth. T,t: fultura inferior (furca) in ventral (T) and lateral (t) view; large, propping the aedeagus rather than holding it. V,P: valve; small, elongated, of fairly normal type (somewhat resembling the palaeotropical genus (*Chilades* Moore) with small bent tapering upper process (P) intermediate between *ceraunus* and *isola*. (The hairs are not shown; they evenly clothe the whole lower process almost to the base of the valve in *huntingtoni*, but are grouped distally in *hanno*.)

The sagum is totally absent in holarctic and palaeotropical *Plebejinae*, but is found at various stages of development in the majority of neotropical species; in its extreme form it produces (i.e. ventrally) two great lobes meeting in front (i.e. ventrally) of the aedeagus and exceeding it in length, each lobe being margin to forty prominent teeth increasing in size proximad. At its present phylogenetic stage, it is very unlike the annellus as found in *Catochrysopinae* and other subfamilies. [VNA]

Notes on Neotropical Plebejinae (Lycaenidae, Lepidoptera)*

Excerpts from lepidopterological paper. Researched and written in late 1944–early 1945. Published in *Psyche* 52 (March–June 1945) [Published October 26, 1945].

In a recent paper† I briefly listed the only *Plebejinæ* (*s.s.*) found in the Nearctic region. Subsequently I decided to see whether any true *Plebejinæ* occurred in the neotropics besides the three or four species the genitalia of which I had happened to examine before. The results proved so unexpected and interesting that it seems worth while to publish the present paper despite its rather superficial and incomplete nature.

In order to cover more ground (and, in some cases, owing to the scantiness of the material at hand) only a very small number of specimens (about 120 in all) have been dissected and drawn (after a few *Catochrysopinæ* and representatives of other subfamilies had been weeded out by the same method). Some of these figures are appended. All the specimens, except a few supplied with his usual kindness by Mr. W. P. Comstock of the American Museum of Natural History, are preserved in the Museum of Comparative Zoology, Harvard.

A rather drastic rearrangement of the species and groups was an inevitable consequence of this investigation. Seven new genera have been introduced; two have been revised and restricted. In several cases it was found that forms had been assigned by recent authors to the wrong species. Some synonyms have been tracked down, others are tentatively suggested but cannot be finally disposed of until the types are examined (or neotypes fixed). The brief bibliographical references given are merely intended to indicate the identity of the forms discussed. Beyond the inclusion of some

*Published with the aid of a grant from the Museum of Comparative Zoology at Harvard College.

†1944 [Feb. 1945] Psyche 51: 104–138, where the following errata should be corrected: line 12, p. 105, instead of "*hanno* Stoll" read "*ceraunus* Fabricius (*nom. spec.*)"; line 28, p. 107, instead of the misprint "*calliopsis*" read "*calliopis*"; p. 111, in the sentence beginning "A complete sequence . . ." transpose "palearctic" and "nearctic."

random notes on certain phases of pattern, macroscopical characters are not discussed, and no attempt has been made to revise in this respect the (fortunately rather few) races that have received names.

In spite of the work accomplished since 1909, by Tutt and Chapman in England and by Stempffer in France, entomologists in this country employ the term "*Plebejinæ*" simply as a euphemism for the "*Lycæna*" of German authors, or "Blues,"* and "*Plebejus*" is used for a number of heterogeneous Nearctic species only *one* of which (*sæpiolus* Boisduval) belongs structurally to the genus of which the Palearctic *Plebejus argus* Linnæus is the type. In a way the initial blunder was Swinhoe's who while correctly giving a subfamilial ending to the group which Tutt's intuition and Chapman's science had recognized ("tribe" *Plebeidi* which exactly corresponds to the *Plebejinæ* of Stempffer) as different from other "tribes" (*i.e.,* subfamilies) within the *Lycænidæ*, failed to live up to the generic diagnoses which he simply copied from Chapman's notes in Tutt and tried to combine genitalic data he had not verified or did not understand with the obsolete "naked *v.* hairy eyes" system (which at Butler's hands had resulted in probably the most ludicrous assembly of species ever concocted, see for example Butler 1900, Entom. 33:124), so that in the case of several Indian forms which Chapman had not diagnosed, Swinhoe placed intragenerically allied species in different subfamilies and species belonging to different Tuttian "tribes" in the same subfamily.

In reality the subfamily *Plebejinæ* is extremely well differentiated in all its genitalic elements (the ædeagus and its appendages, the tegumen, cingula, falces, uncus lobes and valves of the male, and the cervix bursæ and vaginal armature of the female) from the *Catochrysopinæ* (containing the holotropical *Leptotes* Scudder and a huge array of palæotropical species in

---

*Thus McDunnough uses "*Plebeiinæ*" in his "Check List" of Nearctic Lepidoptera (1938 Mem. S. California Acad. Sci. 1:26), and thus Comstock uses "*Plebejinæ*" in his work on Rhopalocera of Porto Rico and the Virgin Islands (1944, *in* Miner, Scient. Survey P. R. and V. Isls. 12:492), but the two references the latter author appends (Swinhoe 1910, Lep. Indica 8:10 and Hampson 1918, Novit. Zool. Tring 25:385) are most misleading: the first, because *Syntarucus* Butler, a genus structurally indistinguishable from *Leptotes* Scudder (which is one of the two genera assigned by Comstock to "*Plebejinæ*" Swinhoe) is placed by Swinhoe in a different subfamily, namely *Lampidinæ* (now known as *Catochrysopinæ*), and the second, because Hampson's (perfectly invalid) use of "*Plebejus*" and "*Plebejinæ*" refers to a section of a different family, namely *Erycinidæ* (now known as *Riodinidæ*).

several genera), the *Glaucopsychinæ* (containing, among others, the three holarctic genera *Glaucopsyche* Scudder, *Scolitantides* Hübner [to which *Phædrotes* Scudder and "*Shijimia* Matsumura" fall as synonyms] and *Philotes* Scudder), the *Everinæ* with the holarctic *Everes*, the *Lycænopsinæ* with the holarctic *Celastrina* Tutt (= *Cyaniris* Scudder, *nec* Dalman), *etc.*

The arrangement proposed in the present paper needs to be prefaced by a few words on taxonomic units. The strictly biological meaning forcibly attached by some modern zoologists to the specific concept has crippled the latter by removing the morphological moment to a secondary or still more negligible position, while employing terms, *e.g.,* "potential interbreeding," that might make sense only if an initial morphological approach were presupposed. What I term species, in my department, can be defined as a phase of evolutionary structure, male and female, traversed more or less simultaneously by a number of, consequently, more or less similar organisms morphologically shading into each other in various individual or racial ways, interbreeding in a given area and separated there from sympatric representatives of any other such phase by a structural hiatus with absence of interbreeding between the two sets. In other words: 1. any two structurally indistinguishable individuals belong to the same species regardless of biological, physiological, geographical or any other factors; 2. structurally distinguishable sympatric non-interbreeding sets represent different species regardless of all other considerations; 3. structurally distinguishable sympatric individuals belong to the same species when they occur within an interbreeding set; 4. structurally distinguishable allopatric sets belong to the same species if the hiatus between their structures is completely bridged by intermediate structures in other, not necessarily intermediate, areas; 5. obviously allied but structurally distinguishable allopatric sets not linked by such intergrades can be said to belong to different or the same species only by analogy, *i.e.,* by analysing the structural gaps between sympatric species or individuals possessing the same general type of structure. Conditions 2 and 4 do not exclude each other and so it may happen that two structurally distinguishable local forms belong to one species allopatrically because they racially intergrade, but at the same time belong to different species sympatrically because in some other region their structural counterparts occur side by side without interbreeding (this incidentally is the position in *Lycæides*). In such cases one should give precedence to the all important sympatric moment and find somewhere in the spirals of racial intergradation a point at which the whole system can be elegantly, in the mathematical sense (for we are dealing with measurable structures), divided into two parts, *i.e.,* two species, using some combination of trinomials to designate this or that interspecific form (*e.g., Lycæides scudderi doei* Roe *trans ad melissa roei* Doe). This state of affairs is not a flaw in the concept of "species" but an indirect result of its dual nature ("structure" plus "reproduction," "male" plus "female" *etc.*) and should be accepted by the taxonomist with perfect equanimity.*

The impact on the eye of a combination of characters in the whole structure or in an element of it, results in the perception of certain structural types. Structures of the same type imply phylogenetic affinities unless it can be proved, as in some cases it is easy to do, that the resemblance is "false" *i.e.,* attained by essentially different means. Such false resemblances are extremely rare and the number of characters involved is small, and this is as it should be, since such "convergence" depends upon the mathematics of chance. False dissimilarities also occur (and are also rare), *i.e.,* the striking difference between one type and another is seen, when analysed, to be due to a simple and brief process of evolution in an unusual direction.

Unless we believe that certain structural resemblances and dissimilarities are not due to chance or to gross adaptional modifications, but can be classified according to their phylogenetic sense, all horizontal genera are artificial groupings – of some practical use to collectors (*e.g.,* the convenient lumping of all small blue butterflies with rounded hindwings and dotted undersides in one "genus") but of no scientific value. This brings us to the question as to whether a classification on the basis of genitalia reflects natural relationships better than do other principles. I think the answer is "yes."

---

* "Subspecies" (on which I hold rather special views which I shall discuss elsewhere) may be briefly defined as a locally constant phase of specific alar characters with or without a local fixation of some stage within the graded variational range of the specific genitalic structure. The days are quite gone when easy-going describers could give names to these things without a detailed study of genitalic and pattern characters throughout the polytypic species or genus involved.

A "polytypic genus" is determined by structural characters which are common to all the species it includes and the particular combination of which, more than the presence of some particular detail, no matter how striking, distinguishes the group from any other. A "monotypic genus" (*i.e.*, a structurally isolated species which does not fit into any known generic group) obviously lacks the first feature while the number of characters entering the distinctive combination is vastly increased by practically coinciding with the whole array of specific characters, so that the only "reality" a monotypic genus has, lies in the implication that the only species it contains is the only one "known" and that if others were "known," a common denominator now "hidden" in the monotypic genus would be revealed. Among polytypic genera, a "natural genus" is one which reflects the flickering, as it were, of a strongly differentiated type of combinational structure within limits as narrow *per se* as, say, the range of continuous variation within a structurally highly polytypic species, and thus consists of specific structures resembling each other more than they do any other species. If h_1, h_2, h_3, h_4 denote the interspecific hiatuses, and H_1, H_2, etc. the intergeneric ones, then the lesser the h's and the larger the H's, the more "natural" the genus is – and the more liable it is to be transformed into a polytypic species by the next reviser with more material at his disposal.

A certain harmony, as yet rather obscure, seems to exist between a particular type of male armature and a particular female one; this has been taken into account in founding the genera discussed below. The impression I have formed so far that with "natural genera" specific differentiation in these organs is more marked (or at least easier to observe) in the male may be due to insufficient investigation, but anyway I cannot find any *exact* correlation between female lock and male key. In what manner and to what extent the sclerotized parts of the sexes in *Plebejinæ* fit each other during copulation is not clear, but I doubt whether the valves, the termination of which is evolutionarily the most vulnerable part, come into any direct contact with such structures in the female organ that might lead to some intersexual adaptation.*

---

*Lorkoviz states (1938, Mitt. Münchner Ent. Ges. 28:231) in an admirable paper on the European representatives of

Adaptation to surroundings, to climate, altitude *etc.*, and hence "natural selection" in its simplest sense, certainly had no direct action whatever on the moulding of the genital armature, and we know nothing of the physiological processes of which that elaborate sculpture is the structural overflow. While accepting evolution as a modal formula, I am not satisfied with any of the hypotheses advanced in regard to the way it works; on the other hand, I am quite certain that repetitions of structure, on the Siberian tundra and on the paramos of the Andes, on a mountain in India and on an island in the Caribbean Sea, cannot be treated as a result of haphazard "convergence" since the number of coincident characters in one element, let alone the coincidence of that coincident number with a set of characters in another element, exceeds anything that might be produced by "chance." Hence the conviction that there is *some* phylogenetic link where there is a recurrence of similar genitalic characters and that certain groupings – the new genera to which we now must turn – may be so devised as to reflect the natural affiliations of the species.   [*Psyche* 52: 1–6]

Parachilades n.g.

Type and only known species *Lycæna titicaca* Weymer 1890 . . .

Five males and one female investigated: prep. 610, "Titicaca [Lake], Bolivia," *ex* coll. Huntington [*ex* coll. Staudinger-Bang Haas], Amer. Mus. Nat. Hist.; prep. 483, 488, 589, 620, ♀ 590, "Sicasica, Bolivia, 1.X.1899" *ex* coll. Weeks, Mus. Comp. Zool.

Ædeagus thickish,* about 1 mm. long, the suprazonal portion subequal to the subzonal one. In general type fairly close to *Chilades* (see pl. 2, CON 1), still more curved, however, with a pronounced bulging of the outline (in lateral view) dorsally at the zone (above the zone and less conspicuous in *Chilades*) and a somewhat different structure of the suprazonal portion. Suprazonal sheath terminating on the ventral side in a point (which is not notched as it is in *Chilades*) with two filament-like lateral portions (struc-

---

Everes (*Everinæ*) that in that genus the median uncal projection (a structure not found in *Plebejinæ* and wrongly, in my opinion, regarded as being formed by the fusion of the uncus lobes) fits exactly the vaginal plate of the female, both varying together according to the species. See also Chapman 1916, Trans. Ent. Soc. London 1916:170.

*In all genera examined the subzonal portion of the ædeagus appears in cross-section as a dorso-ventrad directed oval, the lengthening of which produces the appearance of "thickness" in the organ when the latter is viewed from the side.

turally similar to the spine-like single medial process described by Chapman in other genera and represented in *Chilades**) diverging from it and rimming the vesica, the erected (everted) frothy membrane of which they seem to prop. Vesical opening (on the dorsal side) beginning just above the zone (thus at a more proximal point than in *Chilades*). Vesica very simple and weak as in *Chilades*, *Freyeria*,[†] *Lycæides*, etc. Alulæ considerably more developed than in *Chilades*, forming two petals almost 0.3 long and resembling (or representing) rudiments of the peculiar element (sagum) that exists at various degrees of development in several other neotropical genera where, however, it is well differentiated from the alulæ (except in *Hemiargus*). Furca considerably smaller in relation to the ædeagus than in *Chilades*, singularly thick, pincers-like, connected at its tips with the petals of the alulæ. The whole dorsum (falx + uncus lobe + tegumen) remarkably similar in type to *Chilades*, which type is characterised by the breadth of the robust and long forearm exceeding that of the long finger-shaped uncus lobe,[‡] by the humerulus appearing to be produced (owing to the exiguity of the lobe) not from the base of the lobe but from the tegumen proper, and by the latter being smaller by comparison to the falx and the lobe than in other *Plebejinæ*. Differing from *Chilades* in the greater size of the falx and uncus lobe in relation to the rest of the armature and to the size of the wings.[§] Falx very big, long and thick, fatter than in *Chilades*, and not distinctly separated to the eye into its components (humerulus, elbow, etc.) owing (1) to its not bunching at the shoulder as it does in *Chilades* (in ventral view); (2) to the unusual (unique in *Plebejinæ*, typical in *Catochry-*

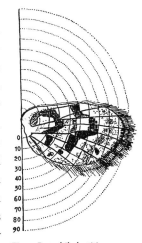

Fig. 1. *Parachilades titicaca*, left hindwing underside.

---

*One wonders whether this medial process in *Chilades* is not, perhaps, merely a lesser stage of development of the pointed part of the sheath of *Parachilades*, while the lateral processes in the latter represent a lesser stage of development in comparison to the latero-ventral pointed sheath portions of *Chilades*. I am not fully satisfied with my observations in regard to the ædeagus of these two genera.

[†]I fail to find in either of the two species of *Freyeria* (*trochilus* and *putli*) the cornuti mentioned in the case of *trochilus* by Stempffer (1937, Bull. Soc. ent. France 42:215).

[‡]In fact Fruhstorfer, the only German writing author of his time who made any attempt to follow the British authors in the study of Lycænid genitalia for systematic purposes, in an enthusiastic, but amateurish, and poorly illustrated paper on *Chilades* (1916 Zool. Meded. Leiden, 2:90–95) mistook the uncus lobes of *lajus* and *cleotas* for an additional pair of falces (besides confusing generic characters with specific ones).

[§]The *titicaca* lobe length is only attained in *Chilades* by one species (*cleotas*, pl. 2, CLE 3) in which the whole alar surface is 5.4 times greater and the forewing 2.5 times longer than in *titicaca*, while in *galba* forms (e.g. pl. 2, CON 3) where dwarfs from Cyprus approach my largest *titicaca* (length of fore wing 8.5 mm.) in wing span (though of course the wings remain always much fuller than in *Parachilades*), the lobe is at least twice smaller than in the latter.

sopinæ) slant in the part that corresponds to the, very upright, forearm of *Chilades,* with a consequently wide and weak falcal arch; and (3) to its even breadth from basal point to almost three-quarters of its length; thus of a limacine appearance increased by the fact (again unique in this subfamily, but frequent in *Catochrysopinæ*) that in ventral view the point of the oblique falx seems twisted away from the lobe instead of curving hookwise toward the latter as it does in *Chilades* (or other genera) where it attains the tip of the lobe. Uncus lobe narrow and long, exceeding the length of the tegumen (from base of falx to beginning of cingula) which is not the case in *Chilades* nor indeed in any other genus of the subfamily; tapering above the humerulus to form a finger-shaped projection of even breadth throughout; slightly excurved (in contrast to the straight "gothic" projection in *Chilades*) and at least $1^1/_2$ narrower than the forearm. Valve exceedingly small and squat, about half the ædeagus and about equal to the falx in length, the first proportion only approached in one other species of *Plebejinæ* (*Hemiargus ramon* Dognin) and the second unique in the subfamily (but common in other Lycænids); of a peculiar stunted appearance, shaped like an elephant, about one and two-fifths as long as broad, thus strikingly different from the elongated shape of *Chilades* and all Old World members of the subfamily; with a strongly and evenly curved processus superior ending in a thickish gradually tapering rostellum (about a third of the valve in length), which continues the even curve of the whole upper margin and comes to rest upon the well-developed, strongly jutting mentum, the tip of which may assume a fluted appearance *in situ.*

Female: fibula of ostium bursæ strongly developed, of the *Chilades* type, with the upper lamella conspicuously long (about 0.3 mm.). Papillæ anales about 0.45 mm. broad and very large in relation to the short-looking rods (about 0.6). [*Psyche* 52: 6, 7–9]

Pseudothecla n.g.*

Type and only known species: *Thecla faga* Dognin 1895, Ann. Soc. ent. Belgique 39: 105–106 "Loja, Ecuador" (= ? *excisicosta* Dyar 1913, Proc.

---

*[Nabokov notes in his *Lepidopterological Papers 1941–1953,* "=*Nabokovia* Hemming (1961 Annot. lep., pt. 2, p. 41)."]

United States Natnl. Mus. 45: 637–638 "Cotahuasi; Chuquibamba, Peru").*

One male investigated: prep. 611, "Peru," *ex* coll. Huntington, Am. Mus. Nat. Hist. (with a somewhat more weakly marked underside than Dognin's description suggests). . . .

This is a very curious addition to the subfamily. . . .   [*Psyche* 52: 11]

Pseudochrysops n.g.

Type, and only known species: *Hemiargus bornoi* Comstock-Huntington 1943 (Ann. New York Acad. Sci. 45 : 102–104, "Pont Beudet, Haiti," pl. 1, figs. 18 ♀, 19 underside; Comstock, 1944, Rhopalocera, *in* Miner, Scient. Survey Porto Rico and Virgin Isls. 12 : 498–499, fig. 16 venation).

Two male paratypes and one female paratype (all *ex* coll. Am. Mus. Nat. Hist., Mus. Comp. Zool.) investigated: prep. 496, 604, ♀ 605, all "Pont Beudet, Haiti, about 100 ft., 3–4-III-1922."

Ædeagus slim, elongated, 1 mm. long, suprazonal portion equal to subzonal one; ventral part of subzonal sheath slightly notched distally, acuminate in lateral view; vesical opening high, about half-way up from the zone, alulæ small, Chapman's process slight, vesica weak, unarmed, the whole organ vaguely intermediate between *Chilades* and *Freyeria.*† Sagum rudimentary, in the form of two weak ill-defined lobes produced from the zone ventrad. Furca well developed, in length subequal to the subzonal portion of the ædeagus, of a conventional subfamilial shape, but with a broad membraneous lining giving it a lobed appearance *in situ.* Falx and uncus lobe different in type from *Chilades* although related to it in general elongation, much more strongly developed than in *Freyeria,* but otherwise definitely allied to the latter. Forearm more than a third of a mm. long, slightly overtopping the uncus lobe, remarkably slender and straight, very gradually tapering to a minutely hooked point, elegantly elbowed, more finely drawn and direct that in *Freyeria,* similar in these features to *Lycæides melissa* Edwards, but combined with a differently shaped, comparatively high shoulder, as in *Freyeria,* only finer in outline. . . .   [*Psyche* 52: 12]

---

*Sylphis Draudt 1921 (*in* Seitz, Macrolep. World 5: 823, "Cuzco (Peru)," pl. 144, n) ought to be also checked in relation to *faga* (*op. cit.*: 823–824, pl. 144, m). Both are doubtfully placed by Draudt in *Scolitantides auct.*

†Freyeria is less close to *Chilades* than to *Lycæides,* its nearest ally.

Valve bearing a false resemblance in shape to *Iolana* Tutt (*Glauco-psychinæ*); in general proportions likewise resembling *Parachilades*; in character of rostellum somewhat allied to *Pseudothecla*; in basic structure truly allied to the next genus; very short, at its broadest (very distal) part about three-quarters as broad as long, shorter than the ædeagus, about sixteen times shorter than the length of the forewing (which is about 11 mm.) [the latter ratio being one-eighth in *Freyeria* (about 7 mm.) where, as in all Old World *Plebejinæ*, the valve is longer than the ædeagus], subtriangular, strongly expanding from its bluntly rounded base to form a buffalo hump; the process superior abruptly sloping from that point to evenly rise again at a point immediately below whence it projects distad as a slender, very slightly incurved, horn-like rostellum, in length just under one-sixth of the whole process. Stretch between rostellum and mentum extensive and steep, lending the valve a gaping appearance, this effect being due not to any special feature of mentum or distal margin of valval membrane, but to the rudimentary or aborted (despite the horn-like free end) condition of the upper process which in all other *Plebejinæ* is long enough to allow the rostellum to rest on the mentum. . . .   [*Psyche* 52: 13]

In pattern characters this rare and remarkable butterfly belongs, together with a few other genera or aberrant species, to what may be termed the "catochrysopoid" pattern group in *Plebejinæ* (some notes on the subject will be found further on and at the end of this paper), none of the members of this group having, however, any structural connection whatever with the *Catochrysopinæ* genitalically. Moreover, the present assignment of *bornoi* and *faga* to the true *Plebejinæ* adds two "tailed" species to the small number (all in *Chilades*) already known (first recognized by Chapman 1916).

Cyclargus n.g.
Type: *Lycæna ammon* Lucas 1857
    Four species known:*

---

*Listed in chronological order. The obvious systematic sequence is: *dominica, ammon, woodruffi, thomasi*. [Nabokov added in his *Lepidopterological Papers 1941–1953*: "A fifth species described by me in Ent. 81 Dec. 1948, *erembis* Nabokov, Little Cayman."]

ammon Lucas . . .
dominica Möschler . . .
thomasi Clench . . .
woodruffi Comstock-Huntington . . .

GENERIC DESCRIPTION

Ædeagus in a very general way allied to *Pseudochrysops*, smaller, stubbier, from just under 0.65 to just over 0.8 long; suprazonal portion about half or just over one-half the subzonal one; ventral side of suprazonal sheath notched distally; vesical opening beginning at about half-way or two-thirds from the zone on dorsal side, at first very narrow, with distinct lateral portions then brusquely allowing the vesica to expand; the latter very plump (facing more or less distad), in lateral view not unlike a pin cushion, in dorsal view resembling a bourbon crown; set with about 120–160 comparatively large (0.003) cornuti in several regular rows of about ten and more or less distinctly divided by the thin point of Chapman's process; alulæ and subzonal portion of the usual type in the subfamily, the former about 0.1 long, the latter compressed laterally, broader in lateral than in ventral or dorsal view. Furca small, slightly shorter than the subzonal portion, more efficiently holding it in the forking than in Old World types. Sagum well developed, consisting of two convex (ventrad) lobes about 0.4 long by 0.2 broad, connected at the zone with the alulæ, and below the zone with the points of the furca, converging in front (*i.e.,* on the ventral side) of the ædeagus in the manner of a stiffly bulging short waistcoat, too ample as it were for the body it encloses, and edged at and along its margins (which appear distally projected in lateral view and thus differ from other sagum bearing genera to be discussed) with conspicuous teeth reaching 0.03 in length. Uncus, especially falces, extremely small and weak. Falx allied in type only to one Old World genus, namely *Aricia;* in shape resembling a beheaded dromedary, the part of the "neck" being taken by the straight, rather bluntly tapering, plain-tipped vertical projection (forearm) of the falx, and the "hump" being represented by the high evenly shaped vertical shoulder of the medially thickish, straight, rather long horizontal extension (humerulus) of the falx (see pl. 1, fig. 4). Uncus lobe subtriangular *in situ,* spoon shaped when slightly compressed in flat ventral view, from slightly to one-fifth longer than the falx and hardly two-thirds the length of the lobe of *Pseudochrysops bornoi.* Valve allied to that of the latter but better developed in the processus superior, thus approaching a more normal (though still very squat) *Plebejinæ* shape which it resembles only insofar as a puffer resembles a pike; very small and short, hardly attaining the length of the ædeagus, twice or less than twice as long as broad, heavily humped; the hollowed outline formed by the mentum (which here seems somewhat upturned *in situ*) and the (strongly receding here) margin of the body of the valve extending laterally (*i.e.,* subparallel to the long axis of the valve) rather than "vertically" as it does in *bornoi* (where the upper process is poorly developed); the free part of the upper process (rostellum) throughout its length snugly resting upon and merging with the hollowed margin, but when manipulated seen to be sinuous, flexible looking and long; ending in a more or less broad coxcomb with well developed or greatly developed teeth oriented along the long axis of the valve, longer relatively to it than in other *Plebejinæ* (except one palearctic species, *Plebejus argus* L. where, however, they point obliquely down as in *Itylos, sensu mihi*), and providing the main characters for distinguishing the four species.

Female: fibula resembling *P. bornoi* but shorter (0.1 long by as much broad distally and twice broader proximally). Everted henia stumpy and short.* Papillæ anales about 0.3 long by 0.3–0.4 broad, with rods 0.7 long, thus shorter (both in relative and absolute size) than in *bornoi.* . . .

[*Psyche* 52: 14–16]

Hemiargus Hübner [revised]
1818, Zuträge Exot. Schmett. 1: 10

Since *Papilio hanno* Stoll 1790, here found to be a different species from *Hesperia ceraunus* Fabricius 1793, is not mentioned in the Zuträge, Scud-

---

*My impression is that the extensibility of the henia and its prop so marked in all *Plebejinæ* (see Chapman, 1916 *op. cit.*) is more limited in *Pseudochrysops, Cyclargus* and *Hemiargus* (*s. mihi*) in contrast to the rest of the neotropical genera examined which conform to the Old World type in this respect. I have dissected, however, only a few females and my results should be checked on more material.

der's selection (1875, Proc. Amer. Acad. Arts Sci., Boston 10: 186) and Hemming's confirmation (1934, Gen. names Holarctic Butt. 1: 104) of the type as *hanno* Stoll cannot stand.

Type: *Hemiargus antibubastus* Hübner 1818 (= *Hesperia ceraunus* Fabricius 1793, subspecies). . . .

Three known species:

ceraunus Fabricius . . .

hanno Stoll . . .

ramon Dognin . . . [*Psyche* 52: 21]

GENERIC DESCRIPTION

Ædeagus very long in relation to the other parts of the armature, with a neck-like suprazonal portion (as if the corresponding part in *Cyclargus* had been telescoped out). Suprazonal sheath in ventral (1), dorsal (2) and lateral (3) view: (1) slightly expanding at its termination where it is slightly notched, each of the resulting portions being armed with five or six ventrolaterally placed spinules; (2) revealing at more than half-way from the zone a narrow vesical fissure, the rather rough margins of which, just before expanding slightly to form the vesical opening proper (which is as long as the fissure), are somewhat drawn together and produce at this point two surculi, one on each side; (3) rather strongly incurved, with the vesical opening facing more or less distad and appearing still shorter than it is owing to the vesical slit not being seen from this angle, so that the eye mistakes the projection in profile of the paired surculi (directed dorsad and proximad) for the protruding nether "lip" of the opening.* Vesica, as seen laterally, pulvinate as in *Cyclargus*, but with smaller cornuti. Alulæ hardly, if at all, differentiated from the sagum, which is rudimentary, with no trace of teeth. Furca small, well adjusted to the ædeagus subzonally as in *Cyclargus*. Falx resembling *Cyclargus* but somewhat stronger and thicker. Uncus lobe evenly tapering to a blunt point. Valve small, shorter than the ædeagus, approaching the *Plebejinæ* shape-norm somewhat better than *Cyclar-*

---

*Moreover, from a certain angle, and especially in *hanno*, these surculi are easily mistaken by the eye for modified alulæ that would have been carried away from the zone by the generic distal extension of the ædeagus.

gus which it resembles only in the shoe-shaped mentum with no trace of a bullula and in the freedom of the rostellum; the latter, however, lacking any serration, with a bluntly tapering tip, and somewhat resembling in curvature (especially in the genotype) the kind of rostellum obtained among Old World genera only in *Chilades galba* Lederer (*sensu mihi*, i.e. including Eastern Mediterranean, Caspian, Arabian and Indian forms considered by authors as being distinct species, i.e. *galba* Lederer, *phiala* Grum Grshmailo, *ella* Butler and *contracta* Butler) and by an aberrant *Albulina* (*auct.*) species, *felicis* Oberthur, of the southern part of the Central Palæarctic region, in which species, however, the tip is toothed.

Female: henia shortish and curiously thick (with apparently reduced extensibility as in *Cyclargus* and thus unlike *Chilades*), strongly chitinized dorsally. Fibula resembling *Chilades*, pistol-shaped in profile (pointing distad), in ventral view seen to consist of a lamellate ventral piece and a horseshoe-shaped dorsal one.   [*Psyche* 52: 21–22]

Hemiargus ceraunus Fabricius . . .
The occurrence of [*H. ceraunus*] anywhere north of Arizona or the Carolinas (and even there the colonies would probably die out if not regularly replenished by the offspring of new arrivals) is due to direct spring immigration from the south in suitable seasons, which in its turn produces a more or less nomadic summer generation or generations. The same refers to *isola*. . . .   [*Psyche* 52: 24]

This [*H. ramon*] is the longest ædeagus in *Plebejinæ* except *Aricia isaurica* Staudinger which is subequal, and *Icaricia icarioides* Boisduval which attains the enormous length of 1.75. Incidentally, in Chapman 1916, *l.c.*, the former species (pl. 29, fig. 2, ædeagus) is wrongly figured as *Albulina pheretes auct.* (*orbitulus* Prunner) and vice versa (pl. 30, fig. 4, ædeagus).

Echinargus n.g.
Type: *Lycæna isola* Reakirt 1866.
   Two species known, one unnamed:*

---

*A third sp., *martha* (Dognin) redescribed by me *Psyche* 52(3–4). [VN note, *Lepidopterological Papers 1941–1953*.]

isola Reakirt (*Lycæna*, 1866, Proc. Acad. Nat. Sci. Philadelphia 1866:332, "Vera Cruz, Mexico"; *Hemiargus isola*, Bethune-Baker, 1916, Ent. News 27:450);

and a new species,* from Trinidad, British W. Indies.

GENERIC DESCRIPTION

Ædeagus shorter and weaker than in *Hemiargus*, intermediate in shape between *Hemiargus* (*hanno*) and *Cyclargus*; much plainer in structure, however, than in either, with very minute cornuti on the similarly shaped vesica. Suprazonal sheath shorter than the subzonal one, weakly notched ventrally, acuminate laterally, with high, rather distad facing vesical opening and small alulæ at the zone. Furca larger or much larger than in *Hemiargus*. Sagum considerably more developed (and reaching in *isola* its maximum for the whole subfamily), consisting of two, ventrally scooped out or fully formed lobes aproning the ædeagus and armed with a set of teeth along the distal part or the whole of the margin. Forearm of falx very slightly curved and sharper than the straight blunt forearm of *Cyclargus* or *Hemiargus*, with a higher and more conical shoulder. Uncus lobe as in *Hemiargus* but slightly more excurved and tending to a hatchet shape under pressure. Valve of a normal subfamilial (fish-like) shape, allied to the *lajus* section in *Chilades*, with a tapering rostellum of the *Hemiargus ceraunus* type but differing from those genera by the presence of a bullula which is typical for holarctic *Plebejinæ* (and also exists in the next three neotropical genera to be discussed). Female: henia long and comparatively thin, thus again differing from *Hemiargus* in a normal "Old-World" direction.

Echinargus isola Reakirt

Seven males and one female investigated:

Prep. 540, "Tancitaro, Michoachan, Mexico, 6,000 ft., on *fæces*, 10-

---

*Shortly after recognizing this as an undescribed species by studying the Thaxter pair (see below), I learnt from Mr. W. P. Comstock that he knew it already from specimens (one of which he gifted to this Museum) taken on the same island by Mr. E. I. Huntington, and was about to publish it. I refrain from using Comstock's MS. name so as not to interfere with his priority in case my paper appears before his.

VII-1941, *leg.* R. Haag: 539 (*forma "nyagora* Boisduval") *id.*; 478, "Round Mt., Texas, X-1930," *ex* coll. Fall; ♀ 587, "Dallas, Texas, *leg.* Boll"; 500, 526, 534, "Texas"; 538, "Half Way House, Pike's Peak, Colorado, 9,000–10,000 ft., 16–18 VII-1902," *ex* coll. Weeks (? *ssp. alce* Edwards; see Field 1941, Kans. Univ. Sci. Bull. 26:347).

Ædeagus very poorly chitinised, very anemic looking when teased out of the prodigious structure of the sagum; just over two thirds of a mm. long, the suprazonal portion less than one third of the subzonal one with the vesical opening at two thirds from the zone. Furca extremely long,* almost reaching one mm. and thus of a very holarctic aspect. Sagum hugely developed, consisting of two convex lobes, in ventral view resembling the parietal bones of a skull; about twice as long as broad, only slightly shorter than the prongs of the flexible furca embracing them: thus twice longer than the subzonal portion of the ædeagus which they envelop from the zone down, their strongly serrated edges meeting in front (e.g. ventrally) of the ædeagus and of an imaginary line prolonging it proximad; these teeth of uneven length but on the whole increasing in size proximad; up to 45 teeth along each margin, the first three or four (at the most distal point where the edges begin to meet) about 0.012 long, then ranging (in the same specimen) from 0.02 to 0.04 (and to 0.055 in some specimens) in an unequal sequence; finally reaching 0.1 at the proximal ends of the parting margins where they become clawlike, with clusters of additional spines on the præmarginal surface of the lobes. Shoulder of falx almost as high as the forearm which is about one third of the ædeagus. Valve twice longer than the ædeagus and more than three times as long as broad itself with a long tapering tail, a rather weak hump, a small mentum and a curved rather than bent, thickish, gradually tapering rostellum about 0.2 long.

Female: henia beautifully developed with its distal half (about 0.6) strongly plated; fibula engulfed as it were in this chitinisation.

---

*This is the only species of the nineteen discussed here that already had been (briefly) described genitalically: namely, Bethune Baker 1916, *l.c.*, refers to "a large toothed hood ... [which] has its origin just above the very short furca." Evidently the greater part of the *very long* furca was screened from the observer by other parts of the armature. In this connection it should be noted that during the time the armatures are studied they should be kept in vials and if mounted at all (subsequently) the parts should be well separated, with the dorsum placed in ventral view. A slide of the whole armature in lateral view (or a photograph of such a preparation) is utterly useless.

Measurements (m mm.): ædeagus 0.6–0.7 (mean 0.69), suprazonal portion 0.15–0.2 (mean 0.18), subzonal 0.45–0.52 (mean 0.49) with breadth (in lateral view) 0.08–0.09; penis mean 0.62. Furca mean 0.9. Sagum 0.85–0.96 (mean 0.93) with breadth 0.41–0.44 (mean 0.42). Vertical/Horizontal extension of uncus: forearm 0.2/0.03–0.22/0.035, humerulus 0.055/0.13–0.065/0.14, shoulder 0.18/0.05; lobe 0.25/0.08. Valve 1.28–1.31, with breadth 0.33–0.39.

Echinargus n.sp.*

Two males and one female investigated: prep. 578, "Port of Spain, Trinidad, XII-1912-V-1913, *leg.* R. Thaxter," Mus. Comp. Zool.; female, prep. 597 *id.*; prep. 614, "Chancellor Rd., Port of Spain, Trinidad, 21-31-III-1929, *leg.* E. I. Huntington," *ex* coll. Amer. Mus. Nat. Hist., Mus. Comp. Zool.

Ædeagus just over half a mm. in length, the suprazonal portion about three fifths of the subzonal one, vesical opening at about two thirds from zone on the ventral side. Furca longer than the subzonal portion of the æedeagus and very thin. Sagum very remarkable: showing a transitional stage of development between *Hemiargus ceraunus* and *Echinargus isola*; each of its twin parts produced ventrad from the zone and embraced by the furca, in shape roughly resembling a high-shouldered falx the forearm of which (copied by the jutting lower portion of each lobe) would terminate in a process resembling a valval comb. For purposes of measurement this peculiar fig-leaf type of sagum may be imagined in the case of each lobe as a roughly equilateral triangle ZPD.[†] (where Z is the præzonal point, P the base of the penis and D the dentate end of each sagum lobe) with ZP (along the æedeagus) and PD (at an angle away from the æedeagus ventrad) and the

---

Echinargus huntingtoni Rindge & Comstock (1953 [June], *J.N.Y. Ent. Soc.* 61, pp. 99–100, Hololo Mountain Road, St. Annis, Trinidad, B. W. I., end III.29. [vn note, *Lepidopterological Papers 1941–1953.*] In this article Frederick Rindge and William Comstock named the butterfly *Echinargus huntingtoni*, explaining: "In his 'Notes on Neotropical Plebejinae' (1945, Psyche, vol. 52, pp. 1–61), Nabokov recognized this species as being undescribed and he included a careful diagnosis of the maculation and the genitalia of both sexes. He refrained from applying a name to this species, as Mr. Comstock had already applied a manuscript name to the series in the collection of the American Museum of Natural History, and was preparing to publish it. However, illness prevented a completion of this project and so it is being done now."

[†]Which following the falcal simile would coincide with BHF (see pl. 1).

imaginary line ZD connecting these points (and in position coinciding with the "filled out" ventral margin of each lobe in *isola*) each about 0.3–0.35 long. Actually a large portion (shaped rather like the falcal arch in high-shouldered falces) is left unfilled in the triangle ZPD so that each sagum lobe consists of an upper portion dorsally curving along the ædeagus, ventrally sinuous with a bulge in its outline, and roughly 0.35 long by 0.15 broad at that bulge, and of a lower portion, jutting in a ventral direction, 0.35 long along its straight basal side, 0.3 along its sinuous and oblique opposite margin and 0.04 broad at the beginning of its free part, then widening to 0.1, and at the very end narrowing again to form a spur 0.05 broad with four teeth 0.01 long. Falx and uncus lobe covered by the generic description and the measurements given below. Valve small but at least a fifth longer than the ædeagus, elongated, slightly more than twice as long as broad, with Bayard's angulation well pronounced. Rostellum bent towards the mentum, thin, tapering, about 0.11 long.

Female: henia extruding (semi-exerted) to a length of 0.25 by 0.12 broad medially in lateral view. Fibula consisting of two lamellate portions one longer by 0.04 than the other which is 0.17 long by 0.12 broad, of a suboval shape. Papillæ anales about 0.33 long by 0.42 broad, with rods 0.7 long.

Measurements (in mm.): ædeagus 0.56–0.58, suprazonal portion 0.2–0.21, subzonal 0.36–0.37 with breadth 0.1; penis 0.5. Furca 0.42–0.43. Sagum 0.35 (see description). Vertical/Horizontal extension of uncus: forearm 0.18/0.035–0.18/0.045, humerulus 0.04/0.12–0.045/0.14, shoulder 0.11/0.065–0.11/0.07, lobe 0.21/0.05. Valve 0.7 by 0.29–0.31 broad. Rostellum 0.11.

Alar characters, underside, ♀, (see plate 8): 0–150: number of concentric scale lines with common center for both wings (as also in *Cyclargus*). Veins ending at following lines: forewing Sc|65, R_1|85, R_2|100, R_3|120, R_4|140, M_1|145, M_2|145, M_3|143, Cu_1|137, Cu_2|128, 1A|124, 2A|118, hindwing Sc|78, R_s|94, M_1|108, M_2|110, M_3|110, Cu_1|108, Cu_2|100, 1A|94, 2A|85, 4A|40. The evenly rounded stretch of termen 94–108–110–110–108–100–94 is a rare character in *Plebejinæ* (also found in *Cyclargus*).

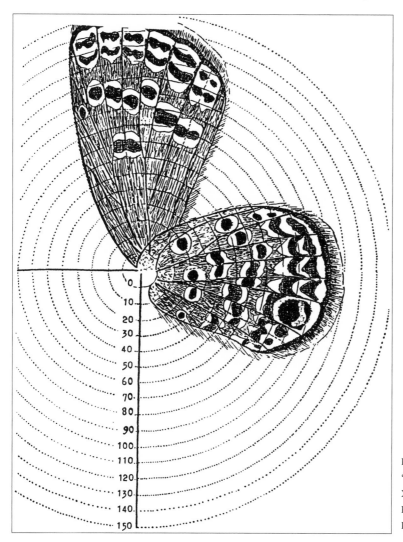

Plate 8. *Echinargus*, n. sp.,
"Port of Spain, Trinidad,
XII-1912–V-1913, *leg.*
R. Thaxter," Mus. Comp. Zool.
Left hindwing underside.

The following markings are represented: forewing, fairly broad terminal line, split macule I (with inner and outer cretules and uncolored interval) in cells R_4 to $1A$, lateral macule in R_2, macule II (with broad halo) in R_4 to $1A$, I discoidal $R + M$ (with broad halo). Example of disposition (on interneural fold); in Cu_1: terminal line 133–136; outer cretule 127–133; præterminal mark (outer part of split macule I) 123–127; interval 116–123; semimacule (inner part of split macule I) 111–116; crescentic inner cretule 104–111 (thus the whole system of macule I extends from 104 to 133); outer part of halo of macule II 88–94; macule II 81–88; inner part of halo of macule II 76–81 (thus the whole system of macule II 76–94). Hindwing, fairly broad terminal line, split macule I (with crescentic inner and outer cretules; interval uncolored except in Cu_1) in cells Sc to $2A$, poorly pigmented except the præterminal mark in Cu_1; macule II in same cells, macule III in Sc and Cu_2; I $R + M$ and II M; lateral macule in $4A$. Observations: præterminal marks in hindwing from Sc increasing tornad and together with the intervals tending to a triangular (basad pointed) shape, especially in M_2, M_3, weakly pigmented; then in Cu_1 greatly developed (20 scale lines), round, strongly pigmented ("black") with a distally placed band-like scintilla consisting of 52 scales and about a fifth the mark in extension (proximo distad), and a narrow crescentic interval faintly flushed with the auroral element; then in Cu_2 to $2A$ mark roundish, but small, decreasing tornad, weakly pigmented. Other catochrysopoid features, shared with *Cyclargus* and *Hemiargus*, can be easily seen from the figure.

Pseudolucia n.g.

Type: *Lycæna chilensis* Blanchard 1852.

Two species known:

chilensis Blanchard (*Lycæna*, 1852, *in* Gay, Hist. Chile, Zool. 7:37–38, "Coquimbo, Chile," pl. 3, figs. 4a ♂, b; *Scolitantides chilensis*, Butler, 1881, Trans. Ent. Soc. 1881:467; ?*Lycæna endymion** Blanchard, 1852 *ibid.*:37 "Coquimbo, Chile," pl. 3, fig. 3a ♂, b; *Polyommatus atahualpa* Wallengren, 1860, Wien. ent. Monatschr. 4:37, "Valparaiso, Chile").

---

*Rechristened "*sibylla*" by Kirby (1871, Cat. Diurn. Lepid.: 377) who wrongly thought Blanchard's name clashed with *Papilio endymion* [Schiff] = *Meleageria meleager* Esper.

PLATE 18 a (top side)

PLATE 18 b (underside)

PL 18 a, b Two views of VN's first important American catch, taken on June 9, 1941, on the South Rim of the Grand Canyon. He named it *Neonympha dorothea* for Dorothy Leuthold, a friend who drove the Nabokovs west on the trip and "kicked up" the first specimen, enabling the butterfly's discovery. It filled in one part of a puzzle that VN solved pertaining to the Satyrs. Later findings revised the name to *Cyllopsis pertepida dorothea* (Nabokov).

(Photographed by Jeff Mermelstein)

PLATE 19

Male (left) and female Mountain Parnassians (*Parnassius smintheus*). This genus of swallowtail relatives had a special appeal for VN. The Eurasian Apollo and Clouded Apollo (*P. apollo*, *P. mnemosyne*) receive many mentions in his fiction. This species occurs in the mountains of the American West. VN collected the female in New Mexico and the male in Telluride, Colorado, a town that provides the landscape for Humbert's vision of the mining town spread below after Lolita's escape in *Lolita*.

(Frank DiMeo, Cornell University Photography)

PL. 20 The Anise Swallowtail (*Papilio zelicaon*) and Mead's Sulphur (*Colias meadii*), both collected by VN in the Rocky Mountains. *P. zelicaon* is very similar to the first butterfly named by Linnæus in 1758, *Papilio machaon* (the Old World Swallowtail), which had enchanted VN as a youth. While the Anise Swallowtail occurs in many habitats all over the West, Mead's Sulphur flies only in the high alpine elevations VN loved to haunt.

(Frank DiMeo, Cornell University Photography)

PL. 21 A male Silvery Blue (*Glaucopsyche lygdamus*) collected by VN in Sierra Madre, Wyoming, in July 1952, and so labeled in VN's hand. This bright blue flies in springtime in the lowlands and is on the wing by midsummer in the arctic-alpine heights.

(Frank DiMeo, Cornell University Photography)

PL. 22 A female of the orange Christina race of Queen Alexandra's Sulphur (*Colia alexandra christina*) that VN collected while crossing the Black Hills of South Dakota in July 1958. It is related to the "rose-margined Sulphurs" he evokes near the end of Chapter 6 of *Speak, Memory*.

(Frank DiMeo, Cornell University Photography)

PLATE 23

PLATE 24

vn's first Karner Blues (*Lycaeides melissa samuelis*), which he had identified in 1943, from museum specimens, as at least a separate subspecies (he and others later came to consider it likely to be a distinct species). After searching for it for years in the American Northeast, he caught these two specimens in the Karner pine-barrens, between Schenectady and Albany, in 1950. Partly through vn's support, this butterfly would become a major symbol of the conservation movement in the Northeast.

(Frank Dimeo, Cornell University Photography)

ABOVE A series of Boisduval's Blue (*Icaricia icarioides*), labeled "race 'kaibabensis' Nabokov ms." vn collected these specimens on the Kaibab Plateau of Arizona in June 1956 and may have intended to name them as a new subspecies. In fact, this name was never applied, and no such race, or manuscript, is known. The brigher blue individuals are males; the specimen in the lower right corner has aberrant spots on the forewings. vn erected the genus *Icaricia* to receive this and several other North American species.

(Frank DiMeo, Cornell University Photography)

PLATE 25 OPPOSITE PAGE Below, vn's numbered drawing showing the elegant scale-row classification system he worked out overlaid on a heavily spotted Melissa Blue. Double digits specify radial scale rows that furnish a grid for mapping individual markings. Letters identify the wing veins according to an established anatomical system. Above, the maculation of a lightly marked subspecies, *L. idas annetta*, for comparison.

(Berg Collection of English and American Literature, The New York Public Library; Astor, Lenox, and Tilden Foundations)

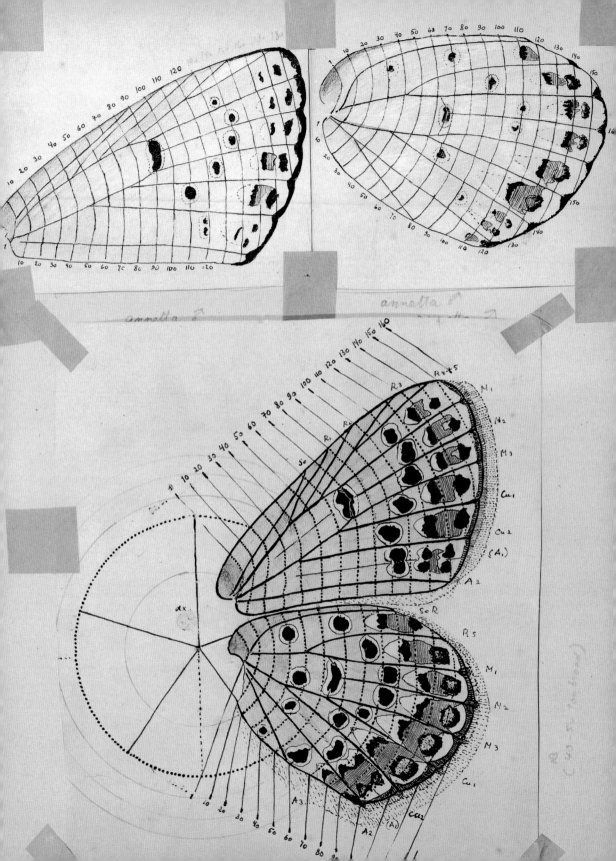

annetta ♂

annetta ♂

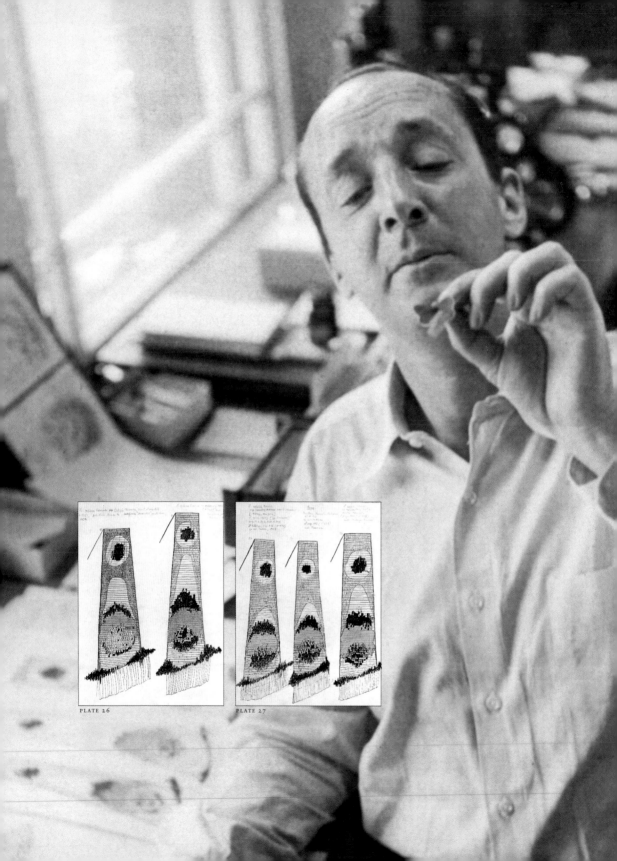

PLATE 26

PLATE 27

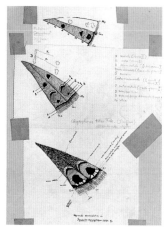

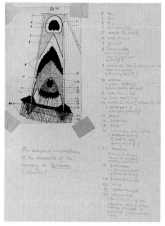

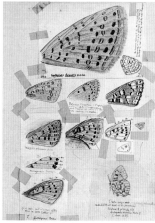

PLATE 28

PLATE 29

PLATE 30

Pairs of ventral hindwing sectors showing VN's fine penwork and the way in
which adjacent markings could be
compared using this means of analysis
as well as the scale rows of plate 25.

OPPOSITE PAGE: inset, PLATES 26, 27

Hindwing sectors with superimposed
scale rows drawn to such a power that
individual scales have been illustrated
in the macules, aurorae, and scintillae.
Such close-up wing mapping enabled
VN to discern and describe fine distinctions among races and colonies of
Blues, and to juxtapose and compare
their microevolutionary details, long
before protein electrophoresis, DNA
sampling, and gene-sequencing arrived.

(Berg Collection of English and American Literature,
The New York Public Library; Astor, Lenox, and
Tilden Foundations)

Background VN at his laboratory bench at
the Museum of Comparative Zoology,
Harvard, November 1946. Visible on
the bench are some of his wing-segment drawings. *(Joffe/Vogue)*

A stylized drawing of one sector of the
ventral hindwing of a blue. VN's handwritten caption and numbers point out
twenty-two distinct features that he
used in the description of these butterflies, from the halo through the aurora,
scintilla, and lacrima, to the outer
fringe. Some of these terms were established, others he created for the purpose.

(Berg Collection of English and American Literature,
The New York Public Library; Astor, Lenox,
and Tilden Foundations)

VN's drawings of the undersides of several lycaenid butterflies related to the
Blues he revised. The central study
illustrates the Harvester, an American
species whose larvae uniquely feed on
aphids. By examining an array of
lycaenids, VN sought an understanding
of the origins, ancestry, and development of their markings, the better to
tease out and characterize their relationships.

(Berg Collection of English and American Literature,
The New York Public Library; Astor, Lenox,
and Tilden Foundations)

OVERLEAF A series of hindwing radial
sectors showing the variation in features named in plate 29 among related
blues from thirteen localities including
Yellowstone and Yakima, Washington.

(Berg Collection of English and American Literature,
The New York Public Library; Astor, Lenox, and
Tilden Foundations)

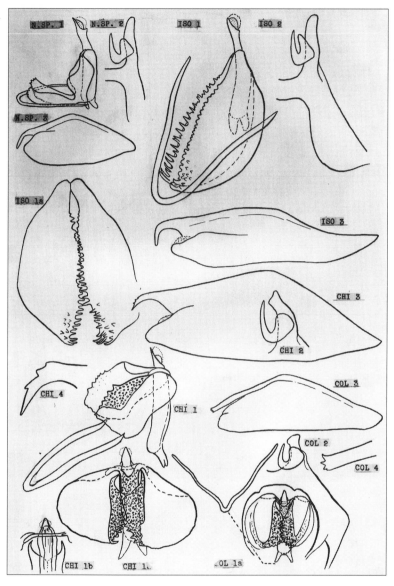

Plate 5. N.SP – *Echinargus* sp. prep. 578, "Port of Spain, Trinidad, XII–1912–V–1913, *leg.* R. Thaxter," Mus. Comp. Zool.

ISO – *Echinargus isola* Reakirt

ISO 1,2 – prep. 540, "Tancitaro, Michoachan, Mexico, 6,000 ft. alt., on *fœces*, 10–VII–1941, *leg.* R. Haag," Mus. Comp. Zool.

ISO 1a, 3 – prep. 478, "Round Mt., Texas, IX–1930, *ex* coll. Fall," Mus. Comp. Zool.

CHI – *Pseudolucia chilensis* Blanchard

CHI 1, a,b – prep. 619, "Central Chile, 1882–1885, *leg.* H. B. James," *ex* coll. Weeks, Mus. Comp. Zool.

CHI 2,3,4 – prep. 534, "Penco, Chile," *ex* coll. Weeks, Mus. Comp. Zool.

COL – *Pseudolucia collina* Blanchard, prep. 536, *Penco, Chile, ex* coll. Weeks, Mus. Comp. Zool.

1 a, b, ædeagus with sagum and furca (ISO 1a, sagum separate)

1 – lateral view, 1 a, ventral view, 1 c, dorsal view

2 – uncus lobe, falx and part of tegumen

3 – valve

4 – comb of valve

collina Philippi (*Lycæna,* 1860, Linn. Ent. 14:270–271 "Santiago, Chile"; *Scolitantides* collina,* Butler, 1881 l.c.; *Lycæna lyrnessa* Hewitson, 1874, Ent. Month. Mag. 11:107 "Chile").

GENERIC DESCRIPTION

Ædeagus thick-set, with strong fat tabs and alulæ, the latter very homogeneous with the subzonal sheath, sepaloid, arched and raised (as in several suprazonally short palæarctic genera e.g. *Agrodiætus*), the zone dipping medially (ventrally slightly more so than dorsally) and coinciding with the beginning of the vesical opening on the dorsal side. Suprazonal portion, as measured from that medial point ventrally, extremely short, about one third the length of the subzonal one (and still shorter if measured from the apices of the "shrugged" alulæ), thus shorter than in any other species restricted to the New World. The short shield of the (ventral) suprazonal sheath deltoid in ventral aspect, acuminate in lateral view and quite straight i.e. lacking the slight excurvation noticeable in *Hemiargus, Cyclargus* etc.; exceeding in length the plain unarmed vesical tip of the penis (which seems sunken between the alulæ). Subzonal sheath thickly lining the penis, curiously shagreened ventrally. Furca strongly developed, its tips connected with the sagum. The latter in shape and position of the *Echinargus isola* type, but considerably smaller (in relation to the ædeagus), its two lobes reaching from the level of the alulæ (to which they are attached) to the level of the base of the penis proper and almost as broad as long; meeting in front (i.e. ventrally) of the ædeagus at about one third of the subzonal portion from the zone, overlapping for a short stretch, then parting again; these front edges coarsely serrated, and the whole præmarginal portion of each lobe strengthened ventrally by an additional sharply localized granulation of the chitinous surface (similar to the shagreened ventrum of the ædeagus as seen in the V-shaped anterior parting of the lobes), a character not found elsewhere in the subfamily. Uncus small, resembling *Pseudothecla* and also the unique plebejinoid uncus[†] of the holotropical

---

*The genus *Scolitantides* Hübner, of which *orion* Pallas is the type, belongs to the *Glaucopsychinæ*. By an amusing coincidence Butler placed almost correctly in that genus the species *plumbea* described *ibid*.

[†]This and the *Catochrysopinæ*-like features of the *Parachilades* (and less distinctly-*Chilades*) falx constitute the only two links between the *Plebejinæ* and other subfamilies.

Zizula gaika Trimen (*Lycæna cyna* Edwards) in *Brephidinæ*. Falx still more curved than in *Echinargus*, differing from *Hemiargus* as a beckoning index does from a warning one; the whole outline from point of forearm to base of humerulus evenly rounded, with a gently sloping shoulder, thus quite different from the "cameloid" falces of the three preceding genera. Uncus lobe still more tending to a hatchet shape than in *Echinargus* (and thus resembling *Eumedonia*). Valve of a typical holarctic shape, with bullula; elongated, nicely angled at Bayard's point, rather exactly three times as long as broad and at least twice longer than the ædeagus, with a sparsely serrated rostellum.

Female: henia long and thin, with a plate-like chitinisation at the tip. . . .

[*Psyche* 52: 27–33]

The high development of the auroral element in the ground of *chilensis* and *collina* is approached among the *Plebejinæ* only by the upperside of the Sonoran *Plebulina emigdionis* and by the intense coloration of the forewing underside in certain individuals of the Spanish *Aricia idas* Rambur (rechristened at one time "*ramburi*" by Verity).* The upperside of the females oddly recalls certain Australian Lycænids belonging to a widely different subfamily. . . .   [*Psyche* 52: 35]

Paralycæides n.g.

Type and only species known: *Itylos inconspicua* Draudt 1921 (*in* Seitz, Macrolep. World 5:822, "Cuzco, Peru," pl. 144, m).

One male investigated: prep. 607 "Cuzco, Peru, 3500 m. alt., *leg.* Fassl," *ex* coll. W. P. Comstock, [*ex* coll. Staudinger-Bang Haas, "*vapa* Stgr*"], Amer. Mus. Nat. Hist.

Extremely close to *Lycæides*, in the falx, furca and valve, and considered here as retaining an ancestral aspect of that genus. . . .   [*Psyche* 52: 36]

In regard to macroscopical characters it may be briefly noted that the wing-shape recalls that of small arctic or high alpine forms of *Lycæides* while the

---

*One would like to suggest that in the future no such renaming, however necessary, should be valid unless the author of the new name redescribes the species or subspecies and selects a holotype.

pattern of the underside (very proximal position of II macule $Cu_2 + 1A$ in forewing and II macule M_3 in hindwing, poverty of pigmentation of macules, strong development of halos and other colorless scales) belongs to the same phase, as traversed by the structurally very different genus *Itylos* (*s.s.*).

Itylos Draudt [revised]
At the end of a jumble of species and forms belonging really to several genera and subfamilies but all crammed into "genus *Lycæna* F, subgenus *Rusticus* Hbn" (whatever that means), Draudt (1921, *in* Seitz, Macrolep. World 5:818) said of *Lycæna ruberrothei* Weeks ["English" text]: "Perhaps better to be placed to *Itylos* beside *moza* and *inconspicua*." This is the first time the genus *Itylos* is "indicated." A few pages further (: 821) *Itylos* Draudt was superficially described and made to include *pelorias* Weymer, *pacis* [Staudinger in commerce] Draudt, *koa* Druce, *vapa* Staudinger [*sp. incert.*], *ludicra* Weymer [*id.*], *moza* Staudinger, *inconspicua* Draudt [*recte Paralycæides sp., supra*], *titicaca* Weymer [*recte Parachilades sp., supra*] and *speciosa* Staudinger [*id.*]. Regarding the two last, however, Draudt said (: 822) that they belonged to "a somewhat deviating group." Under the circumstances, *i.e.*, since *speciosa* Staudinger [= *titicaca* Weymer] is not mentioned in the original list of *Itylos* species (*ruberrothei* Weeks [*fortas.*], *moza* Staudinger and *inconspicua* Draudt [*nom. nud.* at the time]) and is only doubtfully assigned to it when the genus is more fully discussed subsequently, Hemming's selection of *speciosa* Standinger as the type of *Itylos* (1929, Ann. Mag. Nat. Hist. 3: 240) cannot stand.

Type: *Cupido moza* Staudinger 1894.

Four species known:*

moza Staudinger (*Cupido*, 1894, Iris 7: 79–80, "Cocapata and Huallatani, Bolivia"; *Lycæna, ibid.* pl. 2, fig. 5 ♀; *Itylos moza*, Draudt 1921, *op. cit.*: 818 *et*: 821; *Lycæna babhru* Weeks, 1901, Trans. Am. Ent. Soc. 27: 357, "Sicasica, Bolivia"; 1905, Unfig. Lep.: 98, pl. 43, fig. 1 [♀]);

ruberrothei Weeks (*Lycæna*, 1902, Ent. News 12: 104 "Sicasica, Bo-

---

*Listed in systematic sequence.

livia," 1905 *op. cit.* : 99, pl. 43, fig. 2 [♂]; *Itylos?*, Draudt 1921, *op. cit.* : 818);

    pacis Draudt (*Itylos*, 1921, *op. cit.* : 821, "Cuzco, Peru," pl. 144, 1, *pacis* ♂ ♀; ?*Lycæna pelorias* Weymer 1890, *in* Reiss *et* Stübel, Reisen in Sud-America, Lepidoptera : 121–122 "Sajama, Bolivia," pl. 4, fig. 2 ♂);

    koa Druce (*Lycæna*, 1876, Proc. Zool. Soc. London, 1876 : 239–240, "Pozzuzo, Peru," pl. 18, fig. 7 [♂]; ?Weymer, 1890, *op. cit.*: 49 "Antisana, Ecuador"; *Itylos,* Draudt, 1921, *op. cit.*: 821 pl. 144, m; [see also "*Lycæna koa*," Dyar, 1913, Proc. United States Natul. Mus. **45** : 638, who suggests seasonal dimorphism in the tone and density of the blue overlay in Peruvian males].

    My study of the bibliography has been very superficial and my material too scanty for a satisfactory revision of these little known species. *Lycæna ludicra* Weymer 1890 (*op. cit.* : 122, "Tacora, Bolivia," pl. 4, fig. 3 ♂) may be a form of *Itylos moza*, or an allied species, with well developed cyanic overlay, and *Itylos grata* Kohler 1934 (Rev. Soc. ent. Argentina **6** : 38–39 "Las Lajas, Argentina," text fig. [poor phot.] ♂) is apparently close to *pacis* Weymer. *Cupido vapa* Staudinger 1894 (Iris **7** : 79, "Huallatani; Cocapata, Bolivia"; *Lycæna vapa, ibid.* pl. 2, fig. 4 ♂) may turn out to belong to *Itylos*, and the same may be said of *Lycæna martha* Dognin 1887* (Le Naturaliste **9** : 190, "Loja, Ecuador"), which, judging by the woodcut (l.c. fig. 5 ♂ ♀) combines *Hemiargus* and *Itylos* wing characters and very possibly is a form of *koa* (some specimens of which have a well formed, "black," scintillated præterminal mark in Cu_1) with strongly developed ornamentation of the catochrysopoid type.

GENERIC DESCRIPTION

A very holarctic looking genus. Ædeagus acuminate, slightly incurved, in structure and shape closely allied to *Icaricia, Aricia*, and *Lycæides*. Suprazonal portion subequal to the subzonal one; suprazonal sheath in ventral view rather narrow above the zone, then slightly broadening, then tapering to a sharp point, and (in side view) laterally enveloping the vesica

---

Echinargus martha see *Psyche* 52 (3–4). [vn note, *Lepidopterological Papers 1941–1953.*]

only immediately above the zone, then gradually turning into a strictly ventral shield. Vesical opening on the dorsal side beginning immediately above the zone, vesica plain, weakly convex, about as long as the subzonal sheath. Alulæ small. Furca well developed. Sagum absent. Falx resembling an enlarged edition of *Cyclargus*; somewhat allied to *Aricia* but well formed, with a steeper and narrower shoulder. Forearm straight, tapering to a blunt point, falcal arch narrow, shoulder high and conical though not as high in relation to the falx as it is in *Echinargus*. Uncus lobe with *Albulina* affinities, larger than in all preceding groups considerably higher than the forearm. Structure of tegumen at its junction with the uncus more elaborate, than in the preceding genera, of a common holarctic type (*Albulina, Plebulina*, etc.). Valve likewise representing the holarctic norm, longer than the ædeagus, with a well developed bullula. Rostellum, broader than in *Aricia*, serrated, exceeding the mentum in length, differing from *Paralycæides* in the latter character as well as in the receding margin of the comb, the sharp regular teeth of which are directed downward.

Papillæ anales with comparatively short rods. Henia well developed, with an oval fibula (*koa*) somewhat resembling *Aricia*. . . . [*Psyche* 52: 37–40]

Itylos koa Druce
Two males and one female investigated (Mus. Comp. Zool.): prep. 592, 595 and 593 female, "Puno, Peru, 12,500 ft. alt., 1-XI-1898" *ex* coll. Weeks. . . . [*Psyche* 52: 42]

The "vitta" of British authors is a certain combinational pattern element occurring on the hindwing underside of a number of Palæarctic *Plebejinæ* (and especially conspicuous in certain *Agrodiætus* species). It is made up of halo and cretule fusions and can be divided into four phases of development: 1. halo M_2 (its posterior distal part) and cretule M_2 fuse in the posterior part of the cell, *i.e.*, below the interneural fold in M_2, the resulting white streak occupying the whole space between the fold and vein M_3; 2. a similar somewhat weaker fusion is added (not occurring alone) in the anterior part of cell M_3 and blends along vein M_3 with the fusion in the posterior part of cell M_2; 3. halo IM (lower part of first discoidal) fuses with halo

M_2 which is fused with cretule M_2; 4. halo IIM is also involved, this producing a white comet tail traversing most of the wing, "splitting" it longitudinally and widening distally (owing to fusion 2). When, as often happens in *Agrodiætus* the rest of the halos and cretules are reduced while the median macules themselves are "dissolved," so to speak, in the vitta, the effect is very striking. In *Itylos* the vitta effect is produced quite differently and may be termed a *pseudovitta*. At its full development it is formed by the fusion of the halos and cretules in M_3, CU_1, Cu_2, and IA, and would not be distinguishable from similarly formed blendings in *Lycæides, Cyclargus*, etc., had not the following three factors been present: 1. owing to the very proximal ("lagging") position of second macule M_3 the fusion is lengthened in that cell; 2. together with the shorter fusions in the cubital cells it forms an elongated shiny white mark subparallel to the costa; 3. this blending is especially conspicuous because absent in M_2 and M_1.

CONCLUSIONS

The following general remarks may be added. Of the nine neotropical genera none occur elsewhere. Three, namely *Parachilades, Paralycæides* and *Itylos*, have retained in the Andes (whither they brought them) structural shapes closely similar to such structures from which *Chilades, Lycæides* and *Aricia*, respectively, can be easily imagined to have been derived in their Old World homes. Three, namely *Pseudochrysops, Hemiargus* and *Echinargus* reveal certain characters of the palæotropical *Freyeria* (the first) and *Chilades*, but have become strongly differentiated in the neotropics. Still more remote is the relationship between *Cyclargus, Pseudothecla* and *Pseudolucia* on one side and Old World forms on the other. It is to be noted however that *Cyclargus* and *Hemiargus* are allied to *Aricia* and *Itylos* in the falx. The general *Hemiargus – Echinargus – Cyclargus* type of ædeagus is not found in the Old World and apparently represents a very ancient type retained and developed in the neotropics, but extinct or unrecognizably altered elsewhere.

One can assume, I think, that there was a certain point in time when both Americas were entirely devoid of *Plebejinæ* but were on the very eve of receiving an invasion of them from Asia where they had been already evolved. Going back still further, a modern taxonomist straddling a Wellsian time machine with the purpose of exploring the Cenozoic era in a "downward" direction would reach a point – presumably in the early Miocene – where he still might find Asiatic butterflies classifiable on modern structural grounds as Lycænids, but would not be able to discover among them anything definitely referable to the structural group he now diagnoses as *Plebejinæ*. On his return journey, however, he would notice at some point a confuse adumbration, then a tentative "fade-in" of familiar shapes (among other, gradually vanishing ones) and at last would find *Chilades*-like and *Aricia*-like and *Lycæides*-like structures in the Palæarctic region.

It is impossible to imagine the exact routes these forms took to reach Chile, and I have no wish to speculate on the details of their progress, beyond suggesting that throughout the evolution of *Lycænidæ* no two species ever became differentiated from each other at the same time in the same habitat (*sensu stricto*), and that the arrival of *Plebejinæ* in South America preceded the arrival in North America (and differentiation from Old World ancestors) of the genera *Icaricia* and *Plebulina* (and of the species *Plebejus sæpiolus*) while the latter event in its turn preceded the invasion of North America by holarctic species which came in the following sequence: *Lycæides argyrognomon* (subsequently split), *Agriades glandon, Vacciniina optilete*. It is to be noted that only those *Plebejinæ* which breed freely in the far north of Eurasia (besides enjoying an enormous distribution in other, mainly alpine regions) are common to both Eurasia and America.

In regard to certain Lycænids of other subfamilies, such as the holotropical *Zizula gaika* Trimen and the South African and American genus *Brephidium*, the difficulty of making them take the Bering Strait route is very great, but in the case of *Plebejinæ*, the discontinuity in distribution is not so disconcerting, and I find it easier to give a friendly little push to some of the forms and hang my distributional horseshoes on the nail of Nome rather than postulate transoceanic land-bridges in other parts of the world.

The majority of neotropical *Plebejinæ* possess a sagum or rudiments of one. It is completely absent only in *Itylos* as it is absent in all palæarctic, nearctic and palæotropical species. This structure can be loosely defined as a fultura superior in relation to the furca (fultura inferior), but its function, if any, is obscure. One is inclined to assume that at the time of the invasion of the neotropical region from the north there existed Eurasian forms with rudiments of a sagum (possibly allied at that stage to the anellus now possessed by the *Catochrysopinæ* and other subfamilies) which in the subsequent flurry of hectic central palæarctic evolution was lost (and had been already lost by the ancestors of *Itylos*) but in the comparative peace of the neotropics continued to develop owing to that peculiar evolutionary inertia which in the absence of any obstruction keeps a structure tending to its maximum along certain inheritable lines.

In all (80 to 100) Old World and nearctic species the valve is of a very constant general shape.* Among the 19 neotropical species known, "normal" shape occurs in 11 species. The rest show four types of variation unparalleled elsewhere. In this respect the peculiar reduction of the valve in *Parachilades*, *Pseudochrysops* and *Cyclargus* would seem to be a case of stunting rather than the retention of a very short valve from which the normal elongate structure of the subfamily was evolved ("pulled out" as it were). In regard to *H. hanno* and *ramon* one suspects that the unusual shape is due to the irregular dwarfing of a *ceraunus*-like valve which had initially attained a very full shape (suggested by some of the Central American specimens), the "keel" in *hanno* and *ramon* being probably the remnant of an ample lower margin.

The underside wing pattern of neotropical *Plebejinæ* falls into two main types: catochrysopoid and ityloid. The catochrysopoid type (*Pseudochrysops*, *Cyclargus*, *Hemiargus* and *Echinargus*) is shared in the Old World by the small Palæotropical section (*Chilades*† and less strikingly, *Freyeria*) and in result, certain *Hemiargus* and *Echinargus* forms are remarkably similar to *Chilades* forms (especially to the *galba* group), the remarkable point being that while the palæotropical ones are sympatric with the kind of *Catochrysopinæ* which they resemble (and which is especially

---

*A slightly aberrant structure occurs only in *Chilades galba* and *Albulina (auct) felicis* and this leads to a false resemblance to certain *Glaucopsychinæ*.

†Which, moreover, in *Chilades cleotas* (a species ranging from the Malay to the New Hebrides, at least) evolves a likeness to *Talicada nyseus (Everinæ)*, the behavior of which (deducible from a note in Moore) is that of a "protected" species. *Freyeria* on the other hand tends, mainly owing to its small size, to a *Brephidium* aspect.

well represented in Africa, *e.g.,* "*Euchrysops*"*), the latter does not exist in the neotropics (where the sparse representatives of the *Catochrysopinæ* belong, as exemplified by the holarctic *Leptotes,* to a different phase of pattern). The Ityloid pattern group includes: *Itylos,* one of the two *Pseudolucia* species, *Paralycæides* (to a certain extent) and *Parachilades.* At its initial stage the "pseudovitta" of *Itylos* copies the differently formed vitta of certain palearctic *Plebejinæ* (cp. *Agrodiætus damon* or *Aricia donzelli*).

Taking 100 as the minimum number of known *Plebejinæ* (see footnote further on) the following figures may be given for the various regions where these insects occur. Only six species exist in the Palæotropical region proper, one reaching the Palæarctic, another reaching both the Palæarctic and S. Africa and a third extending into Australia. As many as 19 (probably more) exist in the neotropical region (12 of these are restricted to the Andes) and nowhere else, except for the fact that 2 reach the nearctic as 2 do in regard to the Caspian and E. Mediterranean region (these four invaders are not taken into account further on†). As many as 60 occur in the Central Palæarctic (between 40° and 90° longitudes). One half of these, with the addition of only half-a-dozen (most of which are poorly differentiated) not occurring elsewhere, are found in the Western Palæarctic (the whole of C., N.W. and W. Europe having 20, all of which it shares with the Mediterranean area, while 27 can be collected in a narrow area stretching from the southern Alps to the mountains of Spain); but in the Eastern Palæarctic the number dwindles to 12, all of which occur also in the Central Palearctic.

Some 30 (of which only 3 are holarctic) are found in the New World, and of these hardly a dozen exist in N. America. All these occur in its western part; only 5 reach eastern Canada and only one sparsely occurs in a large‡ area between the Atlantic and the Mississippi, while 2 representatives of the neotropical group invade the more southern states.

---

*Provisionally: *Euchrysops* Butler, *sensu mihi = Euchrysops s.* Bethune Baker + *Neochrysops* Bethune Baker minus the *niobe* group, for which the erection of a separate genus is necessary.

†In the eastern part of the Central Palearctic half a dozen palearctic species attain along the mountain chains technically tropical territory.

‡The paucity of true butterflies in the eastern United States is unrivalled in any other general area of the same size in the temperature part of holarctic territory.

In conclusion the following complete list of the genera of the *Plebejinæ* of the world is appended.*

Plebejinæ (s.s.)

100–120 species in 24 genera

I   *Parachilades* Nab.: t. *titicaca* Weymer; 1; Neot. in Andes.

II   *Chilades* Moore: t. *lajus* Cramer; 4–5; PT, one reaching P.

III   *Pseudochrysops* Nab.: t. *bornoi* Comstock-Huntington; 1; Neot. in W.I.

IV   *Cyclargus* Nab.: t. *ammon* Lucas; 5;[†] Neot. in W.I. to Fla.

V   *Hemiargus* Hübner: t. *cerargus* Fabricius; 3; Neot., one reaching S. Nea.

VI   *Echinargus* Nab.: t. *isola* Reakirt; 3;[‡] Neot., one reaching SW Nea.

VII   *Pseudolucia* Nab.: t. *chilensis* Blanchard; 2; Neot. in Andes.

VIII   *Pseudothecla* Nab.: t. *faga* Dognin; 1; *id.*

IX   *Paralycæides* Nab.: t. *inconspicua* Weymer; 1; *id.*

X   *Lycæides* Hübner: t. *argyrognomon* Bergstrasser (Tutt); 6; P, Nea, P + Nea.

XI   *Freyeria* Courvoisier: t. *trochilus*; 2; PT one reaching P, the other[§] reaching AU.

XII   *Plebejus* Kluk: t. *argus* Linnæus; 7–8; P, one in Nea.

XIII   *Plebulina* Nab.: t. *emigdionis* Grinnell; 1; S.W. Nea.

XIV   *Itylos* Draudt: t. *moza* Staudinger; 4; Neot. in Andes.

XV   *Aricia* R.L.: t. *agestis* [Schiff]; 6–8; P.

XVI   *Icaricia* Nab.: t. *icarioides* Boisduval; 5; W. Nea.

XVII   *Polyommatus* Latreille: t. *icarus* Rottemburg; 7–9; P.

XVIII   *Vacciniina* Tutt: t. *optilete*-Knoch; 4; P, one P + Nea.

XIX   *Eumedonia* Forster: t. *eumedon* Esper; 1; P.

---

*Abbreviations: t – type of genus. P – Palearctic Region. PT – Palæotropical (excluding AU – Australia), Nea – Nearctic (excl. Florida), Neot. – Neotropical. The figure after the type refers to the number of species in the genus. When two numbers are given, the second includes additional species which I have not dissected myself, but which have been figured (genitalia) by other observers. I have not taken into account several names in Forster's (1938, *l.c.*) list which in various respects is very unreliable.

[†] vn ms change from printed "4." *Lepidopterological Papers 1941–1953.*

[‡] vn ms change from printed "2." *Lepidopterological Papers 1941–1953.*

[§] The correct name of which is *Freyeria putli* Kollar – granted of course that *Chilades putli* Moore and *Chilades trochilus isophtalma* Waterhouse (*nec* Herrich-Schaffer) which I have dissected are the same as *Lycæna putli* Kollar from North India whence I have no material.

XX   *Albulina* Tutt: t. *orbitulus* Prunner; 6–7; P

XXI   *Agriades* Hübner: t. *glandon* Prunner; 4;* P, one P + Nea.

XXII   *Cyaniris* Dalman: t. *semiargus* Rottemburg; 1;† P.

XXIII   *Meleageria* Stempffer: t. *meleager* Esper; 1; P.

XXIV   *Agrodiætus* Hübner (incl. *Lysandra* Hemming): t. *damon* Schiff; 25–35;
        P . . .

[*Psyche* 52: 42–48]

[Note on "polytypism"]

Written after "Notes on Neotropical Plebejinae."

The current use of term "monotypic" as opposed to "polytypic" is most misleading, since at the hands of a splitter or recombinator a "monotypic" species may turn into a "polytypic" one overnight. Herein, too, lies the danger attending the popular pastime of comparing families and orders on the basis of the number of "monotypic" and "polytypic" species or genera. Since the days of Linnaeus are gone, and the comparative zoologist cannot possibly be a specialist in all groups he has to rely on works, the worth of which he is unable to judge, so that in numerous cases what he is actually comparing are not two groups of organisms, but the abilities and idiosyncrasies of the specialists (or the blunders of [two words illegible] compilators) who worked at them.

This in turn is linked up with the fact that the general concept of "species" in one order or family or even genus is more often than not totally different from that in another order, family or genus. A polytypic genus of butterflies cannot be compared statistically to a polytypic genus of birds or mammals without first defining in what way the idea of "species" in butterflies differs from that of "species" in birds and second in what way the specific idea varies from genus to genus and from reviser to reviser within the

---

*Or more. [VN correction, *Lepidopterological Papers 1941–1953*.]

†*persephatta* Alpheraky which Stempffer (followed by Forster) makes congeneric with *semiargus* (apparently on the strength of a casual note in Chapman) belongs to another subfamily (*Glaucopsychinæ*).

limits of each of the two groups involved. Unless in each separate case (polytypic species or genus) a describer or reviser defines exactly what he means by "species" and "subspecies" . . . .[125] In order not to give the worker in comparative systematics . . . dubious premises I prefer to avoid the term "monotypic" in speaking of little known species only one race of which has been described. In the case of *ammon* for instance "monotypism" is a direct result of 1) no other conspecific form having been described from Cuba and 2) of my separating specifically *ammon* from allopatric forms which had been assigned to its race. This separation I have based on one structural difference, which is of the same order and affects the same part . . . as that separating other species occurring on the same ground and not interbreeding (say, *Agriades glandon* and *Agriades pyrenaica*), this triple (morphological, spatial and biological) concept being the specific idea in its purest form.

But it is quite possible that someone else will 1) find that *ammon* produces well-defined local forms in some corner of Cuba or 2)[126] with facts which were unknown to me – and in result the monotypic *ammon* may revert without any evolutionary activity on its own part whatever to the polytypic aspect it had prior to this paper.　　[VNA, Lepidoptera material, Box 5]

From letter to William T. M. Forbes, August 6, 1945

From Cambridge, Massachusetts. Unpublished.

Thanks for your kind letter. I am very much interested in the material you mention, especially the Plebejinae: *hanno-bogotana-ramon-martha-chilensis-koa-collina-faga-excisicosta.* (*Cassius, callanga, marina* belong to another subfamily *Catochrysopinae*, and *tulliola* is *cyna = Zizula gaika* Trimen). You would do me a great favour indeed if you could send me the specimens.

It was so nice to have you here!　　[CORNELL]

From letter to William T. M. Forbes, September 24, 1945

From Cambridge, Massachusetts.

Dear Professor Forbes:

Many thanks for gifting these excellent little Lycaenids (*faga, ramon,* some *hanno* specimens) and for the loan of the rest. Also, for the return and dissection of the *mollicularia* specimen.

Your material comes out as:

Itylos (sensu stricto) koa Druce, 2 ♂, 2 ♀

Pseudolucia endymion Blanchard (forma *chilensis* Blanchard), 4 ♂, 1 ♀

Pseudolucia collina Philippi, 1 ♂

Pseudothecla faga Dognin, 4 ♂ (one labeled "*excisicosta*")

Echinargus martha Dognin, 1 ♂, "Huacapistana," 1 ♂ *sic*! "Matucana."

Hemiargus ramon Dognin, 2 ♂, 1 ♀

Hemiargus hanno Stoll (various forms, the *Paramaribo* one being the typical one), 10 ♂, 5 ♀

I was especially pleased with the loan of *martha* (I think it *is* the *Lycaena martha* of Dognin, judging by his woodcut etc.). Genitalically (and in a way macroscopically) it is beautifully intermediate between *Echinargus isola* from Central America and *Echinargus n.sp.* from Trinidad. One hind wing (in the ♂) was loose. I shall return the loaned specimens (and genitalia preparation) together with the *Lycaeides* forms previously borrowed, if this is convenient to you.

[SL 55–56]

From letter to Edmund Wilson, September 27, 1945

From Cambridge, Massachusetts.

I am doing the same things I was doing last year: dissecting butterflies at the Museum and teaching Russian to girls in Wellesley. I have forgotten much, Cynara. The urge to write is something terrific but as I cannot do it in Russian I do not do it at all. Cynara is the Russian tongue, not a woman.

We have passed our citizenship examinations. I know all the amendments.

Your article about Greece was most enjoyable especially in regard to the landscape. But where on earth did you see *firs?* I spent a couple of months there in 1919 collecting butterflies in Kephisia and elsewhere. All those marble pillars and statues when painted must have looked atrociously garish. I feel Greece in terms of olives, but that is all. [NWL 156]

From letter to Elena Sikorski,[127] October 25, 1945

From Cambridge, Massachusetts. In Russian.

Four days a week (for four years now) I spend at the microscope in my wonderful entomological laboratory, researching the most touching organs. I have described several species of butterflies, one of which I caught myself, in a perfectly fabulous canyon in the mountains of Arizona. In a certain sense this has realized (rather obliquely, but with singular vividness) my cherished dreams in *The Gift.* [*Perepiska s sestroy* 18]

From letter to Cyril dos Passos, c. November 9,[128] 1945

From Cambridge, Massachusetts. Unpublished.

In 1943 I went to Washington and sorted out (to the vast disgust of Field)[129] the jumbled specimens of *Neonympha* they had. Subsequently I published . . . the following note: The Female of *Neonympha maniola* Nabokov.[130] . . . I begged the U.S. Nat. Mus. to make a gift to the Mus. Comp. Zool. of one of these rare females but they wanted such an exorbitant price (namely a specimen of one of the rarest "psittacoid"[131] S. American *Theclinae* in exchange) that nothing came of it.

I have been enjoying hugely yours and Grey's *Argynninae* papers and have sent Grey some notes on genitalic differences in *sympatric* individuals of *aphrodite* and *cybele.* [AMNH]

From Minutes of the Cambridge Entomological Club, November 13, 1945

Unpublished. Written by G. E. Erikson.

The 614th meeting of the Cambridge Entomological Club was held at the Biological Labs on Nov. 13, 1945 with six members and guests present.

The scientific program of the evening was a series of short papers. . . . Vladamir Nabokov spoke on some peculiar specimens found in M.C.Z. collections – artifacts due to deliberate touching-up or accidental chemical phenomena.[132]

These talks were illustrated by specimens and lantern slides and were followed by interesting discussion.

[MCZ]

From letter to Elena Sikorski, November 26, 1945

From Cambridge, Massachusetts.

At about half-past-nine I too set out, carrying my lunch (a flask of milk, two sandwiches). It is about a quarter hour's walk to the museum, along tranquil streets (we live in a suburb, in the Harvard area), then past the university tennis courts – a multitude of courts, totally overgrown with gigantic weeds during the war years, when there has been no one to care for them. My museum – famous throughout America (and throughout what used to be Europe) – is the Museum of Comparative Zoology, a part of Harvard University, which is my employer. My laboratory occupies half of the fourth floor. Most of it is taken up by rows of cabinets, containing sliding cases of butterflies. I am custodian of these absolutely fabulous collections. We have butterflies from all over the world; many are type specimens (i.e., the very same specimens used for the original descriptions, from the 1840s until today). Along the windows extend tables holding my microscopes, test tubes, acids, papers, pins, etc. I have an assistant, whose main task is spreading specimens sent by collectors. I work on my personal research, and for more than two years now have been publishing piecemeal a study of the classification of American "blues" based on the structure of their genitalia (minuscule sculpturesque hooks, teeth, spurs, etc., visible only under a microscope), which I sketch in with the aid of various marvelous devices, variants of the magic lantern. When the weather is good I take a short break around midday. Other curators, from various floors, of reptiles, mammals, fossils, etc. – all wonderful people – also gather on the steps. My work enraptures but utterly exhausts me; I have ruined my eyesight, and wear horn-rimmed glasses. To know that no one before you has seen an organ you are examining, to trace relationships that have occurred to *no one* before, to immerse yourself in the wondrous crystalline world of the microscope, where silence reigns, circumscribed by its own horizon, a blindingly white arena – all this is so enticing that I cannot describe it (in a certain sense, in *The Gift*, I "foretold" my destiny – this retreat into entomology). Around five I come home, already in the blue darkness of winter, the hour of evening newspapers, the hour when . . . are rolling home, and radio phonographs burst into song in the illumined apartments of large ivy covered buildings. . . .

The school delivers Mityushenka at about the same time . . . he can forget everything in the world to immerge in an aviation magazine – airplanes, to him, are what butterflies are to me; he can unerringly identify types of aircraft by a distant silhouette in the sky or even by a buzz, and loves to assemble and glue together various models. During our travels in the Rocky Mountains and in Utah he accompanied me on my hunts, but he does not have a real passion for butterflies. [SL 58–59]

A Third Species of *Echinargus* Nabokov (Lycaenidae, Lepidoptera)

Lepidopterological note. Researched and written 1945. Published in *Psyche* 52 (September–December 1945).

Since discussing the neotropical *Plebejinae* (Mar.–June, 1945 [publ. 26-X.1945] Psyche 52: 1–61), I have examined a male of *"Lycaena" martha* Dognin 1887 (Le Naturaliste 9: 190. fig. 5) kindly loaned to me by Prof. Wm. T. M. Forbes. The species proves to belong to my genus *Echinargus* and structurally is beautifully intermediate between *isola* and the Trinidad species. The specimen is labeled "Huacapistana, Rio Tarma, Peru, 1-3-VI-1920, [*leg.*] T. M. Forbes," coll. Cornell U.

Measurements (in mm.): aedeagus 0.79, suprazonal portion 0.3, subzonal 0.49, with breadth (lateral view) 0.1; penis 0.67; furca 0.5; sagum 0.52

(see description). $\frac{\text{Vertical}}{\text{Horizontal}}$ extension of uncus: forearm $\frac{0.26}{0.04}$, humerulus $\frac{0.06}{0.19}$, shoulder $\frac{0.16}{0.08}$, lobe $\frac{0.24}{0.07}$. Valve 0.87, with breadth 0.39.

Sagum intermediate between *isola* and the Trinidad species: smaller than in the former, with an "unfilled" portion in the ventral margin as in the Trin. sp., and larger than in the latter, with the "unfilled" portion much less pronounced and armed with teeth as in *isola*: if measured as in the case of the Trin. sp. (*l.c.*: 30) then ZD = 0.52, PD = 0.4, and ZP = 0.45, the jutting "lower portion" being only 0.16 (i.e. about twice shorter than in the Trinidad species) along its "upper" margin, and some of the teeth (the medial ones) with which the side ZD is set (about a dozen in all) reaching almost 0.1 in length.

I take this occasion to note that in *Pseudothecla faga* Dognin the rudimentary sagum (*l.c.*: 11) clings to the furca and is armed with numerous minute teeth averaging 0.014 in length. (A certain roughness suggesting rudimentary teeth is also apparent under a ×360 magnification in the small sagum lobe of *Hemiargus hanno*).

[*Psyche* 52: 193]

From letter from L. Paul Grey, February 2, 1946

In response to "Notes on Neotropical *Plebejinae*," esp. pp. 351–82.

Your general treatment of the subject is so exactly in line with my own ideas of what is needed in this hitherto badly mutilated classification, that criticisms, disagreements or questions can be leveled only at details. In broad outline, you have performed a real service for students who would like to arrange their material along "natural" cleavages. I agree emphatically that a genitalic approach is indispensable. . . .

Your exposition of speciation, beginning on p. 3, certainly pulls no punches. If, faced with the alternative of accepting your philosophy as opposed to that which nervously and timidly accepts everything as "species" which differs on different localities, of course I am on your side of the fence, as you probably know. However, I seem to run up against a solid wall with a bump when I read your blunt statement that "any two structurally indistinguishable individuals belong to the same species regardless of biological, physiological, geographical or any other factors."   [VNA]

vn's notes in response on Grey's letter

Unpublished.

1. "Structural" is not merely "genitalic." Palpi, wing-form, scaling, venation etc. are all "structural."

2. There is no such thing as a difference that cannot be expressed.

3. Thus seven species, *sympatric*, A, B, C, D, E, F, G, *must* differ *inter se* if they can be sorted out;

4. but if you cannot express their structural characters (specific) then I do not see how, taking another group (H, I, J, K, L, M, N) in a remote region you can say that H is a race of A (and not of B or F), I a race of B etc.

5. I feel quite sure that in each sympatric array structural (and probably genit.) differences will be found.   [VNA]

From letter to Edmund Wilson, February 16, 1946

From Cambridge, Massachusetts.

Incidentally, I was wrong in saying that there were no Russians in "Sherlock." Except for two or three stories from the "Case Book" I had read them all, and it is queer that I should have forgotten the lady nihilist who lost her pince-nez or the lovely sentence: " . . . he was an elderly man, thin, demure, and commonplace – by no means the conception one forms of a Russian nobleman" (:493). "Students of criminology will remember the analogous incidents in Godno (Grodno?), in Little Russia." This comes from the *H. of the Baskervilles* (:884) and you may be amused to know that I have named a new butterfly *vandeleuri* in honour of Vandeleur alias Stapleton the villainous entomologist of the story.[133] "I learn at the British Museum that he was a recognized authority upon the subject, and that the name Vandeleur has been permanently attached to a certain moth which he had, in his Yorkshire days, been the first to describe" (say – *Luperina berylae* Vand.) (:893–894).

[signed]

[NWL 162]

From letter to Edmund Wilson, March 24, 1946

From Cambridge, Massachusetts.

many thanks for the lepidoptera:[134] most of them belong to *Ebriosus ebrius*[135] but there is a good sprinkling of the form *vinolentus*.[136] At least one seems to be an authentic *A. luna*[137] seen through a glass (of gin) darkly; the person who drew these insects possessed the following attributes:

1) was not an entomologist;

2) was vaguely aware of the fact that a lepidopteron has four, and not two, wings;

3) in the same vague groping way was more familiar (very comparatively, of course) with moths (Heterocera) than butterflies (Rhopalocera);

4) the latter suggests that at one time he may have spent the month of June (for the *luna* lurking at the back of his mind occurs only in early summer) in a country-house in New York state; warm dark fluffy nights.

5) He was not a smoker since the empty Regent cigarette box with the

sketches would have contained a few crumbs of tobacco if he had been using its contents just before; it had been lying about and he just picked it up.
[In margin] The reasoning here is uh-uh.

6) May have been together with a lady: she lent him the scissors to cut
out of the cigarette wrapping paper the specimen of *Vino gravis*;[138] the scissors were small pointed scissors (because an attempt was made, but not
pursued, to cut out one of the moths on the paper napkin).

7) There is a faint smudge of lipstick on the lid of the box.

8) He had not been eating when he started to sketch – because the first
one (the *pseudo luna*) was drawn on the paper napkin when it was still
folded.

9) He was not a painter but may have been a writer; this is however not
suggested by the presence of a fountain pen; quite possibly he borrowed the
pen from the lady.

10) The whole thing may have started from a curlicue; but the further
development was conscious.

11) There is a *cherteniata* or *diablotins*[139] strain in the general aspect of
the moths.

12) Was under the impression that a moth's body is all belly: he segmented it from tip to top; this *may* mean that he believed in the stomach
rather more than in the heart: e.g., he would be apt to explain this or that
action on material, and not sentimental, grounds.

13) The lady was doing the talking.

Well, Watson, that's about all. I am eagerly looking forward to seeing
you!   [NWL 166–67]

From letter to Edmund Wilson, May 25, 1946

From Cambridge, Massachusetts.

I have discovered a new butterfly among material (sent from Oxford!) collected in the Cayman group of islands (W.I.).   [NWL 169]

Bend Sinister

Excerpts from novel. Written 1941–46. Published in 1947.

He wore a badly creased dark suit and a bow tie, always the same, hyssop violet with (pure white in the type, here Isabella) interneural macules and a crippled left hindwing.[140]   [BS 47]

[Olga, the wife of Adam Krug, the story's hero (but not usually also its narrator), dies just before the novel begins.]

Holding your cupped hands together dear, and progressing with the cautious and tremulous steps of tremendous age (although hardly fifteen) you crossed the porch; stopped; gently worked open the glass door by means of your elbow; made your way past the caparisoned grand piano, traversed the sequence of cool carnation-scented rooms, found your aunt in the *chambre violette* –

I think I want to have the whole scene repeated. Yes, from the beginning. As you came up the stone steps of the porch, your eyes never left your cupped hands, the pink chink between the two thumbs. Oh, what were you carrying? Come on now. You wore a striped (dingy white and pale-blue) sleeveless jersey, a dark-blue girl-scout skirt, untidy orphan-black stockings and a pair of old chlorophyl-stained tennis shoes. Between the pillars of the porch geometrical sunlight touched your reddish brown bobbed hair, your plump neck and the vaccination mark on your sunburned arm. You moved slowly through a cool and sonorous drawing room, then entered a room where the carpet and armchairs and curtains were purple and blue. From various mirrors your cupped hands and lowered head came towards you and your movements were mimicked behind your back. Your aunt, a lay figure, was writing a letter.

"Look," you said.

Very slowly, rosewise, you opened your hands. There, clinging with all its six fluffy feet to the ball of your thumb, the tip of its mouse-grey body slightly excurved, its short, red, blue-ocellated inferior wings oddly protruding forward from beneath the sloping superior ones which were long and marbled and deeply notched –

I think I shall have you go through your act a third time, but in reverse – carrying that hawk moth back into the orchard where you found it.

As you went the way you had come (now with the palm of your hand open), the sun that had been lying in state on the parquetry of the drawing-room and on the flat tiger (spread-eagled and bright-eyed beside the piano), leaped at you, climbed the dingy soft rungs of your jersey and struck you right in the face so that all could see (crowding, tier upon tier, in the sky, jostling one another, pointing, feasting their eyes on the young *rada-barbára*) its high colour and fiery freckles, and the hot cheeks as red as the hind wings basally, for the moth was still clinging to your hand and you were still looking at it as you progressed towards the garden, where you gently transferred it to the lush grass at the foot of an apple tree far from the beady eyes of your little sister.

Where was I at the time? An eighteen-year-old student sitting with a book (*Les Pensées*, I imagine) on a station bench miles away, not knowing you, not known to you. Presently I shut the book and took what was called an omnibus train to the country place where young Hedron was spending the summer. This was a cluster of rentable cottages on a hillside overlooking the river, the opposite bank of which revealed in terms of fir trees and alder bushes the heavily timbered acres of your aunt's estate.

We shall now have somebody else arrive from nowhere – *à pas de loup*,[141] a tall boy with a little black moustache and other signs of hot uncomfortable puberty. Not I, not Hedron. That summer we did nothing but play chess. The boy was your cousin, and while my comrade and I, across the river, poured over Tarrash's collection of annotated games, he would drive you to tears during meals by some intricate and maddening piece of teasing and then, under the pretence of reconciliation, would steal after you into some attic where you were hiding your frantic sobbing, and there would kiss your wet eyes, and hot neck and tumbled hair and try to get at your armpits and garters for you were a remarkably big ripe girl for your age; but he, in spite of his fine looks and hungry hard limbs, died of consumption a year later.

And still later, when you were twenty and I twenty-three, we met at a Christmas party and discovered that we had been neighbours that summer, five years before – five years lost! And at the precise moment when in awed surprise (awed by the bungling of destiny) you put your hand to your mouth and looked at me with very round eyes and muttered: "But that's where *I* lived!" – I recalled in a flash a green lane near an orchard and a sturdy young girl carefully carrying a lost fluffy nestling, but whether it had been really you no amount of probing and poking could either confirm or disprove.

Fragment from a letter addressed to a dead woman in heaven by her husband in his cups. [BS 133–35]

[Krug thinks over odds and ends of information he has stored for an essay he now will never write.]
How I envy Cruquius who had actually seen the Blandinian MSS of Horace . . . Oh, what was it like travelling along the Appian Way in that large four-wheeled coach for long journeys known as the *rhēda*? Same Painted Ladies fanning their wings on the same thistleheads. [BS 156]

Krug blew his nose and while wiping it cast a look at the contents of the shop: mainly books. A heap of *Librairie Hachette* volumes (Molière and the like), vile paper, disintegrating covers, were rotting in a corner. A beautiful plate from some early nineteenth-century insect book showed an ocellated hawk moth and its shagreen caterpillar which clung to a twig and arched its neck. A large discoloured photograph (1894) representing a dozen or so bewhiskered men in tights with artificial limbs (some had as many as two arms and one leg) and a brightly coloured picture of a Mississippi flatboat graced one of the panels. [BS 180–81]

[Sad Krug is on the brink of succumbing to the brash temptations of his young maid Mariette when at last the dictator's thugs, in cahoots with Mariette, arrive to take him and his son away.]
"You know too little or much too much," he said. "If too little, then run along, lock yourself up, never come near me because this is going to be a bestial explosion, and you might get badly hurt. I warn you. I am nearly three times your age and a great big sad hog of a man. And I don't love you."

She looked down at the agony of his senses. Tittered.

"Oh, you don't?"

Mea puella, puella mea.[142] My hot, vulgar, heavenly delicate little *puella.* This is the translucent amphora which I slowly set down by the handles. This is the pink moth clinging –

A deafening din (the door bell, loud knocking) interrupted these anthological preambulations.

"Oh, please, please," she muttered wriggling up to him, "let's go on, we have just enough time to do it before they break the door, please."

He pushed her away violently and snatched up his dressing gown from the floor.   [BS 197]

[Officials attempt to apologize to Krug for the killing of his son, whom they too needed alive as leverage on him.]

(Krug had been brought to a spacious room resplendent with megapod murals, in the Ministry of Justice. A picture of the building itself as it had been planned but not actually built yet – in consequence of fires Justice and Education shared the Hotel Astoria – showed a white sky-scraper mounting like an albino cathedral into a morpho-blue sky.[143] The voice belonging to one of the Elders who were holding an extraordinary session in the Palace two blocks away poured forth from a handsome walnut cabinet. Crystalsen and several clerks were whispering together in another part of the hall.)   [BS 227]

[Driven insane, Krug rushes toward the firing squad, thinking he is back at school, where Paduk is not the nation's tyrant but a drab schoolmate, nicknamed "Toad." This passage ends the novel.]

He saw the Toad crouching at the foot of the wall, shaking, dissolving, speeding up his shrill incantations, protecting his dimming face with his transparent arm, and Krug ran towards him, and just a fraction of an instant before another and better bullet hit him, he shouted again: You, you – and the wall vanished, like a rapidly withdrawn slide, and I stretched myself and got up from among the chaos of written and rewritten pages, to investigate the sudden twang that something had made in striking the wire netting of my window.

As I had thought, a big moth was clinging with furry feet to the netting, on the night's side; its marbled wings kept vibrating, its eyes glowed like two miniature coals. I had just time to make out its streamlined brownish-pink body and a twinned spot of colour; and then it let go and swung back into the warm damp darkness.

Well, that was all. The various parts of my comparative paradise – the bedside lamp, the sleeping tablets, the glass of milk – looked with perfect submission into my eyes. I knew that the immortality I had conferred on the poor fellow was a slippery sophism, a play upon words. But the very last lap of his life had been happy and it had been proven to him that death was but a question of style. Some tower clock which I could never exactly locate, which, in fact, I never heard in the daytime, struck twice, then hesitated and was left behind by the smooth fast silence that continued to stream through the veins of my aching temples; a question of rhythm.

Across the lane, two windows only were still alive. In one, the shadow of an arm was combing invisible hair; or perhaps it was a movement of branches; the other was crossed by the slanting black trunk of a poplar. The shredded ray of a streetlamp brought out a bright green section of wet boxhedge. I could also distinguish the glint of a special puddle (the one Krug had somehow perceived through the layer of his own life), an oblong puddle invariably acquiring the same form after every shower because of the constant spatulate shape of a depression in the ground. Possibly something of the kind may be said to occur in regard to the imprint we leave in the intimate texture of space. Twang. A good night for mothing.

[BS 240–41]

Southern Pierids in New England

Lepidopterological note. Written in 1946. Published in *Psyche* 53 (September–December 1946).

It might be worth placing on record, as a feature of the warm autumn of 1946, that not only was *Eurema lisa* Boisd. and Lec. abundant throughout the fall along the railway line near Wellesley, Mass., but that the very rare visitors, *Eurema nicippe* Cramer and *Phœbis sennæ eubule* Poey (one specimen of each), were seen by the author of this note on October 17th in the streets of Cambridge, Mass.[144] – V. NABOKOV

[*Psyche* 53: 42]

From letter to Edmund Wilson, June 21, 1946

From Cambridge, Massachusetts.

With the feeling I had 1. some serious heart trouble, 2. ulcers, 3. cancer in the gullet and 4. stones everywhere, I had myself thoroughly examined at a good hospital. The doctor (a Prof. Siegfried Tannhäuser) found that I was constitutionally in fine shape but was suffering from acute nervous exhaustion due to the entomology-Wellesley-novel combination, and suggested my taking a two months vacation. So we have rented a bungalow in the middle of New Hampshire (Newfound Lake) and are going there in the middle of next week. [NWL 170]

From letter to Phyllis Smith,[145] July 18, 1946

From Newfound Lake, New Hampshire. Unpublished.

Dear Phyllis,

Many thanks for your neat little letter. I was glad to hear about the visitors we have had. Munro sent me a card "Announcing the Arrival of Donald Douglas."

Collecting here is very poor. The whole place is quite terrible. A horrible highway encircles a swampy lake. Self-consciously "rustic" cottages line the highway. All around are densely timbered slopes. The coarse sand of the "beach" is littered with bits of paper etc. A smell of fried clams comes from Johnson's.

We shall stay here till the 18th of August. Unfortunately we had paid in advance. Never again.

Please, give my best greetings to Mrs. Smith, Dr. Bequaert[146] and (if he happens to be around) Kenny.[147]

My wife and son send you theirs.

> *Faithfully yours,*
> V. NABOKOV
> *Could you please send Ralph L. Chermock, Ent. Dep., Cornell Un., Ithaca, a reprint of my "Notes on New or Little Known Neonympha." Please! In the filing cabinet.*

From letter to Charles Remington,[148] July 20, 1946

From Newfound Lake, New Hampshire. Unpublished.

Many thanks for writing to Miss Schmoll. You can well imagine how attractive her place is to me but unfortunately we shall not be able to go to
Colorado this year. We hope, however, to go there next July and I shall get
in touch with Miss Schmoll before her arrangements for the summer are
made. I would dearly have loved to meet your father. Will he go to Colorado next year?

The collecting (butterflies) here is miserable: 1. *P. glaucus*, 2. *P. rapae*, 3.
C. philodice (and x *eurytheme*), 4. *S. cybele*, 5. *aphrodite*, 6. *atlantis*, 7. *A.
bellona*, 8. *A. selene*, 9. *E. phaeton*, 10. *P. tharos*, 11. *P. faunus*, 12. *progne*,
13. *E. l-album*, 14. *antiopa*, 15. *A. milberti*, 16. *V. atalanta*, 17. *huntera*,
18. *B. arthemis*, 19. *archippus*, 20. *C. alope*, 21. *E. portlandia*, 22. *S. can-
thus*, 23. *C. euritis*, 24. *D. plexippus*, 25. *T. calanus*, 26. *Ch. titus*, 27. *F.
tarquinius*, 28. *L. phlaeas*, 29. *thoe*, 30. *E. comyntas*, 31. *C. argiolus*, 32.
A. samoset (belated), 33. *A. numitor*, 34. *A. zabulon*, 35. *T. otho*, 36. *mys-
tic*, 37. *P. peckius*, 38. *E. tityrus* and 39. *Th. pylades* – the usual dismal as-
semblage (except, perhaps, *thoe*).[149]   [Remington Collection]

From introductory lecture to Wellesley Russian literature class, September 1946

Published in BB, VNAY, 1991.

Whichever subject you have chosen, you must realize that knowledge in it
is limitless. Every subject brims with mysteries and thrills, and no two students of the same subject discover a like amount of delight, accumulate
exactly the same amount of knowledge. . . . Suppose a schoolchild picks
up the study of butterflies for a hobby. He will learn a few things about
the general structure. He will be able to tell you that a butterfly has always
six feet and never eight or twenty. That there are innumerable patterns
of butterfly wings and that according to those patterns they are divided

into generic and specific groups. This is a fair amount of knowledge for a schoolchild. But of course he has not even come near the fascinating and incredible intricacies invented by nature in the fashioning of this group of insects alone. He will not even suspect the fascinating variety of inner organs, the varying shapes of which allow the scientist not only unerringly to classify them, often giving the lie to the seeming resemblance of wing patterns, but also to trace the origin and development and relationship of the genera and species, the history of the migration of their ancestors, the varying influence of the environments on the developments of the species and forms, etc. etc. etc.; and he will not [have] even touched upon other mysterious fields, limitless in themselves, of for instance mimicry, or symbiosis. This example applies to every field of knowledge, and it is very apt in the case of literature. . . .

The more things we know the better equipped we are to understand any one thing and it is a burning pity that our lives are not long enough and not sufficiently free of annoying obstacles, to study all things with the same care and depth as the one we now devote to some favorite subject or period. And yet there is a semblance of consolation within this dismal state of affairs: in the same way as the whole universe may be completely reciprocated in the structure of an atom, . . . an intelligent and assiduous student [may] find a small replica of all knowledge in a subject he has chosen for his special research. . . . and if, upon choosing your subject, you try diligently to find out about it, if you *allow* yourself to be lured into the shaded lanes that lead from the main road you have chosen to the lovely and little known nooks of special knowledge, if you lovingly finger the links of the many chains that connect your subject to the past and the future and if by luck you hit upon some scrap of knowledge referring to your subject that has not yet become common knowledge, then will you know the true felicity of the great adventure of learning, and your years in this college will become a valuable start on a road of inestimable happiness.   [VNA]

From letter to Cyril dos Passos, October 23, 1946

From Cambridge, Massachusetts. Unpublished.

The paper on the *Argynninae* is very impressive.[150] I am delighted to note that it all corresponds so well to what happens in the *Plebejinae* etc.

My congratulations to you and Paul Grey. [AMNH]

From letter to Nancy Flagg,[151] c. October 27, 1946

From Cambridge, Massachusetts. Unpublished. In response to request for interview and photography session at Wellesley on October 31 for publication of *Bend Sinister*.

All right – but I do not go to Wellesley on Thursdays. I could be at your disposal between 9 and 1 A.M. [*sic*] Thursday at my Harvard office, Room 402, Museum of Comparative Zoology (first entrance on the left, facing Oxford Street), Cambridge. [VNA]

From letter to Edmund Wilson, December 19, 1946

From Cambridge, Massachusetts. Published in *Briefwechsel mid Edmund Wilson*.

[YALE]

From letter to Edmund Wilson, April 7, 1947

From Cambridge, Massachusetts.

I have finished my main entomological paper,[152] and butterflies will be more or less shelved for a year or so. We are thinking of going to Colorado or somewhere this summer, if luck lays an egg. [NWL 188]

VN at his laboratory bench in Room 402 of the Museum of Comparative Zoology, Harvard, November 1946. Visible on the bench are some of his detailed wing-segment drawings. *(Vogue/Joffe)*

Letter to Cyril dos Passos, April 16, 1947

From Cambridge, Massachusetts. Unpublished.

Dear Mr dos Passos

Thanks for your interesting paper.[153] I wish I could write with such lucidity. My own style gets constantly entangled in subordinate clauses and brackets.

I think my paper on Lycaenids is coming out soon.

Yours sincerely

V. NABOKOV   [AMNH]

From letter from Francis Hemming,[154] April 29, 1947

Unpublished.

Among the papers which I have now been able to read carefully are yours on the Plebejinae published in *Psyche*. I am particularly pleased about these, for I have realized for a long time that the omnibus genus *Plebejus* as constituted in North American check-lists was totally unnatural. Some years before the war I made dissections from specimens in the British Museum of a number of the species concerned and these sufficed to show that an early revision was badly needed. This clearly could only be done by someone having ample Nearctic material and with access to types. I feel therefore very grateful for your papers. . . .

Pseudothecla Nabokov, 1945. This name is invalid, being a homonym of *Pseudothecla* Strand 1910, *Ent. Rundsch*, 27: 162. I daresay your attention has been drawn to this fact but I mention it in case it has not, as you will wish to give this genus a valid name (if you have not already done so in some recent paper which I have not seen).   [VNA]

From letter from Véra Nabokov to Lee Lerman,[155]
c. July 1, 1947

From a capsule biography.

At the age of 6 [*sic*] he developed a passionate interest in Lepidopterology, which has endured to this day. Through the events in Europe he lost consecutively three valuable collections. He has published numerous scientific papers on butterflies which have no interest whatever for the layman.[156]

[VNA]

From letter to Edmund Wilson, July 24, 1947

From Estes Park, Colorado.

I am having a wonderful, though somewhat strenuous time collecting butterflies here. We have a most comfortable cabin all to ourselves. The flora is simply magnificent, some part of me must have been born in Colorado, for I am constantly recognizing things with a delicious pang.   [NWL 190]

Sphingids over Water

Lepidopterological note. Written in 1947. Published in *Lepidopterists' News* 1 (November 1947).

On a hot August day, from a bridge in Estes Park, Colo., my wife and I watched for almost a minute a striped Hawk Moth (*Celerio*)[157] poised above the water, facing upstream against a swift current, in the act of drinking. The delicate wake produced by the immersion of the proboscis was a special feature of the performance. This should not be confused with the dipping-the-abdomen habit noticed by me – and other Russian collectors – in the case of *Smer. populi* and *S. amurensis*.

V. Nabokov

[*Lepidopterists' News* 1: 82]

From letter to Don Stallings, August 25, 1947

From Estes Park, Colorado. Unpublished.

Those two days of collecting we had together were most delightful. I wish you could have stayed longer.

Despite Dmitri's efforts, no more "pale" *chryxus* have been caught. . . . I do hope that the thing you got near Telluride is what I am describing and figuring under the name of *argyrognomon sublivens*.   [VNA]

From letter to Phyllis Christiansen,[158] August 25, 1947

From Estes Park, Colorado. Unpublished.

How are things at the museum? I shall be back in the second week of September. I have lost some 20 pounds since I hike as many miles daily in search of butterflies.

Véra and Dmitri join me in sending you and Kenny warm greetings. I have a few dragonflies for Kenny.   [VNA]

From letter to Joseph C. Bequaert, August 28, 1947

From Estes Park, Colorado. Unpublished.

The collecting is almost over here. . . .

I have certain plans which I shall discuss with you regarding the re-arrangement of our Lepidoptera. I plan to start on the N. American cabinets incorporating the additional material and bringing the whole in line with the Palearctic collection which I have, in the main, already classified.

[VNA]

From letter to Edmund Wilson, early November 1947

From Cambridge, Massachusetts.

My girls[159] and my bugs are as usual taking a lot of my time.   [NWL 193]

From letter to Elena Sikorski, c. November–December 1947

From Cambridge, Massachusetts. In Russian.

After an amazing sweat-inducing summer in Colorado, from where I brought some wonderful butterflies, I have again got fat and flabby.

[*Perepiska s sestroy 52*]

Letter to Cyril dos Passos and Paul Grey, January 15, 1948

From Cambridge, Massachusetts. Unpublished.

Dear friends dos Passos and Grey,

It is only now that I have had time to read your Systematic Catalogue of *Speyeria*.[160] It is an excellent piece of work. Here are some notes I jotted down in the margin:

1. Sympatrism plus structural distinction – this is the only absolute proof of specific difference. We must however distinguish sympatrism *s. lato* and sympatrism *s. stricto*. The first would imply a day's ramble (on foot). The second the same clump of thistles or horse-mint. Theoretically there ought to exist sympatrism *s. lato* of a maximum of 11 species (i.e. all but *idalia* and *diana*) in some parts of the Rockies (*i.e.* Colorado). Actually, in *s. stricto*, representatives of eight species in one spot would be a number seldom exceeded. I have collected in various parts of California, Colorado, Utah, Arizona, etc. and my maximum is only seven for one clump of flowers visited throughout one season.

2. It is interesting that all the *Semnopsyche* section inhabits the East. I wonder if a race of *aphrodite* will turn up in California. I had hoped that *edwardsi* (one of three monoform species with a limited distribution) would be found to be co-specific with *idalia*, but I see that structurally you place them in different subgenera.

3. There seems to be a good deal still to be done in the Canadian section of *atlantis* and *aphrodite*. Incidentally does *aphrodite* occur

sympatrically with the curious *cybele novoscotiae*? And what do you make of Edwards' remark in Butterflies of North America that Geddes took *lais* at Calgary flying with *atlantis*? And has *cybele pugetensis* F. Cherm. been published?

4. Here and there you have been a little too generous with the retention or erection of subspecies. I know that sometimes it seems convenient to fix an intergradation by means of a subspecific name but I prefer to use numbers (with the term "form") in such cases (of which I discuss many in my final paper on *Lycaeides* soon to appear). I find it difficult to separate subspecifically your b., c., d. races of *nitocris*. I cannot distinguish *atlantis hollandi* or *atlantis canadensis* from *atlantis atlantis* without looking at the locality labels. The *zerene* forms from Utah and Nevada seems to be one subspecies to me ranging sympatrically from rosy (fw. unders.) and fawn (hw. unders.) with large silver spots to very pale blond undersides with average silver spots. *Egleis mcdunnoughi* is very variable in Wyoming grading into *oweni* or *utahensis*.

5. On the other hand I think a Montana form of *aphrodite*, a Yakima River, Washington, form of *callippe* and the pale brick (unders. hw.) Vancouver Island form of *egleis* deserve names.

6. I have noticed a curious thing in the field. In the case of certain subspecies which vary a good deal in one place (*mormonia* and *eurynome*, or *zerene platina* and others) specimens found *in copula* will be generally of the same aspect.

7. I had lots of fun collecting in Estes Park last summer. At 9500 feet where I lived (Columbine Lodge, near Long's Peak Inn) only two species actually bred: *atlantis electa* and *mormonia eurynome* (of which incidentally I got one *completely* black save for a narrow orange bar in RM fw.) but *edwardsi*, *aphrodite ethne* and worn *atlantis hesperis*, often wandered up. At 7000–7500 (Wild Basin, and towards Boulder) *atlantis hesperis* occurred together with *aphrodite ethne*, *zerene sinope* and *callippe meadii* (which later wandered up to the top of knolls at 11,000 feet as the Utah species also does).

Thanks for sending me your paper. I am looking forward to monographs on the various species and then we shall get together and make a new "Butterflies of North America."

> *Very cordially yours*
> VLADIMIR NABOKOV
> *Sorry for this mess. Our new secretary does not understand my long-hand.*

[AMNH]

From letter to William T. M. Forbes, February 12, 1948

From Cambridge, Massachusetts.

I have great pleasure in informing you that I am joining your Faculty (as Associate Professor and Chairman of the Russian Department) and shall come to Cornell some time in the summer.

I want to ask you whether it would be possible for me to go on with my lepidopt. research work at the Agric. Exper. station? Could I have the use of microscopes (binoc. and monoc.)? Do tell me if this is all feasible.

I am looking forward to seeing a lot of you next term.   [SL 80–81]

From letter from William T. M. Forbes, February 17, 1948

Unpublished.

Glad to hear you are to be with us; and trust you will be going on with the Lycaenidae . . . But I will surely try to get you working on the larger groups as well as species and what I call subgenera, – the family needs a classification badly.

As to space, we will certainly be able to find you an alcove in the collection room, but I am afraid you won't have quite so much space as at the M.C.Z. . . . As to microscopes I have talked with Dr. Pate, who has the best knowledge of what we have, and he is not too optimistic, but I imagine he will be able to scratch around and find something if you are satisfied with good practical condition rather than recent design. . . .   [CORNELL]

Letter to William T. M. Forbes, February 26, 1948

From Cambridge, Massachusetts. Unpublished

Many thanks for your kind letter. The arrangement you suggest sounds admirable. I am sure the microscopes will be less old-fashioned than ours.

This winter I have been rearranging the North American collection here. It was in a sad mess. In working on the *Melitaea* and *Phyciodes* I had the pleasure of studying your revision of Hall's revision.[161] I quite agree with you that *nycteis* and *gorgone* are much closer to *Mel. harrisii* than they are to the *tharos* group. But here are a few queries:

1. Strecker says (Cat. Amer. Macrolep.: 123) that the Bdl.–Lec. figures if *ismeria* have been ascertained by Scudder to have been copied (poorly) [with the underside hindwing markings not crenulated enough, I suppose] from John Abbot's unpublished drawings [in the B.M.?] I cannot believe that the picture represents anything more than a lightish form of *gorgone* of which we have fairly typical specimens from Kentucky (i.e. correspond well to Hübner's figure).

2. Unless Holland's photo of *hanhami* is not that of the type, as he says, *hanhami* (of which we have specimens from Manitoba quite close to the figures) is a race of *nycteis* (close in fact to *nycteis drusius*) and *not* of *harrisii*.

3. *Orseis* of which we have pair from Edwards in our short series, seems to be a dark race of *mylitta* (incl. *barnesi*, which comes very close to *orseis* in some loc., on the underside). I have not yet checked the genitalia.

4. *Picta* is, I think, co-specific with *phaon* (we have intermediate specimens) while *vesta* is distinct.

5. I have found, in various odd places, specimens (Albany and Penns.) of *batesi* (which I could not trace when you were here), including the model of Scudder's figure. Does the latter (and Clark's fig.) represent the true *batesi*? I think it does.[162]

Are you going to Europe this summer?

Very cordially yours,

V. NABOKOV

[CORNELL]

From letter to Don Stallings, March 10, 1948

From Cambridge, Massachusetts. Unpublished.

I am preparing a boxful of nice things for you. You have been so very generous and helpful that you really deserve them.   [VNA]

From letter to Alexander B. Klots,[163] April 22, 1948

From Cambridge, Massachusetts. Unpublished.

I am very much interested in your plans for a new book on American butterflies as I, too, have been toying with this idea.

    Freija was practically over when I arrived (in the last week of June 1947): I took five rather faded specimens near Longs Peak Inn, Estes Park, about 9500 ft. alt., aspen zone, on marshy meadows (but *not* the very wet sphagnum bogs where *selene tollandensis* occurred) – the kind of place where *S. eurynome* congregated in huge numbers.   [VNA]

From letter to Edmund Wilson, May 30, 1948

From Cambridge, Massachusetts.

[NWL 200]

From letter to Edmund Wilson, June 10, 1948

From Ithaca, New York.

I am "resting comfortably"[164] and am engaged in preparing for publication a work on butterflies, and then I shall ditch butterflies for at least a year.

[NWL 203]

The Nearctic Members of the Genus *Lycaeides* Hübner (Lycaenidae, Lepidoptera)

Excerpts from lepidopterological paper. Researched and written 1944–48. Published in the *Bulletin of the Museum of Comparative Zoology* 101 (March 1949).

Introduction

The genus *Lycaeides* (*sensu stricto*), belonging to the subfamily *Plebejinae* (also *s. str.*), consists of three polytypic species, of which the first, *argyro-gnomon* (Bergstrasser, Tutt), is holarctic, the second, *ismenias* (Meigen), palearctic, and the third, *melissa* (Edwards), nearctic.

The classification adopted in discussing these organisms is based on the following principles: 1. When we say that a genus consists of species, and that a species consists of subspecies, each of which again consists of smaller units (minor races or strains, alar or genitalic), we are dealing primarily with certain definite and recurrent aspects (within the general aspect of the genus); these "forms" endure in time as preserved material for study and in space as living creatures with a definite habitat. 2. A morphological gap between two forms with spatial (geographical, zonal etc.) coincidence or contact, but no interbreeding, is taken to mean absolute specific distinction between them, even if in some other region the two species to which they belong are linked by intergrades. 3. A morphological gap with no spatial contact means either relative specific distinction (i.e. depending on comparisons with allied sets of sympatric forms) or absolute subspecific distinction. 4. When there is spatial contact between two different forms at the limits of their distribution, with some morphological merging there, we have either relative subspecific distinction between the two (i.e. depending on comparisons with allied isolated forms) or some minor racial distinction not requiring a quadrinomial designation. 5. In order to raise the subspecific criterion a peg or so above the subjective level, I have adopted the following rule: a form in the genus under review is subspecifically distinct if separable from any other intraspecific form, already described, by at least two characters, one of which must be either (*a*) male alar (e.g. underside) or (*b*) male genitalic, and the other either male genitalic (if the first be *a*) or female alar (e.g. upperside or shape).

In the present paper I extend the holarctic specific concept *argyrogno-mon*, as given by me (1944, Psyche for 1943, 50, p. 87, etc.), to include the Central Asiatic *agnata* (Staudinger), the Eastern Asiatic *subsolanus* (Eversmann) with allied races, and the North American group *scudderi* (Edwards, Nabokov). The palearctic concept *ismenias* as given by recent authors is now extended to include the Central Asiatic *christophi* (Staud-inger) and the Aral Sea *bergi* (Kuznetsov).

An ancestral type of *Lycaeides* male armature was deduced by me from a preliminary study of the variation in the genitalia of the palearctic and nearctic forms (1945, Psyche for 1944, 51, p. 109), and was later discov-ered to have survived in a butterfly still inhabiting the mountains of Peru (*Paralycaeides* Nabokov, 1945, Psyche, 52, p. 36). This fact tends to justify the study of the male genitalia for the purpose of tracing the evolution of the various *Lycaeides* forms. Specific formulas for the three species have been worked out by measuring parts (F, forearm, H, humerulus, E, elbow, U, uncus lobe, see Pl. 1, fig. 9) of the male genitalic dorsum (the right half of the uncus as seen from the ventral side) in some 600 specimens. Below is the arrangement I have decided upon. From N ("normal") the *Lycaeides* falx may depart intraspecifically to produce variations W ("weak humeru-lus") and C ("semicircle"). N is characterized by a more or less conspicu-ous, angled or rounded, elbow and a more or less gradual thickening of the humerulus from a breadth slightly exceeding the medium breadth (FM) of the forearm. W is angled at the elbow and conspicuously narrowed along the humerulus (to a breadth equal to, or less than FM) before the latter bulges to form the short shoulder. C is evenly rounded at the elbow with a thin F and an equally thin, or thinner, humerulus, which is shaped as in W, the combined effect being that of a slender semicircle. Excluding for the moment certain transitional forms from Wyoming, the three species show the following measurements (in 1/100 mm. units).

argyrognomon. Falx N, with distinct hook. F short to long (32–52), from equal to H to 1.5 times longer, and from thin to very thick (at el-bow 5.5–11). H short to long (26–44), and from equal to (or in rare ne-arctic cases slightly shorter than) U to 1.5 times longer. U short to medium (25–39).

ismenias. Falx N, W or C (but W or C alone when F less than 55), with more or less distinct hook. F medium to very long (43–74), from 1.1 to not quite 1.5 times longer than H, and from thin to fairly thick (at elbow 6–9). H medium to very long (35.5–56), and from 1.02 to almost 1.2 times longer than U. U short to long (26.5–50).

melissa. Falx W or C, with weak hook. F medium to very long (47.5–69), from 1.5 to almost 1.8 times longer than H, and from very thin to medium (at elbow 4.5–7.5). H short to long (32–45.5), and from 1.4 times shorter than U to (in rare cases) equal to U. U medium to long (37–50).

The valve is poor in diagnostic characters. In all three species it has the same variational range in length (measured from proximal point to tip of mentum, in 1/100 mm. units), namely 120–165. The longer valves correspond to a larger wing expanse, so that among the nearctic valves, for instance, the longest occur in *argyrognomon anna.* Breadth fluctuations are: Eurasian *argyrognomon* 45–55, nearctic *argyrognomon* 45–60, *melissa* 45–65. In the breadth of the comb the *melissa-ismenias* range, 13–20, exceeds that of palearctic *argyrognomon,* which is 16–18. In broad comb races (or individuals) of *melissa* and *ismenias* (e.g. certain altitudinal Chinese forms of the latter, or *melissa annetta*) the valve has a thickset appearance due to the whole rostellum being broadened; but in broad-combed races of *argyrognomon* (West Coast nearctic specimens and especially European forms) it is only the comb proper which is affected, the neck of the rostellum remaining comparatively narrow, so that the dorsal part of its tip appears excurvated at the point where the distinctly toothed comb expands. In other words, an elongated valve with a strongly *retroussé* comb always (as far as my material goes) belongs to *argyrognomon,* while a round-humped, squat valve with an evenly thick rostellum never does. There are, however, a number of less extreme shapes which may occur in any of the three species.

According to my present views, *argyrognomon* is represented in North America by ten multiform intergrading subspecies which may be grouped in three geographical arrays: 1. the Western array (from Central California to British Columbia), consisting of three subspecies (*anna, lotis, ricei*); 2. the Northern or Transcontinental array (from Alaska and British Columbia to the Maritime Provinces), consisting also of three subspecies (*alaskensis, scudderi, aster*); and 3. the Rocky Mts. array (from S.E. British Columbia and S.W. Alberta to S. Colorado) consisting of four subspecies (*ferniensis, atrapraetextus*, and two new subspecies).

The other species, *melissa*, consists of a Western nearctic group of four multiform intergrading subspecies (the widely distributed *melissa*, and three, more local, races, *inyoensis, annetta* and one new subspecies) and of a monoform, isolated Eastern nearctic subspecies (*samuelis*).

While studying the nearctic organs, I have come across an extraordinary case not easily paralleled in the annals of speciation. In the palearctic region *ismenias* and *argyrognomon* occur sympatrically from the Pacific Coast to Central France (only the second reaching Spain), being everywhere separated by a distinct gap in F, a gap which is small (3–7.5) on Honshu Island, medium to large (8–25.5) in East Siberia and very large (17–31) in Europe. In the nearctic region, *melissa* occurs sympatrically with *argyrognomon* from British Columbia eastward to South Manitoba and Minnesota, south-eastward to localities in Montana, Idaho and South Colorado, and southward through the West Coast states to the southern spurs of the Sierra Nevada. They are separated by distinct gaps in F and U; but in the mountains of North-West Wyoming, *argyrognomon*, after producing through a sequence of local forms, a longer F than its palearctic counterpart does, gradually reaches a point of development from which either *ismenias* or *melissa* is evolved, depending on whether it is H or U that grows with F; in other words, a group of intergrading forms is produced, some individuals of which can be classified as "long" *argyrognomon*, others as "medium" *ismenias*, others again as "shortish" *melissa*.

The alar characters of the genus, studied in 2000 specimens, are examined in the light of my work on the morphology of the group (1944, Psyche, for 1945, 51); the subspecific divisions now in use are drastically revised, and a number of new forms, to three of which it was found convenient to give subspecific names, are described from material in the Museum of Comparative Zoölogy. The nomenclature of the macular elements is based on my viewing the evolution of the pattern as an intracellular movement distad, a centrifugal succession of waves, a phenomenon of expansion, in opposition to the old and still widely accepted theory (of which Schwan-witch is the foremost modern exponent) of a fixed number of initial trans-versal lines or bands that break into macules. I am inclined to think that ever since organisms which a modern systematist would have classified as Lycaenids or proto-Lycaenids (or indeed Lepidoptera) have existed macu-lar patterns have been in existence too; while the zebroid patterns, peculiar to certain groups in certain environments, suggest specialized protective adaptations rather than primitive designs. The discovery (see Psyche, 51, p. 112) of the concentric rings or ripples in which the scales are placed, ra-diating from a center more or less coincident with the base of the wing, and which I have termed scale-lines (sls.), continues to yield a convenient method for calculating and describing the position of various elements of the pattern. In this respect the "critical cell," Cu_1 of the hindwing, has proved to be most valuable in giving as it were a summary of the main vari-ational characters in a race (see Pl. 2).

I have spent many happy hours looking up bibliographical matters, and the results are given under each subspecies; it was found unnecessary, how-ever, to clutter the synonymy with references to catalogues (Weidemeyer, 1864; Kirby, 1871, 1877; Edwards, 1872, 1877; Scudder, 1876; Strecker, 1878; Skinner, 1898; Staudinger and Rebel, 1901; Dyar, 1902), mere lists of names (Edwards, 1884; Smith, 1903; Barnes and McDunnough, 1917; Barnes and Benjamin, 1926; McDunnough, 1938; Forster, 1938) and other compilations (Morris, 1862; French, 1886; Maynard, 1891; Draudt in Seitz, 1921, etc.), unless something new or peculiar was added to the his-tory of the forms under discussion.

A number of persons and institutions have loaned me specimens for study, some of which they have allowed this Museum to keep. I have to thank Mr. W. P. Comstock, Mr. E. I. Huntington, Mr. C. F. dos Passos, and the American Museum of Natural History; Professor W. T. M. Forbes and the New York State College of Agriculture at Cornell University; the late R. C. Williams, Jr., and the Academy of Natural Sciences of Philadelphia, for much interesting material. With the utmost generosity Mr. D. B. Stall-ings and Dr. J. D. Turner, Mr. Harry K. Clench, Mr. F. H. Chermock, and Messrs. P. S. and C. L. Remington loaned me their choicest specimens of *Lycaeides*, and donated a number of them to the Museum of Comparative

Zoölogy. Dr. J. McDunnough and Mr. T. N. Freeman most kindly provided me with specimens of *argyrognomon aster* form *empetri* Freeman, Mr. D. Eff with N. Ohio specimens of *melissa samuelis* Nabokov, and Monsieur H. Stempffer of Paris with a series of *argyrognomon calliopis* (Boisduval), the first consignment of butterflies received here from Europe since the end of the war. Among the Mus. Comp. Zoöl. material, the Weeks Collection (especially the beautiful specimens collected by Signor O. Querci) proved of invaluable assistance in pursuing these studies. Professor Oakes Ames kindly determined for me some plants and Dr. W. S. Creighton an ant.   [*Bulletin MCZ* 101: 479–83]

Remarks on the Eurasian Group

Without a study of the material, especially Grum Grshmaïlo's types, in London and Leningrad, it is impossible to undertake a thorough revision

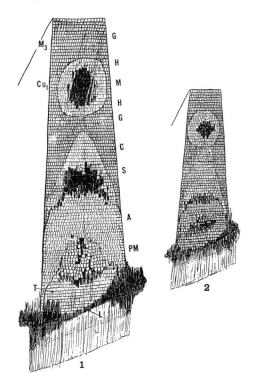

Plate 2. Underside component of hindwing cell Cu$_1$. The measurements are in scale-lines along the interneural fold from the level of the apex of cell M$_3$ to the termen.

Fig. 1. Giant race (forewing length 18.5 mm.) of *Lycaeides ismenias* (Meigen) from Chikoy R., Transbaikalia. Right hindwing of male. G, ground . . . 13 scale-lines. H, halo, prox. part . . . 3. M, macule (belonging to discal series) . . . 12. H, halo, dist. part . . . 4. G, ground . . . 5. C, prox. cretule . . . 10. S, semimacule . . . 11. A, aurora (with cusps reaching the prox. triangles on veins) . . . 15. PM, praeterminal mark (with scintillant scales) . . . 14. T, terminal space (within which the dist. cretule is diffused in this genus) . . . 8. L, terminal line . . . 2 (rising to 8 on veins to form the proximal triangles). The distal triangles are on the fringe and point distad. It should be remembered that the semimacule and praet. mark are the proximal and distal portions of a split macule (belonging to limbal series) and that the cretules correspond to the prox. and dist. parts of its (split) halo.

Fig 2. Dwarf male (fw. length 8 mm.) of *ismenias christophi* (Staudinger) from vic. Samarkand, Turkestan. The corresponding sequence is: 8, 4, 7, 4, 0 (halo and cretule fused), 17, 4, 3, 6, 5, 2.

of the Eurasian group. Forster (1936, Mitt. München. Ent. Ges., 26), who attempted to do so, relied for the revision of Asiatic forms, which had been vaguely described by Russian workers, upon specimens boldly name-labeled by German dealers, with disastrous consequences. I have figured, however, a few Eurasian forms. Some of them are very little known or not known at all. The Japanese forms are instructive, for instance a male specimen (Pl. 1, fig. 39, left; Pl. 3, fig. 13) of *argyrognomon yarigadakeana* (Matsumura, 1929) from Nikko (VI, 1899, *leg.* Hashimoto, M.C.Z.) which is a transition to the form *yagiana* (Sugitani, 1938) of *ssp. subsolanus*. This form, incidentally, is the same as *montinus* (Yagi, 1915), *nom. praeoc.*, dubbed "*yagina*" by Strand (1922) whose farcical nomenclatorial methods I refuse to accept, and yet another candidate here is *Lycaena asamensis* Matsumura, 1929, which is the same as *shiroumana, id., id.*, unless the name applies to a remarkable Karuizawa form of *Plebejus argus* (Linn.) which I have also dissected. Matsumura in this group was as incompetent as he was prolific. This specimen of *yarigadakeana* is less close to the Hokkaido form, *argyrognomon iburiensis* (Butler), 1881 (which is the same as *ishidae* Matsumura, 1929), than it is to forms from N.E. Asia which I group under *argyrognomon kenteana* (Staudinger, 1892); the Hokkaido representative of *Plebejus argus* has been confused with both *argyrognomon iburiensis* and the Honshu representative of *ismenias*.

An undescribed form of *ismenias* (prep. 138, Pl. 1, fig. 40, right, and Pl. 2, fig. 1; Pl. 3, figs. 21, 22; Pl. 7, figs. 105, 106), sold by Bang-Haas to A. G. Weeks under a fancy name, comes from near Troitzkosovsk in Transbaikalia (Chikoy R., 3000 ft. alt., VII, M.C.Z.) and is the largest form of *Lycaeides* I have seen. One of these males (fig. 21), is interesting because of its remarkable resemblance to *ismenias calabricola* (Verity), which I figure (Pl. 3, fig. 18; Pl. 7, fig. 104) from specimens taken by Querci's family in the coastal range of Calabria (San Fili, Cosenza, 3000 ft. alt., 17. VI. 1920, AGW, M.C.Z.), a beech and bracken region very different from harsh Transbaikalia, four thousand miles away, where the subsoil never thaws.

Of the other Asiatic specimens I shall note *ismenias sinica*, Pl. 4, fig. 25, and Pl. 7, fig. 108, E. Kansu, Hwei-si Tsinling Shan Mts., AGW, M.C.Z. (the male of which had a *Plebejus argus* abdomen neatly glued on by the

Staudinger-Bang Haas firm); a curious *ismenias* form (Pl. 4, fig. 26; Pl. 7, fig. 109) from N. Chihli, Tung-Kia-ying-tze, 5000 ft. alt., IX, AGW, M.C.Z., which despite its small size is allied to the Mongolian group; and an altitudinal *ismenias* form (Pl. 4, fig. 27, Szechwan, Tsiling, 11.300–11.500 ft. alt., late VIII, *leg.* Sage, ex A.M.N.H., M.C.Z.) which does not fit the original description of *Lycaena ganssuensis* Grum Grshmaïlo, but is certainly the same as *Lycaena aegina* Leech (preoccupied by *L. aegina* Gr. Grsh., a different form altogether). The most interesting specimen, however, belongs to what is probably a new species linking up this genus with *Plebejus* (see Pl. 1, fig. 41 and Pl. 8,* fig. 28). With its short, fat humerulus, non-hooked forearm and unusually large valve, this unique specimen (labeled "Alai, Fergana" by Bang Haas, sold to Weeks as a "very rare *var.*" of a species with which it has not the slightest affinity, and now in M.C.Z., prep. 495) on the upperside resembles *argyrognomon subsolanus* in the reduction of the cyanic overlay to a mere basal and neural dusting.

[*Bulletin MCZ* 101: 484–85]

Descriptions of the North American Forms

Lycaeides argyrognomon anna (Edwards) . . .
The distribution of this subspecies, which has been confused with more northern races, is very imperfectly known. Intergrades with *ssp. lotis* ought to occur in the mountains to the NE of the Sacramento, and various connections with *ssp. ricei*, some of them very close to *anna*, occur in southern Oregon. It is doubtful that it spreads very far east in Nevada. No Eurasian race of the species can compete with *anna* (and *ricei*) in general loss of pigment, but the other Eurasian species, *ismenias*, produces in Central Asia a form (*ssp. christophi*) which shows considerable homoptic resemblance to the west American forms, in spite of the shorter terminal space and more slender build (and a quite different, blue, female).

[*Bulletin MCZ* 101: 486, 490]

---

*Pl. 4. [VN correction, *Lepidopterological Papers 1941–1953.*]

Lycaeides argyrognomon ricei (Cross) . . .

Throughout a large area comprising the Cascade range (Oregon, Washington), the northern part of Washington and several localities in southern British Columbia, we witness at certain points the little-studied phenomenon of the production of similar (in the present case limbally immaculate) undersides by means of the fading out of the pattern of dissimilar basic forms of *argyrognomon*, each of which is linked up with a different subspecies. The butterfly fauna of the regions involved is so poorly known (despite "check-lists") that for the moment I prefer grouping several forms under one subspecific heading (*ricei*).

A series marked "Oregon" (and sold to Weeks as "*annetta*") is still so close to ssp. *anna* that it might be assigned to either subspecies. Little remains of the underside limbal markings, save the thin semimacules, and the upperside aurorae in the female are reduced, but the general aspect of the specimens, owing to the well-developed wing-shape is still *anna*-like.

Ft. Klamath and Diamond Lake undersides, which are nearest to typical *ricei*, show every transition from what looks like poorly marked *anna* to specimens indistinguishable from Mt. Rainier ones. The whole system I (limbal) followed by macules II (discal) is liable to disappear in hw. (but both sets are more stubborn in fw.). The fw. length dwindles to an average of 13 mm., and the discal set in fw. is on the whole less sinuous. The Kirk female is small and except for a few dull scales in the strong cells of hw., devoid of upperside aurorae. Although the corresponding male, which is also small, has regained the underside limbal system of hw., it has not acquired an "*anna*" aspect but a definite "*scudderi*" look.

In the Rainier region, the starting point, or spring board, for the gradual fading out of the underside hw. markings, is a form (occurring among immaculate individuals but probably racially predominant elsewhere in Wash.) which approaches the Vancouver Isl. race in four characters: 1. extension of turquoise pulvis (basal in fw., well over the disc in hw.); 2. slight elongation of fw. discal macules; 3. fair development of unconnected, or weakly connected, light colored aurorae in hw., and 4. distinctly marked semimacules tending to a pointed shape. From small Californian and Oregon (*anna, prox.*) specimens it differs in a greater amount of pulvis and in the components of the limbal set being less conspicuously spaced. *Ssp. scudderi* undersides look either drabber (in greyish or greyish fawn specimens with reduced pulvis) or whiter (in poorly pigmented forms) and have much heavier proximal triangles even when the other markings are weak.

The Rainier female is a small, comparatively short-winged edition of *ssp. anna*, quite similar to certain Oregon specimens, with the underside ground varying from "dead leaf" (Edwards' term) to white, exactly as in that subspecies. The upperside aurorae are of a dull weak yellowish tint with blurred outlines. They disappear in specimens roughly corresponding to the fade-out males.

In the fade-out underside aspect of the Rainier form the weak pigment of the praeterminal marks seems to be the most liable to go, and in such specimens (with or without the pale scintillae in hw. which may linger after the pigment has vanished) the retention in both wings of well-marked semimacules rimming proximally the narrow aurorae give an interesting supercilious appearance to the limbal part of the wing. At a further stage the semimacules have disintegrated leaving more or less distinct, naked-looking aurorae. When these go, and when the fairly stubborn scintillae follow suit, nothing remains of the limbal markings in either wing save vague traces of proximal cretules and a faint terminal line with or without weak inner triangles. All this hardly affects the fw. discal macules, although there do occur specimens with these macules reduced (to about 1/35) and the colon obsolescent. In the hw., on the other hand, the disappearance of some or most of the discal macules is fairly usual but does not necessarily coincide with the limbal fading. When this does coincide we get the almost immaculate whitish hw. of the extreme form (the "race *fretchini*" of Chermock). Incidentally, the first Mt. Rainier specimens of this form were collected not by Frechin, but by McDunnough in the summer of 1910, above Paradise Valley at an elevation of about 7,000 ft. on an isolated stone ridge jutting over a snowfield.

From Okanagan Co., N.E. Washington, come undersides, of which some are similar to the fade out aspect of the preceding form. The wings, however, seem to tend to a more elongated shape with a higher angle to the hw. In the females, which are larger than the Mt. Rainier ones, the upperside aurorae are somewhat better developed, especially in hw., and are of a warmer shade (approaching in this and in "long" wing shape the Didsbury form of *ssp. ferniensis emend.*). In one of these females (*ex* ST, M.C.Z.) both proximal (short arrowhead) cretule and distal (bar-like) cretule are reproduced on the upperside of the hw. in chalky blue. There is also a tendency to the spreading of some basal blue. The basic aspect of the male underside corresponding to the basic aspect of the Mt. Rainier form, curiously differs from the latter. The ground is dustier with a fawn shade; the cretules are indistinct; partly owing to the blurriness of their haloes the distal macules seem rather weak; but in contrast to the weak semimacules (quite different from those in strong specimens of the Mt. Rainier form) the aurorae though small and unconnected are vividly colored, and the praet. marks as well as the prox. triangles are more distinct than in other Washington specimens. The general effect combined with the "long" wing shape and the strong vadum of the upperside suggests a possible intergradation further east with *ssp. ferniensis*.

Two poorly-marked specimens from the Similkameen district, S. Brit. Col. (Peachland, on Okanogan L., and Coalmont between Okanagan L. and Fraser R.) seem connected with *ssp. scudderi* of the Osoyoos region and central B.C. More material, however, is needed for a fuller analysis.

Under the subspecific heading *ricei* I also place (provisionally) the beautiful and very curious Vancouver Island race, to which presumably Fletcher, 1904 and 1906, refers in the 34th and 36th Ann. Rpts. Ent. Soc. Ontario, 1903, p. 91, and 1905, p. 80, saying that "*Rusticus anna*" is not uncommon on Vancouver Isl. and was taken near Wellington by Tailor. Males 14–15 mm., female 14 mm. Male underside characters: 1. weak greyish ground thoroughly dusted with turquoise blue, the brightness and discal extension of the pulvis being especially conspicuous in hw.; 2. the singular tendency on the part of the fw. discal macules to assume a triangular (basad pointing) shape, this tendency being repeated in the semimacules of both wings; 3. the equally singular arrangement of the discal macules of fw. in a straight row parallel to the limbal series and much closer to the latter than to the discoidal; this is a well known individual extreme in many races and if found to be racially permanent here would be of great interest;

4. the palish, narrow, more or less connected aurorae, the fw. ones being only slightly weaker than the hw. set.

The female, a poor specimen, resembles some of the Wash. specimens on the upperside. The aurorae are difficult to make out in fw.; those in hw. are narrow and, together with the strong insulae, of a conspicuously pointed shape. There is a good deal of bright blue despite the state of the specimen, and in the strong cells the pointed prox. cretules are repeated in blue. The underside is very like that of the male.

[*Bulletin MCZ* 101: 490, 492–95]

Lycaeides argyrognomon lotis (Lintner) . . .
This butterfly has been badly confused with *melissa inyoensis* (Gunder) *emend., q.v.* To the scraps of information about it one may add that the types may have been collected by Hy. Edwards; that Holland (1900, Ent. News, 11, p. 416), possibly thinking of *lotis* Wright (*anna* Edw. *prox.*), suggests the Mt. Shasta region as the true type locality; and that Butler (1882, J. Linn. Soc., 16, p. 469) refers to a female of "*Lycaena anna*," taken in Mendocino Co. by Walsingham, which ought to be checked, if it exists in the Brit. Mus. Since my fixation of the true *lotis* in 1944, as separate from the Californian subspecies of *melissa*, no other specimens of the typical form of *lotis* have come to light. Darkest Africa seems to be better known lepidopterologically than the coastal stretch of Western North America from Mendocino northwards. In consequence of a reexamination of the Pt. Arena pair, I now assign it (as form 2) to this subspecies.

[*Bulletin MCZ* 101: 495–96]

Lycaeides argyrognomon alaskensis (F. H. Chermock) . . .
It is interesting to note that the first specimens were referred to what is now known as *Icaricia shasta* (Edwards). There does exist a curious homoptic resemblance between the two. The name used by Wright, 1906, who assigned it to Edwards (*op. cit.*, p. 63), is preoccupied by *Lycaena kodiak* Edwards (1879, Trans. Amer. Ent. Soc., 3, p. 20), which judging by the description seems to be a form of *Icaricia icarioides* (Boisduval).

[*Bulletin MCZ* 101: 498, 499]

Lycaeides argyrognomon scudderi (Edwards) . . .

I have had to omit a few references which were quite impossible to unravel without seeing the specimens. It may well be, for instance, that a well-marked Washington form near *ssp. scudderi* is disguised as "*Plebeius melissa* var *lotis*" in Leighton's incredibly naive paper (1946, Univ. Washington publ., Biol., **9**, p. 61), where utter confusion is achieved by references, under each item, to Holland's hopelessly unreliable book. In this connection, it is worthwhile repeating that Holland, 1931, figured, as the "type" of *Lycaena scudderi* Edwards, a male of *melissa samuelis* Nabokov (see Psyche **50**, p. 98, footnote), which is one of the reasons why I do not attach any importance to Chermock's vague statement (1945, Can. Ent., for 1944, **76**, p. 213) that in Edwards' Collection (Carnegie Mus.) he found "two males . . . that may be part of the series given to Edwards by Scudder." The confusion between *argyrognomon scudderi* and *melissa samuelis* runs through the whole literature, and from Scudder, 1898, to Macy and Shepard, 1941, biological data referring to *samuelis*, are assigned to *scudderi*. A crucial date is that of Stempffer's (1933) fixation of the genitalic position of *scudderi*. His specimen presumably belonged to the rather well-marked B.C. form which grades into *ssp. ferniensis* eastward and into *ssp. ricei* westward.   [*Bulletin MCZ* 101: 501, 503]

Lycaeides argyrognomon aster (Edwards) . . .

Aster was the first American *Lycaeides* form observed (1834, by Gosse). In 1840 Doubleday wrote to Harris (see Scudder, Ent. Corr. Th. W. Harris, p. 144) that he had seen Gosse's unpublished drawings of a Newfoundland "Blue" resembling what is now known as *Plebejus argus* (Linn.). Both Couper (1872), and Scudder (1877) said they saw no difference between the Lycaenid under review and *scudderi auct* (*melissa samuelis* Nabokov), excepting the Cape Breton material which looked different to Scudder. The blue Labrador females do somewhat resemble small specimens of *melissa samuelis*, and it is not improbable that after Möschler's paper had appeared, and had been referred to in Staudinger's catalogue, German dealers labeled some New York males and females of *samuelis* "Labrador," which would explain the *melissa samuelis* genitalia figured as "*melissa var.*

aster" by Chapman, 1917, Oberthür, Et. Lep. Comp., **14**, Pl. 15, figs. 45, 46. [*Bulletin MCZ* 101: 507]

Lycaeides argyrognomon ferniensis (F. H. Chermock) . . .

The o.d. is very poor. I have, however, the author's types before me and so know what he meant, viz. the form I had previously distinguished as *argyrognomon*, nearctic group B2. The underside ground, which is said to be "almost brown, very much darker than in any member of this whole group of *scudderi, melissa* and *anna*," is really of an extremely ordinary whitish or dusty fawn shade (cropping up throughout the genus); much darker specimens occur in *ssp. scudderi*. The comparison of the "plain brown" female to *S. fuliginosa* (Edwards), of all things, is unfortunate, since in *ferniensis* the hindwing insulae are sufficiently in evidence, which of course is not so in the case of the other Lycaenid. Another comparison, that of the underside markings of *ferniensis* to L. Tahoe (typical) *ssp. anna*, is misleading since the limbal set in the latter is considerably weaker, while the macular radianal slant in the forewing disc is of much more frequent occurrence than in *ferniensis*. It should also be noted that the holotype is slightly aberrant, with reduced macules (to about 1/30 in forewing) and with the forewing Cu_1 II macule in an extremely distal position.

I now propose to extend the name *ferniensis* to include forms from S.E. Brit. Columbia and S.W. Alberta. Vadum in male with a tendency to widen, reaching twelve sls. in fw., with generally conspicuous terminal vadosae. Beneath a whitish or dusty-looking fawn with more or less distinct (often very diluted, as in the holotype) haloes around the usually well-developed macules. Pulvis poor. Proximal cretules short in fw., fairly developed in hw. The main distinction from *ssp. scudderi* undersides (with which it intergrades) is in the limbal set which tends to a full development, with the aurorae more or less well cusped, attaining medially 12 sls. in hw. (and usually exceeding 6 sls.) and often represented in the fw.

These characters would hardly have served to distinguish *ferniensis* from *ssp. atrapraetextus*, had they not been combined with the following: in both sexes the wings tend to an elongated shape with a rather rounded termen in the female (which thus looks quite different from the small, dapper *atrapraetextus*). The upperside aurorae of the female are either absent (Fernie) or barely discernible in hw. (Michel) or diffusely marked in both wings (Cranbrook, Lansdowne) or fully developed and then tending to a warm fulvous (Didsbury) which, in combination with some bright basal blue, curiously recalls the S. Californian *melissa inyoensis* (Gunder), *emend.*

[*Bulletin MCZ* 101: 509, 510–11]

Lycaeides argyrognomon atrapraetextus (Field) . . .
The distinctive character of this subspecies in comparison with *ferniensis* is not so much the increase in vadum breadth (very striking in extreme examples), as the shorter wing shape, which in the female is combined with the following characters: 1. small size; 2. *melissa*-like aspect due to rather sharp forewing and well-angled hindwing; 3. sharp sagittate outline of rather narrow upperside aurora in both wings (the fulvous is of a *scudderi* yellowish tone rather than of the mellow orange found in *melissa* forms and in the Didsbury race of *ferniensis*) and 4. strong development of the hindwing inner triangles, this lending a more or less crenulated appearance to the termen.

In Priest R. males the underside varies from whitish to fawn of a shade perhaps a trifle deeper than in my darkest *ferniensis*; from the latter there is no appreciable difference in maculation, this as well as the ground being extremely variable in both subspecies. However, at what I consider to be the peak of the *atrapraetextus* upperside phase (a phase remarkably paralleling *ssp. subsolanus* forms from Eastern Siberia) there are some interesting peculiarities on the underside too. In one specimen (prep. 625) the combination of strong, distinctly haloed discal macules, intensely pigmented sharp semimacules, black (more or less devoid of scintillae) praeterminal marks and a yellowish cast to the well developed aurorae produces a strong resemblance to the Asiatic subspecies. On the upperside of this largish (just over 14 mm.) individual the deep fuscous vadum is at least 20 sls. broad in both wings with vadosal patches riddling the violet blue to about another score of scale lines basad from the vadum in the forewing and throughout the disc in the hindwing. The vadum is continued distally by an intensely pigmented vadosal fringe and there is a conspicuous RM insula five or six sls. wide in both wings. All this is characteristic of the *subsolanus* upperside and also produces a homoptic resemblance to *Icaricia shasta* (Edwards). In other topotypical males the forewing vadum varies from 12 to 15 sls. My only female specimen has no blue scales above.

Montana and Uranus Peak males vary from 3 to 15 sls. in the vadum, and the females have some blue dusting at the base of the wings.

Lycaeides argyrognomon sublivens subsp. nov.

Male holotype, prep. 142, (Pl. 1, fig. 27, left; Pl. 5, fig. 65) and 7 male paratypes (preps. 175, 176, 205–207, 426, 687), Telluride, San Miguel Mts., S.W. Colorado, alt. 10,000 to 12,000 ft., 28–30. VII. 1902, *ex* coll. Weeks, M.C.Z.

Male paratype, prep. 0469, San Miguel Mts., S.W. Colo., alt. 14,200 ft., VIII, *leg.* Oslar, *ex* coll. Williams, Ac.N.S.-Phila.

Genitalic measurements and forewing length (in $^{1}/_{100}$ mm.)

prep. no.	F	H	U	E	
206	45	36	34	6	1300
426	46	34	35	7	1300
207	47	33	34	6	1300
687	48	35.5	32	7	1350
205	49	38	36	6	1300
175	49	36	39	6	1350
142	50	39	38	6.5	1400
176	52	37	38	8	1400
0469	52	36.5	39	7	1400
mean	48.5	36	35.5	7	1350
range	7	6	7	2	100

Of all the subspecies of *argyrognomon* hitherto discussed, this subspecies has the longest F. As will be seen it is exceeded only by the N.W. Wyoming forms which intergrade with *melissa*. The F length of the shortest individual (206) is reached by the longest (with greater wing-span) individuals of ssps. *atrapraetextus*, *scudderi*, and *ferniensis*, but the mean of any of those series is considerably (by more than 5) lower than the mean of *sublivens*. The relation H/U is curiously unstable. Prep. 687 is in measurements, not unlike a dwarf *ismenias*, and the long uncus lobe in the larger specimens has a *melissa* touch, but the strongly hamate, well formed, fattish falx is quite definitely that of *argyrognomon*.

It is interesting to compare this S. Colorado race to the only other southern subspecies of *argyrognomon*, the Californian *anna*, taking specimens with F min. and F max.

	anna				*sublivens*			
	F	H	U	E	F	H	U	E
min	37	32	29	8	45	36	34	6
mean	40	34.5	33	9	48.5	36	35.5	7
max	43	37	37	9	52	37	38	8

It is tempting to suppose that if *anna*'s dispersal eventually took on an eastward direction and that of *sublivens* a westward one, these two highly specialized subspecies would not interbreed when they met, so that somewhere in the Colorado R. region *anna*, *sublivens*, and *melissa* would occur together, as the first and third do in California.

Underside components of hindwing cell Cu$_1$ (in scale-lines)
Holotype, right hindwing. Ground (greyish fawn with bluish cast) . . . 3. Halo (blurred), prox. part . . . 4. Macule (fairly strong) . . . 7. Halo, dist. part . . . 4. Ground . . . 17. Prox. cretule (blurred, difficult to measure) . . . 10. Semimacule (rather weak) . . . 5. Aurora (fairly bright with one thin neral cusp anteriorly) . . . 5. Praet. mark (strongly developed, with compact scintilla consisting of 115 scales) . . . 14. Term. space . . . 6. Term. line . . . 1 (rather strongly rising to 7 on veins).

The nine specimens with good undersides I have before me are of a conveniently uniform aspect (despite the presence of one aberrational specimen, prep. 426, which lacks some of the discal macules). In general appearance this highly interesting southern Rocky Mts. representative of *argyrognomon* resembles, in the male underside and shape, *ssp. scudderi* forms of the northern Rocky Mts. region much more than it does the geographically intermediate central Rocky Mts. forms, and is very different in general aspect from the only other southern representative of the species, namely *ssp. anna* of the parallel Sierra Nevada in the West. I have not seen McDunnough's "*Plebeius scudderi*" (1916, Contrib. Nat. Hist. Lep. Amer. 3, p. 110) from Silverton, S.W. Colo.

The following combination of characters seems unique: 1. Shape: conspicuous extension and angulation of the hindwing (the hw. termen in the holotype at the end of veins Sc, Rs, M_1, M_2, M_3, Cu_1, Cu_2, 2A, goes through scale-lines 110, 140, 160, 168, 170, 165, 150, 130, respectively) with rather pointed but comparatively underdeveloped forewing (the fw. termen in the holotype at the end of veins R_4, M_1, M_2, M_3, Cu_1, Cu_2, 2A, goes through scale-lines 200, 212, 210, 200, 190, 178, 165, respectively), as if the forewing were less successful in dealing with altitudinal stunting than the hindwing; 2. Underside ground: a curiously bluish, dull, darkish fawn, shading into "livid," due to the fact that the well pigmented scales of the ground are evenly intermixed with a discally extending spread of pulvis and with abundant bluish drab hair scales. The haloes and the pointed but shortish cretules are not conspicuous owing to the blurring effect of the bluish dusting; 3. Small, separate, *scudderi*-like, but fairly bright aurorae in hind wing (see measurements of cell Cu_1 in holotype, *supra*); very weakly represented in forewing; 4. A fair development of all the fuscous markings, even the rare outer triangles of forewing ("checquered" fringe) being represented more or less clearly (in preps. 175 and 687, for instance). In the holotype the discal macules are of generically average size (1/20) in the forewing and above average (1/17) in the hindwing. Their disposition in fw. (holotype: R_4 156–162, M_1 154–162, M_2 150–159, M_3 138–149, Cu_1 111–126, Cu_2 112–121, 1A 116–123) is somewhat affected by the apical strain, the curve of the series R_4 to M_3 being rather "open" and macule Cu_1 lagging behind; 5. The semimacules and praeterminal marks tend to assume a triangular (basad pointed) shape.

It should be noted that the bluish fawn of the ground is approached by one or two N. Alberta (one Laggan male, for instance) individuals of *scudderi* – among the much more usual whiter or greyer or browner ones – but that in such individuals the maculation is less developed than in *sublivens* with none of the *sublivens* tendency (prep. 206 for instance) towards heaviness in the semimacules, and the aurorae though similarly shaped, are less bright. It was this development in intensity of pattern that caused me to provisionally lump the S. Colorado race with other more or less strongly marked forms, such as *lotis* and *atrapraetextus*, in my preliminary notes on the subject (1944, Psyche, for 1943, 50, p. 95).

The somewhat faded specimen prep. 0469 seems less bluish below than the rest (though the livid shade of the dull fawn can be distinguished), and the aurorae in the smaller specimens are still narrower than in the holotype, but otherwise, as already mentioned, the series is very uniform.

The upperside is very conventional; an average vadum, with a suggestion of hindwing insulae in some of the paratypes.

A *Lycaeides* female from San Isabel Forest, mentioned in my preliminary notes (1944, *l.c.*) is an extraordinary looking specimen, shaped like the males (with a "lagging" forewing, 13.5 mm. in length), of a uniform fuscous except for some silky drab bluish hairs in the hw. basally, with a fuscous shade to the fringes and a mere suggestion of small, quite blurred aurorae and insulae in the hindwing. The underside (Pl. 5, fig. 65) is very like the Telluride males with the maculation more pronounced, but whether it really belongs here is not certain.   [*Bulletin MCZ* 101: 511, 512–16]

Lycaeides argyrognomon longinus subsp. nov. . . .
Specimen 144 is somewhat worn, but I select it as the holotype of the whole subspecies (instead of choosing one of the two fresh males 140 and 303), partly because of its genitalic measurements which expose better certain trends that I wish to stress, and partly because of its having been taken *in copula*, with the allotype, thus leaving no doubt as to their being conspecific. Its falx is of the normal (N) type to which *argyrognomon* invariably belongs, with conspicuously hamate tip. In F it exceeds the longest *argyrognomon* from E. Asia by as much as 8 and the longest European *argyrognomon* (from Spain) by even more (11), and equals the F of the smallest *melissa* unci. There is, however, no great hiatus between it and the other longest nearctic *argyrognomon* F (from Colorado) and I do not doubt that the gap will be completely bridged when more material is available. Thus, by rather arbitrarily assigning the present form to *argyrognomon*, we may say that whereas the known range for F of the Eurasian *argyrognomon* group is 32–47, that of the nearctic group is extended to at least 33–55, overlapping Asiatic *ismenias*, individuals of which are already reached by the Coloradian subspecies of *argyrognomon*. In H it has little affinity with *ismenias*, being much shorter in its relation to F and not thinning out as it

tends to do in that species (and to a still greater degree in *melissa*). While equaling the larger nearctic *argyrognomon* individuals, it falls slightly short (by 3) of the longest Asiatic H and by as much as 6 of the longest European one. In U it exceeds the holarctic limit slightly and its ratio U/H is more than 1. This ratio (42/38) is approached by sundry nearctic individuals, and is in keeping with the logic of the evolution of *argyrognomon* in America where H lags behind while U grows with F (it is the other way round in Eurasia). On the other hand, 42/38 is large enough to indicate a true affinity with *melissa*. Indeed a loss in thickness less than the difference between, say, southern and northern individuals of the Cascade Mts. forms of *argyrognomon*, together with a weakening of the hook, would be enough to change *longinus* (holotype) into *melissa*. As will be seen further, in the Jackson Lake region such intergradation actually does occur, apparently within the same colony or array of connected colonies. At this point of its development *argyrognomon* does turn into *melissa* (from which, however, only 300 miles to the west, it is sharply separated in all characters). That it wavers here at the crossroads of evolution and may select another course, is proved by the *ismenias*-like genitalia of the paratypes.

Both paratypes reveal an *ismenias*-like uncus. The falx is of a common (Asiatic) *ismenias* type, intermediate between N and W, well elbowed, with a long slender F, hamate at tip, a slender H from medium to long, somewhat exceeding the length of the U which is by 3–5 shorter than in the holotype (but intergrades with the latter through the sympatric melissoid forms to be discussed further). There is no doubt in my mind whatever that prep. 140 comes from the same colony as the specimen selected as holotype, and this (in conjunction with ismenioid tendencies in the Colorado subspecies of *argyrognomon*) makes me most reluctant to separate the form which the paratypes represent from the bulk of nearctic *argyrognomon* as an American subspecies of *ismenias*. I also suggest that some *ismenias*-like specimens might be produced, among melissoid ones, through pairings between *melissa* and "long" *argyrognomon*, whereas the initial Eurasian *ismenias* was most probably evolved directly from *argyrognomon* by isolation in some very favorable Asiatic nook, after which it spread into regions where less favorable conditions had kept other *argyrognomon* colonies in a more or less short-falx state. Anyhow, the similarity between the genitalia of *longinus* (paratypes) and some of the Asiatic forms (for instance Honshu, prep. 146, F . . . 55, H . . . 44, U . . . 40, E . . . 7.5, or Quelpart Isl.,[165] prep. 438, F . . . 57, H . . . 43.5, U . . . 38, E . . . 7, or Szechwan, prep. 284, F . . . 55.5, H . . . 43.5, U . . . 40, E . . . 7), is most extraordinary.

[*Bulletin MCZ* 101: 516–17]

Alar characters. . . . The Blacktail Butte specimen (695) is intermediate in appearance between the specimens described and *argyrognomon longinus*, the links being (as differing from 427, 252, and 142): a more powdery greyish blue tone of underside ground and a slightly more extended II–I stretch, hw. (in genitalia, however, 695 is a typical "small" *melissa*).

That these transitional specimens came from colonies in which "long" *argyrognomon*, "shortish" *melissa* and "medium" *ismenias* were genitalically represented is a possibility that the taxonomist must face.

[*Bulletin MCZ* 101: 520]

Lycaeides melissa melissa (Edwards) . . .
The typical form is weak fawn below in both sexes with well developed and fairly distinct white elements, producing a general impression of "whitish buff" (Edwards' original description), while the drab look of not-too-fresh specimens (and a comparison with the white ground of *anna*) may have suggested the "grey" in Mead's notes. The pulvis (pale blue) is rather conspicuous, the macules above average strength and size in both wings, the aurorae of average development in the forewing, somewhat reduced and isolated in hindwing, especially in the male. On the brown upperside of the female the blue is reduced to some basal dusting in hw. and the aurorae are connected, forming bands in both wings around 12 scale lines broad in hw. (Cu$_1$, M$_3$), with crenulated prox. margin and well developed cusps, and somewhat broader in fw., with straight prox. margin and shorter cusps that do not reach the terminal line as they do in fw. From other stations in Colorado I have similar females often with the addition of dingy white or bluish distal cretules in hw., bringing out conspicuously the terminal line and the praet. insulae.

In material from lower altitudes in Colorado, N. Mexico and Arizona, the size increases from 13 to 15 mm. (in fw.), the ground ranges from typical to a strong fawn (sometimes almost egg brown, especially in females) the pulvis is much reduced, the cretules tend to be short in both wings (but fuse with the haloes in specimens with reduced space between macules and semimacules) and the macules and aurorae are sometimes very strong. In females of this group, the bright blue overlay is often well developed, spreading (at the maximum of subspecific extension) over the hw., from base to the semimacules (which are left out in strong ground fuscous) and from R_8 to dorsum, and in the fw. more sparsely invading the M part of cell RM, the apices of cells M_3 and Cu_2 and the greater part of cell $Cu_2 + 1A$, where this diffuse dusting may almost reach the semimacular limit. The aurorae are variable, often very rich (S.E. Colorado, Kansas) but in S. California and Arizona a rather distinctive upperside female form is produced by a combination of rich blue overlay on dark ground and blurred, isolated fw. aurorae which are reduced to around 8 scale lines (Cu_1) in both wings.

In the northern western states and in Canada, the underside ground often acquires a smooth greyish fawn shade, with reduced pulvis and rather diffuse cretules, especially in males. In the females the blue overlay is often absent or reduced, the aurorae tend to narrow but they are sharply defined so that blue females do not have the dark blurry look of the Arizona form. Individual females with the auroral band in fw. greatly enlarged, from 15 to 20 scale-lines broad (swamping the semimacular area), occur in Idaho, Utah and elsewhere.

The undersides of specimens from low elevations in Utah and N. and E. California are similar to the northern form but there is an intensification of auroral and macular pigment, and the scintillae are often most brilliant. Intermixed with this form one finds intergrades with the alpine *annetta* and also a whitish form, with bright orange, isolated, but proximo-distally well extended aurorae which differs from *ssp. inyoensis* mainly in heavier terminal markings.

A large, ample-winged, beautiful form collected by Bell, near Fallon, Nevada, has a light, variably tinted underside ground, enlarged macules and isolated aurorae. In the female upperside the auroral band is hypertrophied (attaining 15 sls. in hw. and 25 sls. in fw.), with a straight proximal margin in both wings. The cusps of adjacent aurorae broadly fuse on veins and reach the terminal line. As in females of *inyoensis*, with which these intergrade, the ground is very light, intermixed with fulvous scales (very close to auroral ones) along the veins discally, with a sparse, basal rather light blue dusting. In a few specimens the aurorae are bleached to a creamy white, a pathological phenomenon which occurs also in *ssp. annetta*.

In San Diego, S. California, a small form is common, with a white (grading into *ssp. inyoensis*), whitish grey or greyish fawn (often with the tan effect noted by Chermock in the Gold L. form) underside and not very conspicuous haloes and cretules. The macules are strong and often enlarged, the aurorae cuspless, sometimes well separated, though fairly developed. The females are quite similar to the Arizona form.

Finally there is the Mono Co. and Sierra Co. form ("*fridayi*") which is larger than the San Diego one, but has the same variable underside ground with dull haloes and cretules. The aurorae are somewhat reduced, especially in specimens with beautifully developed greenish-gold scintillae. The upperside ornamentation of the female varies from reduced aurorae to the enlarged ones of *ssp. inyoensis*, with which this form intergrades although very unlike it in extreme individuals.

It is to be noted that typical *melissa* is *not* the low level (sage belt, oak brush, alfalfa, prairie, etc.) form or forms, with richly ornamented underside and female upperside, but an altitudinal, comparatively drab race, little known to collectors. The low level group is much too intricately connected with other, taxonomically existing, subspecific groups at various points of its enormous though patchy dispersal, to be kneaded into a separate subspecific entity. Therefore, I have connected it with the type race and thus have retained, on the whole, the general concept of "*melissa*"; but it may well happen that further research will necessitate a subspecific segregation of some of the richer forms.

In regard to the hypothetical occurrence of *melissa* Edwards in the Palearctic region, the following should be said. The legend started with Alpheraky determining in 1897 (*in* Romanoff, Mém. Lép., **9**, p. 315) as "*Lycaena Argus* L. (Hübner nec L; *argyrognomon auct.*) *var. Melissa* Edw." a single female specimen taken by Herz, 7.VIII.1890, in Kamchatka (apparently in the vic. of Staryi-Ostrog, judging by Herz's own account, *op. cit.*, p. 289). His determination was based on the specimen having a conspicuously broad auroral band on both wings upperside, unlike any other Eurasian specimen of "*Argus*" in the Romanoff collection but similar to three Californian females which the collection contained. He added that on the underside the Californian specimens and the Kamchatka one were absolutely similar to light colored Central Asiatic and South Russian undersides (which he referred to his "*Argus var. planorum*" = a tangle of *Lycaeides argyrognomon* and *ismenias* forms), and to certain specimens from Persia which he referred to "*Hypochiona* Rambur," now known to be a ssp. of the true *Plebejus argus* (L.) (the "*Aegon*" of Alpheraky), but which probably belonged to another ssp. of *argus* L., namely *orientalis* (Verity). It is evident that no weight can be attached to Alpheraky's identification of a single female specimen which might have belonged to an aurorally well marked form of *Lycaeides argyrognomon* or *ismenias*, or *Plebejus argus* much more readily than to *melissa*.

I have little doubt that as soon as Staudinger's "Katalog" (1901) had, on Alpheraky's authority, and possibly, for its own commercial reasons, given "Kamchatka" as a palearctic locality for *melissa*, some thrifty German dealer affixed this label to American specimens, thus greatly increasing their price. Eventually a pair of these got into the Bavarian State Museum and were solemnly studied by Forster (1938). Seitz (1909) also includes "*var. melissa*" from "Kamchatka" among his palearctic Lycaenids (p. 301, English Ed.) but the extent of his knowledge in regard to *melissa* Edwards can be gauged by his inflicting upon it a "broad black margin."

This seems to settle Kamchatka; but another Russian locality, Sarepta, on the lower Volga, causes more trouble. Chapman described as *Plebeius sareptensis*, 1917, in Oberthür, Et. Lép. Comp., **14**, pp. 42–46, 52–53, Pl. 12, figs. (male genitalia) 34–36, and 1918, Ent. Rec., **31**, pp. 2, 4–5, 7–8, text fig. 7 (androconial scale), a *Lycaeides*, genitalically close to *melissa*, from specimens purported to have been taken by Jones who, travelling with Sheldon (see Sheldon, 1914, Ent., **47**, pp. 233, 269, 293, 315), had found what seems to have been *Lycaeides argyrognomon* (Bergstr., Tutt),

1st brood, common at Sarepta, 20 V.1913, and another species, Chapman's *sareptensis*, common there in June. It is useless to discuss the matter in detail until Chapman's material is reinvestigated. The collection of A. H. Jones was sold in 1925 (Sheldon, 1925, Ent., 58, pp. 124–125) and the Lycaenids in question seem to have been in lot 384a.

[*Bulletin MCZ* 101: 520, 525–29]

Lycaeides melissa pseudosamuelis subsp. nov. . . .
Description. Differs in both sexes from other Colorado forms in the combination of the following characters: 1. underside ground (light fawn) with conspicuous greenish-blue pulvis in base of both wings, spreading to disc in posterior part of hindwing; 2. underside aurorae in hindwing bright but greatly reduced; in forewing tending to disappear; 3. female upperside aurorae in hindwing reduced to around 5–7 scale-lines in medial extension; in forewing reduced or obsolescent. There is no trace of blue overlay on female upperside, except some dusting in the distal cretules of some specimens.

I am prompted to give this form subspecific status by the following considerations: it is just sufficiently distinct in alar characters to merit such rank; its fixation helps to delimit the geographically adjacent type form of *melissa melissa* on the negative side of its pattern (*ssp. pseudosamuelis* being the weakest of *melissa* races in Colorado, the Fairplay typical form of *ssp. melissa* coming next, and the S.E. Colo. form bringing *ssp. melissa* to its maximum expansion in Colorado); it has been confused in the past with *argyrognomon alaskensis* ("*kodiak*"); and finally it shows a certain resemblance to *argyrognomon sublivens* of S. Colo., a resemblance which suggests further investigation (it is not unlikely that a state of affairs similar to the Jackson Hole tangle may be discovered in S. Colo.).

[*Bulletin MCZ* 101: 529–30]

Lycaeides melissa inyoensis (Gunder) . . .
It is a pity to have to use a name originally meant to designate an aberration, but I do not see how one can adopt any other course under the present rules. This subspecies had been confused with *Lycaena lotis* Lintner until I

separated it in 1944. Incidentally I doubt that Chermock (1945) dissected specimens of Lintner's form when erecting his *melissa paradoxa*. A pair of his "true *lotis*" (*l.c.*), which he kindly sent me, turns out to belong to the ordinary N. Californian form of *melissa* and thus has nothing to do with *argyrognomon lotis* (Lintner). [*Bulletin MCZ* 101: 530–31]

In what I consider the extreme, and taxonomically most typical, upperside female form, the rather light, silky violet blue varies from "basal" to "maximum" on a weak fuscous ground with auroral intermixture. The upperside aurorae in both wings fuse into warm orange bands with the cusps tending to reach the terminal line and with a more or less straight inner margin which in the fw. is rather diffuse. The general aspect (sometimes on *both* surfaces) bears a striking homoptic resemblance to the sympatric (at least in Kern Co.) *Plebulina emigdionis* (Grinnell). The auroral bands vary in breadth from quite narrow to very broad, often overflowing proximad beyond the semimacular limit, and specimens with little or no blue dusting occur among the most brilliant ones. [*Bulletin MCZ* 101: 532]

Lycaeides melissa annetta (Edwards) . . .

Specimens examined. Utah. Numerous specimens from Alta, Wasatch Mts., 8,500–9,000 ft. alt., 12. VII–20.VIII.1943, *leg.* V and D. Nabokov, M.C.Z., of these males, Pl. 1, fig. 13, Pl. 6, figs. 87, 89, 90, females, Pl. 6, fig. 88, Pl. 9, figs. 133–135. Other specimens from Twin L., above Brighton, Wasatch Mts., 9,000 ft. alt., 13. VIII.1943, *leg.* V. and D.N., M.C.Z. A pair from Park City, male *leg.* Spalding, 1895, female *leg.* Skinner, both Ac.N.S.Phila.

Genitalic measurements. 10 males (Wasatch Mts.) showed the range: F . . . 62–68, H . . . 41–45.5, U . . . 43–49, E . . . 5.5–7.5. The tendency (quite unusual for the species) on the part of H to catch up with U is to be noted. The resulting mean (65, 43, 45, 6.5) is interesting to compare with the mean of *ssp. samuelis* (56, 37, 46, 5.5), where the shortness of H is particularly well marked. That this altitudinal subspecies with an almost pathological reduction in wing pigmentation should have the highest intraspecific F (and a well developed wing shape) is most curious. I suggest that it has arisen from *argyrognomon* with a later admixture of *melissa melissa* blood. . . .

It should be noted that the immaculate disc form is the male type of Edwards' *Lycaena annetta*. Such extreme specimens (of both sexes) occur at the ratio of about 1 to 20 in one colony, so far as my own observations go.

The following upperside female forms are represented in my material: 1. The strongest form of the subspecies. The aurorae of both wings, though richly pigmented, are shorter than in *melissa melissa* of low altitudes in Utah and tend to be disconnected. The cusps are variable. There is some violet blue dusting over the brown ground and the hw.praeterminal insulae are made conspicuous by the presence of whitish or bluish distal cretules; 2. Same as 1, but with fw. aurorae obsolescent; 3. Bleached aurorae occur in 1 and 2, on a rather weak ground, the latter with a "grey-blue" effect due to a sparse overlay. A similar form occurs among individuals of a large Nevada *melissa melissa* form. The fact of this happening both in sagebrush surroundings and at high altitudes seems to preclude a direct environmental cause for this albinistic tendency; 4. Aurorae light colored, intermediate between bright and bleached; 5. The presence of whitish, more or less sagittate, proximal cretules in both wings, with a tendency to be especially pronounced and elongated in the radial cells. All combinations and intergradations between these five forms occur. The taxonomic type form is a very striking combination (see figs. 134 and 135) of more or less bright (almost red in the prettiest specimens) aurorae, light ("silky") blue overlay dusting the weak ground throughout, long whitish proximal cretules and light bluish or pure white distal ones.

This exceptionally interesting subspecies was very little known, when I came across it in the Wasatch Mts. in July 1943. I was assisted in its rediscovery by my son Dmitri, then aged 10. It was extraordinarily local, being found only in small colonies for about a mile or so on both sides of the Little Cottonwood River, between 8,500–9,000 ft. alt., at Alta.[166] Nothing of it was seen on the various hillsides investigated on the other side of the highway, but one colony was found beyond the Pass, above Brighton. In all instances its habitat was characterized by clumps of Douglas fir, ant-heaps (*Formica sanguinea subnuda* Emery) and an abundant growth of *Lupinus*

parviflorus Nuttall (which is the foodplant of the likewise poorly pigmented local form of *Glaucopsyche lygdamus*). It had one protracted generation from at least mid-July to at least the end of August. Once, among a
colony of fresh *ssp. annetta* individuals of both sexes, I took a single very
faded female specimen of the oak-scrub form of *ssp. melissa* which had certainly wandered up from the valley. Such wandering females are presumably responsible for the intergrades (some such *ssp. melissa* looking specimens are mentioned under that *ssp.*) which now and then occur among
typical *annetta*. By hiking some fifteen miles daily I satisfied myself that
neither *melissa* nor *annetta* were present between 6,000 and 8,500 ft. alt.
along the canyon. Below, in the oak-scrub and sage-brush belt, a smallish
form of *ssp. melissa* was common here and there, in at least two generations, and in obvious association with *Hedysarum boreale* Nuttall growing along the roads.   [*Bulletin* MCZ 101: 533, 534–35]

Lycaeides melissa samuelis Nabokov . . .
In perusing the above synonymy it should be kept in mind that Edwards
described as "*Lycaena scudderii*" three different species: in 1861 the male
of *Lycaeides argyrognomon scudderi* (Edwards), *q.v.*, a member of the
short-falced holarctic species; in the same year and paper the female of
Agriades glandon aquilo (Boisduval, 1832), as ascertained by me, in 1944,
from Edwards' description; and finally in 1863 the female of what is now
known as *Lycaeides melissa samuelis* Nabokov, 1944, a member of the
long-falced nearctic species. The confusion, which was started by Edwards
misidentifying the captures of Saunders and Lintner, lasted for more than
eighty years, except that McDunnough in 1915 (in Anderson, Proc. Ent.
Soc. Brit. Columbia, 1915, p. 126) and Blackmore in 1920 (*op. cit.*, Syst.
Ser. 14, p. 7) expressed some vague doubts as to the "Eastern form" being
the "true *scudderi*."   [*Bulletin* MCZ 101: 535, 537]

On the underside the smooth greyish fawn ground with inconspicuous
basal pulvis, the distinctly haloed, average-sized, strongly pigmented
discal macules, the reduced semimacules and short, cuspless, but fairly
bright aurorae (which are often, say in 35 out of 40 specimens from the

same colony, absent in fw.), and last but not least, the absence of fw. cretules and the shortness of the very much reduced crescentic hw. ones, all
this, combined with an ampler outline, especially in hw., and a remarkable
upperside in the female, produces a quite constant subspecific aspect, without any intermediate forms to fill the distinct gap in alar characters between this subspecies and *melissa melissa* from Manitoba or the Dakotas.
In the average female fw. the bright purplish blue overlay very evenly
covers the M cell of RM and the surface dorsad from base to just beyond
the disco-macular limit and is rather more sharply outlined on the dark fuscous ground than in other blue forms of the species; in the hw. the blue in-
vades the whole of RM and the posterior part of the wing from base to the
semimacular limit, with the neural vadosae more or less distinct. In two
specimens the blue is also represented in the discal part of the anterior cells
of fw. In a few specimens the overlay is sparse, but only in one (stunted)
specimen (fig. 121) is it almost absent. The rest of the markings are: fairly
bright crescentic aurorae more or less clearly defined in hw. but absent in
fw.; rather conspicuous discoidal insulae in both wings and rather large
praeterminal ones in hw. In about half of my specimens violet blue distal
cretules enliven the terminal space.

This mysteriously constant subspecies seems to occur only east of the
Mississippi, between latitudes 41° and 44° (I doubt whether the N. Carolina record of "*Lycaena scudderi*" reported by Brimley, 1923, Ent. News,
34, p. 113, to have been taken by Sherman at Blantyre, V.1908, refers to a
Lycaeides). It is sharply cut off from the western bulk of *melissa* (the most
eastern stations of which are in S. Manitoba, Minnesota and Iowa). It is
found in isolated colonies, and only in association with lupine (thus on
sandy soil), here and there along the S.E., S. and possibly S.W. shores of L.
Michigan, at the western end of L. Erie and at both ends (if not extinct in
the western one) of L. Ontario. It patchily follows the Hudson (being still
plentiful in its old haunts near Albany); occurs, or occurred, in N.E. Penn-
sylvania, and is recorded in a very few specimens from the Merrimac, N.H.
(where, however, I searched for it in vain in the summer of 1946). Owing
to various causes (building, farming, fires, etc.) old colonies die out, while
new ones founded by wandering females in quest of lupine, may not always

thrive beyond one season. The Massachusetts' records (Merrimac R.?) have never been repeated, and despite Holland's absurd assertion that this is the "commonest member of the group," its distribution remains as imperfectly known as it was in Scudder's day.

Conclusions

Having examined the forms of *Lycaeides* found in North America, we can now compare their variational range by placing the mean measurements (in 1/100 mm. units) of the falx and uncus according to the length of the forearm. The first nine subspecies belong to *argyrognomon* (Bergstr., Tutt), the last five to *melissa* (Edw.). The tenth, although taxonomically assigned to *argyrognomon*, includes transitions between the latter and *melissa*.

	F	H	U	E
aster	38	30.5	30	6
ricei	39.5	32.5	31	9
alaskensis	40	32.5	29.5	7.5
anna	40	34.5	33	9
lotis	40.5	33.5	34.5	7
atrapraet	42.5	32	33	7
ferniensis	43	33	32.5	7
scudderi	43	33	33.5	7.5
sublivens	48.5	36	35.5	7
longinus	53.5	38.5	39.5	7
samuelis	56	37	46.5	6
pseudosam	57.5	38	44.5	5.5
melissa	58	38	43.5	5.5
inyoensis	58.5	37.5	46	6
annetta	65	43	45	6

In regard to the alar characters displayed by nearctic *argyrognomon* and *melissa*, certain specific tendencies can be distinguished, despite the fact that both species go through much the same racial aspects (from pale, poorly marked, to dark, strongly marked forms). The *argyrognomon* range in forewing length, from the Maritime Provinces races to those of California, is one or two mm. wider at either limit than it is in *melissa*. In shape the *argyrognomon* hindwing tends to be high-angled and strongly developed (in comparison to the forewing especially), while in *melissa* it tends to be shorter and rounder than in the other species, with, on the whole, less ground-space between the pigmentary components of the cells. The male upperside in *argyrognomon* tends to be more infuscated than in *melissa*, with the *argyrognomon* forewing vadum attaining racially as much as 15–20 sls., whereas in *melissa* the forewing vadum is generally very thin and only in one (individual) case attains an extension of some 10 sls. Though the underside ground color of both species goes from white through greyish and fawn to brown, at the fawn stage a more even and vivid tone seems to be associated with *melissa* rather than *argyrognomon*. The male underside aurorae, which may be obsolescent in either species, are seldom strong in *argyrognomon* where they hardly attain 10 sls. in the critical cell (with a mean of 5); in *melissa* they attain a greater development in richness of pigment as well as in medial and neural extension, with a medial range reaching as much as 17 sls. in the critical cell (with a mean of 8). Finally only in *argyrognomon* is the minimum of female upperside ornamentation attained (no trace of aurorae) while only in *melissa* is the maximum (hypertrophied auroral bands) found.   [*Bulletin MCZ* 101: 537, 539–41]

A new species of *Cyclargus* Nabokov (Lycaenidae, Lepidoptera)

Excerpts from lepidopterological paper. Researched in 1946, written in 1948, and published in *The Entomologist*, 81 (December 1948).

Dr. A. S. Corbet, as quoted by Carpenter and Lewis (1943, *Ann. Carnegie Mus.*, **29**: 392), applied (wrongly) the name "*Hemiargus catilina* Fabricius" [Bethune-Baker, *nec* Fabricius] to material in the British Museum from Hispaniola [probably *Cyclargus thomasi noeli* (Comstock and Huntington)] and Nevis Island [possibly *C. woodruffi* (Comstock and Huntington)], and also to specimens, then in the Oxford University Museum, from Little Cayman (3 males) and Cayman Brac (a male and a female). Comstock and Huntington (1943, *Ann. New York Acad. Sci.*, **45**: 112) suspected that the mysterious Cayman specimens belonged to the group which I later defined generically as *Cyclargus*, and showed that Fabricius's description of *catalina* could apply only to the Floridian race of *Leptotes*

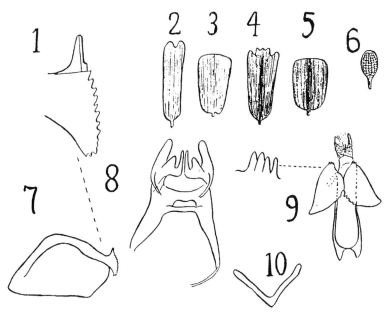

Figs. 1–10. Genitalia of *Cyclargus erembis* Nabokov. (1) comb of valve; (2–5) scales; (6) androconial scale; (7) valve; (8) uncus (9) aedeagus (with teeth of sagum shown separately); (10) furca.

cassius (Cramer) (*ibid.*, 91–92). Professor G. D. Hale Carpenter very kindly sent me from Oxford one of the Little Cayman males for study, and this I find belongs to a new (fifth) species of *Cyclargus*, genitalically intermediate between *C. thomasi* (Clench) and *woodruffi* (Comstock and Huntington). The reader is referred to my paper on the wing-pattern of the sub-family (1944 [20.ii.1945] *Psyche*, 51: 104) and to my revision of its neotropical section (1945 [26.x.1945] *Psyche*, 52: 1) for an explanation of the terminology used here.

Cyclargus erembis, n. sp. (Figs. 1–11)
Genitalia (male). – Aedeagus 0.8 mm. with penis 0.7, thus larger than *thomasi* and very like *woodruffi*. The sagum seems to possess only four distally placed teeth (about 0.03 long) on each lobe (0.36 by 0.2) instead of the ten or so, which can be easily made out in *thomasi*. The measurements of the uncus (forearm 0.19 by 0.03, humerulus 0.055 by 0.12, shoulder 0.14 by 0.05, lobe 0.24 by 0.06) suggest an intermediate stage between *thomasi* (ten males examined) and the only specimen of *woodruffi* I have

measured (cp. *Psyche*, **52**: 18–19, and see Pl. 3, *ibid.*). The same may be said of the valve (0.7 by 0.4). The comb is slightly narrower than in *thomasi* with the first tooth conspicuously prolonged (0.06) as in the latter species but slightly thicker and on the whole shorter than in *thomasi* specimens of the same wing-size, and with the rest of the teeth (15) distinctly smaller and blunter and thus approaching *woodruffi* where, however, they are more numerous.

Androconia. – In all *Cyclargus* this scale resembles a mandolin in shape but in the *thomasi* group its body is oval (0.045 mm. by 0.035 in *erembis*, slightly narrower in *woodruffi* and still narrower in *thomasi*) with only six visible ribs, while in the *ammon* group it is short and round (0.03 by 0.03) with eight ribs in *ammon* and ten in *dominica*. [*The Entomologist* 81: 273–75]

Comparison with allied species. – The presence of macule IIR or second upper discoidal, counting basad, in fore wing, not represented in any other *Cyclargus*, but of common occurrence in the sub-family and family, distinguishes *erembis* from all its congeners. It differs from them further in the following underside characters:

> from *ammon* Lucas and *dominica* Moeschler in a lesser development of cretules and other white elements (there are other distinctions, e.g. the absence of macule Cu_2III in *ammon*, no less obvious);
>
> from *thomasi* races in a slightly longer aurora;
>
> from *thomasi thomasi* Clench (to which it is very similar in darkish ground colour, pigmentation of macules and shape of cretules and halos) and *thomasi noeli* Comstock and Huntington (which is of a much whiter fawn) in larger size;
>
> from *thomasi bethune-bakeri* Comstock and Huntington in the lesser development of cretules (in length and breadth), which in the latter race form band-like fusions in both wings;
>
> and from *woodruffi* Comstock and Huntington (a very poor specimen for comparison) in a paler, slightly smaller aurora, narrower cretules and darker general appearance.

Conclusions. – I am inclined to think that the known *Cyclargus* forms fall into two genitalically very distinct superspecies, the *ammon* group and

Fig. 11. Underside of wings of *Cyclargus erembis* Nabokov, with numbered scale-lines.

the *thomasi* group, the former consisting of two (*ammon* and *dominica*) and the latter of three (*thomasi, woodruffi* and *erembis*) genitalically less differentiated species, one of which (*thomasi*), moreover, consists of at least three genitalically identical subspecies (*thomasi, noeli, bethune-bakeri*).

These relationships are also borne out by the androconia and the pattern.

There is little doubt in my mind that *erembis* will be found to occur (sympatrically with *ammon*) on Cuba – that, in fact, it is the Cuban representative of the *thomasi* group.   [*The Entomologist* 81: 279–80]

From letter to Edmund Wilson, July 23, 1948

From Ithaca, New York.

No tennis or butterfly-hunting for me this year.   [NWL 204]

From letter to Edmund Wilson, September 3, 1948

From Ithaca, New York.

Dmitri has developed a magnificent tennis form owing to the Cornell coach but his chess is still only passable. Véra has bought a car and has learned to drive it in a very short time. I saw, but could not catch, a very rare migrant butterfly (*L. bachmanii*).[167] My health is good. We have rented an enormous, pleasantly furnished house (note new address beginning 10 Sept: 802 Seneca St., Ithaca). Visitors encouraged.   [NWL 205]

From letter to Edmund Wilson, September 21, 1948

From Ithaca, New York.

I also want to draw your attention[168] to the fact that biological and ecological characters have no taxonomic value *per se*. As a systematist, I always give priority to structural characters. In other words two butterfly populations may breed in vastly different environments – one, say, in the Mexican desert and the other in a Canadian bog – and still belong to the same species. Similarly, I do not give a hoot whether a writer is writing about China or Egypt, or either of the two Georgias, – what interests me is his book. The Chinese or Georgian features are intraspecific ones. What you want me to do is to give superiority to ecology over morphology.   [NWL 214]

From draft notes, 1948

Written on an offprint of Austin Clark's "Classification of the Butterflies, with the Allocation of the Genera occurring in North America north of Mexico," *Proceedings of the Biological Society of Washington* 61 (June 1948): 77–81.

Dr. Munroe[169] mentions Clark's classification (1948, Proc. Biol. Soc. Washington, *61*, pp. 77–84). But in that list the "subtribe Plebejina" is a meaningless hodge-podge of meaningless genera, because:

1. If *Plebejus* is used in a broad sense as Clark does (= my Plebejinae) then *Hemiargus* cannot be separated from it. Here Clark is the splitter not I.

2. If one separates and segregates things by their "general facies" as Munroe suggests, then *Hemiargus* must be fused with a mass of African forms, with the great majority of which it has no structural affinity whatsoever (indeed, the whole interest of the matter from a phylogenetic and zoogeographic viewpoint is that they *look* alike, but are structurally as far apart as can be).

3. *Philotes* holarctically grades into *Scolitantides* which is the same as *Phaedrotes* and the latter is much closer to *Glaucopsyche* than say *Plebejus s. str.* to *Lyceaides s. str.* Here again Clark, not I, is a splitter.

4. What *Brephidium* (part of an African subfamily) is doing in *cette galère* as the French say I cannot understand since it is as far removed from Clark's "Theclini" and "Lycaenini" as say his Spalginae. (Incidentally I never said that the "Blues" – a term which means little to me but which may

be rendered by group P . . .) consisted of 5 subfamilies. I listed 5 and said "etc." There are more than 5.

It is easier to handle things that have names.

Genus is a subjective idea. For my classification (classif. by genitalia) it is useful. If it is of no use to the general collector let him use my genera in parentheses.   [VNA]

From letter from Alexander B. Klots, April 2, 1949
Unpublished.

I have been extremely glad to note your synthetic tendency when consider-ing Palearctic and Nearctic forms. Since my own major interest has so largely concerned Holarctic distributions, I am greatly in accord with such work as pointing out relationships. . . . On the other hand, however, I have been wondering how you reconcile to yourself your synthesizing activities in *Lycaeides* with your very definitely disruptive tendencies in the tropical "Hemiargus" genera.   [VNA]

From letter from Charles Remington, April 27, 1949
Unpublished.

Heartiest thanks for your generous check covering your sustaining mem-bership for the [Lepidopterists'] Society.   [VNA]

From letter from Donald Eff,[170] May 8, 1949
Unpublished.

I've also heard many complimentary remarks with regard to your justifi-able thrusts at Frechin and F. Chermock, who by most of those who have had dealings with them, are regarded in the light of "black sheep."   [VNA]

From letter to Alexander B. Klots, May 16, 1949

From Ithaca, New York. Unpublished.

I *am* trying to discover *lygdamus* here (it is said to occur at a couple of miles distance from my house) but so far have not found it. . . . How and where does one obtain a permit to collect in the Teton or Jackson Hole National Forest?

. . . My wife has some timorous questions about grizzlies.[171]   [VNA]

From letter to Edmund Wilson, May 23–25, 1949

From Ithaca, New York.

Just a couple of words between two lectures. This is the last academical week. Around the 20th of June we shall start driving westwards – first to a Writers' Conference in Utah Univ., then to Teton Nat. Forest, Wyo., to look for a butterfly which I have described, named, fondled – but never actually taken myself.   [NWL 227]

From letter from Cyril dos Passos, May 31, 1949

Unpublished.

You have doubtless read Munroe's paper in The Lepidopterists' News (1949, p. 3) on the genus concept in RHOPALOCERA, in which he holds up Warren,[172] Grey, yourself, and myself as horrible examples of splitters and returns to the old outworn ideas of considering superficial characters as the more important.

Warren and I have been having some correspondence on this subject and feel that Munroe should be taken down a peg or two. It is our opinion that you are the person to do this, first, because you have carried this phase of taxonomy further than we – no new genus or subgenus has been erected by us, so far as I can recollect, although Munroe seems to imply otherwise. . . . Secondly, we are both tied up at present, but perhaps you are also!

[AMNH]

Letter to Edmund Wilson, postmarked August 18, 1949

From Wilson, Wyoming. Published in *Briefwechsel mit Edmund Wilson.*

Teton Pass Ranch
Wilson, Wyoming

Dear Bunny,

We have had some wonderful adventures in Utah and Wyoming and are driving back next week. I have lost many pounds and found many butterflies. We send both of you our very best greetings. We *must* see each other somewhere, somehow.

V.

[YALE]

From letter to Alexander B. Klots, August 31, 1949

From Ithaca, New York. Unpublished.

I have just returned from my Wyoming expedition. My headquarters were in Jackson Hole (first in the Hoback R., then near Teton Pass) and I got *everything* I wanted to plus some unexpected things.

Your charming letter was immensely helpful, and so was your paper on the *Brenthis + Colias.*[173] I shall write you much more fully about my captures when I have spread them. The *Boloria selene* race which I got in quantities (together with *L. thoe*) in two bogs near Jackson is *not* ssp. *tollandensis* though the ♀♀ are rather like the latter. I am puzzled by a dark *Oeneis* which seems to belong to the *Jutta* group. I got one *L. phlaeas* in the Shoshone (Beartooth Mts) at about 8000 ft. It was delightful to take lots of my *longinus* (the Blue between *melissa* and *scudderi*) in the Tetons. There are many other matters I shall tell you about later on.

My wife joins me in thanking you for the very helpful tips you gave us.

Sincerely yours

V. NABOKOV

I envy you terribly for obtaining laeta *in Vermont. I looked for it near Brattleboro in 1942 and 1943. Do give me some details (of habitat). I never believed that beech business.*[174]

[University of Connecticut Library]

From letter to George Davis,[175] November 10, 1949

From Ithaca, New York.

Your line about the butterflies *déclancha*[176] a fancy of mine which I have long wished to realize. Old Masters, especially Flemish and Italian, often had butterflies among their flowers. I once determined the country of origin of a painting by identifying the local form of butterfly depicted on it. A very interesting piece might be written on the whole subject (with illustrations) about butterflies in art beginning with the species figured in 1420–1375 B.C. by an Egyptian under Tuthmosis IV or Amenophis III (British Museum No. 37933). I am a pioneer in this subject. It would be lovely to brighten the essay with colored reproductions of butterflies in various pictures through the ages and have photos of real specimens for comparison.

[VNA]

Letter to *Life* magazine, November 12, 1949

From Ithaca, New York. Published in *Life*, December 5, 1949.

Sirs,

It may interest a few of your readers to learn that the butterfly wings in the third panel of the Bosch tryptich, so beautifully reproduced in your issue of November 14, can be at once determined as belonging to a female specimen of the common European species now known as *Maniola jurtina*, which Linnaeus described some 250 years after good Bosch knocked it down with his cap in a Flemish meadow to place it in his Hell.   [SL 93–94]

From letter to Don Eff, December 12, 1949

From Ithaca, New York. Unpublished.

This past summer I started out West by car in June from Ithaca and kept steadily collecting through the Mid-West, Colorado, Utah, Wyoming, Montana and then, on the return way, through Minnesota and Ontario, Canada, arriving home in September.

Except for the latter region I had some beautiful collecting, several strokes of marvelous luck, and made a few highly satisfying discoveries in the Tetons, where I roamed for a month and a half. . . . As soon as I have some spare time, I shall send Charles Remington for the *Lep.'s News* a special paper about my experience and finds.[177]

[VNA]

From letter to John Downey,[178] December 13, 1949
From Ithaca, New York. Unpublished.

As I promised, I am sending my drawings of *all* the Nearctic *Plebejinae* (except the genus *Lycaeides* which is now sufficiently known). These genera (*Plebejus, Agriades, Plebulina, Icaricia*) have never been figured in their Nearctic aspects. The drawings are valuable and perhaps you can copy them and send me back the originals. Apart from this, you are welcome to use them in any way you deem fit.

[VNA]

Conclusive Evidence
Excerpts from autobiography. Written 1947–50. Published serially 1948–50, mostly in the *New Yorker*, and in book form as *Conclusive Evidence* (New York: Harper, 1951) and *Speak, Memory* (London: Gollancz, 1951). Translated into Russian and revised as *Drugie berega* (1954), revised in English 1965–66, published as *Speak, Memory: An Autobiography Revisited* (New York: Putnam, 1967). (See pp. 511–14 and 626–39 for textual additions in revised editions.)

[As an infant walking down a path between his parents, Vladimir suddenly senses what time means.]
Thus, when the newly disclosed, fresh and trim formula of my own age, four, was confronted with the parental formulas, thirty-three and twenty-seven, something happened to me. I was given a tremendously invigorating shock. As if subjected to a second baptism, on more divine lines than the Greek Catholic ducking undergone fifty months earlier by a howling, half-drowned half-Victor (my mother, through the half-closed door, behind which an old custom bade parents retreat, managed to correct the bungling archpresbyter, Father Konstantin Vetvenitski), I felt myself plunged

abruptly into a radiant and mobile medium that was none other than the pure element of time. One shared it – just as excited bathers share shining seawater – with creatures that were not oneself but that were joined to one by time's common flow, an environment quite different from the spatial world, which not only man but apes and butterflies can perceive. At that instant, I became acutely aware that the twenty-seven-year-old being, in soft white and pink, holding my left hand, was my mother, and that the thirty-three-year-old being, in hard white and gold, holding my right hand, was my father. Between them, as they evenly progressed, I strutted, and trotted, and strutted again, from sun fleck to sun fleck, along the middle of a path, which I easily identify today with an alley of ornamental oaklings in the park of our country estate, Vyra, in the former Province of St. Petersburg, Russia. [SM 21–22, CE 3–4]

[*His paternal uncle, Konstantin Nabokov, a diplomat,*] is portrayed, goatee and all (together with Count Witte, the two Japanese delegates and a benevolent Theodore Roosevelt), in a mural of the signing of the Portsmouth Treaty on the left side of the main entrance hall of the American Museum of Natural History – an eminently fit place to find my surname in golden Slavic characters, as I did the first time I passed there – with a fellow lepidopterist, who said "Sure, sure" in reply to my exclamation of recognition.[179] [SM 60–61, CE 35]

[*His maternal uncle, Vasily Rukavishnikov, "Uncle Ruka."*]
"*L'air transparent fait monter de la plaine . . .*" he would sing in his high tenor voice, seated at the white piano in our country house – and if I were at that moment hurrying through the adjacent groves on my way home for lunch (soon after seeing his jaunty straw hat and the black-velvet-clad bust of his handsome coachman in Assyrian profile, with scarlet-sleeved outstretched arms, skim rapidly along the rim of the hedge separating the park from the drive) the plaintive sounds

> *Un vol de tourterelles strie le ciel tendre,*
> *Les chrysanthèmes se parent pour la Toussaint*

reached me and my green butterfly net on the shady, tremulous trail, at the end of which was a vista of reddish sand and the corner of our freshly re-painted house, the color of young fir cones, with the open drawing-room window whence the wounded music came.

7

The act of vividly recalling a patch of the past is something that I seem to have been performing with the utmost zest all my life, and I have reason to believe that this almost pathological keenness of the retrospective faculty is a hereditary trait. There was a certain spot in the forest, a footbridge across a brown brook, where my father would piously pause to recall the rare butterfly that, on the seventeenth of August, 1883, his German tutor had netted for him. The thirty-year-old scene would be gone through again. He and his brothers had stopped short in helpless excitement at the sight of the coveted insect poised on a log and moving up and down, as though in alert respiration, its four cherry-red wings with a pavonian eye-spot on each. In tense silence, not daring to strike himself, he had handed his net to Herr Rogge, who was groping for it, his eyes fixed on the splendid fly. My cabinet inherited that specimen a quarter of a century later. One touching detail: its wings had "sprung" because it had been removed from the setting board too early, too eagerly.[180]   [SM 74–75, CE 42–43]

[Classes at Vyra with his second English governess, Victoria Sheldon ("Miss Clayton").]

The schoolroom was drenched with sunlight. In a sweating glass jar, sev-eral spiny caterpillars were feeding on nettle leaves (and ejecting interest-ing, barrel-shaped pellets of olive-green frass). The oilcloth that covered the round table smelled of glue. Miss Clayton smelled of Miss Clayton. Fantastically, gloriously, the blood-colored alcohol of the outside ther-mometer had risen to 24° Réaumur (86° Fahrenheit) in the shade. Through the window one could see kerchiefed peasant girls weeding a garden path on their hands and knees or gently raking the sun-mottled sand. (The happy days when they would be cleaning streets and digging canals for the State were still beyond the horizon.) Golden orioles in the greenery emitted their four brilliant notes: dee-del-dee-O![181]   [SM 80, CE 46]

[Bathing in Biarritz, helped by paid attendants.]

In the security of a little cabin, one would be helped by yet another attendant to peel off one's soggy, sand-heavy bathing suit. It would plop onto the boards, and, still shivering, one would step out of it and trample on its bluish, diffuse stripes. The cabin smelled of pine. The attendant, a hunchback with beaming wrinkles, brought a basin of steaming-hot water, in which one immersed one's feet. From him I learned, and have preserved ever since in a glass cell of my memory, that "butterfly" in the Basque language is *misericoletea* – or at least it sounded so (among the seven words I have found in dictionaries the closest approach is *micheletea*).[182]

[SM 148, CE 100]

[First Russian tutor, "Ordo" (Ordyntsev).]

On walks with my brother and me in the cool summer of 1907, he wore a Byronic black cloak with a silver S-shaped clasp. In the deep Batovo woods, at a spot near a brook where the ghost of a hanged man was said to appear, Ordo would give a rather profane and foolish performance for which my brother and I clamored every time we passed there. Bending his head and flapping his cloak in weird, vampiric fashion he would slowly cavort around a lugubrious aspen. One wet morning during that ritual he dropped his cigarette case and while helping to look for it, I discovered two freshly emerged specimens of the Amur hawkmoth, rare in our region – lovely, velvety, purplish-gray creatures – in tranquil copulation, clinging with chinchilla-coated legs to the grass at the foot of the tree.

[SM 156, CE 107–18]

[His first adolescent infatuation.]

There are two especially vivid aspects of her that I would like to hold up simultaneously before my eyes in conclusion of her haunting image. The first lived for a long while within me quite separately from the Polenka I associated with doorways and sunsets, as if I had glimpsed a nymphean incarnation of her pitiful beauty that were better left alone. One June day, the year when she and I were both thirteen, on the banks of the Oredezh, I was engaged in collecting some so-called Parnassians – *Parnassius mnemo-*

syne, to be exact – strange butterflies of ancient lineage, with rustling, glazed, semitransparent wings and catkin-like flossy abdomens. My quest had led me into a dense undergrowth of milky-white racemosa and dark alder at the very edge of the cold, blue river, when suddenly there was an outburst of splashes and shouts, and from behind a fragrant bush, I caught sight of Polenka and three or four other naked children bathing from the ruins of an old bathhouse a few feet away. Wet, gasping, one nostril of her snub nose running, the ribs of her adolescent body arched under her pale, goose-pimpled skin, her calves flecked with black mud, a curved comb burning in her damp-darkened hair, she was scrambling away from the swish and clack of water-lily stems that a drum-bellied girl with a shaven head and a shamelessly excited stripling wearing around the loins a kind of string, locally used against the evil eye, were yanking out of the water and harrying her with; and for a second or two – before I crept away in a dismal haze of disgust and desire – I saw a strange Polenka shiver and squat on the boards of the half-broken wharf, covering her breasts against the east wind with her crossed arms, while with the tip of her tongue she taunted her pursuers. [SM 210–11, CE 148–49]

The summer evenings of my boyhood when I used to ride by her cottage speak to me in that voice of hers now. . . . A colossal shadow would begin to invade the fields, and the telegraph poles hummed in the stillness, and the night-feeders ascended the stems of their plants. Nibble, nibble, nibble – went a handsome striped caterpillar, not figured in Spuler, as he clung to a campanula stalk, working down with his mandibles along the edge of the nearest leaf out of which he was eating a leisurely hemicircle, then again extending his neck, and again bending it gradually, as he deepened the neat concave. Automatically, I might slip him, with a bit of his plantlet, into a matchbox to take home with me and have him produce next year a Splendid Surprise, but my thoughts were elsewhere: Zina and Colette, my seaside playmates; Louise, the prancer; all the flushed, low-sashed, silky-haired little girls at festive parties; languorous Countess G., my cousin's lady; Polenka smiling in the agony of my new dreams – all would merge to form somebody I did not know but was bound to know soon.[183]

[SM 212–13, CE 149–50]

[His first full love affair, begun a year earlier.]

That spring of 1916 is the one I see as the very type of a St. Petersburg spring, when I recall such specific images as Tamara, wearing an unfamiliar white hat, among the spectators of a hard-fought interscholastic soccer game, in which, that Sunday, the most sparkling luck helped me to make save after save in goal; and a Camberwell Beauty, exactly as old as our romance, sunning its bruised black wings, their borders now bleached by hibernation, on the back of a bench in Alexandrovski Garden; and the booming of cathedral bells in the keen air, above the corrugated dark blue of the Neva, voluptuously free of ice; and the fair in the confetti-studded slush of the Horse Guard Boulevard during Catkin Week. . . . The excitement in the streets made one drunk with desire for the woods and the fields. Tamara and I were especially eager to return to our old haunts.

[SM 139, CE 174]

[Leaving the Crimea and Russia, Vladimir worries about the letters his old girlfriend will still be trying to send him.]

Over a glassy sea in the bay of Sebastopol, under wild machine-gun fire from the shore (the Bolshevik troops had just taken the port), my family and I set out for Constantinople and Piraeus on a small and shoddy Greek ship carrying a cargo of dried fruit. I remember trying to concentrate, as we were zig-zagging out of the bay, on a game of chess with my father – one of the knights had lost its head, and a poker chip replaced a missing rook – and the sense of leaving Russia was totally eclipsed by the agonizing thought that Reds or no Reds, letters from Tamara would be still coming, miraculously and needlessly, to southern Crimea, and would search there for a fugitive addressee, and weakly flap about like bewildered butterflies set loose in an alien zone, at the wrong altitude, among an unfamiliar flora.

[SM 251, CE 180]

[En route from the Crimea to London, spring 1919.]

We had left our northern home for what we thought would be a brief wait, a prudent perching pause on the southern ledge of Russia; but the fury of the new regime had refused to blow over. In Greece, during two spring months, braving the constant resentment of intolerant shepherd dogs, I searched in vain for Gruner's Orange-tip, Heldreich's Sulphur, Krueper's White: I was in the wrong part of the country.[184]   [SM 153, CE 186]

[Bringing up his son Dmitri, born 1934, Nabokov would wheel or walk with him through public gardens and parks.]

I can name a blooming garden in Paris as the place where I noticed, in 1938 or 1939, a quiet girl of ten or so, with a deadpan white face, looking, in her dark, shabby, unseasonable clothes, as if she had escaped from an orphanage (congruously, I was granted a later glimpse of her being swept away by two flowing nuns), who had deftly tied a live butterfly to a thread and was promenading the pretty, weakly fluttering, slightly crippled insect on that elfish leash (the by-product, perhaps, of a good deal of dainty needlework in that orphanage). You have often accused me of unnecessary callousness in my matter-of-fact entomological investigations on our trips to the Pyrenees or the Alps; so, if I diverted our child's attention from that would-be Titania, it was not because I pitied her Red Admirable (Admiral, in vulgar parlance) but because there was some vaguely repulsive symbolism about her sullen sport. I may have been reminded, in fact, of the simple, old-fashioned trick a French policeman had – and no doubt still has – when leading a florid-nosed workman, a Sunday rowdy, away to jail, of turning him into a singularly docile and even alacritous satellite by catching a kind of small fishhook in the man's uncared-for but sensitive and responsive flesh.   [SM 305–6, CE 235–36]

From Chapter 16 of *Conclusive Evidence*

Published in the *New Yorker*, December 28, 1998. Excerpts from memoir, in form of pseudo-review. Written April–May 1950.

[Nabokov wrote the sixteenth chapter of his autobiography as if it were the first half of someone else's double review of Conclusive Evidence *and an imagined Barbara Braun's* When Lilacs Last. *Although designed as the final chapter of the book version, Nabokov decided the device was too much at odds with the truthfulness of the rest of the autobiography, and left it unpublished.]*

He is out to prove that his childhood contained, on a much reduced scale, the main components of his creative maturity; thus, through the thin sheath of a ripe chrysalis one can see, in its small wing cases, the dawning of color and pattern, a miniature revelation of the butterfly that will soon emerge and let its flushed and diced wings expand to many times their pupal size.

The unravelling of a riddle is the purest and most basic act of the human mind. All thematic lines mentioned are gradually brought together, are seen to interweave or converge, in a subtle but natural form of contact which is as much a function of art, as it is a discoverable process in the evolution of a personal destiny. Thus, towards the end of the book, the theme of mimicry, of the "cryptic disguise" studied by Nabokov in his entomological pursuits, comes to a punctual rendezvous with the "riddle" theme, with the camouflaged solution of a chess problem, with the piecing together of a design on bits of broken pottery, and with a picture puzzle wherein the eye makes out the contours of a new country. To the same point of convergence other thematic lines arrive in haste, as if consciously yearning for the blissful anastomosis provided jointly by art and fate. The solution of the riddle theme is also the solution of the theme of exile, of the "intrinsic loss" running through the whole book, and these lines blend, in their turn, with the culmination of the "rainbow" theme ("a spiral of life in an agate"), and merge, at a most satisfying *rond point*, with the many garden paths and park walks and forest trails meandering through the book. . . .

Today Mr. Nabokov must find it strange to recall the literary vagaries of his young years. With his wife and son, he now lives in this country of which he is a citizen; lives happily, I understand, in the simple disguise of an obscure college professor of literature with spacious vacations devoted to butterfly hunting in the West. In lepidopterological circles, he is known as a somewhat eccentric taxonomist with analytic rather than synthetic leanings. In American scientific circles, he has published various discoveries of his own relating to new species or forms of butterflies; and – a scientific tradition that seems to impress so much lay reporters – other entomologists have named butterflies and moths after him. The American Museum of Natural History in New York and the Museum of Comparative Zoology at Harvard preserve Nabokov's type specimens. On a visit to the latter institution I was shown several tiny moths – belonging to a marvelously multiform genus – which Nabokov discovered in the Wasatch Mountains of Utah in 1943. One of these McDunnough has named *Eupithecia nabokovi*. This is a delightfully satisfying resolution of a certain thematic line of "Conclusive Evidence" where Nabokov tells how passionately he had dreamed in his boyhood of discovering a new member of that particular group.

[SM 1999: 249–50, 256–57]

Remarks on F. Martin Brown's "Measurements and Lepidoptera"

Lepidoptera paper. Written in 1950 and published in *Lepidopterists' News*.

Mr. Brown has devoted most of his article on "Measurements and Lepidoptera" (*Lep. News*, vol. 4: p. 51) to criticizing from the point of view of statistics the measurements used in my paper on "The Nearctic Members of the Genus *Lycaeides*" (*Bull. Mus. Comp. Zool.*, vol. 101: 479–541; 1949). I wish to say a few words in reply.

Under the name of *sublivens* (*l.c.*: p. 513) I described on the basis of nine males a subspecies of *argyrognomon* (Bergstr.) [= *idas* auct.] from the St. Miguel Mts., S.W. Colorado, and, for the sake of completeness, listed the measurements of all the specimens (uncus parts and forewing). This was followed (pp. 516–520) by a description of another, much more complicated, form from the Teton Mts., *argyrognomon longinus*. [See supplementary notes at end.]

"Although a table of data is not presented for [*longinus*]," writes Mr. Brown (who consistently misspells the name of the thing), "measurements on seven specimens are scattered in the text." Of these DELIBERATELY scattered measurements, Mr. Brown gathers into a tidy column the "F" ones (mean length of falx) in order to compare them with my "F" column under *sublivens*.

Now this is the danger of statistics (and "keys," and those jagged lines that are so amusing to plot). Only three of the seven males belong to typical *longinus* (p. 516) in the qualitative sense in which the nine *sublivens* males are typical. The other four specimens I discussed (p. 519) under *longinus* are more or less definite transitions to *melissa*, and I pointed out that the matter is a systematist's nightmare. Nightmares cannot be statistically treated, but they can be very precisely described. If, moreover, Mr. Brown turns to my "Introduction," he will see (pp. 480–481) that I took great pains to define in qualitative terms the specific differences between *melissa* and *argyrognomon*. These specific formulas and the whole of the distal part of the uncus in ventral view ("FHUE") should be taken into account when comparing the seven specimens of *sublivens* with the three typical and four "melissoid" specimens of *longinus*; whereas Mr. Brown jumbles up the all-important qualitative values with quantitative ones and enforces upon me a statistical procedure that I never intended, or intend, to follow.

In explaining his misleading table, Mr. Brown refers to something he calls a "typical population" of *sublivens*. At the moment of description I had only nine old specimens, all males, preserved in a museum collection. In its habitat, *sublivens* during the last fifty years may have become extinct, for all I know, or taxonomically blurred by hybridization. Experience tells me that when I study a series of nine specimens that closely resemble each other, differ from allopatric conspecific sets sufficiently to be assigned to a new subspecies, and some from a region where the species has not been detected before, the specimens may be said to belong to a monoform race (*l.c.*: "Introduction"), probably represented at the station that the series comes from by a certain number of live individuals; but this is as far as I desire to go in this business of "population" – a term the lax use of which leads to the notion that a population IS a subspecies (or species), whereas, in point of fact, a population only represents a subspecies or BELONGS to it.

"The question then is," Mr. Brown continues, "is the apparent difference [between the F means of *sublivens* and *longinus*] real or only a result of a small size of the samples used?" There is no such question here – for the simple reason that F, alone and unqualified, is not what separates the two forms. To estimate the chances of the two series being "samples drawn from the same general population" as Mr. Brown proposes to do "mathematically," would be a loss of time. The term "general population," if it has any meaning at all, presupposes a more or less continuous stretch of inhabited space; but between the St. Miguel Mts. and the Tetons, the only known habitats of *argyrognomon sublivens* and *argyrognomon longinus* respectively, there is a 500 miles gap where nobody has yet found *argyrognomon*; and, anyway, the problem to be solved is not whether *sublivens* and *longinus* overlap in F, but what is the true significance of the alar resemblance between *argyrognomon sublivens* and *melissa pseudosamuelis* (*l.c.*: p. 530).

In conclusion I must object to Mr. Brown's casual condemnation of my "time-consuming counts of scale rows" which to him "mean nothing until the statistical parameter of the data on each subspecies is established." I was not concerned with "statistical parameters" when writing my paper. I was concerned with presenting what my scale-line method allowed to present – an exact description of taxonomic types. I was also concerned with giving examples of its application to the description of phases selected at random within the variational range of a racial wing pattern and of such extremes as complete obliteration of this or that component. I cannot see what part "parameters" could have played here, and how they affect the description of holotypes. Mr. Brown also suggests that future revisers measure a thousand, or more, unci of *sublivens* – a nice batch that the miracle of statistics is somehow supposed to produce. I have dissected, drawn and measured many more specimens of *Lycaeides* than that, and have arrived at the conclusion that the kind of genitalic ranges I have computed illustrate with sufficient clarity racial characters, despite small samples of each race; and that structural (uncal) fluctuation in connection with intra-racial wing-size variability is (if obviously stunted individuals are omitted) a negligible factor. And, finally, I have been concerned with "qualitative" subspecies (since I consider that merely "quantitative" phenomena have no taxonomic status) and with trying to restore the qualitative approach to its position of honor, while placing at its service quantitative values to guide the next man armed with a microscope, a camera lucida, and a finely nibbed pen. After all, natural science is responsible to philosophy – not to statistics.

[*Lepidopterists' News* 4 (1950): 75–76]

Postscript

In July and August, 1949, I searched diligently but in vain, at the sagebrush level in Jackson Hole, for colonies or wandering individuals of the bright-colored, alfalfa-and-*Hedysarum*-feeding *melissa* form that is common in Utah at 6000 ft. alt. [see my discussion of its intergrades with the alpine *melissa annetta* (Edw.) in the Wasatch Mts., *l.c.*: p. 535]; but I did find, in some numbers, the "melissoid" form of *argyrognomon longinus* Nab., which I already knew, on an isolated, well-timbered hill [Blacktail Butte] that rises to about 700 ft. above the floor of the upland valley [6000–7000 ft.alt.] immediately east of Moose, between Jackson and Moran. From July 15 to the end of August I studied typical *longinus* in the mountains west of Jackson (it was especially abundant in the vicinity of Teton Pass, on slopes between 7500 and 9500 ft. alt. where I ascertained its foodplant) and eastward along the Hoback R., at the foot of Battle Mt., from about 6500 ft. up, flying in company with such butterflies as *Speyeria atlantis tetonia* dos Pas. & Grey, *S. callippe meadii* (Edw.), *S. egleis macdunnoughi* (Gund.), *S. hydaspe purpurascens* (H.Edw.), *S. mormonia clio* (Edw.), and *S. zerene garretti* (Gund.) [one of the males I took has the scintillant macules reduced and conspicuously rimmed with fine black]; *Boloria rossicus ingens* (B. & McD.) and *kriemhild* (Stkr.); *Euphydryas anicia* ssp. and *E. gillettii* Barnes [a very sluggish insect in comparison to its vivacious palearctic ally *maturna* (L.)]; *Oeneis jutta* ssp. and *norna* ssp. [one almost typical, others transitional to ssp. *chryxus* (Dbldy. & Hew.)]; "*Coenonympha*" *haydenii* Edw.; "*Philotes*" *enoptes* (Bdv.); and "*Pieris*" *callidice occidentalis* (Reak.). I saw nothing of *longinus* above timberline in the Grand Tetons [around Amphitheatre Lake] where *B. rossicus grandis* (B. & McD.), *Lycaena phlaeas* ssp. [near ssp. *fieldeni* (McLach.), and very much like *snowi* (Edw.) on the wing], *Colias skinneri* Barnes and *Pyrgus centaureae freija* Warr. were taken. Among other things incidentally picked up I may mention the following from around Jackson at about 6500 ft.: *Speyeria cybele letona* dos Pas. & Grey, *Boloria selene* ssp. [between ssp. *albequina* (Holl.) and ssp. *tollandensis* (B. & Benj.) and *toddi* (Holl.) [=? *frigga* (Thun.)] ssp. [hindwing below suffused with bolorian purple]; a colony of darkish *Apodemia mormo* F. & F. on a very dry slope above Wilson at

7500 ft. alt.; *Strymon saepium* (Bdv.), *itys* (Edw.), and *edwardsii* (Saund.); *Mitoura spinetorum* (Hew.) near *johnsoni* (Skin.); *Callipsyche behrii* (Edw.); *Strymon titus* ssp.; "*Phaedrotes*" *piasus* (Bdv.); *Lycaena thoe* ssp. and *mariposa* (Reak.); and *Polites sonora utahensis* (Skin.) and *peckius* (Kby.). The combination *selene-toddi-thoe-peckius* on a marsh north of Jackson reminded one uncannily of, say, West Wardsboro, Vermont.

My material is now in the Cornell University Museum, Ithaca, New York. [*Lepidopterists' News* 4:76]

From letter to Edmund Wilson, June 3, 1950

From Ithaca, New York. Published in *Briefwechsel mit Edmund Wilson.*

Vera and I came back yesternight (вечор – not many Russians know the meaning of this word) from Boston minus my teeth and the Mass. part of her licence . . . and we are again driving thither on the 7th. We stayed at the Vendôme (tall stale rooms). Yesterday morning on our way back, we drove to a certain place between Albany and Schenectady where, in a pine-scrub waste, near absolutely marvelous patches of lupines in bloom, I took a few specimens of my *samuelis*. [YALE]

Letter to Joseph C. Bequaert, July 6, 1950

From Ithaca, New York.

Dear Bequaert,

I am sending you a little memorandum that may be useful to Dr. McDunnough when he arrives. As you know, a serious illness in the spring of 1948 prevented me from winding up my lepidopterological affairs to my satisfaction before I left for Ithaca. I have now looked through my correspondence and notebooks and have jotted down the following items for your and McDunnough's information.

1. I am responsible for the arrangement of the Nearctic butterflies. Very possibly Dr. McDunnough will disagree with some of my taxonomic ideas but at least the series are in good order now. It was not an easy job since

the specimens were scattered all over the place. I also classified most of the Palearctic butterflies of the Weeks collection which were originally in glassless trays when I first examined the collection in 1941–42. As you also know, I was never officially curator of the Lepidoptera, and what I did in that line was solely in appreciation of Barbour's sympathy and generosity in giving me the possibility to indulge in research work dealing with certain Lycaenids, which resulted in various papers published in "Psyche," "The Entomologist" and the "MCZ Bulletin."

2. A chest near the bookcase contains numerous vials with male genitalia (mainly Lycaenids) coated with glycerine in a mixture of alcohol and water. I had hoped to arrange them more permanently (using the jar system, as I do not believe in slides for these things) but I did not have the time to do so before my departure. The numbers affixed to these vials correspond to numbers on *yellow* labels affixed to Lycaenids in the collection. Most of them refer to the *Lycaeides* (the "*scudderi-melissa*" group) that is temporarily set apart with "do-not-disturb" notes (opposite the Nearctic collection) since there are still specimens that I have to return to my correspondents. The numbers in pencil on white labels affixed to the butterflies refer to my files where each specimen has a card of its own, and should not be confused with the aforesaid numbers on yellow labels referring to the vials with genitalia. I shall be in Boston sometime in September and shall finish sorting out the specimens to be returned. The Frank Chermock batch is ready but he does not answer my letters and I do not know where to send it to him (it contains a holotype-allotype pair among other valuable things).

3. Some Lycaenids occurring in North America, but really belonging to the Neotropical group, will be found together with specimens of the latter in one of the cabinets (nearest to the windows) containing West-Indian butterflies. I placed them there temporarily while working on the Neotropical *Plebejinae*.

4. Also temporarily, for safety's sake, while boxes were continuously opened and handled, I removed Scudder's Lycaenidae specimens, among which there are a few types, to the "green" cabinet and attached large labels "Scudder's collection" to the cases.

5. The following material had been loaned through me and I do not

know if it has been returned since I left (there are notes pinned in the corresponding empty spots in the cases):

> To Avinov, Carnegie Museum, 15-VI-1943, 6 females of *Phoebis argante* race from Cuba.
>
> To Franklin Chermock, 18-IV-1945, a specimen of *Colias occidentalis* Scud.
>
> To W. P. Comstock, A.M.N.H., 7-IX-1946, nine specimens of *Anaea* and, in 1945, some sixty or more *Heliconius charithonius* (you should have the list, if I remember correctly).
>
> To R. M. Fox, Carnegie Museum, 25-IX-1946, about 1900 specimens of *Ithomiines* (his count, 1878, is short of ours by 32).
>
> To A. B. Klots, College of the City of New York, Dep. of Biology, 22-IV-1948, 1 *Boloria freija*.

6. I have given to the MCZ all the abundant lepidopterological material spread and incorporated in the Nearctic section, that I collected in 1943 and 1947 in Utah and Colorado besides a smaller collection I made in various Eastern localities.

7. I have been also responsible for obtaining specimens for the Museum from various correspondents of mine (you have the list of these accessions) such as Stallings, Grey, Eff and many others.

There are some other, minor, matters but they can wait until I see you in the fall.

Sincerely yours,

VLADIMIR NABOKOV   [SL 102–4]

From letter to Elena Sikorski, August 3, 1950

From Ithaca, New York. In Russian.

Don't read Sartre – fashionable nonsense, already forgotten, and Miller is talentless obscenity. When I want good reading, I reread Proust's *A la Re-*

cherche du Temps Perdu or Joyce's *Ulysses*. Moth lure: treacle and beer (flat) half in half, prepare in the afternoon, before use add a little glass of rum (per half-bucket), smear at head-height with a painter's brush the bark (coarser) of leafy trees (oldish), 20–30 trees before dark. Cover the moths with a glass or jar, with cotton wool soaked in chloroform at the bottom. Did I write you that I had discovered and described several new species and that there exist several named *nabokovi* in my honor? I must say that I have changed ridiculously little over all these years. [*Perepiska s sestroy* 63]

Letter to Charles Remington, January 8, 1951

From Ithaca, New York. Unpublished.

Dear Charles,

Many thanks for consenting to publish my reply to Brown. I knew you would not let me down (sorry for this rhyme).

Not quite sure what you mean by "your view that sympatric species are equally uncertain." On the contrary! Sympatric species are the only absolute species. But that some such two absolute sympatric species in one locality (whither, perhaps, one arrived later than the other, after complete differentiation) may be linked by intergrades in another, remote, place, is neither their fault nor mine.

Nomenclature. *Scolitantides. I* am the little lumper here, and *Clark* (or Munroe) the little splitter. I have thoroughly investigated the matter and have found that *lygdamus*, the *battoides* group and *piasus* are linked up generically in the Old World by a wonderfully complete chain of alar and genitalic intergrades and thus should all be included in *Scolitantides. Phaedrotes* etc. might be placed in parenthesis as you often do to denote subgenera? Or throw in a footnote pointing out that I consider the three genera in which you, splitters, place *lygdamus, enoptes* and *piasus* as being really one, *Scolitantides* Hübner, of which *Papilio battus* /Schiff./, 1775, is the type.

Skinneri is quite certainly a race of *pelidne* which, in its turn, interbreeds with *palaeno*.

Was sorry not to have been able to come to New York and see you.

Yours,

VLADIMIR NABOKOV

P.S. If this is too repugnant to you editorially, I do not insist on these nomenclatorial points.

P.P.S. Do you know, I was collecting at Steamboat Springs etc. a few days before you were there in 1949?

[Remington Collection]

Letter to Patricia Hunt,[185] February 6, 1951

From Ithaca, New York.

Dear Miss Hunt,

Your suggestion interests me hugely. All my collecting life (45 years – I started at 6) I had been dreaming of somebody's taking photographs of the marvels I saw, and the skill of a Nature Reporter and a photographer from LIFE combined with my knowledge of butterflies and their ways would make a simply ideal team. It is really a wonderful idea and I am absolutely at your service in this matter, if we agree on terms.

There are the following considerations to be taken into account. The environs of Ithaca are hopeless; and so is New England. Indeed, the whole east (except Florida which, however, represents a totally different, tropical, fauna related to the Antilles) is extremely poor in butterflies. There are a few interesting things far up in the north of Maine but none of them are showy. The few showy ones that occur throughout the eastern states (the Monarch, two or three Swallowtails, Admirals) have been pictured ad nauseam. The few rare species, dingy or dazzling, are extremely local and cannot be counted upon to show up at a fixed time and place. There is one little thing [the Early Hairstreak], a perfect jewel (and one of the rarest butterflies in the world) of which only some thirty or forty specimens have been taken since it was turned up by Edwards' Negro gardener almost a hundred years ago; at the present time two or three collectors know of a locality for it in Vermont, in early May – but the exact place is a secret. A very local blue butterfly [the Karner Blue], which I have named myself can be found in a pine barren between Albany and Schenectady but nothing else of popular or scientific interest is to be found in that neighborhood. The only eastern butterfly that combines marvelous beauty with comparative rarity (a good female costs two or three dollars) is a large Fritillary [the Diana Fritillary] which is found here and there in June in the hills of the south-eastern states. To try and get pictures of these things would mean traveling from one place to another and being subject to the whims of weather and collector's luck.

Not so in the west (where I have extensively collected during several summers). I am thinking especially of S. Colorado and Arizona – but some gorgeous things can be easily found in fair numbers anywhere in the Rockies. I would dearly want to have photographs taken of a charming middle-size butterfly that I discovered and named ten years ago in the Grand Canyon, a few minutes walk down the Bright Angel Trail. The Tetons where I collected for two months in 1949 are also splendid. Then, of course, there is Alaska, where I have not been, but which I know to be full of nice things easy to photograph.

I have had in mind for years a list of positions and perching places in regard to various not too shy and very photogenic butterflies. Flowerheads, leaves, twigs, rocks, treetrunks. In certain spots, a number of interesting and gaudy things have, on hot days, a habit of congregating on damp sand and are not easily disturbed in their tippling. Many other species settle with outspread wings on short alpine flowers or bask in the sun on stones. (I take it for granted that your photographer is prepared to do some crawling and wriggling and to ignore completely the possible presence of snakes). Others with closed wings revealing in profile beautiful undersides can be photographed very nicely since dozens of them can be seen at a time on the blossoms of thistles along quite accessible roads in canyons. All these western butterflies can make wonderful pictures and such pictures have never been taken before.

Some fascinating photos might be also taken of me, a burly but agile man, stalking a rarity or sweeping it into my net from a flowerhead, or capturing it in midair. There is a special professional twist of the wrist immediately after the butterfly has been netted which is quite fetching. Then you could show my finger and thumb delicately pinching the thorax of a netted butterfly through the gauze of the netbag. And of course the successive stages of preparing the insect on a setting board have never yet been shown the way I would like them to be shown. All this might create a sensation in scientific and nature-lover circles besides being pleasing to the eye of a layman. I must stress the fact that the whole project as you see it has never been attempted before.

When collecting, my general system is to go by car to this or that locality which may be a bog or a mountain pass or the shore of a lake or the beginning of a trail leading to alpine meadows. I do not care to camp out but usually stay at one of the good motels which abound in the west. The best time to collect is from the end of June to the beginning of August though of course this varies with altitude, latitude etc. I have not quite made up my mind where I shall collect this summer. It will depend to some extent on the money my book – (CONCLUSIVE EVIDENCE to be brought out by Harper on the 14th of this month – you may have seen parts of it in The New Yorker, Harper's Magazine or the Partisan) will bring me. It may also depend on what LIFE would decide to spend on this project.

Sincerely yours,

VLADIMIR NABOKOV   [SL 113–15]

From Nabokov's diary, February 18, 1951

Unpublished.

I see quite clearly now another book, "More Evidence" – something like that – "American" part

1.   Criticism and addenda of "Conclusive Evidence"
2.   Three Tenses[186]
3.   Dreams
4.   MCZ and collecting (merge back into Russia)

5.   St Marks (with full details)[187]

6.   Story I am doing now

7.   Double Talk (enlarged)[188]

8.   Edmund W.[189]

9.   *The assistant professor* who was *never* found out (Cross, Fairbanks)[190]

10

11

12

13

14

15   Criticism and addenda to this   [VNA]

From letter to Elena Sikorski, March 13, 1951

From Ithaca, New York. In Russian.

Somehow – I won't forget – I will send Amer. butts. And one of my works on "blues." In it there's one little thing that flies not far from you, at Versoix, in two generations, *Plebejus ismenias aegus*. I have described many new American butterflies, but only one from Asia and one from Europe (Alpes Maritimes, caught it myself in 1938, in Moulinet). And there are, besides, four *nabokovi*, named by others, and especially dear to me is *Eupithecia nabokovi,* a tiny geometrid, which I caught at a great height (9000ft. – i.e. almost three thousand meters) in the Wasatch mountains in Utah. I think I've already told you all this. *Je suis un peu gaga.*

[*Perepiska s sestroy* 65]

From letter to Edmund Wilson, March 24, 1951

From Ithaca, New York.

Life, a magazine, wants to take photographs of me catching butterflies, and of rare butterflies on flowers or mud, and I am doing my best to give it a strictly scientific twist – nothing of the kind has ever been done with rare

Western species, some of which I have described myself – so they are sending a photographer to be with me, for a week or so, in some productive locality in S.W. Colorado or Arizona (Dmitri is in a great singing voice today,
booming French from *La Juive*, and in a minute he is driving me to the soccer field for some practice and coaching) in July – they do not quite understand what is going to happen.   [NWL 260]

From Nabokov's Cornell lectures, March 1951

Masterpieces of European Fiction lecture, first delivered in March 1951 and until January 1959 normally repeated every year.

[Gogol's The Overcoat, *Stevenson's* Dr. Jekyll and Mr. Hyde, *and Kafka's* Metamorphosis.*]*
"The Carrick," "Dr. Jekyll and Mr. Hyde," and "The Metamorphosis": all
three are commonly called fantasies. From my point of view, any outstanding work of art is a fantasy insofar as it reflects the unique world of a unique
individual. But when people call these three stories fantasies, they merely
imply that the stories depart in their subject matter from what is commonly
called reality. Let us therefore examine what *reality* is, in order to discover
in what manner and to what extent so-called fantasies depart from so-
called reality.

Let us take three types of men walking through the same landscape.
Number One is a city man on a well-deserved vacation. Number Two is a
professional botanist. Number Three is a local farmer. Number One, the
city man, is what is called a realistic, commonsensical, matter-of-fact type:
he sees trees as *trees* and knows from his map that the road he is following
is a nice new road leading to Newton, where there is a nice eating place recommended to him by a friend in his office. The botanist looks around and
sees his environment in the very exact terms of plant life, precise biological
and classified units such as specific trees and grasses, flowers and ferns, and
for him *this* is reality; to him the world of the stolid tourist (who cannot
distinguish an oak from an elm) seems a fantastic, vague, dreamy, never-
never world. Finally, the world of the local farmer differs from the two others in that his world is intensely emotional and personal since he has been
born and bred there, and knows every trail and individual tree, and every
shadow from every tree across every trail, all in warm connection with his

everyday work, and his childhood, and a thousand small things and patterns which the other two – the humdrum tourist and the botanical taxonomist – simply cannot know in the given place at the given time. Our farmer will not know the relation of the surrounding vegetation to a botanical conception of the world, and the botanist will know nothing of any importance to him about that barn or that old field or that old house under its cottonwoods, which are afloat, as it were, in a medium of personal memories for one who was born there.

So here we have three different worlds – three men, ordinary men who have different *realities* – and, of course, we could bring in a number of other beings: a blind man with a dog, a hunter with a dog, a dog with his man, a painter cruising in quest of a sunset, a girl out of gas – – – In every case it would be a world completely different from the rest since the most objective words *tree, road, flower, sky, barn, thumb, rain* have, in each, totally different subjective connotations. Indeed, this subjective life is so strong that it makes an empty and broken shell of the so-called objective existence. The only way back to objective reality is the following one: we can take these several individual worlds, mix them thoroughly together, scoop up a drop of that mixture, and call it *objective reality*. We may taste in it a particle of madness if a lunatic passed through that locality, or a particle of complete and beautiful nonsense if a man has been looking at a lovely field and imagining upon it a lovely factory producing buttons or bombs; but on the whole these mad particles would be diluted in the drop of objective reality that we hold up to the light in our test tube. Moreover, this *objective reality* will contain something that transcends optical illusions and laboratory tests. It will have elements of poetry, of lofty emotion, of energy and endeavor (and even here the button king may find his rightful place), of pity, pride, passion – and the craving for a thick steak at the recommended roadside eating place.

So when we say *reality*, we are really thinking of all this – in one drop – an average sample of a mixture of a million individual realities. And it is in this sense (of human reality) that I use the term *reality* when placing it against a backdrop, such as the worlds of "The Carrick," "Dr. Jekyll and Mr. Hyde," and "The Metamorphosis," which are specific fantasies.

[*Lectures on Literature* 252–3]

[Published in part in Natural History, *July–August 1999.]*

There was a Chinese philosopher[191] who all his life pondered the problem whether he was a Chinese philosopher dreaming that he was a butterfly or a butterfly dreaming that she was a philosopher.

All three stories are concerned with transformation, with metamorphosis. Who can explain the process in entomological terms?

Transformation ... Transformation is a marvelous thing ... I am thinking especially of the transformation of butterflies. Though wonderful to watch, transformation from larva to pupa or from pupa to butterfly is not a particularly pleasant process for the subject involved. There comes for every caterpillar a difficult moment when he begins to feel pervaded by an odd sense of discomfort. It is a tight feeling – here about the neck and elsewhere, and then an unbearable itch. Of course he has moulted a few times before, but *that* is nothing in comparison to the tickle and urge that he feels now. He must shed that tight dry skin, or die. As you have guessed under that skin, the armor of a pupa – and how uncomfortable to wear one's skin over one's armor – is already forming: I am especially concerned at the moment with those butterflies that have carved golden pupa, called also chrysalis, which hang from some surface in the open air.

Well, the caterpillar must do something about that horrible feeling. He walks about looking for a suitable place. He finds it. He crawls up a wall or a tree-trunk. He makes for himself a little pad of silk on the underside of that perch. He hangs himself by the tip of his tail or last legs, from the silk patch, so as to dangle head downwards in the position of an inverted question-mark, and there *is* a *question* – how to get rid now of his skin. One wriggle, another wriggle – and zip the skin bursts down the back, and he gradually gets out of it working with shoulders and hips like a person getting out of a sausage dress. Then comes the most critical moment. – You understand that we are hanging head down by our last pair of legs, and the problem now is to shed the whole skin – even the skin of those last legs by which we hang – but how to accomplish this without falling?

So what does he do, this courageous and stubborn little animal who is already partly disrobed. Very carefully he starts working out his hind legs, dislodging them from the patch of silk from which he is dangling, head down – and then with an admirable twist and jerk he sort of jumps *off* the silk pad, sheds the last shred of hose, and immediately, in the process of the same jerk-and-twist-jump he attaches himself anew by means of a hook that was under the shed skin on the tip of his body. Now all the skin has come off, thank God, and the bared surface, now hard and glistening, is the pupa, a swathed-baby like thing hanging from that twig – a very beautiful chrysalis with golden knobs and plate-armor wingcases. This pupal stage lasts from a few days to a few years. I remember as a boy keeping a hawk-moth's pupa in a box for something like seven years, so that I actually finished high school while the thing was asleep – and then finally it hatched – unfortunately it happened during a journey on the train, – a nice case of misjudgement after all those years. But to come back to our butterfly pupa.

After say two or three weeks something begins to happen. The pupa hangs quite motionless, but you notice one day that through the wingcases, which are many times smaller than the wings of the future perfect insect – you notice that through the horn-like texture of each wingcase you can see in miniature the pattern of the future wing, the lovely flush of the ground-color, a dark margin, a rudimentary eyespot. Another day or two – and the final transformation occurs. The pupa splits as the caterpillar had split – it is really a last glorified moult, and the butterfly creeps out – and in its turn hangs down from the twig to dry. She is not handsome at first. She is very damp and bedraggled. But those limp implements of hers that she has disengaged, gradually dry, distend, the veins branch and harden – and in twenty minutes or so she is ready to fly. You have noticed that the caterpillar is a *he*, the pupa an *it*, and the butterfly a *she*. You will ask – what is the feeling of hatching? Oh, no doubt, there is a rush of panic to the head, a thrill of breathless and strange sensation, but then the eyes see, in a flow of sunshine, the butterfly sees the world, the large and awful face of the gaping entomologist.

Let us now turn to the transformation of Jekyll into Hyde.   [MS, VNA]

[Lecture on Kafka's Metamorphosis.*]*
Now what exactly is the "vermin" into which poor Gregor, the seedy commercial traveler, is so suddenly transformed? It obviously belongs to the branch of "jointed leggers" (*Arthropoda*), to which insects, and spiders, and centipedes, and crustaceans belong. If the "numerous little legs" men-

tioned in the beginning mean more than six legs, then Gregor would not be an insect from a zoological point of view. But I suggest that a man awakening on his back and finding he has as many as six legs vibrating in the air might feel that six was sufficient to be called numerous. We shall therefore assume that Gregor has six legs, that he is an insect.

Next question: what insect? Commentators say *cockroach*, which of course does not make sense. A cockroach is an insect that is flat in shape with large legs, and Gregor is anything but flat: he is convex on both sides, belly and back, and his legs are small. He approaches a cockroach in only one respect: his coloration is brown. That is all. Apart from this he has a tremendous convex belly divided into segments and a hard rounded back suggestive of wing cases. In beetles these cases conceal flimsy little wings that can be expanded and then may carry the beetle for miles and miles in a blundering flight. Curiously enough, Gregor the beetle never found out that he had wings under the hard covering of his back. (This is a very nice observation on my part to be treasured all your lives. Some Gregors, some Joes and Janes, do not know that they have wings.) Further, he has strong mandibles. He uses these organs to turn the key in a lock while standing erect on his hind legs, on his third pair of legs (a strong little pair), and this gives us the length of his body, which is about three feet long. In the course of the story he gets gradually accustomed to using his new appendages – his feet, his feelers. This brown, convex, dog-sized beetle is very broad. I should imagine him to look like this:

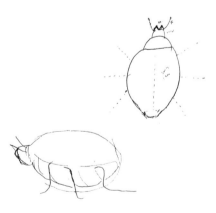

In the original German text the old charwoman calls him *Mistkafer,* a "dung beetle." It is obvious that the good woman is adding the epithet only to be friendly. He is not, technically, a dung beetle. He is merely a big beetle. (I must add that neither Gregor nor Kafka saw that beetle any too clearly.)

[*Lectures on Literature* 258–60]

From letter to Francis Brown,[192] April 19, 1951

From Ithaca, New York.

Yesterday I wrote asking you to let me review Klots' book on butterflies, which I know is an important and interesting work. I hope that this idea will appeal to you.   [SL 119]

Review of Alexander B. Klots, *A Field Guide to the Butterflies of North America, East of the Great Plains*

Written in late April 1951 and published as "Yesterday's Caterpillar" in the *New York Times Book Review.*

Unquestionably this is the finest book on American butterflies to be published since 1889 when Samuel Scudder's great work, "The Butterflies of the Eastern United States and Canada," inaugurated a new era in lepidopterology. It is scientific without being pedantic and up-to-date without being esoteric. The author is an associate of the American Museum of Natural History and Professor of Biology at the College of the City of New York. Marjorie Statham's colored figures of 247 species are admirable, and there are more than two hundred excellent photographs, many of which instructively magnify the subjects of the paintings.

About 450 butterflies are listed by the author for all of North America east of the hundredth meridian. Of this number, only some 150 (including about twenty-five shared with the Old World) can be said, as I see it, to belong truly to the core of the fauna; and many of these are very local. The rest are of Central or South American origin – stragglers from Mexico, Floridian forms, widespread migrants and more or less well established settlers (to which some of our commonest species belong).

The work is divided into three parts, two dealing with general matters, such as collecting techniques and classification, and one, discussing the genera and species, with comparative descriptions and keys. Brevity and clarity are on the whole well combined. Perhaps the geographic references are a little too vague in respect to butterflies that are known only from a few spots within such generous limits as "Quebec to Georgia."

On the other hand, a little too much emphasis has been placed on "Life Zones," and the lists of "Characteristic Species" are misleading. What counts is the exact combination, and no such combination of species as is listed under "Canadian Zone" or "Transition" exists anywhere in one spot. Ecology is a pretty metaphysical business unless it is absolutely accurate.

I note some oversimplifications and a few errors. The Viceroy mimics the Monarch not only in appearance but also in behavior – and the why and the how of the matter still present a great mystery, not solved in terms of "edibility." For years the legend of the Painted Lady's "hibernating" (in the sense the Mourning Cloak does) has been traveling from butterfly book to butterfly book and should have been stopped in this one.

Minor blemishes are unavoidable in the first edition of a work of such scope. The fact remains that here is a wonderfully stimulating and delightfully presented survey of the subject, and one hopes that a companion volume on Western butterflies will follow.

[*New York Times Book Review,* June 3, 1951]

From letter to Edmund Wilson, June 13, 1951

From Ithaca, New York.

We are in the midst of packing. Next fall we shall have another house, smaller but more comfortable. We are starting westward в двадцатых числах сего месяца[193] and shall probably spend July near Telluride in southwestern Colorado where I want to study in the field a butterfly I described

Telluride, Colorado, from Tomboy Mine. Every morning in July 1951 VN would set off in pursuit of *Lycæides idas sublivens*, which he had described from male museum specimens in his 1949 monograph but never caught himself. He was particularly eager to sight the as yet unknown female. On July 15, hiking up Tomboy Road, he found a sole slope with a few males and three days later, on the same slope, the first female. In the afternoons and on wet days he was writing *Lolita*, and he used this setting for the last scene Humbert reports, the sounds of children at play wafting up from the valley floor and Lolita's voice absent "from that concord."

from preserved specimens. I am taking with me copious notes relating to a novel I would be able to finish in a year if I could completely concentrate upon it.

[NWL 264]

From letter to Mark Aldanov, August 15, 1951

From West Yellowstone, Montana. In Russian. Unpublished.

My wife and I are now in Montana, to the west of Yellowstone Park (the firs are groaning!),[194] and our son is a hundred miles away in the Tetons (as a French voyageur called this chain of amazingly jagged mountains), in Wyoming, where he is learning alpinism. All my time goes on butterflies: we spent an unforgettable month at a great height in southwest Colorado where we caught a butterfly[195] which I described myself, though I did not know the female – but now I have twenty of these females no one had ever seen before. I have a footballer's legs but my breasts bounce when I run.

[COLUMBIA]

From letter to V. Siviter Smith, August 29, 1951

From Ithaca, New York. Unpublished.

My specimens of *Lycaena phlaeas feildeni*, prox., were taken in the Teton Mts. (near Amphitheatre Lake), North-West Wyoming, and in the Beartooth Mts., Montana, just north of Yellowstone Park. The species is a great rarity in the Rockies, although of course quite common in the eastern States. When comparing it in my mind to some remembered locotypes of *feildeni* I had seen in New York's American Museum of Natural History (I *think* they were locotypes), I was concerned with the brassy upperside and slaty underside common to both. . . .

Snowi, which I have taken many times in various parts of Colorado, is far from brilliant on the wing (cannot be compared to *virgaureae* or *dispar* forms) and has the brassy look of my *phlaeas* form with the same dull underside flipping through in the *Lycaena* manner. I think the existence of a high-altitude race of the thing most interesting.[196]   [VNA]

From letter to Edmund Wilson, early September 1951

From Ithaca, New York.

I am ill. The doctor says it is a kind of sunstroke. Silly situation: after two months of climbing, shirtless, in shorts, in the Rockies, to be smitten by the insipid N.Y. sun on a dapper lawn. High temperature, pain in the temples, insomnia and an incessant, brilliant but sterile turmoil of thoughts and fancies.

I do not recall if I told [you] of some of my experiences in the San Miguel Mts. (Southwestern Colo., Telluride and vicinity) and near or in Yellowstone Park. I went to Telluride (*awful* roads, but then – endless charm, an old-fashioned, absolutely touristless mining town full of most helpful, charming people – and when you hike from there, which is 9000', to 10000', with the town and its tin roofs and self-conscious poplars lying toylike at the flat bottom of a *cul-de-sac* valley running into giant granite

mountains, all you hear are the voices of children playing in the streets –
delightful!) for the sole purpose, which my heroic wife who drove me
through the floods and storms of Kansas did not oppose, of obtaining more
specimens of a butterfly I had described from eight males, and of discovering its female. I was wholly successful in that quest, finding all I
wanted on a steep slope high above Telluride – quite an enchanted slope, in
fact, with hummingbirds and humming moths visiting the tall green gentians that grew among the clumps of a blue lupine, *Lupinus parviflorus*,
which proved to be the food plant of my butterfly.

We then met some more charming people near W. Yellowstone, Mont.,
and rented for a ridiculously small sum a ranch in the hills, which Véra and
I had absolutely to ourselves, – aspens, pines, more warm-blooded animals
than I have ever seen in one place, not a human for miles around, a distant
gate we had to unlock when we drove through on a road with more flowers
than sand – and all this for a couple of dollars per day.   [NWL 265–66]

From letter to Elena Sikorski, September 6, 1951

From Ithaca, New York. In Russian. Translated by DN.

[Dmitri] left us to take part in the national forensic championship in Los
Angeles, then joined us in Telluride, a little old mining town in the San Juan
Mountains of Southwestern Colorado. I went all that way over unpaved,
broken-up mountain roads in specific search of a butterfly that I myself had
described in 1948 on the basis of nine museum specimens; I had an over-
whelming desire to see it live and discover its unknown female. The altitude of Telluride is 9000 feet (3000 meters), and from there I had to climb
on foot every morning to 12,000 feet (4000 meters), and I am fat and
heavy, although I still have my soccer calves. It will not be hard for you to
understand what a joy it was for me to find at last my exceedingly rare god-
daughter, on a sheer mountainside covered with violet lupine, in the sky-
high, snow-scented silence. *Je fais mon petit Sirine,*[197] as you can see.

[SL 122]

From letter to Edmund Wilson, January 24, 1952

From Ithaca, New York.

We are in the throes of packing. Beebe has sent me a paper on some observed migrations of insects in Venezuela.[198] They passed in a gap between two mountains – bees, flies, beetles, wasps. He sent the bees to a bee expert, the wasps to a wasp expert (to have them identified). Each wrote back – the wasp man, the beetle man, the blackfly man – that in each respective batch there were two or three *moths* admirably mimicking this or that insect. Beautiful little fellow travellers! I have just finished a paper on my finds in Southwest Colorado last summer. [NWL 271]

From letter to Charles Remington, February 15, 1952

From Cambridge, Massachusetts. Unpublished.

Owing to the pressure of work, academic and literary, I have been postponing a paper I wanted to submit to you concerning all kinds of entertaining butterflies I have been collecting in Colorado and West Yellowstone last summer. I now see there is no chance of my finding soon a gap in time for that elaboration. So, not wishing to cancel my plans altogether, I have jotted down a few notes about one little thing. Perhaps you would care to publish this. I have added a few notes about an error or two in Klots' book which he might like to correct in the next edition.

Temporarily – for the spring term – I have transferred my academic activities to Harvard where I am teaching Russian literature and Humanities 2 (the novel). [Remington Collection]

The female of *Lycaeides argyrognomon sublivens*[199]

Lepidopterological paper. Written in January 1952. Published in *Lepidopterists' News* 6 (August 1952).

Last summer (1951) I decided to visit Telluride, San Miguel County, Colorado, in order to search for the unknown female of what I had described as

Lycaeides argyrognomon sublivens in 1949 (*Bull. Mus. Comp. Zool.*, vol.
101: p. 513) on the strength of nine males in the Museum of Comparative
Zoology, Harvard, which had been taken in the vicinity of Telluride half a
century ago. *L. sublivens* is an isolated southern representative (the only
known one south of northwestern Wyoming, southeast of Idaho, and east
of California) of the species (the holarctic *argyrognomon* Bergstr. = *idas*
auct.) to which *anna* Edw:, *scudderi* Edw., *aster* Edw., and six other nearctic subspecies belong. I bungled my family's vacation but got what I
wanted.

Owing to rains and floods, especially noticeable in Kansas, most of the
drive from New York State to Colorado was entomologically uneventful.
When reached at last, Telluride turned out to be a damp, unfrequented, but
very spectacular cul-de-sac (which a prodigious rainbow straddled every
evening) at the end of two converging roads, one from Placerville, the other
from Dolores, both atrocious. There is one motel, the optimistic and excellent Valley View Court where my wife and I stayed, at 9,000 feet altitude,
from the 3rd to the 29th of July, walking up daily to at least 12,000 feet
along various more or less steep trails in search of *sublivens*. Once or twice
Mr. Homer Reid of Telluride took us up in his jeep. Every morning the sky
would be of an impeccable blue at 6 A.M. when I set out. The first innocent
cloudlet would scud across at 7:30 A.M. Bigger fellows with darker bellies
would start tampering with the sun around 9 A.M., just as we emerged from
the shadow of the cliffs and trees onto good hunting grounds. Everything
would be cold and gloomy half an hour later. At around 10 A.M. there
would come the daily electric storm, in several installments, accompanied
by the most irritatingly close lightning I have ever encountered anywhere
in the Rockies, not excepting Longs Peak, which is saying a good deal, and
followed by cloudy and rainy weather through the rest of the day.

After 10 days of this, and despite diligent subsequent exploration, only
one sparse colony of *sublivens* was found. On that one spot my wife found
a freshly emerged male on the 15th. Three days later I had the pleasure of
discovering the unusual-looking female. Between the 15th and the 28th, a
dozen hours of windy but passable collecting weather in all (not counting
the hours and hours uselessly spent in mist and rain) yielded only 54 specimens, of which 16 were females. Had I been younger and weighed less, I

might have perhaps got another 50, but hardly much more than that, and, possibly, the higher ridges I vainly investigated between 12,000 and 14,000 feet at the end of July, in the *magdalena-snowi-centaureae* zone, might have produced *sublivens* later in the season.

The colony I found was restricted to one very steep slope reaching from about 10,500 to a ridge at 11,000 feet and towering over Tomboy Road between "Social Tunnel" and "Bullion Mine." The slope was densely covered with a fine growth of lupines in flower (*Lupinus parviflorus* Nuttall, which did not occur elsewhere along the trail) and green gentians (the tall turrets of which were assiduously patronized by the Broad-Tailed Hummingbird and the White-Striped Hawkmoth). This lupine, which in the mountains of Utah is the food-plant of an alpine race of *L. melissa* (*annetta* Edw.), proved to be also the host of *L. sublivens*. The larva pupates at its base, and in dull weather a few specimens of both sexes of the imago could be found settled on the lower leaves and stems, the livid tone of the butterflies' undersides nicely matching the tint of the plant.

The female of *sublivens* is of a curiously arctic appearance, completely different from the richly pigmented, regionally sympatric, locoweed- and alfalfa-feeding *L. melissa* or from the *melissa*-like females of Wyoming and Idaho *argyrognomon* (*idas*) races, and somewhat resembling *argyrognomon* (*idas*) forms from northwestern Canada and Alaska (see for instance in the above-mentioned work, p. 501 and plate 8, fig. 112). It also recalls a certain combination of characters that crops up in *L. melissa annetta*.

Here is a brief description of *L. sublivens* female: Upperside of a rather peculiar, smooth, weak brown, with an olivaceous cast in the living insect; more or less extensively dusted with cinder-blue scales; triangulate greyish blue inner cretules generally present in the hindwing and often accompanied by some bluish or greyish bleaching in the radial cells of the forewing; aurorae reduced: short and dullish in the hindwing, blurred or absent in the forewing, tending to disappear in both wings and almost completely absent in 3 specimens; lunulate pale greyish blue outer cretules very distinct in both wings; underside similar to that of the male.

Deposited: 20 males and 10 females in the Cornell University collection, and 18 males and 6 females in the Museum of Comparative Zoology, Harvard University.   [SO 315–18]

On Some Inaccuracies in Klots' *Field Guide*

Lepidopterological note. Written in February 1952 and published in *Lepidopterists' News* 6 (August 1952).

In connection with "Blues," I wish to correct two or three slips in Professor Alexander B. Klots' important and delightful book (*A Field Guide to the Butterflies of North America, East of the Great Plains*, Houghton Mifflin, Boston, 1951).

On p. 166 there is a misprint: "Center (formerly Karner)" should be, of course, "Karner (formerly Center)." Incidentally I visit the place every time I happen to drive (as I do yearly in early June) from Ithaca to Boston and can report that, despite local picnickers and the hideous garbage they leave, the lupines and *Lycaeides samuelis* Nab. are still doing as fine under those old gnarled pines along the railroad as they did ninety years ago.

On p. 165, another, more unfortunate transposition occurs: "When fawn colored, more vivid in tone" should refer not to *Lycaeides argyrognomon* [*idas*] but to *L. melissa*, while "wings beneath, when fawn colored, duller in tone" should refer not to *L. melissa* but to *L. argyrognomon* [*idas*] (see my "Nearctic Lycaeides," *Bull. Mus. Comp. Zool.*, vol. 101: p. 541: 1949).

On pp. 162–164, the genus *Brephidium* (in company with two others) is incorrectly placed between *Hemiargus* and *Lycaeides*. I have shown in my paper on Neotropical Plebejinae (*Psyche*, vol. 52: pp. 1–61; 1945) that *Hemiargus* (*sensu lato*) and *Lycaeides* belong to the same group (subfamily Plebejinae – or supergenus *Plebejus*; the rank does not matter but the relationship does). *Brephidium*, of course, stands on the very outskirts of the family, in a highly specialized group, immeasurably further removed from *Hemiargus* or *Lycaeides* than, say, *Lycaena*.[200] This is where my subfamilies come in handy since at least they keep related things in one bunch and eject intruders. Views may differ in regard to the hierarchic element in the classification I adopt, but no one has questioned so far the fact of the structural relationship and phylogenetic circumstances I mean it to reflect. The whole interest of *Hemiargus* is that it is allied to *Lycaeides* etc., while bearing a striking superficial resemblance to an African group with which it does not have the slightest structural affinity. Systematics, I think, should bring out such points and not keep them blurred in the haze of tradition. I am perfectly willing to demote the whole of my "subfamily" Plebejinae to a supergenus or genus *Plebejus* (*Plebejus ceraunus, isola, thomasi, idas, melissa, aquilo, saepiolus,* etc.) but only under the condition that it include exactly the same species, in the same groupings ("subgenera" or numbered sections, as you will) and in the same sequence of groups, without intrusions from groups assigned structurally to other "subfamilies" (and then, of course, *lygdamus, battoides,* and *piasus* should be all in *Scolitantides* or its equivalent). However, I still think that the formality of generic names for the groupings is a better method than going by numbers, etc. Names are also easier to handle in works on zoological distribution when it is important to bring out the way a group is represented in different regions of the world. Generally speaking, systematics is not directly concerned with the convenience of collectors in their dealings with small local faunas. It should attempt to express structural affinities and divergences, suggest certain phylogenetic lines, relate local developments to global ones – and help lumpers to sort out properly the ingredients of their lumps.   [SO 319–21]

From letter from Véra Nabokov to Rosalind Wilson,[201] July 24, 1952

From Dubois, Wyoming.

Vladimir has asked me to answer your letter of July 1st for him, and, even before I do so, to apologize for the lateness of his reply.

The question of mimicry is one that has passionately interested him all his life and one of his pet projects has always been the compilation of a work that would comprise all known examples of mimicry in the animal kingdom. This would make a voluminous work and the research alone would take two or three years. If this sort of thing corresponds to what Houghton Mifflin have in mind, Vladimir is your man. Should they, however, think of a much slighter work for the amusement of the lay reader in his more ambitious "scientific" moments, this, Vladimir says, would not be in his line. . . .

P.S. I don't think I made it sufficiently clear that the book on mimicry Vladimir would like to write would present, in the first place, his own views on this very complicated matter, based on the classified presentation of all the known examples.

[SL 134–35]

From letter from Véra Nabokov to Rosalind Wilson, August 10, 1952

From Afton, Wyoming.

Thanks for your letter of July 28. Perhaps I did not convey to you in mine the exact way Vladimir feels about the possibility of writing a book on mimicry. It is not that he "would rather not even try" to communicate "the mysteries of his field" to a layman. On the contrary, he would not like anything better than having a chance to do so. He wonders, however, if Houghton Mifflin would be inclined to contemplate a *complete* survey (about 1000 pages plus numerous illustrations) and if they would be willing to "foot" the bill for the costs of some two years of research.

    He says he would not blame them if they did not.   [VNA]

From letter to Edmund Wilson, August 10, 1952

From Afton, Wyoming.

. . . this is a lovely little place in southwest Wyoming. We have made it our headquarters, Véra and I, for collecting butterflies in the neighbouring National Forests while Dmitri is climbing the Tetons from Lake Jenny where he camps.   [NWL 277–78]

Letter to Cyril dos Passos, October 9, 1952

From Ithaca, New York.

Dear Mr. dos Passos,

    Many thanks for your letter and the many interesting enclosures concerning the High Brown and the Monarch.

Let me break the news gently. I am not on your side in these matters. My opinion is that in this business of zoological nomenclature there is no middle way: one has either to 1. reject the Rules altogether, and go on applying "traditional" names ("adippe," "amathusia," "aphirape" etc.), or 2. apply the Rules with utter rigidity making no exceptions whatsoever, no matter how inconvenient, in any respect, a change of name might be. Since the first course would be nonsensical ("traditional" generally meaning such names as Staudinger used for commercial purposes) I adopt the second one and cling to it through thick and thin. Incidentally, have you not noticed that when a necessary change in names is made this operation gives the species and sometimes the whole genus a new lease of life and prompts all kinds of interesting research not only taxonomic but biological, so that in the long run science profits from a nomenclatorial shift. I am all for suppressing doubtful names; but first of all let us discuss these names and prove that they *are* doubtful. I also believe in the magic taxonomic virtue of the First Reviser.

Before any action be taken in regard to the High Brown I suggest the following questions be settled:

1. Does a specimen name-labelled in Linnaeus' hand constitute a type, if it conforms exactly to his description?

2. Has Dr. Verity's forty-year-old diagnosis (1913), namely that the butterfly labelled by Linnaeus "*cydippe*" is a silvered *niobe*, been verified, and if so, has his identification been proved correct?

3. Has there been among the "some authors" mysteriously alluded to by Hemming, Riley and Verity (p. 331, Bull. Zool. Nom., 1952) a First Reviser, or a second or third one, who intelligently and intelligibly applied the name *berecynthia* Poda, 1761, to the High Brown?

4. Have the two figures of *phryxa* Bergstrasser (1, 2, pl. 82), 1783, been checked and found to coincide with Verity's statement (1929) that they represent quite certainly the High Brown?

If the answer to 1, 2 and 3 is yes, then the High Brown should be known as *Fabriciana berecynthia* (Poda); if the answer to 1, 2 and 4 is yes, then it should be known as *Fabriciana phryxa* (Bergstrasser); if the answer to 3 and 4 is no, then let us look for the next name available. And when it is found, let us fix it as definite (revising the First Reviser for all eternity).

The other case is much more simple. Obviously the First Reviser of "*plexippus*" is Linnaeus himself, 1764, and this name should be applied to the oriental species (the type locality is inessential for have not we here fritillaries and hawk moths whose home was erroneously given as Jamaica or South America?) Whose comfort are we so anxious about? Who minds what names nature magazines or the boys in applied entomology give to popular or unpopular bugs (which they misidentify anyway), or whether it will distress them to have to switch to other names?(If anything *should* be suppressed, it is Holland's "Blunderfly Book"!)

I see eye to eye with you and Grey and Klots, in so many important issues that I do not feel too contrite at disagreeing with you and them on this comparatively insignificant question. But I do disagree, definitely.

Sincerely,

VLADIMIR NABOKOV

P.S. I take this opportunity to bring up a totally different matter. I have just returned from a very successful expedition to various mountain ranges of Wyoming. Among other things I have collected some remarkable Bolorids, Coliads and Blues. The A.M.N.H. has been exceptionally kind to me when I had some research to do. I would like, therefore, in modest token of my gratitude, to make a gift of some 300 or so rare butterflies, spread and unspread, to them. Would you be so very kind to find out if they have room for them, and tell me to whom I should address my package.

P.P.S. I am sending a copy of this letter (minus the P.S.) to Hemming.

[AMNH]

Review of *Audubon's Butterflies, Moths, and Other Studies,* edited by Alice Ford

Written October 1952. Published as "A World of Butterflies," *New York Times Book Review*, December 28, 1952.

Anyone knowing as little about butterflies as I do about birds may find Audubon's lepidoptera as attractive as his bright, active, theatrical birds are to me. Whatever those birds do, I am with them, heartily sharing, for instance, the openbilled wonder of "Green Heron" at the fantastic situation and much too bright colors of "Luna Moth" in a famous picture of the "Birds" folio. At present, however, I am concerned only with Audubon's sketchbook ("a fifteen-page pioneer art rarity" belonging to Mrs. Kirby Chambers of New Castle, Kentucky) from which Miss Ford has published drawings of butterflies and other insects in a handsome volume padded with additional pictorial odds and ends and an account of Audubon's life. The sketches were made in the 1820s. Most of the lepidoptera which they burlesque came from Europe (Southern France, I suggest). Their scientific names, supplied by Mr. Austin H. Clark, are meticulously correct – except in the case of one butterfly, p. 20, top, which is not a *Hamaeris* but a distorted *Zerynthia*. Their English equivalents, however, reveal some sad editorial blundering: "Cabbage," p. 23, and "Miller," p. 91, should be "Bath White" and "Witch," respectively; and the two moths on p. 64 are emphatically not "Flesh Flies." In an utterly helpless account of the history of entomological illustration, Miss Ford calls Audubon's era "scientifically unsophisticated." The unsophistication is all her own. She might have looked up John Abbot's prodigious representations of North American lepidoptera, 1797, or the splendid plates of eighteenth- and early-nineteenth-century German lepidopterists, or the rich butterflies that enliven the flowers and fruit of the old Dutch Masters. She might have traveled back some thirty-three centuries to the times of Tuthmosis IV or Amenophis III and, instead of the obvious scarab, found there frescoes with a marvelous Egyptian butterfly (subtly combining the pattern of our Painted Lady and the body of an African ally of the Monarch). I cannot speak with any authority about the beetles and grasshoppers in the Sketchbook, but the butterflies are certainly inept. The exaggerated crenulation of hindwing edges, due to a naive artist's doing his best to render the dry, rumpled margins of carelessly spread specimens, is typical of the poorest entomological figures of earlier centuries and to these figures Audubon's sketches are curiously close. Query: Can anyone draw something he knows nothing about? Does there not exist a high ridge where the mountainside of "scientific" knowledge joins the opposite slope of "artistic" imagination? If so, Audubon, the butterfly artist, is at sea level on one side and climbing the wrong foothill on the other.   [SO 329–30]

From Nabokov's diary, 1952

Undated endmatter.

Brit. Mus. N° 37977 Tuthmosis IV or Amenophis III (1420–1375 B.C.)
Fowling in the Marshes

4 identical specimens of a butterfly that looks like an artistic combination of *Danaus chrysippus* (body quite certainly danaid) and *Vanessa cardui* both common in Egypt. [VNA]

From letter to Yuri Ivask,[202] January 1, 1953

From Ithaca, New York. In Russian. Unpublished.

I share your love for both Blok and Mandelstam,[203] and of course for beetles, although it's many years since I've studied beetles. But I devote my spare time to butterflies. [VNA]

Butterfly Collecting in Wyoming, 1952

Lepidoptera paper. Written in January 1953. Published in *Lepidopterists' News* 7 (July 1953).

A visit to Wyoming by car in July–August 1952 was devoted to collecting in the following places:

Southeastern Wyoming: eastern Medicine Bow National Forest, in the Snowy Range, up to approximately 10,500 ft. alt. (using paved road 130 between Laramie and Saratoga); sagebrush country, approximately 7,000 ft. alt., between Saratoga and Encampment, east of paved highway 230; marshes at about the same elevation between eastern Medicine Bow National Forest and Northgate, northern Colorado, within 15 miles from the Wyoming State Line, mainly south of the unpaved road 127; and W. Medicine Bow National Forest, in the Sierra Madre, using the abominable local road from Encampment to the Continental Divide (approximately 9,500 ft. alt.).

Western Wyoming: sagebrush, approximately 6,500 ft. alt. immediately east of Dubois along the (well-named) Wind River; western Shoshone and Teton National Forests, following admirable paved road 26, from Dubois towards Moran over Togwotee Pass (9,500 ft. alt.); near Moran, on Buffalo River, approximately 7,000 ft. alt.; traveling through the construction hell of the city of Jackson, and bearing southeast along paved 187 to The Rim (7,900 ft. alt.); and, finally, spending most of August in collecting around the altogether enchanting little town of Afton (on paved 89, along the Idaho border), approximately 7,000 ft. alt., mainly in canyons east of the town, and in various spots of Bridger National Forest, Southwestern part, along trails up to 9,000 ft. alt.

Most of the material collected has gone to the Cornell University Museum; the rest to the American Museum of Natural History and the Museum of Comparative Zoology.

The best hunting grounds proved to be: the Sierra Madre at about 8,000 ft. alt., where on some forest trails I found among other things a curious form (? *S. secreta* dos Passos & Grey) of *Speyeria egleis* Behr flying in numbers with *S. atlantis hesperis* Edw. and *S. hydaspe purpurascens* H. Edw., a very eastern locality for the latter; still better were the forests, meadows, and marshes about Togwotee Pass in the third week of July, where the generally early emergences of the season were exemplified by great quantities of *Erebia theona ethela* Edw. and *E. callias callias* Edw. already on the wing; very good, too, were some of the canyons near Afton.

Here are a few notes on what interested me most in the field: *Boloria, Colias,* certain Blues, and migratory or at least "mobile" species.

Of *Boloria* I got seven species, of the eight (or possibly ten) that occur within the region. Plunging into the forest south of route 130 on the western slopes of the Snowy Range, I found *B. selene tollandensis* B & McD. not uncommon on a small richly flowered marsh at about 8,000 ft. alt.; also on marshes north of Northgate and on Togwotee Pass. On July 8, I spent three hours collecting a dozen fresh specimens of *B. eunomia alticola* B & McD., both sexes, on a tiny very wet marsh along the eastern lip of the last lake before reaching Snowy Range Pass from the west, possibly the same spot where Klots had taken it in 1935 (*Journ. N.Y. Ent. Soc.* 45: p. 326; 1937). I met with the same form on a marsh near Peacock Lake, Longs Peak, Colorado, in 1947. Forms of *B. titania* Esp. (mostly near ssp. *helena*

Edw.) were abundant everywhere above 7,500 ft. alt. By the end of July *B. freija* Thunb. was in tatters near Togwotee Pass (it had been on the wane in June, 1947, on marshes near Columbine Lodge, Estes Park; and on Hoback River, Tetons, in early July, 1949). Of the beautiful *B. frigga sagata* B. & Benj. I took two ♂♂ (fresh but frayed) near Togwotee Pass. Of *B. toddi* Holland ssp. I took a very fresh ♂ in early July in the Snowy Range at 8,000 ft. alt. and a couple of days later, acting upon a hunch, I visited a remarkably repulsive-looking willow-bog, full of cowmerds and barbed wire, off route 127, and found there a largish form of *B. toddi* very abundant – in fact, I have never seen it as common anywhere in the west; unfortunately, the specimens, of which I kept a score or so, were mostly faded – and very difficult to capture, their idea of sport being to sail to and fro over the fairly tall sallows that encompassed the many small circular areas (inhabited only by *Plebeius saepiolus* Boisd. and *Polites utahensis* Skin.) into which the bog was divided by the shrubs. Another species I had never seen to be so common was *B. kriemhild* Strecker which I found in all the willow-bogs near Togwotee Pass.

In regard to *Colias* I could not discover what I wanted – which was some geographical intergradation between *C. scudderi* Reakirt, which I suggest should be classified as *C. palaeno scudderi* (Reakirt) (common everywhere in the Medicine Bow National Forest), and *C. pelidne skinneri* Barnes (locally common near Togwotee Pass and above Afton). I was struck, however, by the identical ovipositing manners of *C. scudderi* and *C. skinneri* ♀♀ which were common in the densest woods of their respective habitats, laying on *Vaccinium*. I found *C. meadi* Edw. very common on Snowy Range Pass. It was also present at timberline near Togwotee Pass and east of it, below timberline, down to 8,000 ft. alt. in willow-bogs, where it was accompanied by another usually "Hudsonian" species, *Lycaena snowi* Edw., the latter represented by undersized individuals. (In early July, 1951, near Telluride, Colorado, I found a colony of healthy *Colias meadi* and one of very sluggish *Pyrgus centaureae freija* Warren in aspen groves along a canyon at only 8,500 ft. alt.) On a slope near Togwotee Pass at timberline I had the pleasure of discovering a strain of *C. meadi* with albinic ♀♀. The species was anything but common there, but of the dozen ♀♀ or so seen or caught, as many as three were albinic. Of these my wife and I took two, hers a dull white similar to *C. hecla* "pallida," mine slightly tinged with peach (the only other time I saw a white *C. meadi* was at the base of Longs Peak, 1947, where the species was extremely abundant).

In 1949 and 1951, when collecting *Lycaeides* in the Tetons, all over Jackson Hole, and in the Yellowstone, I had found that to the north and east *L. argyrognomon (idas) longinus* Nab. turns into *L. argyrognomon (idas) scudderi* Edw. but I had not solved the problem of the *L. melissa* strain so prominent in some colonies of *L. argyrognomon longinus* (i.e. Black Tail Butte near Jackson). I had conjectured that hybridization occurs or had occurred with wandering low elevation *L. melissa* (the rather richly marked "Artemisian" *L. melissa* – probably in need of some name) that follows alfalfa along roads as *Plebeius saepiolus* does clover. In result of my 1952 quest the situation appears as follows. The most northern point where typical *L. longinus* occurs is the vicinity of Moran, seldom below 7,000 ft. alt. and up to 11,000 at least. It spreads south at those altitudes for more than a thousand [*sic*] miles to the southern tip of Bridger National Forest but not much further (I have not found it, for instance, around Kemmerer). I have managed to find one *L. melissa*, a fresh ♂, in August, 1952, in a dry field near Afton, less than a mile from the canyon into which both sexes of *L. longinus* descended from the woods above. At eastern points of the Bridger and Shoshone Forests, *L. longinus* stops definitely at The Rim, west of Bondurant, and at Brooks Lake (about 7,500 ft. alt.) some twenty miles west of Dubois. Very small colonies (seldom more than half-a-dozen specimens were taken in any one place) of *L. melissa* were found around Dubois at 6,500 ft. alt. or so (agricultural areas and the hot dry hills). A colony of typical (alpine) *L. melissa melissa* as described by Edwards, was found just above timberline in the Sierra Madre. The search for *L. melissa* in various windy and barren localities in the sagebrush zone in mid-July led to the finding of a rather unexpected Blue. This was *Plebeius (Icaricia) shasta* Edw., common in the parched plain at less than 7,000 ft. alt. between Saratoga and Encampment flying on sandy ground with *Phyciodes mylitta barnesi* Skinner, *Satyrium fuliginosa* Edw., and *Neominois ridingsi* Edw. It was also abundant all over the hot hills at 6,500 ft. alt. around Dubois where nothing much else occurred. I have not yet been able to compare my specimens with certain series in the Museum of Comparative Zoology, Harvard, but I suggest that this low-altitude *P. shasta* is the true *P. minnehaha* Scudder while the alpine form which I found in enormous numbers above timberline in Estes Park (especially, on Twin Sisters) and which collectors, following Holland's mislead, call "*minnehaha,*" is really an undescribed race.

As to migratory species observed in Wyoming, 1952, I distinguish two groups: (1) latitudinal migrants – moving within their zones of habitat mainly in a west-east (North America) or east-west (Europe) direction and capable of surviving a Canadian Zone winter in this or that stage. Mobile, individually wandering species of *Plebeius* and *Colias* belong to this group as well as our four erratically swarming *Nymphalis* species which hibernate in the imaginal stage. In early August the trails in Bridger National Forest were covered at every damp spot with millions of *N. californica* Boisd. in tippling groups of four hundred and more, and countless individuals were drifting in a steady stream along every canyon. It was interesting to find a few specimens of the beautiful dark western form of *N. j-album* Boisd. & Lec. among the *N. californica* near Afton. (2) longitudinal migrants – moving early in the season from subtropical homes to summer breeding places in the Nearctic region but not hibernating there in any stage. *Vanessa cardui* L. is a typical example. Its movements in the New World are considerably less known than in the Old World (in eastern Europe, for instance, according to my own observations, migratory flights from beyond the Black Sea hit the south of the Crimea in April, and females, bleached and tattered, reach the Leningrad region early in June). In the first week of July, 1952, this species (offspring mainly) was observed in colossal numbers above timberline in the Snowy Range over which the first spring flock had passed on May 28, according to an intelligent ranger. A few specimens of *Euptoieta claudia* Cramer were in clover fields around Afton, western Wyoming, in August. Of *Leptotes marina* Reakirt, one ♂ was observed near Afton in August, with *Apodemia mormo* Felder and "*Hemiargus*" (*Echinargus*) *isola* Reakirt. Both *A. mormo* and *E. isola* plant very isolated small summer colonies on hot hillsides. The *H. isola* specimens, which I took also in Medicine Bow National Forest, are all tiny ones, an obvious result of seasonal environment, not subspeciation. *H. isola* (incidentally, this is not a Latin adjective, but a fancy name – an Italian noun originally – and cannot be turned into "*isolus*" to comply with the gender of the generic name, as done by some writers) belongs to a neotropical group (my *Echinargus*) with two other species: *E. martha* Dognin, from the Andes, and a new species, described by me but not named, from Trinidad and Venezuela (see *Psyche*, 52: 3–4). Other representatives of neotropical groups (*Graphium marcellus* Cramer, "*Strymon*" *melinus* Hübner, *Pyrgus communis* Grote, *Epargyreus clarus* Cramer – to name the most obvious ones) have established themselves in the Nearctic more securely than *H. isola*. Among the migratory Pierids, the following were observed: single specimens of *Nathalis iole* Boisd. all over Wyoming; one worn ♂ of *Phoebis eubule* L. in the Sierra Madre (Battle Lake), July 9; one worn ♂ of *Eurema mexicana* Boisd., between Cheyenne and Laramie (and a worn ♀ near Ogallala, Neb.), first week of July. [so 322–28]

Collecting Insects in U.S. National Parks

Unpublished. Lepidopterological note. Written January 1953 for *Lepidopterists' News*.

A word to my field-mates in regard to the present regulations in National Parks (forbidding an entomologist to wield his modest net unless he be a government official). One result is the preposterously misidentified and unrepresentative collections in Park museums.

Well, here is a line of behavior: collect whatever insects you want wherever you go. When a Park official (they are all very nice fellows) dutifully remonstrates, just point to the nearest series of parked cars. Let him count the number of butterflies that the radiators have collected while passing through the Forbidden Zone. Have him talk to these motorists, take their license numbers, compute how many cars pass daily through and how many "bugs" they accumulate per day. Ask him when he has last seen any one with a butterfly net. If no cars are in sight, draw his attention to the millions of endemic insect larvae, mostly undescribed, fed to imported fish by imported fishermen. Tell him he has just destroyed a new species of mosquito on his cheek.   [VNA]

From letter to Charles Remington, March 8, 1953

From Cambridge, Massachusetts. Unpublished.

Your letter arrived at the wrong time. I have been frightfully busy with a non-entomological matter,[204] in Cambridge, where I will stay till April, after which my wife and I plan to drive to Portal, Arizona, and probably spend the summer there.

I had decided to postpone my answer until I could thoroughly investigate the *cardui* origin question; but I see that I am as busy as ever and prefer to delete a sentence – and to return to the subject later, when – or if – I have time to visit the MCZ library, which I see from my window but cannot reach.[205]

I have had the papers[205] re-typed (a longhand addict, I have never learned to type myself).

Parks. The bit about poorly-identified specimens refers to the Mammoth Museum in Yellowstone where an inept collection I inspected in 1951 had been made by schoolboys.

Neominois. I cannot remember the exact structural difference between *Neominois* and *Hipparchia* but remember having come to the conclusion when working on Satyrids in 1941 that they were one. Have your own way, however.

N. j-album. OK, since, as you say, the paper is not taxonomic. I am not in favor of biological concepts interfering with morphological ones, and there can be no doubt that structurally *j-album* and *l-album* belong to the same species.

N. antiopa. Although a true hibernator and thoroughly endemic, it is certainly at times migratory (in my first sense) in Europe, e.g. reaching England from Scandinavia.

Echinargus isola. I have explained in my paper why this cannot be "*isolus.*"

Plebeius. I have explained in the Lepidopterists' News, 1952, v. 6, p. 41, my concept of genera. In my 1945 paper, on Neotropical *Plebejinae,* p. 27–28 and footnote, I had shown that Bethune Baker's assigning *isola* to *Hemiargus* in 1916 was based on a blunder; and I had also shown why *isola* should be removed to another genus. What I call *Plebejinae (l.c.,* p. 47–48) consists of 24 genera. As I said in my 1952 paper, I am perfectly willing to demote the subfamily category to a generic one, and to call the group: *Plebejus,* consisting of 24 subgenera, among which should be *Hemiargus* and *Echinargus;* but use "*Hemiargus*" in a sense directly opposite to the spirit of my 1945 paper, I cannot. Hence, the quotes.   [Remington Collection]

Lycaeides argyrognomon in Wisconsin

Letter to Louis Griewisch. Published in *Lepidopterists' News.*

A series of *Lycaeides* was taken near Waubee Lake, in Oconto and Marinette Cos., Wisconsin, on July 1–15, 1952. Specimens were submitted to Professor VLADIMIR NABOKOV. His comments seem to be worth recording, and are given as follows.

"When I realized that the Blue you wanted identified came from Wisconsin, I foresaw it could be either of two species, the closest locality to Wisconsin being in one case S. Michigan and in the other Minnesota.

"S. Michigan specimens that I have studied belonged to the curiously isolated (type loc.: Albany, N.Y.) Great Lakes representative of *melissa* Edw. which I named *melissa samuelis* (Psyche, 1943, and Bull. Mus. Comp. Zool, 1949) (as you know, it used to be called "scudderi" in former days).

"The Minnesota thing, which I described and figured, but did not name, because of scantiness of material (Bull. Mus. Comp. Zool., 1949, p. 505, Pl. 5, fig. 54, male, Pequot, Minn.) is a subspecies of *argyrognomon* (Bergsträsser, Tutt), which I now think is sufficiently distinct from the Canadian (north of 50°) *argyrognomon scudderi* (type loc.: The Pass, west of Winnipeg L., Manit.) to warrant a new subspecific name for it.[206]

"It is this form that your specimens belong to, and you should be congratulated on establishing the interesting Wisconsin range of *argyrognomon*. It comes very near to a point where it should fly together with *melissa samuelis* Nab.

"Your beautiful series will be deposited at the Museum of Comparative Zoology, Harvard College, where I have accumulated the most representative series of American *Lycaeides* in the world. I have nowadays hardly any time at all for working on Lepidoptera, and you may use any information in this letter for your report on your find to a scientific magazine."

LOUIS GRIEWISCH, 114 Gray Street, Green Bay, Wis., U.S.A.

[*Lepidopterists' News* 7 (1953):54]

From letter to Donald Eff, May 1, 1953

From Portal, Arizona. Unpublished.

I am on leave of absence from the university this spring and thought it a good idea to spend it collecting in the Chiricahua Mts – and writing a book. I hope you will have lots of luck in the Wind River Range. I went to Pinedale to reach it, but it was too far and rugged. . . .

I am eager to get here (this is its type locality) my *Neonympha maniola* (which R. Chermock demoted to a subspecies of my *dorothea* – wrongly, I think). It should appear late in May. Another *Neonympha*, *henshawi* Edw., (the northern form of the Mexican *pyracmon*) coexists with *maniola*. The three are readily separated by the females: what Holland figures as "henshawi" male, is *dorothea*, female. The female of *henshawi* is figured by Edwards (it has a slightly tailed and banded appearance, and that of *maniola* (a rather ruddy thing) is figured by Wright (Butt. W. Coast).

I am having some luck here with the local representative of *Erora laeta* and other nice little things. An hour's drive takes me from cactus to aspen.

[VNA]

From letter to Alexander Klots, May 1, 1953

From Portal, Arizona. Unpublished.

Since February I have been wandering all over the States, while my mail dutifully trickled on in my wake; accumulated in little postal pools; and trickled on. Your interesting letter thus reached me after considerable delay.

Humerulus, alula, bullula, mentum, rostellum, sagum, surculus, Bayard's Angulation or Point, Chapman's process – are terms I invented thinking them up as I went. I planned to write a work on the genitalia of the whole family of Blues, and regarded my papers on the Plebejinae as preliminary ones. Around 1949, however, I had to give up serious entomological work, since it encroached fatally upon my literary and academic labors. Hence – the abrupt introduction of those terms. . . .

"Stempffer's Process" is really a euphemism: it is something he saw (a projection of the uncus in *shasta*) and I did not. I think it was merely a hair scale that had got involved in his preparation (he had another mistake in one of his first papers on these things: leaving his falces for too long a period in a corrosive solution which caused structurally not existing serrations which he dutifully figured). . . .

Here, in the Chiricahua Mts., I have great fun collecting the local representative of *Erora laeta* on flowers of the *Robinia* sp., between 6,000–7,000 ft. altitude. We may remain here till midsummer as I am anxious to get some of my *Neonymphas*.   [VNA]

From letter to Harry Levin,[207] May 2, 1953

From Portal, Arizona.

We are in the south-east corner of Arizona, on the border of New and Old Mexico. The nearer mountains are maroon, spotted with the dark green of junipers and the lighter green of mesquites, and the far mountains are purple as in the Wellesley song. From eight A.M. to noon, or later, I collect butterflies (only Wells, Conan Doyle and Conrad have portrayed lepidopterists – all of them spies, or murderers, or neurotics) and from two P.M. to dinner time I write (a novel).[208] . . .

I wonder if your account of your trip will make me Europe-sick, or at least France-sick. I know that every time I come to this dear West, I feel a pang of recognition, and no Switzerlands could lure me away from Painted Canyon or Silver Creek.

[SL 136–37]

From letter to Edmund Wilson, May 3, 1953

From Portal, Arizona.

This is a magnificent place, near Paradise (a ghost town), sixty miles from civilization (Douglas), a ten-minute drive from cactus to pine; and then a short climb to aspen. . . . I spend several hours daily collecting butterflies.

[NWL 280]

From letter from Véra Nabokov to Alice James,[209] May 17, 1953

From Portal, Arizona. Unpublished.

The owners have turned the place into a kind of wildlife preserve, and the profusion of most spectacular birds is incredible (they do not have a chance to wake us: V. gets up at 6 and begins to hope that the day will prove warm and favorable for butterfly collecting, but most of the time is disappointed). Still, V. has written every day, and is satisfied with the results, and he has also picked up a few butterflies, few in numbers but rare and interesting.

[VNA]

Lines Written in Oregon

Poem. Written in early June 1953. Published in the *New Yorker*, August 19, 1953.

> Esmeralda! Now we rest
> Here, in the bewitched and blest
> Mountain forests of the West.
>
> Here the very air is stranger.
> Damzel, anchoret, and ranger
> Share the woodland's dream and danger.

And to think I deemed you dead!
(In a dungeon, it was said;
Tortured, strangled); but instead –

Blue birds from the bluest fable,
Bear and hare in coats of sable,
Peacock moth on picnic table.

Huddled roadsigns softly speak
Of Lake Merlin, Castle Creek.
And (obliterated) Peak.

Do you recognize that clover?
Dandelions, *l'or du pauvre?*
(Europe, nonetheless, is over).

Up the turf, along the burn,
Latin lilies climb and turn
Into Gothic fir and fern.

Cornfields have befouled the prairies
But these canyons laugh! And there is
Still the forest with its fairies.

And I rest where I awoke
In the sea shade – *l'ombre glauque* –
Of a legendary oak;

Where the woods get ever dimmer,
Where the Phantom Orchids glimmer –
Esmeralda, *immer, immer.*

[PP 171–72]

From letter to Edmund Wilson, June 20, 1953

From Ashland, Oregon.

Véra and I drove from Arizona to Oregon through the lake region of California, collecting en route. In the meanwhile, Dmitri, in an old Buick he had put together, was making his way west from Harvard Square. We met in Ashland, a lovely place. From here he will go to British Columbia in July – to climb with his club; and his parents intend to stay on till the end of August here; we have rented the house of a professor (Ashland is a college town) who has gone east for the summer. The collecting is good.   [NWL 282]

From letter to P. Sheldon Remington,[210] June 23, 1953

From Ashland, Oregon.

Tomboy Road is more of a trail than a road. When I was there, you could not drive up it in a passenger car. It starts on the left of the town (if you face the town from the Valleyview Court motel) and meanders up and up till you reach (at about 10,500 ft. alt., approaching timberline) an archway through the stone called "Social Tunnel." Just beyond it you will see the first lupines on the left side of the road. A little further a steep, lupine-covered slope (on the left above you) reaches a ridge. I found *sublivens* occurring only on this slope, from the road to the ridge, in mid-July. (It might be out on the 12th or the 13th.) I think you will easily recognize that slope by the combination of lupines and turret flowers (green gentians) upon it. And there are some pines further up, before reaching the ridge. Opposite the slope, on the right side of the road, there is an abandoned house where I used to take refuge during the daily electric storms. There are some old magazines there.

If you follow the road further, you soon come (in the vicinity of Bullion Mine) to some beautiful tumbling water among which flies the true *smintheus hermodur* (Henry Edwards) as figured by Verity (not Holland).

At timberline, the road abuts at a ghost mining town, and from here the Hudsonian zone is accessible through Marshal Basin, if I remember the name right. Homer Reid, ex-mayor of Telluride, twice took me up there in his jeep. If you don't care to hike up (it used to take me about three hours including collecting *en route*, to reach Social Tunnel), I am sure he will drive you up. He charges a few dollars for the trip. He is a very amiable gentleman and has a thorough knowledge of the region. . . .

I did not find *sublivens* above timberline in July. Let me repeat, its only habitat as known to me is on the left side of the road as described above, between Social Tunnel and Bullion Mine. [VNA]

Long and hazy the evening

Poem ("Vecher dymchat i dolog," in "Nepravil'nye yamby"). Written in Ithaca, September 1953. Published in *Novyy Zhurnal* 46 (1956). Translated by DN.

Long and hazy the evening,
and I stand, as in prayer,
a young entomologist,
with some honeysuckle near.

How I crave, unexpected,
Midst those flowers to glimpse,
With proboscis projected,
a heavenly sphinx!

A quick throb – and I see it.
At an angel I hit,
and a demon's entangled
in the haze of my net.

[*Stikhi* 288]

From letter to Elena Sikorski, September 29, 1953

From Ithaca, New York. In Russian. Translated DN.

The passion for butterflies has turned into a real mania this year, and there have been many interesting discoveries. [SL 139]

Lolita

Excerpts from novel. Written 1950–53. Published in 1955.

[Humbert Humbert defines his terms.]

Now I wish to introduce the following idea. Between the age limits of nine and fourteen there occur maidens who, to certain bewitched travelers, twice or many times older than they, reveal their true nature which is not human, but nymphic (that is, demoniac); and these chosen creatures I propose to designate as "nymphets."

It will be marked that I substitute time terms for spatial ones. In fact, I would have the reader see "nine" and "fourteen" as the boundaries – the mirrory beaches and rosy rocks – of an enchanted island haunted by those nymphets of mine and surrounded by a vast, misty sea. Between those age limits, are all girl-children nymphets? Of course not. Otherwise, we who are in the know, we lone voyagers, we nympholepts, would have long gone insane. Neither are good looks any criterion; and vulgarity, or at least what a given community terms so, does not necessarily impair certain mysterious characteristics, the fey grace, the elusive, shifty, soul-shattering, insidious charm that separates the nymphet from such coevals of hers as are incomparably more dependent on the spatial world of synchronous phenomena than on that intangible island of entranced time where Lolita plays with her likes. Within the same age limits the number of true nymphets is strikingly inferior to that of provisionally plain, or just nice, or "cute," or even "sweet" and "attractive," ordinary, plumpish, formless, cold-skinned, essentially human little girls, with tummies and pigtails, who may or may not turn into adults of great beauty (look at the ugly dumplings in black stockings and white hats that are metamorphosed into stunning stars of the screen). A normal man given a group photograph of school girls or Girl Scouts and asked to point out the comeliest one will not necessarily choose the nymphet among them. You have to be an artist and a madman, a creature of infinite melancholy, with a bubble of hot poison in your loins and a super-voluptuous flame permanently aglow in your subtle spine (oh, how you have to cringe and hide!), in order to discern at once, by ineffable signs – the slightly feline outline of a cheekbone, the slenderness of a downy limb, and other indices which despair and shame and tears of tenderness forbid me to tabulate – the little deadly demon among the wholesome children; *she* stands unrecognized by them and unconscious herself of her fantastic power.

Furthermore, since the idea of time plays such a magic part in the matter, the student should not be surprised to learn that there must be a gap of several years, never less than ten I should say, generally thirty or forty, and as many as ninety in a few known cases, between maiden and man to enable the latter to come under a nymphet's spell. It is a question of focal adjustment, of a certain distance that the inner eye thrills to surmount, and a certain contrast that the mind perceives with a gasp of perverse delight. When I was a child and she was a child, my little Annabel was no nymphet to me; I was her equal, a faunlet in my own right, on that same enchanted island of time; but today, in September 1952, after twenty-nine years have elapsed, I think I can distinguish in her the initial fateful elf in my life.[211]   [*Lolita* 16–18]

[Humbert comes to fetch Lolita (Dolly Haze) early from the summer camp run by Shirley Holmes.]
Let me retain for a moment that scene in all its trivial and fateful detail: hag Holmes writing out a receipt, scratching her head, pulling a drawer out of her desk, pouring change into my impatient palm, then neatly spreading a banknote over it with a bright ". . . and five!"; photographs of girl-children; some gaudy moth or butterfly, still alive, safely pinned to the wall ("nature study"); the framed diploma of the camp's dietitian; my trembling hands; a card produced by efficient Holmes with a report of Dolly Haze's behavior for July ("fair to good; keen on swimming and boating"); a sound of trees and birds, and my pounding heart . . . I was standing with my back to the open door, and then I felt the blood rush to my head as I heard her respiration and voice behind me.[212]   [*Lolita* 110–11]

[Humbert has withheld from Lolita the news of her mother's death, pretending she is merely ill.]
I said the doctors did not quite know yet what the trouble was. Anyway, something abdominal. Abominable? No, abdominal. We would have to hang around for a while. The hospital was in the country, near the gay town of Lepingville, where a great poet had resided in the early nineteenth century and where we would take in all the shows. She thought it a peachy idea and wondered if we could make Lepingville before nine P.M.

"We should be at Briceland by dinner time," I said, "and tomorrow we'll visit Lepingville.[213] How was the hike? Did you have a marvelous time at the camp?"   [*Lolita* 111–12]

[Humbert waits for a sleeping pill to work on Lolita at the Enchanted Hunters Hotel.]
I left the loud lobby and stood outside, on the white steps, looking at the hundreds of powdered bugs[214] wheeling around the lamps in the soggy black night, full of ripple and stir. All I would do – all I would dare to do – would amount to such a trifle. . . .   [*Lolita* 126]

[Humbert singles out details of the year-long tour around America he has imposed on Lolita.]
A patch of beautifully eroded clay; and yucca blossoms, so pure, so waxy, but lousy with creeping white flies.[215] Independence, Missouri, the starting point of the Old Oregon Trail; and Abilene, Kansas, the home of the Wild Bill Something Rodeo. Distant mountains. Near mountains. More mountains; bluish beauties never attainable, or ever turning into inhabited hill after hill; south-eastern ranges, altitudinal failures as alps go; heart and sky-piercing snow-veined gray colossi of stone, relentless peaks appearing from nowhere at a turn of the highway; timbered enormities, with a system of neatly overlapping dark firs, interrupted in places by pale puffs of aspen; pink and lilac formations, Pharaonic, phallic, "too prehistoric for words" (blasé Lo); buttes of black lava; early spring mountains with young-elephant lanugo along their spines; end-of-the-summer mountains, all hunched up, their heavy Egyptian limbs folded under folds of tawny moth-eaten plush; oatmeal hills, flecked with green round oaks; a last rufous mountain with a rich rug of lucerne at its foot.

Moreover, we inspected: Little Iceberg Lake, somewhere in Colorado, and the snow banks, and the cushionets of tiny alpine flowers, and more snow; down which Lo in red-peaked cap tried to slide, and squealed, and was snowballed by some youngsters, and retaliated in kind *comme on dit*. Skeletons of burned aspens, patches of spired blue flowers. The various items of a scenic drive. Hundreds of scenic drives, thousands of Bear Creeks, Soda Springs, Painted Canyons. Texas, a drought-struck plain. Crystal Chamber in the longest cave in the world, children under 12 free, Lo a young captive. A collection of a local lady's homemade sculptures, closed on a miserable Monday morning, dust, wind, witherland. Conception Park, in a town on the Mexican border which I dared not cross. There and elsewhere, hundreds of gray hummingbirds in the dusk,[216] probing the throats of dim flowers.   [*Lolita* 156–57]

[Humbert and Lolita settle at Beardsley.]

Her girl friends, whom I had looked forward to meet, proved on the whole disappointing. There was Opal Something, and Linda Hall, and Avis Chapman, and Eva Rosen, and Mona Dahl (save one, all these names are approximations, of course).[217]   [*Lolita* 189–91]

[Humbert and Lolita suddenly agree to leave Beardsley and her role in the school play. Driving out of town, they stop at traffic lights.]

As we pulled up, another car came to a gliding stop alongside, and a very striking looking, athletically lean young woman (where had I seen her?) with a high complexion and shoulder-length brilliant bronze hair, greeted Lo with a ringing "Hi!" – and then, addressing me, effusively, edusively (placed!), stressing certain words, said: "What a *shame* it was to *tear* Dolly away from the play – you should have *heard* the author *raving* about her after that rehearsal – " "Green light, you dope," said Lo under her breath, and simultaneously, waving in bright adieu a bangled arm, Joan of Arc (in a performance we saw at the local theatre) violently outdistanced us to swerve into Campus Avenue.

"Who was it exactly? Vermont or Rumpelmeyer?"

"No – Edusa Gold – the gal who coaches us."[218]

"I was not referring to her. Who exactly concocted that play?"

"Oh! Yes, of course. Some old woman, Clare Something, I guess. There was quite a crowd of them there."   [*Lolita* 208–9]

[They head westward.]

With Lo's knowledge and assent, the two post offices given to the Beardsley postmaster as forwarding addresses were P.O. Wace and P.O. Elphinstone.[219]   [*Lolita* 222]

[They are pursued westward by an unidentified driver.]

He seemed to patronize at first the Chevrolet genus, beginning with a Campus Cream convertible, then going on to a small Horizon Blue sedan, and thenceforth fading into Surf Gray and Driftwood Gray. Then he turned to other makes and passed through a pale dull rainbow of paint shades, and one day I found myself attempting to cope with the subtle distinction between our own Dream Blue Melmoth[220] and the Crest Blue Oldsmobile he had rented; grays, however, remained his favorite cryptochromism, and, in agonizing nightmares, I tried in vain to sort out properly such ghosts as Chrysler's Shell Gray, Chevrolet's Thistle Gray, Dodge's French Gray . . .

[*Lolita* 222]

[Lolita's tennis.]

Despite her advanced age, she was more of a nymphet than ever, with her apricot-colored limbs, in her sub-teen tennis togs! Winged gentlemen! No hereafter is acceptable if it does not produce her as she was then, in that Colorado resort between Snow and Elphinstone,[221] with everything right: the white wide little-boy shorts, the slender waist, the apricot midriff, the white breast-kerchief whose ribbons went up and encircled her neck to end behind in a dangling knot leaving bare her gaspingly young and adorable apricot shoulder blades with that pubescence and those lovely gentle bones, and the smooth, downward-tapering back.   [*Lolita* 230–31]

Her form was, indeed, an absolutely perfect imitation of absolutely top-notch tennis – without any utilitarian results. As Edusa's sister, Electra Gold,[222] a marvelous young coach, said to me once while I sat on a pulsating hard bench watching Dolores Haze toying with Linda Hall (and being beaten by her): "Dolly has a magnet in the center of her racket guts, but why the heck is she so polite?" Ah, Electra, what did it matter, with such grace!   [*Lolita* 231]

She was hitting hard and flat, with her usual effortless sweep, feeding me deep skimming balls – all so rhythmically coordinated and overt as to reduce my footwork to, practically, a swinging stroll – crack players will understand what I mean. My rather heavily cut serve that I had been taught by my father who had learned it from Decugis or Borman, old friends of his and great champions, would have seriously troubled my Lo, had I really tried to trouble her. But who would upset such a lucid dear? Did I ever mention that her bare arm bore the 8 of vaccination? That I loved her hopelessly? That she was only fourteen?

An inquisitive butterfly passed, dipping, between us.[223]

Two people in tennis shorts, a red-haired fellow only about eight years my junior, with sunburnt bright pink shins, and an indolent dark girl with a moody mouth and hard eyes, about two years Lolita's senior, appeared from nowhere.
[*Lolita* 233–34]

[Humbert drives back from the hospital where he has taken feverish Lolita.]

Wide gravel roads criss-crossed drowsy rectangular shadows. I made out what looked like the silhouette of gallows on what was probably a school playground; and in another wastelike block there rose in domed silence the pale temple of some local sect. I found the highway at last, and then the motel, where millions of so-called "millers,"[224] a kind of insect, were swarming around the neon contours of "No Vacancy"; and, when, at 3 A.M., after one of those untimely hot showers which like some mordant only help to fix a man's despair and weariness, I lay on her bed that smelled of chestnuts and roses, and peppermint, and the very delicate, very special French perfume I latterly allowed her to use, I found myself unable to assimilate the simple fact that for the first time in two years I was separated from my Lolita.
[*Lolita* 241]

[After Lolita escapes, Humbert picks up a mature woman in order to steady himself.]

She was twice Lolita's age and three quarters of mine: a very slight, dark-haired, pale-skinned adult, weighing a hundred and five pounds, with charmingly asymmetrical eyes, an angular, rapidly sketched profile, and a most appealing *ensellure* to her supple back – I think she had some Spanish or Babylonian blood. I picked her up one depraved May evening somewhere between Montreal and New York, or more narrowly, between Toylestown and Blake, at a darkishly burning bar under the sign of the Tigermoth, where she was amiably drunk: she insisted we had gone to school together, and she placed her trembling little hand on my ape paw. My senses were very slightly stirred but I decided to give her a try; I did – and adopted her as a constant companion. She was so kind, was Rita, such a good sport, that I daresay she would have given herself to any pathetic creature or fallacy, an old broken tree or a bereaved porcupine, out of sheer chumminess and compassion.

When I first met her she had but recently divorced her third husband – and a little more recently had been abandoned by her seventh *cavalier servant* – the others, the mutables, were too numerous and mobile to tabulate. Her brother was – and no doubt still is – a prominent, pasty-faced, suspenders-and-painted-tie-wearing politician, mayor and booster of his ball-playing, Bible-reading, grain-handling home town. For the last eight years he had been paying his great little sister several hundred dollars per month under the stringent condition that she would never enter great little Grainball City. She told me, with wails of wonder, that for some God-damn reason every new boy friend of hers would first of all take her Grainball-ward: it was a fatal attraction; and before she knew what was what, she would find herself sucked into the lunar orbit of the town, and would be following the flood-lit drive that encircled it – "going round and round," as she phrased it, "like a God-damn mulberry moth."[225]

[*Lolita* 258–59]

[*Humbert looks up the* Briceland Gazette *in the hope of finding some echo of his first love-making with Lolita, at Briceland's* Enchanted Hunters *hotel.*]

I scanned and skimmed . . . *Brute Force* and *Possessed* were coming on Sunday, the 24th, to both theatres. Mr. Purdom, independent tobacco auctioneer, said that ever since 1925 he had been an Omen Faustum smoker. Husky Hank and his petite bride were to be the guests of Mr. and Mrs. Reginald G. Gore, 58 Inchkeith[226] Avenue. The size of certain parasites is one sixth of the host. Dunkerque was fortified in the tenth century.   [*Lolita* 262]

[*Humbert drives out to the home of the man who took Lolita from him, but finding a number of cars there, decides to shoot him the next day, and returns to town.*]

I started to drive to Grimm Road, twelve miles north of the town. By that time night had eliminated most of the landscape and as I followed the narrow winding highway, a series of short posts, ghostly white, with reflectors, borrowed my own lights to indicate this or that curve. I could make out a dark valley on one side of the road and wooded slopes on the other, and in front of me, like derelict snowflakes, moths drifted out of the blackness into my probing aura. [*Lolita* 292]

Gently I rolled back to town, in that old faithful car of mine which was serenely, almost cheerfully working for me. My Lolita! There was still a three-year-old bobby pin of hers in the depths of the glove compartment. There was still that stream of pale moths siphoned out of the night by my headlights. Dark barns still propped themselves up here and there by the roadside. People were still going to the movies. [*Lolita* 293]

[Humbert points his gun at his "rival," who chatters to stall for time.]
We have here a most reliable and bribable charwoman, a Mrs. Vibrissa – curious name – who comes from the village twice a week, alas not today, she has daughters, granddaughters, a thing or two I know about the chief of police makes him my slave. I am a playwright. I have been called the American Maeterlinck. Maeterlinck-Schmetterling,[227] says I. Come on! All this is very humiliating . . . [*Lolita* 301]

[After killing his "rival," Humbert gives himself up. Just before the police reach him, he reflects.]
I was soon to be taken out of the car (Hi, Melmoth, thanks a lot, old fellow) – and was, indeed, looking forward to surrender myself to many hands, without doing anything to cooperate, while they moved and carried me, relaxed, comfortable, surrendering myself lazily, like a patient, and deriving an eerie enjoyment from my limpness and the absolutely reliable support given me by the police and the ambulance people. And while I was waiting for them to run up to me on the high slope, I evoked a last mirage of wonder and hopelessness. One day, soon after her disappearance, an attack of abominable nausea forced me to pull up on the ghost of an old mountain road that now accompanied, now traversed a brand new highway, with its population of asters bathing in the detached warmth of a pale-blue afternoon in late summer. After coughing myself inside out, I rested a while on a boulder, and then, thinking the sweet air might do me good,

walked a little way toward a low stone parapet on the precipice side of the highway. Small grasshoppers spurted out of the withered roadside weeds. A very light cloud was opening its arms and moving toward a slightly more substantial one belonging to another, more sluggish, heavenlogged system. As I approached the friendly abyss, I grew aware of a melodious unity of sounds rising like vapor from a small mining town that lay at my feet, in a fold of the valley. One could make out the geometry of the streets between blocks of red and gray roofs, and green puffs of trees, and a serpentine stream, and the rich, ore-like glitter of the city dump, and beyond the town, roads crisscrossing the crazy quilt of dark and pale fields, and behind it all, great timbered mountains. But even brighter than those quietly rejoicing colors – for there are colors and shades that seem to enjoy themselves in good company – both brighter and dreamier to the ear than they were to the eye, was that vapory vibration of accumulated sounds that never ceased for a moment, as it rose to the lip of granite where I stood wiping my foul mouth. And soon I realized that all these sounds were of one nature, that no other sounds but these came from the streets of the transparent town, with the women at home and the men away. Reader! What I heard was but the melody of children at play, nothing but that, and so limpid was the air that within this vapor of blended voices, majestic and minute, remote and magically near, frank and divinely enigmatic – one could hear now and then, as if released, an almost articulate spurt of vivid laughter, or the crack of a bat, or the clatter of a toy wagon, but it was all really too far for the eye to distinguish any movement in the lightly etched streets. I stood listening to that musical vibration from my lofty slope, to those flashes of separate cries with a kind of demure murmur for background, and then I knew that the hopelessly poignant thing was not Lolita's absence from my side, but the absence of her voice from that concord.[228]   [*Lolita* 307–8]

Drugie berega

Excerpts from memoirs. Translated into Russian and rewritten from the English *Conclusive Evidence/Speak, Memory*, spring 1953–spring 1954. Published in 1954.

Once, in 1940, in New York, where immediately after my arrival in America I had the happiness of plunging into the sheer heaven of scientific research, I was coming down the elevator from the fifth floor of the American Museum of Natural History, where I spent whole days in the entomological laboratory, and suddenly – with the thought perhaps that I had been overtaxing my brain – I saw my surname, traced out in great golden Russian letters on the fresco in the entrance hall. Looking closer I could see the name belonged with the image of [my uncle] Konstantin Dmitrievich: young, highly colored, sporting an imperial, he was taking part, together with Vitte, Korostovets and the Japanese delegation, in the signing of the Portsmouth Treaty under the kindly aegis of Theodore Roosevelt, in whose memory the museum was built.   [DB 52–53]

In relation to many human feelings – hope sufficient to hinder sleep, and its luxurious fulfilment, despite the snow in the shadows; the alarm of vainglory and the silence of the goal achieved – the half century of my butterfly adventures, collecting and dissecting, stands for me in pride of place. If as an artist I find my only delight in the flash of my private lightnings and in fixing them as best I can, and do not concern myself with fame, then – I confess – I seethe with incomprehensible excitement as I sort out in my mind my entomological discoveries: the exhausting labors; the changes I have introduced in systematics; the revolution – with bloody executions of colleagues – in the bright circle of the microscope; the image and vibration in me of all the rare butterflies I have caught and described myself; and my surname, henceforth immortal behind a Latin name I have invented or, in lower case, with a Roman "i" attached, in the designation of a butterfly called in my honor. And as if on the horizon of this pride, there shine in my memory all the unusual, legendary localities – northern bogs, southern steppes, mountains fourteen thousand feet high – over which I have walked with a muslin net in my hand, as a slender boy in a straw hat, as a young man in rope soles, as a fat and fiftyish man in shorts.

I understood early, as my mother understood so well when collecting mushrooms, that in such cases one must be alone. In the course of my childhood and boyhood, I had a maniacal fear of companions, and of course nothing in the world except rain could prevent my five-hour morning hike. My mother warned my tutors and governesses that the morning was entirely mine, and they prudently stood aside.   [DB 118]

[He chases a butterfly in a bog on the other side of the Oredezh, and catches up with it at last near Longs Peak.]

I have strayed a long way, but all the past is right by my side, and a part of the future too. In the flowering thickets of Arizona canyons, high on the ore-bearing slopes of the San Miguel Mountains, on the lakes of the Teton Range, and in many other harsh and beautiful localities, where I know every path and ravine, there fly and will fly every summer species and subspecies discovered and described by me. "By my name is called – " no, not a river, but a butterfly in Alaska, another in Brazil, a third in Utah, where I took it high in the mountains, on the window of a ski lodge, that *Eupithecia nabokovi* McDunnough which secretly closes the thematic series begun in a Petersburg wood. I admit I do not believe in fleeting time – light, gliding, Persian time. I have learned to fold this magic carpet to superimpose one part of the pattern upon another. Let visitors trip. And for me the highest enjoyment – outside diabolical time, but very much inside divine space – is a randomly selected landscape, no matter what latitude, tundra or wormwood or even amid the remains of some old pinewood by a railroad between the lifeless in this context Albany and Schenectady (where flies one of my favorite namesakes, my blue *samuelis*), in short wherever I can be in company of butterflies and their food plants. [DB 128]

[Late 1917, after the Bolshevik coup.]

A month ahead of time I sat the school-leaving exams, counting on finishing my education in England, and then organizing an entomological expedition into the mountains of western China. All this seemed straightforward and plausible, and in fact much of it did come to pass. [DB 210]

[Early 1918, in the Crimea.]

The pink puffs of blossoming almond trees already enlivened the seashore slopes, and I had long been occupied with the first butterflies, when the Bolsheviks vanished, and the Germans modestly appeared. [DB 215]

[He imagines returning to Russia with a false passport, under an assumed name.]

But I do not think I shall ever do it. I have been dreaming of it too long, too idly, too wastefully. I have squandered my dream. By torturous examination of miniatures, of tiny print, of double light, I have hopelessly spoiled my inner sight. In exactly the same way I wasted my resources when in 1918 I dreamed that in winter, after I had finished my entomological forays, I would join Denikin's army and reach Tamara's hamlet; but winter went by, and I was still making up my mind, and in March the Crimea began to crumble under the pressure of the Reds, and the evacuation began.

[DB 216–17]

From letter to Edmund Wilson, June 30, 1954

From Taos, New Mexico.

I am now collecting butterflies in New Mexico. A dull series of events led us to rent by wire from Ithaca a house here. We are near a superb canyon where I go for my hunting, and twelve miles from Taos which is a dismal hole full of third-rate painters and faded pansies. [NWL 285]

From letter to Katharine White,[229] August 11, 1954

From Taos, New Mexico.

Chance and certain lepic considerations have led us to an adobe house ten miles north of Taos, an ugly and dreary town with *soi-disant* "picturesque" Indian paupers placed at strategic points by the Chamber of Commerce to lure tourists from Oklahoma and Texas who deem the place "arty." There are, however, some admirable canyons where most interesting butterflies occur. [SL 150]

Pnin

Excerpts from novel. Written 1953–55. Published in the *New Yorker* 1953–55, and in book form in 1957.

[Pnin, a guest at the summer home of a fellow Russian émigré in the New England countryside, talks to another, Konstantin Ivanovich Chateau.]

"Look, how pretty," said observant Chateau.

A score of small butterflies, all of one kind, were settled on a damp patch of sand, their wings erect and closed, showing their pale undersides with dark dots and tiny orange-rimmed peacock spots along the hindwing margins; one of Pnin's shed rubbers disturbed some of them and, revealing the celestial hue of their upper surface, they fluttered around like blue snow-flakes before settling again.

"Pity Vladimir Vladimirovich is not here," remarked Chateau. "He would have told us all about these enchanting insects."[230]

"I have always had the impression that his entomology was merely a pose."

"Oh no," said Chateau. "You will lose it some day," he added, pointing to the Greek Catholic cross on a golden chainlet that Pnin had removed from his neck and hung on a twig. Its glint perplexed a cruising dragonfly.

[*Pnin* 128]

[Another school year starts.]

The 1954 Fall Term had begun. Again the marble neck of a homely Venus in the vestibule of Humanities Hall received the vermilion imprint, in applied lipstick, of a mimicked kiss. Again the *Waindell Recorder* discussed the Parking Problem. Again in the margins of library books earnest freshmen inscribed such helpful glosses as "Description of nature," or "Irony"; and in a pretty edition of Mallarmé's poems an especially able scholiast had already underlined in violet ink the difficult word *oiseaux* and scrawled above it "birds." Again autumn gales plastered dead leaves against one side of the latticed gallery leading from Humanities to Frieze Hall. Again, on serene afternoons, huge, amber-brown Monarch butter-flies flapped over asphalt and lawn as they lazily drifted south, their incompletely retracted black legs hanging rather low beneath their polka-dotted bodies.

[*Pnin* 137–38]

[The narrator, a stylized Nabokov, recalls meeting Pnin in their youth.]

Five years later, after spending the beginning of the summer on our estate near St. Petersburg, my mother, my young brother, and I happened to visit a dreary old aunt at her curiously desolate country seat not far from a famous resort on the Baltic coast. One afternoon, as in concentrated ecstasy I was spreading, underside up, an exceptionally rare aberration of the Paphia Fritillary, in which the silver stripes ornamenting the lower surface of the hindwings had fused into an even expanse of metallic gloss, a footman came up with the information that the old lady requested my presence. In the reception hall I found her talking to two self-conscious youths in university student uniforms. One, with the blond fuzz, was Timofey Pnin, the other, with the russet down, was Grigoriy Belochkin.   [*Pnin* 177]

From letter to John Adams Comstock,[231] March 14, 1956

From Cambridge, Massachusetts.

This year, in April, my wife and I plan to drive to South California. I want to revisit *emigdionis*, *neurona*,[232] and a few other things in their haunts. We cannot make up our minds where exactly to establish our headquarters but it will be, I suppose, in the Tehacapi or Kern Counties till June. My dream is a cottage at the entrance of a canyon.   [VNA]

From letter to Jason Epstein,[233] May 25, 1956

From Mt. Carmel, Utah.

Let me confess that your suggestion about a book on butterflies appeals to me tremendously.[234] It would contain my adventures with leps in various countries, especially in the Rocky Mountain States, the discovery of new species, and the description of some fantastic cases of adaptation. I think I could achieve a perfect blend of science, art and entertainment. . . .

[beside inkblot]: Sorry! my fountain pen cannot cope with this altitude although it is a mere 5200'. Amer. collectors use the word "leps" as an abbreviation of "lepidoptera." One lep, two leps, lep by lep! Lepping stones (on which leps settle).[235]   [VNA]

From letter to Jason Epstein, June 13, 1956

From Mt. Carmel, Utah.

I want to ask you to allow me a little more time for pondering the butterfly book. Your conditions suit me; but before definitely committing myself I would like to evolve a precise plan for the book and can only do so after Lermontov is out of the way.[236] When I get back to Cornell, where my papers are, I shall show you some of my own drawings illustrating my theories regarding wing patterns in butterflies.   [SL 187]

From letter to Elena Sikorski, August 6, 1956[237]

From Ithaca, New York.

Over the spring and summer we did 16 and a half thousand kilometers in our good Buick and caught wonderful butterflies in Utah, Arizona and Montana.   [*Perepiska s sestroy* 86]

From letter to Edmund Wilson, August 14, 1956

From Ithaca, New York.

Véra and I have just returned from a marvelous trip to the Rockies. We stayed first at Mt. Carmel, a village in southern Utah where we had hired a house. We collected butterflies in the Grand Canyon, Arizona, and in other national parks in the vicinity. Pink, terra-cotta and lilac mountains formed a sympathetic background to the Caucasus of Lermontov in *A Hero of Our Time* which is now ready to be mailed to Doubleday, with commentaries and a map. In July we moved on to higher altitudes in Wyoming and Montana.   [NWL 299–300]

From letter to Henry Allen Moe,[238] September 24, 1956

From Ithaca, New York.

My other suggestion is in the nature of a query. Would you consider awarding a *third* fellowship to a split personality, Twiddledee and Twiddledum in one, or better say a Dr. Jekyll and Mr. Hyde combined, one half writer, the other half entomologist? I have written the better part of a novel ("Bend Sinister") and a considerable part of a book on Pushkin's "Eugene Onegin," including a translation of the work, on two Guggenheim awards, in 1943 and in 1953, respectively. The Pushkin book has suffered some delays since then but will be ready for publication by Christmas.

On the other hand, I have devoted many years to entomological research and am the author of several monographs and papers on Lepidoptera, a list of which I attach to this letter. I have completely re-classified a group of Lycaenidae (as you can see from "A Field Guide to the Butterflies of North America" by Alexander B. Klots, of the City College of New York and the American Museum of Natural History). I have described and named a number of species and subspecies, and other scientists have named lepidoptera after me.

For several summers now I have been studying the lepidopterous fauna of the Rocky Mts. To complete these studies, I would need to examine certain collections, both in America and Europe, and then do some laboratory work. I might add that for six years I have been a Research Fellow in Entomology on the staff of the Museum of Comparative Zoology, Harvard.

[SL 189]

On a Book Entitled *Lolita*

Excerpts from article. Written in 1956. Published in the *Anchor Review* in 1957 and as an afterword to *Lolita* from 1958.

Every summer my wife and I go butterfly hunting. The specimens are deposited at scientific institutions, such as the Museum of Comparative Zoology at Harvard or the Cornell University collection. The locality labels pinned under these butterflies will be a boon to some twenty-first-century scholar with a taste for recondite biography. It was at such of our headquarters as Telluride, Colorado; Afton, Wyoming; Portal, Arizona; and Ashland, Oregon, that *Lolita* was energetically resumed in the evenings or on cloudy days. I finished copying the thing out in longhand in the spring of 1954, and at once began casting around for a publisher. [*Lolita* 314]

I have not reread *Lolita* since I went through the proofs in the spring of 1955 but I find it to be a delightful presence now that it quietly hangs about the house like a summer day which one knows to be bright behind the haze. And when I thus think of *Lolita,* I seem always to pick out for special delectation such images as Mr. Taxovich, or that class list of Ramsdale School, or Charlotte saying "waterproof," or Lolita in slow motion advancing toward Humbert's gifts, or the pictures decorating the stylized garret of Gaston Godin, or the Kasbeam barber (who cost me a month of work), or Lolita playing tennis, or the hospital at Elphinstone, or pale, pregnant, beloved, irretrievable Dolly Schiller dying in Gray Star (the capital town of the book), or the tinkling sounds of the valley town coming up the mountain trail (on which I caught the first known female of *Lycaeides sublivens* Nabokov).[239] These are the nerves of the novel. These are the secret points, the subliminal co-ordinates by means of which the book is plotted – although I realize very clearly that these and other scenes will be skimmed over or not noticed, or never even reached, by those who begin reading the book under the impression that it is something on the lines of *Memoirs of a Woman of Pleasure* or *Les Amours de Milord Grosvit.*   [*Lolita* 318]

From letter to Katharine White, February 5, 1957

From Ithaca, New York.

Here is a little note for The New Yorker. I shall send you my ballad in the course of this week. Many thanks for your charming letter.

Department of Mimicry

In The New Yorker of February 23, 1957, page 31, Mr. Hellman writes that if the two butterflies he mentions, a skipper and a Lycaenid (the correct genus of this "shasta comstocki" is by the way *Icaricia* Nabokov, 1944), are not named after John Henry Comstock, Professor of Entomology in Cornell University, he will eat his cyanide jar. Since these butterflies are named after Dr. John A. Comstock, renowned for his excellent work in the life history of California lepidoptera, I can only hope that Mr. Hellman's jar is not loaded. Incidentally, pinching the thorax is a much simpler way of dispatching a butterfly.[240]   [SL 199]

From "The Ballad of Longwood Glen"

Poem written in July 1953, rewritten by March 1957. Published in the *New Yorker*, July 6, 1957.

[At a Sunday picnic in a park, Art Longwood shows his son how to toss a ball high. When it does not come down from a tree, Art climbs up after it. He is never seen again.]

Anacondas and pumas were mentioned by some,
And all kinds of humans continued to come:

Tree surgeons, detectives, the fire brigade.
An ambulance parked in the dancing shade.

A drunken rogue with a rope and a gun
Arrived on the scene to see justice done.

Explorers, dendrologists – all were there;
And a strange pale girl with gypsy hair.

And from Cape Fear to Cape Flattery
Every paper had: Man Lost in Tree.

And the sky-bound oak (where owls had perched
And the moon dripped gold) was felled and searched.

They discovered some inchworms,[241] a red-cheeked gall,
And an ancient nest with a new-laid ball.

They varnished the stump, put up railings and signs.
Restrooms nestled in roses and vines. . . .

[PP 178–79]

From letter from William James, March 9, 1957

Unpublished.

"Pnin" arrived this morning. I said to myself, "There *couldn't* be a butterfly on the title page" – but there he was, along with the affectionate inscription, small and exquisite (and of no known species – and all the better for that!) and I said to myself "Only you would remember to do that!"   [VNA]

From letter to Mark Schorer,[242] March 24, 1957

From Ithaca, New York.

I shall be glad to make my contribution to the D. H. Lawrence Fellowship Fund, although, between you and me, I dislike Lawrence as a writer and detest Taos, where, in 1954, I had the misfortune of establishing my headquarters when collecting butterflies in the N. Mexico mountains.

I would like you to know how much I appreciated your eyespot on Pnin's underwing.   [SL 214]

From letter to Katharine White, April 4, 1957

From Ithaca, New York.

I was sorry that The New Yorker decided not to use my entomological correction. The blunder in that article must have grievously hurt the Comstock of California, eminent author of BUTTERFLIES OF CALIFORNIA, – a touchy old man whom I respect. The Cornell Comstock, with whom Helmann confused him, was a much inferior scientist, whose specialty, moreover, was not lepidoptera.   [SL 215]

From letter to Jason Epstein, July 18, 1957

From Ithaca, New York.

This may amuse you: In a book on Colorado butterflies[243] that has just come out, a species that I discovered and described fifteen years ago has now been given the popular name of "Nabokov's Wood Nymph."   [VNA]

From letter to William James, October 15, 1957

From Ithaca, New York. Unpublished.

Your boyhood letter about those great unwieldy moths is perfectly enchanting.[244] Véra and I, and Dmitri, enjoyed and re-enjoyed it. None of those soft monsters was endemic in Northern Russia, but I used to be given pupae of American and Asiatic Saturnids,[245] and went through all the thrills and throes reflected so vividly in your dear old little letter.

[Houghton Library, Harvard]

Eugene Onegin

Excerpt from Nabokov's commentary to his translation of Aleksandr Pushkin's novel in verse, *Eugene Onegin*. Written in 1948–57, published in 1964, revised in 1966, revised edition published in 1975.

[Chapter Five: XXV]

1/ *bagryánoyu rukóyu*: The epithet *bagryanïy*, "crimson," is synonymous with *purpurnïy*, "porphyrous," and implies a rich tone of red, the French *pourpre*, not the English "purple," which is deep violet (Russ. *fioletovïy*). . . .

As far as I can make out (and frankly, I have not gone into the question beyond its shallows), there were two kinds of classical purples: the Tyrian purple, which was crimson, the color of blood and dawn; and the Tarentine dye, said by poets to rival the hue of the violet. French poets in their use of *pourpre* drove the Tyrian idea to a point where sight ceased to be of any moment; and an abstract sunburst replaced the perception of any specific hue; they were followed by the Russians, whose *purpur* is merely the conventional crimson of a heavy curtain in an allegory or an apotheosis; but the once woaded English, with their Saxon cult of color, turned to the plum, and the Purple Emperor butterfly, and the heather in bloom, and remote hills – in short, to "amethyst" and "violet" for their conception of purple. "You violets . . . / By your pure purple mantles known," writes Sir Henry Wotton (1568–1639) in a poem addressed to Elizabeth of Bohemia. Shakespeare's "long purples" (*Hamlet*, IV, vii, 170) become characteristically "fleurs rougeâtres" with Letourneur, which, of course, makes nonsense of the comparison to the bluish fingers of dead men in the same passage. The bright-red variety of purple does crop up as a Europeanism in Shakespeare and other poets of his time, but its real ascendancy, of short duration happily, comes with the age of pseudoclassicism, when Pope seems to have deliberately conformed to the French use of *pourpre*; Pope's pupil, Byron, followed suit. . . . [EO, V. 2: 520–21]

From letter to Richard Schickel,[246] January 1, 1958

From Ithaca, New York.

For many years (1941–1949) I looked after the lepidoptera in the Museum of Comparative Zoology at Harvard. I have been collecting leps during more than fifty summers in many remote regions. I have worked out several taxonomic problems. I have discovered several new American butterflies, one of which is pleasingly called by lepidopterists "Nabokov's Wood Nymph" (a feral cousin of our common friend). Although I do not teach biology at Cornell, I am in touch with the admirable entomological museum here. Moreover, I discuss in detail beetles and their parasites every year around April, when in my literature course, I get to Kafka's "Metamorphosis," after which, in May, I annually attempt to identify the noctuid moth that circles around a lamp in the brothel scene of Joyce's "Ulysses." And there are three butterflies in "Madame Bovary," black, yellow, and white, respectively. So you see that your making me a professor of biology was not only very much to the point, but warmed a cockle which no success in comparative literature can so exquisitely prick. [SL 239]

From letter to Harry Levin, April 28, 1958

From Ithaca, New York.

I enjoyed your treatment of Poe.[247] Not only did he not visualize the death's-head moth,[248] but he was also under the completely erroneous

impression that it occurs in America. In Kafka's case the reader sees the
domed beetle quite clearly. [SL 257]

From Page a Day diary[249]

MAY 20 [1958] Spread Wyoming butterflies, batch taken in 1952. Snowy
Range-Sierra Madre-Dubois-West Wyoming. Prepared analysis of Or-
mond Hotel chapter (in "Ulysses") for tomorrow. Read Notes + Queries,
for 1870, 4th S. VI, July–Dec. . . .

MAY 22 Quiet day. Sorted out the *Speyeria* I caught in Wyoming, Oregon and New Mexico (rare *egleis secreta* from the Sierra Madre, tiny *cybele carpenteri* from Taos, etc.) and composed a chess problem (White:
Kc1, Qf8, Ktd4, e7, Pb4, b7, c7; Black Kab, Ra7, c6, Pb6, cd; mate in two;
key: Q to F3).

JULY 13 [Véra Nabokov entry.] We left Ithaca on June 10 and after 8
days arrived at Glacier Park. Stopped overnight at Babb. It was raining.
Moved next day to a "housekeeping cabin" 5 miles to the south of Babb.
Primitive one-room cabin, electricity (dim), hot shower (cold). Marvelous
meadows full of flowers, coveted butterflies (by V.),[250] practically on the
cabin's doorstep, a small, fairy-tale lake hidden by aspens on all sides, inhabited by numerous waterfowl. . . .

On Friday, the 11th [July], we drove to Elko, B.C., 124 miles and back
in search of *ferniensis*. Landscape disappointing, burnt-out stripes on both
side of road, hardly any flowers, no butterflies. Finally, found some 10
males on an unlikely stretch of sand and gravel (formerly used to obtain
sand for road construction). 250 miles for 10 blues! Drove yesterday to
Logan Pass (hurrying to profit by a sunny morning) where V. climbed a
forbidding-looking scree-slope and, after an hour and a half, came down
with 3 specimens of *damoetas* (a prize!). 120 miles for 3 *Melitaea*. The
weather so distressing we are cancelling plans of going to Banff (and, possibly, Jasper – a point of contention) and driving to Wyoming instead – tomorrow – then Big Horn, the Black Hills of S. Dakota; then – New York.

[VNA]

From letter from Véra Nabokov to Walter Minton,[251] August 13, 1958

From Ithaca, New York.

He is spreading our catches at the rate of fifty or more a day – so I am again in charge of his correspondence.

[VNA]

From Page a Day diary

AUGUST 21 [Véra Nabokov entry.] On Aug. 18 (publication day of *Lolita*) Minton wired:

"Everybody talking of Lolita on publication day yesterdays reviews magnificent and NY Times blast this morning provided necessary fuel to flame 300 reorders this morning and bookstores report excellent demand congratulations on publication day – Walter J. Minton." . . .

V. serenely indifferent – occupied with a new story, and with the spreading of some 2000 butterflies we caught during several trips; he kept them in papers and is now spreading them all.

[VNA]

From interview with Paul O'Neil, September 5–6, 1958

On the brink of the Grand Canyon he saw and netted a new butterfly (which was named, prophetically, Nabokov's Wood Nymph) and from that moment on never had a moment's yearning for the Old World.

Butterflies had a great deal to do with this transition. If he had to give up either writing or lepidopterology, Nabokov says, he would reluctantly abandon writing. The science gives him an indescribable "sense of power, of triumph over nature."

[*Life International*, April 13, 1959: 66]

Interview notes, undated [late February–early March 1959]

Q: And what else [other than teach] did you do?
A: In the second place – I used my knowledge of butterflies. I do not know

if Chehov was a good doctor, or Ingres a good fiddler, but I was certainly an ambitious lepidopterist – oh, for $^1/_2$ a century, ever since my orange-tipped and green-marbled childhood[252] and so, from 1941 to 1948, I combined a Research Fellowship in Entomology at Harvard with the teaching of Russian language and literature at Wellesley. The results were several taxonomic works on American butterflies in scientific journals, and two graduates who really learned Russian out of the hundreds who took it. . . .

My third source of income was literature, but since I needed two or three months to plan a short story, that source was the least reliable one. Unlike Joseph Conrad, I had written in my mother tongue before, and indeed was an established author in Emigravia. The déménagement from my palatial Russian to the narrow quarters of my English was like moving from one darkened house to another on a starless night during a strike of candlemakers and torchbearers. After a period of panic and groping I managed to settle down rather comfortably but now I know what a caterpillar must feel on the rack of metamorphosis, in the straitjacket of the pupa.

[VNA]

From letter to Sergey S. Nabokov,[253] March 15, 1959

From New York City.

[On being told that a Nabokov River in Novaya Zemlya was named after an ancestor associated with a Russian cartographic expedition.]
When I think that my son Dmitri is an alpinist (and has climbed an unclimbed peak in British Columbia) and that I myself have discovered and named a number of butterflies (and a few – an Alaskan rarity, a Utah moth etc. – have been named after me), the Nabokov River in Zembla acquires an almost mystical significance. [VNA]

From letter to Pyke Johnson,[254] March 15, 1959

From New York City.

Many thanks for sending me the designs for jacket and title page of the Collected Poems.

I like the two colored butterflies on the jacket but they have the bodies of ants, and no stylization can excuse a simple mistake. To stylize adequately one must have complete knowledge of the thing. I would be the laughing stock of my entomological colleagues if they happened to see these impossible hybrids. I also want to draw your attention to the fact that nowadays butterflies are being displayed on birthday cards, lampshades, frocks, curtains, candy boxes, wrapping paper and all kinds of ads.

Anyway, the body should look as in the sketch I am enclosing, and not the way they look in your artist's drawing, and the wings should be attached not to the abdomen but to the thorax. I like the texture and tints of these two insects, and the lettering is admirable.

Now, turning to the title-page butterfly, its head is that of a small tortoise, and its pattern is that of a common Cabbage White butterfly (whereas the insect in my poem is clearly described as belonging to a group of small blue butterflies with dotted undersides), which is as meaningless in the present case as would be a picture of a tuna fish on the jacket of *Moby Dick*. I want to be quite clear and frank: I have nothing against stylization but I do object to stylized ignorance.

I suggest therefore either of two courses: 1) Not to have any butterflies, or any pictures, at all or 2) To provide the insects depicted with butterfly bodies and butterfly heads and (in the case of the title-page butterfly) with a different pattern.   [SL 284–85]

From letter to Pyke Johnson, April 15, 1959

From New York City.

Thanks for sending me the designs. The title-page butterfly is now charming – a very natural and stylish little lep in comfortable surroundings. The binding-design swallowtail lacks antennae but otherwise is presentable. The jacket is well drawn but the choice of models (two popular European insects, the Galatea Marbled White and the Machaon Swallowtail) is not apt, and the whole arrangement looks like the jacket of some popular in-

sect book for young collectors. I beg you to give up the idea of a lepidopterological jacket. Let us have it quite plain, with no drawings at all, or perhaps just a duplicate of the title-page lep.   [SL 287]

From letter to Nicholas Nabokov, May 12, 1959

From Big Bend National Park, Texas.

. . . here, in the Big Bend National Park, southwestern Texas, a magnificent
semitropical place, the newest (and wildest) of our national parks. Collecting is difficult but rewarding.   [VNA]

From letter to John Franclemont,[255] May 31, 1959

From Flagstaff, Arizona. Unpublished.

In April we stayed for a week in the Great Smokies, Tenn., where we had a
delightful time with *Pieris virginiensis*. We also spent some time in the Big
Bend National Park, Texas where we found a rather wonderful, apparently undescribed, green hairstreak close to *M. siva*.   [VNA]

From letter to Gleb Struve,[256] June 3, 1959

From Flagstaff, Arizona.

At present my wife and I are in a charming canyon near Flagstaff, where I
am collecting butterflies.   [SL 288]

From interview with Robert H. Boyle, June 1959

Published as "An Absence of Wood Nymphs" in *Sports Illustrated*, September 14, 1959.

. . . Nabokov has had a passionate interest in butterflies since he was a boy
of six in Russia. . . . Shortly after Nabokov arrived in the United States in

1940, he became a Research Fellow at the Museum of Comparative Zoology at Harvard. . . . In 1948 he became a member of the Department of Literature at Cornell, but he has kept his summers free for his beloved butterflies. Net in hand, he roams the West, unmindful of hooting motorists, chiding cowpokes or snarling dogs that, he says, "ordinarily wouldn't bark at the worst bum."

"This, to me," Nabokov explains, "is most pleasurable – to collect on mountain tops or bogs. It is nostalgic perhaps, but there is also the pleasant feeling of being familiar with a place and surprised when you get more than you expect. You can get as close as possible to these living creatures and see reflected in them a higher law. Mimicry and evolution are for me more and more fascinating. . . . I cannot separate the aesthetic pleasure of seeing a butterfly and the scientific pleasure of knowing what it is."

In late May of 1959 Nabokov and his wife, Véra, were staying in a cabin at Forest Houses in Oak Creek Canyon, a sort of watchpocket Grand Canyon, eighteen serpentine miles south of Flagstaff, Arizona. There, tucked away in the woods, Nabokov devoted himself to literature (working on translations of the *Song of Igor's Campaign,* the twelfth-century Russian epic, and *Invitation to a Beheading,* a novel he wrote in Paris during the 1930s) and lepidoptera. For a couple of days, lepidoptera won out.

On a Monday morning, for instance, Nabokov, dressed in dungarees, sport shirt and sweater, emerged from his pine cabin to sniff the air and see the morning sun. "It is now nine o'clock," he said, lying. It was really only eight-thirty, but Nabokov keeps moving all of his clocks and watches ahead to make his wife move faster so he can get to his butterflies all the sooner. "The butterflies won't be up for another hour," he admitted, however. "This is a deep canyon, and the sun has to go some way up the rim of the mountain to cast its light. The grass is damp, and the butterflies generally come out when it's dry. They are late risers. Of course, in the plains they are up earlier at eight o'clock and flying merrily."

He moved inside, sat down on a sofa and picked up a thick brown volume entitled *Colorado Butterflies.* He opened to Nabokov's Wood Nymph on page eleven. "This butterfly which I discovered has nothing to do with nymphets," he said, smiling. "I discovered it in the Grand Canyon in 1941.

I know it occurs here, but it is difficult to find. I hope to find it today. I'll be looking for it. It flies in the speckled shade early in June, though there's another brood at the end of the summer, so you came at the right time." He turned to page 161 showing Nabokov's Blue. "Another group of butterflies I'm interested in are called Blues. This I discovered in Telluride in southwest Colorado." He picked up another book, Alexander Klots's *A Field Guide to the Butterflies*, and opened to the page on the Orange-Margined Blues. Proudly, he pointed to a sentence which read, "The recent work of Nabokov has entirely rearranged the classification of this genus." A look of bliss spread across his face. "The thrill of gaining information about certain structural mysteries in these butterflies is perhaps more pleasurable than any literary achievement," he said. Two pages later he pointed to the entry on *Lycaeides melissa samuelis*, a subspecies known as the Karner Blue, and said, "I discovered it and named it *samuelis* after Samuel Scudder, probably one of the greatest lepidopterists who ever lived. Karner is a little railway station between Schenectady and Albany. People go there on Sundays to picnic, shedding papers and beer cans. Among this, the butterfly."

Mrs. Nabokov called him to breakfast – soft-boiled eggs, toast and coffee. "The Southwest is a wonderful place to collect," he said over his soft-boiled eggs. "There's a mixture of arctic and subtropical fauna. A wonderful place to collect."

At 9:35 (Nabokov standard time), he got up to get his net and a blue cloth cap. The thrill of the chase was upon him as he left the cabin and headed south down a foot trail paralleling Oak Creek. "Good luck, Professor!" the motel manager shouted. Nabokov chuckled. His eyes sweeping the brush on either side of the trail, Nabokov said, "This Nabokov's Wood Nymph is represented by several subspecies, and there's one here. It is in this kind of country that my nymph occurs."

He stopped and pointed with the handle of his net to a butterfly clinging to the underside of a leaf. "Disruptive coloration," he said, noting the white spots on the wings. "A bird comes and wonders for a second. Is it two bugs? Where is the head? Which side is which? In that split second the butterfly is gone. That second saves that individual and that species. You may call it a large Skipper."

Nabokov walked on. At 9:45, he gave a quick flick with the net. "This is a checkered butterfly," he said, looking at his catch. "There are countless subspecies. The way I kill is the European, or Continental, way. I press the thorax at a certain point like this. If you press the abdomen, it just oozes out." He took the butterfly from the net and held it in the palm of his hand. "This," he exclaimed, "is a beauty! Such a beautiful fresh specimen. *Melitaea anicia.*" He took a Band-Aid box from his pocket, shook loose a Glassine envelope and slid *Melitaea anicia* home to rest. "It's safe in the envelope until I can get to a laboratory and spread it."

In good spirits, he pushed on. Something fluttered across the trail. "A common species," he said, walking on, maneuvering the net before him. "The thing is," he said, "when you hit the butterfly, turn the net at the same time to form a bag in which the butterfly is imprisoned." No sooner had he spoken than he darted forward. "A large male!" he cried as he deftly made a backhand volley. He held the net up for examination. "I'm not going to kill it," he said. "A common species." He released the butterfly which flew off.

Nearby, another butterfly was feeding on a flower, but Nabokov ignored it. "A dusky-wing Skipper. Common." At 10:03, he passed a *clarus* sitting on a bare twig. "I've seen that same individual on the same twig since I've been here," he said. "There are lots of butterflies around, but this individual will chase the others from its perch."

Further down the trail, Nabokov swung but missed a Blue. "Thirty-fifteen," he said. He walked off the trail into an apple orchard where he detected a Hairstreak feeding on a flower. He caught it, then released it. "Forty-fifteen," he said.

Nabokov started walking back toward the cabin. He noted a day-flying Peacock moth. "In quest of a female. It only quiets down at certain hours of the day. I have found them asleep on flowers. Oh, this is wretched work. Where is my Wood Nymph? It's heartbreaking work. Wretched work. I've traveled thousands of miles to get a species I never got. We went to Fort Davis, Texas, but there was no Wood Nymph. Toad-like sheep with their razor-sharp teeth had eaten everything. Horrible!"

At 10:45, Nabokov lunged wildly off the trail and raced up a rocky incline. Whatever it was had escaped in the underbrush. As he picked his way down, he sighed, "There I did something I shouldn't have done. I went up there without looking for rattlesnakes, but I suppose God looks after entomologists as He does after drunkards." At 11:00, he stopped short. "Ah," he said, a tremor of delight rocking him ever so slightly. "Ah. Oh, that's an interesting thing! Oh, gosh, there it goes. A white Skipper mimicking a Cabbage butterfly belonging to a different family. Things are picking up. Still, they're not quite right. Where is my Wood Nymph? It is heartbreaking work," he complained. "Wretched work."

Back at the cabin, Mrs. Nabokov, fresh from writing letters, greeted her husband in Russian. "Let us hurry, darling," he said. Mrs. Nabokov smiled indulgently and followed him down the porch steps to their car, a black 1956 Buick, where she got behind the wheel. Nabokov, who does not drive, did not want to go fast, and to be sure that his wife did not exceed forty miles an hour a warning klaxon was attached to the speedometer. But just as he moves clocks forward a half-hour, his wife moves the klaxon up to sixty. "I always put it a little higher so he doesn't know," she said as he listened intently. "Now I'll put it at forty."

The car would not start. "The car is nervous," Nabokov said. "The car?" asked Véra. "The car," said Vladimir. At last it started. Mrs. Nabokov drove onto Highway 89A and headed to a butterfly hunting ground several miles north. The klaxon went off, and Mrs. Nabokov slowed down. A motorcyclist whizzed by in the opposite direction, and Nabokov shuddered discreetly. The Nabokovs wheeled past the Chipmunk Apartments. The name delighted him. "They have considerably improved all the motels across the country," he said. "No comparison with what they were in the early '40s. I shall never forget the motel-keeperess who said, when I complained that they didn't have hot water, 'Was there any hot water on your grandmother's farm?'" A gale of laughter swept over him.

At 11:26 (Nabokov standard time), Mrs. Nabokov swung over to the left side of the road and parked by Oak Creek. Nabokov leaped out. "Now we'll see something spectacular, I hope!" He hopped across the rocks in the creek, slipped and soaked his right leg. He ignored it. His eyes were on a swarm of butterflies flitting around a puddle. "These are all males and this is their pub," he said. "They suck moisture in the ground. In mountains,

European mountains, where the mules have passed and pissed, it's like a flowery carpet. And it's always the males. Always the males."

He waved farewell to his wife who had stayed on the other side of the creek, and he jogged down a rough trail. He stopped. A butterfly was sipping nectar from yellow asters. "Here's a butterfly that's quite rare. You find it here and there in Arizona. *Lemonias zela.* I've collected quite a few. It will sit there all day. We could come back at four, and it would still be here. The form of its wings and its general manner are very mothlike. Quite interesting. But it is a real butterfly. It belongs to a tremendous family of South American butterflies, and they mimic all kinds of butterflies belonging to other families. Keeping up with the Smiths, you know."

He walked on, then stopped. He said softly, "Now here is something I really want." He swung his net, "'One flick, one dart, and it was in his net.' I'm not suggesting anything." He pressed the thorax of the prey and displayed the butterfly in his hand. "A Checker," he said, "but it seems to be another form of the butterfly we took earlier. Quite interesting. I would like to take some more."

He pushed off the trail into a stand of bushes. From behind one, he exclaimed, "*Chort!*" Reappearing he explained, "I have been doing this since I was five or six, and I find myself using the same Russian swear words. *Chort* means the devil. It's a word I never use otherwise." Back on the trail he swung his net in forehand fashion and missed a butterfly. "Fifteen all," he said.

Nabokov clambered up a pile of rocks. "Haha! Haha!" he shouted, backhanding a butterfly. "A prize! One of the best things I've taken so far. That's a darling. Wonderful! Ha, so unexpectedly. Haha, look at it on this fern. What protective coloration. *Callophrys.* I'm not sure of the species." He turned it over in his hand. "Isn't it lovely? You could travel hundreds of miles and not see one. Ha, what luck! That was so unexpected, and just as I was about to say there was nothing interesting here today. A female that has hibernated. That was very nice, very nice indeed. Quite exciting. That was one of those things that make coming here worthwhile. This will go to Cornell, this little green thing. The best way to put it is, 'A green Hairstreak not readily identified in the field.'" Beaming, Nabokov boxed it.

Woosh! Nabokov had suddenly struck again. He grinned savagely. "I took two in one diabolical stroke of my net. A female Blue. A Lygdamus female Blue, one of the many species of Blues in which I am especially interested. This other, by freakish chance, is a male Blue of another species that was flying with it. That's adultery. Or a step toward adultery." He let the offending male fly free unpunished.

Nabokov worked over a dry stream bed. "Quite a number of little things have appeared today which I haven't seen before. It's picking up. The next week will probably go much faster. I give the Wood Nymph a week to be out. I may go to Jerome for my Wood Nymph. It's a ghost town on the side of a mountain. I know of several collectors who were there and brought back my butterfly a few years ago."

He returned down the trail. Just before crossing Oak Creek to join his wife, he swung his net. "Three with one sweep of the net. This one is an Angle Wing. It has a curiously formed letter C. It mimics a chink of light through a dead leaf. Isn't that wonderful? Isn't that humorous?" He discarded the other two butterflies and danced across the creek to Véra where he carefully boxed the Angle Wing. "They won't lose any color," he said. "I saw an Indian moth, probably taken in the middle of the eighteenth century, that had been presented to Catherine the Great, and the color was still fresh. Some of the butterflies of Linnaeus, the first great naturalist, a Swede, are quite fresh. They are less fragile, I suppose, than pickled human beings."

Mrs. Nabokov headed the Buick south to Sedona for lunch. "I lost two butterfly collections," Nabokov recalled as the car sped along (someone had tampered with the klaxon). "One to the Bolsheviks, one to the Germans. I have another I gave to Cornell. I dream of stealing it back."

At 12:15, the Nabokovs drove into Sedona, which a sign proclaimed as the Flying Saucer Capital of the Universe. "It's a kind of quest, but they are going the wrong way," Nabokov said. After gathering their mail and lunching in a local restaurant, the Nabokovs drove south. "We would like to see if I can get a Blue butterfly." His eyes wallowed in the gorgeous windswept buttes. "It looks like a giant chess game is being played around us." At 2:20, Mrs. Nabokov parked the car by the side of the road. Net at the ready, Nabokov was off like an eager boy. "Mind the snakes," his wife called. "I'm going to inspect the grove," he said, "It interests me." Mrs. Nabokov took a net from the back seat and joined him. "You should see my wife catch butterflies," he said. "One little movement and they're in the net."

The grove was disappointing. "*Rien,*" Nabokov muttered. He probed some bushes. "There is nothing," he said. "A hopeless place." He cautiously inspected a rocky area. " 'Suddenly we heard an ominous rattle, and Mr. Nabokov fell like a log.' " He went back to the car. "I'm sorry this was not a very great show," he said. "Sad." Still, he couldn't leave quite yet. He moved down the edge of the highway peering into bushes. "In Alberta you have to watch for bear." At 2:35, he got in the car, and Mrs. Nabokov drove back to Sedona to shop. There he followed her into the supermarket. "When I was younger I ate some butterflies in Vermont to see if they were poisonous," he said as his wife hovered over the cold-cuts counter. "I didn't see any difference between a Monarch butterfly and a Viceroy. The taste of both was vile, but I had no ill effects. They tasted like almonds and perhaps a green cheese combination. I ate them raw. I held one in one hot little hand and one in the other. Will you eat some with me tomorrow for breakfast?"

Back in their cabin, the Nabokovs set up drinks and hors d'oeuvres for the owners of Forest Houses, Robert Kittredge and his wife. The Kittredges arrived promptly at four (4:30 NST) and Nabokov excused them for being late. He and Kittredge, a fledgling novelist, have the same publisher in England. . . . Occasionally the talk would alight upon butterflies. In delight, Nabokov recalled a pregnant White butterfly that came all the way from Ireland by ship ("She laid her eggs immediately in a kitchen garden in Quebec in 1860"), a marvelous day in Alberta when he found a "treasure, a Nitra Swallowtail, sitting there on bear dung."

When the Kittredges left at 6:30, Nabokov burrowed into a pile of scientific papers and pulled out the thickest one, his article on the Nearctic members of the Genus *Lycaeides* Hübner. "The most interesting part here," he said, settling himself on the sofa, "was to find the structural differences between them in terms of the male organ. These are magnified thirty-four times. These are hooks which the male has to attach to the female. Because of the differences in the size of the hooks, all males cannot copulate with all females. Suddenly in Jackson Hole, I found a hook intermediate between the two. It has the form of the short-hooked species, but the length of the long-hooked species. It is almost impossible to classify. I named it *longinus*. This work took me several years and undermined my health for quite a while. Before, I never wore glasses. This is my favorite work. I think I really did well there." Yes, the Soviets were aware of his work on butterflies. Only in November of last year, one Lubimov had attacked him in the *Literary Gazette*. "He said that I was starving in America, compelled to earn a precarious existence selling butterflies." Nabokov laughed merrily and picked up another paper, this one dealing with an elaborate count of wing scales. "It's impossible to understand," he said, beaming. "But I proved my point, and it will stand forever."

The next morning, Nabokov was as chipper and as restless as ever. "Come on, darling," he called to his wife during breakfast. "The sun is wasting away! It's a quarter to ten." Mrs. Nabokov took her time. "He doesn't know that everyone is wise to him," she said. At 10:10, Nabokov at last succeeded in luring her behind the wheel. "We are going to Jerome, a ghost town," he said happily as the car moved south on 89A. "We are looking for my butterfly, the Wood Nymph, which should be out, I hope, on Mount Mingus." While the car sped through a veritable Lolitaland ("See Tuzigoot Ruins," "See Historic Fort Verde"), Nabokov said, "Butterflies help me in my writing. Very often when I go and there are no butterflies, I am thinking. I wrote most of *Lolita* this way. I wrote it in motels or parked cars. . . .

Nabokov reached Jerome ("Welcome to Ghost City. 3 Places to Eat") at 11:10. "Shall we catch my butterfly today?" Nabokov asked. . . . "We're getting into oaks and pines," he said, joyfully. "The greatest enemy of the lepidopterist is the juniper tree. Charming! Charming! Charming butterfly road!" Mrs. Nabokov swung off the road and parked by a marker announcing the elevation to be 7,023 feet. Both took nets from the back seat and walked up a dirt road bordered by pines. A yellow butterfly danced crazily by. Nabokov swung and missed. "Common," he said. "I'm just getting warmed up." A fifteen-minute search of the terrain revealed nothing.

At 12:20, Mrs. Nabokov drove to the Potato Patch Picnic Ground, a quarter of a mile back down the mountain. Nabokov headed toward an iris-covered meadow. "I can't believe there won't be butterflies here," he said. He was mistaken. "I'm very much disappointed," Nabokov said after searching the meadow. "*Rien. Rien.* Iris is not very attractive to butterflies anyway. It's rather ornamental, and that's it." On the way back to the car, Mrs. Nabokov called excitedly. "Here's a yellow! Here's a yellow!" "I saw it, darling," Nabokov replied calmly. "It is very common. Just an orange Sulphur."

Nabokov got in the car. "It was very sad. 'And then I saw that strong man put his head on his forearms and sob like a woman.'" At 12:40, Mrs. Nabokov stopped again. "This will be our last stop today," Nabokov said. Véra took a net, and they walked up a dirt road. "It is this kind of place that my nymph should be flying, but with the exception of three cows and a calf, there is nothing." "Do we have to mix with cows?" asked Mrs. Nabokov.

They got back in the car and drove back to Jerome. "Sad," said Nabokov. "'His face was now a tear-stained mask.'" Five minutes later, he had Véra stop at Mescal Canyon. "We may be in for a surprise here," he said. Nabokov walked up a dirt road alone. Mrs. Nabokov lent her net to their visitor. With a whoop of joy, the visitor snared a white-winged beauty. Cupping it in his hands, he showed it to Nabokov who dismissed it. "A winged cliché," he said. It had been a poor day for hunting. There would be other days to come, but the visitor wouldn't be there. As the car swung out for the journey home, Nabokov spread his arms and said sadly, "What can I say? What is there to say? I am ashamed for the butterflies. I apologize for the butterflies." [Robert H. Boyle, *At the Top of Their Game*, 124–32]

From letter to George Hessen,[257] July 10, 1959

From Flagstaff, Arizona. In Russian. Unpublished.

In reply to your sweet but short note I am writing you a few lines from a marvelous canyon in Arizona, where since the end of May we have had a charming wooden chalet. Here I finished my translation of *The Song of*

Igor. Here I looked over Mityusha's translation of *Invitation to a Beheading*[258] with great satisfaction. Here a talented reporter from *Sports Illustrated* visited me. Here Vera and I have caught some wonderful butterflies. Here I have refreshed my spirits. [VNA]

From letter to Harry Levin, July 10, 1959

From Flagstaff, Arizona.

I am writing you from the depths of a marvelous, green and red, well watered Arizona canyon where the mingling of deciduous trees with desertic elements of flora forms a fascinating ecological paradox. . . .

I am getting some wonderful butterflies here. The beautiful place where we are staying has been inhabited by Max Ernst and Cholishchev in the past, but we got here by pure chance. [SL 294]

From letter to Francis Hemming, July 14, 1959

From Flagstaff, Arizona. Unpublished.

I would much prefer *you* to rename the genus *Pseudothecla* Nabokov (*Psyche*, vol. 52, page 11, 1945, type *faga* Dognin.[259]

I hope to be in London this autumn and it would be a great pleasure to see you. [VNA]

The Admirable Anglewing

Story. Written 1959–66. Unfinished.

[A blank line indicates a new index card.]
The Admirable Anglewing
notes for a short story[261]

artificial copy — *Danaus plexippus* with
margin cut out with scissurs 260

THE ADMIRABLE ANGLEWING

Polygonia
♂ *Basilarchia* n.sp.

del. V.N.
Feb. 6, 1966

Oliver Smith, curator of insects at the New England Museum of Natural History, had been laid up for three days with a New England cold and when, on a frosty Friday, he resumed his investigation of the genitalia of Sulphurs an unwelcome visit interrupted his work.

A few weeks earlier Dr   the celebrated biologist who

An extraordinary – and irreplaceable – aberration of the Diana Fritillary. In that species the black-dotted ground colour is brownish-orange in the male (as retained marginally, the inner two-thirds of both wings being heavily melanized), cindery and dark blue in the female. The precious freak was a female that happened to have the cindery part of the forewings re-placed by the bright fulvous of the male coloration, in striking contrast with the blue of the secondaries.

In the series where it had stood there was now a gap with a telltale pinhole. Momentarily thinking that the specimen might have got misplaced, Smith pulled halfway out and thrust back in rapid succession several adjoining trays, two above, three below – a mechanical outburst of futile search which petered out at once in that world of ordered wings and classified patterns.

He marched to another cabinet and got rid of the smiling banker and im-passive child by showing them some South American moths freckled and eyed with six-inch tails ending in orchid petals.

that the eminent Professor Burroughs (a visiting biologist who had been dropping in recently) had died   while walking from his hotel to the museum. Everybody agreed that he had looked the picture of health on the day before. He was to lecture that night on Chance and Change in the museum amphitheater.

Re letter

What was done about the Diana? He recalled that he had allowed Dr Burroughs to borrow it for his lecture – he had no doubt returned it by now.

L̶i̶b̶e̶l̶u̶l̶a   ~~Libelula~~

He talked to gloomy Lavrov the coleopterist, and to Bill Uhler the dragonfly man and to Miss Little, the learned old lady who was in charge of
the spiders and it was decided that nothing should be done before
Dr   return

sand paper – spreading board   February 1959
          frock coat's skirts
   the abdomen enveloped by the inner margin
   the black clubbed, tawny tipped antenna
   Pinned it. Had trouble separating the close wettish wings
   Tweasers
   Inserted pin to keep body in place
   Tracing cloth (paper). Taut. But left fore wing came down when started
        on right wing.
   Push up, slight crackle, vein
   Arranged antenna
   Crucified

                                                             June 1959
I have your paper. it is very interesting but I am afraid nothing can be done
before the editorial staff sees your type specimen. The very poor photograph is of no use as evidence although it does show some enigmatic features; and, anyway, you certainly should not have retouched it.

   Claims to the discovery of extraordinary new species of lepidoptera
have not seldom been made and frequently have turned out to refer to
pathological individuals or rare freaks. I question whether your butterfly

is not a *Basilarchia* (*wiedemeyerii* or *arthemis*) with a symmetrically repeated defect in the development of the margins (hence their angularity)
or else an aberration of *Polygonia interrogationis* combining portions of
bleached ground colour with a melanic coalescence of macules. But again,
I can say nothing without seeing the actual specimen. Hybridization between two so widely separate species is certainly out of the question. Let

me add however that the chances of digging up a perfectly new American Vanessid in our times are fantastically small. The December issue will come out Monday the 15th. I suppose you could just make it if you rushed the specimen and it proved to be all you say it is.

[in margin] We had a specimen which you may have seen (alas, it is lost) of a gynandromorph

carpet beetle – *Anthrenus scrophulariae* also called "buffalo bug"
two other species are the museum pests *Anthrenus varius* and *A. musaeorum*

Burzels

1) She had married the barber   the widow of a
        next door   German cobbler
            and *manicure*

The "fascinating collection" her brother had spoken of reduced itself to three oversized old-fashioned showcases with glassed lids secured by hooklets. The dustiest of the three housed more than a score of huge, faded, fat-bodied moths some of which had lost their abdomens or heads or even, in a few instances, had completely disintegrated at their pins; it was the only box hung up picturewise and after scanning its crippled contents and the bits of fawn fluff in the lower corners, Mrs Burzel angrily denounced the *Anthrenus* beetles which she called "grey ladybugs" that had somehow got in and fed on the "spinners"

Burzels

2) The German cobbler's widow was a Russian

A tear burned her eyelid – often she helped to spread some of those freshly hatched beauties. And now the havoc . . .

That showcase looked like an ancient battlefield full of tattered banners, dismembered corpses and wide-open dead eyes. She turned to the other two boxes stacked on a chest of drawers. One contained dragonflies and hawkmoths; in the other were specimens of showy local butterflies. Among them the least practised   could distinguish a series of the black-and-white Admirables one could have seen earlier in the year sailing along forest lanes.

The boy eagerly helped his mother to loosen the tight hooks and tease off the lid. She sneezed. Then she slapped his hand aside

3)

and delicately took out one of those handsome nymphs. She carried it to the kitchen, holding it aloft by the pinhead, fingers bunched like those of a Russian about to bless someone.

Despite her dexterity with scissors, she managed to break off a silky wing, and another specimen had to be fetched. This time she was more successful.

She did her best   4)

trying to copy the jagged outline of what was left of the unique and invaluable rarity, by snipping at the wavy fringes of the fairly tough old "admiral" to indent them more deeply and produce the semblance of a "tail" on each hindwing. You'll bust it, you'll bust it, the jittery children kept crying until told to stop jumping up and down and "shaking the whole house." A second specimen was sacrificed. The third, as in a fairy tale, was a success.

4)

One antenna had come off during the operation. The   of the margins, right and left, were roughly symmetrical but to any entomologist that particular White Admirable could look only like an old mouldy specimen of that species whose shape had been altered by an idiot with a pair of manicure scissors. The children, one must add in all fairness, had some intuitive misgivings and hoped their uncle would not notice the box had been rewrapped and check its contents. He did not. He slipped it into

5

the pocket of his overcoat and left for New York. The children clapped their breastbones, exhaling relief. Their mother, very pleased with herself, went to the house of a woman friend whose turn it was to serve coffee and cake to her friends that Sunday.

a mimic of *Limenitis arthemis* Drury, the White Admirable
shape practically the same as that of the Question Mark Anglewing

Atman thought:

The "h" was distressing: his classical education forbid [sic] him to call
it *"arthemoides."* He tried and rejected the other names connected with
Artemis (such [as] Orthia or Laphria). "Diana" would be confusing because of that famous American fritillary. What about the synonyms of
Drury's *arthemis*? *lamina* Fabricius? But there was the awful possibility of
getting into some synonymic trouble. Though perhaps the sinking of *lamina* to *atmanii* by the first reviser was not unpleasant?

　　　exclamationis?　　　*Limenitis arthemis* & (the closest)

Polygonia interrogationis F.

The Question Mark

The possibility of its being a hybrid of the two was excluded by the latter
not occurring where it was captured; by its shape and structure being limited to that of a typical *Polygonia*; by its differing from *P. interrog.* in an
obviously specific rather than aberrational way

maroon marked underside with a silvery exclamation mark beneath on
the hindwing

[VNA]

Lolita: A Screenplay

Written in 1960. Published in 1974.

*[Humbert tours Lolita around the American West to keep her from boredom and from making friends
who could challenge his monopoly.]*

CUT TO:

The Route now offers spectacular scenery
as it snakes up a gigantic mountainside. At the top of the pass, tourists take pictures and feed the marmots. In the next valley we inspect

the collection of frontier lore in a Ghost Town museum. We have a little trouble when the car stalls on a steep incline but some kind youths help. The radiator grill is plastered with dead butterflies.

CUT TO:
A Dirt Road in a Canyon
Humbert pulls up at the bloomy and lush wayside.
HUMBERT: I should not have attempted to take a short cut. We're lost.
LOLITA: Ask that nut with the net over there.
The Butterfly Hunter. His name is Vladimir Nabokov. A fritillary settles with outspread wings on a tall flower. Nabokov snaps it up with a sweep of his net. Humbert walks toward him. With a nip of finger and thumb through a fold of the marquisette Nabokov dispatches his capture and works the dead insect out of the netbag onto the palm of his hand.
HUMBERT: Is that a rare specimen?
NABOKOV: A specimen cannot be common or rare, it can only be poor or perfect.
HUMBERT: Could you direct me –
NABOKOV: You meant "rare species." This is a good specimen of a rather scarce subspecies.
HUMBERT: I see. Could you please tell me if this road leads to Dympleton?
NABOKOV: I haven't the vaguest idea. I saw some loggers (*pointing*) up there. They might know.

[LS 127–28]

From letter to John G. Franclemont, October 3, 1960
From Los Angeles.

I am mailing you three round tins of papered leps which I collected this year in California (mainly Mandeville Canyon, Los Angeles and Glacier Lodge, Inyo County) in between working on the screenplay of LOLITA.

Therein you will find two subspecies of an interesting *Cercyonis* (conspecific with *behri, paula* and *masoni*) from both localities, and some good examples of *P. emigdionis* from above San Bernardino. The names on the envelopes are provisional jottings since I had no time to study the material, had no reference works with me and have no memory for names.   [VNA]

From letter to Edmund Wilson, October 10, 1960
From Los Angeles. Published in *Briefwechsel mit Edmund Wilson.*

Our stay here, under the jacarandas, has been most enjoyable. The screenplay I have been working on since March is now ready, and the job is nicely done. I had seclusion and freedom, and a canyon full of butterflies.   [YALE]

From letter to Samuil Rosov,[262] October 10, 1960
From Los Angeles. In Russian. Unpublished.

You invite us over [to Israel], but look how things stand. Since *I* can't imagine that I could visit Israel, Iran or Tibet and not hunt for butterflies there, and since on the other hand *my wife* vividly imagines that some border guard could fire at or drag away any such hunter, the result is that we'll hardly get to these countries soon.   [VNA]

Interview with Anne Guérin, January 1961
In French. Published in *L'Express.*

When I start to dismantle a butterfly, I suddenly develop very delicate hands and fine fingers and can do everything. Otherwise I'm "all thumbs," as they say in English.   [*L'Express*, January 26, 1961]

Interview with Janine Colombo, January 1961

In French. Published in *L'Information d'Israel*.

– Yes, I'll go to Israel in February.

– In a few weeks?

– Impossible, you see, since I am in the middle of writing a new novel and that will take me some time still, two or three months perhaps.

– So you will come to Israel. Let's see, I'm counting, two, three . . . April? or May?

– In February, I tell you.

– ???

– In February or not at all, and I really mean to go, so it will be in February and only in February!

– Why especially in February? . . .

– Because of the butterflies. . . . And don't look at me with those great big saucer eyes. No, I'm not mad. For me, you see, every country I see in terms of butterflies and in shades of butterflies. I am a collector and I know that a species of butterflies, butterflies of a pastel tone, very rare, can be found on the hills of Jerusalem in February. That's why I want to go there only in February.   [*L'Information d'Israel*, February 3, 1961]

From letter from Véra Nabokov to Laura Mazza,[263] February 20, 1961

From Nice. Unpublished.

Please bear in mind that neither my husband nor I know Italian. Inevitably some of our queries will prove superfluous. But all we are trying to do[264] is to make the sense of the lines as clear as possible to the translator so that he may correct his text accordingly wherever necessary. . . .

One more thing I would like to add. My husband is extremely precise in all his botanic, zoological or scientific terms and attaches great importance to a correct translation of these terms. Here too he will be happy to help with any useful information or elucidation that may make the translator's task easier. . . .

Una scoperta[265]

line 8. "dingy underside" – something like "scolorito roverscio" (not "blackish abdomen"); "chequered fringe" – could it be "frangia a scacchi"? Chequered means in little checks.

line 9. "teased out" means merely "extracted." This is important.

line 10. "corroded" means just that: could it be "corrosi"? The dead butterfly is immersed into a solvent to make dissection possible.

line 12. "piattino." Is it clear that "slide" is a narrow strip of glass used in laboratories for inserting small particles in a drop of liquid under the microscope for examination? . . .

line 22. This is an allusion to the biblical "moth and rust." "Creeping relatives" are the destructive moths with which every curator of insects in a museum has to lead a ceaseless battle to protect the collections. Is "rust" adequately rendered by "sudicio"? We cannot express an opinion because we do not know how the passage is rendered in Italian translations of the Bible.

line 23. Not "rare specimens" but "type specimens." Type specimens are those from which the original description has been made. There must be an accepted term for this in science.

line 28. "Red label." "Red" is the key word because in museums, at least in American museums, the labels on type specimens are red, on ordinary specimens, white.

[VNA]

From letter to Robert Crane,[266] March 15, 1961

From Nice.

As a novelist, I have, I think, imagined some of my characters driving through New Jersey. As a lepidopterist, I see maps and visualize regions in terms of the butterflies found in this or that place; and New Jersey is for me the State from which have been described certain exciting butterflies, such as Hessel's Hairstreak (type locality: Lakehurst) or Aaron's Skipper (type locality: Cape May). [SL 327]

Interview with Claude Mercadié, April 1961

In French. Published in *Nice-Matin*. *(See also* LS *xii.)*

"I spent the day in the hills around Villeneuve-Loubet," he told us. "Come and see what I caught."

We followed him into his study.

"Look."

He opened a cardboard container, from that he took out a silk pouch, and from that he took out . . .

"Look. I managed to capture this at the foot of a strawberry tree after four hours of stalking. It's marvelous."

Under our eyes, he spread out a minute butterfly, hardly as big as a fingernail.

"It's a *Callophrys avis*," he told us. "Careful, you must write *avis* without a capital. It's a very rare species, very important. I was very lucky."[267]

[*Nice-Matin*, April 13, 1961]

Pale Fire

Excerpts from novel. Written in 1960–61. Published in 1962.

[In his poem "Pale Fire" the American poet John Shade, at sixty-one, sums up his life and confronts the suicide, two years previously, of his twenty-three-year-old only child, Hazel. Here he describes the garden of the house he has lived in all his life.]

> I had a favorite young shagbark there
> With ample dark jade leaves and a black, spare,
> Vermiculated trunk. The setting sun

Bronzed the black bark, around which, like undone

Garlands, the shadows of the foliage fell.

It is now stout and rough; it has done well.

White butterflies turn lavender as they

Pass through its shade where gently seems to sway

The phantom of my little daughter's swing.

[PF 34]

[Shade addresses his wife Sybil, whom he has known since high school.]

Come and be worshiped, come and be caressed,

My dark Vanessa, crimson-barred, my blest

My Admirable butterfly! Explain

How could you, in the gloam of Lilac Lane,

Have let uncouth, hysterical John Shade

Blubber your face, and ear, and shoulder blade?

[PF 42–43]

[Shade sets the scene for his sadly unattractive-looking daughter's last year.]

Another winter was scrape-scooped away.

The Toothwort White[268] haunted our woods in May.

Summer was power-mowed, and autumn, burned.

Alas, the dingy cygnet never turned

Into a wood duck. And again your voice:

"But this is prejudice! You should rejoice

That she is innocent. Why overstress

The physical? She *wants* to look a mess.

Virgins have written some *resplendent* books. . . ."

[PF 44]

[Reporting the night Hazel committed suicide, Shade alternates between recounting his daughter's blunt rejection by a blind date and his watching television at home with his wife while they wonder how Hazel's first date is turning out.]

> *He took one look at her,*
> *And shot a death ray at well-meaning Jane.*

A male hand traced from Florida to Maine
The curving arrows of Aeolian wars.
You said that later a quartet of bores,
Two writers and two critics, would debate
The Cause of Poetry on Channel 8.
A nymph came pirouetting, under white
Rotating petals, in a vernal rite
To kneel before an altar in a wood
Where various articles of toilet stood.[269]

[PF 47–48]

[Pondering whether his vision in a near-death experience is genuine, Shade compares it to the deceptions of natural mimicry.]

> In life, the mind
Of any man is quick to recognize
Natural shams, and then before his eyes
The need becomes a bird, the knobby twig
An inchworm, and the cobra head, a big
Wickedly folded moth.[270]

[PF 59]

[Shade spends a term at "I.P.H., a lay/Institute (I) of Preparation (P)/For the Hereafter (H)."]

That tasteless venture helped me in a way.
I learnt what to ignore in my survey
Of death's abyss. And when we lost our child
I knew there would be nothing: no self-styled
Spirit would touch a keyboard of dry wood
To rap out her pet name; no phantom would
Rise gracefully to welcome you and me
In the dark garden, near the shagbark tree.

[PF 57]

[Shade concludes his poem serenely, confident that the harmonies of his art can resolve the discords of his life.]

> I'm reasonably sure that we survive
> And that my darling somewhere is alive,
> As I am reasonably sure that I
> Shall wake at six tomorrow, on July
> The twenty-second, nineteen fifty-nine,
> And that the day will probably be fine;
> So this alarm clock let me set myself,
> Yawn, and put back Shade's "Poems" on their shelf.
>
> But it's not bedtime yet. The sun attains
> Old Dr. Sutton's last two windowpanes.
> The man must be – what? Eighty? Eighty-two?
> Was twice my age the year I married you.
> Where are you? In the garden. I can see
> Part of your shadow near the shagbark tree.
> Somewhere horseshoes are being tossed. Click. Clunk.
> (Leaning against its lamppost like a drunk.)
> A dark Vanessa with a crimson band
> Wheels in the low sun, settles on the sand
> And shows its ink-blue wingtips flecked with white.
> And through the flowing shade and ebbing light
> A man, unheedful of the butterfly –
> Some neighbor's gardener, I guess – goes by
> Trundling an empty barrow up the lane.

[PF 69]

[In his commentary to "Pale Fire," Shade's neighbor and university colleague, Charles Kinbote, recently arrived from Zembla, often explains how he tried to inspire Shade to write the story of the recent flight from Zembla of the country's deposed king, Charles II ("the Beloved"). Note to line 49, "shagbark."]

A hickory. Our poet shared with the English masters the noble knack of transplanting trees into verse with their sap and shade. Many years ago

Disa, our King's Queen, whose favorite trees were the jacaranda and the maidenhair, copied out in her album a quatrain from John Shade's collection of short poems *Hebe's Cup,* which I cannot refrain from quoting here (from a letter I received on April 6, 1959, from southern France):

THE SACRED TREE

The ginkgo leaf, in golden hue, when shed,

    A muscat grape,

    Is an old-fashioned butterfly, ill-spread,

    In shape.[271]

[PF 93]

[Note to line 71, "parents." Kinbote describes Charles II's father, Alfin the Vague].
King Alfin's absent-mindedness was strangely combined with a passion for mechanical things, especially for flying apparatuses. In 1912, he managed to rise in an umbrella-like Fabre "hydroplane" and almost got drowned in the sea between Nitra and Indra.[272]

[PF 103]

[Note to lines 90–93, "Her room," etc., where Shade describes the bedroom of his Aunt Maud, who brought him up after his parents' early death.]
In the draft, instead of the final text:

    . . . . her room

    We've kept intact. Her trivia for us

    Retrace her style: the leaf sarcophagus

    (A Luna's dead and shriveled-up cocoon)

The reference is to what my dictionary defines as "a large, tailed, pale green moth, the caterpillar of which feeds on the hickory." I suspect Shade altered this passage because his moth's name clashed with "Moon" in the next line.

[PF 114]

[Note to line 130. After the Zemblan revolution, King Charles II is imprisoned in a room in his own palace.]

The fleeting and faint but thousands of times repeated action of the same sun that was accused of sending messages from the tower, had gradually patinated this picture which showed the romantic profile and broad bare shoulders of the forgotten actress Iris Acht, said to have been for several years, ending with her sudden death in 1888, the mistress of Thurgus. . . .

[PF 121]

[The King escapes through a secret tunnel leading from this room that he had once explored, but not found the exit from, in his childhood. After closing the tunnel entrance behind him, he switches on a flashlight.]

The dim light he discharged at last was now his dearest companion, Oleg's ghost, the phantom of freedom. He experienced a blend of anguish and exultation, a kind of amorous joy, the like of which he had last known on the day of his coronation, when, as he walked to his throne, a few bars of incredibly rich, deep, plenteous music (whose authorship and physical source he was never able to ascertain) struck his ear, and he inhaled the hair oil of the pretty page who had bent to brush a rose petal off the footstool, and by the light of his torch the King now saw that he was hideously garbed in bright red.[273]

[PF 133]

[Note to line 149, "one foot upon a mountain." Kinbote describes Charles II's escape from imprisonment and his flight over the mountains. After a night's refuge with a peasant couple, their daughter points him on his early way.]

A sepulchral chill emanated from the sheer cliff along which the trail ascended; but on the opposite precipitous side, here and there between the tops of fir trees growing below, gossamer gleams of sunlight were beginning to weave patterns of warmth. At the next turning this warmth enveloped the fugitive, and a black butterfly came dancing down a pebbly rake.

[PF 142]

The King, now at the most critical point of his journey, looked about him, scrutinizing the few promenaders and trying to decide which of them might be police agents in disguise, ready to pounce upon him as soon as he vaulted the parapet and made for the Rippleson Caves. Only a single sail dyed a royal red marred with some human interest the marine expanse. Nitra and Indra (meaning "inner" and "outer"), two black islets that seemed to address each other in cloaked parley, were being photographed from the parapet by a Russian tourist, thickset, many-chinned, with a general's fleshy nape. [PF 145]

[Note to line 238, "empty emerald case."]

This, I understand, is the semitransparent envelope left on a tree trunk by an adult cicada that has crawled up the trunk and emerged. Shade said that he had once questioned a class of three hundred students and only *three* knew what a cicada looked like. Ignorant settlers had dubbed it "locust," which is, of course, a grasshopper, and the same absurd mistake has been made by generations of translators of Lafontaine's *La Cigale et la Fourmi* (see lines 243–244). The *cigale's* companion piece, the ant, is about to be embalmed in amber.

During our sunset rambles, of which there were so many, at least nine (according to my notes) in June, but dwindling to two in the first three weeks of July (they shall be resumed Elsewhere!), my friend had a rather coquettish way of pointing out with the tip of his cane various curious natural objects. He never tired of illustrating by means of these examples the extraordinary blend of Canadian Zone and Austral Zone that "obtained," as he put it, in that particular spot of Appalachia where at our altitude of about 1,500 feet northern species of birds, insects and plants commingled with southern representatives. As most literary celebrities, Shade did not seem to realize that a humble admirer who has cornered at last and has at last to himself the inaccessible man of genius, is considerably more interested in discussing with him literature and life than in being told that the "diana" (presumably a flower) occurs in New Wye together with the "atlantis" (presumably another flower), and things of that sort.[274] [PF 168–69]

[Note to line 270, "My dark Vanessa."]

It is *so* like the heart of a scholar in search of a fond name to pile a butterfly genus upon an Orphic divinity on top of the inevitable allusion to *Van*homrigh, *Esther!* In this connection a couple of lines from one of Swift's poems (which in these backwoods I cannot locate) have stuck in my memory:

> When, lo! *Vanessa* in her bloom
> Advanced like *Atalanta's* star

As to the Vanessa butterfly, it will reappear in lines 993–995 (to which see note). Shade used to say that its Old English name was The Red Admirable, later degraded to The Red Admiral. It is one of the few butterflies I happen to be familiar with. Zemblans call it *harvalda* (the heraldic one) possibly because a recognizable figure of it is borne in the escutcheon of the Dukes of Payn. In the autumn of certain years it used to occur rather commonly in the Palace Gardens and visit the Michaelmas daisies in company with a day-flying moth. I have seen The Red Admirable feasting on oozy plums and, once, on a dead rabbit. It is a most frolicsome fly. An almost tame specimen of it was the last natural object John Shade pointed out to me as he walked to his doom (see, see now, my note to lines 993–995).

[PF 172]

[Note to line 316, "The Toothwort White haunted our woods in May."]
Frankly, I am not certain what this means. My dictionary defines "toothwort" as "a kind of cress" and the noun "white" as "any pure white breed of farm animal or a certain genus of lepidoptera." Little help is provided by the variant written in the margin:

> In woods Virginia Whites occurred in May

Folklore characters, perhaps? Fairies? Or cabbage butterflies?[275]

[PF 183–84]

[Note to line 347, "old barn."]
The light never came back but it gleams again in a short poem "The Nature of Electricity," which John Shade had sent to the New York magazine *The Beau and the Butterfly*,[276] some time in 1958, but which appeared only after his death . . .

[PF 192]

[Note to line 408, "A male hand." Kinbote describes the advance from Zembla of Gradus, the designated assassin of King Charles, and coordinates it with the composition of Shade's poem. Here Gradus has been seeking the king's traces in a villa in Lex, above Lake Geneva.]

Gradus as he stood there, and moodily looked down at the red tiles of Lavender's villa snuggling among its protective trees, could make out, with some help from his betters, a part of the lawn and a segment of the pool, and even distinguish a pair of sandals on its marble rim – all that remained of Narcissus. One assumes he wondered if he should not hang around for a bit to make sure he had not been bamboozled. From far below mounted the clink and tinkle of distant masonry work, and a sudden train passed between gardens, and a heraldic butterfly *volant en arrière,*[277] sable, a bend gules, traversed the stone parapet, and John Shade took a fresh card.

[PF 202]

[Note to line 470, "Negro."]

The juxtaposition of the phrases "a white" and "a colored man" always reminded my poet, so imperiously as to dispel their accepted sense, of those outlines one longed to fill with their lawful colors – the green and purple of an exotic plant, the solid blue of a plumage, the geranium bar of a scalloped wing. "And moreover [he said] we, whites, are not white at all, we are mauve at birth, then tea-rose, and later all kinds of repulsive colors."[278]

[PF 218]

[Note to line 678, "into French." Kinbote discusses the translations of Sybil Shade, the poet's wife.]

The other poem, Andrew Marvell's "The Nymph on the Death of her Fawn," seems to be, technically, even tougher to stuff into French verse. . . . And finally, the lovely closule:

> Had it lived long it would have been
> Lilies without, roses within

. . . How magnificently those two lines can be mimed and rhymed in our magic Zemblan ("the tongue of the mirror," as the great Conmal has termed it)!

Id wodo bin, war id lev lan,
Indran iz lil ut roz nitran.

[PF 242]

[Note to line 691, "the attack."]

amid an ovation of crickets and that vortex of yellow and maroon butterflies that so pleased Chateaubriand on *his* arrival in America[279]   [PF 247]

[Note to line 949, "and all the time."]

We know already some of his gestures, we know the chimpanzee slouch of his broad body and short hindlegs. We have heard enough about his creased suit. We can at last describe his tie, an Easter gift from a dressy butcher, his brother-in-law in Onhava: imitation silk, color chocolate brown, barred with red, the end tucked into the shirt between the second and third buttons, a Zemblan fashion of the nineteen thirties – and a father-waistcoat substitute according to the learned.[280]   [PF 277]

[Note to lines 993–995, "A dark Vanessa," etc. Just after writing this final passage of his poem, Shade has accepted Kinbote's invitation for a drink, but before they get inside Kinbote's rented home, a gunman shoots and kills Shade.]

One minute before his death, as we were crossing from his demesne to mine and had begun working up between the junipers and ornamental shrubs, a Red Admirable (see note to line 270) came dizzily whirling around us like a colored flame. Once or twice before we had already noticed the same individual, at that same time, on that same spot, where the low sun finding an aperture in the foliage splashed the brown sand with a last radiance while the evening's shade covered the rest of the path. One's eyes could not follow the rapid butterfly in the sunbeams as it flashed and vanished, and flashed again, with an almost frightening imitation of conscious play which now culminated in its settling upon my delighted friend's sleeve. It took off, and we saw it next moment sporting in an ecstasy of frivolous haste around a laurel shrub, every now and then perching on a lacquered leaf and sliding down its grooved middle like a boy down the banisters on his birthday. Then the tide of the shade reached the laurels, and the magnificent, velvet-and-flame creature dissolved in it.   [PF 290]

[From Index.]

Botkin, V., American scholar of Russian descent, *894;* King-bot, maggot of extinct fly that once bred in mammoths and is thought to have hastened their phylogenetic end, *247;* bottekin-maker, *71; bot,* plop, and *botelïy,* big-bellied (Russ.); botkin or bodkin, a Danish stiletto.   [PF 306]

Disa, Duchess of Payn, of Great Payn and Mone; my lovely, pale, melancholy Queen, haunting my dreams, and haunted by dreams of me, b. 1928; her album and favorite trees, 49; married 1949, 80; her letters on ethereal paper with a watermark I cannot make out, her image torturing me in my sleep, 433.

Embla, a small old town with a wooden church surrounded by sphagnum bogs at the saddest, loneliest, northmost point of the misty peninsula, 149, 433.[281]   [PF 306]

Kinbote, Charles, Dr., an intimate friend of S, his literary adviser, editor and commentator; first meeting and friendship with S, *Foreword;* his interest in Appalachian birds, *1;* his good-natured request to have S use his stories, *12;* his modesty, *34;* his having no library in his Timonian cave, *39;* his belief in his having inspired S, *42;* his house in Dulwich Road, and the windows of S's house, *47;* Prof. H. contradicted and corrected, *61, 71;* his anxieties and insomnias, *62;* the map he made for S, *71;* his sense of humor, *79, 91;* his belief that the term "iridule" is S's invention, *109;* his weariness, *120;* his sports activities, *130;* his visit to S's basement, *143;* his trusting the reader enjoyed the note *149;* boyhood and the Orient Express recalled, *162;* his request that the reader consult a later note, *169;* his quiet warning to G, *171;* his remarks on critics and other sallies endorsed by S, *172;* his participation in certain festivities elsewhere, his being debarred from S's birthday party upon coming home, and his sly trick next morning, *181;* his hearing about Hazel's "poltergeist" phase, *230;* poor who? *231;* his futile attempts to have S get off the subject of natural history and report on the work in progress, *238;* his recollection of the quays in Nice and Mentone, *240;* his utmost courtesy towards his friend's wife, *247;* his limited knowledge of lepidoptera and the sable gloom of his nature marked like a dark Vanessa with gay flashes, *270;*   [PF 308]

Nitra and Indra, twin islands off Blawick, 149.   [PF 311]

Vanessa, the Red Admirable (*sumpsimus*), evoked, *270*; flying over a parapet on a Swiss hillside, *408*; figured, *470*; caricatured, *949*; accompanying S's last steps in the evening sunshine, *993*.   [PF 314]

From letter from Véra Nabokov to Morris and Alison Bishop,[282] November 4, 1961

From Montreux.

Vladimir misses the States very much, the language, the general atmosphere, everything, including the American lepidoptera. However, there are certain things right now that make it necessary for him to be in Europe.

[SL 331]

From interview with Phyllis Meras, spring 1962

For seven years, you see, I was responsible for the butterflies at Harvard. I was practically curator there. There's a butterfly in every one of my novels. One of the first things I ever wrote in English was a paper on lepidoptera I prepared at the age of 12. It wasn't published because a butterfly I described had been described by somebody else. But the paper itself was written in beautiful, precise English.   [*Providence Sunday Journal*, May 13, 1962]

[From Phyllis Meras's typescript.]

"Do I have anything in mind next? No, I'm closing up the workshop for a while. I'm a little tired now, I must say."

"Except that every now and then he talks about wanting to write a book on butterflies," Mrs. Nabokov said.

"Yes, and what I would really like to do is have a special institute for breeding a certain genus of caterpillar that lives on special breeds of violets in North America, but there is one insurmountable obstacle. My wife hates caterpillars."   [VNA]

From interview by New York journalists, June 5, 1962

From VN's notes, as published by him in SO.

Q: When did you start writing in English?

A: I was bilingual as a baby (Russian and English) and added French at five years of age. In my early boyhood all the notes I made on the butterflies I collected were in English, with various terms borrowed from that most delightful magazine *The Entomologist.* [SO 5]

From interview by Peter Duval-Smith and Christopher Burstall, July 1962

For BBC program *Bookstand.* Published in *The Listener*, November 22, 1962.

Q: You're a professional lepidopterist?

A: Yes, I'm interested in the classification, variation, evolution, structure, distribution, habits, of lepidoptera: this sounds very grand, but actually I'm an expert in only a very small group of butterflies. I have contributed several works on butterflies to the various scientific journals – but I want to repeat that my interest in butterflies is exclusively scientific.

Q: Is there any connection with your writing?

A: There is in a general way, because I think that in a work of art there is a kind of merging between the two things, between the precision of poetry and the excitement of pure science.

Q: In your new novel, *Pale Fire,* one of the characters says that reality is neither the subject nor the object of real art, which creates its own reality. What is that reality?

A: Reality is a very subjective affair. I can only define it as a kind of gradual accumulation of information; and as specialization. If we take a lily, for instance, or any other kind of natural object, a lily is more real to a naturalist than it is to an ordinary person. But it is still more real to a botanist. And yet another stage of reality is reached with that botanist who is a specialist in lilies. You can get nearer and nearer, so to speak, to reality; but you never get near enough because reality is an infinite succession of steps, levels of perception, false bottoms, and hence unquenchable, unattainable. You can

VN and Véra on a hunt staged for *Life* magazine. (*Vogue/Joffe*) VN in wet parka but still with net in hand, Zermatt, Switzerland, late July 1962. (*Horst Tappe*)

know more and more about one thing but you can never know everything about one thing: it's hopeless. So that we live surrounded by more or less ghostly objects – that machine, there, for instance. It's a complete ghost to me – I don't understand a thing about it and, well, it's a mystery to me, as much of a mystery as it would be to Lord Byron.   [SO 10]

From letter from Vladimir and Véra Nabokov to Peter and Joan de Petersen,[283] July 24, 1962

Last week a team of very brilliant young television men who put on "The Bookman" show for the BBC came over for a televised interview with Vladimir. Since they brought a kind of girl Friday with them from London and a three-man team of technicians from Zurich, and since the six of them with all their photographic and sound-track equipment followed Vladimir for two days all over Zermatt, mostly in cabs, unpacking, putting up camera and mikes, repacking, moving to another location, and all the time shooting pictures of V. catching butterflies or talking, this occasion, I'm afraid, became for many tourists the highlight of their stay here. They followed in droves! [SL 339]

Letter to Elena Sikorski, August 8, 1962

In Russian.

Hotel Ermitage Napoleon
**** DIGNE (Basses-Alpes) France
   8.VIII.1962

Hello, my dear.
   We're spending the night here after *glorious* collecting near Gap (H-A). We go down to Cannes tomorrow.

[*Perepiska s sestroy* 105]

From Nabokov's 1962 diary, undated end pages

If a lepid. . . . and if there is one small cloud in the sky, that cloud. . . .

The two remarkable differences between Eur. and Amer. butt. faunas

Local species. Overcollecting [VNA]

From interview with Alvin Toffler, March 1963

Published in *Playboy*, April 1964.

Q: Can you tell us something more about the actual creative process involved in the germination of a book – perhaps by reading a few random notes for or excerpts from a work in progress?

VN below and Véra above,
on a hot day in Zermatt,
late July 1962.

A: Certainly not. No fetus should undergo an exploratory operation. But I can do something else. This box contains index cards with some notes I made at various times more or less recently and discarded when writing *Pale Fire*. It's a little batch of rejects. Help yourself. . . . "Berry: the black knob on the bill of the mute swan" . . . "Dropworm: a small caterpillar hanging on a thread" . . . "Place-name in the Orkneys: Papilio" . . . "Not 'I too, lived in Arcadia,' but 'I,' says Death, 'even am in Arcadia' – legend on a shepherd's tomb (*Notes and Queries*, June 13, 1868, p. 561)." . . . "Marat collected butterflies" . . . "From the aesthetic point of view, the tapeworm is certainly an undesirable boarder. The gravid segments frequently crawl out of a person's anal canal, sometimes in chains, and have been reported a source of social embarrassment" (*Ann. N.Y. Acad. Sci.* 48:558).

[SO 29–31]

Q: You have been quoted as saying: My pleasures are the most intense known to man: butterfly hunting and writing. Are they in any way comparable?

A: No, they belong essentially to quite different types of enjoyment. Neither is easy to describe to a person who has not experienced it, and each is so obvious to the one who has that a description would sound crude and redundant. In the case of butterfly hunting I think I can distinguish four main elements. First, the hope of capturing – or the actual capturing – of the first specimen of a species unknown to science: this is the dream at the back of every lepidopterist's mind, whether he be climbing a mountain in New Guinea or crossing a bog in Maine. Secondly, there is the capture of a very rare or very local butterfly – things you have gloated over in books, in obscure scientific reviews, on the splendid plates of famous works, and that you now see on the wing, in their natural surroundings, among plants and minerals that acquire a mysterious magic through the intimate association with the rarities they produce and support, so that a given landscape lives twice: as a delightful wilderness in its own right and as the haunt of a certain butterfly or moth. Thirdly, there is the naturalist's interest in disentangling the life histories of little-known insects, in learning about their habits and structure, and in determining their position in the scheme of classification – a scheme which can be sometimes pleasurably exploded in a dazzling display of polemical fireworks when a new discovery upsets the old scheme and confounds its obtuse champions. And fourthly, one should not ignore the element of sport, of luck, of brisk motion and robust achievement, of an ardent and arduous quest ending in the silky triangle of a folded butterfly lying on the palm of one's hand.   [SO 39–40]

Q: What is your reaction to the mixed feelings vented by one critic in a review which characterized you as having a fine and original mind, but "not much trace of a generalizing intellect" and as "the typical artist who distrusts ideas"?

A: In much the same solemn spirit, certain crusty lepidopterists have criticized my works on the classification of butterflies, accusing me of being more interested in the subspecies and the subgenus than in the genus and the family. This kind of attitude is a matter of mental temperament, I suppose. The middlebrow or the upper Philistine cannot get rid of the furtive feeling that a book, to be great, must deal in great ideas. Oh, I know the type, the dreary type!   [SO 41]

From notes for interview with Jacob Bronowski, August 1963

For an interview scheduled for British television but canceled before filming because of Bronowski's health.

BRONOWSKI: Are you the same character when you are working with butterflies as when you are working on a novel?

NABOKOV: No, not quite. In ordinary life, for example, I'm strictly righthanded but when manipulating butterflies, I use my left hand more than my right. I am also much more nervous, much gloomier and greedier when hunting them. I omit strange sounds, curses and entreaties. Finally, we should all remember that a lepidopterist reverts in a sense to the ancient apeman who actually fed on butterflies and learned to distinguish the edible from the poisonous kinds.

BRONOWSKI: Do you think scientists are as deeply and personally involved in their work as the novelist is?

NABOKOV: I think it all depends on what scientists or novelists you have in view. Darwin or Gauss were as deeply and rapturously involved in their work as Browning or Joyce. On the other hand, in both camps we have those crowds of imitators, those technicians and administrators and career boys who cannot really be called scientists and artists. They, of course, dismiss their work from their minds after office hours.

BRONOWSKI: Is there something personal and revealing about your choice of butterflies as a subject of study?

NABOKOV: They chose me, not I them. It all started on a cloudless day in my early boyhood – started as a passion and a spell, and a family tradition. There was a magic room in our country house with my father's collection – the old faded butterflies of his childhood, but precious to me beyond words – now almost a hundred years old, if they still exist. My mother taught me to spread my first swallowtail, my first hawkmoth. That enchantment has always remained with me. I have spoken of this much better in my memoir *Speak, Memory*.   [VNA]

From Introduction to Time Reading Program
edition of *Bend Sinister*

Written in September 1963. Published in 1964.

Bend Sinister was the first novel I wrote in America, and that was half a dozen years after she and I had adopted each other. The greater part of the book was composed in the winter and spring of 1945–1946, at a particularly cloudless and vigorous period of life. My health was excellent. My daily consumption of cigarettes had reached the four-package mark. I slept at least four or five hours, the rest of the night walking pencil in hand about the dingy little flat in Craigie Circle, Cambridge, Massachusetts, where I lodged under an old lady with feet of stone and above a young woman with hypersensitive hearing. Every day including Sundays, I would spend up to 10 hours studying the structure of certain butterflies in the laboratorial paradise of the Harvard Museum of Comparative Zoology; but three times a week I stayed there only till noon and then tore myself away from microscope and camera lucida to travel to Wellesley (by tram and bus, or subway and railway), where I taught college girls Russian grammar and literature.

The book was finished on a warm rainy night, more or less as described at the end of Chapter Eighteen. [BS xi]

I reread my books rarely, and then only for the utilitarian purpose of controlling a translation or checking a new edition; but when I do go through them again, what pleases me most is the wayside murmur of this or that hidden theme.

Thus, in the second paragraph of Chapter Five comes the first intimation that "someone is in the know" – a mysterious intruder who takes advantage of Krug's dream to convey his own peculiar code message. The intruder is not the Viennese Quack (all my books should be stamped Freudians, Keep Out), but an anthropomorphic deity impersonated by me. In the last chapter of the book this deity experiences a pang of pity for his creature and hastens to take over. Krug, in a sudden moonburst of madness, understands that he is in good hands: nothing on earth really matters, there is nothing to fear, and death is but a question of style, a mere literary device, a musical resolution. And as Olga's rosy soul, emblemized already in an earlier chapter (Nine), bombinates[284] in the damp dark at the bright window of my room, comfortably Krug returns unto the bosom of his maker. [BS xviii–xix]

From Foreword to *The Defense*

Written December 1963. Published in *The Defense* (1964).

The Russian title of this novel is *Zashchita Luzhina,* which means "the Luzhin defense" and refers to a chess defense supposedly invented by my creature, Grandmaster Luzhin: the name rhymes with "illusion" if pronounced thickly enough to deepen the "u" into "oo." I began writing it in the spring of 1929, at Le Boulou – a small spa in the Pyrenees Orientales where I was hunting butterflies – and finished it the same year in Berlin. I remember with special limpidity a sloping slab of rock, in the ulex- and ilex-clad hills,[285] where the main thematic idea of the book first came to me. Some curious additional information might be given if I took myself more seriously. [*Defense* 7]

The Butterflies of Europe

Unfinished lepidopterological book. Researched and written September 1963–August 1965.

Letter to George Weidenfeld,[286] September 18, 1963

From Montreux. Unpublished.

I am even more tempted to do the book of European butterflies than I was when we first discussed it. As I see it, there would be about 3000 specimens represented (counting important subspecies, females when different, and undersides when necessary for identification). Small specimens (expanding, say, one inch or less) should be enlarged. The process of compiling the pictorial material would involve work at the Museum of Natural History in London (at least two months) and possibly some additional research, though not much, in Paris. I would need a research assistant (a trained lepidopterist) to help with the bibliography, the tracking down of specimens, their careful removal from cabinets for photographing, etc.

The volume should stay open when opened, and there should be no tissue paper cover on the plates. Names (not merely numbers) should be *on* the plates, under each figure.

I would have to devote all my time and thought to this which means that all my present projects must be completed first. I think I could begin the museum and library part of the work sometime late in 1964 or early 1965. And, of course, you and Mr. Nicolson would have to make it worth my while undertaking this spectacular job.   [VNA]

Notes for book plan

[A blank line indicates a new index card.]

Sept. 19 [1963]

Notes for Butterfly Picture Book   (1)

(NB) Illust. capable of being magnified by glass without showing confetti dots

33 × 25 centimeters

Plate size: 13 × 10 inches   Background white, of mat texture or appearance (like "pasty" aquarelle paper so as to give the color photographs a semblance of paintings). *No* tissue paper on plates. There are about 300 species of butterflies in Europe, and *all* will be figured, including important subspecies, females when different from males, and undersides (of same specimens as uppersides if possible?) when helping identification. This will make about 2000 specimens in all to be figured. Of these the largest are about 3 inches from tip to tip, the smallest around 1 inch. There would be a minimum of *eight* and a maximum of *fifty* figures per plate, making some 85 plates in all.

Notes . . .   Sept. 19

(2)

The name of the genus will head the plate. The butterflies will be placed in two or three vertical rows (as "series" of specimens are pinned in glass trays) of four to eight specimens in each row. Specimens belonging to the same species will follow each other in a downward sequence (wherever possible) commencing with a male locotype and followed by a female locotype or the locotype's underside, followed in turn by examples of the main local races (subspecies) with their females and or underside if significant. Under every specimen on the plate or under every series of specimens representing the same subspecies, there will be a label-like rectangle enclosing the name of the figured form.

Notes . . .   Sept. 19

(3)

This label will not indicate the subgenus or the describer of the species or subspecies, but will give both latter and former preceded by the first letter of the genus and followed by the mark of the specimen's sex. Thus:

> *P. machaon sphyrus*
> ♂

When this label refers to two or more specimens of the same subspecies in the downward series these specimens will be placed closer together than specimens representing each a different species. Numbers following the vertical sequence will head them, and on the page facing the plate full data will be given for the specimens figured including full generic, subgeneric (in parens.) specific subspecific and authorial names, with sex, locality, date of capture etc., and ref to page of description.   [VNA]

From 1963 diary

OCTOBER 1 Began arranging European butterflies on plates for Weidenfeld edition[.]

NOVEMBER 2 Completed 50 pages of European butterflies (more than a 1000 figures) in outline. Some 25 remain.

NOVEMBER 13 Finished outline drawings of Butterflies of Europe, 2000 figures on 80 plates.   [VNA]

Letter to George Weidenfeld, December 31, 1963

From Montreux. Unpublished.

Dear George,

   I am now able to give you a fairly definitive description of my butterfly book in addition to what I wrote to you on September 18, 1963.

There are about 310 different species of butterflies in Europe. These I have split into 652 subspecies figuring uppersides, and when necessary undersides, of male, and when necessary female, with some examples of variation within the subspecies. I add one plate of striking individual forms. This makes in all 88 plates 13 × 10 inches with 2250 figures (thus an average of 25 figures per plate) arranged in series as done in the glass-topped trays of cabinets containing collections.

European butterflies come roughly in five sizes: 1) large (about 3 inches from tip to tip of forewings); 2) large-medium; 3) medium; 4) small medium; and 5) small (expanding about 1 inch or less). I am sending you samples of sizes 1 and 4. There are not more than half-a-dozen plates of size 1 but at least two dozens of size 5. Some of the plates showing small butterflies have four or five vertical rows of nine or more specimens but the average plate has three rows of around nine specimens.

Now a few words about the two sample plates I enclose. Disregard the jottings in the margins – they are merely my own working memos. The sign ♂ means male; the sign ♀ means female. R stands for underside (Reverse), and the roman numerals, for the broods (spring brood and summer brood, for instance). I would like if possible to have the same individual show upperside and underside. Note in figures 1 and 2 of Plate One the damaged wing and the bent antenna (also the point of the pin). This does not mean that rubbed or torn or badly prepared specimens will be photographed; on the contrary, whenever possible, the freshest examples will be photographed; but on the other hand if only one specimen of a race from a needed locality is available, and that specimen is slightly damaged, it will be used rather than a fresher specimen of the same race from another locality. By "needed" I mean that I plan to have specimens come from the exact locality whence the subspecies was originally described. We shall always sacrifice "beauty" to science with the result that genuine beauty will be achieved. Of course, the great majority of specimens in collections are very fine ones, not chipped as the *machaon machaon* figured here is.

The photographed label on the plate gives the four names of every butterfly: genus (e.g. *Erebia*), subgenus (e.g. *simplicia* – generally placed in parentheses after the genus), species (e.g. *flavofasciata*), and subspecies (e.g.

thiemei) to which the usually abbreviated name of the author of the first description is added. The name of the genus is again used for the first subgenus to be described under it, and the name of the species is again used for the first subspecies to be described under it: e.g. *Papilio (Papilio) machaon machaon* L. On the left page facing the plate full data will be given for each specimen, e.g.: Fig.1: *Papilio (Papilio) machaon machaon* Linnaeus, ♂, Stockholm, Sweden, 14 June, 1924, B.M. ex coll. Tullgren; fig.2: same, underside.

There will be about 200 pages of text; it is too early to discuss the text in any detail but I think it would be nice to have it interpolated with the plates.

I am not sure I have supplied you with all the information you want in regard to the plates. Tell me what else you would like to know.

I wish you a very happy New Year.

As ever,

VLADIMIR NABOKOV   [VNA]

Letter to Nicholas Thompson,[287] February 6, 1964

From Montreux. Unpublished.

Dear Mr. Thompson,

Thanks for your clear and satisfying letter of January 22.

Yes, it would be splendid if the Museum Photographic Department undertook the work.

I would also need a lepidopterist on the museum staff to assist me in various matters, such as the actual handling of boxes etc.

As to the two ways of organizing the illustrations – that of taking a transparency of each individual butterfly (method A) and that of taking a large transparency for a plateful of properly arranged specimens (method B) – I certainly prefer method A, even if an aesthetic blending of backgrounds is not always achievable. In fact, in some instances method A is the only possible one as for example, when there is available in the collection only one cotype or locotype (a specimen coming from the type locality, i.e.

from the same area or exact place – a mountain range in Spain or a village in Croatia – from which came the type specimen of the original description). I do not know how frequently this may happen but it is a possibility to be taken into account, and there are others, such as the necessity of reversing the same individual when certain details of transparent pattern cannot be exactly matched in two examples. On the other hand, there may be entire plates containing more accommodating butterflies (less variable or less rare) where method B might be used without impairing scientific accuracy, but how many such plates there may be, I cannot say without examining the museum's series.

You ask me about getting to London such specimens as are not available at the B.M. This is not so difficult as it sounds. For example, I have set my heart on illustrating Linnaeus' species with Swedish specimens, and since all the butterflies he described are very common ones, mostly found around Uppsala, there would be no difficulty whatsoever of obtaining them from Sweden if necessary.

Yes, I would like to find out more about the Langer book although I doubt very much that it is on the same lines as mine would be.

Yours sincerely,
VLADIMIR NABOKOV   [VNA]

Draft notes for Introduction to *Butterflies of Europe*

[Index card notes on taxonomic and other principles, and selected other notes. A blank line indicates a new index card.]

Classification: I do not see any real necessity for more than ten categories. Category first from bottom to top is the subspecies – *idas bellieri*, second the species, *idas*, third the subgenus, *Lycaeides*, fourth the genus, *Plebejus*, fifth the subfamily, *Plebejinae*, sixth the family, *Lycaenidae*, seventh, suborder, *Rhopalocera* (butterflies), eighth order, *Lepidoptera* (butterflies and moths), ninth subphylum (or class), *Insecta* (insects), tenth phylum, *Arthropoda* (animals with jointed limbs). A given butterfly is known by its first four names in reverse sequence: *Plebejus Lycaeides idas bellieri*. The name of its author is added to the name of the butterfly and the name of subgenus is given[288] (by typographic tradition) in parentheses

Individual forms (aberrations, seasonal forms, female forms etc.) are really generic (or even subfamilial) variations e.g. the aberration interspatial distension and fusion of macules in Lycaeninae and Plebejinae

The family at one end of the taxonomic chain and the subspecies at the other have some objective reality. It is when we move down from the family to the genus that divergences of opinion arise.

A family falls into groups and it is a purely subjective matter whether we call each such group a "subfamily" a "tribe" or a "genus." We gradually get closer again to the realities of nature when we subdivide the genus into subgenera, the subgenera into species and the species into subspecies, provided of course that the genitalic, or in the case of subspecies, alar, distinctions are constant.

The larger the group the blurrier its limits. It matters little whether we place *Danaus* or *Charaxes* (with *Apatura*) or *Satyrus* in separate families or arrange them as subfamilies within *Nymphalidae*. The same in regard to "Riodinidae" or "Riodininae in Lycaenidae"

March 3, 1964

I have avoided using suprageneric names such as the very subjective "subfamily" and "tribe" for the divisions I call "groups" which can be simply denoted by Roman numbers after the name of the family. Within the genus, the nominal subgenus naturally comes first and is always the oldest name (e.g. *Cupido* includes *Cupido* and *Everes* and not *Everes* with *Everes* and *Cupido*); but for the names of the families I have preserved the names employed by all lepidopterists i.e. not deriving rigidly such names from the oldest genus (i.e. not changing *Lycaenidae* to *Cupidinidae*)

June 15, 1964

As of now, I prefer substituting the word "group" with a number only, or a name ending in "-a" for the subfamily (which is much too rigid in the case of many groups) – or perhaps eliminating the level betw. family and genus altogether (?)

The purpose of subgeneric and subfamilial classification is not to make things easier or harder for the collector; its sole purpose is to bring out affinities and distinctions by forming and separating groups of species and groups of genera.

The only real use of subgenera, genera and higher divisions is their enabling one to express in classificatory terms that species A belongs to the same as, or to another than, B, and that both belong to another, higher, group than C

It should be borne in mind that any accepted subdivision of one family may not necessarily be equal in its structural implications to some other subdivision although both are termed genus or subfamily.

Subgenera

We now come to the vexed question of subgenus. It is quite true that when it mascarades as a regular genus (i.e. when hoisted to the same classificational level as some time-honored, "natural" genus in another group) it puzzles and distresses the butterfly collector who (partly because only a few members of a given group – consisting of hundreds of species elsewhere – occur in the locality where he collects) deplores the necessity of placing every catch in a different genus, instead of having all the Blues in one genus and all the Hairstreaks in another. It is true that the expert in one group who has spent a lifetime studying its genitalic structures and on the strength of which he splits it into genera or subgenera which are as familiar and natural things to him, will naively recoil in indignation upon finding the familiar genus in another group of whose structure he knows next to nothing, split into a subgenus by a fellow worker. And finally, it is also true that this expert after splitting an old genus into[289] several genera in one subfamily, will find a certain pleasure – as does an artist who rubs out the pencilled lines of perspective and other delimiting marks in his completed drawing – a certain pleasure in bracketing the subgenera, and using the subfamily as a generic name (the point being that the "level" of this grouping is an illusion, the only thing is to be *consistent* throughout a family of organisms)

The drawbacks of generic splitting are obvious (they are mostly of an esthetic and mnemonic [nature],[290] really). What are their value? First of all by the very act of analyzing a genus (or species) and splitting it into smaller groups, the organisms it treats of are more closely and thoroughly studied. Secondly: this structural genus (or subgenus) tells the zoogeographer things about the distribution and evolution of a group which would otherwise be obscured by the employment of a vague groupment.

In a region where, say, five *Plebejus* (or *Plebejina*) species occur (say, *P. argus, P. idas, P. icarus, P. bellargus*, and *P. arstrache*) the collector may find it a nuisance that each of these Blues is assigned to a different subgenus (or genus). But for the taxonomist who is concerned with world distribution it is of the greatest interest to know that of the so many *Plebejus, Lycaeides* etc these are represented in a given region.

Subgenera
Ponder this
The need of splitting a genus into subgenera depends very much upon the number of monotypic groups in it. If this number is one half (?one third) or more than one half (?one third) of the entire number of groups in the genus, then it is wise not to give these groups subgeneric names.

subgenera mentioned on plate and in text
microgenera
(e.g. *Charcharodus* = *Charcharodus* + *Reverdinus* + *Lavatheria* and *Pyrgus* = *Pyrgus* (t. *malvae*) + *Scelotrix* (t. *sidae*) + *Ateleomorpha* (t. *onopordi*)
not to be mentioned on plates but mentioned in text

When both generic and subgeneric names are given the latter is placed in parentheses after the former eg *Papilio (Papilio)*. The last word in the parenthesis following the name of the species and of its author refers to the place whence the first specimen of the species or subspecies came.

The first, and sometimes only subgenus, given under the genus, and the first, sometimes only subspecies, given under the name of the species are identical with those of the genus and the species and are termed nomino-typical, meaning that they were the first to be described.

If not otherwise stated the type of a genus or subgenus is the first species placed under it. (In a few cases the type is a non-European species, which is then mentioned)

A species is an abstraction represented somewhat more concretely by a subspecies or group of subspecies (geographical races) anatomically dis-tinct from and not interbreeding with other organisms.

for example, when we say that the species *machaon* of the genus *Papilio* is found not only on the continent but in England we mean that England is inhabited by a comparatively small population of the endemic subspe-cies *machaon britannicus* and is moreover visited by vagrants from the continent belonging to *machaon gorganus* or *machaon machaon*

The structural distinction between *P. machaon* and *alexanor* is absolute, and indeed subgeneric, between *machaon* and *alexanor* or between either of them and *podalirius*, it is somewhat less between *machaon* and *hospiton* and still less, in fact teetering on the brink of subspecific between *podalirius* and *feisthamelii*. Thus degrees of which there are an infinite number in Lepid [optera] cannot be represented taxonomically.

The enthusiastic reliance on biological data with meagre morphological characters has led to the erection of many very doubtful species.

There are about   species ("I say "about" because at least ten teeter on the subspecies borderline). As to the number of existing subspecies the question has to be resolved by every new reviser, in this case myself. The great majority of forms described as subspecies during these last fifty years are actually very minor local races within the varietal range of a known subspecies or represent merely arbitrary points in the so-called "cline" between two geographically intergrading subspecies. I have thus chosen only what I consider to be the most important and interesting subspecies, not the minor local forms.

Subspecies   see Van Son Lep. News 1955, p. 7

A true subspecies is a form conditioned by geographical or host [foodplant] isolation. If A and B are such forms occurring in two small areas far apart, a third form C, occurring in another such area may prove to be transitional in markings or structure independent of whether its area is intermediate or not. A second kind of subspecies is the extreme or final geographical product of a cline connecting it with another extreme subspecies. Reversible variation and random transitions are not subspecies.

Infrasubspecific names such as those given to seasonal varieties, individual forms, aberrations, etc. are not used in this [catalogue]

e s p e r i

s e r i p e

I would make it a rule when replacing a preoccupied name by a new one, to base whenever possible on the name (or on the anagram of the name) of the author of the first name. Thus *Boloria alethea* should have been *Brenthis (Boloria) esperi*[291] and *(Clossiana) titania rossica* should have been *Brenthis (Clossiana) titania seripe*.

Caterpillars

Blind compilation impossible. E.g. one author describes the larva of a species as greyish-blue with yellowish stripe, another describes that of an allied species as violet with reddish brown stripe. Actually the colors in both are exactly alike, but *both* describers have missed the fact that in one larva there is always [illegible] pale dot[s?] which the other never has.

Special plate or plates (two?) illustrating albinic forms, melanic aberrations and hybrids.

possible species in the making or hybrids:

Lysandra cormion Nab. (*coridon* × *daphnis*)

Lysandra polonus Zell. = "calydonius," "haffneri" etc (*coridon* × *bellargus*)

Brinteria etc.

Neither Fruhstorfer nor Verity were sufficiently experienced in genitalic studies to settle adequately the taxonomic problem of what to consider a generic, subgeneric or specific difference in regard to the general structure of valve or   in a given group.

Fritillaries

Interesting tendency in the entire group: two forms of melanism: 1) enlargement of dark markings (*not* the aberrational blotching and radiation but a harmonious growth of black pigment) which culminates in the specific melanism of *M. didyma*, and 2) a dusting over of the fulvous areas with dark scales in females resulting in the "valesina" and *M. didyma* or *B. napaea* dark female forms (with the paradoxical result of an albinic appearance when the fulvous pigment fails before the melanic dusting has thoroughly taken over).

Europe:

From the Arctic Ocean to the Mediterranean Sea (except Turkey) and to the Black Sea (except the Caucasus) and from the Atlantic Ocean to (approximately) the meridian of Astrakhan.

The concept of "Europe" is a much more discrete one than that of the "Palearctic" or "N. America." In the Palaearctic there is a bothersome encroachment of tropical forms in N. India and N. Africa and in the Nearctic [the] picture is spoiled by the fact that a good deal of collecting was done at Farr,[292] S. Texas. It will be noted that Europe is connected with certain exotic elements only in the Southern Balkans, while on the other hand, Western Siberia is too poor in endemic forms to encroach much on N.E. Russia.

Nearctic & European

Among non-migrants all the species that are common to Europe and N. America are either arctic or range to the arctic zone. These species are: (list)

Sweden

The Uppsala and Stockholm region (Upps. is about 60 kils. NNW of Stock.), especially the first (consult a Swedish lepidopterist and check in Nordstr) should be the selected locality of Linnaeus' types from Sweden.

See also Nordström-Wahlgren, ed. Tullgren

When writing to Sweden for specimens 1. ask for average, normal things from *that* region 2. Preferably bred specimens? (with wild ones for comparison?) 3. representatives of *both* broods when different and, of course, both sexes 4. Three or four specimens of each sex. 5 Also – dimorphic ♀ – alb. *Colias* & "valesina"   [VNA]

From draft catalogue of *The Butterflies of Europe*

[The following notes are selected from the approximately 1400 index cards of the catalogue, a work in progress whose classification system (especially at the levels between family and genus) was in partial flux. A blank line marks a new card, an ellipsis a series of cards omitted.]

An Illustrated Catalogue of the Butterflies of Europe with 88 Plates representing all known European species of diurnal Lepidoptera with their main geographical races

Systematically arranged and annotated by Vladimir Nabokov

~~about 150 pages of text~~ ——————————— ~~85 plates (13 × 10 inch)~~

~~about 2000 figures)~~

Family I: *Papilionidae*

A large, world-wide family of showy butterflies. It is represented in Europe by a relatively small number of species in four subfamilies.

Subfamily I: *Papilioninae*

Comprising two genera:

Genus I: *Papilio* Linnaeus (1758) & Latreille (1810; type: *Papilio machaon* L.)

Comprising two subgenera:[293]
Subgenus I: *Papilio* L.

Comprising two species:
Species I: *Papilio* (*Papilio*) *machaon* Linnaeus (1758, Syst. Nat., ed. X, p. 1662 [Sweden])

Common throughout the Palearctic, from Lapland to N. Africa and from England to Alaska and Japan, at sea level and high altitudes (up to almost 6000 m. in the Himalayas), and represented in the Nearctic by some extraordinary subspecies and allied species. It has a strong purposeful flight and shares with certain tropical members of the family a habit of avidly fanning its wings when sampling flowers. Larval foodplant: various umbellifers. . . .

Subspeciation in Europe is weak and incoherent and seems mainly dependent on climatic conditions. *P. machaon sphyrus* Hbn as figured by Verity from S. Italy (type locality *probably* Sicily) goes from dark, heavy, richly colored specimens from Palermo (which *he* says cannot be distinguished from *machaon britannicus* Seitz) to very light, slender, pale ones (from Sardinia, but I have taken such specimens also in Cannes, in August). Incidentally: if in the early 19th c. *machaon* was widely distributed in England was it the migrant (*P. machaon gorganus*) now taken sometimes on the coast, or the present fen race from Cambridgeshire and Norfolk? . . .

Papilio (Papilio) machaon alpica Verity

. . . Up to 2000m. in the Maritime Alps. An altitudinal form hardly worth naming, had it not been for its slight resemblance to Asiatic alpine races of the species. Its ground color is paler than that of any other European race, with broadened black markings and shorter tails. The marginal pale yellow spots are narrower than in *bigenerata*. . . .

Iphiclides (Iphiclides)

Species II: *Papilio feisthamelii* Duponchel

. . . A curious subspecies (or species in the making) ranging from N. Africa northward through Spain to Portugal and to Perpignan where I have seen it haunting orchards in March in close proximity to *podalirius podalirius*, the ordinary Pyrenean form. . . .

Subfamily II: *Zerynthinae*

represented in Europe by one genus and subgenus: *Zerynthia* Ochsenheimer (1816) & Scudder (1875; type: *Papilio polyxena* Schiffermüller which is *P. hypsipyle* Schulzens), which replaces the better known but preoccupied *Thais* Fabricius (1807).

A West Palaearctic group with three species. They appear in spring, skimming over grass, rocks & ditches, & settling on the ground when fresh but later dawdling, flat and inert, on flowers. They are sluggish fliers with a curious air of not belonging to their surroundings. Larval food: *Aristolochia*. . . .

Archon (Archon) apollinus Herbst (1798, see next card)

This butterfly looks like a *Parnassius* in fancy dress.

Subfamily IV: Parnassiinae

Species I: *Parnassius (Parnassius) apollo* Linnaeus (1758, Syst. Nat. ed. X, p. 465, *Papilio* sp.; "common in Sweden")

One of the most popular European butterflies equally at home in Scandinavia and Sicily with a wide palearctic range from the mountains of Spain, Portugal and France to the plains and mountains of N. and Cen. Asia, from N. Norway to Sicily and Armenia. It is not found either in England or in N. Africa and does not reach the Pacific (as *phoebus* does).

Hundreds of "subspecies" have been described, most of which (especially those named by Bryk, Fruhstorfer and Verity) have no taxonomic or biological standing whatever. . . .

One of the most comic escapades in the *apollo* nomenclatorial farce is a batch of eight "subspecies" all from Tyrol (!) named by a Herr H. Belling of Berlin-Pankow and carefully preserved in his collection (they all sink with a number of others to *brittingeri* Reb. & Rghf)*

---

*besides about ten other "subspecies" named from the Tyrol making of that small but touristically very accessible region a perfect paradise for race-names

The "Phalaena prima" of Moufet in 1634, the "Papilio alpinus" of Petiver in 1704 and the "Papilio alpicola" of Geer in 1752 (see Bryk, 1935, p. 325)

Bryk, 1935: "Mittelschweden mit den angrenzenden Inseln"

Type ♂ in coll. Linnean Soc. London

I have selected ten races which seemed to me important, representative, distinct, and convenient out of the approximately 200 named subspecies, doomed to be carried for ever in complete catalogues.

A Central Palaearctic species restricted to mountains in Central, Southern and Eastern Europe, extending to Asia Minor and Central Asia, and from the lowland of Scandinavia and Russia far into Siberia, but not reaching the Pacific.

It has been steadily dying out in a number of its Western European habitats (and this phenomenon is seldom due to overcollecting, especially in the case of mountain butterflies).

I know of several large areas in the Swiss mountains (e.g. in the Valais and in the Vaud) where the species is now very rare. You can walk miles without seeing one specimen. . . .[294]

Parnassius apollo provincialis Kheil . . .

Specimens from Digne or Thorens (10 km. from type loc.) should do for fig.

Under this convenient flag I group the several named forms from S. France: A.M., B.A., Lozère, Auvergne, the Pyrenees, etc., all of them showing a family air unless specially selected to conform to the type specimens. Bryk (1935) darkly points out that the types were bred by Kheil in Prag, but a true subspecies does not change *pour si peu* unless subjected to experimental temperatures when, however, the resulting aberration should still retain the ssp. basis. . . .

P. (P.) phoebus cervinicolus Fruhstorfer . . .

I have found it common in July, 1961, along the western bank of Visp R, just N of Zermatt at 1650m.

Family II: *Pieridae*
Subfamily I: *Pierinae*
Genus I: *Pieris* Schrank (1801) & Latreille (1810); type: *Papilio brassicae* L.)
Subgenus* *Pieris* Schr.

P. (P.) brassicae brassicae L.

Rarer in Western Europe now than a century ago when it was considered the commonest European butterfly. Well known for its migratory properties. Two broods in Northern Europe and up to four in the South. I have seen fairly fresh females on wallflowers in Taormina as late as November 25. Ranges from N. Africa and the Azores to N. Scandinavia, E. Siberia and N. India.

. . . Has a curious propensity of developing striking insular races, Canaries, Madeira, Azores, Cyprus. . . .

Pieris (Pieris) brassicae azorensis Rebel . . .

[The inclusion of Azoran forms may complicate the book too much. Think. . . .]

Pieris (Pieris) mannii Mayer (1851 . . .)

One of the most interesting Palaearctic butterflies. It remained unrecognized and neglected (mainly owing to Staudinger's Catalog (1901) considering it as an insignificant variety of *rapae*) for fifty-six years after the publication of its description. . . .

Pieris napi

Such races as *flavescens* and other similar strains (from Italy and elsewhere) should be regarded, I think, as lingering *remnants* of old transitions between *napi* and its possible ancestor *bryoniae* Hub. . . .

---

*The genus *Pieris* has been recently split into subgenera but too many transitions exist between the latter to make them either rational or convenient.

P. napi flavescens Wagner . . .

One of the many intermediate local froms intergrading variously into *bryoniae*, which occur at moderate elevation in Austria, North Italy and elsewhere. I have seen strikingly dark, grayish or tawny females among more or less typical ones, in May, in the gardens of Stresa. . . .

P. napi bryoniae Hübner . . .

Considered by some as a distinct species but certainly interbreeding with *napi napi* in suitable zones (e.g. at circa 1500 ft on mountain trails ascending from the Rhone valley in the Valais, SW. Switzerland).

Genus II: *Pontia* Fabricius (1807), & Curtis (1824; type: *Papilio daplidice* L.)

Three subgenera in Europe:

subgenus I: *Pontia* F.

species I: *Pontia (Pontia) daplidice* Linnaeus (1758, Syst. Nat., X ed., p. 468; *Papilio* sp, citing Petiver, 1702, Gazophylacii naturae, Pl. 1, fig. 7; Ford, 1945, Butterflies, Pl. 1, fig. 4, ♀, Cambridge, England, May, 1702).

reaching N. to about Lat. 60° where it still breeds but is very rare: in twelve years collecting near St. Petersburg I took only one specimen, a small fresh male of the spring form, on the Oredezh R. in 1915. . . .

By a taxonomic fluke the type locality is in a country where the butterfly, a migrant from France, breeds very seldom. Petiver's female specimen is a spring specimen that might have emerged in England.

Genus III: *Euchloe*

. . . of the five European species, one (*ausonia*) is widely distributed throughout the Palaearctic Region and West America, two are confined to the eastern Mediterranean, the fourth is insular and the fifth, alpine. Some more research is needed, however, to establish quite definitely the specific limits within this group. The old entomologists saw only three species here, "*belia*," *tagis* and *belemia*, and perhaps they were right.

E. (E.) ausonia ausonia Hüb. . . .

This is the alpine race (sometimes treated as a separate species), the "*simplonia* Freyer." . . . It occurs on grassy slopes, seldom below 1000m; commonly at 1500 m, and reaching 2500m, in one protracted generation (as early as April and as late as August, according to altitude) in the Piedmont, Valais, Bernese Oberland, and Tessin. . . .

Delias

Subgenus: *Aporia* Hübner: . . . one species in Europe: *crataegi* Linnaeus. . . . The blood drops noticed by ancient historians on the white walls of doomed cities. . . .

Colias (Colias) . . .
hyale & australis

1950, Lamb. 50, pp. 90–98, pl. 5 & 6
Warren figured photographs of the ♂ gen. of both – but photographs of these parts are of very little use or lucidity: a sharp outline drawing of the parts detached yields incomparably better results! The differences he found are very slight and vague.

hyale, or not at all

aucun de ces critères n'est absolu[295] but hindwing characters more stable than others

Colias (Colias) chrysotheme schugurowi Krulikovski

. . . I remember the thrill of taking this form on the lawns of the estate Kamenka, a few miles from Popelyuha, Prov. of Podolsk in August, 1911.

Pieridae

Subfamily IV: *Dismorphiinae* . . .
Genus: *Leptidea* Billberg . . .

As many fragile-looking butterflies the members of this genus are great wanderers.

L. sinapis corsica Verity

Corsica . . . I observed this curious race in a wood near Calvi, at about 500m., in late April, 1963.

Family III: *Satyridae*

A large family of mostly dark butterflies, with ocellated undersides and fish-shaped mostly grass-feeding caterpillars, well represented in Europe where it greatly surpasses the entire Nearctic in number of species (excepting *Oeneis*). Comprises subfamilies: *Satyrinae, Erebiinae, Lethinae* & *Ypithiminae.*

Subfamily I: *Satyrinae*

Brisk snappy flyers settling on treetrunks and stones (e.g genus *Hipparchia*) or floppy indolent grassland dwellers (e.g. genus *Satyrus, Brinthesia*)

With six genera: *Satyrus, Hipparchia, Aulocera, Oeneis, Maniola, Aphantopus.* . . .

I have more or less followed Lesse, and to a certain extent Verity, but the classification is simplified by means of some lumping.

Satyrus (cont)

This difference in habitat and flight sometimes differs between two subspecies (e.g. the Nearctic *Minois pegala pegala* F. and *pegala nephele* Kirby)

Two subgenera in Europe. . . .

Species II: *ferula* Fabricius . . .

It is very conspicuous along roads, in the hayfields of the Valais, where it emerges in late June at elevations of c. 500–1000m. . . .

Genus II: *Hipparchia* Fabricius . . .

A large handsome group of dark, white-banded or tawny patterned Palaearctic butterflies [represented in the W. Nearctic by a single drab degenerate species?] . . .

Hipparchia (Neohipparchia) statilinus statilinus Hufn.

Very local but here and there common, in sandy localities, from N. Germany to Switzerland & to N. Italy (where it grades here and there into the next race) and along the Atlantic coast southwards at least to Biarritz (where I remember taking it as a boy, in September 1909, in a pinewood).

Hipparchia (Neohipparchia) statilinus australis

. . . I am inclined to lump under this name all the large strains of *statilinus* (formerly known as "*fatua* Freyer") such as *fidiaeoformis* Verity . . . and *onosandrus* Fruhstorfer. . . . When one sees for the first time this large *fidia*-like butterfly (for instance in the environs of Mentone where it flies with *H. (N.) fidia*) one does tend to mistake it for a distinct species from typical *statilinus*. . . .

Hipparchia (Chazara) hippolyte euxinus Kuznetsov

(1909, Ann. Zool. Petersb. 14, p. 140, plates   figs.   , *Hipparchia* sp. Ay Petri (?) Crimea)

The most interesting member of the meager Crimean butterfly fauna. Rocky escarpments topping the pine-clad slopes of the Yayla mountains on the southern coast are its favourite haunts. It flies for brief indolent spells frequently on the ground and on rocks. . . .

Aulocera (Brinthesia)

Species: *circe* Fabricius . . .

A lazy and clumsy flier, haunting hayfields and oak groves. . . .

Maniola (Pyronia)

Species III.* *bathseba* Fabricius (; *pasiphae* Esper, name preocc.)

West Mediterranean reg.

Maniola (Pyronia) bathseba bathseba F.

I have found it fairly common near Toulon in mid-May 1923. It prefers shady nooks and settles with open wings on the leaves of shrubs, relinquishing the flowers of the meadow to its two congeners which emerge later.

Genus VI: *Aphantopus* Wallengren (1853; type: *Papilio hyperantus* L.)

Three species, of which two limited to Asia.

---

*unnecessarily placed by Lesse in *Pasiphana* (1952) with *janizoides* H.-S of Algeria. In such small genera as *Pyronia* there is no room and no basis for other than specific distinctions.

Species *hyperantus* Linnaeus (1758, Syst. Nat. X ed., p. 471, *Papilio* sp.; 1761, Fauna Suecica; Sweden)

Throughout the Palaearctic, in Europe from central Scandinavia to the Mediterranean area. In central Europe it prefers shady lanes and the outskirts of woods but in North Russia it is a typical denizen of open fields where it occurs in countless numbers.

Aphantopus (Aphantopus) hyperantus hyperantus L.

A "ganz kleine form des höchsten Nordens *arctica form. nov.*" thus "described" by Dr. Seitz, 1, p. 137, 1908, cannot exist taxonomically wherever it was found. . . .

Subfamily II: *Erebiinae*

In all five parts of the world, from the Arctic Circle to Spain, Africa, India, New Zealand and Patagonia.

Two genera are represented in Europe.

Genus I: *Erebia* Dalman (1816; type: *Papilio ligea* L.) reaches its great development in Europe – especially in the mountains of Europe.*

My arrangement of European species [of *Erebia*] Dec. 1964[296]

I.   *Ligea Erebia*[297] 1. *ligea* 2. *euryale* 3. *eriphyle* 4. *manto* 5. *claudina* 6. *flaviofasciata* 7. *christi* 8. *pharte* 9. *epiphron* 10. *melampus* 11. *sudetica* 12. *serotina*

II.   *Medusa Medusia* 1. *medusa* 2. *triarius* 3. *rossi*

III.   *Fasciata* 1. *fasciata* Name

IV.   *Edda* 1. *edda* Name

V.   *Alberganus Gorgo* 1 *alberganus* 2 *dabanensis*

VI.   *Epistygne Phorcis* 1. *epistygne* 2. *pluto* 3. *gorge* 4. *gorgone* 5. *rhodopensis* 6. *aethiopella* 7. *mnestra*

VII.   *Tyndarus* 1. *tyndarus* 2. *hispania* 3. *cassioides* 4. *ottomana* 5. *pandrose*

---

*The splitting of the European *Erebia* into several subgenera on the basis of their genitalia helps to sort out and gather most of the species rather neatly into distinct groups. It is, in any case, a more logical and objective arrangement than the subgeneric splitting proposed in the case of *Coenonympha* (see note, p.   ).

VIII.   *Pronoe Syngea 1. pronoe 2. lefebvrei 3. scipio 4. styrius 5. styx 6. monta-*
        nus 7. neoridas 8. zapateri 9. melas

IX.   *Meolans Monica 1. meolans 2. palarica*

X.   *oeme 1. oeme* Name

XI.   *aethiops Truncaefolia 1. aethiops*

XII.   *embla 1. embla 2. disa 3. cyclopius* Name

XIII. *Atramentaria*

XIV.   *Callerebia*

Erebia (Erebia)
Species III: *manto* Schiffermuller (1775)...

Although a sluggish flier, it needs very little sunshine to leave the deep, damp grass of mountain meadows on summer mornings. . . .

Species VI: *flavofasciata* Heyne (1895 . . . Campolungo Pass, near Fusio, Tessin)

The first specimen was taken in July 1893 on that romantic pass by a German lieutenant colonel a certain von Nolte, a mysterious traveller whom as a child I envied and venerated with poignant unforgettable force.

Species VII: *christi* Rätzer (1890 . . . Simplon region)

The type locality is a narrow valley, with a beautiful waterfall at its head, on the west side of the Simplon highway just below Simplondorf.

In late June or early July, walking up the trail along the north bank of the torrent one may see as low as 1350 m. the males dribble down the southfacing steep slopes, flying low over grass and scree and often settling on flowers. *Christi* also occurs at a number of other points between 1500m and 2000 m on the southern side of the Simplon, between Laquintal and the Pass. . . .

Erebia (Edda) cassioides murina Reverdin:

. . . Odd: the smaller the country the longer and more complicated the titles of scientific journals!

Erebia (Phorcys)

Species III: *gorge* Hübner . . .

As alert as a *Dira*; haunts ridges at & above timberline up to 10,000 ft settling on slabs of rock with half-open wings, but always near grass, unlike *pluto*. . . .

Erebia (Phorcys)

Species VI: *mnestra* Hübner . . .

Its favorite zone is around 2000m but I have found it locally common (above Champex and elsewhere in the Valais) among larches on slopes at much lower altitudes (1500–1600m.) . . .

Erebia (Phorcys)

Erebia rhodopensis[Mrs] Nicholl

. . . the only species of European butterfly described by a woman [1900].

Erebia

Subgenus VII[298]

Species I: *pandrose* Borkhausen . . .

Typical of the rhododendron belt, but ascending to almost 3000 ft. "short Alpine pastures" – Warren. The skipping, zigzagging flight of the species and of those of the *tyndarus* group is quite different from other *Erebias*. The independent-looking motion and, in fresh specimens, underside bluish-grey flash of the hindwing are especially remarkable. . . .

Erebia

Subgenus VIII: *Syngea* Hübner (1818) & Hemming (1933) . . .

Species I: *pronoë* Esper (1780 . . .)

Ranges at elevations from 600 to 2600 ft. from the Caucasus and Turkey westward to the Pyrenees.

Its favorite zone is 1200–1500ft. Emerges late (in some places at 1500 ft only in mid-August). Males, very abundant in limited areas (e.g., steep bank of a torrent) skipping all over the grass in search of females. . . .

Erebia (Truncaefalcia) aethiops altivaga Fruhstorfer . . .

An altitudinal form, rather than a subspecies, occurring at high elevation throughout the central Alps. Eggs brought down from 2500m to 250m would probably produce individuals belonging to ssp. *sapaudia* or *rubria* or *aethiops*. . . .

Erebia

Subgenus XII: *embla* Thunberg

In N. Asia extending to Kamchatka. In Europe only in N. Scandinavia & N. Russia, S. to about 60°. In ten years (1907–17) of assiduous collecting near Leningrad[299] I found only two males and one female, all three in late June, flying singly in birchwood clearings between Rozhestveno and Batovo. . . .

Erebia

Subgenus XI[II]: *Callerebia* Butler.

Species: *phegea* Borkhausen, long known as *afer* Esper ( ), preocc.

A prairie insect dancing in and out of the grass of southern Russian steppes locally in great numbers (i.e. on the Yayla plateau in the Crimea in June). . . .

Subfamily III: *Lethinae*

. . . There is much work still to be done in regard to the proper arrangement of the subfamilial, generic and subgeneric elements in this part of the family.

Pararge (Pararge)

egeria

The southern subspecies is especially at home in sun-speckled groves but also occurs in the open, along low hedges etc.

The northern subspecies, on the other hand, is with *Lopinga achine* one of the very few exclusively woodland butterflies of Europe.

Pararge (Lasiommata)
maera

very common in rocky places and in flowery fields. Fresh individuals are curiously gaudy on the wing, as they dance by with a flash of blue ~~here~~ and a flash of red ~~there~~; one remembers Tutt's pleasing account of how completely baffled he was by the first *maera* he saw on trip to the continent

Pararge (Lasiommata)
Species III: *petropolitana* Fabricius . . .
Dira (Dira) petropolitana petropolitana F.

One of the first Spring butterflies in Northern Russia, where it emerges as early as mid-May, and is completely replaced by *D. maera* by the end of June.

Dira (Dira) petropolitana calidia Fruhstorfer . . .

Ascends up to timberline along mountain trails. I have never found it very abundant in the Alps where fresh specimens can be found from late April (at 500m) to early July (at 2000m) flitting here and there among bushes or sunning themselves on stones.

~~Genus V: *Agapetes* Billberg (1820) & Scudder (1875; type *Papilio galathea* L~~

  replace –>

Long known as *Melanargia* Meigen (1828) *< – now placed on official list* 1956 opinion 400

Palaearctic (and partly tropical) and particularly characteristic of Europe where its range is southern except in the case of the species (*galathea* and *russiae*) which reach lat. 55°. The subgenus *Argeformia* Verity (1953) has been suggested for some of the species but its acceptance would only throw out of balance this compact and well-defined little group.

Species I: *galathea* Linnaeus (1758, Syst. Nat., ed. X, p. 474, *Papilio* sp.; Germany)

Throughout central and especially southern Europe, northward to N. Germany? and Yorkshire in England. Extremely abundant in some places, such as hayfields in the Alps, where it flutters from flower to flower; up to about 1500 m. in Switzerland but to much greater altitudes when indulging in the half-hearted migratory flights which I have observed in the case of this species. . . .

A. *russiae*

. . . It is a much stronger flier than *galathea* or *psyche*. I have seen wandering females of ssp. *cleanthe* on mountain ridges 2000m. high. . . .

Subfamily IV: *Ypthiminae*

A large tropical group represented in Europe by two genera, the first nearctic, the second palearctic.

Genus I: *Coenonympha* Hübner (1823) & Butler (1868; type: *Papilio oedippus* F.)

Well stocked with species in Europe; represented by a dozen more in Asia and N. Africa; and only by two in N. America, the holarctic *tullia* Müll. and the nearctic *haydeni* Edw.

Except for a few hours after emergence when they are singularly alert, the members of this genus are weak fliers flitting in and out of grass or scrub, in meadows, marshes, and wastes and forest clearings. The splitting of this genus into subgenera seems to me utterly useless. . . .

Coenonympha (Coenonympha) tullia suevica Hemming (1936, Proc. Ent. Soc. London, 5, p. 123, replacing preoccupied *isis* Thunberg, 1791, Dissert. Insect. Suecica, 2, p. 31, *Papilio* sp.; Sweden, Roslagia (not checked)

I suspect that this and other forms of *tullia* are not true geographic races but occur in an intricate mosaic of distribution in response to surroundings.

Is not *isis* Thunb = *scotica* Staudinger (1901, Cat. Lep. Pal. p. 66, found in Aberdeenshire, Sutherlandshire etc and in the Orkneys & Shetland Isles)?

It is the only indigenous butterfly in the Shetlands. . . .

Coenonympha (Chortobius)
Species III: *hero* Linnaeus

(1761, Fauna Suecica, p. 274   ) (check)

Local and rare in central Europe, as far W. as Belgium and NW France, commoner northward and eastward. Very abundant with *iphis* in the fields of N. Russia (e.g. near Leningrad), and ranging eastward to Japan. . . .

Coenonympha (Coenonympha) corinna elbana Staudinger . . .

The only known butterfly it would seem with a range limited to this small island. The fact of its absence from coastal Italy, if true, is incomprehensible. . . .

Family V: *Nymphalidae*

Nymphalis (Nymphalis)
Species IV: *antiopa* Linnaeus . . .

Throughout the Palaearctic, except England* and the Mediterranean islands, especially abundant in the birchwoods of the North; much less so among the willows of southern streams. Ranges southward to N. Africa and eastward to N. India and Japan. Widely distributed but not particularly common in the Nearctic, southward to Mexico. 'Rarity' among butterflies works in inverse ratio to size, and if *antiopa* were no bigger than a Blue it would be considered rare in Switzerland or S. France. (transfer this to Foreword)

Nymphalis (Nymphalis) urticae ichnusa Hübner . . .

Common throughout Corsica and Sardinia. From an evolutionary point of view, it has not quite reached the specific status that *P. hospiton* or *A. elisa* (or *Nymphalis caschmirensis*) have just managed to make. . . .

Genus II:
Vanessa† Fabricius (1807) . . .

Long known as *Pyrameis* Hübner (1818) . . .

---

*where however migrants from Scandiniavia are observed every year, from one or two to more than four hundred (in 1872).

†On a strict and in my opinion necessary application of the law of priority the name *Cynthia* F. (1807) & Westwood (1840; type: *Papilio cardui* L.) should take precedence of *Vanessa* F. The I.C.Z.N. has decided otherwise [for sentimental reasons].

Vanessa (Vanessa)

Species II: *cardui* Linnaeus

(1758, Syst. Nat., ed X, p. 475, Papilio sp.; Europa [Sweden] & Africa)

Despite statements to the contrary, does not hibernate in any stage anywhere in the Old World where there is frost.

A subtropical species, regularly invading Europe from Africa, and N. America from Mexico. It is found in the whole world except S. America. I have observed in Russia migrants hitting the Crimea in April and breeding in the Yayla plateau. Bleached and tattered their progeny reached Leningrad early in June, producing there one generation in late August. I have observed a tentative southward ebbing in the autumn, but the first frosts soon kill off the night travellers. . . .

Araschnia (Araschnia) levana levana L.

Seasonally dimorphic. Not generally realized what a strong migrant this is. Hibernates in the chrysalid stage as far north as Leningrad. One day in the Spandau Forest (Berlin), in late July 1934 or 1935, I observed a swarm of exhausted *levanas*, of the summer form, resting on flowers and shrubs.

The species founds small colonies as far Southwest as Portugal (one series) and the Piedmont (rare). Local and sporadic throughout Central Europe, more abundant in the east, from the Balkans to Siberia and Japan.

These July or August travellers have been mistaken for a third generation.

Subfamily II: *Melitaeinae*

Genus I: *Melitaea* Fabricius (1807) & Westwood (1840: type: *Papilio cinxia* L.)

Subgenus I: *Melitaea* F . . .

Melitaea (Melitaea) cinxia pallidior Oberthur

. . . Hardly a true subspecies. Similar strains, due to accidental seasonal conditions, occur elsewhere. . . .

Melitaea (Melitaea) phoebe minoa Fruhstorfer

. . . I am not sure this is a true subspecies which would not turn into the nominal form if bred at sea level. . . .

Melitae (Melitaea) diamina aurelita Fruhstorfer

. . . A curious little race from N. Italy ranging from Bellinzona to Bolzano, it repeats in a smaller and weaker form the *vernetensis* idea. . . .

Melitae (Melitaea) diamina vernetensis Oberthür . . .

I have taken it at Saurat, in the Ariège, in May 1929. Extreme specimens reveal affinities with the rest of the subgenus. . . .

Melitaea (Athaliaeformia)
athalia Spanish and Balkan groups

The task of naming and grouping the races of *Athalia* is pretty hopeless. The splitter has a field day and the lumper is balked by the fact that one finds small dark forms collected a few miles away from the type localities of large bright ones. . . .

Melitaea (Athaliaeformia) deione berisalii Rühl . . .

~~I came across a small colony only a couple of miles W. of Berisal, on a flowery slope at about 1400m. in early June 1961.~~ I ~~also~~ found it in some numbers in June 1963 at 800m. near Varen (in the Rhone valley, about 50 kilom. E. of Martigny). . . .

Melitaea britomartis melathalia Rocci

. . . I am not convinced that the difference in presence or absence of uncus between *britomarti* and *parthenie*, which is much the same as between races of *athalia*, is a specific one. There exist variations. . . .

M. parthenie mendrisiota Fruhstorfer . . .

This is the form I took in the vicinity of Gardone, along a stream running from Lavino, at c. 300m., in May 1965. . . .

Melitaea (Athaliaeformia) parthenoides sphines Fruhstorfer

(1917, Arch. Naturges, 82, A, 2, p. 12; Gex, near Geneva)

In the Bernese Oberland, in Savoy, in the Valais and in the Cevenees, I have found it at 1500–1600ft. Rare in August above Les Diablerets (Vaud), and in a smaller form, swarming on meadows in late June above Zermatt (Valais) from 1700 m. up to timberline.

Melitaea (Athaliaeformia) parthenoides beata Caradja

(1894, Iris 6, p. 181; near Bagnères de Luchon, 622m.)

I remember finding it in great profusion, fifty five years ago,[300] on dry waste ground among dusty bramblebushes, in autumn, in Biarritz. At higher altitudes in the Pyrenees it develops a form resembling *varia* but with a *parthenoides* male armature. I think it is hardly separable from the following and varies as does the latter.

Melitaea (Athaliaeformia)
Species VII: *varia* Herrich-Schäffer

(1851, Syst. Bearb. Schm. Eur., 6, p. 2, name given to *athalia var.*, 1845, loc. cit . . .

In August 1961 I found it occurring in small restricted colonies here and there on high slopes above the Simplon Pass. This I would fix as its type locality. Found also in Maritime Alps, Switzerland, Mts. of North and Central Italy, Austria and Tyrol.

varia

It differs from *parthenoides* in the same way as *parthenie* differs from *britomartis*, or *deione* from *athalia*, that is in the rudimentary state of the uncus.

Alp Grüm, July 1965
on slopes near station
Large specimens, very like *parthenoides*.
Sluggish . . .

Melitaea
Subgenus III: *Didymaeformia* Verity . . .

Species I: *didyma* Esper . . .

The ridiculous number of subspecific names! Here is a representative selection of European races. . . .

(worth while?)
Melitaea (Didymaeformia) trivia catananoides Verity
  (1918, . . .)
hardly a ssp., merely a dwarfish form of the second generation, which can be exactly duplicated in other localities. The forms *nana* Staudinger (1871) from S. Turkey and *catapelia* Staudinger (1886) from the vicinity of Samarkand, belong here.

[perhaps figure a pair of dwarf individuals of any of these "races" without a subspecific name]

(worth while?) *a controversial form* (See Higgins)
Melitaea (Didymaeformia) trivia aabaca Fruhstorfer
  (1917 . . . Castile)
This name should do, despite its ugliness, for the Iberian subspecies, including *ignasiti* Sagaria (1926) from Catalonia and *microignasiti* Verity (1950) from Portugal

[Should be examined closer]

Dismiss – but figure Spanish specimens . . .

Euphydryas (Euphydryas)
Species II: *maturna* Linnaeus
  . . . Common for a few days in June in aspen glades near St. Petersburg . . .

Euphydryas (Euphydryas) aurinia glaciegenita Verity
  (1928 . . . Ortalio, Rhaetian Alps)
  Long known as *merope* de Prunner (1798), a primary homonym.
  (also above Stresa)
  In June 1963 I found a small colony of a form intermediate between this and *aurinia aurinia* on a marshy spot near a brook at 1350 m. just below

Leukerbad in the Valais. Typical *glaciegenita* (which some deem a distinct species) was fairly common on marshy ground just N. of the Simplon Pass, at c. 2000m in June 1961. . . .

Euphydryas (Euphydryas) aurinia provincialis Boisduval
 . . . I have found it common here and there in the hills between Mentone and Roquebrune in April, 1938. . . .

Genus II: *Issoria* Hübner (1818)
 . . . *Iathonia* Linnaeus . . . the several "subspecies" described by Verity and others are purely an environmental and climatic affair of no taxonomic value. . . .

Brenthis (Brenthis)
Species III: *daphne* Schiffermüller
 (1775 . . . Vienna)
 Note resemblance to underside and ♀ of *A. laodice*!
 When just emerged it flies high over hedges and along roads, with an '*Argynnis*' zest if not vigor. But very soon, though still fresh, it slows down, and lingers on bramble flowers, disregarding the approaching net. . . .

Boloria (Boloria) pales mixta Warren
 (1944 . . . Briançon, Hautes Alpes) [types in B.M.]
 Widely distributed in the Cottian and Maritime Alps, at 1700–3000m. In the Val du Boreon and elsewhere is apparently sympatric* with *graeca* (*are* they distinct?) which can be separated only genitalically (check this!)
 Transitional between *pales* & *pyrenes miscens*!

Boloria (Boloria)
sifonica aquilonaris Stichel . . . In late July, 1965, I collected 17 ♂ & 6 ♀ at

---

figure sympatric individuals

Torfweisen (peat bogs) on the E shore of the St. Moritz Lake in the Grisons at 1820m. Sluggish quite unlike the two other species which occurred on slopes not far off. Dark female!

Boloria (Boloria)
aquilonaris alethea Hemming
   . . . I would be inclined to sink this to the preceding. . . .

Limenitis (Limenitis) populi semiramis Schrank
   (1801 . . . vicinity of Banz Convent, Upper Franconia)
   Central Europe, W. Czechoslovakia, Germany, (e.g. Baden (completely replaced banded)) Switzerland, France
   I saw it in a wood near Marienbad, settling on the flowers of a bush, quite unlike the northern *bucovinensis*

Limenitis (Limenitis)
Species II: *anonyma* Lewis = *reducta* Staudinger
   (1872, Zoologist, p. 3074, new name for preoccupied *camilla* Schiffermüller [nec. Linnaeus], 1775, Schm. Wien., p. 172, *Papilio* sp.; Chemnitz, Saxony; Bernardi, 1947, Miscellanea entomoligca, 44, p. 81; *rivularis* Stichel [nec Scopoli], 1907, Ent. Z., 21, p. 35)
   This delicate butterfly has had a stormy nomenclatorial career of which only the important stages are given above. It was known for more than a century as "camilla" . . .

Neptis Fabricius . . .
   Languidly gliding, rather eerie, butterflies of glades and groves, where they sail through sunbeams and settle on shrubs. . . .

Family VI: *Danaidae*
Subfamily: Danainae
Genus: *Danaus* Kluk 1802 & Hemming (1933 . . .)
Species: *chrysippus* Linnaeus . . .
Danaus chrysippus

This butterfly has the distinction of being the oldest known to have been represented by man. Seven specimens of it (with a typical white-dotted *Danaus* body but somewhat *Vanessa cardui* like wingtips) are shown flitting over the papyrus swamp in a fowling scene from a Theban tomb (XVIII Dynasty, 1580–1350 BC), Brit. Mus

Family VII: *Libytheidae*

Subfamily: *Libytheinae*

Genus: *Libythea* Fabricius (1807) & Latreille (1810; type: *Papilio celtis* Laich)...

A remarkable genus, containing the remnants, perhaps, of a much greater group, with species scattered over different parts of the world with only one or two species in each, sometimes insular.

(give details)

Species: *celtis** Laicharting

(1782 ... along the main road to Unteratzwang [Campodazzo, commune of Bolzano, N.E. Italy])

Spain, Italy, Greece, Asia Minor

The butterfly is a migrant and is only sporadically common in the more northern parts of S. Europe, wherever *Celtis australis* grows. Verity (1950, Farf. d. Ital, 4, pp. 6–8) lists a number of N. Italian localities and Wheeler (1903) gives the southern slopes of the Simplon. It occurs here and there throughout Italy. I never saw much of it on the Riviera, but found it in great profusion settling with tattered individuals of *N. polychloros* on catkins everywhere in the neighborhood of Perpignan, Pyr.-Or., in February, 1929. I have seen it appear regularly [in] spring on the south coast of Crimea, and it is widely distributed throughout N. Africa and Asia. It has been observed congregating in enormous numbers on *celtis* shrubs in Greece, somewhat like *D. plexippus* on pines. Its northernmost capture is Czechoslovakia (Povolny, Act. Mus. Moraviae 39).

The mechanism of its movement is obscure.

---

*often attributed to Füsslin (= Fuessly)

These early spring species are somewhat faded in comparison to the June and October broods. They have all the appearance of hibernated examples, or of exhausted new arrivals while there is no doubt a southward exordium in autumn, as I have observed in the case of the American species one early morning, in [illegible], in a field [illegible] with weary breakfasting travellers.

. . . The American species is *Libythea bachmanii* Kirtland . . .

Family VIII: *Riodinidae*

A resplendent and bizarre family, especially rich in American genera and species. Poorly represented in the Palearctic. . . .

Family IX: *Lycaenidae . . .*

Lycaena (Lycaena)

Species II:* *helle* Schiffenmüller

(1775 . . . Saxony)

Long known as *amphidamas* Esper (1779)

Very local in Central and N. Europe, west to Belgium, S. to the Pyrenees, east to E. Sibera. Austria, Hungary. Belgium: Liege & Luxemburg. France: Doubs; Pyr. Or.

I wonder if it still common in May, as it was forty years ago among the pines and flowering brambles on the sandy banks of Lake Grunewald, Berlin.[301]

1. *Lycaena (Lycaena) helle helle* Schiff.

Larval food: *Polygonum bistorta, Rumax acetosa.*

Lycaena (Heodes) alciphron gordius Sulzer

(1776 . . . Engadine)

The type locality has been limited by Verity (1943) to Chiavenna, N. of L. Como

---

*I cannot see the need of removing *helle* to a separate subgenus (*Helleia*) as does Verity (1943, F. d'Ital, 2, p. 20)

Common in the hills and mountains of S. Switzerland (up to 2000m. in the Simplon), S. Tirol, Italy & S. France.

A number of local forms of this subspecies have been described, some transitional in regard to the nominal race.

I can see no subspecific difference between the individuals I took at Menton and Moulinet (A.M.)[302] and those I took on the Simplon road and elsewhere in S. Switzerland[303] . . .

Lycaena (Thersamolycaena)
Species II: *dispar* Haworth

The butterfly was first taken in a Huntingdonshire fen in the early 1790s. It was discovered in Cambridgeshire in 1797 or 1798. It was later found in Norfolk and Suffolk, and in other English fens. By 1835, it had become very scarce. One of the last specimens was taken at Holme Fen, Cambridgeshire in 1847 or 1848 and a very last one was caught in the Somersetshire marshes in 1857 (see E.R. 1958). The artificial establishment of the Dutch race at Wicken in 1929–30 since when it has unfortunately thrived is to be deplored. . . .[304]

Lycaenidae
Cupidinae = Blues

A somewhat loose aggregation (serviceable mainly for the Holarctic fauna) corresponding to the popular notion of "Blues," "Coeruleae,"* Germ. Bläulinge, Fr. Azures, Russ. Golubyanki, etc. It also corresponds to the old group *Lycaena* (auct. nec F & Curtis), to the *Polyommatini* of Forster (1938) [check] and to the *Plebejinae* of authors e.g. of Verity, 1943 (but not of Stempffer or Nabokov). It could have been made to comprise the Lycaeninae ("Coppers") had it not been important to stress certain distinctions between the two groups such as the structural gap separating blue *Lycaena heteronea* Boisduval of N. America from genuine "Blues"

Genus IV: *Scolitantides* Hübner (1823) & Tutt (1906; type: *Papilio battus* Schiff., 1775 = *Papilio orion* Pall., 1771)

---

*Check the scope of *Coeruleae* Haworth, 1803, Lep. Brit., pp. 37–49. Used by Eversmann, 1844, "*Lycaenae coeruleae*" as distinguished from "*rutilae*" and "*caudatae*" . . .

Another very distinct genus. Equivalent to subfamily *Glaucopsychinae* of Forster (1936) and the tribe *Glaucopsychidi* of Hemming (1931).

Five subgenera: *Scolitantides, Glaucopsyche, Zizeeria, Maculinea & Iolana.*

Subgenus I: *Scolitantides* . . .

Species I: *orion* Pallas

(1771 . . . Syzran, E. Russia)

From Belgium to Korea, and N. Tibet, and from Finland (62°) to Spain and Cen. Italy. Rare in N. Europe and rather local further south.

It is still to be taken (in the company of *Agrod. thersites* and *Pieris manni*) on sunny May days, with an icy wind, in the vineyards near Martigny whence it was reported almost a century ago. . . .

Scolitantides (Glaucopsyche) alexis aeruginosa Staudinger

(1881, . . .)

From W. Asia to S. Russia. I have found it common near Yalta, on seaside lawns. . . .

Scolitantides (Maculinea)

Species II: *nausithous* Bergsträsser

(1779 . . . Frankfort on the Main)

Central Europe to Siberia and Armenia. It appears to be rare in Italy, and is local everywhere.

In a sense intermediate between *alcon* and *arion*. I have never seen it flying with either. (has anybody? check) . . .

Both *nausithous* and *teleus* frequent marshes and like to settle on the dense brownish flower-clusters of the tall herb *Sanguisorba officinalis* (Amat. Pap., 1937)

Scolitantidea (iolana)

Species: *iolas* Ochsenheimer . . .

Have taken perfectly typical in Forêt des Finges = Pfynwald
Colutea arborescens (Fr. baguenaudier Engl. bladder senna)[305]
In flight like a giant *argiolus*. Not forget ants in common with Blues! . . .

Genus V: *Plebejus* Kluk (1802) & Hemming (1933; type: *Papilio argus* L.)

A large, clear-cut genus equivalent to the subfamily *Plebejinae* of Stempffer 1937, 1938, and Nabokov 1944, 1945 (but not to the *Plebejinae* of authors, e.g. Verity); also equivalent to the "tribe" *Plebejidi* or *Plebeiidi* of Tutt & Chapman, 1909; and to the subfamily *Polyommatinae* of Forster, 1938. It includes twenty-four worldwide subgenera,* twelve of which are represented in Europe [add from Nabokov 1945, pp. 45–48]

Plebejus (Plebejus) argus aegidion Meisner

(1818 . . . Vallée d'Unseren, St. Gothard)

At high elevations in Switzerland and elsewhere; more of an environmental, altitudinal form (reducible downward to various lowland races of the correspondent regions!) than a regular subspecies especially as it is repeated pretty exactly in Lappland and Arctic Russia. . . .

Plebejus (Plebejus) argus corsica Bellier

. . . As with many Corsican subspecies (cp. *P. idas bellieri*) this one is the most striking of the species. . . .

Plebejus (Plebejus) pylaon trappi . . .

In mid-July 1962 I found a few near Berisal.

On June 28, 1963, I found it flying in great numbers on the slopes of the Genter valley, and around Schallberg† (about 6 kil. from Brig on the Simplon Rd.) both sexes settling on the leaves of *Astragalus exscapus*.

I never saw any near the Pass.

Also found in the Saastal.

---

*Thus demoted here from the rank of the twenty-four genera listed in my Notes on Neotropical Plebejinae 1945 Psyche, p. 47.

†Probably the exact type locality of *lycidas* Trapp.

Plebejus (Lycaeides) idas valesiaca Oberthür . . .

It grades into the altitudinal race *argulus* on the Simplon road at c. 2000m. and into *calliopsis* in the Piedmont.

Plebejus (Lycaeides) idas argulus Frey

(1882 . . . type (check it) [in BM] labelled "Simplon")

As with other altitudinal forms of butterflies it is not easy, taxonomically speaking, to cope with the close resemblance between alpine forms (from widely separate localities) which turn into quite different subspecies as they gradually descend into their respective valleys. On the other hand I cannot distinguish extreme *argulus* from W. Switz. and extreme *haefelfingeri* from E. Switz. . . .

Plebejus (Lycaeides) idas corsica Tutt . . .

As many Corsican races, it looks like a distinct species, but the male structure is that of other small forms of *idas*. . . .

Note: *Plebejus (Agrodiaetus) bellargus vestae* Verity: Relegate the hybrids to Aberrations plate. . . .

Lycaeides (Lycaeides) argyrognomon

Two gen. (*idas* generally but not always or everywhere has one)

Its home is certainly Asia, where it attains its greatest size and beauty in Transbaikalia and occurs in a number of striking subspecies in China, N. India and Central Asia. From the Aral Sea and the Volga region it radiates in a westward direction the westernmost points of its distribution being in Norway, Germany, N. and E. France and the Piedmont. It is local in central Europe occurring at low or moderate elevations in Switzerland and Italy (S. to Calabria), Austria and Hungary, Poland, S. Russia and the Northern Balkans. It does not reach S.E. France (beyond Isère), the Pyrenees or Spain but has not yet been recorded from Turkey or Greece.

In other words it has not spread westward as far and as densely as *idas* nor has it produced altitudinal forms and its distribution should be regarded as the second wave of *Lycaeides*, of a structurally more developed species than the first.

Plebejus (Aricia)

　(omit)

Aricia montensis debrosi Beuret

　. . . Merely a small well-marked *allous* with the ♂ uncus lobe (pl. 2, fig. 2) less affected by pressure in mounting (as also the figure of *montens montensis*) and thus looking "narrower" than *allous* & *agestis*. . . .

Plebejus (Agriades) glandon zullichi Hemming . . .

　Considered by some as being a good species on the strength of the different androconia [*not* a reliable specific characteristic in *Plebejus*] . . .

A presumable cross between *Plebejus (Agrodiaetus) coridon* Poda and *Plebejus (Meleageria) daphnis* Schiffermuller was described from SE France as *Lysandra cormion* Nabokov (1941, Journal New York Ent. Soc, 49, p. 265, Moulinet, Alpes Maritimes, two ♂; 1945, *Psyche*, 52, p. 48; Pl. 1, figs. 1 & 5, ♂ paratype, genitalia) and reported from Czechoslovakia as a hybrid by Smelhaus (1947, Act. Soc. Ent. Czechosloveniae, 44, p. 44, fig.,　　　). . . .

Plebejus

Subgenus XII: *Polyommatus* Latreille (1804 . . .)

Species I: *icarus* Rottemburg

　(1775 . . . Halle, E. Germany)

　The commonest European Blue; found throughout the palaearctic region. Esper's figures represent a rare aberration without basal ocelli.

　It is very sensitive to climatic conditions; and seasonal forms cut across local ones in a most haphazard way. We can speak of racial tendencies rather than of true subspecies, and it is from this point that a number of the "races" described by Verity should be viewed. . . .

Plebejus (Polyommatus) icarus septentrionalis Fuchs

　. . . I figure this Arctic form which is climatic rather than genetic mainly to counterbalance the southern forms illustrated below. . . .

Plebejus (Polyommatus) icarus flavocincta Rowland Brown (1909 . . .)

An attempt on the part of the species to establish a rather constant local form in Corsica.

I have taken it in late April, near Calvi in 1963.

(figure one underside) . . .

Thecla (Strymon)

acaciae Fabricius (1787 . . .)

Here and there in Cen. & S. Europe east to Asia minor N. to Thuringia, E. Germany.

The only spot on which I ever found it common was a Tatar village cemetery on the S. coast of the Crimea, in June, 1918.

Thecla

Strymon (Strymon) ilicis inalpina Verity

(1911 . . . Martigny, Valais)

I include this very minor race (cropping up in various southern localities) for a personal reason: in the Forêt des Finges a few miles E. of Martigny I have observed females flying over patches of thyme and revealing such an expanse of fulvous in the curiously non-*ilicis*-like flight they adopted as to mimic the *Melitaeas* that visited the same flowers.

Callophrys (Callophrys)

avis Chapman[306] . . .

Hyères. Amélie-les-Bains. Puységur found ♂ betw. Villeneuve-Loubet & le Colombier (R.N. 85) [30.iv.1938] I found it there in April, 1961.

Family X:* *Hesperidae*

Four groups in the world of which one (*Ismenina*) is strictly nocturnal (Verity, p. 3). Two groups represented in Europe.

---

*The "skippers" are sometimes separated from the rest of the butterflies (*Rhopalocera*) by removing them to an equivalent superfamily (*Grypocera*); but *Rhopalocera* (or *Heterocera*, "moths") itself is not a sufficiently homogeneous group to be segregated from the *Hesperidae*; and I dislike "superfamilies."

Equivalent to the subfamily *Hesperiinae* of Barnes & Benjamines (*1926*) *and Verity (1940)* (check) and to the subfamily *Pamphilinae* of Butler 1870 (Proc. Zool. Soc. London). Five genera in Europe: (*Hesperia, Adopoea, Gegenes, Carterocephalus* & *Heteropterus*)

check also Tutt's *Urbicolidae* p. 728

Adopoea (Adopoea)

Species III: *actaeon* Rottemburg . . .

The egg is said to be different – but museum specimens (the basis of taxonomy) do not lay eggs . . .

Heteropterus (Heteropterus)

Species: *morpheus* Pallas

(1771 . . . orchards (check) near Samara)

Throughout central Europe, here and there in damp meadows, on the edge of marshes and ponds etc. Reported from Holland and Belgium (very local in most western regions). I have taken it only in Berlin & Stresa. Strays N. to the Gulf of Finland, as *laodice* & *xanthomelas* do.

Describe flight. Hindwing appears to move separately from forewings. Jerky, "mechanical," rather rapid. Settles on rushes and ground.

figure also large specimens

Heteropterus (Heteropterus) morpheus morpheus . . .

Pyrgus

Subgenus II: *Scelotrix* Rambur (1858) & Plötz (1879 . . .) . . .

Species I: *carthami*

. . . Smallish (but I took a gigantic individual at Moulinet, A.M.!) . . .

Pyrgus (Ataleomorpha)

Species V: *armoricanus* Oberthür . . .

Central and S. cen Europe. N. to Denmark, straying to S. Sweden and Leningrad (I took one specimen in 1913 or 1914). . . .

Pyrgina
Genus II: *Carcharodus* Hübner
Subgenus: *Carcharodus** Hbn

Carcharodus (Carcharodus)
Species IV: *lavatherae* Esper
. . . I have often seen it in the Valais along footpaths in the vineyards between Varen and Susten.

Genus III: *Erynnis* Schrank (1801)
. . . Species I: *tages* Linnaeus
. . . has been observed folded mothlike at rest (see Ford, 1945, Butts., pl. xiv, fig. 4), a fitting position for the last genus in the butterfly list.

[VNA, Lepidoptera material, Boxes 1–4]

---

*Monotypical, according to recent authors.

The differences in value between the species, though striking, are specific, not generic or subgeneric. It is hardly useful to split into subgenera such a small genus as *Carcharodus*.

From interview with Jane Howard, September 1964

Published in *Life*, November 20, 1964.

Q: Have you ever seriously contemplated a career other than in letters?
A: Frankly, I never thought of letters as a career. Writing has always been for me a blend of dejection and high spirits, a torture and a pastime – but I never expected it to be a source of income. On the other hand, I have often dreamt of a long and exciting career as an obscure curator of lepidoptera in a great museum. [SO 46–47]

A: Butterflies are like grapes in that some years are much better for them than others. Sometimes rare specimens hide under stones and I find myself hunting them on all fours. It's a pity to have to kill them – I despise bull-fighting, subscribe to an antivivisection journal and don't like hunting or hunters – but it's done very simply and quickly by pinching their thoraxes. Look at that wasp – it's horrible the way the relatives crowd around the bedside of the dead, isn't it? [*Life*, November 20, 1964, p. 62]

VN in his bedroom at the Montreux Palace Hotel, his main writing space from 1962 to 1977, with a printed page of butterflies, working on his own *Butterflies of Europe*, 1964. (*Horst Tappe*)

From letter to Jane Howard, October 5, 1964

From Montreux.

Thanks for letting me see your jottings. I am returning them with my notes and deletions. I do hope you won't find the latter too discouraging. You have done your job extremely well, but I didn't. Much of what I said was idle talk, mainly and lamely meant to entertain you and Mr. Grossman[307] in between business.

I am a poor *causeur*, and this is why I prepare my answers to interviewers in writing; and since this method takes up time, I very seldom grant interviews. Several things that I said, and that you took down, are quite unfit for publication. I cannot discuss my obesity in public. I do not want to embarrass a heroic, and now ailing, cosmonaut by recalling a fishy television program. I find it unseemly to speak of my pedigree or of the butterflies bearing my name. I cannot be made to criticize contemporary writers.

[SL 359]

From letter from Véra Nabokov to George Weidenfeld, October 27, 1964

From Montreux.

Vladimir has now heard indirectly from you (via Dmitri) and from Mr. Thompson (via Walter Minton) that the British Museum has informed you they have available about 50% of Vladimir's butterfly list. He considers this good news. But he has been waiting in vain to hear from your office *which* are the species on his list that are represented in the BM collection. Of those subspecies they don't have, some could be replaced by others, and many might be found in the Museum d'Histoire Naturelle in Paris. He would like to be put now in direct touch with the person who did the research for you at the BM. He would then also get in touch with the French museum.

It has now been more than a year since you first mentioned this project. As you know, Vladimir is very much interested. On the other hand, he has been putting off many other things because of it (things that by now would have been accomplished), and the delays and silences are keeping him, he says, "in a constant state of perplexity and irritation." He thinks that if you still intend to go on with the project, some schedule ought to be worked out *now*. For instance, he finds it rather odd that more than a fortnight has elapsed since Minton told him of your having received the BM report without his having received a copy of it. [SL 360–61]

From letter from Nicholas Thompson, November 3, 1964
Unpublished.

Mr Howarth has now put on one side 768 specimens which represent about half of those required to complete the present list. There are 776 names on the list, each of which should be represented by a male and female, giving a total of 1552 specimens. The specimens which Mr Howarth has selected cover 407 names but of these 46 are represented by only one sex. [VNA]

Letter to Nicholas Thompson, November 9, 1964
From Montreux. Unpublished.

Dear Mr. Thompson,

Thanks for sending me the list of specimens checked at the BM. I found the percentage of available, or potentially available, things very encouraging. Here are some points I would like to make:

1. BM: I think Mr. Howarth[308] has done a grand job in checking the specimens and I would like him to know how much I appreciate his labor. I have also a number of special questions I would like to put to him. Some of my localities might be expanded to accommodate certain specimens. It was awfully nice of him to put those 768 on one side. How long can he keep them that way? What are his initials? At the moment I cannot decide when exactly I could be in London.

VN with net and butterfly,
September 1964.
VN at his lectern in the Montreux
Palace bedroom, with the butterfly
he has added to the floral decora-
tion on the hotel lampshade
visible on the right, 1966.
(*Philippe Halsman*)

2. Sweden: A number of common European butterflies were first described by Linnaeus from Sweden. It will be quite easy for me to send a list of these common topotypes to a Swedish collector and have him mail me, for a few pennies each, fresh specimens of these topotypes freely obtainable in the Uppsala or Stockholm countryside.

3. Musée d'Histoire Naturelle, Paris: A number of topotypes should certainly be there. If you would like to get in touch with the Museum, I would beg you to enclose a letter from me to Bernardi of the Lepidoptera department. All photographs should be taken by the same operator and with the same equipment as the BM ones (otherwise, there may be fatal differences in coloration, light, background, etc.); either the BM photographer should go to Paris or the specimens be borrowed and shipped to the BM. The second course would be preferable. In your letter to them (enclosing mine) I suggest you explain that the BM has already set aside specimens etc. If they accept either of the two procedures, we might ask them to check the list that I shall attach to my letter. I would probably have to visit the museum myself – but first let us get in touch with them.

4. My own collections: I have been hunting in southern France, Italy and Switzerland during the last four seasons, and I shall be collecting, I

hope, in Spain in the coming spring and summer. This will take care of several topotypes. Tring and perhaps other collections in England should be investigated, but this can wait.

5. The type localities of a hundred butterflies or so are marked "to be settled" in the list I sent the BM. Many, if not all, of these will probably be found to be either in the BM or in the Paris museum. I used the term "to be settled" either because I hoped in due course to dig up a more precise locality than the "Greece" or "Lapland" of the original description, or (more often) because I did not have the original description before me.

6. Some of the Russian things may prove unobtainable; I shall give up trying to get them when I have exhausted the Paris Museum possibilities and written to a Russian lepidopterist at the Bavarian Museum at Munich.

Incidentally, did I send you an additional copy of my list? If so, I would appreciate your returning it to me since I have to make some changes therein.

May I hope that things will develop at a more normal rate now? Please acknowledge this letter at your earliest convenience.

Sincerely yours,
VLADIMIR NABOKOV

[VNA]

Dream report, November 23, 1964

Published in the *New Yorker*.

November 23, 1964, 6:45 A.M.: End of a long "butterfly dream" that started after I had fallen asleep following upon a sterile awakening at 6:15 A.M. Have arrived (by funicular?) to a collecting ground of timberland (in Switzerland? in Spain?), but in order to get to it have to cross the hall of a large gay hotel. Very spry and thin, dressed in white, skip down the steps on the other side and find myself on the marshy border of a lake. Lots of bog flowers, rich soil, colorful, sunny, but not one single butterfly (familiar sensation in dream). Instead of a net, am carrying a huge spoon—cannot understand how I managed to forget my net and bring this thing—wonder how I shall catch anything with it. Notice a kind of letter box open on the right side, full of butterflies somebody has collected and left there. One is alive – a marvellous aberration of the Green Fritillary with unusually elongated wings, the green all fused together and the brown of an extraordinary variegated hue. It eyes me in conscious agony as I try to kill it by pinching its thick thorax – very tenacious of life. Finally slip it into a morocco case – old, red, zippered. Then realize that all the time a man camouflaged in some way is seated next to me, to the left in front of the receptacle in which the butterflies are; and prepares a slide for the microscope. We converse in English. He is the owner of the butterflies. I am very much embarrassed. Offer to return the fritillary. He declines with polite half-heartedness.   [VNA]

From notes for French translation of *Pale Fire*,[309] January 11, 1965
Unpublished.

two hundred years ago collectors spread the butterflies thus:

and not the modern way which is: [VNA]

From letter to Oakley Shields,[310] January 13, 1965
From Montreux. Unpublished.

As to [*Mitoura*] *spinetorum* [Hewitson], I certainly had great fun with it in Estes Park, Colo., in 1947, last week of May, where I used to observe numerous specimens very early in the morning (i.e. as early as any butterfly started to stir) settling on the ground of trails etc. or on bald patches along the fringe of a pine forest, and later in the day on flowers, between Columbine Lodge and Lily Lake. A short series of these specimens is in the MCZ,

Harvard. It was much less sluggish on a late May day, or early June day, in 1953, on a winding road above Portal, Arizona, where I caught three or four that were playing in the sun very wildly.   [VNA]

Letter to William H. Howe,[311] January 25, 1965
From Montreux.

Dear Mr. Howe,

I thank you very much for sending me a copy of your *Our Butterflies and Moths.*

As an illustrator of lepidoptera you reveal a rare and splendid talent. Although some of the subjects of the watercolor paintings are strongly stylized, there is always a smiling brightness about them, and in certain cases the stylization brings out nicely an otherwise inconspicuous detail. Most of the black-and-white wash drawings of butterflies and moths in various stages are equally delightful (my only criticism here would be that in the settled butterflies the position of the legs in profile is not always correct). On the other hand, the drawings of non-entomological objects – and especially those deliberately "comic-strip" little people – are banal and irritating.

My two main objections to the book are: The higgledy-piggledy arrangement of specimens and the enormous preponderance of common, showy species, sometimes repeated, among the North-American butterflies. The worthwhile youngster, the passionate novice (for whom your work is presumably meant) will demand first of all some kind of classification and comparison, and good pictures, of rare, drab, small, precious bugs. He cannot be expected to chase *Papilio glaucus* for very long. It is curious how authors and publishers of so-called "popular" butterfly books never seem to realize that the only reader who matters – the bright, eager, gifted boy (generally called "a sissy" by his schoolmates) will toss aside with bored disgust the book in which he cannot find that bizarre little thing he has just caught in a Vermont beechwood, or any of the *Colias, Boloria* and *Plebeius* that he sees in the willow bog of his Wyoming home. Why not figure for a change only the *less known* North-American butterflies?

I refrain from dwelling on the text of your work; it is not on the level of the paintings. Your genuine enthusiasm seldom finds the right word, and your science errs not infrequently. I also cannot imagine what or who induced you to insert all those stale anecdotes, pseudo-Indian legends and samples of third-rate poetry (in this respect, old Dr. Holland was a notorious offender).

Let me add in conclusion that instead of doing the rather bleak-sounding portfolio you plan – depicting feeding habits and migrations – your gifts entitle you to concentrate on something where art and science can really meet, such as an illustrated monograph on *Polygonia* or on the various races (both sexes and undersides) of *Papilio indra* (for a real thrill you should go one day to hunt the Grand Canyon subspecies).[312]

> *Sincerely yours,*
>
> VLADIMIR NABOKOV
>
> *ps. I have no special connection with the NY Times Book Review, but if they ask me, I can send them a copy of this letter, provided this is what you would like.*

[SL 367–69]

From letter to William McGuire,[313] February 13, 1965
From Montreux. Unpublished.

I would indeed welcome the opportunity of publishing a collection of my lepidopterological papers and it is extremely kind of you to suggest it.

All of these papers . . . I have had bound in a volume for my own convenience. I am not sure at what stage it was when you saw that bunch. There are in all 24 plates, of which three are unpublished photographs, and a few line drawings. [VNA]

From letter to Jean Bourgogne,[314] February 24, 1965

From Montreux. In French. Unpublished.

The publisher Weidenfeld and Nicolson has asked me to do a book on the butterflies of Europe, and I have been so rash as to accept, although I haven't seriously engaged in lepidopterology since the forties. This work will be an illustrated catalogue with short notes and large plates showing color photographs of all European species (both sexes, upper and under-side, seasonal dimorphism, etc.) with a selection of geographic races. Bibliographical and biological references will be given for each species and subspecies. I would like, as much as possible, all the examples illustrated to come from their type localities. The British Museum has not only agreed to verify how many topotypes they can put at my disposition, but also to photograph them in color for my plates.

I have therefore drawn up a list (very provisional and with lacunae due to the fact that I do not have all the necessary sources here in Montreux) of species and subspecies with their type localities and have sent it to my publisher who has handed it on to the British Museum. They have sent it back to me indicating all the topotypes they have there, male and female, and telling me that they have set them aside for me. The BM has a lot of material, but not everything. That's why I would like to ask the help of the Musée d'Histoire Naturelle to complete my list, in other words to find the missing examples. [VNA]

From letter from Véra Nabokov to James Page,[315] April 2, 1965

From Montreux. Unpublished.

It would interest him very much to publish a collection of his lepidoptero-logical papers.

. . . he has crossed out the works which he would like to omit; this leaves eleven articles (all marked with a cross) that he would like to publish.[316] Some of these papers are illustrated in black and white, and he could supply additional photographs in the case of two papers. He would also like to reproduce an unpublished colored plate of small wing patterns referring to the *Lycaeides* genus. [VNA]

From letter to George Hessen, July 16, 1965

From St. Moritz. In Russian. Unpublished.

Now we are in the charming Engadine, where there are lots of butterflies despite the big-bellied clouds and rain. Yesterday I was on Alp Grüm, behind Potresina. There with cries and whoops of delight, I caught, on a steep slope covered with alpine lilies, a very local *Erebia* with a golden stripe on black on the underside of its hindwings. [VNA]

Letter to E. P. Wiltshire,[317] August 22, 1965

From Montreux.

Published in part in *Proceedings of the British Entomological and Natural History Society*, 1969, 35.

Dear Mr. Wiltshire,

Sorry to answer your letter so late but both it and I have travelled about a lot. Although I cannot be of much help, it was awfully nice hearing from you: I am a great admirer of your papers in the Ent. Rec. (into whose editor, with his little black net for micros, I happened to run in the Engadine this summer) and of your delightful "Lepidoptera of Iraq" (which gave me the keenest pangs of hunter's envy).

I am far from being a *Pyrgus* specialist but with one thing and another am inclined to consider *malvoides* Elw. and Edw. conspecific with *graeca* Obthr., *tutti* Verity and *malvae* L. I have not dissected any of them but know from some experience in other groups that genitalic structures can fluctuate geographically within a given specific range, which only thousands of preparations can establish or at least suggest. When collecting at various seasons in the Vaud, the Valais, the Engadine, Lake Maggiore and Garda Lake, I have certainly come across individuals that *looked* like intergrades between *malvae* and *malvoides*, but the few samples I kept are not available at this moment. I have been lately wrestling in the field with similar problems in the *Melitaea* group and *so far* believe that *parthenie* Borkh. (= "*aurelia*") is conspecific with *britomartis* Assm., and – as old writers thought – *parthenoides* Kef (= "*parthenie*") is conspecific with *varia* H.-S. (in the large sense), just as *helvetica* Ruhl. (= *pseudoathalia* Rev.) belongs to *athalia* Rott., despite structural variation. But the more one learns the less one knows. Taxonomy is human, nature demonian. Just below Leukerbad, on its westside slope, in a tiny marsh at 1350 m., in June 1963, near a steep meadow full of St. Bruno's lilies and *mnemosyne* males, I found a small colony of perfect intergrades between *Euph. aurinia* Rott. and *glaciegenita* Vrty (= "*merope*"). On the other hand, I have had the rare pleasure of taking a beautiful dark race of *Bol. aquilonaris* Stichel (= "*arsilache*") flying practically side by side with *napaea* Hoffmgg and *pales* Schiff. on a peatbog near Pontresina, at 1820 m., this July. I don't know if it has been described.

I list these rambling analogies for what they are worth. I regret I do not know any Vaudois entomologists (except de Beaumont who strictly speaking is not a lepidopterist, head of the Zoological Museum in Lausanne). Anyway, it would be of great interest to establish that *malvae* and *malvoides* are sympatric in Switzerland or elsewhere.

Sincerely yours,

VLADIMIR NABOKOV   [VNA]

From letter from Véra Nabokov to George Weidenfeld, September 9, 1965

From Montreux. Unpublished.

More than two years ago you asked Vladimir if he would like to prepare for you a picture book of European butterflies, and he agreed. According to your wish Vladimir prepared a list of the butterflies to be figured. To work this out Vladimir spent numerous hours in libraries and at his desk.

During the last two years the book remained constantly in his thoughts greatly interfering with his other projects. Some of the delays were due to the leisurely working methods of the British Museum and the Musée National, but many could have been eliminated if you had shown more interest, and your office more energy, in this matter. During all this time you have been keeping him in a state of suspense which as he says was "at first irritating, and then became insupportable." He now asks me to advise you that he will not have anything more to do with this project. This decision is final.

As he wrote you on January 30, 1965, and again on April 15, 1965, he wants to be paid for the actual hours he devoted till now to the butterfly project, and this fee would be $500.00

I was in the process of finishing this letter when you telephoned from London. I told you over the phone what this letter was about. But Vladimir wants me to send it anyway so that you have it all in writing.   [VNA]

From letter from George Weidenfeld, September 10, 1965

On my return from abroad and after my telephone conversation with Véra, I am writing to you about the Butterfly book, on the subject of which I gather you are about to write to me. . . .

I would like to put it on record that in spite of apparent slowness in coming to decisions or bringing the project to a conclusive stage, we did work hard on the book and the difficulty, which you might not perhaps have always realised, was to translate your idea of a rather systematic and scientific book for the specialist market without any concessions to the general reader in presentation and more popular "layout," which brought us sharply up against enormous problems of cost. Also it was essential to get all of the various co-publishers, American and European, to guarantee his [*sic*] certain minimum edition. So there was a great deal of work that had to be done at all events. Nevertheless, we were and still are prepared to commission such a book on the basis of an advance of $10,000 against royalties covering the first initial edition of 10,000 copies and further payment pro rata in the event of reprints. But, as I tried to explain during our last meeting, it would be impossible for us to make additional payments with regard to expenses or travelling because the figure of $10,000 is already a very high one in relation to this particular project.   [VNA]

From letter from Véra Nabokov to George Weidenfeld, September 15, 1965

From Montreux.

Vladimir thanks you for the offer of a contract for the butterfly book that he was to write. At the present he cannot renew his interest in the project, mainly because he already has started working on another one. Sometime he still hopes he may go back to it. For the present he wants me to repeat that he would like you to settle for the time already spent by him on preliminary work on the butterfly book.   [VNA]

From interview with Robert Hughes, September 1965

Filmed for Television 13 educational program, New York. Broadcast February 1966. Published in part in *Strong Opinions*.

[From typed transcript.]

Q: Is there anything you miss from your teaching days in the United States?

NABOKOV: Perhaps I miss the United States more than my teaching days. I preferred summers to winters, so it's really summers I connected in my mind, as a kind of rainbow. And they were really quite wonderful.   [VNA]

[Nabokov's selection from transcription of interview, cameras rolling.]

Late September in Central Europe is a bad season for collecting butterflies. This is not Arizona, alas.

In this grassy nook near an old vineyard above the Lake of Geneva, a few fairly fresh females of the very common Meadow Brown still flutter about here and there – lazy old widows. There's one.

Here is a little sky-blue butterfly, also a very common thing, once known as the Clifden Blue in England.

The sun is getting hotter. I enjoy hunting in the buff but I doubt anything interesting can be obtained today. This pleasant lane on the banks of Geneva Lake teems with butterflies in summer. Chapman's Blue and Mann's White, two rather local things, occur not far from here. But the white butterflies we see in this particular glade, on this nice but commonplace autumn day, are the ordinary Whites: the Small White and Green-Veined White.

Ah, a caterpillar. Handle with care. Its golden-brown coat can cause a nasty itch. This handsome worm will become next year a fat, ugly, drab-colored moth.

[SO 60]

From Foreword to *The Waltz Invention*, December 8, 1965

The main revisions in the present text are based upon intentions more than a quarter of a century old, stemming as they do from the summer of 1939 (at Seytenex, Haute Savoie, and Frejus, Var) when, between butterfly hunting and moth luring, I was preparing the thing for the stage.

[*Waltz Invention* ii]

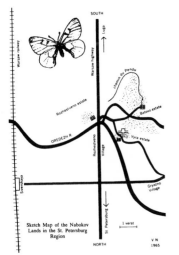

Sketch Map of the Nabokov
Lands in the St. Petersburg
Region

Speak, Memory: An Autobiography Revisited

Excerpts from additions to autobiography. Revised 1965–66, published 1967. For Chapter 6, "Butterflies," see pp. 81–97. For earlier versions of the remainder of the autobiography, see *Conclusive Evidence / Speak, Memory* (pp. 450–56) and *Drugie berega* (pp. 511–14).

[Foreword: Nabokov explains the choice of title.]

I had no trouble therefore in assembling a volume which Harper & Bros. of New York brought out in 1951, under the title *Conclusive Evidence*; conclusive evidence of my having existed. Unfortunately, the phrase suggested a mystery story, and I planned to entitle the British edition *Speak, Mnemosyne*[318] but was told that "little old ladies would not want to ask for a book whose title they could not pronounce." I also toyed with *The Anthemion* which is the name of a honeysuckle ornament, consisting of elaborate interlacements and expanding clusters, but nobody liked it; so we finally settled for *Speak, Memory* (Gollancz, 1951, and The Universal Library, N.Y., 1960). [SM 11]

[Nabokov explains why he decided to revise his autobiography, although he had already aimed at complete factual accuracy when he first wrote it: in America, he lacked details about family history; and he decided to elaborate on certain asides.]

Or else an object, which had been a mere dummy chosen at random and of no factual significance in the account of an important event, kept bothering me every time I reread that passage in the course of correcting the proofs of various editions, until finally I made a great effort, and the arbitrary spectacles (which Mnemosyne must have needed more than anybody else) were metamorphosed into a clearly recalled oystershell-shaped cigarette case, gleaming in the wet grass at the foot of an aspen on the Chemin du Pendu, where I found on that June day in 1907 a hawkmoth rarely met with so far west, and where a quarter of a century earlier, my father had netted a Peacock butterfly very scarce in our northern woodlands.

In the summer of 1953, at a ranch near Portal, Arizona, at a rented house in Ashland, Oregon, and at various motels in the West and Midwest, I managed, between butterfly-hunting and writing *Lolita* and *Pnin*, to translate *Speak, Memory*, with the help of my wife, into Russian. Because of the psychological difficulty of replaying a theme elaborated in my *Dar* (*The Gift*), I omitted one entire chapter (Eleven). On the other hand, I revised many passages and tried to do something about the amnesic defects of the original – blank spots, blurry areas, domains of dimness. I discovered that sometimes, by means of intense concentration, the neutral smudge might be forced to come into beautiful focus so that the sudden view could be identified, and the anonymous servant named. For the present, final, edition of *Speak, Memory* I have not only introduced basic changes and copious additions into the initial English text, but have availed myself of the corrections I made while turning it into Russian. This re-Englishing of a Russian re-version of what had been an English re-telling of Russian memories in the first place, proved to be a diabolical task, but some consolation was given me by the thought that such multiple meta-morphosis, familiar to butterflies, had not been tried by any human before.

[SM 12–13]

[In describing his close links with his mother, VN points out that, unlike her, he was unresponsive to music from early childhood.]

Despite the number of operas I was exposed to every winter (I must have attended *Ruslan* and *Pikovaya Dama* at least a dozen times in the course of half as many years), my weak responsiveness to music was completely overrun by the visual torment of not being able to read over Pimen's shoul-der or of trying in vain to imagine the hawkmoths in the dim bloom of Ju-liet's garden.

[SM 36]

[The new tennis court at Vyra, the Nabokov summer estate.]

By then, an excellent modern court had been built at the end of the "new" part of the park by skilled workmen imported from Poland for that pur-pose. The wire mesh of an ample enclosure separated it from the flowery meadow that framed its clay. After a damp night the surface acquired a brownish gloss and the white lines would be repainted with liquid chalk from a green pail by Dmitri, the smallest and oldest of our gardeners, a meek, black-booted, red-shirted dwarf slowly retreating, all hunched up, as his paintbrush went down the line. A pea-tree hedge (the "yellow aca-cia" of northern Russia), with a midway opening, corresponding to the court's screen door, ran parallel to the enclosure and to a path dubbed *tro-pinka Sfinksov* ("the path of the Sphingids") because of the hawkmoths visiting at dusk the fluffy lilacs along the border that faced the hedge and likewise broke in the middle. This path formed the bar of a great T whose vertical was the alley of slender oaks, my mother's coevals, that traversed (as already said) the new park through its entire length. Looking down that avenue from the base of the T near the drive one could make out quite dis-tinctly the bright little gap five hundred yards away – or fifty years away from where I am now. Our current tutor or my father, when he stayed with us in the country, invariably had my brother for partner in our temperamental family doubles. "Play!" my mother would cry in the old manner as she put her little foot forward and bent her white-hatted head to ladle out an assiduous but feeble serve. I got easily cross with her, and she, with the ballboys, two barefooted peasant lads (Dmitri's pug-nosed grandson and the twin brother of pretty Polenka, the head coachman's daughter). The northern summer became tropical around harvest time. Scarlet Sergey would stick his racket between his knees and laboriously wipe his glasses. I see my butterfly net propped against the enclosure – just in case.

[SM 41–42]

[Family background.]

My great-great-grandfather, General Aleksandr Ivanovich Nabokov (1749–1807), was, in the reign of Paul the First, chief of the Novgorod garrison regiment called "Nabokov's Regiment" in official documents. The youngest of his sons, my great-grandfather Nikolay Aleksandrovich Nabokov, was a young naval officer in 1817, when he participated, with the future admirals Baron von Wrangel and Count Litke, under the leadership of Captain (later Vice-Admiral) Vasiliy Mihaylovich Golovnin, in an expedition to map Nova Zembla (of all places) where "Nabokov's River" is named after my ancestor. The memory of the leader of the expedition is preserved in quite a number of place names, one of them being Golovnin's Lagoon, Seward Peninsula, W. Alaska, from where a butterfly, *Parnassius phoebus golovinus* (rating a big *sic*), has been described by Dr. Holland; but my great-grandfather has nothing to show except that very blue, almost indigo blue, even indignantly blue, little river winding between wet rocks; for he soon left the navy, *n'ayant pas le pied marin* (as says my cousin Sergey Sergeevich who informed me about him), and switched to the Moscow Guards.

[SM 52]

I can feel upon my skin and in my nostrils the delicious country roughness of the northern spring day which greeted Pushkin and his two seconds as they got out of their coach and penetrated into the linden avenue beyond the Batovo platbands, still virginally black. I see so plainly the three young men (the sum of their years equals my present age) following their host and two persons unknown, into the park. At that date small crumpled violets showed through the carpet of last year's dead leaves, and freshly emerged Orangetips settled on the shivering dandelions. For one moment fate may have wavered between preventing a heroic rebel from heading for the gallows, and depriving Russia of *Eugene Onegin*; but then did neither.[319]

[SM 62]

My Rukavishnikovs belonged (since the eighteenth century) to the landed gentry of Kazan Province. Their mines were situated at Alopaevsk near Nizhni-Tagilsk, Province of Perm, on the Siberian side of the Urals. My father had twice traveled there on the former Siberian Express, a beautiful train of the Nord-Express family, which I planned to take soon, though rather on an entomological than mineralogical trip, but the revolution interfered with that project.

[SM 66]

[VN's mental roll call of his English nurses and governesses.]

There was dim Miss Rachel, whom I remember mainly in terms of Huntley and Palmer biscuits (the nice almond rocks at the top of the blue-papered tin box, the insipid cracknels at the bottom) which she unlawfully shared with me after my teeth had been brushed. There was Miss Clayton, who, when I slumped in my chair, would poke me in the middle vertebrae and then smilingly throw back her own shoulders to show what she wanted of me: she told me a nephew of hers at my age (four) used to breed caterpillars, but those she collected for me in an open jar with nettles all walked away one morning, and the gardener said they had hanged themselves. There was lovely, black-haired, aquamarine-eyed Miss Norcott.

[SM 86–87]

[VN's drawing teachers.]

He was replaced by the celebrated Dobuzhinski who liked to give me his lessons on the *piano nobile* of our house, in one of its pretty reception rooms downstairs, which he entered in a particularly noiseless way as if afraid to startle me from my verse-making stupor. He made me depict from memory, in the greatest possible detail, objects I had certainly seen thousands of times without visualizing them properly: a street lamp, a postbox, the tulip design on the stained glass of our own front door. He tried to teach me to find the geometrical coordinations between the slender twigs of a leafless boulevard tree, a system of visual give-and-takes, requiring a precision of linear expression, which I failed to achieve in my youth, but applied gratefully, in my adult instar, not only to the drawing of butterfly genitalia during my seven years at the Harvard Museum of Comparative Zoology, when immersing myself in the bright wellhole of a microscope to record in India ink this or that new structure; but also, perhaps, to certain camera-lucida needs of literary composition. [SM 92]

[A ride through a bright St. Petersburg spring day.]

In the open landau I am joined by the valley of a lap rug to the occupants of the more interesting back seat, majestic Mademoiselle, and triumphant, tear-bedabbled Sergey, with whom I have just had a row at home. I am kicking him slightly, now and then, under our common cover, until Mademoiselle sternly tells me to stop. We drift past the show windows of Fabergé whose mineral monstrosities, jeweled troykas poised on marble ostrich eggs, and the like, highly appreciated by the imperial family, were emblems of grotesque garishness to ours. Church bells are ringing, the first Brimstone[320] flies up over the Palace Arch, in another month we shall return to the country; and as I look up I can see, strung on ropes from housefront to housefront high above the street, great, tensely smooth, semitransparent banners billowing, their three wide bands – pale red, pale blue, and merely pale – deprived by the sun and the flying cloud-shadows of any too blunt connection with a national holiday, but undoubtedly celebrating now, in the city of memory, the essence of that spring day, the swish of the mud, the beginning of mumps, the ruffled exotic bird with one bloodshot eye on Mademoiselle's hat. [SM 111]

[Biarritz, fall 1909, aged ten.]

The rich-hued Oak Eggars questing amid the brush were quite unlike ours (which did not breed on oak, anyway), and here the Speckled Woods haunted not woods, but hedges and had tawny, not pale-yellowish, spots. Cleopatra,[321] a tropical-looking, lemon-and-orange Brimstone, languorously flopping about in gardens, had been a sensation in 1907 and was still a pleasure to net.

Along the back line of the *plage,* various seaside chairs and stools supported the parents of straw-hatted children who were playing in front on the sand. I could be seen on my knees trying to set a found comb aflame by means of a magnifying glass. Men sported white trousers that to the eye of today would look as if they had comically shrunk in the washing; ladies wore, that particular season, light coats with silk-faced lapels, hats with big crowns and wide brims, dense embroidered white veils, frill-fronted blouses, frills at their wrists, frills on their parasols. The breeze salted one's lips. At a tremendous pace a stray Clouded Yellow came dashing across the palpitating *plage.* [SM 147]

Two years before, on the same *plage,* I had been much attached to Zina, the lovely, sun-tanned, bad-tempered little daughter of a Serbian naturopath – she had, I remember (absurdly, for she and I were only eight at the time), a *grain de beauté* on her apricot skin just below the heart, and there was a horrible collection of chamber pots, full and half-full, and one with surface bubbles, on the floor of the hall in her family's boardinghouse lodgings which I visited early one morning to be given by her as she was being dressed, a dead hummingbird moth found by the cat. But when I met Colette, I knew at once that this was the real thing. [SM 149]

During the two months of our stay at Biarritz, my passion for Colette all but surpassed my passion for Cleopatra. . . .

I had a gold coin that I assumed would pay for our elopement. Where did I want to take her? Spain? America? The mountains above Pau? "*Là-bas, là-bas, dans la montagne,*" as I had heard Carmen sing at the opera. One strange night, I lay awake, listening to the recurrent thud of the ocean and planning our flight. The ocean seemed to rise and grope in the darkness and then heavily fall on its face.

Of our actual getaway, I have little to report. My memory retains a glimpse of her obediently putting on rope-soled canvas shoes, on the lee side of a flapping tent, while I stuffed a folding butterfly net into a brown-paper bag. The next glimpse is of our evading pursuit by entering a pitch-dark *cinéma* near the Casino (which, of course, was absolutely out of bounds). There we sat, holding hands across the dog, which now and then gently jingled in Colette's lap, and were shown a jerky, drizzly, but highly exciting bullfight at San Sebastián. [SM 150–51]

[Nabokov's father's passion for butterflies.]

Till the age of thirteen he was educated at home by French and English governesses and by Russian and German tutors; from one of the latter he caught and passed on to me the *passio et morbus aureliani.* . . . [SM 173]

[On discovering at school that his father has called someone out to a duel, and imagining him perhaps already dead, Nabokov recalls his most cherished images of his father.]

I remembered that summer afternoon (which already then seemed long ago although actually only four or five years had passed) when he had burst into my room, grabbed my net, shot down the veranda steps – and presently was strolling back holding between finger and thumb the rare and magnificent female of the Russian Poplar Admirable that he had seen basking on an aspen leaf from the balcony of his study. [SM 192]

[His cousin Yuri Rausch von Traubenberg, best friend of his youth.]

In the country, Yuri got up late, and I did not see him before my return to lunch, after four or five hours of butterfly hunting. From his earliest boyhood, he was absolutely fearless, but was squeamish and wary of "natural history," could not make himself touch wriggly things, could not endure the amusing emprisoned tickle of a small frog groping about in one's fist like a person, or the discreet, pleasantly cool, rhythmically undulating caress of a caterpillar ascending one's bare shin. He collected little soldiers of painted lead – these meant nothing to me but he knew their uniforms as well as I did different butterflies. He did not play any ball games, was incapable of pitching a stone properly, and could not swim, but had never told me he could not, and one day, as we were trying to cross the river by walking over a jam of pine logs afloat near a sawmill, he nearly got drowned when a particularly slippery bole started to plop and revolve under his feet. [SM 196]

[Berlin, 1910, aged eleven.]

My brother loved the museum of wax figures in the Arcade off the Unter den Linden – Friedrich's grenadiers, Bonaparte communing with a mummy, young Liszt, who composed a rhapsody in his sleep, and Marat, who died in a shoe; and for me (who did not know yet that Marat had been an ardent lepidopterist) there was, at the corner of that Arcade, Gruber's famous butterfly shop, a camphoraceous paradise at the top of a steep, narrow staircase which I climbed every other day to inquire if Chapman's new Hairstreak or Mann's recently rediscovered White had been obtained for me at last. [SM 204–5]

[The shock of creating his first poem.]

That summer I was still far too young to evolve any wealth of "cosmic synchronization" (to quote my philosopher again). But I did discover, at least, that a person hoping to become a poet must have the capacity of thinking of several things at a time. In the course of the languid rambles that accompanied the making of my first poem, I ran into the village schoolmaster, an ardent Socialist, a good man, intensely devoted to my father (I welcome this image again), always with a tight posy of wild flowers, always smiling, always perspiring. While politely discussing with him my father's sudden journey to town, I registered simultaneously and with equal clarity not only his wilting flowers, his flowing tie and the blackheads on the fleshy volutes of his nostrils, but also the dull little voice of a cuckoo coming from afar, and the flash of a Queen of Spain settling on the road, and the remembered impression of the pictures (enlarged agricultural pests and bearded Russian writers) in the well-aerated classrooms of the village school which I had once or twice visited; and – to continue a tabulation that hardly does justice to the ethereal simplicity of the whole process – the throb of some utterly irrelevant recollection (a pedometer I had lost) was released from a neighboring brain cell, and the savor of the grass stalk I was chewing mingled with the cuckoo's note and the fritillary's takeoff, and all the while I was richly, serenely aware of my own manifold awareness.[322] [SM 218–19]

[His first full love-affair, at sixteen.]

Autumn came early that year. Layers of fallen leaves piled up ankle-deep by the end of August. Velvet-black Camberwell Beauties with creamy borders sailed through the glades. The tutor to whose erratic care my brother and I were entrusted that season used to hide in the bushes in order to spy upon Tamara and me with the aid of an old telescope he had found in the attic; but in his turn, one day, the peeper was observed by my uncle's purple-nosed old gardener Apostolski (incidentally, a great tumbler of weeding-girls) who very kindly reported it to my mother. She could not tolerate snooping, and besides (though I never spoke to her about Tamara) she knew all she cared to know of my romance from my poems which I recited to her in a spirit of praise-worthy objectivity, and which she lovingly copied out in a special album.   [SM 231–32]

[November 1917, immediately after the Bolshevik coup, Nabokov and his next oldest brother are sent from St. Petersburg to the Crimea, in the first stage of exile.]

As far as I remember, the main reason for sending my brother and me off so promptly was the probability of our being inducted into the new "Red" army if we stayed in town. I was annoyed at going to a fascinating region in mid-November, long after the collecting season was over, having never been very good at digging for pupae (though, eventually, I did turn up a few beneath a big oak in our Crimean garden). Annoyance changed to distress, when after making a precise little cross over the face of each of us, my father rather casually added that very possibly, *ves'ma vozmozhno*, he would never see us again; whereupon, in trench coat and khaki cap, with his briefcase under his arm, he strode away into the steamy fog.   [SM 242]

[Mount Ay-Petri, above Yalta, summer 1918.]

One morning, on a mountain trail, I suddenly met a strange cavalier, clad in a Circassian costume, with a tense, perspiring face painted a fantastic yellow. He kept furiously tugging at his horse, which, without heeding him, proceeded down the steep path at a curiously purposeful walk, like that of an offended person leaving a party. I had seen runaway horses, but I had never seen a walkaway one before, and my astonishment was given a still more pleasurable edge when I recognized the unfortunate rider as Mozzhuhin, whom Tamara and I had so often admired on the screen. The film *Haji Murad* (after Tolstoy's tale of that gallant, rough-riding mountain chief) was being rehearsed on the mountain pastures of the range. "Stop that brute [*Derzhite proklyatoe zhivotnoe*]," he said through his teeth as he saw me, but at the same moment, with a mighty sound of crunching and crashing stones, two authentic Tatars came running down to the rescue, and I trudged on, with my butterfly net, toward the upper crags where the Euxine race of the Hippolyte Grayling was expecting me.

[SM 247]

My wife took, unnoticed, this picture, unposed, of me in the act of writing a novel in our hotel room. The hotel is the Établissement Thermal at Le Boulou, in the East Pyrenees. The date (discernible on the captured calendar) is February 27, 1929. The novel, *Zashchita Luzhina* (*The Defense*), deals with the defense invented by an insane chess player. Note the pat pattern of the tablecloth. A half-empty package of Gauloises cigarettes can be made out between the ink bottle and an overful ashtray. Family photos are propped against the four volumes of Dahl's Russian dictionary. The end of my robust, dark-brown penholder (a beloved tool of young oak that I used during all my twenty years of literary labors in Europe and may rediscover yet in one of the trunks stored at Dean's, Ithaca, N.Y.) is already well chewed. My writing hand partly conceals a stack of setting boards. Spring moths would float in through the open window on overcast nights and settle upon the lighted wall on my left. In that way we collected a number of rare Pugs in perfect condition and spread them at once (they are now in an American museum). Seldom does a casual snapshot compendiate a life so precisely.

[SM, facing p. 256]

[His brother Sergey.]

He is a mere shadow in the background of my richest and most detailed recollections. I was the coddled one; he, the witness of coddling. Born, caesareanally, ten and a half months after me, on March 12, 1900, he matured earlier than I and physically looked older. We seldom played together, he was indifferent to most of the things I was fond of – toy trains, toy pistols, Red Indians, Red Admirables. At six or seven he developed a passionate adulation, condoned by Mademoiselle, for Napoleon and took a little bronze bust of him to bed. As a child, I was rowdy, adventurous and something of a bully. He was quiet and listless, and spent much more time with our mentors than I. [SM 257]

[Caption to most unusual European butterfly catch, 1938.]

The small butterfly, light blue above, grayish beneath, of which the two type specimens (male holotype on the left, both sides, one hindwing slightly damaged; and male paratype on the right, both sides), preserved in the American Museum of Natural History and figured now for the first time from photographs made by that institution, is *Plebejus (Lysandra) cormion* Nabokov. The first name is that of the genus, the second that of the subgenus, the third that of the species, and the fourth that of the author of the original description which I published in September 1941 (*Journal of the New York Entomological Society*, Vol. 49, p. 265), later figuring the genitalia of the paratype (October 26, 1945, *Psyche*, Vol. 52, Pl. 1). Possibly, as I pointed out, my butterfly owed its origin to hybridization between *Plebejus (Lysandra) coridon* Poda (in the large sense) and *Plebejus (Meleageria) daphnis* Schiffermüller. Live organisms are less conscious of specific or subgeneric differences than the taxonomist is. I took the two males figured, and saw at least two more (but no females) on July 20 (paratype) and 22 (holotype), 1938, at about 4,000 ft. near the village of Moulinet, Alpes Maritimes. It may not rank high enough to deserve a name, but whatever it be – a new species in the making, a striking sport, or a chance cross – it remains a great and delightful rarity. [SM, facing p. 274]

[The fourth stage of exile, Germany, 1922–37.]

Somehow, during my secluded years in Germany, I never came across those gentle musicians of yore who, in Turgenev's novels, played their rhapsodies far into the summer night; or those happy old hunters with their captures pinned to the crown of their hats, of whom the Age of Reason made such fun: La Bruyère's gentleman who sheds tears over a parasitized caterpillar, Gay's "philosophers more grave than wise" who, if you please, "hunt science down in butterflies," and, less insultingly, Pope's "curious Germans," who "hold so rare" those "insects fair"; or simply the so-called wholesome and kindly folks that during the last war homesick soldiers from the Middle West seem to have preferred so much to the cagey French farmer and to brisk Madelon II. [SM 278]

[Writing in the emigration.]

By 1928, my novels were beginning to bring a little money in German translations, and in the spring of 1929, you and I went butterfly hunting in the Pyrenees. [SM 281]

[First Index entries beginning with "L."]

[SM 313]

From letter from Véra Nabokov to Bud McLennan,[323] February 8, 1966

From Montreux.

THE GIFT, jacket design: This is one of the things on which my husband makes his own decisions. In the present case he asks me to say the following:

"The design for the jacket seems to me tasteless in the extreme. The only symbol a broken butterfly is of is a broken butterfly. Moreover, there is a grotesque clash between that particular peacock butterfly (which does not occur in the St. Petersburg region) and the Petersburg spring poem, while, on the other hand, in regard to the explorer father the peacock butterfly is pretty meaningless because it is one of the commonest butterflies in Asia, and there would have been no point in rigging up an expedition to capture it. The girl does not look like Zina Mertz at all. The entire conception is artistically preposterous, wrong and crude, and I cannot understand why they are not using the subtle and intelligent sketch I sent them, with the keys on the floor of the hall."

I am sorry that he should feel so strongly about this, but he does.

[SL 384]

From letter from Véra Nabokov to Filippa Rolf,[324] April 11, 1966

From Montreux. Unpublished.

My husband is working on a new novel[325]. . . .

We shall look for a very quiet and secluded spot, and shall not budge from there, dividing our time between butterflies and work. Butterflies are conducive to writing, at least it is so in his case, because he can think in complete concentration while following them.   [VNA]

From notes for *Butterflies in Art* project
Unpublished.

[Index card accompanying postcard.]
Linard, Jacques c. 1600–45
    Basket with Flowers. *Louvre Mus.*
  An interesting *pyri?*   in r. lower corner
      quercus?[326]
     (check)   [VNA, MTRX]

From Nabokov's diary, June 25, 1966
Unpublished.

In catching butterflies, we distinguish: the forehand stroke; the backhand; and the lowly "pudder" – popping the net over the butterfly settled on the damp ground.   [VNA]

From letter to Elena Sikorski, July 21, 1966
From Ponte di Legno, Italy. In Russian.

PONTE DI LEGNO m. 1260
   Panorama [Hotel]
. . . It's so cold here, that my legs are like marble under their bronze bloom. But there are not bad butterflies and one Italian entomologist, whom I brilliantly avoid on my walks (he lies in wait in a tin car).   [*Perepiska s sestroy 106*]

From interview with Alfred Appel, Jr.,[327] September 25–29, 1966

Published in *Wisconsin Studies in Contemporary Literature* 8 (Spring 1967).

My passion for lepidopterological research, in the field, in the laboratory, in the library, is even more pleasurable than the study and practice of literature, which is saying a good deal. Lepidopterists are obscure scientists. Not one is mentioned in Webster. But never mind. I have re-worked the classification of various groups of butterflies, have described and figured several species and subspecies. My names for the microscopic organs that I have been the first to see and portray have safely found their way into biological dictionaries (compare this to the wretched entry under "nymphet" in Webster's latest edition). The tactile delights of precise delineation, the silent paradise of the camera lucida, and the precision of poetry in taxonomic description represent the artistic side of the thrill which accumulation of new knowledge, absolutely useless to the layman, gives its first begetter. Science means to me above all natural science. Not the ability to repair a radio set; quite stubby fingers can do that. Apart from this basic consideration, I certainly welcome the free interchange of terminology between any branch of science and any raceme of art. There is no science without fancy, and no art without facts. Aphoristicism is a symptom of arteriosclerosis. [so 78–79]

In my lectures I tried to give factual data only. A map of three country estates with a winding river and a figure of the butterfly *Parnassius mnemosyne* for a cartographic cherub will be the endpaper in my revised edition of *Speak, Memory*. [so 90]

From Alfred Appel, Jr., note in the *Annotated Lolita*

While I was visiting him in 1966, he took from the shelf his copy of Alexander B. Klots's standard work, *A Field Guide to the Butterflies [of North America, East of the Great Plains]* (1951), and, opening it, pointed to the first sentence of the section on "*Genus* Lycaeides Scudder: The Orange

Margined Blues," which reads: "The recent work of Nabokov has entirely rearranged the classification of this genus" (p. 164). "That's real fame," said the author of *Lolita*. "That means more than anything a literary critic could say."

[*Annotated* Lolita (1970), 327–28]

From interview with Herbert Gold, September 1966

Published in the *Paris Review*, October 1967.

Q: Are you a lepidopterist, stalking your victims? If so, doesn't your laughter startle them?

A: On the contrary, it lulls them into the state of torpid security which an insect experiences when mimicking a dead leaf. Though by no means an avid reader of reviews dealing with my own stuff, I happen to remember the essay by a young lady who attempted to find entomological symbols in my fiction.[328] The essay might have been amusing had she known something about Lepidoptera. Alas, she revealed complete ignorance and the muddle of terms she employed proved to be only jarring and absurd.

[so 96]

Q: Besides writing novels, what do you, or would you, most like to do?

A: Oh, hunting butterflies, of course, and studying them. The pleasures and rewards of literary inspiration are nothing beside the rapture of discovering a new organ under the microscope or an undescribed species on a mountainside in Iran or Peru. It is not improbable that had there been no revolution in Russia, I would have devoted myself entirely to lepidopterology and never have written any novels at all.

[so 100]

From interview with Dieter E. Zimmer,[329] October 1966

Published in *Die Zeit*, November 1, 1966.

I have chosen Switzerland because it is an especially charming and comfortable country. There are fascinating butterflies in the mountains. Collecting in the Simplon region or the Grisons is a marvelous pleasure, and some of these renowned localities – Pontresina, Zermatt, Laquintal, the Rhone valley – are classical haunts that still yield unexpected discoveries despite the generations of English and German collectors who roamed there in the past. . . .

Yes – my wife and I imagine very clearly the quiet sunny spot in America where we would like to settle down. But I also intend to collect butterflies in Peru or Iran before I pupate. . . .

Had the Revolution not happened the way it happened, I would have enjoyed a landed gentleman's leisure no doubt, but I also think that my entomological occupations would have been more engrossing and energetic and that I would have gone on long collecting trips to Asia. I would have had a private museum, and a large library, comfortably housed. . . .

The butterfly book has been postponed but I have worked out the draft of a complete catalogue of European butterflies. . . .

[Lepidopterist of renown?] Let us not exaggerate: Actual publication of scientific papers is limited in my case to one hectic decade, roughly from 1940 to 1950, when I tackled relatively narrow problems in lepidopterology. [TS, VNA]

From letter to Page Stegner,[330] October 14, 1966

From Montreux.

You should have been warned that Mrs. Butler's article[331] is pretentious nonsense from beginning to end. [SL 393]

From letter from Véra Nabokov to Page Stegner, October 21, 1966

From Montreux.

My husband asks me to list some other little errors we have noticed in your book. . . .

p. 26–29   My husband wants to repeat that there is no connection whatsoever, either in his work or his mind, between entomology and humbertology. He says "Good thing Diana Butler did not know that there is a butterfly called (long before Lo) 'Nabokov's Nymph.' There is a famous American butterfly called 'Diana,' and there was a celebrated British lepidopterist called Butler."

[SL 394]

King, Queen, Knave

Excerpts from revisions to novel. Written 1928 in Russian. Revised and expanded translation 1966–67. Published in 1968.

[Franz, Martha and Dreyer visit Pomerania Bay.]

Sitting around in cafés was not unpleasant although it could be overdone too. There was the Blue Terrace café where the pastry, he thought, was so good. The other day as they were having ice chocolate there, Martha counted at least three foreigners among the crowd. One, judging by his newspaper, was a Dane. The other two were a less easily determinable pair: the girl was trying in vain to attract the attention of the café cat, a small black animal sitting on a chair and licking one hind paw rigidly raised like a shouldered club. Her companion, a suntanned fellow, smoked and smiled. What language were they speaking? Polish? Esthonian? Leaning near them against the wall was some kind of net: a bag of pale-bluish gauze on a ring fixed to a rod of light metal.

"Shrimp catchers," said Martha. "I want shrimps for dinner tonight." (She clicked her front teeth.)

"No," said Franz. "That's not a fisherman's net. That's for catching mosquitoes."

"Butterflies," said Dreyer, lifting an index finger.

"Who wants to catch butterflies?" remarked Martha.

"Oh, it must be good sport," said Dreyer. "In fact, I think to have a passion for something is the greatest happiness on earth."

"Finish your chocolate," said Martha.

"Yes," said Dreyer. "I think it's fascinating, the secrets you find in most ordinary people. That reminds me: Piffke – yes, yes, fat pink Piffke – collects beetles and is a famous expert on them."

"Let's go," said Martha. "Those arrogant foreigners are staring at you."

[KQK 232–33]

The foreign girl in the blue dress danced with a remarkably handsome man in an old-fashioned dinner jacket. Franz had long since noticed this couple; they had appeared to him in fleeting glimpses, like a recurrent dream image or a subtle leitmotiv – now at the beach, now in a café, now on the promenade. Sometimes the man carried a butterfly net. The girl had a delicately painted mouth and tender gray-blue eyes, and her fiancé or husband, slender, elegantly balding, contemptuous of everything on earth but her, was looking at her with pride; and Franz felt envious of that unusual pair, so envious that his oppression, one is sorry to say, grew even more bitter, and the music stopped. They walked past him. They were speaking loudly. They were speaking a totally incomprehensible language.   [KQK 254]

From letter to Andrew Field,[332] February 3, 1967

From Montreux. Unpublished.

[Nabokov wrote correcting and amplifying the galleys of Field's Nabokov: His Life in Art.*]*
The 1916 collection of poems was on sale in bookshops but the little brochure of 1914 was only distributed among a few friends and enthusiastic relatives: all it contained was one terrible lyrical poem about the first of the moonlit gardens, with a motto from *Romeo and Juliet*, and the only line I remember is *Nád rododéndronom v'yótsya oná* (your loathing lepidoptera is a special question which I will discuss with you when we meet again).   [VNA]

From letter to Morris Bishop, February 7, 1967

From Montreux.

. . . *Passio et morbo aureliana* occurs in the work of an old aurelian (chrysalid lover), and thus is stamped in my mind. I tried to turn it into your better

Latin in the British edition of my book but it resulted in a hideous misprint.[333] . . .

One of my young biographers[334] has visited you in Ithaca – lucky fellow! He saw my *Papilio waterclosetensis*!   [SL 400]

From letter to Alfred Appel, Jr., March 28, 1967

From Montreux.

[Nabokov wrote correcting Appel's draft notes for The Annotated Lolita.*]*

"bears Nabokov's name." An improper phrase. Although a genus (*Nabokovia* Hemming) and several new species (e.g., *Eupithecia nabokovi* McDunnough) do bear my name, no *Lycaeides* species or subspecies happens to be named after me. I have described, however, several new members of that genus, and my name is *appended* to the names I have given them (e.g. *L. sublivens* Nabokov) in the same way as that of the great Canadian lepidopterist is appended to the name of a moth I discovered (see above). . . .

I shall check all your notes but please do leave out all reference to lepidoptera, a tricky subject (which led the unfortunate Diana so dreadfully astray).[335] There are a couple of passages where lep notes are quite necessary but these I shall supply myself.   [SL 407–8]

From letter to Alfred Appel, Jr., April 3, 1967

From Montreux.

Re Reds and Blues. I protest vehemently against the lycaenization of my common use of the epithet "blue." In the p. 265 passage, what Rita does not understand is that a white surface, the chalk of that hotel, does look blue in a wash of light and shade on a vivid fall day, amid red foliage. H. H. is merely paying a tribute to French impressionist painters. He notes an optical miracle as E. B. White does somewhere when referring to the divine combination of "red barn and blue snow." It is the shock of color, not an intellectual blueprint or the shadow of a hobby. H. H. knows nothing about lepidoptera. In fact, I went out of my way to indicate (p. 112 and p. 159) that he cannot distinguish a butterfly from a moth, and that he confuses the hawkmoths visiting flowers at dusk with "gray hummingbirds." But on the other hand, I confess that Miss Phalen's name attracted me because *phalène* means moth in French.

Re French. Ormonde is a Joycean double-bottomed pun for it not only alludes to his bar but also means, in comic translation, "out-of-this-world" (*hors [de ce] monde*). The Dubliner's rainbow of children on p. 223 would have been a meaningless muddying of metaphors had I tried to smuggle in a Pierid of the Southern States and a European moth. My only purpose here was to render a prismatic effect. May I point out (at the risk of being pretentious) that I do not see the colors of lepidoptera as I do those of less familiar things – girls, gardens, garbage (similarly, a chessplayer does not see white and black as white and black) and that, for instance, if I use "morpho blue" I am thinking not of one of the many species of variously blue *Morpho* butterflies of South America, but of the ornaments made of bits of the showy wings of the commoner species. When a lepidopterist uses "Blues," a slangy but handy term, for a certain group of Lycaenids, he does not see that word in any color connection because he knows that the diagnostic undersides of their wings are not blue but dun, tan, grayish etc., and that many Blues, especially in the female, are brown, not blue. In my case, the differentiation in artistic and scientific vision is particularly strong because I was really born a landscape painter, not a landless escape novelist as some think.   [SL 410–11]

From letter to Jason Epstein, May 19, 1967

From Camogli, Italy.

> Camogli (Genova), Italy
> Cenobio dei Dogi

. . . We are staying at a charming place (address above) where we shall remain till June 15th. A new novel I am writing takes up a good deal of my time but I manage to walk up to 15 kilometers daily on the steep paths in search of butterflies.   [SL 411–12]

From letter to Alfred Appel, Jr., May 23, 1967

From Camogli.

p. 48.[336] Pisky is another form of pixy (fairy, elf) and also means "moth" in rural England. Maturin's Melmoth the Wanderer is O.K. It was also Wilde's alias after prison. Melmoth may come from Mellonella Moth (which breeds in beehives) or, more likely, from Meal Moth (which breeds in grain). . . .

Counting "Phalen" (Fr. *phalène*, moth), "Melmoth" and "Pisky," I can glean only eleven lep references in LOLITA (less than there are references to dogs or birds). I may have forgotten two or three, but there are certainly not fifty references!

p. 54. Falter (German for "butterfly"), one of Lo's schoolmates.

p. 112. I think I have given you earlier this "moth-or-butterfly" example of Humbert's complete incapacity to differentiate between Rhopalocera and Heterocera.[337]

p. 123. The "powdered bugs" wheeling around the lamps are noctuids and other moths which look floury on the wing (hence "millers," which, however, may also come from the verb) as they mill in the electric light against the damp night's blackground. Bugs is an Americanism for *any* insect. In England, it means generally bedbugs.

p. 158. The insects that poor Humbert mistakes for "creeping white flies" are the biologically fascinating little moths of the genus *Pronuba* whose amiable and indispensable females transport the pollen that fertilizes the yucca flowers (see, what Humbert failed to do, "Yucca Moth" in any good encyclopedia).

p. 159. The gray hummingbirds at dusk etc. are, as I have mentioned in an earlier communication, not birds but hawkmoths which do move exactly like hummingbirds (which are neither gray nor nocturnal).

p. 191. When naming incidental characters I like to give them some mnemonic handle, a private tag: thus "Avis Chapman" which I mentally attached to the South-European butterfly *Callophrys avis* Chapman (where Chapman, of course, is the non-italicizable name of that butterfly's original describer).

p. 213. This "patient bug" is not necessarily a moth – it could be some clumsy big fly or miserable beetle.

p. 236. Butterflies are indeed inquisitive, and the dipping motion is characteristic of a number of genera.

p. 252 & 303. "Schmetterling" (German "butterfly") blended with the author of L'Oiseau Bleu.[338]

p. 294. Moths like derelict snowflakes.

p. 260. Under the sign of the Tigermoth (an Arctiid).

p. 261. Rita's phrase "Going round and round like a mulberry moth" combines rather pleasingly the "round and round the mulberry tree" of the maypole song and the silk moth of China which breeds on mulberry.[339]

p. 318. Footnote to *Lycaeides sublivens* Nabokov.

This Coloradan member of the subgenus *Lycaeides* (which I now place in the genus *Plebejus*, a grouping corresponding exactly in scope to my former concept of *Plebejinae*) was described by me as a subspecies of Tutt's "*argyrognomon*" (now known as *idas* L.), but is, in my present opinion, a distinct species. V.N.   [SL 413–14]

From letter to Alfred Appel, Jr., July 27, 1967

From Limone Piemonte. Unpublished.

[Still correcting Appel's draft notes for The Annotated Lolita.*]*

Moth holes. An irrelevant and misleading note. You confuse the familiar, domestic, non-scientific connotation of "moth" as limited in cliché phrases ("moth holes," "moth eaten," "moth and rust") to the larva of a clothes moth with the nonbutterfly division Heterocera of Lepidoptera. Moths in that sense are as graceful and often as gaudy as true butterflies. In INVITATION TO A BEHEADING I have a saturnid moth which represents grace and beauty and art at their highest. And there is another charming moth in BEND SINISTER (cupped in a girl's hands).   [VNA]

From interview with Pierre Dommergues, September 7, 1967

In French.

In summer, [my life] is calmer. My wife and I set off travelling in search of butterflies. I adore mountains, in Switzerland, in Italy, in the south of France. I like staying at a thousand meters and climbing every day up to at least two thousand meters to chase alpine butterflies there. I know few things sweeter than to go out early in the morning with my net and take the chairlift towards a cloudless sky, following underneath myself, at the side, the shadow of the airborne chair with my seated silhouette, the shadow of my net in my fist, sliding along the slopes, waving under the alders, still climbing, slim, supple, rejuvenated and stylized by the effect of projection, crawling graciously in an almost mythological ascension. The return isn't so pretty, since the sun has changed place, and you see the shadow stunted, you see two big knees, everything has changed.

[*Les Langues modernes* 62 (January–February 1968)]

From interview with Archbishop Ioann (Strannik),[340] September 22, 1967

In Russian.

During our conversation I expressed the thought (with a clearly "apologist" deviation in V.V.'s direction) that throughout his whole life he had sought after butterflies and his pursuit of this half-real creature was perhaps linked with the highest stage of spiritual consciousness. Vladimir Vladimirovich did not agree with this too-light conjecture and energetically said that a butterfly is not a semi-angelic being. "Sometimes it even alights on corpses."

[*Russkaya mysl'*, June 1, 1978, 10]

From interview with Martin Esslin, February 17, 1968

Published in the *New York Times Book Review*, February 17, 1968.

. . . Between eleven and midnight begins my usual fight with insomnia. Such are my habits in the cold season. Summers I spend in the pursuit of lepidoptera on flowery slopes and mountain screes; and, of course, after my daily hike of fifteen miles or more, I sleep even worse than in winter. My last resort in this business of relaxation is the composing of chess problems.

[so 110]

From letter to Ernst Mayr,[341] April 17, 1968

From Montreux. Unpublished.

I was extremely glad to receive your letter. The pleasure is not unmingled with certain pangs because my love for lepidopterological research has remained as keen as ever. I still collect passionately butterflies every summer in Switzerland and Italy. If I ever visit Cambridge again it will be a treat to call on you. I know there is a new staircase, the pictures of the two or three Liberties are no longer there – but is French still there, I wonder.

Will you please give my warm greetings to anybody who remembers me. I enjoy recalling our conversations about overlapping subspecies and clines. [VNA]

From letter to Heather Mansell,[342] November 25, 1968

From Montreux.

SPEAK, MEMORY: Would like to see the blurb. The butterfly part of the cover design is not acceptable. Those two *meleagers* (?) have nothing to do with the Russian background of the book since they do not occur in the north of Europe; and the female is quite incorrectly colored. Please, no butterflies at all on the cover unless you want to use the white-and-black *mnemosyne* of the Weidenfeld jacket (also facing their page 19). [SL 436]

Letter to Heather Mansell, November 28, 1968

From Montreux.

Dear Miss Mansell,

I have your telegram

"IN VIEW BUTTERFLIES ON PROPOSE SPEAK MEMORY COVER FEATURED IN PLATE OPPOSITE PAGE 228 / sic / WEIDENFELD EDITION COULD YOU RECONSIDER YOUR OBJECTION? WILL SUBMIT NEW DESIGN PNIN/DOZEN STOP BLURB MEMORY FOLLOWS MANSELL PENGUIN BOOKS"

You are mistaken. The butterfly you figure on your cover for SPEAK, MEMORY is the one called *daphnis* by Schiffermüller and *meleager* by Esper and belongs to the subgenus called *Meleageria* by Sagarra, whilst the butterfly I figure on the plate facing p. 288 of the Weidenfeld edition of the book is the one called *cormion* by me, and belongs structurally to the subgenus called *Lysandra* by Hemming. My butterfly differs in male organ, wing shape, upperside coloration and underside pattern from your butterfly. Yours is a butterfly widely distributed throughout the southern part of central Europe and Russia; mine is an extremely rare freak, possibly a hybrid between *Meleageria daphnis (meleager)* and *Lysandra coridon*. The upper of your two figures is presumably a female of the *Meleageria* species (the colored photograph gives it an impossible green shade of blue and a revolting red rim); the female of my butterfly remains unknown to me (my two types are both males). And finally your butterfly is precisely one of the two, *M. daphnis (meleager)*, from which I separate my *L. cormion* as a distinct organism!

To recapitulate: You illustrate the wrong butterfly on your cover. This adds a gratuitous pictorial muddle to an obscure and subtle taxonomic problem. I cannot reconsider my objection. [SL 437–38]

Ada

Excerpts from novel. Written 1965–68. Published in 1969.

[Twelve-year-old Ada shows her "cousin," fourteen-year-old Van, around Ardis Manor for the first time.]

On the first floor, a yellow drawing room hung with damask and furnished in what the French once called the Empire style opened into the garden and now, in the late afternoon, was invaded across the threshold by the large leaf shadows of a paulownia tree (named, by an indifferent linguist, explained Ada, after the patronymic, mistaken for a second name or surname of a harmless lady, Anna Pavlovna Romanov, daughter of Pavel, nicknamed Paul-minus-Peter, why she did not know, a cousin of the non-linguist's master, the botanical Zemski, I'm going to scream, thought Van). A china cabinet encaged a whole zoo of small animals among which the oryx and the okapi, complete with scientific names, were especially recommended to him by his charming but impossibly pretentious companion.

[ADA 43]

[An Andalusian architect comes to dinner.]

"Oh, we'll dazzle the old boy with shop talk!"

They did not. Alonso, a tiny wizened man in a double-breasted tuxedo, spoke only Spanish, while the sum of Spanish words his hosts knew scarcely exceeded half a dozen. Van had *canastilla* (a little basket), and *nubarrones* (thunderclouds), which both came from an *en regard* translation of a lovely Spanish poem in one of his schoolbooks. Ada remembered, of course, *mariposa*, butterfly, and the names of two or three birds (listed in ornithological guides) such as *paloma*, pigeon, or *grevol*, hazel hen. Marina knew *aroma* and *bombre*, and an anatomical term with a "j" hanging in the middle.

[ADA 46]

[Ada continues the tour of Ardis Manor.]

["]We can *squirm* from here into the front hall by a secret passage, but I think we are supposed to go and look at the *grand chêne* which is really an elm." Did he like elms? Did he know Joyce's poem about the two washerwomen? He did, indeed. Did he like it? He did. In fact he was beginning to like very much arbors and ardors and Adas. They rhymed. Should he mention it?

"And now," she said, and stopped, staring at him.

"Yes?" he said, "and now?"

"Well, perhaps, I ought not to try to divert you – after you trampled upon those circles of mine; but I'm going to relent and show you the real marvel of Ardis Manor; my larvarium, it's in the room next to mine" (which he never saw, never – how odd, come to think of it!).

She carefully closed a communicating door as they entered into what looked like a glorified rabbitry at the end of a marble-flagged hall (a converted bathroom, as it transpired). In spite of the place's being well aired, with the heraldic stained-glass windows standing wide open (so that one heard the screeching and catcalls of an undernourished and horribly frustrated bird population), the smell of the hutches – damp earth, rich roots, old greenhouse and maybe a hint of goat – was pretty appalling. Before letting him come nearer, Ada fiddled with little latches and grates, and a sense of great emptiness and depression replaced the sweet fire that had been consuming Van since the beginning of their innocent games on that day.

"*Je raffole de tout ce qui rampe* (I'm crazy about everything that crawls)," she said.

"Personally," said Van, "I rather like those that roll up in a muff when you touch them – those that go to sleep like old dogs."

"Oh, they don't go to *sleep, quelle idée,* they *swoon,* it's a little syncope," explained Ada, frowning. "And I imagine it may be quite a little shock for the younger ones."

"Yes, I can well imagine that, too. But I suppose one gets used to it, by-and-by, I mean."

But his ill-informed hesitations soon gave way to esthetic empathy. Many decades later Van remembered having much admired the lovely, naked, shiny, gaudily spotted and streaked sharkmoth caterpillars, as poisonous as the mullein flowers clustering around them, and the flat larva of a local catocalid whose gray knobs and lilac plaques mimicked the knots and lichens of the twig to which it clung so closely as to practically lock with it, and, of course, the little Vaporer fellow, its black coat enlivened all along the back with painted tufts, red, blue, yellow, of unequal length, like those of a fancy toothbrush treated with certified colors. And that kind of smile, with those special trimmings, reminds me today of the entomological entries in Ada's diary – which we must have somewhere, mustn't we, darling, in that drawer there, no? you don't think so? Yes! Hurrah! Samples (your round-cheeked script, my love, was a little larger, but otherwise nothing, nothing, nothing has changed):

"The retractile head and diabolical anal appendages of the garish monster that produces the modest Puss Moth belong to a most uncaterpillarish caterpillar, with front segments shaped like bellows and a face resembling the lens of a folding camera. If you gently stroke its bloated smooth body, the sensation is quite silky and pleasant – until the irritated creature ungratefully squirts at you an acrid fluid from a slit in its throat."

"Dr. Krolik received from Andalusia and kindly gave me five young larvae of the newly described very local Carmen Tortoiseshell. They are delightful creatures, of a beautiful jade nuance with silvery spikes, and they breed only on a semi-extinct species of high-mountain willow (which dear Crawly also obtained for me)."

(At ten or earlier the child had read – as Van had – *Les Malheurs de Swann*, as the next sample reveals):

"I think Marina would stop scolding me for my hobby ('There's something indecent about a little girl's keeping such revolting pets . . . ,' 'Normal young ladies should loathe snakes and worms,' et cetera) if I could persuade her to overcome her old-fashioned squeamishness and place simultaneously on palm and pulse (the hand alone would not be roomy enough!) the noble larva of the Cattleya Hawkmoth (mauve shades of Monsieur Proust), a seven-inch-long colossus, flesh colored, with turquoise arabesques, rearing its hyacinth head in a stiff 'Sphinxian' attitude."

(Lovely stuff! said Van, but *even* I did not quite assimilate it, when I was young. So let us not bore the boor who flips through a book and thinks: "what a hoaxer, that old V.V.!")

At the end of his so remote, so near, 1884 summer Van, before leaving Ardis, was to make a visit of adieu to Ada's larvarium.

The porcelain-white, eye-spotted Cowl (or "Shark") larva, a highly prized gem, had safely achieved its next metamorphosis, but Ada's unique Lorelei Underwing had died, paralyzed by some ichneumon that had not been deceived by those clever prominences and fungoid smudges. The multicolored toothbrush had comfortably pupated within a shaggy cocoon, promising a Persian Vaporer later in the autumn. The two Puss Moth larvae had assumed a still uglier but at least more vermian and in a sense venerable aspect: their pitchforks now limply trailing behind them, and a purplish flush dulling the cubistry of their extravagant colors, they kept "ramping" rapidly all over the floor of their cage in a surge of prepupational locomotion. Aqua had walked through a wood and into a gulch to do it last year. A freshly emerged *Nymphalis carmen* was fanning its lemon and amber-brown wings on a sunlit patch of grating, only to be choked with one nip by the nimble fingers of enraptured and heartless Ada; the Odettian Sphinx had turned, bless him, into an elephantoid mummy with a comically encased trunk of the guermantoid type; and Dr. Krolik was swiftly running on short legs after a very special orange-tip above timberline, in another hemisphere, *Anthocharis ada* Krolik (1884) – as it was known until changed to *A. prittwitzi* Stümper (1883) by the inexorable law of taxonomic priority.[343]

"But, afterwards, when all these beasties have hatched," asked Van, "what do you do with them?"

"Oh," she said, "I take them to Dr. Krolik's assistant who sets them and labels them and pins them in glassed trays in a clean oak cabinet, which will be mine when I marry. I shall then have a big collection, and continue to breed all kinds of leps – my dream is to have a special Institute of Fritillary larvae and violets – all the special violets they breed on. I would have eggs or larvae rushed to me here by plane from all over North America, with their foodplants – Redwood Violets from the West Coast, and a Pale Violet from Montana, and the Prairie Violet, and Egglestone's Violet from Kentucky, and a rare white violet from a secret marsh near an unnamed lake on an arctic mountain where Krolik's Lesser Fritillary flies. Of course, when the things emerge, they are quite easy to mate by hand – you hold them – for quite a while, sometimes – like this, in folded-wing profile" (showing the method, ignoring her poor fingernails), "male in your left hand, female in your right, or vice versa, with the tips of their abdomens touching, but they must be quite fresh and *soaked* in their favorite violet's reek."

[ADA 53–57]

[*Van cannot stop thinking about Ada.*]

He swore wretchedly in the hopelessness of his bed as he focused his swollen senses on the glimpse of her he had engulfed when, on their second excursion to the top of the house, she had mounted upon a captain's trunk to unhasp a sort of illuminator through which one acceded to the roof (even the dog had once gone there), and a bracket or something wrenched up her skirt and he saw – as one sees some sickening miracle in a Biblical fable or a moth's shocking metamorphosis – that the child was darkly flossed.

[ADA 59]

[*The picnic on Ada's twelfth birthday.*]

Marina came in a red motorcar of an early "runabout" type, operated by the butler very warily as if it were some fancy variety of corkscrew. She looked unwontedly smart in a man's gray flannels and sat holding the palm of her gloved hand on the knob of a clouded cane as the car, wobbling a little, arrived at the very edge of the picnic site, a picturesque glade in an old pinewood cut by ravishingly lovely ravines. A strange pale butterfly passed from the opposite side of the woods, along the Lugano dirt road, and was followed presently by a landau from which emerged one by one, nimbly or slowly, depending on age and condition, the Erminin twins, their young pregnant aunt (narrationally a great burden), and a governess, white-haired Mme Forestier, the school friend of Mathilde in a forthcoming story.

[ADA 79]

[*The end of the picnic.*]

Lying on his stomach, leaning his cheek on his hand, Van looked at his love's inclined neck as she played anagrams with Grace, who had innocently suggested "insect."

"Scient," said Ada, writing it down.

"Oh no!" objected Grace.

"Oh yes! I'm sure it exists. He is a great scient. Dr. Entsic was scient in insects."

Grace meditated, tapping her puckered brow with the eraser end of the pencil, and came up with:

"Nicest!"

"Incest," said Ada instantly.

"I give up," said Grace. "We need a dictionary to check your little inventions."

But the glow of the afternoon had entered its most oppressive phase, and the first bad mosquito of the season was resonantly slain on Ada's shin by alert Lucette. The charabanc had already left with the armchairs, the hampers and the munching footmen, Essex, Middlesex and Somerset; and now Mlle Larivière and Mme Forestier were exchanging melodious adieux. Hands waved, and the twins with their ancient governess and sleepy young aunt were carried away in the landau. A pale diaphanous butterfly with a very black body followed them and Ada cried "Look!" and explained it was closely related to a Japanese Parnassian. Mlle Larivière said suddenly she would use a pseudonym when publishing the story.

[ADA 85]

[Van explores the shattal tree with Ada.]

Van, in his blue gym suit, having worked his way up to a fork just under his agile playmate (who naturally was better acquainted with the tree's intricate map) but not being able to see her face, betokened mute communication by taking her ankle between finger and thumb as *she* would have a closed butterfly.

[ADA 94]

[Van meets Ada for their first assignation as lovers in Ardis Park.]

Van reached the third lawn, and the bower, and carefully inspected the stage prepared for the scene, "like a provincial come an hour too early to the opera after jogging all day along harvest roads with poppies and bluets catching and twinkle-twining in the wheels of his buggy" (Floeberg's *Ursula*).

Blue butterflies nearly the size of Small Whites, and likewise of European origin, were flitting swiftly around the shrubs and settling on the drooping clusters of yellow flowers. In less complex circumstances, forty years hence, our lovers were to see again, with wonder and joy, the same insect and the same bladder-senna along a forest trail near Susten in the Valais. At the present moment he was looking forward to collecting what he would recollect later, and watched the big bold Blues as he sprawled on the turf, burning with the evoked vision of Ada's pale limbs in the variegated light of the bower, and then coldly telling himself that fact could never quite match fancy.   [ADA 128–29]

[Van and Ada's farewell tryst at the end of their first summer at Ardis.]

Ada, doing her feminine best to restrain and divert her sobs by transforming them into emotional exclamations, pointed out some accursed insect that had settled on an aspen trunk.

(Accursed? *Accursed?* It was the newly described, fantastically rare vanessian, *Nymphalis danaus* Nab., orange-brown, with black-and-white foretips, mimicking, as its discoverer Professor Nabonidus of Babylon College, Nebraska, realized, not the Monarch butterfly directly, but the Monarch *through* the Viceroy, one of the Monarch's best known imitators. In Ada's angry hand.)

"Tomorrow you'll come here with your green net," said Van bitterly, "my butterfly."

She kissed him all over the face, she kissed his hands, then again his lips, his eyelids, his soft black hair. He kissed her ankles, her knees, her soft black hair.   [ADA 158]

[Van meets Ada for the first time in months, chaperoned by another schoolgirl, at a railway station tearoom near her boarding school.]

As Ada reached for the cream, he caught and inspected her dead-shamming hand. We remember the Camberwell Beauty that lay tightly closed for an instant upon her palm, and suddenly our hand was empty. He saw, with satisfaction, that her fingernails were now long and sharp.   [ADA 170]

Pedantic Ada once said that the looking up of words in a lexicon for any other needs than those of expression – be it instruction or art – lay somewhere between the ornamental assortment of flowers (which could be, she conceded, mildly romantic in a maidenly headcocking way) and making collage-pictures of disparate butterfly wings (which was always vulgar and often criminal). [ADA 222]

[Van's father, Demon, visits Ardis Park for dinner with Van, Ada, and his cousin and former lover, Marina.]

The tablecloth and the candle blaze attracted timorous or impetuous moths among which Ada, with a ghost pointing them out to her, could not help recognizing many old "flutterfriends." Pale intruders, anxious only to spread out their delicate wings on some lustrous surface; ceiling-bumpers in guildman furs; thick-set rake-hells with bushy antennae; and party-crashing hawkmoths with red black-belted bellies, sailed or shot, silent or humming, into the dining room out of the black hot humid night. [ADA 250]

[Dreading Ada is unfaithful, Van receives an anonymous note advising him that he is being deceived. He deduces that it must be written by one of the French servants at Ardis.]

To interview them all – torture the males, rape the females – would be, of course, absurd and degrading. With a puerile wrench he broke his best black butterfly on the wheel of his exasperation.[344] The pain from the fang bite was now reaching his heart. He found another tie, finished dressing and went to look for Ada. [ADA 287–88]

[Foul-tempered after discovering Ada's infidelity, Van storms from Ardis and provokes a duel with a stranger.]

At the moment his foot touched the pine-needle strewn earth of the forest road, a transparent white butterfly floated past, and with utter certainty Van knew that he had only a few minutes to live.

He turned to his second and said:

"This stamped letter, in this handsome Majestic Hotel envelope, is addressed, as you see, to my father. I am transferring it to the back pocket of my pants. Please post it at once if the Captain, who I see has arrived in a rather funerary-looking limousine, accidentally slaughters me." [ADA 310]

[Van writes a pseudonymous novel obliquely reflecting Ada's letters.]

Letters from Terra, by Voltemand, came out in 1891 on Van's twenty-first birthday, under the imprint of two bogus houses, "Abencerage" in Manhattan, and "Zegris" in London.

(Had I happened to see a copy I would have recognized Chateaubriand's *lapochka* and hence your little paw, *at once.*)³⁴⁵ [ADA 342]

[Lucette reports to Van about her nightly lesbian frolics with Ada.]

"... So the day passed, and then the star rose, and tremendous moths walked on all sixes up the window panes, and we tangled until we fell asleep. And that's when I learnt – " concluded Lucette, closing her eyes and making Van squirm by reproducing with diabolical accuracy Ada's demure little whimper of ultimate bliss. [ADA 376]

[Ada writes to Van that if he will not let her come and live with him she will marry.]

*If you scorn the maid at your window I will aerogram my immediate acceptance of a proposal of marriage that has been made to your poor Ada a month ago in Valentine State. He is an Arizonian Russian, decent and gentle, not overbright and not fashionable. The only thing we have in common is a keen interest in many military-looking desert plants, especially various species of agave, hosts of the larvae of the most noble animals in America, the Giant Skippers*³⁴⁶ *(Krolik, you see, is burrowing again).*

[ADA 385]

[Van and Ada are ecstatically reunited. His infertility simplifies their incestuous love.]

What laughs, what tears, what sticky kisses, what a tumult of multitudinous plans! And what safety, what freedom of love! Two unrelated gypsy courtesans, a wild girl in a gaudy lolita, poppy-mouthed and black-downed, picked up in a café between Grasse and Nice, and another, a part-time model (you have seen her fondling a virile lipstick in Fellata ads), aptly nick-named Swallowtail by the patrons of a Norfolk Broads floramor,³⁴⁷ had both given our hero exactly the same reason, unmentionable in a family chronicle, for considering him absolutely sterile despite his prowesses. Amused by the Hecatean diagnose, Van underwent certain tests, and although pooh-poohing the symptom as coincidental, all the doctors agreed that Van Veen might be a doughty and durable lover but could never hope for an offspring. How merrily little Ada clapped her hands! [ADA 393–94]

[Van and Ada pore over an album of photographs taken at Ardis, some for blackmail purposes, by kitchenhand Kim Beauharnais.]

Drama and comedy. Blanche struggling with two amorous *tsigans* in the Baguenaudier Bower. Uncle Dan calmly reading a newspaper in his little red motorcar, hopelessly stuck in black mud on the Ladore road.

Two huge common Peacock moths, still connected. Grooms and gardeners brought Ada that species every blessed year; which, in a way, reminds us of you, sweet Marco d'Andrea, or you, red-haired Domenico Benci, or you, dark and broody Giovanni del Brina (who thought they were bats) or the one I dare not mention (because it is Lucette's scholarly contribution[348] – so easily botched after the scholar's death) who likewise might have picked up, at the foot of an orchard wall, not overhung with not-yet-imported wisteria (her half-sister's addition), on a May morning in 1542, near Florence, a pair of the Pear Peacock *in copula*, the male with the feathery antennae, the female with the plain threads, to depict them faithfully (among wretched, unvisualized insects) on one side of a fenestral niche in the so-called "Elements Room" of the Palazzo Vecchio. [ADA 399–401]

[After making love, Van and Ada continue with the album.]

"Well," said Van, when the mind took over again, "let's go back to our defaced childhood. I'm anxious" – (picking up the album from the bedside rug) – "to get rid of this burden. Ah, a new character, the inscription says: Dr. Krolik."

"Wait a sec. It may be the best Vanishing Van but it's terribly messy all the same. Okay. Yes, that's my poor nature teacher."

Knickerbockered, panama-hatted, lusting for his *babochka* (Russian for "lepidopteron"). A passion, a sickness. What could Diana know about *that* chase?[349]

"How curious – in the state Kim mounted him here, he looks much less furry and fat than I imagined. In fact, darling, he's a big, strong, handsome old March Hare! Explain!"

"There's nothing to explain. I asked Kim one day to help me carry some boxes there and back, and here's the visual proof. Besides, that's not *my* Krolik but his brother, Karol, or Karapars, Krolik. A doctor of philosophy, born in Turkey."

"I love the way your eyes narrow when you tell a lie. The remote mirage in Effrontery Minor."

"I'm not lying!" – (with lovely dignity): "He *is* a doctor of philosophy."

"Van *ist auch* one," murmured Van, sounding the last word as "*wann.*"

"Our fondest dream," she continued, "Krolik's and my fondest dream, was to describe and depict the early stages, from ova to pupa, of all the known Fritillaries, Greater and Lesser, beginning with those of the New World. I would have been responsible for building an argynninarium (a pestproof breeding house, with temperature patterns, and other refinements – such as background night smells and night-animal calls to create a natural atmosphere in certain difficult cases) – a caterpillar needs exquisite care! There are hundreds of species and good subspecies in both hemispheres but, I repeat, we'd begin with America. Live egg-laying females and live food plants, such as violets of numerous kinds, airmailed from everywhere, starting, for the heck of it, with arctic habitats – Lyaska, Le Bras d'Or, Victor Island. The magnanery would be also a violarium, full of fascinating flourishing plants, from the *endiconensis* race of the Northern Marsh Violet to the minute but magnificent *Viola kroliki* recently described by Professor Hall from Goodson Bay. I would contribute colored figures of all the instars, and line drawings of the perfect insect's genitalia and other structures. It would be a wonderful work."

"A work of love," said Van, and turned the page.

"Unfortunately, my dear collaborator died intestate, and all his collections, including my own little part, were surrendered by a regular warren of collateral Kroliks to agents in Germany and dealers in Tartary. Disgraceful, unjust, and so sad!"

"We'll find you another director of science. Now what do we have here?" [ADA 403–5]

[Van and Ada are in bed with their half-sister Lucette between them; the scene has been described in detail from above, as if for a travel brochure.]

The scarred male nude on the island's east coast is half-shaded, and, on the whole, less interesting, though considerably more aroused than is good for him or a certain type of tourist. The recently repapered wall immediately west of the now louder-murmuring (*et pour cause*) dorocene lamp is ornamented in the central girl's honor with Peruvian "honeysuckle" being visited (not only for its nectar, I'm afraid, but for the animalcules stuck in it) by marvelous Loddigesia Hummingbirds, while the bedtable on that side bears a lowly box of matches, a *karavanchik* of cigarettes, a Monaco ashtray, a copy of Voltemand's poor thriller, and a Lurid Oncidium Orchid in an amethystine vaselet. The companion piece on Van's side supports a similar superstrong but unlit lamp, a dorophone, a box of Wipex, a reading loupe, the returned Ardis album, and a separatum "Soft music as cause of brain tumors," by Dr. Anbury (young Rattner's waggish penname). Sounds have colors, colors have smells. The fire of Lucette's amber runs through the night of Ada's odor and ardor, and stops at the threshold of Van's lavender goat. Ten eager, evil, loving, long fingers belonging to two different young demons caress their helpless bed pet. Ada's loose black hair accidentally tickles the local curio she holds in her left fist, magnanimously demonstrating her acquisition. Unsigned and unframed.

That about summed it up (for the magical gewgaw liquefied all at once, and Lucette, snatching up her nightdress, escaped to her room). It was only the sort of shop where the jeweler's fingertips have a tender way of enhancing the preciousness of a trinket by something akin to a rubbing of hindwings on the part of a settled lycaenid or to the frottage of a conjurer's thumb dissolving a coin; but just in such a shop the anonymous picture attributed to Grillo or Obieto, caprice or purpose, *ober-* or *unterart,* is found by the ferreting artist.

"She's terribly nervous, the poor kid," remarked Ada stretching across Van toward the Wipex. "You can order that breakfast now – unless . . . Oh, what a good sight! Orchids. I've never seen a man make such a speedy recovery."   [ADA 419–20]

[Hypercharged, perhaps drugged, art connoisseur Demon elaborates on the news of his cousin's Dan's "odd Boschean death," a visual echo of a detail from Bosch's "Last Judgment." As he expatiates on two panels from Bosch's triptych The Garden of Earthly Delights, *Van wants only to shut him up and divert him from discovering that he, Van, Demon's son, is living with Demon's daughter Ada.]*

"If I could write," mused Demon, "I would describe, in too many words no doubt, how passionately, how incandescently, how incestuously – *c'est le mot* – art and science meet in an insect, in a thrush, in a thistle of that ducal bosquet. Ada is marrying an outdoor man, but her mind is a closed museum, and she, and dear Lucette, once drew my attention, by a creepy coincidence, to certain details of that other triptych, that tremendous garden of tongue-in-cheek delights, circa 1500, and, namely, to the butterflies in it – a Meadow Brown, female, in the center of the right panel, and a Tortoiseshell in the middle panel, placed there as if settled on a flower – mark the 'as if,' for here we have an example of exact knowledge on the part of those two admirable little girls, because they say that actually the *wrong* side of the bug is shown, it should have been the underside, if seen, as it is, in profile, but Bosch evidently found a wing or two in the corner cobweb of his casement and showed the prettier upper surface in depicting his incorrectly folded insect. I mean I don't give a hoot for the esoteric meaning, for the myth behind the moth, for the masterpiece-baiter who makes Bosch express some bosh of his time, I'm allergic to allegory and am quite sure he was just enjoying himself by crossbreeding casual fancies just for the fun of the contour and color, and what we have to study, as I was telling your cousins, is the joy of the eye, the feel and the taste of the woman-sized strawberry that you embrace *with* him, or the exquisite surprise of an unusual orifice – but you are not following me, you want me to go, so that you may interrupt her beauty sleep, lucky beast!   [ADA 436–37]

[Van writes to Ada, whom he has been barred from seeing, about her performance in the film Don Juan's Last Fling.*]*

Artistically, and ardisiacally, the best moment is one of the last – when you follow barefoot the Don who walks down a marble gallery to his doom, to the scaffold of Dona Anna's black-curtained bed, around which you flutter, my Zegris butterfly, straightening a comically drooping candle, whis-

pering delightful but futile instructions into the frowning lady's ear, and then peering over that mauresque screen and suddenly dissolving in such natural laughter, helpless and lovely, that one wonders if any art could do without that erotic gasp of schoolgirl mirth. And to think, Spanish orange-tip, that all in all your magic gambol lasted but eleven minutes of stop-watch time in patches of two- or three-minute scenes! [ADA 500–01]

[Van is impatient to meet Ada, now married to Andrey Vinelander, in Mont Roux, after twelve years of separation.]

When he reached at long last the whitewashed and blue-shaded Bellevue (patronized by wealthy Estotilanders, Rheinlanders, and Vinelanders, but not placed in the same superclass as the old, tawny and gilt, huge, sprawling, lovable Trois Cygnes), Van saw with dismay that his watch still lagged far behind 7:00 P.M., the earliest dinner hour in local hotels. So he recrossed the lane and had a double kirsch, with a lump of sugar, in a pub. A dead and dry hummingbird moth lay on the window ledge of the lavatory. Thank goodness, symbols did not exist either in dreams or in the life in between.

[ADA 510]

[Van and Ada stroll along the promenade by Lake Geneva. It is the middle of an extraordinarily warm October.]

The last butterflies of 1905, indolent Peacocks and Red Admirables, one Queen of Spain and one Clouded Yellow, were making the most of the modest blossom. [ADA 524]

[Van drives from Dalmatia toward Mont Roux, where Ada will meet him.]

The pale flush of dawn in his rear-vision mirror had long since turned to passionately bright daylight when he looped south, by the new Pfynwald road, near Sorcière, where seventeen years ago he had bought a house (now Villa Jolana).[350] [ADA 552]

[The final paragraph of the novel ends its built-in blurb.]

Not the least adornment of the chronicle is the delicacy of pictorial detail: a latticed gallery; a painted ceiling; a pretty plaything stranded among the forget-me-nots of a brook; butterflies and butterfly orchids in the margin of the romance; a misty view descried from marble steps; a doe at gaze in the ancestral park; and much, much more. [ADA 589]

From letter to Hugh Hefner,[351] December 28, 1968

From Montreux. Published in part in *Playboy*, January 1972.

Have you ever noticed how the head and ears of your Bunny resemble a butterfly in shape, with an eyespot on one hindwing?

Happy New Year.

Yours sincerely,

VLADIMIR NABOKOV [SL 439–40]

From interview with Martha Duffy and R. Z. Sheppard, March 1968

Published in *Time*, May 23, 1969.

In the summer of 1915, in northern Russia, I, an adventurous lad of sixteen, noticed one day that our chauffeur had left the family convertible throbbing all alone before its garage (part of the huge stable at our place in the country); next moment I had driven the thing, with a sickly series of bumps, into the nearest ditch. That was the first time I ever drove a car. The second and last time was thirty-five years later, somewhere in the States, when my wife let me take the wheel for a few seconds and I narrowly missed crashing into the only car standing at the far side of a spacious parking lot. Between 1949 and 1959 she has driven me more than 150,000 miles all over North America – mainly on butterfly-hunting trips. [SO 125]

From interview with Alden Whitman, April 1969

Published in the *New York Times*, April 19, 1969.

My Harvard experience consisted of seven blissful years (1941–1948) of entomological research at the wonderful and unforgettable Museum of

Comparative Zoology and of one spring term (1952) of lecturing on the European novel to an audience of some 600 young strangers in Memorial Hall.   [SO 132]

From interview with Philip Oakes, June 1969

Published in the *Sunday Times*, June 22, 1969.

Q: As a distinguished entomologist and novelist do you find that your two main preoccupations condition, restrict, or refine your view of the world?
A: What world? Whose world? If we mean the average world of the average newspaper reader in Liverpool, Livorno, or Vilno, then we are dealing in trivial generalities. If, on the other hand, an artist invents his own world, as I think I do, then how can he be said to influence his own understanding of what he has created himself? As soon as we start defining such terms as "the writer," "the world," "the novel," and so on, we slip into a solipsismal abyss where general ideas dissolve. As to butterflies – well, my taxonomic papers on lepidoptera were published mainly in the nineteen forties, and can be of interest to only a few specialists in certain groups of American butterflies. In itself, an aurelian's passion is not a particularly unusual sickness; but it stands outside the limits of a novelist's world, and I can prove this by the fact that whenever I allude to butterflies in my novels, no matter how diligently I rework the stuff, it remains pale and false and does not really express what I want it to express – what, indeed, it can only express in the special scientific terms of my entomological papers. The butterfly that lives forever on its type-labeled pin and in its O.D. ("original description") in a scientific journal dies a messy death in the fumes of the arty gush. However – not to let your question go completely unanswered – I must admit that in one sense the entomological satellite does impinge upon my novelistic globe. This is when certain place-names are mentioned. Thus if I hear or read the words "Alp Grum, Engadine" the normal observer within me may force me to imagine the belvedere of a tiny hotel on its 2000-meter-tall perch and mowers working along a path that winds down to a toy railway; but what *I* see first of all and above all is the Yellow-banded Ringlet settled with folded wings on the flower that those damned scythes are about to behead.   [SO 135–36]

Nowadays I write my stuff on index cards, in pencil, at a lectern, in the fore-noon; but I still tend to do a lot of work in my head during long walks in the country on dull days when butterflies do not interfere. Here is a disap-pointed lepidopterist's ditty:

> It's a long climb
> Up the rock face
> At the wrong time
> To the right place.[352]

[so 139–40]

From interview with Allene Talmey, June 1969

Published in *Vogue*, December 1969.

Q: Magic, sleight-of-hand, and other tricks have played quite a role in your fiction. Are they for your amusement or do they serve yet another purpose?
A: Deception is practiced even more beautifully by that other V.N., Visible Nature. A useful purpose is assigned by science to animal mimicry, protec-tive patterns and shapes, yet their refinement transcends the crude purpose of mere survival. In art, an individual style is essentially as futile and as or-ganic as a fata morgana. The sleight-of-hand you mention is hardly more than an insect's sleight-of-wing. [so 153]

A: Whatever the mind grasps, it does so with the assistance of creative fancy, that drop of water on a glass slide which gives distinctness and relief to the observed organism. [so 154]

From interview with James Mossman, September 8, 1969

Broadcast on *Review*, BBC-2, October 4, 1969.

Q: Doesn't giving away past memories to your characters alleviate the bur-den of the past?
A: Items of one's past are apt to fade from exposure. They are like those richly pigmented butterflies and moths which the ignorant amateur hangs

up in a display case on the wall of his sunny parlor and which, after a few years, are bleached to a pitiful drab hue. The metallic blue of so-called structural wing scales is hardier, but even so a wise collector should keep specimens in the dry dark of a cabinet. [so 143]

A: My existence has always remained as harmonious and green as it was throughout the span dealt with in my memoirs, that is from 1903 to 1940. The emotions of my Russian childhood have been replaced by new excitements, by new mountains explored in search of new butterflies, by a cloudless family life, and by the monstrous delights of novelistic invention.

[so 145]

From letter to Michael Walter,[353] September 8, 1969

From Montreux. Unpublished.

The project you write me about is most fascinating. I realize the tremendous labour involved since half-a-dozen years ago I was in contact with the Brit. Mus. about a similar project. Riley and Higgins are great men.

I extremely regret that I am too busy with non-lepidopterological work to write the kind of introduction which would please me and be worthy of the book. [VNA]

From interview with Robert Tabozzi, October 16, 1969

Published in *Panorama*.

Q: A definite autobiographical factor comes out in all your works (LOLITA, THE GIFT, PNIN). Is this factor also present in ADA?
A: The only autobiographical feature in LOLITA is a bunch of motels having some resemblance to those my wife and I stayed at in the forties and fifties, during the several summers we spent, when covering fifty thousand miles of America, in hunting butterflies. There is no such factor in ADA save maybe the rearing of interesting caterpillars that I conducted in my boyhood very assiduously and successfully. [From TS, VNA]

From interview with Gaetano Tumiati, October 30, 1969

In French. Published in *La Stampa*(?).

Q: How can you reconcile the sense of perfect harmony that you experience when you find yourself alone in a wood among the trees, in contact with nature, with the "mini-aggressiveness" and the scientific pedantry of the entomologist, who does not limit himself to looking at butterflies, but kills them, in fact collects and classifies them?

A: First, let me tell you that to enjoy something you have to see it and know it. A man who walks alone, as you put it, "in a wood among the trees," will not see a single butterfly (there's too much shade), unless I, who know them, indicate the moth whose wing design blends with the arabesques of the bark it clings to. I don't understand how one can call the knowledge of natural objects or the vocabulary of nature "pedantry." Is it the relative smallness of an insect which makes entomology seem comic or profane? Because everyone can tell a cat from a lion or a lepoard, and no one finds catalogues of rare books ridiculous. Not only do we collect butterflies, but we examine under the microscope their minuscule organs whose form helps to classify the creature more certainly than the color of its wings. And believe me, the emotion of recognizing in an alpine meadow a butterfly one knows to be different from another and whose special comportment one observes – this emotion is a feeling in which the scientific and the artistic sides join in an apex of sharp pleasure unknown to the man walking under trees he cannot even name.   [From TS, VNA]

From letter from Jaqueline Callier to Charles Monaghan,[354] October 31, 1969

From Montreux.

Mr. Vladimir Nabokov asks me to tell you that of all the books he happened to read in the course of 1969, he liked best

Tukio Tabuchi	The Alpine Butterflies of Japan
Philip Oakes	The God Botherers
Sam Beckett	Molloy

[SL 462]

From letter to Oliver Caldecott,[355] November 17, 1969

From Montreux.

Your artist's Cyprideum looks like a ghastly vulva, and the Puss Moth caterpillar is all wrong (and, moreover, does not breed on orchids). I am emphatically against this symbolic design. I want three or four non-anatomical genuine orchids, prettily colored, garlanded around "A D A". Why don't you simply use the drawing of the three species I made for you – possibly multiplying and stylizing them (but not freudianizing those innocent blossoms)?

[SL 463]

Anniversary Notes

Written February 1970. Published as a supplement to *Triquarterly* 17 (1970).

[At the request of Alfred Appel, Jr., Nabokov wrote a response to every contributor in the 1970 Tri-quarterly special issue devoted to him.]

Butterflies are among the most thoughtful and touching contributions to this volume. The old-fashioned engraving of a *Catagramma*-like insect is delightfully reproduced twelve times so as to suggest a double series or "block" of specimens in a cabinet case; and there is a beautiful photograph of a Red Admirable (but "Nymphalidae" is the family to which it belongs, not its genus, which is *Vanessa* – my first bit of carping).

[SO 284–85]

SIMON KARLINSKY

Mr. Karlinsky's "N. and Chekhov" is a very remarkable essay, and I greatly appreciate being with A.P. in the same boat – on a Russian lake, at sunset, he fishing, I watching the hawkmoths above the water. Mr. Karlinsky has put his finger on a mysterious sensory cell. He is right, I do love Chekhov dearly. [SO 286]

From letter to Dmitri Nabokov,[356] May 30, 1970

From Montreux.

If you fly high over the tropical forest, you may notice what looks like shimmering little light-blue mirrors – *Morpho* butterflies flying above the trees. [SL 468]

From interview with Andrew Field,[357] June 12, 1970

Unpublished.

Q: Would you tell me something of what you remember of your friend Rozov? Where is he now, Tel Aviv or Jerusalem?

A: Samuil Izrailevich Rozov (now an architect in Jaffa), my best friend at school . . . came to see me at Zermatt [in July 1962], and we went for a long walk with my wife, my sister (who had just arrived from Geneva), her dog (an Appenzeller, now no more) and a German photographer (who had also arrived that same day of artistic coincidences). A steady drizzle hampered butterfly hunting but the gray light seemed to be just right for pictures. R. said he did not know what amazed him more, the quantities of wild flowers (he had not seen any Northern ones since boyhood) or the amount of film Herr Tappe was wasting by clicking his camera every few seconds. One of his pictures, the one in the gnomish hood on PALE FIRE and elsewhere, amply repaid all those clicks and remained a memento of that day, that rain, those wet flowers. . . .

Q: Can you tell me something about your friend W. T. M. Forbes who died last year?

A: When I knew him in the Forties and early Fifties he was a corpulent, carp-shaped, white-whiskered eccentric, with a pink complexion that gradually deepened to a frightening carmine as he pottered about, wearing several layers of wool, in his overheated laboratory among the glass trays with spread butterflies, volumes of entomological journals, remnants of a messy snack, and an accumulation of mystery paperbacks of which he was inordinately fond. He was not a talented scientist but a learned and opinionated one with a prodigious memory for butterfly names and localities, and although taxonomic discussions with him gradually turned into a droning monologue which swept over all the obstacles one tried to put in its way, it was fun talking to him about lepidoptera. Unfortunately, he much preferred to propound his views (in the same monotonous uncontrollable flow of words, his eyes moving as if watching tennis) about more worldly matters such as politics, genetics, "Niggers and Hebrews," comic strips, his sister's books and the history of the music hall in America. Being culturally *nicht stubenrein*,[358] he was never invited to our small parties in Ithaca, but I saw a lot of him in the museums (my own collections generally ended up in the MCZ, Harvard or the Comstock Hall, Cornell, where he also worked). And I confess that sometimes, upon seeing his pink pate within its crown of white fluff bent over a distant desk, I would try to slip into my corner as quietly as possible. I am sorry to say that the above is part of my SPEAK ON, MEMORY[359] and cannot be quoted yet.

From interview with Alfred Appel, Jr., August 1970

Published in *Novel* 4 (1971).

Q: How are you progressing with your book on the butterfly in art?
A: I am still working, at my own pace, on an illustrated *Butterflies in Art* work, from Egyptian antiquity to the Renaissance. It is a purely scientific pursuit. I find an entomological thrill in tracking down and identifying the butterflies represented by old painters. Only recognizable portraits interest me. Some of the problems that might be solved are: were certain species as common in ancient times as they are today? Can the minutiae of evolutionary change be discerned in the pattern of a five-hundred-year-old wing? One simple conclusion I have come to is that no matter how precise an Old

Master's brush can be it cannot vie in artistic magic with some of the colored plates drawn by the illustrators of certain scientific works in the nineteenth century. An Old Master did not know that in different species the venation is different and never bothered to examine its structure. It is like painting a hand without knowing anything about its bones or indeed without suspecting it has any. Certain impressionists cannot afford to wear glasses. Only myopia condones the blurry generalizations of ignorance. In high art and pure science detail is everything.

Q: Who are some of the artists who rendered butterflies? Might they not attribute more symbolism to the insect than you do?

A: Among the many Old Masters who depicted butterflies (obviously netted, or more exactly capped, by their apprentices in the nearest garden) were Hieronymous Bosch (1450–1516), Jan Brueghel (1568–1625), Albrecht Dürer (1471–1528), Paolo Porpora (1617–1673), Daniel Seghers (1590–1661), and many others. The insect depicted is either part of a still-life (flowers or fruit) arrangement, or more strikingly a live detail in a conventional religious picture (Dürer, Francesco di Gentile, etc.). That in some cases the butterfly symbolizes something (*e.g.*, Psyche) lies utterly outside my area of interest.

Q: In 1968 you told me you hoped to travel to various European museums for research purposes. Have you been doing that?

A: Yes, that's one reason we've been spending so much time in Italy, and in the future will be traveling to Paris and the Louvre, and to the Dutch museums. We've been to small towns in Italy, and to Florence, Venice, Rome, Milano, Naples, and Pompeii, where we found a very badly drawn butterfly, long and thin, like a Mayfly. There are certain obstacles: still-lifes are not very popular today, they are gap-fillers, generally hanging in dark places or high up. A ladder may be necessary, a flashlight, a magnifying glass! My object is to identify such a picture if there are butterflies in it (often it's only "Anonymous" or "School of ———"), and get an efficient person to take a photograph. Since I don't find many of those pictures in the regular display rooms I try to find the curator because some pictures may turn up in their stacks. It takes so much time: I tramped through the Vatican Museum in Rome and found only one butterfly, a Zebra Swallowtail,[360] in a quite conventional *Madonna and Child* by Gentile, as realistic as though it were painted yesterday. Such paintings may throw light on the time taken for evolution; one thousand years could show some little change in trend. It's an almost endless pursuit, but if I could manage to collect at least one hundred of these things I would publish reproductions of those particular paintings which include butterflies, and enlarge parts of the picture with the butterfly in life-size. Curiously, the Red Admirable is the most popular; I've collected twenty examples.

Q: That particular butterfly appears frequently in your own work, too. In *Pale Fire,* a Red Admirable lands on John Shade's arm the minute before he is killed, the insect appears in *King, Queen Knave* just after you've withdrawn the authorial omniscience – killing the characters, so to speak – and in the final chapter of *Speak, Memory,* you recall having seen in a Paris park, just before the war, a live Red Admirable being promenaded on a leash of thread by a little girl. Why are you so fond of *Vanessa atalanta?*

A: Its coloring is quite splendid and I liked it very much in my youth. Great numbers of them migrated from Africa to Northern Russia, where it was called "The Butterfly of Doom" because it was especially abundant in 1881, the year Tsar Alexander II was assassinated, and the markings on the underside of its two hind wings seem to read "1881." The Red Admirable's ability to travel so far is matched by many other migratory butterflies.

[SO 168–70]

Letter to Elena Sikorski, September 1970[361]

From Montreux. In Russian. Translated by DN.

To My Sister Elena,

> We are distinguished by wings of black hue,
> wine-iridescence, and granules of blue
> following yellowish, crenulate borders.
> Copses of birch are our favorite quarters.

[SL 473]

L. C. Higgins and N. D. Riley, *Field Guide to the Butterflies of Britain and Europe*

Review. Written in 1970. Published as "Rebel's Blue, Bryony White," *Times Educational Supplement* 23 (October 1970).

In my early boyhood, almost sixty-five years ago, I would quiver with help-less rage when Hofmann in his then famous *Die Gross-Schmetterlinge Europas* failed to figure the rarity he described in the text. No such frustration awaits the young reader of the marvelous guide to the Palaearctic butter-flies west of the Russian frontier now produced by Lionel C. Higgins, au-thor of important papers on Lepidoptera, and Norman D. Riley, keeper of insects at the British Museum. The exclusion of Russia is (alas) a practical necessity. Non-utilitarian science does not thrive in that sad and cagey country; the mild foreign gentleman eager to collect in the steppes will soon catch his net in a tangle of barbed wire, and to work out the distribu-tion of Eversmann's Orange Tip or the Edda Ringlet would have proved much harder than mapping the moon. The little maps that the Field Guide does supply for the fauna it covers seem seldom to err. I note that the range of the Twin-spot Fritillary and that of the Idas Blue are incorrectly marked, and I think Nogell's Hairstreak, which reaches Romania from the east, should have been included. Among minor shortcomings is the somewhat curt way in which British butterflies are treated (surely the Norfolk race of the Swallowtail, which is so different from the Swedish, should have re-ceived more attention). I would say that alder, rather than spruce, charac-terizes the habitat of Wolfensberger's and Thor's Fritillaries. I regret that the dreadful nickname "Admiral" is used instead of the old "Admirable." The new vernacular names are well invented – and, paradoxically, will be more attractive to the expert wishing to avoid taxonomic controversy when indicating a species than to the youngster who will lap up the Latin in a trice. The checklist of species would have been considerably more ap-pealing if the names of authors had not been omitted (a deplorable practice of commercial origin which impairs a number of recent zoological and bo-tanical manuals in America).

The choice of important subspecies among the thousands described in the last hundred years is a somewhat subjective matter and cannot be discussed here. In deciding whether to regard a butterfly as a race of its closest ally or as a separate species the *Field Guide* displays good judgment in re-attaching Rebel's Blue to Alcon, and in tying up the Bryony White with the Green-veined White: anyone who has walked along a mountain brook in the Valais, the Tessin, and elsewhere must have noticed the profusion and almost comic muddle of varicolored intergrades between those two Whites. In a few cases, however, the authors seem to have succumbed to the blandishments of the chromosome count. For better or worse our present notion of species in Lepidoptera is based solely on the checkable structures of dead specimens, and if Forster's Furry cannot be distinguished from the Furry Blue except by its chromosome number, Forster's Furry must be scrapped.

In many groups the *Field Guide* accepts the generic splitting proposed by various specialists. The resulting orgy of genera may bewilder the innocent reader and irritate the conservative old lumper. A compromise might be reached by demoting the genitalically allied genera to the rank of subgenera within one large genus. Thus, for instance, a large generic group, called, say, *Scolitantides,* would include 6 subgenera (pp. 262–271 of the *Field Guide*, from Green-underside Blue to Chequered Blue) and a large generic group, called, say, *Plebejus,* would include 15 subgenera (pp. 271–311, Grass Jewel to Eros Blue); what matters, of course, is not naming or numbering the groups but correctly assorting the species so as to reflect relationships and distinctions, and in that sense the *Field Guide* is logical and scientific. On the other hand, I must disagree with the misapplication of the term "f." (meaning "form"). It is properly used to denote recurrent aberrations, clinal blends, or seasonal aspects, but it has no taxonomic standing (and available names for such forms should be quote-marked and anonymous). This the authors know as well as I do, yet for some reason they use "f." here and there as a catchall for altitudinal races and minor subspecies. Particularly odd is "*Boloria graeca balcanica* f. *tendensis,*" which is actually *Boloria graeca tendensis* Higgins, a lovely and unexpected subspecies for the sake of which I once visited Limone Piemonte where I found it at about 7000 ft. in the company of its two congeners, the Shepherd's and the

Mountain Fritillaries. Incidentally, the drabbish figure hardly does justice to the nacreous pallor of its underside.

These are all trivial flaws which melt away in the book's aura of authority and honesty, conciseness and completeness, but there is one fault which I find serious and which should be corrected in later printings. The explanation facing every plate should give the exact place and date of capture of every painted or photographed specimen – a principle to which the latest butterfly books rigidly adhere. This our *Field Guide* omits to do. In result the young reader will not only be deprived of a vicarious thrill but will not know if the specimen came from anywhere near the type locality, whilst the old lepidopterist may at once perceive that the portrait does not represent an individual of the typical race. Thus one doubts that the bright female of the Northern Wall Brown (Pl. 49) comes from the North, and it is a pity that the Poplar Admirable shown on Pl. 15 should belong to the brownish, blurrily banded West European sub-species rather than to the black Scandinavian type race with pure white markings.

The red-stained Corsican Swallowtail (front end-paper) is surely a printer's freak, not the artist's fancy, and no doubt will be repaired in due time. Many of Brian Hargreaves' illustrations are excellent, some are a little crude, a few are poor; all his butterflies, however, are recognizable, which after all is the essential purpose. His treatment of wing shape is sometimes wobbly, for instance in the case of the Heaths (Pl. 47); and one notes a displeasing tendency to acuminate the hind-wing margins of some Ringlets (Plates 37, 41, 44). In some groups of closely allied butterflies Nature seems to have taken capricious delight in varying from species to species the design of the hind-wing underside, thinking up fantastic twists and tints, but never sacrificing the basic generic idea to the cunning disguise. Brian Hargreaves has not always followed this interplay of thematic variations within the genus. For example, in the *Clossiana* hind-wing undersides the compact jagged rhythm of the Polar Fritillary's markings, which intensifies and unifies the Freya scheme, is weakly rendered. The artist has not understood the affinity with Frigga that dimly transpires through the design of the Dusky-winged, nor has he seen the garlands of pattern and the violet tones as connecting the Arctic Fritillary with Titania, and the latter with Dia. Otherwise, many such rarely figured butterflies as the Atlas White, the Fatma Blue, and Chapman's Hairstreak, or such tricky creatures as the enchanting Blues on Pl. 57 came out remarkably well. The feat of assembling all those Spanish and African beauties in one book is not the least glory of Higgins' and Riley's unique and indispensable manual.

[SO 331–35]

From letter to Michael Walter, November 23, 1970

From Montreux.

Many thanks for your kind letter with Dr. Higgins's remarks.

No, I was not alluding to the Balkans in connection with the Twinspot Fritillary's map, but to peninsular Italy (where I have found it common in oak scrub country on the border of Tuscany and Umbria).

I still think that in his drawings of Ringlets Mr. Hargreaves' faithfulness is handicapped by his incomplete grasp of the subject. The pointed hindwing may occur in underdeveloped individuals of some Ringlets (e.g. in small specimens of E. *pluto*) but it is neither a diagnostic nor natural feature of that round-winged genus and looks rather absurd when shown only on one side of the butterfly (p. 37, 7d; pl. 41, 2b and 3a).

As for the Norfolk Swallowtail what I had in view was precisely its resemblance to the first generation of certain Mediterranean races of the species (as noted long ago by Verity) and its striking difference from the typical single-brooded Swedish race.

I shall be grateful to you for transmitting these little clarifications to Dr. Higgins. I also wish to thank you for promising to send me a copy of the revised edition, though let me repeat that even without any revisions, it remains a marvellous and delightful book.

[SL 473–74]

From letter to Arye Levavi,[362] December 31, 1970

From Montreux.

I wish to thank you and your Government very warmly for inviting my wife and me to visit Israel. We shall be delighted to do so. Would April 1972 be an acceptable time? . . .

I would be happy to give one or two readings of my works, I would enjoy visiting museums, libraries and universities, and I would like to take advantage of this wonderful occasion to do some butterfly hunting.   [SL 476]

From interview with Andrew Field, January 1971

[Nabokov recalls his teacher's hostility to a pupil's chasing butterflies on a school trip to Finland, May 1915.]

He should have been rather pleased to have a young boy who knew everything about butterflies. He didn't like it. . . . It would have been all right if I had been a group collecting butterflies. But one boy who was totally immersed in collecting butterflies – that was abnormal.

[Field, *Nabokov: His Life in Part* (1977), 122]

From letter from Véra Nabokov to Roderick Irwin, January 25, 1971

From Montreux. Unpublished.

[H]e does not have any new information on the occurrence of *Lycaeides samuelis* in Illinois (incidentally, he is now inclined to consider it a separate species, and this, of course, would be confirmed if it happened that *L. melissa melissa,* which is gradually spreading eastward, does not interbreed with it where they occur together).   [VNA]

From letter to Samuil Rosov, January 28, 1971

From Montreux. In Russian.

I have, however, gotten an official invitation to visit Israel from your ambassador, who called on us, so perhaps next year or so we shall see both you as a venerable old man, and your country's spring butterflies.   [SL 478]

Letter to Peter Haines,[363] February 3, 1971

From Montreux. Unpublished.

Re: Butterflies of Formosa in Colour by Takashi Shirôzu, 1960
Dear Mr. Haines,

The beauty of the thing is that amidst the Chinese scroll on pp. 3, 5 & 6, I found my name in English mentioned in connection with special terms which I thought up thirty years ago for certain parts of certain anatomical structures and which Shirôzu uses throughout his very fine and very complete account of Formosan butterflies.

Your good letter and splendid gift have touched me greatly.

[VNA]

From letter to Arye Levavi, February 28, 1971

From Montreux.

We certainly hope to come to Israel, unofficially, before I am too decrepit to chase butterflies!

[SL 480]

From interview with Alden Whitman, April 1971

Published in the *New York Times*, April 23, 1971.

At the age of twelve my fondest dream was a visit to the Karakorum range in search of butterflies. Twenty-five years later I successfully sent myself, in the part of my hero's father (see my novel *The Gift*) to explore, net in hand, the mountains of Central Asia.

[SO 177–78]

From letter to Michael Walter, April 14, 1971

From Montreux.

I thank you for Barcant's *Butterflies of Trinidad and Tobago* which I found here on my return from a trip to S. Portugal.

The photographs are good and, generally speaking, the book should be of considerable help to the butterfly hunter in those parts. Too much stress, however, is laid on "habitat" and "rarity" (and even "semi-rarity") of numerous strays, or chance colonies founded by strays of species that come from the mainland where those species are common. In itself Barcant's work is very amateurish, the style is trivial and redundant, and the higgledy-piggledy arrangement of the material, in the text and on the plates, is an absolute nightmare. Among obvious blunders I note: on p. 210, *P barcanti* should be *P. barcanti* Tite, not "*P barcanti* sp. nov.", and on p. 229, *N. maravalica* should be *N. maravalica* Seitz, not "*N. maravalica* sp. nov."

I continue to be distressed by the illiterate vogue of omitting the names of genus-describers – and this not because my own name is omitted (in the case of *Echinargus* Nabokov to which I assigned *huntingtoni,* p. 84, which I was the first to dissect and figure) but because no taxonomic term is clear and correct unless its author's name is affixed to it. One wonders what the beginner will make of the last paragraph on p. 21, implying, as it does, that Linnaeus is the author not only of the species *iphicla* but also of the genus *Adelpha,* which is wrong.

Anyway I read the book with interest and remain gratefully yours.

[SL 480–81]

From letter to Michael Walter, April 16, 1971

From Montreux.

Your very charming note of March 25, with a copy of Dr. Higgins' response to my correction, reached me only to-day in a batch of correspondence that had gone to look for me in Algarve and has now wandered back to Montreux.

Entomologists are the most gentle people on earth – until a taxonomic problem crops up: it then transforms them into tigers. In the present case I can only repeat that the type locality of the butterfly described as *aurelia* by Nickerl in 1850 is "Böhmen." The fact that the type locality of the same butterfly under another, much earlier but invalid name (*parthenie* Borkhausen 1788) is Erlangen, a hundred kilometers W. from the Bohemian border seems to me irrelevant. It is not a question of library but of logic. A "first reviser" may and should assign a definite locality to a species that has been given none, or only a very vague general region, in the original description; but "Böhmen" is definite enough, and if the reviser wants to pin down the locus, he stakes off his moor or mountainside in W. Czechoslovakia and not in Bavaria.

I feel that all this exciting lepidopterological correspondence passing through your kind hands will finally infect you with the aurelian madness! The best stuff for a butterfly net is marquisette. [SL 483–84]

From Nabokov's diary, June 21, 1971

Unpublished.

Collected between 11:30 & 2:00 at Martigny above Plan Cerisier (c. 2½ kl. W. of M.) c. 650. little flowery niches near little vineyards. Below c. 650 no flowers, no butterflies, only pesticide treated vineyards down to the village of Plan Cerisier. [VNA]

From interview with Israel Shenker, June 1971

Published in the *New York Times Book Review*, January 9, 1972.

Q: What struggles these days for pride of place in your mind?
A: Meadows. A meadow with Scarce Heath butterflies in North Russia, another with Grinnell's Blue in Southern California. That sort of thing.

[SO 182]

Rowe's Symbols

Excerpt from review of William Woodin Rowe, *Nabokov's Deceptive World*. Written August 28, 1971. Published in the *New York Review of Books*, October 7, 1971.

The jacket of Mr. Rowe's book depicts a butterfly incongruously flying around a candle. Moths, not butterflies, are attracted to light but the de-

VN on the hunt, above
Gstaad, summer 1971.
(*Dmitri Nabokov*)

signer's blunder neatly illustrates the quality of Mr. Rowe's preposterous and nasty interpretations. And he will be read, he will be quoted, he will be filed in great libraries, next to my arbors and mists! [so 306–7]

From Nabokov's diary, August 30, 1971

Written in Gstaad, Vaud. Unpublished.

Cloudy. 13 fine mornings out of 28 since arrival. Dreary region. Wretched butterfly-hunting.

[VNA]

From letter from Véra Nabokov to Paul Anbinder,[364] September 21, 1971

From Montreux. Unpublished.

It is much too early to discuss his butterfly [in art] book. He has been working on it for years, on and off, and it may take him several more years to finish it. [VNA]

From interview with Kurt Hoffman, October 1971

For Bayerischer Rundfunk.

Upon moving to Berlin I was beset by a panicky fear of somehow flawing my precious layer of Russian by learning to speak German fluently. . . . Later I read Goethe and Kafka *en regard* as I also did Homer and Horace. And of course since my early boyhood I have been tackling a multitude of German butterfly books with the aid of a dictionary. [so 189]

My actual work on lepidoptera is comprised within the span of only seven or eight years in the nineteen forties, mainly at Harvard, where I was Research Fellow in Entomology at the Museum of Comparative Zoology.

vn butterfly hunting for a photographer near Montreux, fall 1971. (*Horst Tappe*)

This entailed some amount of curatorship but most of my work was devoted to the classification of certain small blue butterflies on the basis of their male genitalic structure. These studies required the constant use of a microscope, and since I devoted up to six hours daily to this kind of research my eyesight was impaired for ever; but on the other hand, the years at the Harvard Museum remain the most delightful and thrilling in all my adult life. Summers were spent by my wife and me in hunting butterflies, mostly in the Rocky Mountains. In the last fifteen years I have collected here and there, in North America and Europe, but have not published any scientific papers on butterflies, because the writing of new novels and the translating of my old ones encroached too much on my life: the miniature hooks of a male butterfly are nothing in comparison to the eagle claws of literature which tear at me day and night. My entomological library in Montreux is smaller, in fact, than the heaps of butterfly books I had as a child.

I am the author or the reviser of a number of species and subspecies mainly in the New World. The author's name, in such cases, is appended in Roman letters to the italicized name he gives to the creature. Several butterflies and one moth have been named for me, and in such cases my name is incorporated in that of the described insect, becoming *"nabokovi,"* followed by the describer's name. There is also a genus *Nabokovia* Hemming, in South America. All my American collections are in museums, in New York, Boston, and Ithaca. The butterflies I have been collecting during the last decade, mainly in Switzerland and Italy, are not yet spread. They are still papered, that is kept in little glazed envelopes which are stored in tin boxes. Eventually they will be relaxed in damp towels, then pinned, then spread, and dried again on setting boards, and finally, labeled and placed in the glassed drawers of a cabinet to be preserved, I hope, in the splendid entomological museum in Lausanne.   [SO 190–91]

[*Why Switzerland?*] Exquisite postal service. No bothersome demonstrations, no spiteful strikes. Alpine butterflies. Fabulous sunsets – just west of my window, spangling the lake, splitting the crimson sun! Also, the pleasant surprise of a metaphorical sunset in charming surroundings.   [SO 192]

It is odd but I have never quite made up my mind how much the various elements of sport, science, and nameless delight combine in the soul of a butterfly collector.   [VNA]

Transparent Things

Excerpts from novel. Written 1969–72. Published in 1972.

[Hugh Person, visiting the family home of Armande Chamar, with whom he has just fallen in love, looks through her mother's photograph albums.]

VN extricates a butterfly from his net while being filmed for a German television documentary on the lakeshore promenade, Montreux, October 1971.

Toward the end of the second album the photography burst into color to celebrate the vivid vestiture of her adolescent molts. She appeared in floral frocks, fancy slacks, tennis shorts, swimsuits, amidst the harsh greens and blues of the commercial spectrum. He discovered the elegant angularity of her sun-tanned shoulders, the long line of her haunch. He learned that at eighteen the torrent of her pale hair reached the small of her back. No matrimonial agency could have offered its clients such variations on the theme of one virgin. In the third album he found, with an enjoyable sense of homecoming, glimpses of his immediate surroundings: the lemon and black cushions of the divan at the other end of the room and the Denton mount[365] of a birdwing butterfly on the mantelpiece. The fourth, incomplete album began with a sparkle of her chastest images: Armande in a pink parka, Armande jewel-bright, Armande careening on skis through the sugar dust.   [TT 41]

[Revisiting Switzerland after Armande's death, Hugh, a poor climber, again tries to take the mountain trail on which sporty Armande had first suggested they make love.]

He now ascended through that wood, panting as painfully as he had in the past when following Armande's golden nape or a huge knapsack on a naked male back. As then the pressure of the shoecap upon his right foot had soon scraped off a round of skin at the joint of the third toe, resulting in a red eye burning there through every threadbare thought. He finally shook the forest off and reached a rock-strewn field and a barn that he thought he recalled, but the stream where he had once washed his feet and the broken bridge which suddenly spanned the gap of time in his mind were nowhere to be seen. He walked on. The day seemed a little brighter but presently a cloud palmed the sun again. The path had reached the pastures. He noticed a large white butterfly drop outspread on a stone. Its papery wings, blotched with black and maculated with faded crimson, had transparent margins of an unpleasant crimped texture, which shivered slightly in the cheerless wind.[366] Hugh disliked insects; this one looked particularly gross. Nevertheless, a mood of unusual kindliness made him surmount the impulse to crush it under a blind boot. With the vague idea that it must be tired and hungry and would appreciate being transferred to a nearby pincushion of little pink flowers, he stooped over the creature but with a great shuffle and rustle it evaded his handkerchief, sloppily flapped to overcome gravity, and vigorously sailed away.   [TT 89–90]

From interview with Simona Morini, February 1972

Published in *Vogue*, April 15, 1972.

Q: *Lolita* is an extraordinary Baedecker of the United States. What fascinated you about American motels?

A: The fascination was purely utilitarian. My wife used to drive me (Plymouth, Oldsmobile, Buick, Buick Special, Impala – in that order of brand) during several seasons, many thousands of miles every season, for the sole purpose of collecting Lepidoptera – all of which are now in three museums (Natural History in New York City, Comparative Zoology at Harvard, Comstock Hall at Cornell). Usually we spent only a day or two in each motorcourt, but sometimes, if the hunting was good, we stayed for weeks in one place. The main *raison d'être* of the motel was the possibility of walking out straight into an aspen grove with lupines in full bloom or onto a wild mountainside. We also would make many sorties on the way between motels. All this I shall be describing in my next memoir, *Speak On, Memory*, which will deal with many curious things (apart from butterfly lore) – amusing happenings at Cornell and Harvard, gay tussles with publishers, my friendship with Edmund Wilson, et cetera.

Q: You were in Wyoming and Colorado looking for butterflies. What were these places like to you?

A: My wife and I have collected not only in Wyoming and Colorado, but in most of the states, as well as in Canada. The list of localities visited between 1940 and 1960 would cover many pages. Each butterfly, killed by an expert nip of its thorax, is slipped immediately into a little glazed envelope, about thirty of which fit into one of the Band-Aid containers which represent, with the net, my only paraphernalia in the field. Captures can be kept, before being relaxed and set, for any number of years in those envelopes, if properly stored. The exact locality and date are written on every envelope besides being jotted down in one's pocket diary. Though my captures are now in American museums, I have preserved hundreds of labels and notes. Here are just a few samples picked out at random:

Road to Terry Peak from Route 85, near Lead, 6500–7000 feet, in the Black Hills of South Dakota, July 20, 1958.

Above Tomboy Road, between Social Tunnel and Bullion Mine, at about 10,500 feet, near Telluride, San Miguel County, W. Colorado, July 3, 1951.

Near Karner, between Albany and Schenectady, New York, June 2, 1950.

Near Columbine Lodge, Estes Park, E. Colorado, about 9000 feet, June 5, 1947.

Soda Mt., Oregon, about 5500 feet, August 2, 1953.

Above Portal, road to Rustler Park, between 5500 and 8000 feet, Chiricahua Mts., Arizona, April 30, 1953.

Fernie, three miles east of Elko, British Columbia, July 10, 1958.

Granite Pass, Bighorn Mts., 8950 feet, E. Wyoming, July 17, 1958.

Near Crawley Lake, Bishop, California, about 7000 feet, June 3, 1953. Near Gatlinburg, Tennessee, April 21, 1959. Et cetera, et cetera.

Q: Where do you go for butterflies now?

A: To various good spots in the Valais, the Tessin, the Grisons; to the hills of Italy; to the Mediterranean islands; to the mountains of southern France and so forth. I am chiefly devoted to European and North American butterflies of high altitudes, and have never visited the Tropics.

The little mountain trains cogwheeling up to alpine meadows, through sun and shade, along rock face or coniferous forest are tolerable in action and delightful in destination, bringing one as they do to the starting point of a day-long hike. My favorite method of locomotion, though, is the cableway, and especially the chairlift. I find enchanting and dreamy in the best sense of the word to glide in the morning sun from valley to timberline in that magic seat, and watch from above my own shadow – with the ghost of a butterfly net in the ghost of a fist – as it keeps gently ascending in sitting profile along the flowery slope below, among dancing Ringlets and skimming Fritillaries. Some day the butterfly hunter will find even finer dream lore when floating upright over mountains, carried by a diminutive rocket strapped to his back. . . .

As a youth of seventeen, on the eve of the Russian Revolution, I was seriously planning (being the independent possessor of an inherited fortune) a lepidopterological expedition to Central Asia. [SO 198–200]

Q: What is a "perfect trip" for you?

A: Any first walk in any new place – especially a place where no lepidopterist has been before me. There still exist unexplored mountains in Europe and I still can walk twenty kilometers a day. The ordinary stroller might feel on sauntering out a twinge of pleasure (cloudless morning, village still asleep, one side of the street already sunlit, should try to buy English papers on my way back, here's the turn, I believe, yes, footpath to Cataratta), but the cold of the metal netstick in my right hand magnifies the pleasure to almost intolerable bliss. [SO 204]

From letter to William McGuire, May 10, 1972

From Montreux. Unpublished.

We have just returned from a butterfly trip in the Eastern Pyrenees – three weeks of grey and windy weather spangled with just enough sun for allowing the capture of a few remarkable species.   [VNA]

Letter to William Field,[367] May 25, 1972

From Montreux.

Dear Mr. Field,

Many thanks for your kind letter and the five splendid papers. I hasten to respond to your query about those Vienna examples of *V. atalanta*.

If it is only, or mainly, a reduction of the subapical white bar that gives those specimens an American look, and if the series is fairly short (say, three or four individuals), the narrowing of that bar might be regarded as a chance variation not uncommon in Europe (it is represented, for instance, in photographic figures of *V. atalanta*: South's Brit. Butts, pl. 47, female, and Verity's Farf. d'Italia, pl. 52, fig. 8, " *italica*" – which you have correctly sunk), for it is quite impossible to believe that such a wanderer as our Red Admirable could have evolved a stable race right in the center of its European dispersal (incidentally, all attempts to split it into several European races is doomed from the start, the Swedish type itself being but the summer offspring of May newcomers from the south). Anyway, I shall be collecting soon in a corner of Switzerland not too far from Austria and will try to take specimens of the thing here and there in chalet gardens.

I have been hunting butterflies in the Alps and the Mediterranean area every season since 1961 but everything is still papered and stored, and awaiting a favorable pause in my literary labors to get nicely set for study. I would certainly be delighted to give some of the rarer stuff to the National Museum and shall send a list for approval.

I am looking forward to your Catalogue of New World Lycaenidae. It will, I trust, straighten out the unfortunate nomenclatorial confusion which has resulted from American lepidopterists' ignoring the change of two specific names in *Lycaeides* (Int. Comm. Zool. Nom, 1954). Since the time I wrote about that subgenus (see Bull. NCZ vol. 101, Feb. 1949) the name of the short-falx Holarctic species, which I and others used to call "*L. argyrognomon* (Bergstr., Tutt)", has been changed to "*L. idas* (L)", whilst the name "*L. argyrognomon* (Bergstr.)" has been shifted to the long-falx Palaearctic species, which I and others used to call "*L. ismenias* (Meigen)."

I have also arrived at the conclusion that my "*L. melissa samuelis*" should be treated as a distinct species – but that is another story.

Sincerely yours,

VLADIMIR NABOKOV   [SL 500–01]

How I loved the poems of Gumilyov!

Poem in Russian ("Kak lyubil ya stikhi Gumilyova!"). Written July 22, 1972.

> How I loved the poems of Gumilyov!
> Reread them I cannot,
> But traces have stayed in my mind,
> such as, on this think-through:
>
> ". . . And I will die not in a summerhouse
> from gluttony and heat,
> but with a heavenly butterfly in my net
> on the summit of some wild hill."

[*Stikhi* 297]

From Introduction to interview for *Strong Opinions*

Written in late 1972. Published in 1973.

In mid-July, 1962, Peter Duval-Smith and Christopher Burstall came for a BBC television interview to Zermatt where I happened to be collecting that summer. The lepidoptera lived up to the occasion, so did the weather. My visitors and their crew had never paid much attention to those insects and I was touched and flattered by the childish wonderment with which they viewed the crowds of butterflies imbibing moisture on brookside mud at various spots of the mountain trail. Pictures were taken of the swarms that arose at my passage, and other hours of the day were devoted to the reproduction of the interview proper.   [SO 9]

From letter to Gordon Lish,[368] October 13, 1972

From Montreux.

Do I understand correctly that you are thinking of reprinting *The Potato Elf* in your 40th Anniversary Issue (Sep. 14, 1973)?

In preparing a collection of some of my Russian stories in English translation for McGraw-Hill I have had to retranslate entirely that Elf (first published in Russian in 1929).

The version by Serge Bertenson and Irene Kosinska in *Esquire,* Dec. 1939, is, alas, abominable, with innumerable errors, such as howlers, illiteracies, omissions, and so forth. It cannot be corrected, and must not be reprinted. My new translation, a very beautiful and faithful one, is scheduled to appear sometime next year in my publisher's collection of thirteen stories which is already in their hands. If you want the new, and lovely, Potato Elf, untouched by the Death's Head Moth of mistranslation, I would be delighted to have you prepublish it; but you should discuss the matter with McGraw-Hill.   [SL 503]

From letter to Dan Lacy,[369] January 31, 1973

From Montreux.

To-day I can only try to answer the second part of your letter, pertaining to my literary plans.

The only two kinds of "butterfly books" that I could contemplate writing are: 1. a learned work with a minimum of text and a maximum of colored photographs on the 400 species (and about 1500 subspecies) of European butterflies; this, however, would take three or four years to complete (I had begun it for Weidenfeld but for various reasons the project was given up): this could hardly be a commercial success in the United States; and 2. a picture book, with notes, devoted to the evolution of butterfly painting from ancient times and through the Renaissance, to 1700, with reproductions of still-life pictures of flowers and insects by Dutch, Italian, Spanish, etc. masters. This is a fascinating, never-before attempted and not too complicated project (I have already collected more than a hundred samples) but it would mean your providing me with a photographer who could travel with me to several European picture galleries. I could probably finish the job within a couple of years.

That takes care of the bugs. [SL 507–8]

Letter from Véra Nabokov to Robert Michael Pyle,[370] February 5, 1973

From Montreux. Unpublished.

My husband thanks you for your kind letter of January 27 offering him an Honorary Counsellorship in the Xerces Society. He is very much in sympathy with your aims but has made it a rule not to accept any honorary titles or memberships. [Robert Michael Pyle collection]

From letter to Andrew Field, February 20, 1973

From Montreux. Unpublished.

[Nabokov wrote requesting corrections to the manuscript of Field's Nabokov: His Life in Part. *Field had written that Nabokov visited Dr. Barbour of the Museum of Comparative Zoology seeking part-time work.]*

"Dr. Barbour"

REPLACE BY: "Dr. Nathaniel Banks, Head of the Entomological Department"

"in the hope that some parttime work might be found . . ."

REPLACE BY: "to complain that the Weeks collection of butterflies was improperly preserved: the trays in their numerous cabinets were not glazed and there were other dangerous defects. . . ."

. . .

REPLACE BY: "It was arranged that the necessary number of glass-topped trays would be ordered, and that Nabokov would transfer the thousands of specimens into their new, spacious, clean, and secure abodes. Dr. Barbour, the genial director of the Museum (who greatly admired Nabokov's stories in the *Atlantic Monthly*) offered a remuneration that gradually was transformed into a part-time job under the auspices of Harvard. The salary was not particularly grand but even without any, Nabokov would have kept rapturously examining and classifying butterflies in the MCZ."

(Your version is wrong in all particulars)   [VNA]

From interview with Mati Laansoo, March 1973

For the Canadian Broadcasting Corporation.

It is my entomological hunts in Canada that come to my mind as my voice is being projected onto Canadian air. One of my favorite spots remains a ravine smothered in flowers, near Fernie, three miles east of Elko, British Columbia, where on a summer day in 1958 I collected specimens of a very local little blue butterfly (*Lycaeides idas ferniensis*) which I badly wanted for the Cornell University Museum.

[*Vladimir Nabokov Research Newsletter* 10 (Spring 1983): 47]

From letter to Andrew Field, May 25, 1973

From Montreux.

You can be assured (in case a hijacker takes me to Russia or a dancing butterfly leads me over the brink of a precipice) that your typescripts, my comments to the first version, and our entire correspondence will remain in steel-safe hands.   [SL 516]

From letter from Véra Nabokov to Roy du Cros, June 14, 1973

From Cervia, Italy. Unpublished.

He asks me to tell you that his favorite locality for both *M. deione berisali* and *I. iolas* in the Valais is just SW of Saillon, some 15 kilometers NE of Martigny. It is a path through and up the scrubby hillslope above the "Sarvaz" (so marked) vineyard. He saw dozens of individuals of both species and both sexes there on June 23 1971. *Berisali* is easy to net but *iolas* is a swift flier settling only on the yellow flowers of its foodplant, "false senna" (*baguenaudier*), of which there are stunted remnants near the vines (and some large plants in the forests of the valley).

He also advises you to keep your eye on the arbutus shrubs and ripe figs for *Ch. jasius* when you are in the Provence.[371]   [VNA]

From Foreword to *Lolita: A Screenplay*

Foreword written December 1973.[372]

Sometime at the end of July 1959 (my pocket diary does not give the exact date), in Arizona, where my wife and I were hunting butterflies, with headquarters at Forest Houses (between Flagstaff and Sedona), I received through Irving Lazar who was representing me a message from Messrs. Harris & Kubrick. They had acquired the film rights of *Lolita* in 1958, and were now asking me to come over to Hollywood and write the script. The honorarium they offered was considerable, but the idea of tampering with my own novel caused me only revulsion. A certain lull in the activity of the local lepidoptera suggested, however, that we might just as well drive on to the West Coast. After a meeting in Beverly Hills (at which I was told that in order to appease the censor a later scene should contain some pudic hint to the effect that Humbert had been secretly married to Lolita all along), followed by a week of sterile meditation on the shores of Lake Tahoe (where a calamitous growth of manzanita precluded the presence of good butterflies), I decided not to undertake the job and left for Europe.

[LS vii]

[Months later VN *saw a solution to the artistic problem of adapting the novel and agreed to write the screenplay. He reached Hollywood in March 1960.]*

I worked with zest, composing mentally every morning from eight to noon while butterfly hunting in the hot hills, which, except for some remarkably skittish individuals of a little-known Wood Nymph, produced nothing noteworthy, but *per contra* teemed with rattlers whose hysterical performance in the undergrowth or in the middle of the trail was more comical than alarming. After a leisurely lunch, prepared by the German cook who came with the house, I would spend another four-hour span in a lawn chair, among the roses and mockingbirds, using lined index cards and a Blackwing pencil, for copying and recopying, rubbing out and writing anew, the scenes I had imagined in the morning. [LS ix]

By the end of June, after having used up over a thousand cards, I had the thing typed, sent to Kubrick the four hundred pages it made, and, needing a rest, was driven by my wife in a rented Impala to Inyo County for a short stay at Glacier Lodge on Big Pine Creek, where we collected the Inyo Blue and other nice bugs in the surrounding mountains. Upon our returning to Mandeville Canyon, Kubrick visited us to say that my screenplay was much too unwieldy, contained too many unnecessary episodes, and would take about seven hours to run. He wanted several deletions and other changes, and some of these I did make, besides devising new sequences and situations, when preparing a shorter script which he got in September and said was fine. [LS x–xi]

On May 31, 1962 (almost exactly twenty-two years after we emigrated from St.-Nazaire aboard the *Champlain*), the *Queen Elizabeth* took us to New York for the opening of *Lolita*. Our cabin (main deck, cabin 95) was quite as comfortable as the one we had on the *Champlain* in 1940 and, moreover, at a cocktail party given by the purser (or surgeon, my scribble is illegible), he turned to me and said: Now you, as an American businessman, will enjoy the following story (story not recorded). On June 6 I revisited my old haunts, the entomological department at the American Museum of Natural History, where I deposited the specimens of Chapman's Hairstreak I had taken the previous April between Nice and Grasse, under strawberry trees. The première took place on June 13 (Loew's State, BW at 45, E2 + 4 orchestra, "horrible seats" says my outspoken agenda). Crowds were awaiting the limousines that drew up one by one, and there I, too, rode, as eager and innocent as the fans who peered into my car hoping to glimpse James Mason but finding only the placid profile of a stand-in for Hitchcock.   [LS xii]

Letter from Véra Nabokov to Jeannine Oppewall,[373] January 28, 1974

From Montreux. Unpublished.

My husband asks me to acknowledge to you the receipt of your letter with the picture and to convey his thanks for your kindness. He enjoyed the picture despite the two butterflies' being unidentifiable and too recent by a century. He says their necks are much too long.[374]   [VNA]

Letter to Michael Walter, February 22, 1974

From Montreux.

I thank you very much for sending me the excellent *Field Guide to the Insects of Britain and Europe.*[375] It is quite a feat to present so much so varied material in a comparatively small book, and to do this in an admirably scholarly way and with first-rate illustrations. If I were an all-round entomologist, I would have certainly reviewed it.   [VNA]

Look at the Harlequins![376]

Excerpts from novel. Written 1973–74. Published in 1974.

[Vadim's parents divorce and remarry at a rapid rate, neglecting him.]
An extraordinary grand-aunt, Baroness Bredow, born Tolstoy, amply replaced closer blood. As a child of seven or eight, already harboring the se-

crets of a confirmed madman, I seemed even to her (who also was far from normal) unduly sulky and indolent; actually, of course, I kept daydreaming in a most outrageous fashion.

"Stop moping!" she would cry: "Look at the harlequins!"

"What harlequins? Where?"

"Oh, everywhere. All around you. Trees are harlequins, words are harlequins. So are situations and sums. Put two things together – jokes, images – and you get a triple harlequin. Come on! Play! Invent the world! Invent reality!"

I did. By Jove, I did. I invented my grand-aunt in honor of my first daydreams, and now, down the marble steps of memory's front porch, here she slowly comes, sideways, sideways, the poor lame lady, touching each step edge with the rubber tip of her black cane. [LATH 8–9]

[Vadim visits Iris on the French Riviera.]

By the way what was the nationality of the bronzed old man with the hoary chest hair who was wading out of the low surf preceded by his bedraggled dog – I thought I knew his face.

It was, she said, Kanner, the great pianist and butterfly hunter, his face and name were on all the Morris columns. [LATH 30]

Suddenly there came from somewhere within the natural jumble of our surroundings a roar of unearthly ecstasy.

"Goodness," said Iris, "I do hope that's not a happy escapee from Kanner's Circus." (No relation – at least, so it seemed – to the pianist.)

We walked on, now side by side: after the first of the half-dozen times it crossed the looping main road, our path grew wider. That day as usual I argued with Iris about the English names of the few plants I could identify – rock roses and griselda in bloom, agaves (which she called "centuries"), broom and spurge, myrtle and arbutus. Speckled butterflies came and went like quick sun flecks in the occasional tunnels of foliage, and once a tremendous olive-green fellow, with a rosy flush somewhere beneath, settled on a thistlehead for an instant. I know nothing about butterflies, and indeed do not care for the fluffier night-flying ones, and would hate any of them to touch me: even the prettiest gives me a nasty shiver like some float-ing spider web or that bathroom pest on the Riviera, the silver louse.

On the day now in focus, memorable for a more important matter but carrying all kinds of synchronous trivia attached to it like burrs or in-crustated like marine parasites, we noticed a butterfly net moving among the beflowered rocks, and presently old Kanner appeared, his panama swinging on its vest-button string, his white locks flying around his scarlet brow, and the whole of his person still radiating ecstasy, an echo of which we no doubt had heard a minute ago.

Upon Iris immediately describing to him the spectacular green thing, Kanner dismissed it as *eine* "Pandora"[377] (at least that's what I find jotted down), a common southern *Falter* (butterfly). "*Aber* (but)," he thundered, raising his index, "when you wish to look at a real rarity, never before ob-served west of Nieder-Österreich, then I will show what I have just caught."

He leant his net against a rock (it fell at once, Iris picked it up reverently) and, with profuse thanks (to Psyche? Baalzebub? Iris?) that trailed away accompanimentally, produced from a compartment in his satchel a little stamp envelope and shook out of it very gently a folded butterfly onto the palm of his hand.

After one glance Iris told him it was merely a tiny, very young Cabbage White. (She had a theory that houseflies, for instance, *grow*.)

"Now look with attention," said Kanner ignoring her quaint remark and pointing with compressed tweezers at the triangular insect. "What you see is the inferior side – the under white of the left *Vorderflügel* ('fore wing') and the under yellow of the left *Hinterflügel* ('hind wing'). I will not open the wings but I think you can believe what I'm going to tell you. On the up-per side, which you can't see, this species shares with its nearest allies – the Small White and Mann's White, both common here – the typical little spots of the fore wing, namely a black full stop in the male and a black *Doppel-punkt* ('colon') in the female. In those allies the punctuation is reproduced on the underside, and only in the species of which you see a folded speci-men on the flat of my hand is the wing blank beneath – a typographical ca-price of Nature! *Ergo* it is an Ergane."[378]

One of the legs of the reclining butterfly twitched.

"Oh, it's alive!" cried Iris.

"No, it can't fly away – one pinch was enough," rejoined Kanner soothingly, as he slipped the specimen back into its pellucid hell; and presently, brandishing his arms and net in triumphant farewells, he was continuing his climb.

"The brute!" wailed Iris. She brooded over the thousand little creatures he had tortured, but a few days later, when Ivor took us to the man's concert (a most poetical rendition of Grünberg's suite *Les Châteaux*) she derived some consolation from her brother's contemptuous remark: "All that butterfly business is only a publicity stunt." Alas, as a fellow madman I knew better. [LATH 34–36]

[Vadim and his first wife, Iris, join her brother Ivor at dinner.]

The Paon d'Or no longer exists. Although not quite tops, it was a nice clean place, much patronized by American tourists, who called it "Pander" or "Pandora" and always ordered its "putty saw-lay," and that, I guess, is what we had. I remember more clearly a glazed case hanging on the gold-figured wall next to our table: it displayed four Morpho butterflies, two huge ones similar in harsh sheen but differently shaped, and two smaller ones beneath them, the left of a sweeter blue with white stripes and the right gleaming like silvery satin. According to the headwaiter, they had been caught by a convict in South America.

"And how's my friend Mata Hari?"[379] inquired Ivor turning to us again, his spread hand still flat on the table as he had placed it when swinging toward the "bugs" under discussion. [LATH 67]

[Just after Vadim's proposal to Annette.]

She never had met anyone like me. Whom then did she meet, I inquired: trepanners? trombonists? astronomists? Well, mostly military men, if I wished to know, officers of Wrangel's army, gentlemen, interesting people, who spoke of danger and duty, of bivouacs in the steppe. Oh, but look here, I too can speak of "deserts idle, rough quarries, rocks" – No, she said, they did not *invent*. They talked of spies they had hanged, they talked of international politics, of a new film or book that explained the meaning of life. And never one unchaste joke, not one horrid risqué comparison. . . . As in my books? Examples, examples! No, she would not give examples. She would not be pinned down to whirl on the pin like a wingless fly.

Or butterfly.

We were walking, one lovely morning, on the outskirts of Bellefontaine. Something flicked and lit.

"Look at that harlequin," I murmured, pointing cautiously with my elbow.

Sunning itself against the white wall of a suburban garden was a flat, symmetrically outspread butterfly, which the artist had placed at a slight angle to the horizon of his picture. The creature was painted a smiling red with yellow intervals between black blotches; a row of blue crescents ran along the inside of the toothed wing margins.[380] The only feature to rate a shiver of squeamishness was the glistening sweep of bronzy silks coming down on both sides of the beastie's body.

"As a former kindergarten teacher I can tell you," said helpful Annette, "that it's a most ordinary nettlefly (*krapivnitsa*). How many little hands have plucked off its wings and brought them to me for approval!"

It flicked and was gone.

[LATH 108–9]

[When Annette leaves him, Vadim drives across the United States in consolation.]

I spent what remained of the summer exploring the incredibly lyrical Rocky Mountain states, getting drunk on whiffs of Oriental Russia in the sagebrush zone and on the North Russian fragrances so faithfully reproduced above timberline by certain small bogs along trickles of sky between the snowbank and the orchid. And yet – was that all? What form of mysterious pursuit caused me to get my feet wet like a child, to pant up a talus, to stare every dandelion in the face, to start at every colored mote passing just beyond my field of vision? What was the dream sensation of having come empty-handed – without what? A gun? A wand? This I dared not probe lest I wound the raw fell under my thin identity.

Skipping the academic year, in a kind of premature "sabbatical leave" that left the Trustees of Quirn University speechless, I wintered in Arizona where I tried to write *The Invisible Lath,* a book rather similar to that in the reader's hands. No doubt I was not ready for it and perhaps toiled too much over inexpressible shades of emotion; anyway I smothered it under too many layers of sense as a Russian peasant woman, in her stuffy log house, might overlay (*zaspat'*) her baby in heavy oblivion after making hay or being thrashed by her drunken husband.

I pushed on to Los Angeles – and was sorry to learn that the cinema company I had counted upon was about to fold after Ivor Black's death. On my way back, in early spring, I rediscovered the dear phantasmata of my childhood in the tender green of aspen groves at high altitudes here and there, on conifer-clothed ridges. For almost six months I roamed again from motel to motel, several times having my car scratched and cracked by cretinous rival drivers and finally trading it in for a sedate Bellargus sedan of a celestial blue that Bel was to compare with that of a Morpho.[381]

Another odd thing: with prophetic care I took down in my diary all my stops, all my motels (*Mes Moteaux* as Verlaine might have said!), the Lakeviews, the Valley Views, the Mountain Views, the Plumed Serpent Court in New Mexico, the Lolita Lodge in Texas, Lone Poplars, that if recruited might have patrolled a whole river, and enough sunsets to keep all the bats of the world – and one dying genius – happy. LATH, LATH, Look At The Harlequins! Look at that strange fever rash of viatic tabulation in which I persevered as if I knew that those motor courts prefigured the stages of my future travels with my darling daughter.   [LATH 155–57]

[Vadim Vadymich tours the West with his daughter Bel.]

The education she got in Quirn's best private school for Young Ladies (you, her coeval, were there for a few weeks, in the same class, but you and she somehow missed making friends with each other) was supplemented by the two summers we spent roaming all over the Western states. What memories, what lovely smells, what mirages, near-mirages, substantiated mirages, accumulated along Highway 138 – Sterling, Fort Morgan (El. 4325), Greeley, well-named Loveland – as we approached the paradise part of Colorado!

From Lupine Lodge, Estes Park, where we spent a whole month, a path margined with blue flowers led through aspen groves to what Bel drolly called The Foot of the Face. There was also the Thumb of the Face, at its southern corner. I have a large glossy photograph taken by William Garrell who was the first, I think, to reach The Thumb, in 1940 or thereabouts, showing the East Face of Longs Peak with the checkered lines of ascent superimposed in a loopy design upon it. On the back of this picture – and as immortal in its own little right as the picture's subject – a poem by Bel, neatly copied in violet ink, is dedicated to Addie Alexander, "First woman on Peak, eighty years ago." It commemorates our own modest hikes:

Long's Peacock Lake:
the Hut and its Old Marmot;
Boulderfield and its Black Butterfly;
And the intelligent trail.

[LATH 170–71]

[Vadim meets his last and ideal love, whose name we never learn.]

Coincidence is a pimp and cardsharper in ordinary fiction but a marvelous artist in the patterns of fact recollected by a non-ordinary memoirist. Only asses and geese think that the re-collector skips this or that bit of his past because it is dull or shoddy (that sort of episode here, for example, the interview with the Dean, and how scrupulously it is recorded!). I was on the way to the parking lot when the bulky folder under my arm – replacing my arm, as it were – burst its string and spilled its contents all over the gravel and grassy border. You were coming from the library along the same campus path, and we crouched side by side collecting the stuff. You were pained you said later (*zhalostno bylo*) to smell the liquor on my breath. On the breath of that great writer.

I say "you" retroconsciously, although in the logic of life you were not "you" yet, for we were not actually acquainted and you were to become really "you" only when you said, catching a slip of yellow paper that was availing itself of a bluster to glide away with false insouciance:

"No, you don't."

Crouching, smiling, you helped me to cram everything again into the folder and then asked me how my daughter was – she and you had been schoolmates some fifteen years ago, and my wife had given you a lift several times. I then remembered your name and in a photic flash of celestial color saw you and Bel looking like twins, silently hating each other, both in blue coats and white hats, waiting to be driven somewhere by Louise. Bel and you would both be twenty-eight on January 1, 1970.

A yellow butterfly settled briefly on a clover head, then wheeled away in the wind.

"*Metamorphoza*," you said in your lovely, elegant Russian.

Would I care to have some snapshots (additional snapshots) of Bel? Bel feeding a chipmunk? Bel at the school dance? (Oh, I remember that dance – she had chosen for escort a sad fat Hungarian boy whose father was assistant manager of the Quilton Hotel – I can still hear Louise snorting!)

We met next morning in my carrel at the College Library, and after that I continued to see you every day. I will not suggest, LATH is not meant to suggest, that the petals and plumes of my previous loves are dulled or coarsened when directly contrasted with the purity of your being, the magic, the pride, the reality of your radiance. Yet "reality" *is* the key word here; and the gradual perception of that reality was nearly fatal to me.

Reality would be only adulterated if I now started to narrate what you know, what I know, what nobody else knows, what shall never, never be ferreted out by a matter-of-fact, father-of-muck, mucking biograffitist.

[LATH 225–26]

From interview with Helga Chudacoff, June 20, 1974

Published in *Die Welt*, September 26, 1974.

I cannot imagine what interest there could be for you in seeing me between the rain and the butterfly on a muddy mountain trail. There is nobody more gloomy, silent, and edgy than a lepidopterist in the pursuit of his task. . . .

I have breakfast at 7.30. A quarter to eight I saunter out of the hotel with my net, choosing one of the possible four or five trails. Depending on the weather, my hike can last three hours or five. On the average I walk 15 kilometers a day. Quite often, later in the season, I use a cable car. By the way, the chairlift is a beautiful invention, you just glide along. Once in Italy I used a chairlift with music – and not only music, but Puccini and "La Traviata." Often I spend two or three hours on the same meadow waiting for a certain 'Falter.' Then perhaps I would find a friendly little 'Stube' where I would have a drink. . . .

Butterflies keep quiet for some time after the rain. This morning it was cloudless, the sun was shining after yesterday's rain and nevertheless they did not come out until ten o'clock. . . .

[Does the aesthete in you sometimes prevent the scientist Nabokov from killing a butterfly because it happens to be especially beautiful?]

Not because it is beautiful. All butterflies are beautiful and ugly at the same time – like human beings. I let it go if it is old and frayed, or if I don't need it for my collection. I hate to kill a butterfly which is useless to me. It is an unpleasant feeling – you pinch it automatically and you feel guilty afterwards.

[From TS, VNA]

From Alfred Appel, Jr., memoir of June 1974

From "Remembering Nabokov," in *Vladimir Nabokov: A Tribute*, ed. Peter Quennell (1979).

. . . it had rained the first two days of our stay in Zermatt. "Oh, when will it clear, *when* will it clear?" groaned Nabokov, pacing the hotel lobby as though the world had been created the previous night, and he had to examine at once its resplendent marvels, describe and name them. On the third day there was light; and early that morning – far too early that morning – we accompanied the seventy-five-year-old writer-naturalist on a butterfly hunting trip ("lepping" he always called it) into the mountains. His sedentary guests walked along quite stoically, their thin-skinned office shoes no help at all, as amply soled Nabokov, squinting and scanning the horizon, talked on steadily, mainly about the flora and fauna around us. "Tolstoy saw that [dense shrubbery] best" – these eyes, School of Nabokov, saw a black-green base splashed by brilliant orange flowers, a Fauvist bush – "and you remember how Chekhov described those berries in – *ah*! There's one, what I've been looking for [name in Latin]"; and Nabokov was off, up and over some boulders, net aloft, an assault squad of one in pursuit of a pale-yellow butterfly. After depositing his capture ("Wonderful specimen, wonderful!") in the worn old Johnson & Johnson Band-Aid tin that had served him since the forties, the climb continued ("That hostel has the sweetest of Alpine butters, I speak as an expert, we can stop on the way down"), Nabokov's good spirits rising with the altitude, save for one quiet moment during our ascent when he paused on the path and gestured towards the hillside. "This is the timberline of my youth. See those trees." . . .

"Look, *I* caught a butterfly," I proudly exclaimed a few minutes later,

VN with net while walking with Alfred Appel, Jr., Zermatt, July 1974. (*Nina Appel*)

holding aloft the cupped hands that contained an insect I had picked off a very low shrub. "Actually, that's a moth," said Nabokov, his tone kind, almost apologetic. But I feigned humiliation, slumped abjectly, and the game was on. "Moreover," Nabokov added, with a mock frown, "it is a common species." I slumped even lower. [*Timidly*]: "But I caught it with my bare hands." "Which is easy to do!" thundered Nabokov, his tone very dark now. "They are drawn to the warmth of human hands" – he drew a breath, I slumped some more – "and furthermore [theatrical pause before the final lethal thrust] this wingèd fellow was gaga from sleep." I fell against a boulder and grabbed it for support as the bored and patient creature earned its freedom. The shimmering snow-walled Matterhorn behind me had provided an adequate backdrop for this genre scene, an old-fashioned *rencontre* in St Petersburg or Rio. "*Utterly defeated!*" proclaimed Nabokov, and we laughed. [*Vladimir Nabokov: A Tribute* 26–27]

From interview with Bernard Safarik, c. August 1974

For Swiss-German television.

Nothing has ever influenced me overmuch. I'm a *self-contained* organism. But I must confess that for sheer physical well-being a summer day spent hunting butterflies in the Valais, the Ticino, or the Grisons is only comparable to the delights of Colorado, Montana, Utah. [From TS, VNA]

From interview with George Feifer, August 1974

Q: Is there a person, place, or situation that haunts you, in the sense that you have not used it to your own satisfaction in your work?
A: A strange streak of kindness in my nature prevented me from depicting in a contemplated memoir (*Speak on, Memory*) many burlesque characters I have filed away in the last three decades. As to "places and situations" that "haunt" one, as you put it, there exists in my mind a long series of trails, valleys, mountain slopes, rocky debris, bewitching little peat bogs associ-

ated with certain difficult butterflies that I longed to see alive, and saw at last, in natural motion or at rest, among the plants of their exiguous breeding places. Yet what can I do with that heavenly stuff as a writer? I am certainly not afraid to bore readers with nature notes worked into a memoir or story. I am afraid to trim my science to size or – what is much the same – not to take full advantage of my art in speaking of "scientific" details. . . .

Q: In your recent experience, has pollution affected the life and existence of butterflies?

A: Pollution in itself is a lesser enemy of butterfly life than, say, climatic changes. One sees Skippers and Blues relish black filth near country garages and camping grounds. In the case of very local species whose numbers are not kept up by wide-wandering impregnated females the destruction of an uncommon foodplant by some idiot vineyardist can of course wipe out a habitat. But nature is hardy and certain delicate semitransparent little larvae are known to have outmaneuvered the most modern pesticides. It is wonderful to pick out in the crazy quilt of an agricultural area as seen from an airplane the number of green holes where a lovely insect can safely breed. The gloomiest lepidopterist perks up when he thinks that butterflies have survived milleniums of reckless farming, overgrazing and deforestation.

Q: What do you want to do most in the next two years?

A: Hunt butterflies, especially certain Whites, in the mountains of Iran and in the Middle Atlas. Quietly take up tennis again. Have three new suits made in London. Revisit landscapes and libraries in America. Find a harder *and* darker pencil.　　　[*Saturday Review*, November 27, 1976, 22–24]

From interview with Gerald Clarke, September 17, 1974

If any goal has eluded me, it must be sought in another domain, that of lepidopterology. At the middle point of my life (1940–48) I used to devote many hours daily, including Sundays, to the working out of taxonomic problems in the laboratories of two great museums. Since my years at the Museum of Comparative Zoology in Harvard, I have not touched a microscope, knowing that if I did, I would drown again in its bright well. Thus I have not, and probably never shall, accomplish the greater part of the entrancing research work I had imagined in my young mirages, such as "A monograph of the Eurasian and American *machaon* group," or "The *Eupithecias* of the World." Gratitude for other pleasures leaves, really, no room in my mind for that ghost of regret.   [*Esquire*, July 1975, 69]

From letter to Teddy Kollek, January 15, 1975

From Montreux. Unpublished.

The very name of the place[382] is so enticing – and I will not only admire but certainly visit for butterfly hunting the Moab Hills.

Life – laborious, literary life – has been most complicated this winter and I still cannot decide quite for sure when I could come to Israel.   [VNA]

Letter to Véra Nabokov, April 15, 1975

From Montreux. Translated by DN. "VN's fiftieth-anniversary greeting to Véra Nabokov on 2″ × 4″ section cut from a checked index card, perhaps attached to a present, and illustrated with a beautiful iridescent butterfly" – DN.

Here we are at last, my darling
15.iv.1925–15.iv.1975

[SL 546]

Letter to Robert Wool, April 18, 1975

From Montreux. Published in the *New York Times Magazine*, July 27, 1975.

Dear Mr. Wool,

To my great regret I shall not be able to write on Lepidoptera (at least this year) as you kindly suggest in your letter of March 27. I would be delighted however if, in reference to the recent note on Endangered Butterflies, you could print the following:

To the Editor:

By a nice coincidence the so-called "Karner Blue" illustrating Bayard Webster's note on insects needing protection (N.Y. Times, March 21) is a butterfly I classified myself. It is known as *Lycaeides melissa samuelis* Nabokov or more properly *Lycaeides samuelis* Nabokov (I considered it at first to be a race of the western *melissa* Edwards, but have concluded recently that it is a distinct species). My original description will be found in *Psyche*, Vol. I, 1943, followed by a more elaborate paper in the Bulletin of the Museum of Comparative Zoology, Harvard College, Vol. 101, 1949. It is a very local butterfly attached to extensive growths of lupine, in isolated colonies, from Michigan (probably its original habitat) to at least Albany, N.Y. Readers of my fiction may have found it settled on damp sand in a vacational scene of my novel *PNIN*.

Yours sincerely,

VLADIMIR NABOKOV   [SL 547]

From letter to Robert Dirig,[383] April 23, 1975

From Montreux.

The story of *Lycaeides samuelis* Nabokov, which I separated in 1943 (Psyche, Vol. I) from the W. American race of another species, now known (after a nomenclatorial readjustment) as *Lycaeides idas scudderi* Edwards, is told in detail in my paper on the genus in the *Bulletin of the Museum of*

Comparative Zoology, Harvard College, Vol. 101 (1949). The name I gave it alludes to Scudder's Christian name. When thirty years ago I attempted to classify *samuelis*, I regarded it as a subspecies of *melissa* Edw. on the basis of the length of its falx but now I know better. There are additional structural differences, there are larval differences (which I hope you will find and publish) and there is the crucial fact of *samuelis* and *melissa* not interbreeding at their meeting point which must surely exist already given the inexorable progression of *melissa* from Illinois eastward during the last decades.

This is why I am delighted by your project of writing about it and the celebrated Pine Barrens which I remember as a sandy and flowery little paradise the last time I visited them when commuting between Cornell and Harvard.

[SL 549–50]

From letter to Alfred Appel, Jr., April 23, 1975

From Montreux.

I see I have not thanked you for the clipping about the protection of leps. In a sense I am the Endangered Species illustrating the article, for it is no other than *Lycaeides samuelis* Nabokov named by me in 1943! But what must tickle some of my best readers an iridescent pink is that it is precisely the butterfly which settles on damp sand at the feet of Pnin and Chateau!

[SL 550]

From interview with Sophie Lannes, April 30, 1975

In French. For *L'Express*.

Q: Why Switzerland? . . .

A: Why Switzerland? Why not? Its mountains, the diversity of its flora, its smooth roads, its charming inns remind me of my favorite countryside, the American West. The only thing that really annoys me in Switzerland is that people mow too often and too soon the beautiful medium-altitude meadows, since I need the wildflowers – which all my translators want to translate as "fleurs sauvages"[384] – I need them for my entomological excursions, the greatest delight of my life. But naturally I can always climb in a magic chair to 2000 meters to find my wild butterflies, taking care to avoid certain high mountain slopes where cowpats replace edelweiss. Dialogue on an alpine path with a so-called "protector of nature": He: "You know hunting butterflies is not permitted?" I: "What do you call a butterfly?" (I show him one, rather small.) "No, that's a sort of fly, I mean the ones they make jewels of, the Big Blues." The poor man thought he was in Brazil. . . .

Q: [Why butterflies?]

A: A pastime once as banal as music or watercolor lessons became for me, from my tender childhood, a passion, a study and finally a profession pursued in the laboratories of Harvard and in voyages of discovery. It is pure science with no esthetic side: if one happens to prefer a series of fresh and well-spread specimens, it is in order to study the wing design all the better. And when one has made preparations of organs to examine under the microscope, the india-ink portrait one makes in the radiance of the camera lucida has all the more enchantment for being executed in a manner which technically satisfies the needs of such research. I have discovered several American butterflies and published their portraits and descriptions in obscure journals more lasting than my novels.   [From TS, VNA]

From interview with Bernard Pivot, May 30, 1975

In French. Live broadcast in series *Apostrophes,* French television Channel 2.

Q: So writing has always been the great love of your life? Could you conceive of another life in which you did not write?

A: Yes, I can very easily picture another life: a life in which I would be not a writer, happily renting an ivory tower of Babel, but someone just as happy in another fashion – which I have tried, by the way – an obscure entomologist who spends the summer hunting butterflies in fabulous lands and the winter classifying his discoveries in a museum lab.

Q: Do you feel more Russian or American or, since you live in Switzerland, more Swiss?

A: . . . Our estate was located in the northern wooded lowland; it is rather close in its flora to the northwest corner of America: forests of light aspen and dark pine, lots of birches and splendid peat-bogs with a multitude of more or less arctic flowers and butterflies. . . .

Q: Are you in favor of the protection of nature?

A: The protection of certain rare animals is an excellent thing; it becomes absurd when ignorance and pedantry join in. It's perfectly right to report a curio-seller who collects for resale to amateurs a remarkable moth, the French race of a Spanish species, one of whose scarce colonies risks extinction in the valley of the Durance where these merchants go to harvest this beautiful creature's caterpillars on a common conifer.[385] But it is absurd when a gamekeeper forbids an old naturalist to move about with his old net in a restricted area where there flies a certain butterfly, whose sole food-plant is the bladder-senna – which means nothing to the gamekeeper – a bush with yellow flowers and large pods, which often grows around vineyards. Wherever the bush is, this butterfly can also be found, and it's the bush which should be protected since a million collectors could not destroy this sky-blue insect if only the vineyardists stopped destroying, for some mysterious reason, the bladder-sennas in their vineyards all along the Rhine.

In other cases the rarity of species varies according to the seasons or depends on a more or less sustained succession of migrations. Farmers with their infernal pesticides, road construction, the cretins who burn tires and mattresses on empty fields – these are the real culprits, and not the scientist without whom a policeman could not tell a butterfly from an angel or a bat.

[VNA]

From letter from Véra Nabokov to Irving Lazar,[386]
July 31, 1975
Unpublished.

He thanks you very much for the truly beautiful butterflies book. The photographs are stunning. The method of depiction of the magnified scales was inaugurated by Vladimir.

[VNA]

From letter to Glenn Collins,[387] August 20, 1975

From Montreux.

I had been looking forward eagerly to that delightful essay.[388] For more than a month I hunted butterflies around Davos. Then I took a bad tumble down a steep slippery slope and was laid up for several days. Other worries cropped up in the meantime. When I returned to Montreux in the beginning of August a landslide of correspondence had to be disposed of. And my butterfly net remains hanging on the branch of a fir at 1900 metres like Ovid's lyre.   [SL 552]

Letter to Pyke Johnson, December 8, 1975

From Montreux. Unpublished.

Dear Mr. Johnson,

I was overjoyed and tremendously excited to get THE BUTTERFLIES OF NORTH AMERICA which is the kind of work that we, American lepists, have been awaiting ever since Holland's wretched and dishonest compilation appeared in the "revised" edition of 1932. William Howe is an admirable illustrator, combining the artistic and the scientific. The text is up-to-date and full of wonders.

I have two little scraps of criticism: one, concerning the nine quite unrepresentative tropical strays on the jacket (they occur only in the southernmost fringe of North America); and the other, the fact that the name *argyrognomon* as used here should be replaced *everywhere* by *idas*, as ruled by the International Commission on Zoological Nomenclature twenty years ago (a fact John Downey should have been aware of). A note in the next edition could take care of the matter.

I have been almost literally *feeding* on this beautiful book for the last ten evenings or so. The orgy of subspecific puzzles in the North-American *Papilio* and *Speyeria* groups has no counterpart in the European fauna, and though the mystery is not yet solved it is at least wonderfully depicted and described.

I am most grateful for your gift.

Cordially,
VLADIMIR NABOKOV   [VNA]

From letter to Alfred Appel, Jr., April 26, 1976

From Montreux.

Your big gift and its satellites arrived safely, many, many thanks for your kind thoughts and congs. I am deep in *The New Golden Land*[389] and thrilled by those first American butterflies, some of which are quite recognizable.

[SL 559]

From letter to Victor Lusinchi,[390] October 30, 1976

From Montreux. Published in the *New York Times Book Review*, December 5, 1976.

Three Books

Here are the three books I read during the three summer months of 1976 while hospitalized in Lausanne:

1. Dante's *Inferno* in Singleton's splendid translation (Princeton, 1970) with the Italian *en regard* and a detailed commentary. What triumphant joy it is to see the honest light of literality take over again, after ages of meretricious paraphrase!

2. *The Butterflies of North America* by Howe, coordinating editor and illustrator (1975, 633 pages). It describes and pictures in marvelous color all the nearctic species and many subspecies. Nothing like it has ever appeared here. The indifference of our philistine public to it is scandalous especially as all kinds of non-scientific coffee books—opalescent morphos and so on—are paraded yearly and presumably sell.

3. *The Original of Laura,* the not quite finished manuscript of a novel

which I had begun writing and reworking before my illness and which was completed in my mind: I must have gone through it some fifty times and in my diurnal delirium kept reading it aloud to a small dream audience in a walled garden. My audience consisted of peacocks, pigeons, my long dead parents, two cypresses, several young nurses crouching around, and a family doctor so old as to be almost invisible. Perhaps because of my stumblings and fits of coughing the story of my poor Laura had less success with my listeners than it will have, I hope, with intelligent reviewers when properly published. [SL 561–62]

The butterfly motif in Nabokov book design. *Poems* (1959), which included the poem "A Discovery," was the first to use this motif. The most recent volume, *The Stories of Vladimir Nabokov* (1994, 1995), shows it becoming even more prominent. (*University of Auckland Photographic Studio*)

From letter to Teddy Kollek, December 10, 1976

From Montreux. Unpublished.

I was delighted to learn from my cousin Nicholas that you still want me to come to Israel. I have been eager for quite a time to make this journey. This year has been a bad one for me. I have been hospitalized for several months with a grave illness and only now have begun to resume my usual mode of life.

If convenient I would like to come with my wife in the second week of May for a month or so. I am afraid you will not find me as stimulating a guest as Nicholas. For my part I shall look forward to making your acquaintance after hearing so much about your superb activities. I am also looking forward to the museums and libraries, and, of course, to some butterfly collecting (in the company of an experienced and robust male guide).

[VNA]

From interview with Robert Robinson, February 14, 1977

For the BBC-2 *Book Programme*. Published in *The Listener*, March 24, 1977. Reprinted in *Vladimir Nabokov: A Tribute,* ed. Peter Quennell.

Q: Do you find that you re-read your own earlier work, and if you do, with what feelings?

A: Re-reading my own works is a purely utilitarian business. I have to do it when correcting a paperback edition riddled with misprints or controlling a translation, but there are some rewards. In certain species – this is going to be a metaphor – in certain species, the wings of the pupated butterfly begin to show in exquisite miniature through the wing-cases of the chrysalis a few days before emergence. It is the pathetic sight of an iridescent future transpiring through the shell of the past, something of the kind I experience when dipping into my books written in the twenties. Suddenly through a drab photograph a blush of colour, an outline of form, seems to be distinguishable. I'm saying this with absolute scientific modesty, not with the smugness of ageing art. . . . .

Q: The world knows that you are also a lepidopterist but may not know what that involves. In the collection of butterflies, could you describe the process from pursuit to display?

A: Only common butterflies, showy moths from the tropics, are put on display in a dusty case between a primitive mask and a vulgar abstract picture. The rare, precious stuff is kept in the glazed drawers of museum cabinets. As for pursuit, it is, of course, ecstasy to follow an undescribed beauty, skimming over the rocks of its habitat, but it is also great fun to locate a new species among the broken insects in an old biscuit tin sent over by a sailor from some remote island.

Q: . . . Have you any sense of having narrowly missed some other role? What substitute could you endure?

A: Oh, yes, I have always had a number of parts lined up in case the muse failed. A lepidopterist exploring famous jungles came first, then there was the chess grand master, then the tennis ace with an unreturnable service, then the goalie saving a historic shot, and finally, finally, the author of a pile of unknown writings – *Pale Fire, Lolita, Ada* – which my heirs discover and publish.   [*Vladimir Nabokov: A Tribute* 123–24]

Letter to E. W. Classey Ltd.,[391] February 21, 1977

From Montreux.

I wish to order the following books:

 C. F. Cowan. "Annotationes Rhopalocerologicae" Part 1 and 2 (addenda etc. to Hemming's "Generic Names" etc.) 1968–70.

 Torben B. Larsen. "Butterflies of Lebanon" 1974. Bound.   [VNA]

From Dmitri Nabokov memoir, July 21, 1977

Read at memorial gathering, New York City, July 21, 1977. Published in *In Memoriam Vladimir Nabokov 1899–1977* (New York: McGraw-Hill, 1977) and in revised form as "On Revisiting Father's Room" in Quennell.

A few days before he died[392] there was a moment I remember with special clarity. During our penultimate farewell, after I had kissed his still-warm forehead – as I had for years when saying goodnight or goodbye – tears suddenly welled in Father's eyes. I asked him why. He replied that a certain butterfly was already on the wing; and his eyes told me he no longer hoped that he would live to pursue it again.   [*Vladimir Nabokov: A Tribute* 136]

Notes

NABOKOV, LITERATURE, LEPIDOPTERA

1. Ronald S. Wilkinson, perhaps the foremost recent historian of lepidopterology, had planned in the 1970s and 1980s to republish Nabokov's collected scientific papers. In the course of the project he wrote this to Edward Tenner of Princeton University Press (February 16, 1979, Princeton University Press archives).

2. PF 225.

3. Adalbert Seitz (1860–1938) began publishing his book on *The Butterflies of the World*, the most comprehensive ever attempted, in 1906. A last (sixteenth) installment was published in 1954, but the work was never quite finished.

4. As the lepidopterist Kurt Johnson has remarked to me, "There is no better place to get on a 'thought-wave' that just carries itself" than "out wandering about, collecting."

5. D. Barton Johnson, "That Butterfly in Nabokov's *Eye*," *Nabokov Studies* 4 (1997): 1–14.

6. Alexander Klots (1951), 164. Klots (1903–1989) was a professor of biology at the City College of New York and Research Associate at the American Museum of Natural History (AMNH).

7. Kurt Johnson letter to BB, July 24, 1995.

8. Diana Butler (1960) was the first to link the scene where Nabokov captured the female of *Lycaeides sublivens* with the scene in the novel, but she opted to read into the connection a strained symbolic rather than a plain topographical similarity.

9. The chapter in which this exchange occurs was rejected by the *New Yorker* for political reasons: Nabokov's frank criticism of Soviet prisons.

10. Or, in a more explicit earlier formulation, "a seemingly incongruous detail over a seemingly dominant generalization" (LL 374).

11. *Stikhi* 3.

12. For the case of *The Gift*, see Boyd (1990), 468–78. I naively presumed *Thecla bieti* an invented butterfly discovered by Fyodor's father; Zimmer 1998: 153 corrects and explains.

13. For the case of *Pale Fire*, see Boyd (1999), chapters 9–10.

14. Nabokov had previously admired Howe's skill as an illustrator of Lepidoptera but was critical of his science (SL 367–69), as were many lepidopterists – including some of the volume's contributors – of his editing of *Butterflies of North America*. But the section on Plebejinae, by Howe, Robert L. Langston, and John C. Downey, was technically one of the best in the book.

15. Kurt Johnson and Steven L. Coates (1999), 87.

16. See p. 208.

17. Johnson and Coates (1999), 87.

18. Johnson and Coates (1999), 84.

19. Johnson and Coates (1999), 89.

20. Stallings and Turner (1947), 135.

21. Klots (1951), 164. Klots would later write to William McGuire at Princeton University Press (November 22, 1981): "I know that I (not alone) was a bit worried as to what he might do when I first learned of his intention to work in the butterflies. It would have been so easy for an inspired, but untrained amateur to do a lot of damage that it would take more plodding workers years to repair. . . . I was greatly pleased with the intelligence and thoroughness of his work, which was published in a format that made it usable. (We have gifted amateurs who couldn't be bothered with such things as accurate references and bibliographies.) . . . Certainly we gained from his imaginative ability to see relationships and to trace postulated evolutionary trends. In fact I don't know anybody else who could have done this. . . . My own relations with Nabokov were always cordial. The inaccuracies he pointed out in my Field Guide were just that and needed to be exposed. And [in the 1960s] he very kindly collected for us some species in the south of France that we needed at the Museum."

22. Dos Passos (1964), iv. In a letter to Edward Tenner of Princeton University Press (February 21, 1979), dos Passos commented that Nabokov was "unfortunately not well known to most American entomologists."

23. Downey to Kurt Johnson, August 12, 1996.

24. Reported in Johnson and Coates (1999), 98.

25. Obituary, *Journal of the Lepidopterists' Society* 34 (1980).

26. BB interview with Kurt Johnson, June 1996; Johnson to BB, August 16, 1996.

27. Johnson and Coates (1999), 290.

28. Johnson and Coates (1999), 90.

29. Kurt Johnson and David Matusik (1988); Albert Schwarz and Kurt Johnson (1992); and D. S. Smith, L. D. Miller and J. Y. Miller (1994); the preferability of Nabokov's Caribbean terminology to Riley's is summarized most recently in Johnson and Bálint (1995) and Johnson and Coates (1999).

30. Bálint and Johnson (1994: *Itylos* section), 54, 57.

31. Bálint (1993), 2.

32. "Nearctic Forms . . . ," 88; see p. 280.

33. Robert Michael Pyle adds the caveat of an experienced field naturalist: "Cladistic analysis sometimes suggests likely paths that might nonetheless be artificial because of plastic characters: exactly why Nabokov would have been likely to have stuck, as other good taxonomists do, to conservative traits observed precisely. Although cladistics uses *more* 'individuating details,' it is far less selective in doing so. Quantity of data is in, the 'good eye' is out."

34. Kurt Johnson to BB, July 24, 1995.

35. Now considered to be not *Lysandra cormion*, a new species, but a cross between *Lysandra coridon* and *Meleageria daphnis*; see Schurian (1989) and (1991) and Zimmer (1998), 53.

36. See pp. 273–74.

37. Edward O. Wilson, *The Diversity of Life* (1993), 132–33.

38. SO 153.

BETWEEN CLIMB AND CLOUD

1. Taxonomists try to choose *conservative* characters by which to judge relationships. In Lepidoptera, color, shape, and pattern can evolve fairly rapidly, while the veins of the wings and the sclerotized parts of the genitalia are slow to change – they are thus conservative traits that often furnish reliable clues about phylogenetic relationships.

2. Remington (1995).

3. Lee D. Miller, *Journal of the Lepidopterists' Society* 34, no. 2 (1980).
4. Remington (1995), 277–79.
5. Written August 18, 1949, NWL.
6. Written October 23, 1953, NWL 284.
7. Remington (1995), 277–78.
8. Field (1977), 202.
9. Dmitri Nabokov, in a footnote to a letter from VN to Robert Dirig, April 23, 1975 (SL 550), writes, "VN was a member of the Xerces Society."
10. Brown (1950); VN, "Remarks" (1950) and "Postscript" (1950); FMB, "In Response to Prof. Nabokov," *Lep. News* 4:76.
11. Johnson, Bálint, and Whittaker (1996).
12. Zaleski (1986), 34–38.
13. VNAY, 114–15.
14. Remington (1995), 278.
15. Miller (1974), 1–98.
16. Johnson, Bálint, and Whittaker (1996), 132.
17. Remington (1995), 282.
18. Dirig (1994), 24.
19. See K. Johnson and S. Coates, *Nabokov's Blues*, for full details.
20. Chet Raymo, "The Butterflies' Choice," *Boston Globe*, February 17, 1992.
21. George Feifer, "Vladimir Nabokov: An Interview," *Saturday Review,* November 27, 1976, 20–26.
22. Butler (1960), 58–84.
23. Karges (1985).
24. Herbert Gold, interview with VN, *Paris Review,* October, 1967, 100.
25. Raymo, "The Butterflies' Choice."
26. Karges (1985), 68.

NABOKOV'S BUTTERFLIES

1. The text follows the revised, 1967, edition. Major additions there to the 1948 *New Yorker* version and 1951 *Conclusive Evidence* version include section 2, first half of paragraph 3 ("Retrospectively" to "rarities recently described"); section 3, paragraphs 1–2, 6 ("One summer afternoon" to end), 8–10; section 4, first half of paragraph 2; section 5, paragraph 1; section 6, paragraph 3.
2. Nabokov's father, the leader of the Constitutional Democratic Party in the First State Duma (parliament) in 1906, was imprisoned for three months for signing the Vyborg Manifesto, calling for the Russian people to resist conscription and taxes to protest Tsar Nicholas II's sudden dissolution of the Duma. See also SM 175–76.
3. The Mourning Cloak or Camberwell Beauty, now known as *Nymphalis antiopa* (L.).
4. She and VN married in 1925.
5. Probably *Staurophora celsia* (L.) (no English name), which infrequently abounds but normally is local and rare in central Europe.
6. Nikolay Kardakov (1885–after 1942).
7. Arnold Moltrecht (1874–19??).

8. The Russian word for "pupa" means, literally, "little doll."

9. This manuscript, whose text is here translated in full, is the only known evidence of such a poem.

10. Suggests *Saturnia pavonia* (L.), the large, eye-spotted Emperor Moth.

11. Commonly known as Red Admiral, but Nabokov pointedly preferred the older name Red Admirable.

12. The butterfly in question is *Lycaena virgaureae* Linnaeus, the Scarce Copper. In researching his paper on the butterflies he had caught in the Pyrenees, which would be published in *The Entomologist*, Nabokov came across a recent article considering this case: P. P. Graves and A. F. Hemming, "The Geographical Variation of *Lycaena virgaureae* Linn." The Entomologist 61 [777] (February 1928): 24–31, 56–62, 89–90, 104–9, 128–35. For a detailed treatment, see D. Barton Johnson (1998).

13. Nikolay Raevsky. See the next selection.

14. Eugenia Konstantinovna Hofeld, the former governess of Nabokov's sisters, who remained with the family as a friend in exile.

15. From Rudyard Kipling, "The Feet of the Young Men" (1897), lines 40–47.

16. From Kipling, "The Butterfly That Stamped" (1897), lines 9–12.

17. The Old World Swallowtail, *Papilio machaon* L.

18. VN's cousin, the composer Nicholas Nabokov, and his first wife, Natalie, with whom VN had just stayed on their estate in Kolbsheim, near Strasbourg.

19. See pp. 135–46.

20. Dmitri Nabokov, born April 1934.

21. *Kamni* in Russian.

22. Nabokov became embroiled in an affair with this Russian émigrée in Paris between February and May 1937.

23. "So you raise butterflies?"

24. A copy of the collected works of Pushkin.

25. Grigoriy Efimovich Grum-Grzhimaylo (1860–1936), Russian geographer who several times explored Central Asia for its geography, geology, flora, and fauna.

26. Grand Duke Nikolay Mikhailovich Romanov (1859–1919), historian, amateur geographer and entomologist, editor of *Mémoires sur les lépidoptères* (9 vols., St. Petersburg, 1884–1901), in French, English, and German.

27. Andrey Avinoff (1884–1949), entomologist and painter, who amassed a large collection of Central Asian Lepidoptera in Russia before World War I and from 1917 was a curator and then director of the Carnegie Museum of Natural History in Pittsburgh.

28. Roger (Ruggero) Verity (1883–1959), Italian physicist and lepidopterist.

29. Andreas Bang-Haas (1846–1925), senior partner in the powerful German entomological firm of Staudinger and Bang-Haas. His son Otto (1882–1948), also a lepidopterist, owned the firm after his death.

30. The Tring Museum, as the Walter Rothschild Zoological Museum is popularly known, in Tring, Hertfordshire, a zoological museum built up in the late nineteenth and early twentieth centuries by Lionel Walter Rothschild. Bequeathed to the British Museum on his death in 1937, it is now administered by the Natural History Museum.

31. From Pushkin's poem "Khudozhniku" ("To an Artist," 1836). Pushkin of course has in mind figures from Greek mythology, not butterflies.

32. Gotthelf Fischer von Waldheim (1771–1853), German natural historian, became a professor at Moscow University and Russia's foremost entomologist.

33. Édouard Ménétriès (1802–1861), lepidopterist, curator of the Museum of the Academy of Sciences in St. Petersburg.

34. Eduard von Eversmann (1794–1861), professor of zoology and botany at the University of Kazan, author of *Fauna Lepidopterlogica Volgo-Uralensis* (1844).

35. Nikolay Kholodkovski (1858–1921), zoologist, poet, translator.

36. Charles Oberthür (1845–1924), French lepidopterist, editor of *Études d'Entomologie* (1876–1902) and *Études de Lépidoptérologie comparée* (1904–1925).

37. John Henry Leech (1862–1900), British entomologist, explorer of the Lepidoptera of Asia, author of *Butterflies from China, Japan and Corea* (London, 1892–94).

38. See p. 4 and p. 723, n. 3.

39. Otto Staudinger (1830–1900), influential owner of German entomological store and author of a catalogue of the Lepidoptera of Europe and Asia damned by people like Grum-Grzhimaylo for its lack of scientific precision.

40. A short novel (1836) by Pushkin.

41. The hero of a trilogy (1872–90) by Alphonse Daudet (1840–1897), a boaster who believes his own stories; in the first, *Tartarin de Tarascon*, he overequips himself to shoot lions in the North African desert.

42. "Hello children . . . I have just seen IN the garden, NEAR the cedar, ON a rose a really beautiful butterfly: it was blue, green, purple, golden – and this big."

43. Jean-Paul Claris de Florian (1755–1794), in his fable "Le Grillon," shows a bright butterfly, Petit-maître (Fop), dying through its own thoughtlessness.

44. Jean-Henri Fabre (1823–1915), French amateur entomologist, author of *Souvenirs entomologiques* (1879–1907), widely respected by writers but not by scientists.

45. This is one of the Large Blues (genus *Maculinea*), whose members have coevolved with ants in essentially the manner described here.

46. James William Tutt (1858–1911), English teacher and lepidopterist, author of *A Natural History of the British Lepidoptera*, 4 vols. (London, 1899–1904).

47. This acquired appendage is called the *sphragis*. Several groups of butterflies have it, but none are as large as in Parnassians.

48. Roborovski's White: *Pieris deota* (the name *Pieris roborowskii* proved invalid). Vsevolod Roborovski (1856–1910), Russian explorer, Przhevalski's assistant on his last two expeditions.

49. From Pushkin's poem "Prorok" ("The Prophet"): a seraph touches the poet's eyes, which open wide like a frightened eagle's as visions flood in.

50. Nearby Huntingdonshire (now part of Cambridgeshire) was the type locality of the Large Copper, a butterfly specially adapted to the Fens. Extensive drainage for agriculture, with collecting perhaps a *coup de grace*, extirpated *Lycaena dispar dispar* in the mid-1850s, though other subspecies survive on the continent.

51. A typically Tyutchevian locution, not from "Storm" but from the untitled lyric "*Vchera v mechtakh obvorozhonnikh . . .*"

52. Mikhail D. Skobelev (1843–1882), general of infantry, esp. Central Asia.

53. Small brown Satyrs, the first fictional, the second real.

54. vn had not yet invented a co-author.

55. Evokes King Lear's last speech to the living Cordelia ("Come let's away to prison: / We two alone will sing like birds i' th' cage. / . . . So we'll live, / And pray, and sing, and tell old tales, and laugh / At gilded butterflies, and hear poor rogues / Talk of court news," *King Lear* 5.3.8–14) but pointedly avoids Lear's "gilded butterflies" (which has been taken to mean either literal butterflies, as he prolongs his unreal dream of future idylls, or foppish courtiers).

56. Mikhail Karpovich (1899–1959), professor of history at Harvard. He had invited the Nabokovs to spend the summer with his family in Vermont.

57. Elizaveta and Marussya Marinel, émigré friends in Paris whom Nabokov was trying to help immigrate to the United States.

58. The Marinels were still trying to escape from France after the German invasion.

59. In English. Nabokov had begun research at the AMNH in the fall.

60. Hans Rebel (1861–1940), co-author of the 1901 edition of Otto Staudinger's *Catalog der Lepidopteren des Palearctischen Faunengebiets*.

61. William P. Comstock (1880–1956), Research Associate of the AMNH.

62. Edmund Wilson (1895–1972), critic, editor, novelist, poet, Nabokov's close friend in the 1940s and 1950s.

63. *Atlantic Monthly*.

64. Composer Sergey Rachmaninov's cantata *The Bells* (1913) sets to music a free adaptation of Poe's poem by the Symbolist poet Konstantin Balmont.

65. Russian poets Mikhail Lermontov (1814–1841) and Fyodor Tyutchev (1803–1873).

66. Editor of the *Atlantic Monthly*.

67. If this work ever was written, the manuscript has not been located. Although VN talked on the subject more than once (see pp. 265, 269, 278), his notes have not survived.

68. Thomas Barbour (1884–1946), director of the MCZ, Harvard University. After consulting the MCZ collections for his own work, VN visited the Head of Entomology, Dr. Nathan Banks, to complain about the state of the Lepidoptera material. Banks invited him to rearrange the collection.

69. Mark Aldanov (1889–1957), Russian émigré novelist recently arrived in the United States.

70. Andrey Avinov, see n. 27.

71. Walter R. Sweadner of the Carnegie Museum, Pittsburgh.

72. *Parnassius apollo*, greatest of the waxy-white, red-spotted Swallowtail relatives known as Parnassians.

73. James Laughlin (1914–1997), founder of New Directions and publisher of the first three VN books – *The Real Life of Sebastian Knight* (1941), *Nikolai Gogol* (1944), and *Three Russian Poets* (1945) – to appear after Nabokov's arrival in the United States.

74. During the 1941–42 academic year, Nabokov held the title of Visiting Lecturer in Comparative Literature at Wellesley College.

75. VN correction from "gemmate," *Lepidopterological Papers 1941–1953*.

76. Gladys McCosh of Horton House, Wellesley College.

77. See n. 67.

78. To Wilson's Cape Cod cottage.

79. This was a significant find. Butterfly collectors consider it a major coup whenever they find a new "state record" for a species. It was especially notable for Nabokov to find a new state record for a butterfly named by Scudder in Scudder's own backyard of New England.

80. *Phoebis sennae eubule* (L.), the Cloudless Giant Sulphur.

81. Edgar Fisher of the Institute for International Education, which was organizing VN's lecture tour.

82. A "Hesperid" (or hesperiid) is a Skipper in the family Hesperiidae. Here he refers to the Long-tailed Skipper (*Urbanus proteus* [L.]).

83. Nabokov's friend C. Bertrand Thompson, who had studied music, law, and social science, wrote books on management, sociology and economics, would later study biochemistry, and had read widely in mysticism.

84. Florence Read, president of Spelman College, Atlanta.
85. See pp. 449 and 603.
86. Frank Morton Carpenter, an expert in fossil insects at Harvard's MCZ.
87. In Valdosta, Georgia, on October 13.
88. William Forbes (1885–1968), professor of entomology, Cornell University Agricultural Experimental Station. For VN's character sketch, see pp. 673–74.
89. Henry Allen Moe, Secretary of the John Simon Guggenheim Memorial Foundation.
90. See pp. 547–48.
91. "On Discovering a Butterfly."
92. Charles Pearce, poetry editor of the *New Yorker*. (VN's spelling is incorrect.)
93. In manuscript, line 9 of the poem "A Discovery" (p. 274) had read, "My needles have teased out its horny sex."
94. "Some New or Little Known Nearctic *Neonympha*."
95. In his novel *Bend Sinister*, on which he was working at this time, Nabokov renames James Joyce's *Finnegans Wake* "Winnipeg Lake" (114).
96. L. Paul Grey (1909–1994), a distinguished amateur lepidopterist still regarded as the greatest authority ever on American Fritillaries.
97. What book is meant is unclear; there is no other evidence that he was planning a wholly lepidopterological book at this time. See p. 265, for the first reference to this talk.
98. VN correction from "102," *Lepidopterological Papers 1941–1953*.
99. Mstislav Dobuzhinsky (1875–1957), a celebrated St. Petersburg and then émigré painter, draftsman, and stage designer, VN's drawing master from about 1912 to 1914.
100. Russian for "spent the night."
101. The Irish-American novelist Captain Mayne Reid (1818–1883), whose westerns were wildly popular in Russia.
102. See n. 99.
103. He had just had a large number of teeth extracted.
104. By Gerald Heard (Henry Fitzgerald Heard), published in 1941.
105. The writer Mary McCarthy, Wilson's wife at the time.
106. Katherine Reese was a Wellesley College student.
107. "It's about landscape verse, love verse, political verse and real verse" (VN to Charles Pearce, January 8, 1944, VNA).
108. Austin Clark of the Smithsonian Institution.
109. The text breaks off here, in mid-card.
110. The sentence breaks off here.
111. Continuation missing.
112. Cf. "Notes on the Morphology," p. 334.
113. Robert C. Williams was a lepidopterist at the Academy of Natural Science, Philadelphia.
114. Butterfly genitalia.
115. Cyril dos Passos (1887–1986), Research Associate of the American Museum of Natural History.
116. *Disa* is *Erebia disa* Thunberg, called the Arctic Ringlet in Europe and the Disa Alpine in North America.
117. D-Day, June 6, 1944.
118. That this request was apparently successful is indicated by the identifications of the plant and the ant that appear on pp. 436–37.
119. William Comstock had written to VN on December 20, 1943: "Referring to our discussion of

the varied definitions of a species you might read Chapter 10, 'Species as Natural Units,' in Dobzhansky's *Genetics and the Origin of Species*, 1937 Edition" (VNA). Unlike the two preceding
sets of notes, this is clearly marked up for oral delivery.

120. Russian for "Cross to article."

121. Cf. p. 559.

122. Franklin Chermock (1906–1967), an American butterfly collector active in Western butterfly
taxonomy.

123. For "II."

124. Don Stallings (1910–1987), a lawyer and lepidopterist from Caldwell, Kansas, specialist in the
Giant Skippers.

125. Sentence unfinished.

126. Line cut off.

127. Elena Sikorski (1906–   ), the younger of Nabokov's two sisters, who had just written him from
Prague after losing contact during the war.

128. Marked as received on "10/11/45"; the system seems to be day/month/year.

129. William Field (1914–1992), curator of entomology at the United States National Museum,
Smithsonian Institution, Washington, D.C.

130. See p. 277.

131. Psittacines are woodpeckers; "psittacoid" may refer to a unique beak-like process on the genitalia of the hairstreaks he speaks of.

132. Cf. VN's story "The Admirable Anglewing," pp. 538–44.

133. No such name occurs in any of VN's lepidopterological works.

134. Wilson had sent VN some drawings of Lepidoptera.

135. "Drunk drunkard."

136. "Full of wine."

137. *Actias luna* (L.), the American Luna Moth, has large pale green wings, long tails, and a leading
edge of heliotrope.

138. "Heavy with wine."

139. "Little devils" (Russian and French).

140. Véra Nabokov explained to Charles Timmer (September 27, 1949): the "bow tie is treated as a
butterfly and described in entomological terms, as a new species would have been described in
an entomological journal: the interneural macules, which would have been white in the typical
species, are of Isabella color (dirty white, approaching very, very pale flesh color) in this particular form or subspecies." *Pyrrharctia isabella*, the Isabella Tiger Moth, is the adult of the Woolly
Bear caterpillar.

141. "Stealthily" (French).

142. "My girl" (Latin).

143. The genus *Morpho* holds the large, brilliant blue butterflies of the American Tropics that have
traditionally been used for sky background in jewelry. Their wings, shimmering like Mylar, are
covered with structural scales that refract the light in a prismatic fashion, but go dull under
cloudy skies. See also VN's letter to Alfred Appel, April 3, 1967 (pp. 646–47).

144. These butterflies' common names are the Little Yellow, the Sleepy Orange, and the Cloudless
(Giant) Sulphur. The author of *P. s. eubule* is Linnaeus, not Poey as indicated by Nabokov.

145. Since 1944 a high-school volunteer at the MCZ who after school would carry out routine work
in the entomology lab. See also n. 147 and pp. 42–43.

146. Joseph Bequaert (1886–1982), curator of recent insects at the MCZ from 1945 to 1951.

147. Kenneth Christiansen, a student volunteer at the MCZ, who later married Phyllis Smith.

148. Charles Lee Remington (b. 1922). A Ph.D. student at the MCZ while Nabokov was there; in 1947 cofounded the Lepidopterists' Society with Harry Clench and was founding editor of the *Lepidopterists' News*. Population geneticist; Professor of Biology and Curator of Entomology at Yale University since 1949.

149. He had been looking for the very local Eastern U.S. subspecies *Lycaeides melissa samuelis*, which he had described in "The Nearctic Forms of *Lycaeides* Hübner (Lycaenidae, Lepidoptera)," pp. 278–88.

150. Cyril F. dos Passos and L. Paul Grey, "A Genitalic Survey of *Argynninae* (Lepidoptera, Nymphalidae)," *Amer. Mus. Novit.*, 1927 (1945), 1–17.

151. Nancy Flagg of *Vogue* magazine.

152. "The Nearctic Members of the Genus *Lycaeides* HÜBNER (Lycaenidae, Lepidoptera)."

153. Probably dos Passos and Grey, "Systematic Catalogue of *Speyeria* (Lepidoptera, Nymphalidae) with designations of types and fixations of type localities," *Amer. Mus. Novit.*, 1370 (1947), 1–30, which he responds to in detail on pp. 405–7.

154. Francis Hemming (1893–1964), distinguished British entomologist and taxonomist, Secretary to the International Commission on Zoological Nomenclature, was in his time the world authority on generic names in butterflies.

155. Lee Lerman of *Vogue*.

156. See *Vogue*, August 15, 1947.

157. Now known as *Hyles lineata* (Fabricius), the White-lined Sphinx.

158. See nn. 145 and 147.

159. VN's Wellesley College students.

160. See n. 153.

161. William T. M. Forbes, "The Genus *Phyciodes* (Lepidoptera, Nymphalinae)," *Entomologica Americana*, 24 (1945), 139–207.

162. This letter gives Nabokov's views and guesses on the relationships of several similar species-pairs of Crescent butterflies.

163. See n. 6 to BB, "Nabokov, Literature, Lepidoptera."

164. He had been seriously ill in the spring.

165. Taunting Humbert Humbert for his inability to trace him after he has absconded with Lolita, Clare Quilty signs his address in one hotel register "Quelquepart Island" (*Lolita* 251), "Somewhere Island." Quelpart Island is an old Western name for the island of Cheju do, South Korea.

166. For a more detailed description of Nabokov's collecting *L.m. annetta*, see pp. 315–16.

167. The Snout, so called because of its pronounced, forward-pointing palpi. It emigrates from the South, some years in enormous numbers, but rarely reaches New York.

168. Wilson had written on November 15: "I have never been able to understand how you manage, on the one hand, to study butterflies from the point of view of their habitat and, on the other, to pretend that it is possible to write about human beings and leave out of account all question of society and environment" (NWL 211).

169. Eugene Munroe of the Canadian Department of Agriculture, one of the leading authorities on pyralid moths and systematics.

170. [James] Don[ald] Eff (1914–1994), butterfly collector, Boulder, Colorado, and in the 1950s co-author of *Colorado Butterflies* with F. M. Brown and Bernard Rotger. "Frechin" in text is Don Frechin, an amateur lepidopterist then active in the Puget Sound region.

171. In Teton National Park, where they were headed. Klots replied: "I am told that it is just another damned touristed-out National Park. . . . I am perfectly certain that Mrs N. has nothing to fear from grizzlies nor, for that matter, from black bears, either. The only people hurt by bears in the

Parks are the stupid ones who feed them or tease them. If you are doing any collecting in swampy areas, however, and run across a moose (they are relatively common) give it a wide berth and let it have the trail. I would rather meet ten bears with cubs. . . . Again, reassurance for Mrs. Nabokov. Tourist traps are much more dangerous." (To VN, July 2, 1949, VNA)

172. B. C. S. Warren, a British lepidopterist who wrote the major revision of the genus *Erebia*, a group of Satyrs much liked by Nabokov.

173. Alexander B. Klots, "Some Notes on *Colias* and *Brenthis* (Lepidoptera, Pieridae and Nymphalidae)," *Journal of the New York Entomological Society*, 45 (1937), 311–33.

174. This refers to *Erora laeta* (W. H. Edwards), the Early Hairstreak, long considered a great rarity among eastern collectors. Nabokov is doubting old lore connecting the butterfly to beechwoods. It is now known to feed in the hardwood forest on the fruits of beaked hazel, birches, and American beech, after all.

175. George Davis was an editor at *Flair* magazine whom VN had met in July at a Utah writers' conference and who now asked him for one of his memoir essays (just appearing in the *New Yorker*) or something on butterflies.

176. "Released" (French).

177. He published this paper in 1950 as a very short "Postscript" to another short article (see p. 461–62).

178. John Downey (1926–) was then a student doing his master's thesis on butterflies at the University of Utah. He collected with VN in 1943 and 1949. See pp. 22–25, 49–52.

179. The clauses following "golden Slavic characters" appeared first in the 1967 revision.

180. The word "handsome," the end of the sentence after "poised on a log," and the last two sentences were added in 1967.

181. The second-to-last sentence and the "dee-del-dee-O!" were added in 1967.

182. The Basque word is, in fact, *misirikote*.

183. The caterpillar goes "Nibble, nibble, nibble" in *Conclusive Evidence* but becomes bolder still in *Speak, Memory*. VN here insists with particular force on the link between women and butterflies evident in the structure and the titles of *Speak, Memory* (originally to have been *Speak, Mnemosyne*) and its parodic echo in the novel *Look at the Harlequins!*

184. The *Conclusive Evidence* version ends the sentence, after "shepherd dogs," simply "I collected butterflies."

185. Patricia Hunt, of *Life* magazine's Nature Department, had written VN on January 21 asking for his asistance with a projected article about his butterfly collecting. It was never written.

186. A projected short story, of which Nabokov never wrote more than an outline (quoted in VNAY 189–90).

187. St. Mark's, the private school to which Dmitri had been sent in 1948, and which Nabokov satirized obliquely in Chapter 4 of *Pnin*.

188. A story published in 1945.

189. Edmund Wilson.

190. Samuel Hazzard Cross, a Slavist at Harvard, and Gordon Fairbanks, a linguist and Russian instructor at Cornell.

191. Lao Tzu.

192. Francis Brown, editor of the *New York Times Book Review*.

193. "After the twentieth of this month."

194. A pun on "Yellowstone" and "yeli stonut!" (Russian for "the firs are groaning").

195. *Lycaeides argyrognomon* (now *idas*) sublivens (see pp. 425–28 and 519).

196. This paragraph refers to four bright Copper butterflies: *Lycaena cupreus snowi* (W. H. Ed-

wards), the Lustrous Copper of the American West; *L. virgaureae* (L.), the Scarce Copper, and *L. dispar* (Haworth), the Large Copper, both European; and *L. phlaeus* (L.), known as the Small Copper in Europe, and the American Copper in North America. *L. phlaeus feildeni* (M'Lachlan) is a northwestern Canadian race of the latter. The specimens Nabokov had in hand are now known as *L.p. arctodon* Ferris, named for the Beartooth Mountains.

197. "I am doing my little Sirin." "Vladimir Sirin" was Nabokov's pen name as a Russian writer from 1921 until the 1950s.

198. C. W. Beebe, "Migration of Nymphalidae (Nymphalinae), *Brassolidae*, *Morphidae*, *Lybetheidae*, *Satyridae*, *Lycaenidae* and *Hesperiidae* (butterflies) through Portachuelo Pass, Rancho Grande, north-central Venezuela," *Zoologica*, 36:1 (1951), 1–16.

199. Nabokov added a footnote to the title when he reprinted this piece in *Strong Opinions*: "Now known as *Plebejus (Lycaeides) idas sublivens* or *Lycaeides sublivens* Nab.; it has been dubbed 'Nabokov's Blue' by F. Martin Brown (1955)." The common name did not catch on, however, and another butterfly is now known as "Nabokov's Blue"; see n. 206.

200. Klots later wrote to William McGuire of Princeton University Press (November 22, 1981): "The inaccuracies he pointed out in my Field Guide were just that and needed to be exposed."

201. Rosalind Wilson, the daughter of Edmund Wilson, was an editor at Houghton Mifflin.

202. Yuri Ivask, an émigré poet, critic, and professor of Russian.

203. Aleksandr Blok (1880–1921) and Osip Mandelstam (1891–1938), leading Russian poets of the early twentieth century.

204. Research for the commentary to his translation of Aleksandr Pushkin's verse novel, *Eugene Onegin*. The four-volume translation and commentary was published in 1964.

205. See previous two items.

206. Now *Lycaeides idas nabokovi* Masters 1972, "Nabokov's Blue."

207. Harry Levin, professor of English and comparative literature, Harvard, and a friend since Nabokov's arrival in the United States.

208. *Lolita.*

209. Alice James, wife of William ("Billy") James, the son of philosopher William James and nephew of Henry James. The Jameses had been warm friends of the Nabokovs since the early 1950s.

210. A noted teacher and lepidopterist, and father of Charles L. Remington.

211. Dieter Zimmer points out that "nymphet" owes much of its force to one lepidopterological sense of the word *nymph*. In classical Greek, the word means "maiden, bride"; it can also mean a minor natural divinity, a female demon or spirit such as a wood nymph or dryad, and in this sense is used as the popular name for various butterflies of the subfamily Satyrinae, such as "Nabokov's Wood Nymph" (Nabokov's 1941 Grand Canyon discovery, which he named *Neonympha dorothea*), although Nabokov did not learn of the name until after writing *Lolita* (see p. 521, letter to Jason Epstein, July 18, 1957). But *nymph* can also refer, as the OED notes, to any "insect in that stage of development which intervenes between the larva and the imago; a pupa." In French, *nymphe* is the regular word for "pupa" or "chrysalis," and in German entomology, *Nymphe* "designates the last pre-imaginal state . . . which already shows the outlines of the wings the adults will possess." Zimmer then comments: "With all of these meanings, if Lolita is a little nymph, she is a young individual on the very verge of turning into an adult, already showing the adult's wings, but not yet sexually mature." (Zimmer, "Nabokov's Lepidoptera," p. 121.)

212. See VN gloss, p. 648.

213. See VN gloss, p. 516.

214. See VN gloss, p. 648.

215. See vn gloss, p. 648.
216. See vn gloss, p. 648.
217. See vn gloss, p. 648.
218. Named after *Colias edusa* (now *Colias crocea*), the Clouded Yellow, a butterfly of north Africa, southern and central Europe, and west Asia.
219. *Elphinstonia* is a genus of pierid butterflies.
220. See vn gloss, p. 648.
221. Snow's Copper (*Lycaena cupreus snowi*) and the Greenish Black-tip (*Elphinstonia charlonia*), from the Rockies and the Atlas mountains, respectively, are both butterflies at home on high cliffs and rocks. See p. 73.
222. Nabokov explained to Alfred Appel: "The name is based on that of a close ally of the Clouded Yellow butterfly and has nothing to do with the Greek Electra" (Appel, *Annotated Lolita* 417). Zimmer adds: "Zsolt Bálint suggests that the ally is *Colias electo* Linnaeus, the Afrotropical sister species of *edusa*" (1998, 91).
223. See vn gloss, p. 649.
224. See vn gloss, p. 648. "Miller" is a common vernacular term for moths of the family Noctuidae, the owlets, because of the meal-like scales they shed copiously while battering around porchlights.
225. See vn gloss, p. 649. The Mulberry Moth, or common silkworm, has been domesticated so long that the adults are usually flightless.
226. "Inchkeith" is an obsolete term for *inchworm*, the caterpillar of a geometrid moth or looper.
227. Maurice Maeterlinck (1862–1949), Belgian dramatist; *Schmetterling*, "butterfly" (German).
228. The landscape described here is based on Telluride, where Nabokov caught the first known female of *Lycaeides argyrognomon* (now *idas*) *sublivens* Nabokov. See pp. 425–28, p. 518, and pp. 476–77.
229. Katharine White (1892–1977), fiction editor at the *New Yorker*.
230. Nabokov wrote to Edmund Wilson on February 18, 1957: "One exquisite point about PNIN is the little conversation between Pnin and Chateau about me and the blue butterflies at their feet. I actually described and named that particular Lycaenid (*Lycaeides samuelis* Nabokov, type locality Karner, near Albany, N.Y.)" (nwl 307). See pp. 287–88, 437–39, 462, and 681.
231. John Adams Comstock, Jr. (1883–1970), of San Diego, physician, amateur lepidopterist, author of *Butterflies of California* (1927). See p. 519.
232. *Plebulina emigdionis* F. Grinnell, the San Emigdio Blue, and *Icaricia neurona* (Skinner), the Veined Blue, are uncommon species restricted to Southern California. Nabokov had described and named both genera.
233. Jason Epstein of Doubleday.
234. On May 3, 1956, Epstein had written vn: "You may remember that last summer when I saw you in Ithaca I proposed that you might someday like to write a little book for the layman on butterflies. You gave me very good reasons for rejecting the proposal, but I want to prevail upon you again to think further about the idea."
235. Published in sl 186 without the last paragraph.
236. Nabokov was cotranslating (with Dmitri) and writing an introduction and notes for Mikhail Lermontov's novel *A Hero of Our Time* (Garden City, N.Y.: Doubleday, 1957).
237. Nabokov has mistakenly dated this letter "July 6."
238. See n. 89.
239. See pp. 425–28 and 511, and p. 477.
240. The *New Yorker* did not publish the note.

241. Inchworms are the larvae of moths of the family Geometridae, which includes the genus *Eupithecia* or the Pugs, a favorite group of Nabokov's. "Red-cheeked gall" refers to the round "oak-apples" or galls formed by oak leaves in response to eggs laid by certain wasps, whose larvae will feed within them. See also n. 226.

242. Mark Schorer, Department of English, University of California at Berkeley.

243. *Colorado Butterflies* by F. Martin Brown, Donald Eff, and Bernard Rotger, Denver Museum of Natural History, 1957.

244. James had copied out for VN, spelling mistakes intact, a letter he had written his brother in 1894, at age eleven, about hatching moths.

245. Saturnids, now usually called saturniids, are the family known as the Giant Silk Moths. See the end of the story "Christmas."

246. Schickel had written a piece on *Lolita*, "A Review of a Novel You Can't Buy" (*The Reporter*, November 28, 1957, 45–47).

247. In Levin's *The Power of Blackness* (New York: Knopf, 1958).

248. The hawk or sphinx moth *Acherontia atropos* (L.) bears a skull-like pattern on its thorax and is known as the Death's Head. It migrates from Africa into Europe, leaving five-inch, horned larvae that feed on potato leaves and many other plants. The large adult visits beehives for honey and adds to its alarming presence by making crackles and squeaks.

249. Such a diary was unusual for Nabokov; for 1958 he also had his customary small agenda book.

250. Parenthetical comments added by VN.

251. Walter Minton was the head of Putnam's, which was about to publish the long-awaited American edition of *Lolita*.

252. Orange-tips and Marblewings are the related pierid genera *Anthocharis* and *Euchloe*.

253. Sergey S. Nabokov (1902–1999): VN's cousin and a keen genealogist.

254. Pyke Johnson was an editor at Doubleday.

255. John G. Franclemont (b. 1912), lepidopterist and professor of Entomology at Cornell University with whom VN had searched in vain for *P. virginiensis* near Ithaca.

256. Gleb Struve (1898–1985), professor of Russian literature, University of California, Berkeley, and a friend since 1919.

257. George Hessen (1902–1971), Nabokov's closest friend since the 1920s.

258. Dmitri's translation of his father's novel, written in 1934 and published in 1935–36.

259. Hemming renamed the genus – which Nabokov had defined and named *Pseudothecla*, unaware it was invalid because used in 1910 for a genus of Hairstreaks – *Nabokovia*: "When in the course of my work on the families and genera of butterflies, I observed that the Plebejid genus *Pseudothecla* was without a valid name, I drew Dr. Nabokov's attention to the matter in accordance with the precepts of the Code of Ethics enjoined by the Ninth International Congress of Zoology, Monaco, 1913 and suggested that he should replace this name as soon as he conveniently could do so. In a reply (dated 14th July 1959), Dr. Nabokov invited me to provide this genus with a valid name, and I agreed to do so. I accordingly now establish the following genus LYCAENIDAE required: *Nabokovia* gen. nov. . . . I have much pleasure in naming this genus for Dr. V. Nabokov who has done so much to increase our knowledge of the Sub-Family PLEBE-JINAE." Francis Hemming, "Establishment of the genus 'Nabokovia' gen. nov. [LYCAENIDAE]," *Annotationes lepidopterologicae,* part 2 (London: Hepburn, 1960).

260. *Danaus plexippus* is the Monarch; in the story text the butterfly manicured to mimic another is *Basilarchia* (now *Limenitis*) *arthemis*, the White Admirable.

261. Cf. Minutes of the Cambridge Entomological Club for November 13, 1945, p. 386.

262. Samuil Rosov was Nabokov's closest friend at Tenishev School, St. Petersburg, 1910–17.

263. Laura Mazza was an editor at Mondadori, Nabokov's Italian publisher.

264. For an Italian volume of a selection of Nabokov's Russian and English poems, *Poesie*, trans. Alberto Pescetto and Enzo Siciliano (Milan: Il Saggiatore, 1962).

265. The poem "A Discovery": see pp. 273–74.

266. Robert Crane, chairman of the State of New Jersey Tercentenary Commission, had asked VN to recall a "New Jersey experience."

267. Captured for the AMNH, which Nabokov revisited for the last time on June 6, 1962, leaving this Chapman's Hairstreak (LS xii). Commenting on the cordial relations between Nabokov and lepidopterists at the AMNH, Alexander B. Klots recalled: "And he very kindly collected for us some species in the south of France that we needed at the Museum." (Letter to William McGuire, Princeton University Press, November 22, 1981)

268. This is the West Virginia White (*Pieris virginiensis* W. H. Edwards), whose larval hostplant is Toothwort (*Dentaria*). Lepidopterist Robert Dirig, who tried unsuccessfully to change the common name to Woodland White because its habitat is not confined to West Virginia, thinks Nabokov's (or Shade's) proposed name far superior, since its close ally the Cabbage White (*Pieris rapae*) is named after its occasional hostplant, the Mustard White (*Pieris napi*) after its usual hostplant, and the larva of this butterfly itself almost always feeds on Toothwort.

269. Although no butterfly is apparent here, Nabokov in this "nymph . . . in a wood" is referring extremely obliquely to the butterfly whose popular name was "Nabokov's Wood Nymph" (which in 1942 he named *Neonympha dorothea dorothea* and is now known as *Cyllopsis pertepida dorothea*). In a draft version of this line, according to Kinbote's Commentary, Shade had written not "A nymph came pirouetting" but "A nymphet pirouetted." Since Nabokov revived the word "nymphet" in *Lolita* and quite rightly felt that the word was in a special sense his own personal mark, this is enough in itself to show him signing "Nabokov's Wood Nymph" into the "nymph in a wood." But he reinforces the *Lolita* connection in another way. This passage in the poem is introduced with a rhyme in -ANE/-AINE (here, JANE/MAINE), a special kind of structural marker throughout "Pale Fire." The winds advancing "from Florida to Maine" just before the verse paragraph with the "nymph in the wood" recur later in another couplet with the same marker rhyme, and again with a wind sweeping "from Florida to Maine": "Hurricane/ Lolita swept from Florida to Maine" (ll. 679–80). (Shade is here characterizing 1958, the year *Lolita* swept to the top of the U.S. bestseller lists.) Since Nabokov never repeats phrases in this way without inviting us to interpret the connection, and since Shade here seems not to know Lolita except as the name of a hurricane, Nabokov is again winking at us behind Shade's back through the "hurriCANE Lolita"/"MAINE" rhyme, again asserting his special ownership over the earlier paragraph introduced by the "JANE"/"MAINE" rhyme, with its "nymphet" and "nymph in a wood." See also BB, *Nabokov's Pale Fire: The Magic of Artistic Discovery* (Princeton: Princeton Univ. Press, 1999, pp. 191–95, 238–42).

270. Several species of giant silk moths in the family Saturniidae (such as the Atlas Moth described in the story "Christmas," and the Cecropia and Emperor moths) possess drawn-out, crinkled, and orchidaceous forewing tips with eyespots. The great British naturalist Sir Peter Scott was among those who pointed out that these patterns resemble snakes' heads, and that this mimetic form may furnish protection from birds that spot them.

271. See p. 618.

272. Nitra is the name of a town in the Slovak Republic and Intra of a town on Lago Maggiore, Italy, but this pairing derives from the Nitra Swallowtail, *Papilio zelicaon nitra* (W. H. Edwards) (perhaps a species, *Papilio nitra*, rather than a subspecies), and the Indra Swallowtail (or Short-Tailed Black Swallowtail), *Papilio indra* Reakirt, two related black butterflies of the American West. For entomologist Jean-Henri Fabre, see n. 44.

273. The tunnel in fact will turn out to lead to the door of what had once been Iris Acht's dressing room. Throughout the note the reader faces a kind of riddle: where will the tunnel lead? The reader who is a lepidopterist has one more clue than others; *Apatura iris* is the conspicuously colored Purple Emperor butterfly, as if to mark where the garishly garbed Red King will emerge.

274. Not flowers but Fritillaries, these names refer to *Speyeria diana* (Cramer) and *S. atlantis* (W. H. Edwards).

275. See n. 268.

276. *The New Yorker* (after the dandy Eustace Tilley who, on one of the February covers each year, peers through his monocle at a butterfly, in honor of the magazine's first cover); Nabokov uses the name again in *Ada* and in *Look at the Harlequins!*

277. "Flying backwards" (French).

278. See Kinbote's Index entry on *Vanessa atalanta*, p. 560.

279. Although the writer François-René de Chateaubriand (1768–1848) did travel to America and write about his travels, this scene is invented.

280. See Kinbote's Index entry on *Vanessa atalanta*, p. 560.

281. *Erebia disa* Thunberg is a butterfly, the Arctic Ringlet, found in Europe in the northern parts of Finland, Sweden, and Norway, its habitat wet moorland and bogs; it is similar in appearance to *Erebia embla* Thunberg, the Lapland Ringlet, found in Europe in Finland and northern Sweden, whose main habitat is moorland.

282. Morris Bishop, Professor of Romance Languages at Cornell, and his wife, Alison, a painter, were the Nabokovs' closest friends at Cornell.

283. Peter de Peterson was the son of VN's paternal aunt, Natalia de Peterson.

284. To bombinate is to hum or boom; VN plays here on Bombycidae, the family of the silk moths.

285. *Ulex* is gorse, *Ilex* is holly.

286. George Weidenfeld was head of Nabokov's English publisher, Weidenfeld and Nicolson.

287. Nicholas Thompson of Weidenfeld and Nicolson.

288. In MS, "taken."

289. In MS "it."

290. Word missing from MS.

291. *Brenthis (Boloria) esperi* after the great lepidopterist Eugen Esper (1742–1810).

292. Pharr.

293. After this card comes another:
   "Hemming 1934
   'Linnaeus used *Papilio* for all the species of butterfly known to him (192 in all)'
   (how many of these occur in Europe? check)
   'All later fixations [after Latreille] fall to the ground.'"

294. The Apollo is now considered endangered over most of its range due to afforestation with conifer plantations and other habitat alterations.

295. "None of these criteria is absolute."

296. In his "List of European Rhopalocera," Nabokov notes below *Erebia*: "The subgeneric arrangement is provisional throughout the genus."

297. In this private listing, the first name after each Roman numeral is of the first species in a subgenus; the second is the subgenus name. In the usual order, the scientific name of the first entry would be *Erebia (Erebia) ligea,* where the bracketed name indicates the subgenus.

298. At this point without a name, though by December 1964 Nabokov had decided on *Tyndarus* for the subgenus (see p. 590).

299. Outside his lepidopterological work, Nabokov tended to call the city "St. Petersburg," especially when referring to his childhood.

300. In 1909.
301. This image, though not this butterfly, appears in *The Gift*: see p. 193.
302. In 1938.
303. In the 1960s.
304. Actually, the reintroduction of Dutch Large Coppers to Britain has taken hold at Woodwalton Fen National Nature Reserve, not Wicken Fen. Not really thriving, they are maintained through aggressive care and habitat management, and are said to resemble the extinct British race now more than the Dutch founder race, by some measures.
305. Both the species and its food plant occur in Nabokov's *Ada* (see pp. 659, 661, 666).
306. Nabokov gave the name "Avis Chapman" to an incidental character in *Lolita*: see p. 506 and p. 648.
307. Harry Grossman, photographer.
308. Graham Howarth, Curator of Butterflies at the British Museum (Natural History), and editor of a revised version of the classic *South's British Butterflies*.
309. *Feu Pâle*, trans. Raymond Girard and Maurice-Edgar Coindreau (Paris: Gallimard, 1965). See p. 553.
310. A well-respected American lepidopterist who specialized in lycaenids, systematics, and migration, all interests of Nabokov's, while residing in the suitably named Mariposa, California. *Mitoura spinetorum* (Hewitson) is the Thicket Hairstreak.
311. The most highly regarded American butterfly painter. Nabokov's modest advice to him in this letter was followed not by a monograph on anglewings, but by *The Butterflies of North America*, edited and illustrated by Howe, and "full of wonders" according to Nabokov.
312. For *P. indra kaibabensis*, see *Pale Fire* (above, pp. 553, 555, 558, 560). In *Ada* Nabokov names the "skybab squirrel" after the "Kaibab" Swallowtail (the Kaibab Plateau ends at the North Rim of the Grand Canyon).
313. William McGuire, of Bollingen Press and Princeton University Press.
314. Jean Bourgogne, of the Musée d'Histoire Naturelle, Paris.
315. James Page, of the Natural History Press.
316. He wished to include all his technical papers: all his Lepidoptera papers of the 1940s and "The Female of *Lycaides sublivens* Nabokov" (1952).
317. British lepidopterist in colonial service and the author of papers and books on the butterflies of Asia Minor.
318. After Mnemosyne, Greek goddess of memory and mother of the Muses, and the butterfly, *Parnassius mnemosyne*, the butterfly featured on his endpaper sketch.
319. In his research for his monumental annotated translation of Pushkin's *Eugene Onegin,* Nabokov came to the conclusion that Pushkin's duel with the minor poet Kondratiy Ryleev took place in the park of Batovo, Ryleev's estate, in mid-May 1820. In Nabokov's childhood, Batovo, just across the river from his parents' Vyra, belonged to his grandmother, Maria Nabokov.
320. The Brimstone is *Gonepteryx rhamni* (L.), a Sulphur unusual in that it hibernates as an adult, and is therefore one of the first harbingers of spring.
321. Cleopatra is *Gonepteryx cleopatra* (L.), a Mediterranean relative of the Brimstone that Nabokov knew in northern Europe.
322. In revising this paragraph from *Conclusive Evidence*, Nabokov added one element to the tabulation: the Queen of Spain, a Fritillary (*Issoria lathonia*).
323. Bud McLennan, of Weidenfeld and Nicolson.
324. Filippa Rolf, a Swedish writer who had visited the Nabokovs in 1961.

325. *Ada.*

326. These names belong to *Saturnia pyri* (L.), the Greater Emperor Moth, and *Quercusia quercus* (L.), the Purple Hairstreak.

327. Alfred Appel, Jr. (b. 1934), literary and cultural critic and professor at Stanford University, a student of Nabokov's at Cornell, would become editor of the *Annotated Lolita* (1970, 1991) and a friend.

328. Diana Butler, "Lolita Lepidoptera," in *New World Writing* (Philadelphia: Lippincott, 1960); repr. in *Critical Essays on Vladimir Nabokov,* ed. Phyllis A. Roth (Boston: G. K. Hall, 1984).

329. Dieter E. Zimmer (b. 1934), an essayist, editor of *Die Zeit,* and at this time already the translator of several Nabokov books, would become general editor of the 24-volume annotated Nabokov collected works in German (Rowohlt, 1989–). His experience as translator and editor of Nabokov led him to prepare "Nabokov's Lepidoptera: An Annotated Multilingual Checklist" (1993), which would expand into his invaluable *A Guide to Nabokov's Butterflies and Moths* (1996, 1998).

330. Page Stegner, son of noted American writer Wallace Stegner, had just sent Nabokov his book *Escape into Aesthetics: The Art of Vladimir Nabokov* (New York: Dial Press, 1966).

331. See p. 642 and n. 328.

332. Andrew Field (b. 1938) would write *Nabokov: His Life in Art* (1967), *Nabokov: A Bibliography* (1973), *Nabokov: His Life in Part* (1977), and *VN: The Life and Art of Vladimir Nabokov* (1986).

333. See p. 633. The incorrect Latin *passio et morbo aureliana* of the 1967 American edition was corrected by Nabokov for the English edition but misread by the printer to produce *et passio morbus aureliana* before being corrected to *morbus et passio aureliani* for the 1969 Penguin edition and finally corrected to *passio et morbus aureliani* in the 1989 Vintage edition.

334. Alfred Appel, Jr.

335. See above, p. 642 and n. 328.

336. Page references are to the first American edition (1958) and its many reprints. Appel's *Annotated Lolita* retained pagination in its first (1970) edition but not in its 1991 revision.

337. See pp. 646–47.

338. See above, n. 227.

339. Nabokov did not press home the point of his joke. See n. 225.

340. Archbishop Ioann (1902–89), émigré clergyman and writer, born Prince Dmitri Alekseevich Shakhovskoy, wrote under the name Strannik.

341. Ernst Mayr, an eminent biologist, at that time director of the Museum of Comparative Zoology, Harvard; author of the standard text *Systematics and the Origin of Species.*

342. Heather Mansell of Penguin Books, London.

343. While *Anthocharis ada* Krolik is a fiction, there actually is a butterfly named *A. prittwitzi* – not an *Anthocharis* named by Stümper, but *Adopaeoides prittwitzi* (Plötz), the Sunrise Skipper of Mexico and Southwest Texas. Prittwitz was a spectacularly unsuccessful German general at the beginning of World War I, replaced by Hindenburg only three weeks after hostilities commenced. German *Stümper* means "bungler, blunderer."

344. A butterfly tie (tied with the loop of the bow spread apart like the expanded wings of a butterfly); an echo of Alexander Pope, "Epistle to Dr. Arbuthnot" (1732), lines 307–308: "Satire or sense, alas! can Sporus feel? / Who breaks a butterfly upon a wheel?"

345. Abencerage: *Pseudophilotes* (previously *Philotes*) *abencerragus,* the False Baton Blue, a lycaenid of Southern Spain, Morocco and Tunisia. Zegris: *Zegris eupheme,* the Sooty Orange Tip, a pierid butterfly of eastern Spain and Morocco. Both are named after families of Moors, who,

after their expulsion from Granada, settled in Tunis and Morocco, respectively. Their feud inspired Chateaubriand's story *Le dernier Abencérage* (written 1809, published 1826).

346. Giant Skippers, family Megathymidae, burrow into the rootstocks of yuccas and agaves as larvae. The handsome black, white, and gold adults span two to three inches, have powerful bodies, and are thought to be able to fly at freeway speeds.

347. The nickname of the "broad" in the Norfolk sex club is a play not only on her sexual specialty but also on the name, location, and ecological niche of the butterfly *Papilio machaon*, the Swallowtail. Although present in Europe from North Africa to North Cape, it is "in England now confined to Norfolk, very local in fens [ancient cuttings known as the Norfolk Broads], formerly more widely distributed" (Higgins and Riley [1970], 35).

348. Van's half-sister Lucette studied art history.

349. Partly an allusion to Diana Butler's 1960 essay "Lolita Lepidoptera" (see above, p. 642, 643–44, 646), which argues that "in *Lolita* Nabokov has transposed his own passion for butterflies into his hero's passion for nymphets. At least on one level . . . little Dolores Haze is a butterfly" (Butler, in Roth, p. 60).

350. The villa's name honors the butterfly *Iolana iolas*, the iolas blue, which in Switzerland occurs only in the Valais; Nabokov caught it there for the first time in the Fôret des Finges, or Pfynwald, in July 1963.

351. Hugh Hefner, founder and publisher of *Playboy* magazine.

352. In his diary on July 6, 1967, Nabokov recorded the weather as "cloudy" then added this "ditty."

353. Michael Walter of Collins in London, which was about to publish Lionel Higgins and Norman Riley's *Field Guide to the Butterflies of Britain and Europe.*

354. Jaqueline Callier was Nabokov's secretary and Charles Monaghan the editor of *Book World*, where Nabokov's choice appeared December 7, 1969.

355. Oliver Caldecott was editor at Penguin Books, London.

356. Dmitri was performing in Colombia at the time.

357. Field had begun researching his *Nabokov: His Life in Part.*

358. "Not housetrained" (German).

359. Never completed.

360. This is not the Zebra Swallowtail of the United States (*Eurytides marcellus* (Cramer)), but the Scarce Swallowtail of Europe (*Iphiclides podalirius* (L.)), which is also zebra-striped.

361. Written on a picture postcard of *Nymphalis antiopa.*

362. Arye Levavi was the Israeli Ambassador to Switzerland.

363. Peter Haines was a keen Nabokov reader from Auckland, New Zealand.

364. Paul Anbinder, of publisher Harry N. Abrams.

365. Véra Nabokov wrote to J. B. Blandenier (August 18, 1978): "This is a 'monture' made of plaster of Paris for exposing a butterfly. It is very decorative but is scorned by scientists" (VNA).

366. A Parnassian, probably *Parnassius apollo.*

367. See n. 129. Field had revised the genus *Vanessa.*

368. Gordon Lish, *Esquire* editor.

369. Dan Lacy was an editor at McGraw-Hill. Lacy had suggested a butterfly book, personal, with vignettes or esthetic or literary digressions.

370. At that time a postgraduate student at Yale University with Charles Remington and executive director of the Xerces Society.

371. *Charaxes jasius* (L.), the Two-tailed Pasha, is the only European representative of a group of spectacular African nymphalids.

372. For excerpt from LS, see pp. 544–45.

373. A Santa Monica, California, lepidopterist and Hollywood production designer.
374. While designing the U.S. government exhibition on Franklin and Jefferson for the American Bicentennial in 1976, Ms. Oppewall came across two early American primitive portraits with butterflies in the background. Aware of Nabokov's interest in butterflies in art, she sent him copies. One of the prints depicts Rufus Hathaway's *Lady with Her Pets*, painted in Massachusetts in 1790 and now in the Metropolitan Museum of Art, New York. The two butterflies depicted appear to be roughly inspired by Satyrs. Since he was interested in the possibility that there might be some evolutionary changes detectable in artistic renditions over the centuries, Nabokov planned to go back to 1350 B.C. but he also wanted to keep his examples pre-Linnaean, to prevent any influence from anything like modern taxonomics.
375. Written by Michael Chinery (London: Collins, 1974).
376. "Harlequin" is a name often given to brightly patterned animals, such as three species of Caribbean butterfly (it was expected at the time Nabokov wrote this novel, and proven true a few years later, that a fourth harlequin would be discovered).
377. *Pandoriana pandora* (Schiffermueller) is a large, bright Fritillary known as the Cardinal. The character Iris shares her name with *Apatura iris* (L.), the Purple Emperor.
378. Kanner holds a Mountain Small White, *Pieris ergane* Geyer, a close relative of the Cabbage White restricted in France to the Southeast and the Pyrenees.
379. "Mata Hari" is an ara, a brightly colored macaw brought to mind by the Morphos.
380. It is *Aglais urticae* (L.) the Small Tortoiseshell, widespread throughout Europe.
381. Bellargus derives from *Lysandra bellargus* (L.), the Adonis Blue of Europe, which many feel is the loveliest and bluest of all the Blues. Morphos are brilliant neotropical butterflies of shimmering metallic blue.
382. Nabokov had previously turned down Kollek's invitation, as mayor of Jerusalem, to the visiting artists' apartments in the restored Mishkenot Sha'ananim ("Peaceful Dwellings").
383. Robert Dirig of the Karner Blue Project, Xerces Society, Cornell University, currently of the Bailey Hortorium Herbarium at Cornell.
384. Instead of "fleurs des champs."
385. This rare moth is the long-tailed, pale green Spanish Moon Moth (*Graellsia isabellae*), which feeds on pine as a larva yet is endangered by habitat change throughout its limited Iberian realm.
386. Irving Lazar, Nabokov's agent in Hollywood, was by now a good friend.
387. Glenn Collins of the *New York Times Magazine*.
388. The "ultimate interview," VN interviewing VN for the *New York Times Magazine*.
389. Hugh Honour, *The New Golden Land* (New York: Pantheon, 1975).
390. Victor Lusinchi of the *New York Times Book Review*.
391. E. W. Classey Ltd., located near Oxford, is the major supplier of entomological literature.
392. On July 2, 1977.

Bibliography

BRIAN BOYD

I. PRIMARY MATERIAL

Nabokov Publications

ALL CITATIONS ARE, WHEREVER POSSIBLE, FROM THE CORRECTED VINTAGE TEXTS.

Ada or Ardor: A Family Chronicle. New York: McGraw-Hill, 1969. Repr. New York: Vintage, 1990.

"Audubon's *Butterflies, Moths and Other Studies.*" Repr. SO as "A World of Butterflies."

"Authors' Authors." *New York Times Book Review,* December 5, 1976.

Bend Sinister. New York: Henry Holt, 1947. Repr. with VN introduction, New York: Time, 1964; New York: Vintage, 1990.

"Butterfly Collecting in Wyoming 1952." *Lepidopterists' News* 7 (1953): 49–52. Repr. SO.

Conclusive Evidence. New York: Harper and Bros., 1951. See also *Speak, Memory.*

The Defense. 1929–30. Trans. Michael Scammell with VN. New York: Putnam, 1964. Repr. New York: Vintage, 1990.

Despair. 1934. Trans. VN. New York: Putnam, 1966. Repr. New York: Vintage, 1989.

Details of a Sunset and Other Stories. Trans. DN with VN. New York: McGraw-Hill, 1976.

Drugie berega. New York: Chekhov Publishing House, 1954. See also *Speak, Memory.*

The Enchanter. 1939. Trans. DN. New York: Putnam, 1986. Repr. New York: Vintage, 1991.

Eugene Onegin. Trans. with commentary by VN. 4 vols. New York: Bollingen, 1964. Rev. ed. Princeton: Princeton University Press, 1975.

The Eye. 1930. Trans. DN with VN. New York: Phaedra, 1965. Repr. New York: Vintage, 1990.

"The Female of *Lycaeides argyrognomon sublivens.*" *Lepidopterists' News* 6 (1952): 35. Repr. SO.

"A Few Notes on Crimean Lepidoptera." *Entomologist* 53 (February 1920): 29–33.

The Gift. 1937–38, 1952. Trans. Michael Scammell and DN with VN. New York: Putnam, 1963. Repr. New York: Vintage, 1991.

Glory. 1931. Trans. DN with VN. New York: McGraw-Hill, 1971. Repr. New York: Vintage, 1991.

Gorniy put'. Berlin: Grani, 1923.

Grozd'. Berlin: Gamayun, 1922.

Invitation to a Beheading. 1935–36. Trans. DN with VN. New York: Putnam, 1959. Repr. New York: Vintage, 1989.

King, Queen, Knave. 1928. Trans. DN with VN. New York: McGraw-Hill, 1968. Repr. New York: Vintage, 1989.

Laughter in the Dark. 1932–33. Trans. and rev. VN. Indianapolis: Bobbs-Merrill, 1938.

Lectures on Literature. Ed. Fredson Bowers. New York: Harcourt Brace Jovanovich/Bruccoli Clark, 1980.

Lepidopterological Papers 1941–1953. Nabokov's privately bound collection of his Lepidoptera papers, with his MS corrections, given to Véra Nabokov, August 31, 1964.

Lolita. Paris: Olympia, 1955. Repr. New York: Putnam, 1958; corr. ed., New York: Vintage, 1989.

Lolita: A Screenplay. New York: McGraw-Hill, 1974.

Look at the Harlequins! New York: McGraw-Hill, 1974. Repr. New York: Vintage, 1990.

"*Lycaeides argyrognomon* in Wisconsin." *Lepidopterists' News* 7 (1953): 54.

"*Lysandra cormion,* A New European Butterfly." *Journal of the New York Entomological Society* 49 (September 1941): 265–67.

Mary. 1926. Trans. Michael Glenny with VN. New York: McGraw-Hill, 1970. Repr. New York: Vintage, 1989.

"Migratory Species Observed in Wyoming, 1952." *Lepidopterists' News* 7 (1953): 51–52. Repr. SO.

(With Edmund Wilson.) *Nabokov-Wilson Letters.* Ed. Simon Karlinsky. New York: Harper and Row, 1979. Rev. ed. *Briefwechsel mit Edmund Wilson 1940–1971.* Ed. Simon Karlinsky and Dieter E. Zimmer. Trans. Eike Schönfeld. Reinbek bei Hamburg: Rowohlt, 1995.

Nabokov's Dozen. New York: Doubleday, 1958.

"The Nearctic Forms of *Lycaeides* Hüb[ner]. (Lycaenidae, Lepidoptera)." *Psyche* 50 (September–December 1943): 87–99.

"The Nearctic Members of the Genus *Lycaeides* Hübner." *Bulletin of the Museum of Comparative Zoology* 101 (1949): 479–541.

"A New Species of *Cyclargus* Nabokov (Lycaenidae, Lepidoptera)." *The Entomologist* 81 (December 1948): 273–80.

Nikolay Gogol. Norfolk, Conn.: New Directions, 1944.

"Notes on Neotropical Plebejinae (Lycaenidae, Lepidoptera)." *Psyche* 52 (March–June 1945): 1–61.

"Notes on the Lepidoptera of the Pyrénées Orientales and the Ariège." *The Entomologist* 64 (1931): 255.

"Notes on the Morphology of the Genus *Lycaeides.*" *Psyche* 51 (September–December 1944): 104–38.

"Notes to *Ada* by Vivian Darkbloom." In *Ada,* Harmondsworth: Penguin, 1970, and New York: Vintage, 1990.

"On a Book Entitled *Lolita.*" *Anchor Review* 2 (June 1957). Repr. in *Lolita,* New York: Putnam, 1958.

"On Some Inaccuracies in Klots' *Field Guide.*" *Lepidopterists' News* 6 (1952): 41. Repr. SO.

"Painted Wood." *Karussel* 2 (1923): 9–10.

Pale Fire. New York: Putnam, 1962. Repr. New York: Vintage, 1989.

Perepiska s sestroy. Ann Arbor: Ardis, 1985.

Pnin. Garden City, N.Y.: Doubleday, 1957: Repr. New York: Vintage, 1989.

Poems and Problems. New York: McGraw-Hill, 1971.

"Postscript." *Lepidopterists' News* 4 (1950): 76.

The Real Life of Sebastian Knight. Norfolk, Conn.: New Directions, 1941. Repr. New York: Vintage, 1992.

"Rebel's Blue, Bryony White." *Times Educational Supplement,* October 23, 1970, 19. Repr. as "L. C. Higgins and N. D. Riley, *Field Guide to the Butterflies of Britain and Europe*" in SO.

"Remarks on F. Martin Brown's 'Measurements and Lepidoptera.'" *Lepidopterists' News* 4 (1950): 75–76.

"Reputations Revisited." *Times Literary Supplement,* January 21, 1977, 66.

A Russian Beauty and Other Stories. Trans. DN and Simon Karlinsky with VN. New York: McGraw-Hill, 1973.

Selected Letters 1940–1977. Ed. DN and Matthew J. Bruccoli. New York: Harcourt Brace Jovanovich / Bruccoli Clark Layman, 1989.

"Some New or Little-Known Nearctic *Neonympha*." *Psyche* 49 (September–December 1942): 61–80.

Speak, Memory: An Autobiography Revisited. New York: Putnam, 1966. Repr. New York: Vintage, 1989.

Speak, Memory: An Autobiography Revisited. With new appendix ("Chapter 16"), and introduction by BB. London: Everyman and New York: Knopf, 1999.

"Sphingids Over Water." *Lepidopterists' News* 1 (1947): 82.

Stikhi. Ann Arbor: Ardis, 1979.

The Stories of Vladimir Nabokov. New York: Knopf, 1995.

Strong Opinions. New York: McGraw-Hill, 1973.

Transparent Things. New York: McGraw-Hill, 1972. Repr. New York: Vintage, 1989.

Tyrants Destroyed and Other Stories. Trans. DN with VN. New York: McGraw-Hill, 1975.

The Waltz Invention. Trans. DN with VN. New York: Phaedra, 1966.

"A World of Butterflies." *New York Times Book Review*, December 28, 1952. Repr. as "Audubon's Butterflies, Moths and Other Studies, Compiled and Edited by Alice Ford" in SO.

"Yesterday's Caterpillar." *New York Times Book Review*, June 3, 1951.

Interviews (see also Strong Opinions*)*

Boyle, Robert H. "An Absence of Wood Nymphs." *Sports Illustrated*, September 14, 1959, E5–E8. Repr. in Robert H. Boyle, *At the Top of Their Game*.

Bronowski, Jacob, August 1963. Not filmed. TS, VNA.

Chudacoff, Helga. "Schmetterling sind wie Menchsen." *Die Welt*, September 26, 1974. TS, VNA.

Clarke, Gerald. "Checking in with Vladimir Nabokov." *Esquire*, July 1975, 67–69, 131, 133.

Colombo, Janine. "Si Nabokov vient en Israël ce sera à cause des papillons de Jérusalem." *L'Information d'Israel*, February 3, 1961.

Dommergues, Pierre. "Entretien avec Vladimir Nabokov." *Les Langues modernes*, 62 (January–February 1968): 92–102.

Feifer, George. "Vladimir Nabokov: An Interview." *Saturday Review*, November 27, 1976, 20–26.

Guérin, Anne. "Entretien: Vladimir Nabokov." *L'Express*, January 26, 1961.

Howard, Jane. "Vladimir Nabokov: Lolita, Languages, Lepidoptera. The Master of Versatility." *Life*, November 20, 1964.

Hughes, Robert. National Educational Television, January 1966. TS, VNA.

Laansoo, Mati, Canadian Broadcasting Corporation, 1973. Published in *Vladimir Nabokov Research Newsletter* 10 (1983).

Levy, Alan. "Understanding Vladimir Nabokov – A Red Autumn Leaf Is a Red Autumn Leaf, Not a Deflowered Nymphet." *New York Times Magazine*, October 31, 1971, 20–22, 24, 28, 30, 32, 36, 38, 40–41; and TS, VNA.

Meras, Phyllis. "V. Nabokov Unresting." *Providence Sunday Journal*, May 13, 1962.

Mercadie, Claude. "Sur la Promenade des Anglais Vladimir Nabokov le père de 'Lolita' à planté sa tente de nomade." *Nice-Matin*, April 13, 1961.

O'Neil, Paul. "*Lolita* and the Lepidopterist: Author Nabokov is Awed by Sensation He Created." *Life International*, April 13, 1959, 63–69.

Pivot, Bernard. French television, "Apostrophes," TF-1. May 30, 1975. TS, VNA.

Reese, Katharine. "Alias V. Sirin." *We* (Wellesley College), December 1943, 32.

Robinson, Robert. "A Blush of Colour – Nabokov in Montreux." *The Listener*, March 24, 1977.

Repr. in *Vladimir Nabokov: A Tribute*, ed. Peter Quennell. London: Weidenfeld and Nicolson, 1979, 119–25.

Safarik, Bernard. Swiss German television, 1974. MS, VNA.

Strannik [Archbishop Ioann Shakhovskoy]. "Nachalo Nabokoviani." *Russkaya mysl'*. June 1, 1978.

Tabozzi, Roberto. *Panorama*. Conducted October 16, 1969. TS, VNA.

Zimmer, Dieter E. "Despot in meiner Welt: Ein Gespräch mit Vladimir Nabokov." *Die Zeit*, November 1, 1966. TS, VNA.

Archival Collections

American Museum of Natural History
    Cyril F. dos Passos Papers
    Nabokov butterfly catches, 1938–1961
Columbia University, Butler Library
    Bakhmeteff Collection
        Mark Aldanov Papers
        Mstislav Dobuzhinsky Papers
Cornell University
    William Forbes Papers
    Nabokov butterfly catches, 1949–1958
Harvard University, Museum of Comparative Zoology
    Minutes of the Cambridge Entomological Society
    Nabokov butterfly catches, 1941–1959
Library of Congress
    Vladimir Nabokov Papers
Musée Cantonal de Zoologie, Lausanne
    Nabokov butterfly catches, 1961–1975
New York Public Library, Henry W. and Albert A. Berg Collection
    Vladimir Nabokov Archives (some materials still held by DN)
University of Texas, Austin, Harry Ransom Humanities Research Center
    Edward Weeks Papers
Yale University, Beinecke Library
    Edmund Wilson Papers

II. SECONDARY MATERIAL

Appel, Alfred, Jr., ed. 1970; rev. ed. 1991. *The Annotated Lolita*. New York: McGraw-Hill.

———. 1979. "Remembering Nabokov." In *Vladimir Nabokov: A Tribute*, ed. Peter Quennell. London: Weidenfeld and Nicolson, 11–33.

Bálint, Zsolt. 1993. "A Catalogue of Polyommatine Lycaenidae (Lepidoptera) of the Xeromontane Oreal Biome in the Neotropics As Represented in European Collections," *Reports of the Museum of Natural History, University of Wisconsin*, No. 29, 1–42.

———. 1995. "A Review of Recent Literature and Taxonomic Synonymy in the Neotropical Polyommatinae (Lycaenidae)." *Reports of the Museum of Natural History, University of Wisconsin (Stevens Point)*, No. 49.

——. 1996. "Oh High Andes – You Were My Ardis Park." *News of the Lepidopterists' Society* 38: 27–29.

Bálint, Zsolt, and Kurt Johnson. 1993. "A New Genus of Thecline-like Polyommatinae from the Andean Region of South America (Lepidoptera: Lycaenidae, Polyommatinae." *Reports of the Museum of Natural History, University of Wisconsin*, No. 28.

——. 1993. "New Species of *Pseudolucia* Nabokov from Chile and Patagonia (Lepidoptera: Lycaenidae, Polyommatinae)." *Reports of the Museum of Natural History, University of Wisconsin*, No. 32.

——. 1994. "Polyommatine Lycaenids of the Oreal Biome in the Neotropics, Part 1: The Thecline-like Taxa (Lepidoptera: Lycaenidae)." *Acta Zoologica Academiae Scientiarum Hungariae* 40: 109–23.

——. 1994. "Polyommatine lycaenids of the oreal biome in the Neotropics, part II: The *Itylos* section (Lepidoptera: Lycaenidae, Polyommatinae)." *Annales Historico-Naturales Musei Nationalis Hungarici* 86: 53–77.

——. 1995. "Neotropical polyommatine diversity and affinities. I. Relationships of the higher taxa (Lepidoptera: Lycaenidae). *Annales Historico-Naturales Musei Nationalis Hungarici* 87: 103–22.

——. 1995. "Description of a New *Madeleinea* (Lepidoptera, Lycaenidae) Species from Ecuador." *Acta Zoologica Academia Scientiarum Hungaricae* 41: 25–34.

——. 1995. "Polyommatine lycaenids of the oreal biome in the Neotropics, part V: Synopsis of the High Andean and Austral Polyommatine Genus *Madeleinea* Bálint 1993 (Lepidoptera, Lycaenidae)." *Reports of the Museum of Natural History, University of Wisconsin (Stevens Point)*, No. 43.

——. 1995. "Polyommatine Lycaenids of the Oreal Biome in the Neotropics, Part 6: Species Diagnostics of the Genus *Leptotes* in Continental South America (Lepidoptera, Lycaenidae)." *Reports of the Museum of Natural History, University of Wisconsin (Stevens Point)*, No. 44.

——. 1995. "Neotropical polyommatine diversity and affinities. I. Relationships of the higher taxa [Lepidoptera, Lycaenidae, Polyommatini]." *Acta Zoologica Academiae Scientiarum Hungaricae* 41: 211–35.

——. 1995. "Polyommatine Lycaenids of the Oreal Biome in the Neotropics, Part 7: The Argentine Fauna of *Pseudolucia* Nabokov (Lepidoptera, Lycaenidae)." *Reports of the Museum of Natural History, University of Wisconsin (Stevens Point)*, No. 45.

——. 1995. "Polyommatine Lycaenids of the Oreal Biome in the Neotropics, Part 8: A New Species of *Pseudolucia* Nabokov from the Coastal Region of Chile (Lepidoptera, Lycaenidae)." *Reports of the Museum of Natural History, University of Wisconsin (Stevens Point)*, No. 46.

——. 1995. "Taxonomic Synopsis of the High Andean and Austral Lycaenid Genus *Paralycaeides* Nabokov, 1945 (Lepidoptera: Lycaenidae, Polyommatini)" ("Polyommatine lycaenids of the oreal biome in the Neotropics, part IX"). *Annales Historico-Naturales Musei Nationales Hungarici* 87: 103–22.

——. 1995. "Additional Historical Data for Neotropical Polyommatinae Lycaenid Butterflies in European Collections (Lepidoptera)." *Reports of the Museum of Natural History, University of Wisconsin (Stevens Point)*, No. 50.

——. 1997. "Reformation of the Polyommatus Section (Lycaenidae, Polyommatini) with a Taxonomic and Biogeographic Overview." *Neue entomologische Nachrichten* 40: 1–40.

Bálint, Zsolt, Kurt Johnson, et al. 1995. *A Special Compilation: Neotropical "Blue" Butterflies. Reports of the Museum of Natural History, University of Wisconsin (Stevens Point)*, Nos. 43–54.

Bálint, Zsolt, and G. Lamas. 1994. "Polyommatine Lycaenids of the Oreal Biome in the Neotropics, Part 3: Descriptions of Three New Species (Lepidoptera, Lycaenidae)." *Acta Zoologica Academiae Scientiarum Hungaricae* 40: 231–40.

———. 1996. "On the taxonomy of the Neotropical Polyommatine Lycaenids (Lepidoptera: Lycaenidae, Polyommatini)" ("Polyommatine lycaenids of the oreal biome in the Neotropics, part XI"). *Annales Historico-Naturales Musei Nationalis Hungarici* 88: 127–44.

Baum, David A., and Michael J. Donoghue. 1995. "Choosing among Alternative 'Phylogenetic' Species Concepts." *Systematic Botany* 20: 561–73.

Bell, Ernest L., and William P. Comstock. 1948. "A New Genus and Some New Species and Subspecies of American Hesperiidae (Lepidoptera, Rhopalocera)." *American Museum Novitates* 1379 (June 28): 19–23.

Benyamini, Dubi, Zsolt Bálint, and Kurt Johnson. 1995. "Additions to the Diversity of the Polyommatine Genus *Madeleinea* Bálint (Lepidoptera, Lycaenidae)." *Reports of the Museum of Natural History, University of Wisconsin (Stevens Point)*, No. 47.

———. 1995. "Two New *Pseudolucia* Species from the High Andean Region of Temperate South America." *Reports of the Museum of Natural History, University of Wisconsin (Stevens Point)*, No. 48.

———. 1995. "Recently discovered New Species of *Pseudolucia* Nabokov (Lepidoptera, Lycaenidae) from Austral South America." *Reports of the Museum of Natural History (Stevens Point)*, No. 53.

Boyd, Brian. 1990. *Vladimir Nabokov: The Russian Years*. Princeton: Princeton University Press.

———. 1991. *Vladimir Nabokov: The American Years*. Princeton: Princeton University Press.

———. 1995. "Nabokov's Lepidoptera: A Review-Article on Dieter E. Zimmer's 'Nabokov's Lepidoptera.'" *Nabokov Studies* 2: 290–99.

———. 1999. *Nabokov's Pale Fire: The Magic of Artistic Discovery*. Princeton: Princeton University Press.

Boyd, Brian, and Kurt Johnson. 1999. "Nabokov, Scientist." *Natural History* (July–August): 46–53.

Boyle, Robert H. 1983. "An Absence of Wood Nymphs." In *At the Top of Their Game*. New York: Nick Lyons Books/Winchester Press, 123–33.

Brown, F. Martin. 1950. "Measurements and Lepidoptera." *Lepidopterists' News* 4: 51.

Brown, F. Martin, Donald Eff, and Bernard Rotger. 1957. *Colorado Butterflies*. Denver: Denver Museum of Natural History.

Brown, William L. 1984. In "Remembering Nabokov," in Gibian and Parker, eds., *Achievements*, 224–26.

Butler, Diana. 1960. "Lolita Lepidoptera." In *New World Writing* 16: 58–84. Repr. in *Critical Essays on Vladimir Nabokov* ed. Phyllis A. Roth. Boston: G. K. Hall, 1984, 59–73.

Coates, Steve. 1997. "Nabokov's Work, on Butterflies, Stands the Test of Time." *New York Times*, May 27, C4.

Cracraft, Joel. 1983. "Species Concepts and Speciation Analysis." *Current Ornithology* 1: 159–87.

Dirig, Robert. 1994. "Historical Notes on Wild Lupine and the Karner Blue Butterfly at the Albany Pine Bush, New York." In *Karner Blue Butterfly: A Symbol of a Vanishing Landscape*, ed. D. A. Andow, R. J. Baker, and C. P. Lane. St. Paul: University of Minnesota Misc. Publ. 84-1994, 23–36.

———. 1999. "Nabokov's Rainbow." *American Butterflies* 7:3 (Fall): 4–10.

dos Passos, Cyril F. 1964. *A Synonymic List of the Nearctic Rhopalocera*. New Haven: The Lepidopterists' Society Memoir No. 1.

Downey, John C. "Plebejinae," with William H. Howe and Robert L. Langston. In Howe, ed., 1975, 337–50.

Dujardin, Francis. 1969. "Qu'est-ce que *Lysandra cormion* Nabokov?" *Entomops* [Nice] 2: 241–44.

Field, Andrew. 1977. *Nabokov: His Life in Part*. New York: Viking.

Franclemont, John G. 1984. In "Remembering Nabokov," in Gibian and Parker, eds., *Achievements*, 227–28.

Funke, Sarah, and Glenn Horowitz, eds. 1999. *Véra's Butterflies*. New York: Glenn Horowitz Bookseller.

Gibian, George, and Stephen Jan Parker, eds. 1984. *The Achievements of Vladimir Nabokov*. Ithaca: Cornell Center for International Studies.

Gould, Stephen Jay. 1999. "No Science without Fancy, No Art without Facts: The Lepidoptery of Vladimir Nabokov." In Funke and Horowitz, eds., *Véra's Butterflies*, 84–114.

Hemming, Francis. 1960. "Establishment of the Genus 'Nabokovia' gen. nov. [LYCAENIDAE]," *Annotationes lepidopterologicae*, Part 2. London: Hepburn, November 25.

———. 1967. *The Generic Names of the Butterflies and Their Type-Species (Lepidoptera: Rhopalocera)*. London: Bulletin of the British Museum (Natural History): Entomology, Supplement 9.

Higgins, Lionel G., and Norman D. Riley. 1970. *A Field Guide to the Butterflies of Britain and Europe*. 5th. rev. ed. London: Collins, 1983.

Hodges, Ronald W., et al., eds. 1983. *Check List of the Lepidoptera of America North of Mexico*. London: E. W. Classey.

Hofmann, Ernst. 1887. *Die Gross-Schmetterlinge Europas*. Stuttgart; rev. 1894.

Howe, William H., ed. 1975. *The Butterflies of North America*. Garden City, N.Y.: Doubleday.

Johnson, D. Barton. 1998. "The Butterfly in Nabokov's *Eye*." *Nabokov Studies* 4: 1–14.

Johnson, Kurt, and Zsolt Bálint. 1995. "Distinction of *Pseudochrysops, Cyclargus, Echinargus* and *Hemiargus* in the Neotropical Polyommatini (Lycaenidae)," *Reports of the Museum of Natural History, University of Wisconsin (Stevens Point)*, No. 54.

Johnson, Kurt, and Brian Boyd. 1999. "Naturally Playful – An Introduction." In Funke and Horowitz, eds., *Véra's Butterflies*, 13–20.

Johnson, Kurt, and Steve Coates. *Nabokov's Blues*. Cambridge, Mass.: Zoland, 1999.

Johnson, Kurt, and David Matusik. 1988. "Five new species and one new subspecies of Butterflies from the Sierra de Baorucco of Hispaniola," *Annals of the Carnegie Museum* 57: 221–54.

———. 1992. "Additions to the Hispaniolan Fauna." *Reports of the Museum of Natural History, University of Wisconsin (Stevens Point)*, No. 23: 3–5, ill.

Johnson, Kurt, Zsolt Bálint, and G. Warren Whitaker. 1996. "Nabokov as Lepidopterist: An Informed Appraisal." *Nabokov Studies* 3: 123–44.

Jór, John Mylius. 1977. "Dødsfald i international lepidopterologi: Vladimir Nabokov, Forfatter og sommerfugleforsker, 1899–1977." *Lepidopterologiske Meddelelser fra Instituttet i Adal* 6 (October).

Juliar, Michael. 1986. *Vladimir Nabokov: A Descriptive Bibliography*. New York: Garland.

Karges, Joann. 1985. *Nabokov's Lepidoptera: Genres and Genera*. Ann Arbor: Ardis.

Klots, Alexander B. 1951. *A Field Guide to the Butterflies of North America, East of the Great Plains*. Boston: Houghton Mifflin.

Kuznetsov, Nikolay. 1915. *Fauna Rossii: Nasekomye cheshuekrylye*. Petrograd.

Levy, Alan. 1984. *Vladimir Nabokov: The Velvet Butterfly*. Sag Harbor, N.Y.: Permanent Press.

Luquet, Gérard-Christian. 1995. "Les Publications scientifiques de Vladimir Nabokov." *Europe* 791 (March): 144–51.

Masters, John M. 1972. "A New Subspecies of *Lycaeides argyrognomon* (Lycaenidae)." *Journal of the Lepidopterists' Society* 26: 150–54.

Mayr, Ernst. 1942. *Systematics and the Origin of Species*. New York: Columbia University Press.

McDunnough, James H. 1945. "New North American Eupithecias [Lepidoptera, Geometridae]." *Canadian Entomologist* 77: 168–76.

Miller, Jacqueline Y., ed. 1992. *The Common Names of North America Butterflies.* Washington, D.C., and London: Smithsonian Institution Press.

Miller, Lee D. 1974. "Revision of Euptychiini [Satyridae]. 2. *Cyllopsis* R. Felder." *Bulletin of the Allyn Museum* 20: 1–98.

Miller, Lee D., and F. Martin Brown. 1981. *A Catalogue/Checklist of the Butterflies of America North of Mexico.* New Haven: The Lepidopterists' Society, Memoir No. 2.

NABA. 1996. *Checklist and English Names of North American Butterflies.* Morristown, N.J.: North American Butterfly Association.

Nabokov, Dmitri. 1977. "On Revisiting Father's Room." Rev., in *Vladimir Nabokov: A Tribute*, ed. Peter Quennell. London: Weidenfeld and Nicolson, 1979, 126–36.

———. 1984. "Translating with Nabokov." In Gibian and Parker, eds., *Achievements*, 145–77.

Nabokov, Vladimir Dmitrievich. 1964. "Pis'ma V. D. Nabokova iz Krestov k zhene. 1908g." *Vozdushnye puti* 4: 265–75.

Opler, Paul, and George O. Krizek. 1984. *Butterflies East of the Great Plains.* Baltimore: Johns Hopkins University Press.

Packer, Laurence, John S. Taylor, Dolores A. Savignano, Catherine A. Bleser, Cynthia P. Lane, and Laura A. Somers. 1998. "Population biology of an endangered butterfly, *Lycaeides melissa samuelis* (Lepidoptera; Lycaenidae): Genetic variation, gene flow, and taxonomic status." *Canadian Journal of Zoology* 76: 320–29.

Pyle, Robert Michael. 1981. *The Audubon Society Field Guide to North American Butterflies.* New York: Knopf.

Raevsky, Nikolay. 1989. "Vospominaniya o Vladimire Nabokove." *Prostor* 2 (February): 112–17.

Remington, Charles. 1995. "Lepidoptera Studies." In *The Garland Companion to Vladimir Nabokov*, ed. Vladimir E. Alexandrov. New York: Garland, 274–83.

Riley, Norman D. 1975. *A Field Guide to the Butterflies of the West Indies.* London: Collins.

Rindge, Frederick H., and William Comstock. 1953. "An Unnamed Lycaenid from Trinidad (Lepidoptera)." *Journal of the New York Entomological Society* 61: 99–100.

Sartori, Michael, ed. 1993. *Les Papillons de Nabokov.* Lausanne: Musée cantonal de Zoologie.

Schurian, Klaus G. 1989. "Bermerkungen zu '*Lysandra cormion*' Nabokov 1941 (Lepidoptera: Lycaenidae)." *Nachrichten des entomologischen Vereins Apollo* [Frankfurt], N.S. 10: 183–92.

———. 1991. "Nachtrag zu den 'Bermerkungen zu "*Lysandra cormion*" (Lepidoptera: Lycaenidae).'" *Nachrichten des entomologischen Vereins Apollo* [Frankfurt], N.S. 12: 193–95.

Schwarz, Albert, and Kurt Johnson. 1992. "Two New Butterflies (Lepidoptera: Lycaenidae) from Cuba," *Caribbean Journal of Science* 28: 149–57.

Seitz, Adalbert. 1906–54. *Die Gross-Schmetterlinge der Erde.* 16 vols. Stuttgart: Lehmann, then Alfred Kernen.

Senderovich, Saveliy, and Elena Shvarts. 1998. "V krayu makhaonov (Nabokov i Blok)," *Novyy zhurnal* 211: 243–52.

Smelhaus, Jiri. 1947. "*Polyommatus meleager* Esp. X *P. coridon* Poda (Lep. Lyc.), Predbezna zprava-Note préliminaire." *Casopis ceskoslovenské Spolecnosti entomologické* (Acta Societatis entomologicae cechosloveniae) 44: 1–2, 44–47.

Smith, D. S., L. D. Miller, and J. Y. Miller. 1994. *The Butterflies of the West Indies and South Florida.* Oxford: Oxford University Press.

Stallings, D.B., and J. R. Turner. 1947. "New American Butterflies." *Canadian Entomologist* 78: 134–37.

Tilden, James W., and Arthur C. Smith. 1986. *A Field Guide to Western Butterflies*. Boston: Houghton Mifflin.

Wiley, E. O. 1981. *Phylogenetics: The Theory and Practice of Phylogenetic Systematics*. New York: John Wiley and Sons.

Wiley, E. O., D. Siegel-Causey, D. R. Brooks, and V. A. Funk. 1991. *The Compleat Cladist: A Primer of Phylogenetic Procedures*. Lawrence, Kans.: Museum of Natural History.

Wilson, Edward O. 1993. *The Diversity of Life*. New York: Norton.

Zaleski, Philip. 1986. "Nabokov's Blue Period." *Harvard Magazine* 88: 36–38.

Zimmer, Dieter E. 1993. "Nabokov's Lepidoptera: An Annotated Multilingual Checklist." In Sartori, ed., 25–171.

———. 1996; rev. 1998. *A Guide to Nabokov's Butterflies and Moths*. Hamburg [privately printed].

Butterflies and Moths Named by and for Vladimir Nabokov

ROBERT MICHAEL PYLE

I. BUTTERFLY TAXA DESCRIBED BY VLADIMIR NABOKOV

Listed in order of publication. The sources may be found by checking the date of the name against the chronology of his scientific publications in the text.

1. *Lysandra cormion* Nabokov, 1941. Although he began and finished his days as a lepidopterist in Europe, Nabokov named but a single butterfly entity from that continent. In July 1938, he collected two male blues in the Alpes Maritimes of southern France that were different from any named species, bearing traits of both the Chalk-hill and Meleager's Blues. Though recognizing that these individuals might represent "the freakish outcome of . . . evolutionary gropings," Nabokov overcame his reluctance to describe this blue and gave it a name blended from *L. coridon* and *Meleageria daphnis*. This blue turned out to be a hybrid of the two species, so the name "*Lysandra cormion*" has no formal status today. Before its hybrid nature had been established, Nabokov figured the two specimens he had caught in Moulinet in *Speak, Memory*, which covers only his first European decades but covertly peeks ahead to America and especially to the numerous new butterflies he named there.

2. *Carterocephalus canopunctatus* Nabokov, 1941. As a youth, Nabokov planned to explore Central Asia for its butterflies, perhaps in the company of Grigoriy Grum-Grzhimaylo. He never did, except in fiction (in chapter 2 of *The Gift*), but he did name one species from this area, not by traveling east, but after sailing west to New York. There, among the AMNH collections he was frequenting in order to ascertain the status of *Lysandra cormion*, he noticed a singular specimen, its place of capture designated "Ost-Tibet," which often meant China on early collectors' labels. Nabokov gave this pale-spotted, olive-brown skipper, related to what is known as the Arctic Skipper in North America and the Chequered Skipper in Britain (*Carterocephalus palaemon* (Pallas) 1771), a name that means "having hoary dots." In W. E. Evan's *Catalogue of Hesperia* (1949), it is listed as a junior synonym of, ironically, *Carterocephalus christophi* Grum-Grzhimaylo, 1891.

3. *Neonympha dorothea* Nabokov, 1942. When Vladimir and Véra crossed the country for a lecture engagement at Stanford in June 1941, they were driven by his student Dorothy Leuthold. On a hike down Bright Angel Trail at the Grand Canyon, she "kindly kicked up the first specimen." Nabokov named both the species and the type subspecies (see below) in her honor. This event caused him to investigate the genus, and he found two pairs of "geminate" species in Arizona, "one pair unnamed, the other neglected." In sorting these out, he named this and the next three taxa. Later transferred to *Euptychia* Hübner, then to *Cyllopsis* Felder by Miller (1974), and subsumed under the species *C. pertepida* as a valid subspecies: *C. pertepida dorothea* (Nabokov).

4. *Neonympha dorothea dorothea* Nabokov, 1942. Because he subdivided Dorothy's Satyr into several subspecies, Nabokov designated the original variety as the *type* subspecies that all others would thereafter be compared against. As these are all now regarded as races of *C. pertepida*, the second "*dorothea*" became superfluous.

5. *Neonympha dorothea edwardsi* Nabokov, 1942. A second phenotype recognized by Nabokov and named after W. H. Edwards, who had described the closely related *N. henshawi*, confusing it with *N. dorothea*. Now it is considered merely a seasonal color "form," a category without formal status, and listed as *C. p. dorothea* f. "edwardsi."

6. *Neonympha dorothea avicula* Nabokov, 1942. Nabokov named this butterfly *avicula* ("little bird"), considering it a subspecies of *N. dorothea* from Texas. He liked these southwestern satyrine butterflies partly because they combined the "quiet velvet" of "boreal-alpine" Satyrs, or Browns, of which he was fond, with "the glitter on the under surface" of his beloved Blues. This subspecies, which he found especially reddish, stands recognized in the current checklist as *Cyllopsis pertepida avicula* (Nabokov).

7. *Neonympha maniola* Nabokov, 1942. While revising the southwestern Satyrs in this group, Nabokov picked out certain males from southeastern Arizona as being distinct from the other varieties on the Colorado Plateau and in Texas. Working only from these males, he "reluctantly" described them as the new species *N. maniola*; later he added a note describing the female, which had since turned up. The general aspect seemed "manioloid" to him, reminiscent of the commonest satyrine in Europe, the Meadow Brown (*Maniola jurtina* Schrank), which he knew as a boy and much later found in a painting by Hieronymus Bosch. In the description, Nabokov gave credit to the biologist and writer Marston Bates for noticing the difference between *N. maniola* and *N. dorothea* (both of which Bates had dissected) before he himself did. Now this taxon is considered a solid subspecies, *Cyllopsis pertepida maniola* (Nabokov).

8. *Lycaeides melissa samuelis* Nabokov, 1943. Certainly the Karner Blue, as this species is commonly known, is Nabokov's most famous butterfly. Mentioned in *Pnin* and in several of Nabokov's letters in this volume, it is a conservation *cause célèbre* in the Northeast and Upper Midwest, and has been listed as an Endangered Species by the U.S. Fish and Wildlife Service. Nabokov did not discover it, but as he unraveled the nomenclatural tangles of American Blues, he found that the name it had long been known by, *Plebejus scudderi* (W. H. Edwards), 1861, properly applied to a northern race of the related species now called *L. idas*. That left the only eastern subspecies of the Melissa Blue nameless. A great admirer of Samuel Hubbard Scudder, he gave the butterfly another Scudderian patronym, this time from the lepidopterist's first name. Though the consensus is that it comprises a good subspecies of *L. melissa*, Nabokov came to regard it as a distinct species, and Karner Blue authority Robert Dirig of Cornell University also feels strongly inclined toward the specific identity of *Lycaeides samuelis*. Laurence Packer et al. (1998) conducted electrophoretic studies of Karner and Melissa Blues and failed to find genetic proof of their specific distinctness. However, the Karner Blue nowhere seems to interbreed with expanding populations of the common western *L. melissa melissa*, and demonstrates differences in appearance, genitalia, and ecology. The authors urge "further classical morphological analyses," such as Nabokov conducted, but "using modern cladistic methods, to clarify the taxonomic status of the Karner Blue."

9. *Icaricia* Nabokov, 1944. Recognizing a lack of adequate discrimination in the large genus *Plebejus*, which encompassed many Nearctic Blues, Nabokov erected *Icaricia* to contain several of them. Whether it is considered a full genus or subgenus today depends upon the work consulted. But the most recent authoritative list, *A Catalogue / Checklist of the Butterflies of America North of Mexico* (Miller and Brown, 1981), considers five species to belong to *Icaricia*: *I. icarioides* (Boisduval), *I. shasta* (W. H. Edwards), *I. acmon* (Westwood and Hewitson), *I. lupini* (Boisduval), and *I. neurona* (Skinner). *Icaricia* combines Icarus, son of Daedalus, the wax-and-feather fliers of mythic fame, with *Aricia*, a genus of Blues. *I. icarioides* (designated by Nabokov as the type) resembles genitalically *Polyommatus icarus* (Linnaeus), the Common Blue of Europe.

10. *Plebulina* Nabokov, 1944. A new species of Blue from San Emigdio Canyon in the Mojave region of southern California was described by Grinnell in 1905 as *Lycaena emigdionis*. J. A. Comstock, author of *California Butterflies*, considered it rare and placed it in *Plebejus*. Nabokov, working with American Museum of Natural History specimens, discerned its peculiarity and gave it a brand-new genus that is monotypic (contains only the type species). Its name, *Plebulina*, distilled from *Plebejus* and *Albulina*, recognizes that it "remarkably amalgamates" male genitalic characters of both genera. The genus continues to be recognized as distinct and valid.

11. *Parachilades* Nabokov, 1945. After examining the Nearctic members of the subfamily Plebejinae, Nabokov undertook to revise the plebejiine Blues of the New World tropics. Based on his examination of specimens in the museums to which he had access, he concluded that the existing genera did not adequately contain or define them all. He erected the new genus *Parachilades* (relating it to *Chilades*) for the Bolivian species called *Lycaena titicaca* Weymer, 1890. It has since been sunk as a synonym of *Itylos* Draudt, 1921.

12. *Pseudothecla* Nabokov, 1945. The butterfly described as *Thecla faga* by Dognin in 1895 bears little tails on its hindwings like a Hairstreak. But Nabokov recognized it as a plebejiine Blue and erected the new genus *Pseudothecla* for it. This name turned out to be inadmissible, as it had already been used by Strand in 1910 for a genus of Hairstreaks. Hemming, who had noted the need for a new name and wished to honor Nabokov's work, provided the alternative in 1960 by renaming it *Nabokovia*.

13. *Pseudochrysops* Nabokov, 1945. Erected to receive one "rare and remarkable" Haitian species previously called *Hemiargus bornoi* Comstock-Huntington, 1943. This genus resembles the "catochrysopoid" group of Blues outwardly but not genitalically. It remains valid (Johnson and Bálint, 1995).

14. *Cyclargus* Nabokov, 1945. *Cyclargus* was described for several species previously placed in *Hemiargus*. Argus, Hera's watchman in Greek mythology, had a hundred eyes. His name has been used since Linnaean times for common names, for scientific species names, and as a suffix for scientific names of several genera, usually pertaining to Blues. The genus, combining Cyclops and Argus for "big-eyed" species, is recognized as valid in contemporary taxonomy (Johnson and Bálint, 1995).

15. *Echinargus* Nabokov, 1945. The name means a "spiny argus," perhaps referring to a distinguishing genitalic structure "armed" with teeth. Nabokov placed within it two species of Blues formerly classed in the genus *Hemiargus*. One of these he declined to name as it had already been discerned by W. P. Comstock, who, with Fred Rindge, named it *E. huntingtoni* for their colleague in 1953. As type

species, Nabokov designated *E. isola* (Reakirt) 1866, a northward summer immigrant in North America commonly called the Reakirt's, or Solitary, Blue. Johnson and Bálint (1995) reconfirmed the validity of the genus.

16. *Pseudolucia* Nabokov, 1945. The genus *Lycaena* now consists of coppers, but originally it was an umbrella genus for various types of lycaenids including many Blues. Nabokov removed the Chilean species *L. chilensis* Blanchard, 1852 and *L collina* (Phillipi), 1860 to this new and still-valid genus. He gave no clue as to the identity of the "Lucia" that these bright, delicate butterflies are supposed to resemble, but it might refer to *Polyommatus lucia*, Kirby's 1837 name for the Spring Azure (another name of which is *Argus pseudargiolus* Boisduval and Leconte 1833): as Brian Boyd suggests, the *pseudo* and the *lucia*-as-Spring-Azure anticipate "I was the shadow of the waxwing slain / By the *false azure* in the windowpane," in the famous opening couplet of John Shade's poem in *Pale Fire*, a novel in which Nabokov often signs himself by way of his butterflies. Or, as Boyd also notes, Nabokov always called his first love, Valentina Shulgina, the "Tamara" of *Speak, Memory*, by the nickname "Lyussya"; her figure always haunted his imagination.

17. *Paralycaeides* Nabokov, 1945. Sorting through museum specimens, VN set up this new genus to accommodate a Peruvian species known as *Itylos inconspicua* Draudt, 1921. He saw only a single specimen, but its male genitalic structure and wing shape convinced him that it retained "an ancestral aspect" linking the Neotropical Blues with the Holarctic *Lycaeides* Blues that were his specialty. It is still a valid genus.

18. *Cyclargus erembis* Nabokov, 1948. When he examined a specimen of this Caribbean Blue, sent him from Oxford, Nabokov recognized it as a heretofore unnamed species in the genus he erected in 1945. It had been mistakenly labeled as *Hemiargus catalina* (Fabricius). The name *C. erembis*, which is cryptic, remains valid.

19. *Lycaeides argyrognomon sublivens* Nabokov, 1949. Nabokov's most intimate taxonomic involvement was with the silver-studded Blues of the genus *Lycaeides* Hübner, 1819. He traveled and hiked widely in the West to work out the various geographic varieties, attempting to untangle "the fantastic misadventures" the names had undergone. The term "*sublivens*" implies an unusual degree of bluishness on the underside. This southwest Colorado race was described entirely from male specimens. In 1951, Nabokov found the missing female in the San Juan Mountains near Telluride, in a setting described in his afterword to *Lolita*: "the tinkling sounds of the valley town coming up the mountain trail (on which I caught the first known female of *Lycaeides sublivens* Nabokov)." This scene, he wrote, was one of those that made up "the nerves of the novel." Now this butterfly is listed *as Lycaeides idas sublivens* Nabokov.

20. *Lycaeides argyrognomon longinus* Nabokov, 1949. Not yet having met this subpecies in the wild, Nabokov named it from old museum specimens. The subspecific name refers to the long falx (a male genitalic process) that approaches the dimensions of the same organ on *L. melissa*. In fact, Nabokov felt the two North American species of *Lycaeides* actually met and intergraded around Jackson Hole, Wyoming, where he finally collected this variety himself in the summer of 1949, while Dmitri climbed the Tetons. These American Blues were later correctly allied to the Holarctic species *L. idas* rather than to the far more unpronounceable *L. argyrognomon*. *Lycaeides idas longinus* is still valid.

21. *Lycaeides melissa pseudosamuelis* Nabokov, 1949. The Melissa Blue is closely related and in some forms quite similar to the Northern Blue (*L. idas*). This subspecies, named by VN while cleaning up the taxonomy of these two orange-bordered Blues, reminded him of his own Karner Blue (*Lycaeides melissa samuelis*) in its reduced pattern and coloration. Described from the high country of Colorado, it can be difficult to distinguish in the field from *L. i. sublivens*. It has since been consigned to the synonymy of *L. m. melissa* (W. H. Edwards), 1873, also described from the Colorado mountains.

22. *Lycaeides melissa inyoensis* (Nabokov), 1949. While working on the screenplay for *Lolita* in southern California in 1960, Nabokov stole away to the field in Inyo County to collect a butterfly Jean Gunder had described as aberrational form "inyoensis" in 1927. Nabokov had raised it to subspecies status in 1949, but it was later sunk as a junior synonym under the subspecies *L. melissa paradoxa* (F. H. Chermock), 1945.

II. BUTTERFLY AND MOTH TAXA NAMED IN HONOR OF VLADIMIR NABOKOV

Scientific Names

1. *Eupithecia nabokovi* McDunnough, 1945. In *Speak, Memory* Nabokov expressed his dreamy adolescent hopes of discovering a new "pug" – an inchworm moth of the genus *Eupithecia*: "delicate little creatures that cling in the daytime to speckled surfaces, with which their flat wings and turned-up abdomens blend." His chance came many years later, on a "blessed black night in the Wasatch Range," when he collected not one, but two unknown pugs. He sent them to J. A. McDunnough from Utah, who named one of them for him.

2. *Clossiana (= Boloria) freija nabokovi* Stallings and Turner, 1947. The vigorous amateur lepidopterist Don Stallings, most noted for his work with giant skippers, went afield with Nabokov in Rocky Mountain National Park in July 1947. Subsequently Stallings and his colleague J. R. Turner named this rare subspecies of Freya's Fritillary from northern British Columbia for him. Related to the bog fritillaries Nabokov evokes in *Speak, Memory*, recalling a youthful chase, this subspecies has since been synonymized under *C. f. natazhati* (Gibson), 1920.

3. *Hesperia nabokovi* Bell and Comstock, 1948. All Nabokov did to receive this patronym was to send the specimen from the MCZ collection at Harvard to Comstock at the AMNH. Comstock and Bell recognized it as an undescribed branded skipper and named it for him. A Haitian species, it is the only *Hesperia* from the West Indies.

4. *Nabokovia* Hemming, 1960. As noted above, Francis Hemming promulgated the generic name *Nabokovia* to replace Nabokov's preoccupied *Pseudothecla*. It contains the species *N. faga* Dognin of Ecuador and *N. chilensis* Blanchard of Chile, as well as a new species with a Nabokovian name described by Bálint and Johnson in 1993: *Nabokovia ada*.

5. *Lycaeides idas nabokovi* Masters, 1972. Carrying Nabokov's work on the genus *Lycaeides* still further, John Masters named this Minnesota subspecies for "Dr. Nabokov, who first recognized its distinctness and whose papers on Nearctic *Lycaeides* . . . have provided a background to make this description possible" (from original description).

6. *Cyllopsis pyracmon nabokovi* Miller, 1974. In revising the New World euptychiine satyrs, Lee D. Miller described this respectful patronym from Ramsey Canyon, Arizona. He noted that Nabokov "first pointed out that both *pyracmon* and *henshawi* occurred in the desert southwest of the United States" and that "his work on United States *Cyllopsis* . . . as *Neonympha*, too long has been ignored."

7. Nabokovia Bálint and Johnson, 1995. A section of the Neotropical Polyommatines, consisting of Infratribes Pseudochrysopsina and Nabokovina.

8. Nabokovina Bálint and Johnson, 1995. An infratribe consisting of genera *Echinargus* Nabokov, 1945; *Nabokovia* Hemming, 1960; and *Eldoradina* Balletto, 1993.

English Names

While scientific names are governed by a strict set of rules under the *International Code of Zoological Nomenclature*, common names are not yet standardized. A Xerces Society list (Miller, 1992) gives most names available for both species and subspecies; the North American Butterfly Association (NABA, 1996) lists authorized names for each species.

1. Nabokov's Blue. F. Martin Brown (1956) introduced the name Nabokov's Blue for *Lycaeides idas sublivens* (Nabokov), 1949. Given subsequent to Brown's debate with Nabokov over statistical techniques, this compliment gave Nabokov obvious pleasure. Dark Blue, introduced by Tilden and Smith (1986), has been used more recently.

2. Nabokov's Blue. The name was again applied by Opler and Krizek (1984), this time to *Lycaeides idas nabokovi* Masters, 1972. It is maintained in the Miller/Xerces list.

3. Nabokov's Fritillary. Tilden and Smith applied this name to *Boloria freija nabokovi* Stallings and Turner, 1947. It has since been sunk within Natazhati's Fritillary.

4. Nabokov's Brown. Tilden and Smith called *Cyllopsis pyracmon nabokovi* Miller, 1974 by this name, and it is found as such in the Miller/Xerces list.

5. Nabokov's Wood Nymph. "Wood Nymph," "Brown," and "Satyr" are used somewhat interchangeably for an array of eye-spotted satyrines, and common names may repeat the species patronym or the author's name, or describe other traits. So it happens that *Cyllopsis pertepida dorothea* (Nabokov), 1942 has been dubbed the Canyonland Satyr, the Grand Canyon Brown, Dorothy's Satyr, and Nabokov's Wood Nymph. In his 1956 *Colorado Butterflies*, F. M. Brown called *Euptychia dorothea*, then considered a full species, Nabokov's Wood Nymph. A favorite honorarial, Nabokov referred to it in interviews and letters, sometimes contracting it to Nabokov's Nymph.

6. Nabokov's Satyr. Pyle (1981) designated the full species *Cyllopsis pyracmon* (Butler), 1866 as Nabokov's Satyr. The Miller/Xerces list followed Tilden and Smith in calling it the Pyracmon Brown, but the NABA list selected Nabokov's Satyr. It ranges from Arizona and New Mexico south to Guatemala.

7. Nabokov's Pug. One of the new species of moths collected by Nabokov at publisher James Laughlin's lodge near Alta, Utah, was named *Eupithecia nabokovi* (Nabokov's Pug) by J. H. McDunnough in 1945. The only moth to bear his name, this species completes the circle of his boyhood desire to discover a new type of pug in Russia.

III. MODERN NAMES HONORING NABOKOV'S LIFE AND WORK

In recent years, a number of neotropical Blues have been named after characters or places significant to Nabokov's own past or his fiction. The full references for these are given in the bibliography, under the names and dates of the species' descriptions. G. Warren Whitaker suggested most of the etymologies; the names of prominent Nabokovians who suggested other names are given here in brackets. The dedicatees are identified according to their occurrence in Nabokov's work.

Eldoradina (= Polytheclus) cincinnatus Bálint and Johnson, 1993: Cincinnatus in *Invitation to a Beheading*

Itylos luzhin Bálint, 1993: Luzhin in *The Defense*

Itylos pnin Bálint, 1993: Professor Timofey Pnin in *Pnin*

Leptotes delalande Bálint and Johnson, 1995: Nabokov's philosopher alter-ego in *The Gift* and the epigraph to *Invitation to a Beheading*

Leptotes krug Bálint, Johnson, Salazar and Velez, 1995 [Dieter E. Zimmer]: Professor Adam Krug in *Bend Sinister*

Madeleinea ardisensis Bálint and Lamas, 1996: The suffix "-ensis" on a species name suggests that it belongs to the place named, here Dan Veen's country seat in Ardis

Madeleinea cobaltana Bálint and Lamas, 1994: Kobaltana, a mountain resort in *Pale Fire*

Madeleinea lolita Bálint, 1993: Dolores Haze (Dolly, Lo, Lolita) in *Lolita*

Madeleinea mashenka Bálint, 1993: Mashenka in *Mashenka (Mary)*

Madeleinea nodo Bálint and Johnson, 1995: Nodo in *Pale Fire*

Madeleinea odon Bálint and Johnson, 1995: Odon in *Pale Fire*

Madeleinea tintarrona Bálint and Johnson, 1995: Tintarron, the precious blue glass in *Pale Fire*

Madeleinea vokoban Bálint and Johnson, 1995: "Nabokov" reversed as if in a mirror

Nabokovia ada Bálint and Johnson, 1994: Ada Veen in *Ada*

Paralycaeides hazelea Bálint and Johnson, 1995 [Brian Boyd]: Hazel in *Pale Fire*

Paralycaeides shade Bálint, 1993: John Shade in *Pale Fire*

Plebejus ardis Balint and Johnson, 1997 [Ellendea Proffer]: The bucolic Veen estate in *Ada*, located in Ladore County, Estotiland; and a publishing house set up by Carl and Ellendea Proffer that printed many of Nabokov's books in Russian and a number of books about him in English

Plebejus pilgram Balint and Johnson, 1997 [Simon Karlinsky]: Paul Pilgram is the butterfly collector in "The Aurelian"

(Polytheclus cincinnatus = Eldoradina cincinnatus)

Pseudolucia aureliana Bálint and Johnson, 1993: Denotes a butterfly collector, as in "The Aurelian"

Pseudolucia charlotte Bálint and Johnson, 1993: Charlotte Haze in *Lolita*

Pseudolucia clarea Bálint and Johnson, 1993: Clare Quilty in *Lolita*

Pseudolucia hazeorum Bálint and Johnson, 1993: Of the Haze women, Charlotte and Dolores, in *Lolita*

Pseudolucia humbert Bálint and Johnson, 1995: Humbert Humbert in *Lolita*

Pseudolucia kinbote Bálint and Johnson, 1993: Kinbote, Shade's commentator in *Pale Fire*

Pseudolucia sirin Bálint, 1993: Sirin, Nabokov's youthful pen name

Pseudolucia tamara Bálint and Johnson, 1995 [D. Barton Johnson]: Tamara, Nabokov's early love in *Speak, Memory*

Pseudolucia vera Bálint and Johnson, 1993: Véra Evseevna Slonim, vn's beloved wife

Pseudolucia zembla Bálint and Johnson, 1993: Zembla, the mythical kingdom in *Pale Fire*

Pseudolucia zina Bálint and Johnson, 1995 [Stephen Jan Parker]: Zina Mertz, Fyodor's love in *The Gift*

Acknowledgments

Without the initiative, enthusiasm, and patient forbearance of Deanne Urmy, our editor at Beacon Press, such a comprehensive collection of Nabokov's writings on butterflies would never have been attempted, let alone brought to fruition. At an early stage of the project Walter Lippincott and Emily Wilkinson of Princeton University Press gracefully relinquished rights to publish Nabokov's scientific papers in the face of a much more ambitious butterfly book; Ms Wilkinson kindly supplied information from her files that had been gathered at a still earlier stage by Ronald S. Wilkinson.

Lepidopterists Charles Remington, John Franclemont, John Downey, Oakley Shields, Zsolt Bálint, Robert Dirig, and Kurt Johnson supplied information about Nabokov the lepidopterist with great generosity. Kurt Johnson in particular has spent many hours explaining taxonomic principles and lepidopterological details with passionate lucidity.

Robert Michael Pyle and I want to express our warmest gratitude to Dieter E. Zimmer for the successive, ever more exhaustive versions of his *Guide to Nabokov's Butterflies and Moths* (1993, 1996, 1996, 1998), and for his unstinting readiness to investigate further problems as they were posed. Without his work, *Nabokov's Butterflies* would be poorer in too many ways to admit to. Readers fascinated by the butterflies in Nabokov will want to have access to Zimmer's *Guide*. For conscientious translators of Nabokov it is essential.

Jane Grayson, and especially Alexander Dolinin, made it possible to decipher the inferno of revisions in the manuscript of the "Second Addendum to The Gift" at the Library of Congress. Dmitri Nabokov then spared time from the many demands on his attention to translate this complicated text and a number of his father's butterfly poems. Gavriel Shapiro kindly provided a translation of another poem.

Lisa Browar, Rodney Phillips, Stephen Crook, and Philip Millito of the Henry W. and Albert A. Berg Collection of the New York Public Library, where Nabokov's lepidopterological as well as most of his literary papers are housed, were steadfastly helpful. The staff of the Harvard Museum of Comparative Zoology, the American Museum of Natural History, the Cornell University Insect Collection, and the Musée Cantonal de Zoologie, Lausanne, have also helped as needed. Bookseller Glenn Horowitz kindly made available photographs of some of Nabokov's outstanding butterfly inscriptions on dedication copies of his books. Terry Myers sent the text and photographs of a previously unpublished butterfly poem that would otherwise have been overlooked.

Robert Michael Pyle's enthusiasm for Nabokov and butterflies and for nature and language, fortified by his gusto and unfailing good grace, have made it a pleasure to work with him. – BB

My involvement in this book grew out of the joint vision at Beacon Press of Deanne Urmy and Wendy Strothman (now of Houghton Mifflin), for whose confidence and prescience I am grateful. Ms. Urmy, with her colleagues, including Margaret Park Bridges and David Coen, deftly managed and tamed an extremely challenging manuscript.

From my mentor Charles L. Remington of Yale University came invaluable recollections of the personal relationship he enjoyed with Vladimir Nabokov, as well as essential review of the scientific aspects of this book. Kurt Johnson's enthusiastic, informed assistance, and his promptness in sharing relevant new publications, have also been crucial to me.

Lepidopterist and friend Joann Karges excited my serious interest in the butterflies and moths of Nabokov's texts through her pioneering book *Nabokov's Lepidoptera: Genres and Genera*. Other lepidopterists who lent me their aid during this project include John Franclemont, Frederick H. Rindge, Robert Dirig, Andy Warren, Boyce Drummond, Clyde Gillette, Brian O. C. Gardiner, Lee Miller, Kent Wilson, David Wagner, Jeannine Oppewall, Vladimir Krivda, Robert Robbins, John Hinchliff, Jon Pelham, Charles V. Covell, Jr., and especially John Downey, who kindly recorded his reminiscence of his encounter with vn. Jon Shepard, Lars Crabo, and John Talmadge helped me investigate the origins of Esmeralda and other points concerning moths.

I am also grateful to Phyllis and Kenneth Christiansen and to Paul Brooks for sharing their personal histories with Nabokov. Harry Foster of Houghton Mifflin kindly facilitated my meeting with Paul Brooks and with curators at Wellesley College Libraries. Thanks to Ruth R. Rogers, Special Collections Librarian, and Wilma R. Slaight, Archivist, of the Margaret Clapp Library, Wellesley College, Richard C. Fyffe of the Homer Babbidge Library, University of Connecticut Library at Storrs, and the Rare Book and Manuscript Collections at Cornell University for finding and furnishing letters. To have had free play in Nabokov's Lepidoptera archives at the Henry W. and Albert A. Berg Collection, New York Public Library, was an immense boon for which I am deeply indebted to the curators and to Dmitri Nabokov. Gavriel Shapiro of Cornell was most encouraging and helpful, as were Jane Fenton, David Campbell, Cathy Maxwell, Roseann Hanson, Mary Willy, and Chet Raymo.

While it may not be commonplace to acknowledge one's co-editor, I must make note of the phenomenal knowledge, wisdom, generosity, and sheer industry of Brian Boyd, attributes that made this ambitious project both possible and a great pleasure. – RMP

Index

Butterflies and moths are listed by species name (the most stable form), always in lowercase, and followed if needed by the subspecies name; the name of the genus, always capitalized; the namer of the species; and, if needed, the common name: thus *Lycaeides melissa samuelis* Nabokov, the Karner Blue, appears as *melissa samuelis* Nabokov, *Lycaeides* (Karner Blue). Important common names (Karner Blue, Red Admirable) will be cross-referenced to the species name. When a genus is discussed as a whole, it is listed under the genus name, such as *Lycaeides*.

Titles of Nabokov's literary works are listed under the main entry "Nabokov works." The page numbers of works reproduced or excerpted as selections appear in bold.